THE PEOPLE'S REVOLT

THE PEOPLE'S REVOLT

TEXAS POPULISTS AND THE ROOTS
OF AMERICAN LIBERALISM

Gregg Cantrell

Yale UNIVERSITY PRESS   NEW HAVEN AND LONDON

Yale University Press books may be purchased in quantity
for educational, business, or promotional use. For information, please e-mail sales.press@yale.edu (U.S. office) or
sales@yaleup.co.uk (U.K. office).

Set in Scala type by Westchester Publishing Services.
Printed in the United States of America.

Library of Congress Control Number: 2019941027
ISBN 978-0-300-10097-6 (hardcover: alk. paper)

A catalogue record for this book is available from the
British Library.

This paper meets the requirements of ANSI/NISO
Z39.48-1992 (Permanence of Paper).

10 9 8 7 6 5 4 3 2 1

To Stephanie

Contents

PREFACE

The book is the culmination of an interest in Populism that began more than three decades ago, when in my first graduate seminar at Texas A&M University, my professor, Martin V. Melosi, gave me the assignment of reading Lawrence Goodwyn's brilliant book, *Democratic Promise: The Populist Moment in America.* Although I had grown up in small-town Texas and came from a family with deep rural roots—both of my grandfathers were West Texas cotton farmers—I was surprised to learn that a movement as significant as Populism had originated in my part of the country, and even more surprised that in Texas white Populists had sometimes made common cause with African Americans. The next semester, the late Robert A. Calvert, who himself had written on agrarian politics, encouraged me to write a paper on John B. Rayner, the black Populist leader who had lived just thirty miles up the road in Calvert. That led to my dissertation and later a published biography of Rayner. I eventually set Populism aside for a decade to pursue other scholarly interests, but I knew that someday I would return to the topic that had so fascinated me when I was still in my twenties.

One reason I waited so long to revisit Populism was that I had remained perplexed by it. Goodwyn, whose work I greatly admired and who had generously welcomed me as his houseguest for a week in 1987 while I did research in North Carolina, made a compelling argument that Populism had offered a radical alternative to the course of liberal capitalism in America. In keeping with academic trends in the 1980s, I became convinced that while Goodwyn may have been right, the movement also owed large debts to the older ideas of republicanism and, as Robert C. McMath Jr. had so effectively argued, to American religious and communal traditions. These were elements

ix

of Populism that I assumed I would emphasize when, more than a decade ago, I decided to return to the study of the agrarian revolt. As I waded into the sources, I was struck by how modern many of the ideas seemed, even if the Populists frequently couched those ideas in the only political vocabulary they had available, which drew on the traditional language of American republicanism and Protestantism. The work of Charles Postel, which appeared when I was already deep into my research, reinforced my developing understanding of Populist modernity. But I resisted calling the proverbial spade a spade—that is, acknowledging that Populists had actually helped to pioneer the thing we would later call modern liberalism—until the evidence appeared so convincing to me that it seemed undeniable. Hence the subtitle and main theme of this book.

A word about the organization of the book: although this is a history of the People's Party in Texas, and thus it has a narrative to tell, the subject matter did not lend itself to a purely chronological treatment. What readers will find is a mixture of chronological and topical chapters. The chronological chapters (1, 2, 6, 8, 10, and 11), which tell the story of the party's origins, analyze elections and a legislative session, and relate the party's collapse, are interspersed with topical chapters (3, 4, 5, 7, and 9) that explore ideology, religion, race, gender, and the border. The topical chapters necessarily depart from a strict chronology of events, although I've tried my best to avoid spoiling the plot. The conclusion, which I originally thought would be a brief summary of what had gone before, ended up being a full chapter, wherein I make a tentative effort to trace Populist ideas into the twentieth century.

Throughout, I have sought to communicate something of the flavor of the 1890s by allowing Populists and others to speak in their vernacular as much as possible. Thus, I have left their often nonstandard spelling, grammar, and punctuation as it appears in the sources, using *sic* only when necessary to avoid confusion. White newspaper editors sometimes rendered the words of African Americans in dialect that some readers may find objectionable, but I have chosen to render such passages as they were published; doing so tells us something more about the writer of the quotation. In keeping with what seems to be modern scholarly convention, I have used the labels "African American" and "black" interchangeably, and occasionally I have used "Negro" when referring directly to the words or thoughts of contemporaries who used that now outdated term. I bow to modern convention and use the term "Tejano" to refer to Texas-born people of Mexican descent, although such people usually referred to themselves simply as "Mexicans" or "Mexicanos" regardless of their place of birth (and they sometimes employed their own invented terms such as "Mexicano-Texano"). I use "ethnic Mexicans" or "Mexicanos" to refer to people of Mexican ancestry when I am not specifying their country of birth.

Readers who are not specialists in the history of American politics may occasionally get confused by the terms "Republican" and "republican," "Democratic" and "democratic," "Populist" and "populist" and the many permutations of these terms. To make matters worse, nineteenth-century writers rarely capitalized any portion of formal party names. Furthermore, the Democratic Party was frequently referred to as "the democracy," a usage that did not survive long into the twentieth century. Readers should be aware that I have lowercased the terms when referring to the generic concepts of republicanism, democracy, and so on, and have capitalized them when referring to party names. However, I have allowed the nineteenth-century practices to stand, occasionally substituting a capital letter in brackets for the original lowercase letter when I thought readers were apt to be confused.

As I neared completion of the manuscript, events took an unanticipated turn with the election cycle of 2016. Applied both to Republican candidate Donald Trump and to one of the principal Democratic candidates, Bernie Sanders, the term "populist" (with a small p) suddenly reappeared with a vengeance. With the surprise election of Trump, it became a ubiquitous feature of American political discourse. Although I did not set out to explain how this nineteenth-century label got applied to twenty-first-century politicians, that also became a necessary task, although there are others far more capable that I am of explaining modern populism, especially in its transnational perspective. I am not sure what S. O. Daws, William Lamb, Thomas Nugent, Jerome Kearby, Stump Ashby, Henry Bentley, Charles Jenkins, Bettie Gay, Ellen Dabbs, Melvin Wade, and John B. Rayner would think about their country today and the phenomenon of Trumpian "populism," but I wish they were here to offer their perspectives. I am sure they would have some choice words.

ACKNOWLEDGMENTS

It is possible that the study of Populism attracts unusually generous and intelligent scholars, or it may be that the study of Populism somehow makes them that way. In either case, it has been my good fortune for many years to be able to count myself among the small fraternity of historians who research and write about the agrarian revolt. Of these, my greatest debt is to Worth Robert Miller. Bob first befriended me as a graduate student, and over the ensuing decades he has read my work, shared hard-to-find sources, and answered countless questions about Populism in general and Texas Populism in particular. Bob McMath, Matt Hild, and Charles Postel have also made contributions that I will never be able to repay. Their books and articles have educated me, their formal criticism and informal advice at scholarly meetings has focused my thinking, and their friendship has sustained me. I likewise owe scholarly debts to Donna Barnes, Rebecca Edwards, Alicia E. Rodriquez, James Hunt, James Beeby, Omar Ali, and Ana Martinez-Catsam, among the many historians whose works on the Populist era have served as building blocks for my own. It is a safe bet that all of the above-mentioned scholars will disagree with some (or in some cases, much) of what I say in this book, but I know from experience that they will be gracious in their criticisms.

Like all students of Populism, I also owe a profound debt to the late Larry Goodwyn. My interpretation would have driven him more than a little crazy, and I know that if he had lived to read the final product, he would not have been slow to tell me how wrong I am. Nevertheless, I have had to reckon with his work at every turn, and I feel enormously fortunate to have known him.

At Texas Christian University, I have had the good fortune to have several graduate students who, either willingly or unwillingly, were dragged into the vineyard of Populism and made to labor there. Two of those students, Jeff Wells and Brooke Wibracht, wrote fine dissertations on aspects of the agrarian revolt, and I now count them as valued colleagues. Jeff also shared hundreds of pages of his own notes and images from Texas newspapers, which were invaluable. Brook Poston, Jonathan Perry, Bird Burriss, Brennan Gardner Rivas, Michael Green, and Bob Oliver all contributed to the research that went into this book. Professors often say that they learned more from their students than the students learned from them, but in my case it is literally true.

My colleagues in the History Department at Texas Christian University have been supportive in many ways. I should name them all, but I owe particular thanks to my Americanist colleagues Clayton Brown, Allan Gallay, Todd Kerstetter, Max Krochmal, Celeste Menchaca, Rebecca Sharpless, Gene Smith, Ken Stevens, Kara Vuic, and Steve Woodworth. By pulling their weight in the department, they have left me more time for research, and I count them all as valued friends. It is the national pastime of professors to grouse about college administrators, but over the years that I've worked on this book, I have been blessed to have four excellent department chairs—Ken Stevens, Peter Worthing, Jodi Campbell, and Bill Meier—and two outstanding deans—Mary Volcansek and Andy Schoolmaster—who made the academic ship sail smoothly. Provost Nowell Donovan and Chancellor Victor Boschini have set the standard for how to run a university; rather than telling faculty what they can't do, they consistently have asked, "How can we help?" and then left us alone to concentrate on our work. This is a rare thing in modern universities, and it is appreciated. Outside the History Department, Scott Williams and Juan Carlos Sola-Corbacho helped me with translations from German- and Spanish-language sources, and Robyn Reid of the Mary Couts Burnett Library worked magic in marshaling resources that have facilitated my research. Special thanks go to Mary Ralph Lowe, whose generous endowment of the Erma and Ralph Lowe Chair in Texas History made it possible for me to be at TCU.

I am also exceedingly fortunate to be a part of an unusually close-knit community of scholars in the Dallas–Fort Worth Metroplex. Several times over the years the Dallas Area Society of Historians (DASH) allowed me to present portions of my work at our monthly meetings, and I am a better historian for it. I also owe a special thanks to Keith Volanto, who tutored me on twentieth-century farm policy and the New Deal, and to Paul J. Sugg, who explained the mysteries of the Texas legislative process on many occasions. Alexis McCrossen, Stephen Duffy, and Ty Cashion read portions of the manuscript, making those parts stronger. The critiques of Ben Johnson, Ed Linenthal, and Matt Garcia all made major contributions to the *Journal of American History* article that formed the basis for Chapter 9. Lara Heimert, formerly of Yale University Press, believed in this project at its inception, and she and Chuck Grench, Kent Calder, Andrew Davidson, and Elizabeth Sherburn Demers offered valuable advice in the late stages of the project. My editor at Yale, Adina Popescu Berk, has been wonderfully supportive and accommodating of a miscreant author who asked far more of her and of the press than I had any right to ask.

A number of descendants of Texas Populists have shared information, documents, and photos of their ancestors. Those descendants (and their ancestors) include: Susan Orton (Charles H. Jenkins), Bobby Cain (Robert and Andrew Cain), Mike Dawes (S. O. Daws), Wesley Boyd and Mark Richardson (Joe Eagle), Wiley Clarkson (A. C. Isaacs), James Bellamy (C. A. McMeans), John Meitzen (E. O. Meitzen), Frank Cox and Bentley Kerfoot (Henry L. Bentley), George Booker (Sam Ely Johnson), Billie Ritter Ford (Van Buren Ritter), Debra Munn (Bettie Munn Gay), and the late Charles W. Macune Jr. (C. W. Macune). I am grateful to all of them.

We university-based historians often rely on the generosity and valuable work of local historians outside of academe, and I am no exception. Gary Borders of Lufkin, Judy Falls of Cooper, Ruth Karbach of Fort Worth, Mike Hazel of Dallas, and Jay Moore of Abilene all provided materials and knowledge from their corners of Texas; they deserve more thanks than just this acknowledgment. The same is true for the many librarians and archivists who have assisted me over the years, but one of them, Donaly Brice, now retired from the Texas State Library and Archives, deserves special thanks for being my go-to source at that great institution. The folks at the University of North Texas's Portal to Texas History not only constructed the single most valuable source for my research and made it available online for free, but also went beyond the call of duty in several instances and approved the digitization of several newspapers at my request, including three rare Populist papers: the *Southern Mercury,* the *McKinney Democrat,* and the *Dublin Progress.* If that were not enough, they also awarded me a generous fellowship that facilitated my research in its final stages. Likewise, in digitizing the *Handbook of Texas,* the Texas State Historical Association provided me with a treasure trove of information, as evidenced by the many dozens of *Handbook* citations found in the book. The staff at the Legislative Reference Library have done remarkable work in making biographical information on state legislators and legislative journals available online.

If it takes a village to raise a child, it takes something like that to raise a historian. For their mentorship during the formative part of my career, I thank

Dale T. Knobel, Mike Campbell, Jim Olson, and Tom Camfield. I regret that Bob Calvert and David Weber are no longer here for me to thank, but they are always with me in spirit. A special word of thanks goes to Walter L. Buenger, my mentor and friend for thirty-five years, whose own work has cast a long shadow, not just over my work but over the entire enterprise of Texas history. Every state should be so lucky to have a Walter Buenger guiding its historical fortunes.

Several good friends didn't contribute to the book itself, but they helped keep me sane during the long process of research and writing. My TCU racquetball partners Scott Williams, J. Todd Moye, David Ferrell, Kenton Watt, and Max Krochmal provided competition, camaraderie, and bruises on the weekdays, and the long-suffering Tokalon tennis crew—F. Todd Smith, Guy Chet, Chris Morris, Aaron Navarro, Ben Johnson, Sam Haynes, Lisa Siraganian, Jill Montgomery, Neilesh Bose, Geoff Wawro, and Ben Wright—tolerated my wretched forehand on the weekends.

My family has been a source of love and support, and I want to thank them all. My parents, Jimmie and Mary Lynn Cantrell, have always believed in me, even when I gave them little reason to do so. My sons, Calvin and Nolan Cantrell, grew from toddlers to grown men during the long gestation of this book, and they are my proudest accomplishments. Brenda Cantrell shouldered the burdens of parenthood when I was off doing battle with Populists. Technically, Mike Connor may be my brother-in-law, but he is really the brother I never had, and I am grateful for him. It will be a lasting regret that my remarkable sister, Diana Connor, did not live to see this book completed, but she was always my biggest fan. I thank her in absentia.

During the writing of this book, I had the pleasure of acquiring two terrific stepchildren, Farley Morris and Emily Morris, whose presence in my life has enriched it immeasurably. My greatest debt of gratitude, however, goes to their mother, Stephanie Cole. A far abler historian than me, over the years she has willingly listened to never-ending tales of obscure Texas Populists, accompanied me on research trips, shared her encyclopedic knowledge of women's history, and, in the final stages of the book, read the entire manuscript and expertly critiqued it. *The People's Revolt* is not her style of history, and there is much in it that she would have done differently, but whatever merits it may possess owe much to her contributions. It is with love, gratitude, and admiration that I dedicate this book to her.

THE PEOPLE'S REVOLT

Introduction • On Liberalism and Populism

I have never been frightened by that scarecrow, strong government.
I believe in a government strong enough to protect the lives,
liberty and property of its citizens.
A government that cannot do this is useless, burdensome
and unworthy of support.
—Populist Charles H. Jenkins, 1894

One way of understanding the continuity of liberal history . . . is to see
liberalism as a perennial protest against all forms of absolute authority.
—Alan Ryan, *The Making of Modern Liberalism*

In September 2009, eight months into his presidency, Barack Obama addressed a joint session of Congress. The subject was the need for universal
health care, and the purpose was to explain the administration's plan, which
was still in the process of being drafted. The president understood that many
Americans opposed any plan for federally mandated health care, both on fiscal grounds and, perhaps more ominously for the administration, on ideological grounds. Any new law as sweeping as the one taking shape would run
afoul of conservatives' well-known opposition to "big government." In making his case to the American people, then, Obama outlined what he believed
to be essential elements of "the American character": "our ability to stand in
other people's shoes; a recognition that we are all in this together, and when
fortune turns against one of us, others are there to lend a helping hand; a
belief that in this country, hard work and responsibility should be rewarded

by some measure of security and fair play; and an acknowledgment that sometimes government has to step in to help deliver on that promise." In support of this contention, he offered a history lesson. He reminded his listeners that in 1935, when the Great Depression had swept away the savings of millions and impoverished more than half of the nation's elderly people, Congress enacted Social Security, despite the howls of critics that it "would lead to socialism." Likewise, he noted, in 1965, when opponents argued that Medicare "represented a government takeover of health care," Congress "did not back down." "This," Obama declared, "has always been the history of our progress."[1]

The president, who had studied history and political theory in college, also sought to explain the philosophical underpinnings of his beliefs in the role of government. Acknowledging that "our predecessors understood that government could not, and should not, solve every problem," he admitted "that there are instances when the gains in security from government action are not worth the added constraints on our freedom." But he likewise contended "that the danger of too much government is matched by the perils of too little; that without the leavening hand of wise policy, markets can crash, monopolies can stifle competition, the vulnerable can be exploited." Obama portrayed this pragmatic balancing of the need for curbs on both government power and corporate power as a fundamental part of the nation's political tradition and the key to America's greatness. If enough of his fellow Americans would share this vision, he promised, "we can do great things. . . . That is our calling. That is our character."[2]

The president used the word "liberalism" only once in his speech, and that was in a reference to the recently deceased Sen. Ted Kennedy. Like most twenty-first-century liberals, Obama was more likely to use the word "progressive" to describe his brand of politics. But whatever label he chose to use, in his call for universal health care made possible by the federal government, Obama was urging Americans to embrace the dominant political philosophy of the past eighty years; his speech was a classic expression of American liberalism.

Eight years later, Obama's successor, Donald Trump, embarked on a crusade to overturn the health-care law that was arguably the Obama administration's crowning achievement. Trump's initial effort to repeal "Obamacare" failed, but within the first two years of his presidency he mounted assaults on virtually every cause that his predecessor had championed: liberal immigration laws, environmental policy, financial regulation, gay rights, gun control, and many others. By most policy measures, Trump, who was elected on the Republican ticket, should have been considered a conservative, and indeed, the act that most endeared him to conservatives in the early part of his presidency was his appointment of conservatives Neil Gorsuch and Brett Kavanaugh to the US Supreme Court. But the label affixed to Trump was rarely "conservative"; instead, to friend and foe alike, the controversial Republican president was branded a "populist."

Clearly, political labels are strange and malleable things. The "progressive" label that most American liberals embrace today first rose to prominence in the early twentieth century, when it was applied to reformers from both major parties, most famously Republican Theodore Roosevelt and Democrat Woodrow Wilson. The "populist" label predates it by a few years, hearkening back to the People's Party of the 1890s, whose members were called Populists. This book is a history of that party (and the movement it represented) in the state of Texas, and as I set out to tell the story of the original Populists, readers might reasonably assume that I will be relating the history of the political antecedents of Trump and others who today have inherited that label. But like most things in political history, appearances can be deceiving, and logic does not necessarily hold. So while I will indeed address the question of how the "populist" label survived into our own time, this book is not about Donald Trump's political forebears. Rather, it is the story of the men and women who pioneered the ideas that Barack Obama so clearly enunciated in that 2009 health-care speech; it is, as the book's subtitle suggests, a history of the origins of modern American liberalism.

∼

It is no accident that liberals today rarely use the word for the ideology Obama was espousing in his 2009 speech, because liberalism has gotten something of a bad name in the decades since 1980. Conservatives, arguing that liberalism was sending the country down the road to socialism or worse, seized the rhetorical high ground in the liberal-versus-conservative debates, at least since Ronald Reagan declared that "government is not the solution to our problem; government is the problem." Hence liberals' usual self-identification today as "progressives." Conversely, many on the socialist left spurn the term because they are convinced that liberalism's acceptance of capitalism renders it incapable of addressing capitalism's most intractable problems. In socialists' view, conservatives have bought off liberals with the modest comforts of the welfare state, shipwrecking the "socialist ideal" of true equality, as the German social scientist Werner Sombart famously put it, on shoals of "roast beef and apple pie."[3]

So successful have been the assaults on liberalism from both the right and the left that many observers—and in this number I would include many political historians—have come to the conclusion that modern American liberalism is not really a coherent political philosophy at all. Political labels such as "liberal" or "conservative" are always problematic, because they reduce complex, multifaceted, and often contested ideas to a word or two. In the case of liberalism, definition has been particularly difficult because there have been two distinct historical incarnations of the term, often going by the names "classical" and "modern" liberalism. At the risk of oversimplifying a complex history, a brief summary of the history of these two liberalisms is in order.

Classical liberalism, sometimes called "constitutional liberalism," first emerged in the seventeenth century, an outgrowth of the Enlightenment. No two historians would agree on a settled list of its leading theorists, but many would include John Locke, Adam Smith, Montesquieu, Thomas Paine, James Madison, Alexis de Tocqueville, and Friedrich von Hayek. Its core principles include the rule of law, limited government, separation of powers, private property rights, freedom of contract, religious toleration, freedom of conscience and expression, and personal responsibility for one's actions. In these respects it can be regarded as "the common heritage" of today's liberals and conservatives alike. Classical liberalism, it should be noted, is not necessarily synonymous with democracy, although it did provide for a necessary precondition, the institution of representative assemblies as a means of securing the consent of the governed. In America, classical liberalism mixed with Protestant precepts and the republican ideals coming out of the English Whig tradition to shape the political ideology of the Revolutionary and Constitutional eras. This same potent (if messy) brew, spurred by the particular economic trajectory of the nation in the early nineteenth century, eventually led to the incorporation of political democracy into the greater liberal project. As one recent historian of liberalism has noted, "Liberalism lays out the feast, democracy draws up the guest list."[4]

The twentieth century witnessed the emergence of "modern" liberalism, which took the elements of classical liberalism and modified them to suit the changing circumstances of the nation, particularly the rise of industrial capitalism and the modern corporation. The hallmarks of modern liberalism include not just the rule of law, respect for the rights of the individual, and the other elements of classical liberalism, but also additional aspirations that fall under the heading of freedom. Scholars identify two types of freedom that modern liberalism seeks to secure. On one hand, *negative* freedoms seek to

free people *from* fear and want; social insurance programs such as Social Security, Medicare, unemployment insurance, and a minimum wage exemplify
policies designed secure these negative freedoms. *Positive* freedoms, on the
other hand, seek to help individuals achieve their full potential—public education and the guarantee of civil rights are two of the most prominent examples. In practice, the relationship between positive and negative freedoms is
symbiotic, as each category necessitates, and is necessitated by, the other. Be
that as it may, the expansion of governmental power to secure these freedoms
was never an end unto itself but rather a pragmatic means, resorted to when
the growth of unchecked corporate power in the late nineteenth century threatened individual freedom in new and disturbing ways.[5]

The roots of modern liberalism have proven harder to trace than those of
classical liberalism. Some historians point to the writings of the nineteenth-
century English political economist and philosopher John Stuart Mill as the
intellectual starting point of modern liberalism. It would probably be more accurate to say that Mill is a key transitional figure in its development. As historian James Kloppenberg affirms, Mill's iconic treatise *On Liberty* "stands
among the most ringing proclamations" of classical liberalism's belief that government must be restrained to protect the rights of individuals. Yet, as Mill
scholar Alan Ryan also contends, Mill's work "exemplified" modern liberalism "with its appeal to 'man as a progressive being' and its romantic appeal to
an individuality that should be allowed to develop itself in all its 'manifold diversity.'" Whether one views Mill as the last classical liberal, the first modern
liberal, or something in between, it is a stretch to believe that any one English
intellectual—especially one as skeptical of democracy as Mill—could have
single-handedly crafted a new version of liberalism destined to become the
dominant political philosophy of the Western world in the twentieth century.
With all due credit to Mill, the roots of modern liberalism must lie elsewhere.[6]

Searching for those roots in actual political movements, as opposed to individual thinkers, seems more promising. It is true that some precursors of modern liberalism can be found in the Federalists of the 1790s, the Whigs of the
1830s and 1840s, and Lincoln's Republicans in the 1850s and 1860s, all of whom
departed from the strict laissez-faire of classical liberalism and were willing in
some very limited and specific ways to use the power of government to assist
economic development. Even so, in the late nineteenth century, America remained committed to laissez-faire far more than other Western societies did,
and there were few indications of a willingness to limit the power of corporations, embrace social insurance programs, or protect the rights of minorities.[7]

Scholars are more willing to identify the Progressive Era of the early twentieth century as the starting place for modern liberalism. In supporting antitrust legislation, regulating big business, and creating agencies such as the Federal Reserve, the Department of Labor, and the Federal Trade Commission, progressives for the first time decisively rejected the laissez-faire gospel of classical liberalism. But in the battle of ideas *within* the progressive movement, it is also true that those who would have gone farther toward embracing a fuller range of the tenets of modern liberalism—Robert La Follette comes to mind—never gained the prominence of more moderate progressives like Theodore Roosevelt and Woodrow Wilson. And in its refusal to protect civil rights for minorities and civil liberties for dissenters, its state-enforced moralism on issues such as alcohol and sexual heterodoxy, and its stubborn resistance to any sort of social safety net for the poor, progressivism fell far short of embracing many of the major tenets of modern liberalism. Even the New Deal evoked sharp criticism from many old progressives who survived into the 1930s, as they balked at its collectivist impulses.[8]

It was only after World War I that some former progressives in America began to adopt the label "liberal," in part because they identified with the British Liberal Party of that era and possibly to remind people of American progressives' many continuing political blind spots. The liberalism of this period found its clearest intellectual expression in the works of John Dewey, the psychologist, philosopher, and educational reformer. Dewey was perhaps the first to make the explicit connection between liberalism and democracy, arguing that the goals of liberalism could never be attained merely by political democracy in the narrow sense of universal suffrage; rather, his liberalism called for extending the principles of democracy from the strictly political realm to the family, the workplace, and society in general, using educational and other institutions to knit people into a cohesive national community. Although Dewey never truly incorporated his ideas into a comprehensive philosophy of liberalism, his ideas represented an important elaboration of the evolving concept of modern liberalism in the twentieth century.[9]

The most important expression of modern liberalism in American public policy, though, came in the 1930s, more or less by accident. To meet the economic emergency of the Great Depression and the political threat that desperate Americans might turn to socialism or fascism, Franklin D. Roosevelt embarked on the New Deal. For the first time, the federal government melded the regulatory impulses of progressivism with the negative and positive definitions of freedom that would become hallmarks of modern liberalism. New

Deal liberals took the progressives' anti–laissez-faire economic principles and extended them even further to meet the crisis of a collapsing economy, creating, for the first time in any meaningful way, large-scale programs that secured collective economic rights. The result was a robust organized labor movement, social security, a safety net for farmers, and many other programs. The New Deal also departed from progressive reform, as sociologist Paul Starr points out, by curbing the moralism of the progressives by ending Prohibition, and FDR appointed Supreme Court judges who "confirmed the movement toward strong protections of free speech and a liberalized culture." Although the New Deal failed to expand civil rights for minorities in very many significant ways—indeed, there would have been no New Deal without the devil's pact that FDR made with the segregationist southern wing of his party—the political forces that it set in motion, urged on by grassroots activists, inadvertently led to the first meaningful black civil rights actions under Truman and Eisenhower, and eventually, to even more sweeping reforms under the rubric of LBJ's Great Society.[10]

By the 1970s modern liberalism had found its principal theorist in the person of John Rawls, whose magisterial *A Theory of Justice* (1971) presented a philosophical argument that governments have a moral and ethical obligation not only to operate as democratically as possible but also to promote the economic opportunities and safeguard the civil rights of its most disadvantaged citizens. Rawls's work has inspired much criticism and praise in the decades since its publication, but it went far to elevate modern liberalism to the status of a formal political philosophy. As Alan Ryan perceptively notes, Rawls's achievement lay in showing that "liberalism is not a patched-up compromise between conservatism and socialism, but a distinctive creed with solid foundations."[11]

Perhaps unsurprisingly, the political philosophers and theorists of liberalism and the intellectual historians who write about them have paid little attention to the Populist movement of the 1890s as a potential source of modern liberalism. I say unsurprisingly because as a grassroots farmer-labor movement with its origins in the rural South and Midwest, Populism seems an unlikely source for original or innovative political thought. It had no John Stuart Mill, no John Dewey, no John Rawls. The brevity of its existence and its failure actually to govern at the national level or even in many locales have made it easy to overlook. Of scholars who write about the broad history of American political economy without paying much attention to Populism, Joyce Appleby seems typical. In her sweeping history of capitalism, *The Relentless Revolution,* discussing how Americans first "realize[d] the need for a government equipped to monitor and curtail the great industrial enterprises," she mentions Populism only in passing: "Populists, as the radicals were called, and the more cerebral Progressives, who followed in their reform path . . . finally succeeded in alerting the public to the dangers of unchecked economic power." If the progressives were but the pale progenitors of modern liberalism, then at the hands of scholars like Appleby, the Populists were merely their less "cerebral" forerunners, barely meriting notice.[12]

Historians of Populism have similarly failed to place the movement in the context of the history of liberalism, or certainly of *modern* liberalism. This seems strange. Although many twentieth-century historians have often found much to admire in Populism (many of them are of a liberal bent personally), they have displayed an almost unnatural aversion to even considering the possibility that Populists might have pioneered many of the tenets of the modern liberal creed. The first major academic study of Populism, John D. Hicks's *The Populist Revolt,* appeared in 1931 and thus was written just as the nation was sliding into depression. With the liberalism of the New Deal still ahead, Hicks identified Populism with progressivism, portraying it as interest-group politics mounted in response to the depression of the 1890s. A few years later, C. Vann Woodward, writing about Populist hero Tom Watson, similarly situated southern Populism in the progressive tradition, while anticipating future historians who would see race as the Achilles heel of liberalism in the South.[13]

Constrained as they were by their temporal proximity to the Populist era and by the all-too-real Depression in which they were living, progressives like Hicks and Woodward can be excused for whatever interpretive limitations their work may have displayed. The next major interpreter of Populism, Richard Hofstadter, was likewise affected by the times in which he lived and wrote. In his influential *The Age of Reform* (1955), Hofstadter denied the progressive impulses that Hicks and Woodward had detected in Populism and instead depicted Populists as naive, anxiety-ridden provincials who, fearing they were being left behind by the new industrial order, indulged in conspiracy theories that led them down the paths of nativism, anti-Semitism, and anti-intellectualism. Influenced by the rise of totalitarian governments in Europe and by the paranoia of the McCarthy era, Hofstadter and like-minded scholars of the Cold War era projected their own concerns onto the Populists, seeing, as had Hicks and Woodward in the 1930s, reflections of their own times in the politics of the 1890s.[14]

Hofstadter's influence was such that the next generation of Populist scholars spent much of its energy refuting his specific charges of narrow-
mindedness, provincialism, and even paranoia in the third-party movement.
By the end of the 1960s Hofstadter's interpretation lay in tatters, but new in-
terpretations were slow in arriving. It took the rise of the New Left—inspired
by the civil rights movement, the trauma of Vietnam, and the general cultural
ferment of the 1960s—to produce new understandings of Populism. Again,
historians found what they hoped to find, and Populism in this latest guise
once more became a sort of Rorschach test for enterprising historians. Norman Pollack, for one, turned Hofstadter's interpretation on its head, finding
that Populists not only constructed a radical critique of industrial America but
also developed a class consciousness akin to Marxian socialism. But the most
original account of Populism to come from the New Left tradition was Lawrence Goodwyn's *Democratic Promise* (1976), which became the dominant interpretation for the ensuing generation. In Goodwyn's telling of the story, the
Southern Farmers' Alliance developed a "movement culture" that envisioned
a "cooperative commonwealth," a communitarian or collectivist alternative to
industrial capitalism. When its cooperative efforts failed, the Alliance entered
politics, creating the People's, or Populist, Party. Once headed down the path
of third-party action, the Populists made the centerpiece of their platform the
innovative Subtreasury Plan, an ambitious scheme in which the federal government would build a national network of warehouses where farmers could
deposit their crops and receive low-interest government loans, thus taking the
country off the gold standard, democratizing credit, and effectively subsidiz-
ing agriculture. In Goodwyn's telling of the story, however, the forces of capitalist hegemony defeated the "democratic promise" of Populism by backing a
liberal "shadow movement" based on the illusory promise that silver coinage
would solve the nation's problems. The shadow movement co-opted true Populism, and America lost its last real opportunity for an alternative other than
a watered-down, bourgeois liberalism.[15]

For New Left scholars such as Goodwyn, liberalism was as much an enemy
as conservatism—maybe even more so, since at least conservatives had the
courage of their convictions. One of the interesting features of Goodwyn's account is that the epicenter of his tragic morality tale was Texas, where the
Farmers' Alliance originated and where "Middle-of-the Road" Populists—those
true believers who were schooled in the movement culture of the Alliance—
resisted the lure of the silver "shadow movement" and remained faithful to
true Populism till the bitter end. But while Goodwyn focused a great deal of

his attention on the Alliance antecedents of Populism in Texas, his account largely ignored the actual history of the People's Party in Texas after its founding in 1891. This book aims to remedy that shortcoming.

Populist historiography seemed to have arrived in something of a cul-de-sac after Goodwyn's work. Numerous state studies and two well-crafted syntheses refined or took issue with elements of Goodwyn's interpretation without offering a comprehensive interpretive replacement for it. By the end of the twentieth century, however, scholars were beginning to reexamine Goodwyn's central thesis that when Populism died, so did America's last best hope for meaningful reform. Elizabeth Sanders's *The Roots of Reform* (1999) contended that the agrarian movements of the late nineteenth century, of which Populism was the best known, played a central role in the evolution of the national state as it emerged at the end of the Progressive Era. Populism itself, however, is not the main focus of Sanders's book, although I find much to commend in her interpretation, which I will revisit in this book's Conclusion. Likewise, in Connie Lester's innovative study of Tennessee, *Up from the Mudsills of Hell* (2006), Populists play an important role in state-level progressive agricultural programs in the Progressive Era. Both of these books pointed the way toward a reexamination of the question of tradition versus modernity in Populism.[16]

That theme occupies a central place in the first general reassessment of Populism since Goodwyn, Charles Postel's *The Populist Vision* (2007). A nuanced and sophisticated book that defies easy summary, it argues that Populists were modernizers who not only believed in progress and accepted large-scale enterprise and bureaucratic organization but also sought to use modern "business principles" to push back against corporate power. Instead of seeing the Alliance cooperative movement as a phenomenon outside the mainstream of American capitalist development, Postel views the cooperatives as a sort of "farmer's trust," designed to beat the industrial trusts at their own game. Among his conclusions is the assertion that with their "impulse toward Progressive Era state building," as well as in their support for racial segregation, "the callous-handed Populist shared much ideological ground with the university-groomed Progressive of the next generation."[17]

I agree with much of what Postel has to say, particularly his emphasis on Populist modernity. However, Postel, like Goodwyn before him, ends up being far less interested in the politics of the People's Party than in the organizational and economic activities of the Farmers' Alliance. This book, by contrast, is primarily a study of Populist politics from the founding of the party in 1891 to its dissolution in the years after 1896, with an extended Conclusion that follows Populists and their ideas well into the twentieth century. The tendency to characterize the Alliance and other farmer-labor organizations as somehow the essence of Populism, while treating the actual Populist political party as almost an afterthought—or, as Goodwyn would have it, an enterprise that ultimately betrayed Populist principles—strikes me as a bit odd. Although I analyze elections, political strategy, party structure, and other elements that comprise any institutional history of a political party, I am far more interested in the ideas that motivated the men and women who supported the Texas People's Party, what they believed about the nature of society and government, and how those beliefs shaped their politics. I am also very interested in the Populists themselves: what sort of people they were, where their political ideas came from, why they were attracted to third-party politics, and how they behaved at moments of trial and adversity. One thing Goodwyn was right about was the idea that Populism became a social movement with its own "movement culture," and it is difficult to explain that culture without becoming acquainted with a broad cross-section of its adherents. Readers will meet many real Populists in the coming pages.

As the title indicates, this is a study of the People's Party in one state, Texas, although I hope that it proves instructive on Populism as a whole. There are good reasons, I think, for focusing on the Lone Star State. Texas was the birthplace of the Farmers' Alliance, and to the extent that the Alliance produced the People's Party, the state can be said to be the birthplace of Populism. In the party's heyday, Texas was home to more Populists than any other state; almost 240,000 Texans cast Populist ballots in 1896. As a state that straddles the divide between the South and the West, Texas partook of the political culture of both sections, although its southern heritage remained the dominant strain. But more so than most of the old Confederacy, the state by the 1890s featured a complex ethnic diversity that included not just the traditional southern dyad of blacks and native-born whites but also sizable numbers of ethnic Mexicans in South Texas, Germans in the central Texas Hill Country, and a crazy quilt of other ethnic groups scattered throughout the countryside.[18]

The state was also increasingly diverse economically. Although agriculture remained the backbone of the economy in the 1890s, cities and industry had begun to grow, spurred on by the completion of modern rail and telegraph networks. The state's population nearly quadrupled in the last three decades of the century. None of this is to say that Texas was a microcosm of the nation, but it was a far cry from the frontier that it had been a generation earlier, and its politics likewise diverged in significant ways from those of Louisiana, Alabama, and South Carolina. Labor unions organized in Galveston, woman suffragists demonstrated in Austin, and the Freethinkers' Society of Dallas met monthly to debate the existence of God and other heretical propositions. Texans might be fond of touting their state's heroic, individualistic, frontier past—a mythic story of the Alamo, the Texas Rangers, the Indian wars, and the cattle drives—but the reality for most Texans by the 1890s was that they lived in a rapidly modernizing society, with all of the challenges and insecurities that come with it. Populism was their political response to those challenges and insecurities.[19]

~

Which brings us back to the central question of this book: What marks Populists in Texas (and elsewhere) as the progenitors of modern liberalism? Although I will explore this question in greater detail in the coming chapters, a few basic points should be made here to emphasize conceptions of the state and the relationship between the state and the individual. Classical liberalism saw its mission primarily as protecting the rights of the individual against encroachments of state power. Among these individual rights were the rights of Englishmen against the power of the Crown, a contest that produced Britain's Glorious Revolution and the American Revolution; the rights of citizens against the US central government, a conflict that created both the Constitution and especially the Bill of Rights; and the rights of both slaves and slaveholders against the constitutional structure of the proslavery nation-state, a struggle that brought on the Civil War. For most white antebellum Americans, "big government," to borrow a modern phrase, constituted the only genuine threat to personal liberty. In preindustrial America; widespread land ownership guaranteed a certain degree of control over one's economic fate. The scale of industry was still small enough that an ambitious apprentice or journeyman craftsman might reasonably expect someday to become the owner of his own shop. Little was needed from government except to guarantee basic individual rights and remain weak enough to avoid ruinous taxes, military conscription, or abuse at the hands of state-sanctioned monopolies like a Bank of the United States. The limited-government philosophies of Jefferson and Jackson seemed to embody this sort of liberalism, and it is little wonder that most Populists—at least at the inception of the People's Revolt—instinctively viewed them as their political patron saints.[20]

But even as Populists held up Jefferson and Jackson as the avatars of American democracy, they came to realize that government was not the only tyranny that the common person need fear. With the rise of the large-scale modern corporation in the years after the Civil War, private economic interests arose as a new threat to individual rights. What Populists came to realize in the late nineteenth century—indeed, their great genius and their principal contribution to the history of American political thought—is that modern forms of capitalist enterprise rendered the classical liberal model obsolete. First the great railroads, then mammoth pools and trusts in everything from steel, oil, and the telegraph to sugar, tobacco, jute, and barbed wire, presented new forms of concentrated power that rivaled any threat that the arbitrary authority of King George III might have ever posed to liberty. As millions became wage laborers or tenant farmers, the classically liberal protections of free speech, freedom of religion, and the other individual freedoms guaranteed by the Bill of Rights seemed wholly inadequate. As abstract propositions, limited government and low taxes still seemed desirable, as Jefferson and Jackson had preached, but increasingly these traditional safeguards of liberty seemed to disproportionately benefit the captains of big business who could run roughshod over workers and consumers and through their power corruptly manipulate the government to their own benefit. Jefferson and Jackson notwithstanding, a liberalism that protected citizens against *government* tyranny but not against *economic* tyranny seemed like thin gruel indeed to a starving man or woman.[21]

Hicks and other progressive historians identified hard times as the impetus behind Populism, and their point is valid as far as it goes. It is no accident that the high point of Populism coincided with the bottoming out, in the mid-1890s, of the worst depression in American history up to that time. Hard times were a necessary precondition for sparking the Populist revolt, but that alone was not enough. It took a particular historical context to bring together the sufficient ingredients. That context found expression in places like Kansas and North Carolina and in farming regions throughout the South, the Great Plains, and the Rocky Mountain West. It also found expression among the ranks of the new industrial working class. And it particularly manifested itself on the hardscrabble plains of west-central Texas. In such places, working Americans first sought redress through large-scale self-help organizations—trade unions like the Knights of Labor and agricultural groups like the Farmers' Alliance. The turn to self-help in the face of economic hardship should come as no surprise; the classically liberal aversion to an activist government was part of the received political culture of the day. It was only when self-help proved inadequate, when the unions were busted and the Alliance cooperatives went broke, that people came to realize that the laissez-faire liberalism of their fathers and grandfathers, of Jefferson and Jackson, was inadequate to the new economic order of Gilded-Age America.

That realization manifested itself in a number of ways. For industrial workers, starvation wages, long hours, and inhumane working conditions drove home the need to have the state level the playing field by guaranteeing collective bargaining rights and regulating working hours and conditions. For farmers, collapsing crop prices and the exorbitant cost of land, credit, transportation, supplies, and processing convinced them that the government must intervene to curb the abuses of monopolized industry. When the political system itself seemed to have fallen under the sway of these powerful economic interests, Populists added political reforms to their lists of demands.

Attention to the specific reforms that the Populists devised has done more to obfuscate the fundamental meaning of their movement than to reveal it. Small oceans of ink have been spilled, in the Populist era and among latter-day historians, arguing the relative merits of the Subtreasury Plan, fiat money, government ownership of the railroads, the graduated income tax, and dozens of other policy positions. Some of these policies, as we shall see, were good ideas; others were shortsighted or simplistic. Policy is important and will be dealt with in some detail in the coming pages, but more important is what the Populists' reforms show us about their philosophy of government, or more specially, what those reforms reveal about the Populists' conception of the relationship between the individual and the state. Conservatives had been taught to fear the tyranny of a powerful government, and they viewed power as a sort of zero-sum game: the more state power, the less personal freedom, and vice versa. Populists developed a more sophisticated, more modern understanding of power. Responding to their lived experiences in the new capitalist order, they came to realize that a strong state was not the only potential threat to liberty. Monopoly power, wielded by corporate interests, was at least as dangerous.

That the old laissez-faire liberalism of the past no longer suited modern America became a major theme of Populist rhetoric. As early as 1889, Texas Alliance leader and future Populist congressional candidate Evan Jones of Erath County explained that the government of the Founders "was a simple republic, in which the sovereign will of the people was supreme. . . . But time and circumstances have changed it, so that even Washington and Jefferson would scarcely recognize it." That same year, Allianceman T. M. Smith of Blooming Grove elaborated on Jones's thesis, noting that "the rapid concentration of wealth" was a "process, begun during the late war," and this process had been "surely and systematically carried out till little is left to the producers of the country, but to submit to the dictation of capital." In 1894, at the height of the Populist revolt in Texas, the state party chairman, H. S. P. "Stump" Ashby, offered a more technical explanation of how things had changed. "But with the progress of invention," he noted, "with machinery destroying the trades and transferring labor to congested centers, with the locomotive displacing the oxcart and the electric telegraphy destroying distance in communication, collusion had become the life of trade and in fact of all political economy. Things had so changed that the principles of government which were best adapted a century ago could not possibly be suitable to-day."[22]

The notion that large-scale capitalist enterprise could threaten liberty every bit as much as a tyrannical government could was an idea that met with great resistance. When conservative Democrat George W. Clark campaigned for governor in 1892 on the libertarian slogan "Turn Texas Loose," Populist and Knights of Labor member James Baker Cone charged that what Clark really wanted to do was "to turn the vampires loose upon Texas, and turn them loose unrestricted!" According to Cone, when Clark invited "'capitalists everywhere to come in and help us develop the resources of this great state!' He would just as well have added, 'and make slaves of your children'; for everybody who has been watching the drift of things in this country for the past thirty years, knows that this is just what this policy has been."[23]

According to Populists like Cone, the proper response to the newfound power of corporations was for the people to exert a countervailing power. With private self-help having failed, the way to exert that countervailing power was through the one institution the people controlled in a democracy: the government. It was the act of calling for state power to offset the power of big business and special interests that marked the Populists as political innovators. Campaigning for Congress in 1894, Populist Charles Jenkins explained, "I have never been frightened by that scarecrow, strong government. I believe in a government strong enough to protect the lives, liberty and property of its citizens. A government that cannot do this is useless, burdensome and unworthy of support." Viewed this way, Populist liberals actually shared more in common with conservatives than either group would admit. Both held the fundamental ideological position that individual liberty must be protected from the threats posed by concentrated power. Where they differed was in their estimation of what forms of concentrated power posed such threats. Where conservatives saw the threat only in big government, Populists saw it in both big government *and* in big business. As a leading scholar of liberalism, Alan Ryan, explains, "One way of understanding the continuity of liberal history . . . is to

see liberalism as a perennial protest against all forms of absolute authority."
Another recent student of liberalism, Edmund Fawcett, elaborates on this idea:
"Looked at from the point of view of citizens, liberalism is a practice of politics for people who will not be bossed about or pushed around by superior
power, whether the power of the state, the power of wealth or the power of society. Looked at from the point of view of government, liberalism is a practical
response by state and law to the predicament of capitalist modernity."[24]

Explaining the divide between Populists and their opponents grows more
difficult when we turn from matters of political economy to the social realm.
One of the hallmarks of modern liberalism has been its dedication to the concept of equality of rights and opportunities for all individuals regardless of
race, ethnicity, gender, religion, or (more recently) sexual orientation. This dedication has set modern liberals apart both from their classically liberal forebears and, historically, from most conservatives. When the abovementioned
Charles Jenkins, a Brownwood, Texas, lawyer and prominent Populist, professed his belief "in a government strong enough to protect the lives, liberty
and property of its citizens," he was giving voice not only to the Populist or
liberal conception of government but also to a modernist notion of society,
wherein social relations are governed by constitutionally defined rights rather
than traditionally defined notions of patriarchy. Most Texas Populists were the
historical products of a hierarchical world in which the household was the basic unit of society. The male head of household governed, supported, and protected his subordinates—wife, children, slaves, and other dependents—who
recognized and deferred to his authority. But patriarchy had taken some hard
hits in the nineteenth century. In the Jacksonian era, political rights for common white men had diluted the authority of traditional elites. Emancipation
had removed African Americans from the authority of masters. A few daring
voices were now calling for greater rights for women. Challenges to religious
orthodoxy were more common and more open. The Populist revolt came at a
time of heightened concern over the nation's, and society's, direction.[25]

Texas Populists grappled mightily with these issues. On the racial front, the
party extended the hand of political alliance, if not full brotherhood, to African Americans and Mexican Americans. The People's Party needed black and
brown votes, a fact that opens it to charges of opportunism. Yet, in their calls
for interracial cooperation and in the actual policy positions they took, many
white Populist leaders went well beyond what might reasonably have been expected if their outreach had been purely pragmatic. Some white Populist

sheriffs heroically protected the lives and property of black citizens in their counties. Whites placed African Americans in leadership positions in the party, including the state executive committee. Populist state legislators fought bills that would extend racial segregation in public accommodations and disfranchise black voters, while championing bills that increased funding for African American schools and placed those schools under the control of black trustees. No white Populist would have ever measured up to twenty-first-century liberal standards, and many shared thoroughly in the standard prejudices of their time and place. But taken as a whole, the distinctions between Populists and Democrats were both qualitative and quantitative when it came to race.

Much the same holds true for the Populist position on women and gender. Most Populists were neither radicals nor revolutionaries, and few were equipped to analyze the social bases of patriarchy, much less challenge them directly. Yet, as in the case with race, Populists displayed more than just glimmerings of what we would recognize as a more modern position on the question of women's rights. Some Populist leaders, including the party's two-time standard-bearer Thomas L. Nugent, advocated female suffrage, and those who opposed it did so on pragmatic grounds rather than ideological ones, arguing that action on suffrage should wait until the People's Party was actually in power. Perhaps even more important, Populists consciously distanced themselves from many of their society's overtly patriarchal customs, seeking to redefine what passed as traditional "manly" behavior. Populists eschewed and condemned politically inspired violence, which was an all-too-common feature of late nineteenth-century Texas politics. They welcomed women's counsel and their active participation in party affairs, featuring their speeches at conventions and opening the editorial pages of their newspapers to female writers. In the area of policy, they sought to extend legal protections to women in state asylums and to underage female victims of sexual violence. In all these actions, they endured much ridicule and vituperation from conservatives. But in Texas Populists' reformulation of gender, the whole proved greater than just the sum of the parts. Without ever fully realizing or articulating it, they mounted an assault on the traditional southern code of honor, seeking to replace it with a more restrained and not exclusively male idea of dignity. In both their words and their deeds, then, Populists pointed the way to a conception of masculinity and femininity that clearly presaged the modern liberal position.

Racial, ethnic, and gender norms were often rooted in traditional religious beliefs, and it should come as no surprise that Populists defied many of those norms. This is not to say that Populists were not religious. Indeed, they earned a well-deserved reputation among their political opponents as being overly religious—except, of course, when they were being derided as infidels. Both charges, as it turns out, were true. The great majority of Texas Populists, reflecting the state as a whole, were evangelical Protestants. Their political beliefs were part and parcel of their religious beliefs. They found in Populism a modern-day expression of Jesus' identification with the poor and downtrodden, and they saw in the People's Party organization an expression of Christianity's emphasis on a community of believers. What set many of them apart from their political adversaries (who also professed to be Christians) was their critique of mainstream American Christian practice. Populists believed that materialism and capitalism had permeated and perverted the spirit of true Christianity, leading many of them to deride modern Christianity, with its arcane doctrines and elaborate church buildings and ceremonies, as "Churchianity." As a consequence, Populists were disproportionately represented in the ranks of the so-called restorationist denominations such as the Disciples of Christ and the Primitive Baptists, reform-minded denominations that sought to restore the ancient purity and simplicity of the first-century church. Populists, like modern liberals, believed in the strict separation of church and state, yet they also vehemently believed that religious principles should inform public discourse and that religious people, including ministers of the Gospel, had a responsibility to play an active part in politics. Several prominent Texas ministers ran for political office as Populists, and the party defended their decision to do so.[26]

Yet, the party also made ample room for those with less conventional religious beliefs, or with no religious beliefs at all. When they were not criticizing the People's Party for its religious fanaticism, Democrats were condemning it as the political home of religious nonconformists and even infidels. They had a point; spiritualists, Swedenborgians, atheists, and other "freethinkers" numbered among the party faithful, including several major party leaders. Religious Populists displayed a surprising tolerance for such religious heterodoxy, much as they tolerated the Single Taxers and avowed socialists on the economic-policy fringes of the party. Their commitment to toleration was such that they even ignored it when their two most prominent African American leaders, John B. Rayner and Melvin Wade, both publicly criticized organized religion. The People's Party was, to use another modern term, a "big tent," in social, religious, and even ideological terms—qualities that mark it as a forerunner of modern liberalism.

~

No book about Populism can ignore the term itself, and what that word has come to mean in modern political discourse. Donald Trump, of course, was not the first politician after the original Populists to be called a populist. In the century since the original Populists, the term has been applied variously to Huey Long, Joseph McCarthy, George Wallace, Ross Perot, Howard Dean, Sarah Palin, and Bernie Sanders, among many others. Outside the United States, observers have designated as a populist everyone from Benito Mussolini on the right to Hugo Chavez on the left. But no political development in a century has done more to effect a revival in the usage of the word than the election of Donald Trump. During the 2016 presidential race, a quick internet keyword search produced 4.6 million hits for the word "populism" and 6.9 million for "populist"; after Trump's first year in office, those numbers had risen to 23.8 and 25.6 million, respectively. If, as I shall argue, the original Populists pioneered the prototype of modern liberalism, how could the term be so flexible that it applies to the likes of George Wallace and Donald Trump? Historian Michael Kazin has offered the most useful definition of what we Populist scholars refer to as "small-p" populism, calling it not an ideology but a "persuasion," a style of political rhetoric. In the political language of populism, "speakers conceive of ordinary people as a noble assemblage not bounded narrowly by class, view their elite opponents as self-serving and undemocratic, and seek to mobilize the former against the latter." By Kazin's definition, the original American Populists of the 1890s were certainly small-p populists, although the same can be said for the common folk who elected Andrew Jackson. But Jackson's followers morphed into a permanent American political party, adopting the word "Democrat," an act which rendered that word unavailable, if not inappropriate, for any future movement that might claim to embody the will of the people against the elites. In contrast, because the Populist Party failed to become a permanent institutional entity, its name was available (and convenient) after the turn of the century as a label for any and all groups or movements that defined themselves, or were defined by others, as populist. Hence the confusing and dualistic nature of the term: because "populism" now denotes a *style* of politics, we can have populisms of the right and the left, from fascists to socialists and some positions in between. Whatever their actual politics, such politicians' direct appeals to "the people" and their disdain toward a corrupt establishment elite are the characteristics that mark them as populists.[27]

Because of these attributes, small-p populism in modern political parlance has often become a close synonym for demagoguery—that is, cynical appeals to the fears, prejudices, or other base instincts of the masses by unscrupulous, self-interested political leaders. All parties and movements produce the occasional demagogue, and a few Texas Populists of the 1890s *were* demagogues— James Harvey "Cyclone" Davis foremost among them. But most were not. Indeed, most Texas Populists thought of themselves as simply defenders of true democracy, champions of the common man against the "interests," and they prided themselves on appealing to reason and logic rather than fear or bigotry. They would be horrified to learn that the term "populist" has become associated with demagoguery and antidemocratic politics.

Ask most educated Americans today to name an actual large-*p* Populist and they are likely to say William Jennings Bryan. This, too, would drive the actual Populists of the 1890s a bit crazy, because Bryan, despite his embrace of some Populist policy positions, was never a Populist. The three-time Democratic Party nominee for president became associated with Populism because in 1896 the Populists, in an ill-fated move that destroyed their party, nominated the Democrat Bryan for president in a political maneuver known as fusion. Bryan never accepted the Populists' nomination, and he remained a lifelong Democrat. What most Americans remember about Bryan, however, is not his 1896 nomination by the Populists, his two subsequent runs for president, or his service as Woodrow Wilson's secretary of state. What they remember is the closing act of his long public career, his role in the infamous 1925 Scopes "Monkey" Trial. In that trial, Bryan squared off against the iconoclastic attorney Clarence Darrow, with Bryan supporting Tennessee's law banning the teaching of the theory of evolution and Darrow defending it. As audiences of the various stage and screen depictions of the trial know, Darrow placed Bryan himself on the stand as an authority on the Bible, and Darrow thoroughly humiliated Bryan by exposing the inconsistencies between modern science and Bryan's fundamentalist reading of the scriptures. Bryan won the case anyway, but five days later he died in his sleep, presumably from the stress of the trial.

In the public mind, Bryan would be forever associated with the antiscience, antimodernity, religious fundamentalist stance he took in the Scopes Trial. And since Bryan has been so commonly misidentified as a Populist, Populism itself has become associated with the ignorance and demagoguery of the antievolution crusade. Mostly lost in the story of Bryan, Darrow, Populism, and the Scopes Trial is one supreme irony: there *was* an actual 1890s Populist in the Tennessee courtroom that day when Bryan declared that he was more interested in the Rock of Ages than the age of rocks. The former Populist was

the avowed agnostic Clarence Darrow, who in the 1890s had helped to organize the People's Party in Illinois.[28]

~

If nothing else, then, the following study should help to restore a sense of
historical perspective to the label "populist." When closely scrutinized, most
of the men and women who founded and supported the People's Party in Texas
defy the various stereotypes of what constituted a Populist (or a populist). Many
were plain farmers, and more than a few sported the shaggy beards of Populist lore, but a sizable number of businesspeople, doctors, lawyers, engineers,
educators, and scientists zealously also supported the party. Most were committed Christians, but a diverse assortment of religious nonconformists and
nonbelievers also found a political home in the Populist ranks. African Americans, Mexican Americans, immigrants, and women pledged their loyalty.
Two interconnected beliefs united them. First, they shared a sense that a rapidly modernizing America required a modern political system. But they also
maintained a fervent belief in democracy, a conviction that a government of
the people, by the people, and for the people could meet whatever new challenges were presented by the new corporate order. The Populists took these
two beliefs and fashioned a new form of liberalism in which the people would
use the power of their democratically controlled government to counterbalance
the undemocratic power of the corporations, while simultaneously using the
power of that government to safeguard individual liberty.

In 1892 a Populist named J. M. Washburn published a long editorial in the
Dallas Populist newspaper the *Southern Mercury*. Washburn was attempting
to explain why the conservatives of the nation were so adamant in opposing
the government ownership and operation of the railroads. He had a laundry
list of explanations: "the curse of party; the love of self; the laziness to think;
the opposition to what is novel; blind adherence to the past, together with the
innate love of wrangling to humbug the people—all these stand in the way of
this and of all progress. In religion, in science, in politics, in law, in medicine,
in the arts, men hate what is novel worse than they hate what is evil. The principle is a nightmare on the world's progress." Washburn was right. The novelty
of the Populists' political ideas, not the logic or efficacy or those ideas, is what
doomed Populism, although the opposition of powerful economic interests
certainly contributed to the party's demise. But if the Populists failed politically, their ideas survived. When FDR in 1941 proclaimed the nation's dedication to the "four freedoms"—freedom of expression, freedom of religion,
freedom from fear, and freedom from want; when the grandson of a Texas

Populist, Lyndon Johnson, called for a Great Society that would witness "an end to poverty and racial injustice"; when the nation's first black president called for universal health care by reminding Americans that "we are all in this together"; these leaders were invoking a political ideology first enunciated by Populists, and particularly by those in Texas.[29]

To tell their story, I have had to adopt what may seem an idiosyncratic organizational scheme that intersperses chronological with topical chapters. The first two chapters follow a conventional chronology, chronicling the origins of Populism in the 1870s and 1880s, rooted in the Farmers' Alliance, the Knights of Labor, and the various independent political movements of those decades. The next three chapters depart from a strict chronological scheme to sketch out the Populists' ideological views and policy prescriptions, the role that religion played in the movement, and the party's approach to African Americans and race. Next, I pick up the history of the party with the 1894 election cycle, which in many ways marked the heyday of Populism in Texas. As the party matured, so did its position on women and its conceptions of femininity and masculinity, which are dealt with in Chapter 7. The remaining chapters are mostly, though not exclusively, chronological: Chapter 8 takes a deep dive into Populist legislation at the state level, focusing on the 1895 legislature, which contained twenty-four elected Third-Party members. Chapter 9 examines Populism in the border region of South Texas, with a special focus on Populist efforts to deal with the problems of election fraud in 1895 to 1896. Finally, the last two chapters tell the story of the momentous state and national elections of 1896 and the subsequent fate of the party in the years thereafter. The Conclusion traces Populist ideas—and a number of actual Texas Populists—well into the twentieth century. With regard to those portions of the book that do not follow a strict narrative, chronological order, I ask the reader's indulgence, with the promise that I've tried not to play the spoiler any more than can be avoided. Apart from all that the Populists have to tell us about American political development, theirs remains a compelling human story, and I hope that I do justice to it in the pages that follow.

1 · The Roots of Texas Populism

We are living in an age of organization and co-operation.
—Farmers' Alliance lecturer W. L. Martin, 1890

On an April evening in 1890, some thirty men and at least one woman assembled in the courtroom of the rustic limestone courthouse in Fredericksburg, Texas, for the monthly meeting of the Gillespie County Farmers' Alliance. As their organization's name suggests, all these people made their living directly or indirectly from agriculture, most of them as small farmers or ranchers. They had traveled on primitive roads by buggy or horseback from every corner of the county, from places with names like Nebo, Tivydale, Willow City, and Squaw Creek; you would be hard-pressed to find any of these obscure settlements on a map today. The state's capital at Austin, with its massive new domed statehouse built from pink granite quarried in nearby Burnet County, lay eighty miles to the east, but for most of Gillespie County's residents, the capital might as well have been a thousand miles away, because of both the difficulty of travel and the poverty of the county's inhabitants. Neither the railroad nor electricity had made it to the Hill Country, and at times it seemed like the rapidly modernizing world was passing them by.[1]

True, the countryside was beautiful this time of the year, as bluebonnets and Indian paintbrushes blanketed the hills with gaudy splashes of blue and red. But local farmers knew that the soil beneath the wildflowers was poor; in most places if you plowed much deeper than six inches you would hit solid rock. The weather was crazily unpredictable, and the clear-running rivers and streams were prone to violent flooding. After the introduction of cattle earlier in the century, large stretches of the countryside that had once supported lush stands of native grass had suffered erosion to the point that scrub cedar, mesquite, and prickly pear had taken over large swaths of the landscape. Worse still, since the Civil War, farm prices had declined for so many years in a row that younger farmers had never known what it was like to see prices improve. As if things weren't bad enough, Texas was just beginning to recover from the worst drought in its recorded history. For most of the residents of the remote region, then, life was a constant struggle, if not for outright survival then at least to achieve some measure of comfort and dignity. Membership in the Farmers' Alliance had given them hope for better times.[2]

Fredericksburg and much of the Hill Country had been settled originally by Germans, and names like Striegler, Meitzler, and Luckenbach could be found on the county Alliance membership rolls alongside names like Carter, Jennings, and Lee. At the meeting that night in April 1890, one figure stood out as he circulated among the crowd. Described by a contemporary as a "tall, lithe, well-built, rangy man, six feet in height, with black wavy hair and blue eyes," Sam Johnson had a reputation as a man who "attended all the neighborhood gatherings and met his friends with a handshake, friendly greetings and a hearty resounding laugh" (plate 1). Representing his neighborhood Alliance chapter, the Stonewall "suballiance," the fifty-one-year-old Sam was still a relative newcomer to Gillespie County, having moved there just a year earlier from the flatlands on the other side of Austin, near Lockhart. Already, though, his fellow Alliancemen had elected him to the post of assistant county lecturer, which meant that he needed to be prepared to make a speech if called on.[3]

When the session was gaveled to order, the first item of business was to discuss the matter of the Alliance Exchange, the ambitious statewide farmers' cooperative in Dallas that had recently suffered financial collapse, dealing a serious blow to the Alliance. Some members wanted the Gillespie County Alliance to participate in a proposed resurrection of the Exchange, and "quite a discussion" on this point ensued, ending only when a motion carried to "cease to discuss the affairs of Exchange until the Institution went down or up." The next speaker spoke on the topic of education, but the thrust of his remarks was not recorded. Up to this point, the meeting had proceeded along lines that most Alliancefolk would have approved, focusing on private self-help strategies intended to better the farmer's lot. The Alliance, after all, was an avowedly nonpartisan organization. Many Alliance members, however, believed that "nonpartisan" did not imply non*political*, and Sam Johnson was one of them. When he finally rose to speak it was not to tout the virtues of self-help, but rather to discuss a new plan that would require unprecedented political action

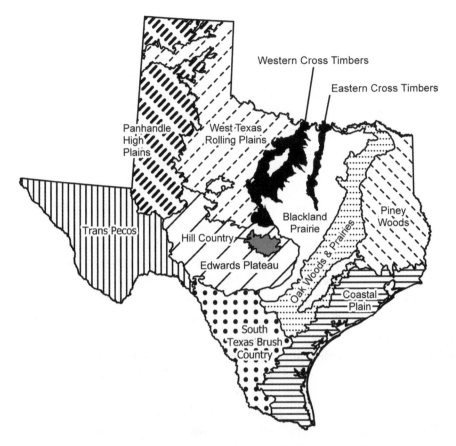

Figure 1 Physiographic regions of Texas. Map by Claire Holland.

on the part of the nation's farmers. Sam then delivered a "talk on the Sub Treasury plan," which he supplemented "by reading lengthy articles" from the *National Economist,* the Alliance's Washington, D.C.–based national organ. The plan, first outlined by Alliance national president (and Texan) Charles Macune a few months earlier, proposed that the federal government build throughout the country a network of warehouses where farmers could deposit their crops and take out low-interest loans in government-issued paper money (popularly known as "greenbacks"), effectively taking the country off the gold standard, improving and stabilizing crop prices, and providing affordable farm credit. No single federal undertaking of this magnitude, short of the postal service and the Union war effort during the Civil War, had ever been seriously proposed.[4]

If somebody had accused Sam of being "liberal," he would have welcomed the label, but not because he championed what a later generation would call "big government." The word "liberal" had not yet been applied to American politics in any specific way. According to *Webster's* dictionary, in Sam's day the term had several meanings. At its most basic it meant "generous," "bounteous," or "open-handed," and by all accounts, Sam was all of these things. But it also meant "not narrow or contracted in mind; not selfish; enlarged in spirit; catholic," and Sam exemplified these descriptions as well. Finally, among several other definitions, *Webster's* defined "liberal" as "not bound by orthodox tenets or established forms in political or religious philosophy," "independent in opinion," and "friendly to great freedom in the constitution or administration of government." He would have embraced all of these descriptions. It is no accident that decades later the term would be applied to a specific political ideology, of which Sam Johnson was something of an inadvertent pioneer.[5]

Sam's biography offers tantalizing clues to how people like him became the progenitors of modern political liberalism. Born in Alabama and brought to Texas as a child, he had joined the Confederate cavalry in 1861 and had seen hard action at the bloody Battle of Pleasant Hill in Louisiana, where he had a horse shot from under him and saved the life of a wounded comrade. After the battle he helped to hold down wounded men while the regimental surgeon amputated their limbs. By the time he marched home to Texas in 1865, he had seen terrible things in the long conflict, which perhaps kept him from taking life too seriously after it was over. He had also witnessed firsthand the might of the Union government, which may have helped him realize the potential, for good or for ill, that that government possessed.[6]

Relocating to Blanco County in the Hill Country after the war, he married a beautiful, raven-haired, high-spirited young woman named Eliza Bunton and went into the cattle business with his older brother Tom. For four years the Johnson brothers, accompanied at least once by Eliza, drove herds north along the fabled Chisholm Trail to Kansas, amassing a fortune that made the brothers the two richest men in the county. But in 1871 and 1872 they borrowed heavily to finance yet more cattle drives, only to meet with financial disaster when the market for Texas cattle experienced an unexpected downturn. With help from Eliza's family, the couple bought a farm south of Austin and cultivated it for sixteen years but never prospered, as the nation's long agricultural depression gradually set in. By the time he was in his forties, Sam had seen how unrestrained capitalism could produce staggering wealth but also how the capriciousness of unregulated markets could just as quickly take that wealth away. He also knew from his subsequent years as a dirt farmer that in Gilded-Age America, hard work and virtuous living by no means guaranteed success.[7]

But Sam remained an optimist, and in 1889 he purchased a nine-hundred-acre spread on the Pedernales River in Gillespie County near the hamlet of Stonewall and moved there with Eliza and their nine children. Life there proved no easier than in the flatlands, as he soon learned the hard truth about farming in the rocky Hill Country soil. But somewhere along the way Sam had nourished a keen intellect, and those dictionary definitions of the word "liberal"—"not narrow or contracted in mind," "independent in opinion"—increasingly came to characterize him.[8]

His religious odyssey may partly explain this part of his independence of opinion. Raised a Baptist, in "early manhood" he joined the Disciples of Christ, or Christian Church.[9] As a part of the "restorationist" movement of the nineteenth century, Disciples hoped to restore the supposedly pure practices of the first-century church. Critical of the excessive materialism and artificiality of modern Protestantism, they also stressed the equality of men and women in the eyes of God; Sam's marriage to the resilient, energetic Eliza had surely demonstrated to him that women could do the same things that men could. Indeed, the Disciples generally disdained social hierarchies of all sorts, and one of their key tenets was a belief that faith, as a response to testimony, was based in rationality. Thus, they took the Bible as the only true guide to faith, arguing that each person possessed the freedom, as well as the responsibility, to study the scriptures and determine God's will.[10]

His membership in the Disciples would have marked Sam as something of a religious "liberal," but Sam was a seeker, never entirely satisfied with the status quo, even when it came to religion. In the fall of 1879 a traveling minister of the Christadelphian faith visited Central Texas. The Christadelphians were an offshoot of the same restorationist movement that had given birth to the Disciples, but they parted ways with the Disciples on various doctrinal issues, including belief in the Trinity. The Christadelphian preacher stopped at the Johnson farm for the night, and after discussing the Bible during and after dinner, Sam arranged an all-day biblical debate the following day between the traveling preacher and a local minister. When in Sam's judgment the Christadelphian bested the local preacher, Sam converted. But it is noteworthy that he never forced his religious views on his children; four of his six daughters eventually followed him in joining the Christadelphian church, and the remaining children chose other paths.[11]

The Christadelphian faith urged its followers to abstain from worldly politics, but unsurprisingly, Sam chose not to follow this particular bit of his denomination's orthodoxy, again signaling his independence of thought. His descendants recalled that throughout his life, he stood ever ready to engage friends or strangers in arguments about politics, philosophy, or theology. His daughter Jessie recalled that even when his children were young, he encouraged them "to engage in games that required them to think, such as dominos, hearts, pitch, and whist." It might be a stretch to call Sam an intellectual, but by Hill Country standards, he came pretty close.[12]

After moving to the ranch on the Pedernales, Sam subscribed to multiple newspapers (including, surely, Charles Macune's Alliance organ, the *National Economist*). His children recalled that the papers were so important to him that he forded the Pedernales on horseback every other day to go to the nearest post office in Stonewall to pick them up. At another meeting of the county Alliance he delivered a lecture titled "The Importance of Mental Culture," about an early form of psychology. A leading 1883 treatise on the subject, quite possibly one Sam had read, defined the "object of mental culture" as being "the fullest development and highest activity of the faculties of the mind." It went on to compare the mind to "a field, and mental culture like the culture of the soil. Left to itself, a farm may be overrun with weeds and briers, while if subjected to the careful culture of the husbandman, it will teem with golden harvest. So the mind, if left to itself, may waste its energies and acquire incorrect habits of activity; while if subjected to the guiding hand of culture, it may develop in normal strength and vigor, and bring forth rich harvests of precious knowledge." Equating the brain to a muscle, mental culture warned against the onset of "mental flabbiness" and recommended "a constant and judicious exercise" of one's intellectual "faculties." Sam Johnson would never be caught with a case of mental flabbiness.[13]

The year after he delivered his lecture on the Subtreasury Plan to his fellow Alliancemen in Fredericksburg, Sam attended the founding convention of the Texas People's Party, where his fellow Populists elected him to the party's first state executive committee. In 1892 he ran, unsuccessfully, against his conservative son-in-law for a seat in the state legislature, with the two men traveling together by buggy to joint campaign appearances, arguing politics the entire way. Sam Johnson never became a major statewide leader of the Texas Populists, but from his biography we can begin to see at least the glimmerings of how otherwise ordinary people might come to embrace a new (and in the eyes of some, radical) vision of American politics.[14]

Of course, drawing a direct line between Populists in the 1890s and American liberals of a later era is a difficult enterprise fraught with intellectual peril. In Sam's case, though, the line is a bit easier to trace: as an old man he sat on the front porch of his home on the Pedernales and regaled his young grandson with tales of the Civil War and the cattle drives. Sometimes, however, the talk turned to politics, and many years later that grandson recalled "hearing my grandfather talk about the plight of the tenant farmer, the necessity for the worker to have protection for bargaining, the need for improvement of our transportation to get the farmer out of the mud." By the time Sam Johnson's grandson, Lyndon, became president of the United States, the term "liberal" had a well-known political meaning. In Lyndon Johnson's case, the roots of his liberalism clearly lay in the rocky soil of the Texas Hill Country, a soil seeded with Populist ideas in the 1890s.[15]

~

In reality, Sam Johnson was better-off than most of his neighbors and certainly more prosperous than the great mass of southern farmers in the late nineteenth century. American agriculture in general, and southern agriculture in particular, had entered into a long, disastrous, downward slide beginning around 1870 and continuing for the next quarter-century. Overall, the wholesale price index for American farm products declined by 50 percent from 1870 to 1896. Cotton, the commodity grown by most Texas and southern farmers, followed this trend, dropping from about sixteen cents a pound in 1870 to eight cents by 1890. Its decline continued until the mid-1890s, when it reached around a nickel a pound, a price below the break-even point for all but the most efficient growers.[16]

The reasons for this decline were complex. Part of the problem was the rise of foreign competition; when the Civil War had interrupted the flow of American cotton to textile manufacturers in Europe and elsewhere, production of the fleecy staple had ramped up in places like India and Egypt. Following the disruptions caused by the war, production in the South resumed and rapidly expanded along with the growing population. The construction of an integrated, statewide system of railroads in Texas in the 1880s made it possible to grow cotton and other commercial crops in parts of the state that had previously been too isolated from national and world markets. Those same railroads brought immigrants by the hundreds of thousands into Texas from the war-devastated states of the old Confederacy. The statistics are staggering: between 1870 and 1890, the state's population grew by 173 percent, from 818,579 to 2,235,527. The number of farms in the state nearly quadrupled, the number of improved acres rose from 3 million to 21 million, and the amount of cotton produced skyrocketed from 351,000 bales to 1.5 million bales. But even as over-production drove down crop prices, the population explosion kept land prices high. Meanwhile, the railroads, processors, commission agents, and other middlemen—often organized into what were effectively monopolies—always seemed to get their profitable cut, no matter how low crop prices might be.[17]

Small farmers had always practiced a "safety first" strategy, in which they sought to be self-sufficient in homegrown food, homemade clothing, and many other home-produced domestic goods before growing a cash crop with what-ever time and resources they had left. Even a poor farmer, or one just starting out, could reasonably expect to climb the "agricultural ladder," meaning that he might start his adult life as a farm laborer, then become a sharecropper, working a landlord's land in return for half of the crop. As he acquired some assets, he might become a share tenant, furnishing his own seed, draft ani-mals, and equipment, and having to pay only a quarter of his cotton crop and a third of his corn in rent. With some luck he might next move into the ranks of the cash tenants, renting a farm for cash and thus retaining full control of the crop and all his operations. The final rung of the ladder was achieved when the farmer had saved enough money to buy land of his own. Climbing each step of the ladder meant a corresponding rise in respect and status, a process consistent with farmers' traditional Jeffersonian belief in the nobility of agri-culture.[18]

For most Texas farmers, the agricultural ladder ceased to function in the years following Reconstruction. By 1890 only 58 percent of Texas farmers worked their own farms, and of the remaining 42 percent who rented, only one in five could pay their rent in cash. When a farmer had to share the pro-ceeds of his crop with his landlord, he normally relinquished control over what, and how much, could be grown on the farm, and it was in the interest of the landlord for every possible square foot of the farm to be planted in cash crops, usually cotton. Fast disappearing were the days when a farmer could grow corn, raise hogs, cattle, and chickens, and feed his family from the bounty of his farm. Most farmers, therefore, had to turn to a local merchant to "furnish" him with the food and other supplies needed to sustain life and keep the farm running. For the poorer farmer who had little or no cash, that meant buying these goods on credit, often for an unspecified price that translated into astro-nomical interest rates, often upward of 50 percent per annum or more. Banks were few and far between, and they did not normally loan to farmers anyway, so to secure their credit with the furnishing merchant, farmers often were forced to mortgage their growing crops. At harvest time, if crops were short, or prices down—which they invariably were—the farmer often was unable to settle his debt to the merchant, in which case the merchant often agreed to "carry" the farmer for another year, beginning a cycle of mounting debt. For those farmers of limited means who were fortunate enough to own their own land, the land itself was often mortgaged to buy food and supplies, and the eventual result was foreclosure. Draconian laws enacted at the behest of land-lords made it almost impossible for a tenant to skip out on a contract, and in-debted farmers were excluded from the operation of bankruptcy laws. As bad as all this was for white farmers, it was far worse for African Americans, most of whom started with nothing after emancipation and had to fight discrimi-nation and injustice every day of their lives. For whites, one of the most dis-turbing and humiliating aspects of the ongoing agricultural depression was that it threatened to reduce them to an economic status that many believed was reserved for blacks.[19]

Farm women of all races and ethnicities led lives shaped not only by grind-ing physical labor but also by the added burdens of a patriarchal system that rendered them subservient to their husbands or fathers. The typical farm wife's day began before sunup and did not end until after dark. If she were lucky enough to be spared work in the fields, she spent her day drawing water; tend-ing a garden; feeding chickens and hogs; milking cows; processing food; cooking meals; cleaning a drafty, dusty house; washing and ironing clothes without the modern conveniences of washer, dryer, and electric iron; caring for young children and seeing to their education; nursing sick family mem-bers; sewing and mending clothes; and lending a hand to neighbors—all of it often done while pregnant or nursing an infant. As the agricultural economy worsened in the last two decades of the nineteenth century, more and more white women found themselves working alongside their husbands or fathers in the fields, a degrading fate long shared by black and brown women. Formal education, if had at all, usually ended with the primary grades. More affluent farm women led somewhat easier lives; they might enjoy the occasional trip to town, with the prospect of a store-bought dress, some canned food or a few fresh oranges, or a musical program at the local opera house. But such luxu-ries were rare indeed for the wives and daughters of the poorer tenants or sharecroppers. And the numbers of renters were steadily on the rise: though a relative rarity before the Civil War, by 1880 (the first year that such records are available) 38 percent of Texas farmers worked farms they did not own, and 80 percent of these farmers were sharecroppers, the lowest rank of tenants.

By 1890 the number of tenants had risen to 42 percent, and in the decade of the 1890s it rose to a full 50 percent.[20]

Through sins of both omission and commission, the government had exacerbated the crisis. Congress effectively returned the country to the gold standard in the 1870s, a deflationary move that contributed to the acute shortage of money and credit. Moreover, the structure of the National Banking System favored northeastern commercial interests at the expense of southern and western agriculture. For their part, Texas Democrats had always harbored a Jacksonian fondness for low taxes and limited government. But their attachment to that philosophy had grown more doctrinaire after the experience of Reconstruction, with its brief but radical experiment in racial equality, and the Democrats institutionalized the laissez-faire dogma when they overthrew the state's Republican government in the mid-1870s. By then, the Republican Party was irrevocably fixed in the minds of most white southerners as the party of "Negro domination" and the "horrors" of Reconstruction, and to the Democrats' thinking, any government (sporting whatever party label) that was strong enough to regulate the economy or provide relief to distressed farmers might also be strong enough to disrupt the South's white-supremacist racial arrangements. As early as the late 1870s, then, Texas farmers knew that they were in financial trouble, but their political beliefs—reinforced and necessitated by their racial prejudices—forestalled any meaningful action beyond private self-help.

~

That self-help took the form of the Farmers' Alliance. It was founded in 1877 some sixty miles to the north and east of Sam Johnson's ranch, on the farm of J. R. Allen in Lampasas County, a place where three major physiographic regions—the Edwards Plateau, the Blackland Prairie, and the Western Cross Timbers—come together. The county lies in what scholars have called Texas's "shatterbelt," an ecological and cultural transition zone where the South meets the West but neither regional pattern dominates. Most of the Anglo settlers in the two-hundred-mile-wide zone had southern cultural roots, but they had to adapt to a very different climate and topography if they wanted to survive. The Comanche Indians had met their final defeat only a few years earlier, and in the mid-1870s farmers were just beginning to settle in what had until recently been an open cattle range. The railroad would not traverse the region until the 1880s.[21]

The 1870s and early 1880s were a particularly wet period, which falsely led settlers to believe that the region would be productive for the sort of agriculture practiced back East. The introduction of barbed wire would soon spell an end to the open range, and for some years to come farmers and ranchers would coexist in considerable tension with one another, which occasionally erupted into violent episodes of fence cutting and gunplay. The original Alliance was founded as a sort of fraternal, protective, and benevolent society for small land-owners, aimed at protecting against rustlers, helping to track down strays, and providing a social outlet for these self-uprooted folk who found themselves cast together on an isolated, alien, sometimes dangerous frontier. Replete with secret rituals and oaths, the Alliance combined aspects of a fraternal lodge, a school, a church, and a literary society, all of which were familiar institutions to Americans of that era. The organization particularly stressed education. Like the much larger and better-known Patrons of Husbandry (also known as the Grange), it taught better farming and housekeeping techniques to farm men and women. The order soon spread from Lampasas to neighboring counties.[22]

To some, the early Alliance would have seemed almost indistinguishable from the Grange, but by the late 1870s the Grange was a national organization, with a rule against participation in partisan politics. This did not prevent the Texas state Grange from endorsing a list of political demands in 1878 or pass-ing a resolution in support of the Democratic administration of Gov. Oran M. Roberts two years later, but such actions were controversial among its mem-bers, and the Grange was nearly moribund in the state by 1880. By contrast, from the very start, the Alliance's educational efforts overtly included politi-cal education, a feature that would have momentous consequences in the com-ing years.[23]

In August 1878 a short newspaper notice informed readers that a Farmers' Alliance had been established in San Saba County, the next county west of Lampasas. If the report was to be believed, politics, not self-help, lay at the cen-ter of that county's Alliance. "The object of the order is to elect good men to county offices," the item read, "and to see that farmers have an equal repre-sentation with other classes." Immediately to the north, in Hamilton County, Alliancemen also "nominated a full county ticket." That same year the Alli-ance created an umbrella "Grand State Alliance" organization. Among its stated objects were "To develop a better and higher state politically and finan-cially"; "To [foster] a better mutual understanding to sustain our laws"; and "To suppress personal, local, sectional and national prejudices, all unhealthy rivalry and all selfish ambitions." Nine counties were said to be represented in the state organization. It is unclear whether any of these local Alliance political efforts in 1878 met with success, but Alliance chapters continued

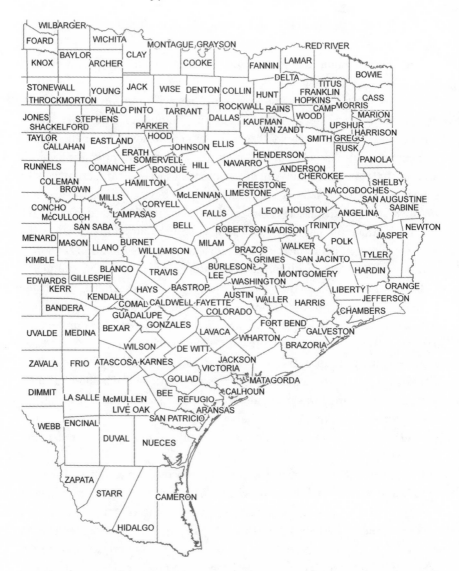

Figure 2 Texas counties, 1890. Excludes counties in the sparsely settled western portion of the state. Map by Claire Holland.

to dabble in politics. Lampasas Alliance members endorsed Democrats Thomas A. Hendricks and Wade Hampton for president and vice president, and a Tarrant County chapter caused a stir in 1881 when it called for the resignation of Texas US senator Samuel Bell Maxey for his alleged role in a Post Office Department corruption scandal.[24]

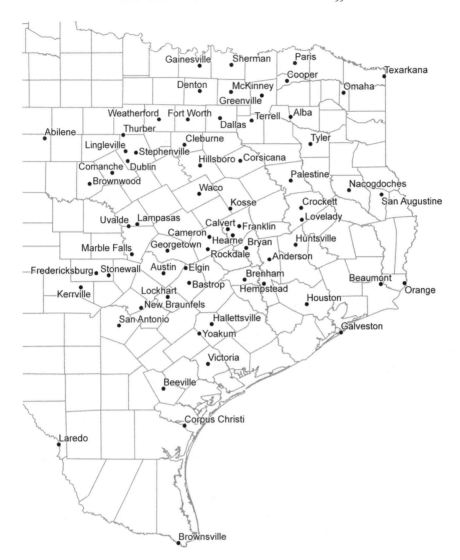

Figure 3 Cities and towns relevant to *The People's Revolt*. Map by Claire Holland.

These early Alliance forays into politics coincided with the emergence of the Greenback-Labor Party, which was founded nationally in the mid-1870s and spread to Texas by 1878. Greenbackers took their name from the irredeemable paper currency that had been used to finance the Civil War. When the Union government began issuing greenbacks in 1861, it effectively took the nation off a metallic, or "hard money," standard. Farmers who needed easy credit and low interest rates loved the greenback system, but in 1875 Congress passed the

Specie Resumption Act, which returned the nation to the gold standard over a four-year period. Farmers' concerns proved well-founded; the country entered a long deflationary spiral that punished debtors—whose ranks included most farmers—and rewarded creditors, most notably the large Wall Street banks.[25]

Over the previous two decades Texas had followed the basic southern political pattern, seceding after the election of Abraham Lincoln, contributing thousands of soldiers to the Confederate war effort, undergoing Reconstruction, and then being "redeemed" from the alleged evils of Republican rule in the early 1870s. By 1876 Democrats held all statewide political offices, enjoyed large majorities in the legislature, and wrote a new state constitution severely limiting the powers of state government. The state, by all appearances, was part of the so-called Solid South. Appearances, however, can deceive, and the reality is that Texas Democrats never had a firm hold on power. The Greenback-Labor Party, along with numerous local independent political movements, repeatedly challenged the Democrats.[26]

The Greenbackers held their first official statewide convention in Waco in August 1878, and by the fall the party boasted nearly five hundred Greenback clubs, of which seventy were African American. Like many of the era's third-party and independent movements, the Greenbackers often joined forces with the Republicans, who had no hope of winning elections on their own. Members of the Grange furnished much of the party's support, and indeed, the Greenbacker state platform closely resembled one promulgated by the state Grange. In addition to its appeal to abandon the metallic standard, the party called for increased funding for public schools, abolition of the convict lease system, and reforms in the administration of county government, all of which would become Populist platform planks in the 1890s. In 1878 the new party elected one congressman—George Washington "Wash" Jones of Bastrop—and, with Republican help, fourteen members of the legislature. Two years later, with less aid from Republicans, the Greenbackers' support dwindled, although they did reelect Jones to Congress. The party faded quickly thereafter.[27]

Disputes over politics dealt a death blow to the Texas Grange, as some Grangers avoided politics altogether (as the national bylaws required) while others feuded over whether to support the Greenbackers or the Democrats. Fragmentary evidence from the tiny new Farmers' Alliance suggests that it suffered much the same fate. In places like Lampasas County, where the local Alliance apparently endorsed the Greenback Party, the move into insurgent politics effectively destroyed the organization. But the impact of the Greenback movement on future politics in Texas can scarcely be overstated. Greenback monetary theories and other reforms embraced by the party would survive and even flourish, and thousands of Texans who had supported the Greenback-Labor Party would later identify with the Populists. Jerome C. Kearby, Eben L. Dohoney, William E. Farmer, Harry Tracy, Charles H. Jenkins, Sam Evans, James Madison Perdue, and Henry L. Bentley were but a few of the Green-backers who went on to become prominent Populists. The Greenbacker experience, however, proved to be a double-edged sword for Alliancefolk. While some embraced the party's political positions and would be watching for future opportunities to pursue them, others read the lessons and concluded that farmers' organizations should strictly avoid partisan politics and stick to self-help. These arguments would test Alliance solidarity repeatedly over the coming years.[28]

~

The Alliance struggled along in the early 1880s, with little support outside the shatterbelt region west of the ninety-eighth parallel. By 1883 only 30 of 130 suballiances were active. That would change in 1884, when the order's president, William L. Garvin, appointed S. O. Daws to the newly created post of traveling lecturer (plate 2). A thirty-eight-year-old native of Mississippi, Daws sparked a revival of the Alliance, mainly by encouraging members to establish local cooperatives. At first these cooperatives took the form of buying committees that negotiated exclusive deals with local merchants who would offer reduced prices in return for the exclusive patronage of Alliancefolk. Daws also promoted the "bulking" of Alliance-grown cotton, whereby farmers would combine their harvested and ginned crops and negotiate with buyers for better prices. Soon some county Alliances were establishing their own cooperative cotton yards to better facilitate the joint marketing of members' crops.[29]

Later in 1884, Daws met another man who was to play a major role in the Alliance and Populism. William Robert Lamb, born in Tennessee in 1850, had worked as a rail-splitter, hired hand, and tenant farmer in several North Texas counties before finally settling in Montague County, in the shatterbelt region on the Red River. Although he was said to have had only twenty-five days of formal education, the plainspoken, redheaded Lamb was elected president of that county's Alliance, and his success in organizing the county brought him to the attention of Daws. At the 1884 state meeting, Daws had him appointed to a new post, state lecturer. Lamb's work over the next year led to astonishing growth in the order. Even more than Daws, Lamb aggressively championed cooperation, urging the order's expansion into member-owned stores, gins, and mills. In 1885 the Alliance gave him the additional job of state purchasing agent, in hopes that he could negotiate bulk purchases of farm implements and machinery for Alliance members.[30]

Under Lamb's guidance, the cooperative movement exploded across Texas. At first, county Alliances simply appointed representatives to negotiate better prices with local merchants in exchange for the exclusive patronage of Alliance members. This led to the establishment of member-owned cooperative stores where farmers could purchase their farming supplies and household provisions at or near wholesale prices. Soon, cooperation extended to the marketing of crops, as farmers began bulking their cotton and wheat harvests and using their collective clout to negotiate better prices with wholesale buyers. This in turn led to the establishment of Alliance-owned cotton yards with their own weighing platforms and, sometimes, storage warehouses. Cooperative gins followed. In the wheat-growing regions north and west of Dallas, Alliancemen began executing ambitious plans to construct cooperative grain mills and elevators. The movement caught the attention of African American farmers, and because the Alliance barred black members, in 1886 they established the Colored Farmers' National Alliance and Cooperative Union, which soon enjoyed rapid growth itself.[31]

In those places where the cooperative movement met with some early success, farmers waxed giddy over the prospect of an escape from the high prices and astronomical interest rates charged by local furnishing merchants and middlemen in the marketing system. "When the Alliance of our county adopted its trade house at ten per cent profit for cash and twelve per cent on a credit the prices astonished the people," an Allianceman from Brazos County wrote. "They were so far below anything they had ever seen, it amused and excited them. They say it is a wonder that the farmers ever had anything. Now let me say to the brotherhood that the grand work is rolling on, and let us all put our shoulders to the wheel." John L. Mooney of Gonzales believed that the cooperative stores "hold in check the rapacity of the commercial classes by reducing profits to the minimum."[32]

Stories from the early days of the cotton-bulking movement illustrate Alliancefolk's staunch dedication to the cooperative program. When Dallas County cotton growers could not get the price they wanted from buyers in their own county seat, they hauled their crop twenty miles northward to Plano, where prices again proved unsatisfactory. Undeterred, they trekked another fourteen miles to McKinney, placing them more than thirty miles from where they had started. Down in Central Texas, Alliancefolk from three counties sold twelve thousand dollars' worth of cotton at Caldwell in 1886, and the cotton yard at

Mexia drew farmers from four counties. An observer hostile to the Alliance complained from the southeast Texas town of Lovelady that "a few unfortunate individuals who reside so remote from an alliance store that it has taken up so much of their time visiting the alliance store that their crops have become so weedy that it is not impossible to save them." A Grayson County couple held their local Alliance cooperative store in such high esteem that they chose it as the venue for their wedding.[33]

The excitement over cooperation led to ever-more-ambitious schemes. In several towns the Alliance operated wagon yards where members who lived more than a day's round-trip away from the nearest Alliance cooperative could camp out for the night before making the long trip home. In Dallas, Alliancefolk built a factory to manufacture agricultural implements, and out in the German Hill Country at New Braunfels they purchased and refurbished a woolen mill to manufacture cloth. At Lingleville in the Cross Timbers, the Erath County Alliance opened an Alliance high school, and 120 miles to the south in Marble Falls the order established an Alliance "University," headed by a respected educator and featuring departments of fine arts, business, and engineering, an industrial department, plus "special courses" in elocution, Spanish, and German. Alliancefolk opened three leather tanneries, two lumberyards, and a cottonseed oil mill. Ambitious plans for a factory at Marble Falls to manufacture textiles, leather, paper, glassware, woodenware, pottery, farm implements, machinery, furniture, and shoes proceeded as far as incorporation, the subscription of stock, and the purchase of a site, although it apparently never opened for business. Even the Colored Alliance managed to establish some cooperative stores, although records are sketchy.[34]

No records of the state Alliance organization survive, and even if they did, they would likely not offer a comprehensive picture of the cooperative movement because it was so decentralized and many local cooperative ventures so ephemeral. However, incorporation records, credit-rating agency reports, and a thorough search of extant newspapers make possible at least a partial reconstruction of the movement's scope. All told, more than three hundred Alliance cooperative ventures can be documented in Texas with reasonable certainty, the great majority of these founded between 1885 and 1890. Among these were 130 stores, 50 gins, 49 cotton yards, 28 grain mills, and 15 warehouses. Thirty records indicate the establishment of cooperative "associations" or the appointment of Alliance business agents or trade committees who negotiated agreements with "preferred trade houses." One North Texas county organization employed its own Alliance fruit tree agent.[35]

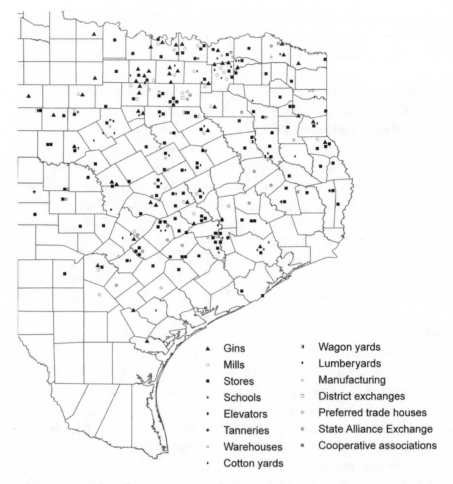

▲	Gins	◦	Wagon yards
○	Mills	•	Lumberyards
■	Stores	△	Manufacturing
✳	Schools	□	District exchanges
'	Elevators	◇	Preferred trade houses
+	Tanneries	⊛	State Alliance Exchange
⁕	Warehouses	○	Cooperative associations
'	Cotton yards		

Figure 4 Farmers' Alliance cooperatives. Placement in each county is approximate.
Map by Claire Holland.

Alliancefolk looked to the cooperative system as a modern solution to the modern problems of credit, commodity prices, and concentrated corporate power. As Hood County Alliance lecturer W. L. Martin wrote, "We are living in an age of organization and co-operation. Look abroad over the land and you can scarcely find an occupation which has not its leagues or associations. The main object is to combine so as to defeat the natural laws of competition. Thus, the interest of one calling is built up at the expense of another. If one should be left unorganized, it of course, becomes the victim of all the others. The only hope, the only safety for the farmers, is in organization. It is no longer a ques-

tion of policy, but one of necessity." For a Navarro County Allianceman, cooperation seemed to be the inescapable wave of the future: "Cooperation has built
all the fine cities in the land. Co-operation has banded our fair Union together
with steel rails and the iron steed sweeps across the hesperian continent faster
than the wind. Co-operation built the mighty ships that plow the briny deep.
Co-operation redeemed the country that we now live in [and transformed it]
from a howling wilderness of barbarism to the grandest nation on the globe."
If cooperation could do all that, surely it could rescue the farmer from his dire
predicament, and do it in a manner that preserved the commitment to individual liberty and limited government that most Texans still saw as the sacred
ideological legacy of Jefferson and Jackson.[36]

But a cooperative system founded on private association soon revealed its
limitations. In a market often awash in cotton at harvest time, selling in bulk
often failed to secure farmers significantly higher prices. When the abovementioned Dallas Alliancefolk drove their cotton-laden wagons to Plano and then
all the way to McKinney, they failed to secure the better prices they thought
they would find, and returned home with their crops unsold. On another occasion the entire Ellis County Alliance, representing eight hundred farmers,
converged on Waxahachie with twenty-three hundred bales of cotton, but buyers would only offer 8.38 cents a pound instead of the 8.75 cents the growers
demanded. Local leaders decided to abandon Waxahachie and take the crop to
Ennis, whereupon a majority of the members refused, tempted by an offer of
better prices if they would abandon the cooperative effort. The buyers' divide-
and-conquer plan succeeded, and the bulking plan collapsed into recrimina-
tion and bitterness. Variations on this theme played out across the state. In
the Alliance stronghold of Wise County, cotton buyers simply refused to pay a
higher price for bulked Alliance cotton, with the clear intent of driving the Alliance out of the market. From McLennan County, a member reported that
rival cotton yards had begun offering "superior inducements" in order to un-
dercut the Alliance yard, a problem for which "there is no remedy."[37]

The experience of the Delta County Alliance further illustrates the sort of
problems inherent in the organization's self-help strategy. Situated between
the two forks of the Sulphur River in northeast Texas, Delta County had rich
black soil that produced high-quality cotton, and Delta Alliancemen typically
bulked their cotton for sale at Paris, the county seat of neighboring Lamar
County. One year, however, lured by the prospect of a better deal, Delta farmers were "beguiled" into taking their crop to Sulphur Springs, where the
Hopkins County Alliance operated a warehouse and cotton yard. However,

the Delta cotton was bulked along with the crops of Alliance cotton from the "poor sand ridges" of Wood and Hopkins Counties, and when the full crop was sold, the Delta farmers got the same "middling" price that the inferior cotton from the other counties received. The lesson, according to an unsympathetic newspaper report, was that cooperation did not necessarily work.[38]

The cooperative stores faced their own set of challenges. Most were undercapitalized, because cash-strapped farmers found it difficult to subscribe to the required shares of stock. Moreover, because the Alliance storekeepers had to pay the same wholesale prices for their goods that commercial stores paid, many undoubtedly learned to their chagrin that the profit margins realized by the for-profit merchants were not nearly as high as they had imagined. This is not to say that merchants welcomed Alliance competition; sometimes when the Alliance came to a county, local merchants simply refused to extend credit to members, a move that a Wilson County tenant farmer believed was calculated "to crush the Alliance." Alliancefolk also sometimes became victims of their own success. In Lampasas, one of the birthplaces of the Alliance, farmers were said to be "deserting the Alliance store and trading with regular merchants because the regular merchants undersell the Alliance store." Of course, one of the goals of the cooperatives was to force merchants and middlemen to behave, but farmers knew too well what would happen to prices once the Alliance enterprises had been run out of business.[39]

Whether or not individual cooperatives managed to succeed as business enterprises, their principal limitation soon became obvious: private self-help failed to solve the problem of credit. In a commercial farming system, all but the wealthiest farmers need credit, for the simple reason that farmers must wait till harvest time each year to be paid for their year's labor. In the meantime, they had to buy seed and supplies, obtain and maintain draft animals, and feed, clothe, and house their families. In Texas, as in most of the South, banks were scarce and rarely made agricultural loans, leaving farmers to finance their operations with a local storekeeper or a "furnishing merchant," who often required a lien on the still-unharvested crop to secure the loan. Merchants maintained a dual system of pricing—one price for cash purchases, another for credit, sometimes as much as 50 percent higher. The interest rates for such loans then often ranged between 30 and 60 percent.[40]

This system took a crushing financial and psychic toll on hardworking farmers. Writing to the *Southern Mercury*, a Falls County Allianceman asked, "Farmer, when you go to town with your 5 cent cotton and turn it over to your merchant, who has furnished you the past year, and by pleading with him you manage to get a few dollars in cash to buy your wife or child some coveted gift—a dress perhaps, or shoes for the little feet of your prattling boy or dimpled-cheek daughter—do you think of what a humiliating position you occupy? Have you realized that you are looked upon as but little better than the professional beggar?" Another Allianceman called the system "an overwhelming curse placed upon the poor people of the country," a characterization with which legions of Texas farmers would have wholeheartedly agreed. It became commonplace for Alliancefolk to complain that they were but a step away from "abject peonage" or "perpetual serfdom."[41]

To truly benefit most poorer farmers—especially those who worked rented farms—the Alliance stores needed to extend credit, but if they did so, they faced the prospect of employing the same practices as the furnishing merchants. Most, therefore, operated on a strictly cash basis. Farmers who could afford to do so enthusiastically supported their local cooperative store; those who could not remained in thrall to the merchants. As a Dallas County farmer explained, "We must begin at the root of the evil; we must first enable the poor to avail themselves of the advantages of co-operation before it can benefit them." By 1887 some Alliance leaders were arriving at the realization that local cooperatives alone would never solve the deepening farm crisis.[42]

For such people, the pull of politics proved nearly irresistible. As we have seen, the Alliance had been "political" from the start. From the neighborhood suballiance all the way up to the annual state meetings, Alliancefolk had always discussed political economy, with greenback monetary theory usually at the center of those discussions. Actual participation in electoral politics as an organization, however, was more controversial. In most of the counties where the early Alliance had fielded its own slates of candidates, the move into politics had divided and destroyed local Alliance organizations. The lessons of these early forays into third-party politics were not lost on many members. For others, allegiance to the Democratic Party—the so-called Party of the Fathers, the party of low taxes, limited government, and the guarantor of white supremacy—was a sacred obligation, a sort of birthright of southerners.

William Lamb was not among the hesitant. His experiences in spreading the gospel of cooperation had shown him firsthand the power—he would say monopoly power—that business—especially big business—held against farmers and laborers. By 1885 he probably already knew in his heart of hearts that self-help alone would never be able to address the structural problems that tilted the economic system so strongly in favor of the rich and powerful. Yet, even Lamb seems to have known that the Alliance was not ready to enter politics directly as a third-party movement. A correspondent for the Alliance newspaper in Wise County captured the basic logic that Lamb undoubtedly understood, explaining that "political action is almost useless until the workers and producers are educated to understand and see clearly and distinctly what principles and policies are necessary to be carried into effect. . . . When farmers and all laborers are thus educated, true political action will naturally and inevitably follow." At the midpoint of the 1880s, Lamb and a small coterie of like-minded leaders were urging their fellow Alliancemen to think, and increasingly to act, in political ways. As that education proceeded, however, the events of 1885 to 1886 suddenly brought politics to the fore in dramatic fashion.[43]

The catalyst for Alliance political activism came from the labor movement, particularly from the Knights of Labor. In February 1885 railroad workers on Jay Gould's sprawling Southwest System walked off the job in protest over an increase in work hours without a corresponding increase in pay. The strike ended in March with a favorable settlement, spurring tremendous growth for the Knights. The union chartered 112 locals in 1885 alone. Many farmers and farm laborers, some of whom were already members of the Alliance, joined the Knights, as did workers in the mining communities west of Fort Worth. Lamb and other Alliance radicals were quick to recognize the potential power of a farmer-labor coalition against common foes like the Gould lines.[44]

In the summer of 1885 the Knights and Alliance held a series of joint rallies, picnics, and barbecues celebrating the Knights' victory in the strike, hailing the successes of the Alliance cooperative program, and calling for solidarity between the two organizations. When more than five hundred delegates convened for the state Alliance meeting in Decatur in August, representatives of the Knights attended, asking for Alliance support in an ongoing labor dispute against the Mallory steamship line by Knights longshoremen in Galveston and in a conflict with the state government over the use of convict labor in the construction of the new state capitol building. Although such causes were not political in the sense of endorsing slates of candidates or creating a new party, they were qualitatively different from the strictly private self-help embodied by the cooperatives. Strikes and boycotts might be aimed at private companies, but they invariably involved the government, which could issue injunctions, arrest strikers, pass all sorts of legislation touching on labor issues, and call out troops to intervene in strikes. Political parties regularly took sides in strikes, rendering support for labor or for the companies matters of party policy. Any signs that the Alliance intended to make common cause with the Knights of Labor was a significant step in a political direction. In response to the Knights' plea, at its state convention the Alliance formally endorsed "unity of action" between the Knights and the Alliance. This was likely the work of William Lamb. Apparently, Lamb's immediate superior in the order, S. O. Daws, also approved of cooperation with the Knights, because in early September he spoke at a joint Alliance-Knights meeting in Dallas, before a crowd described as "both male and female, white and colored." He shared the podium with Knights leader William E. "Bill" Farmer, and both men "urged union and cooperation." The press soon reported a formal merger of the two organizations, a rumor that sent both groups scrambling to deny it.[45]

The newfound solidarity would soon be tested. In late 1885 the Knights struck the Mallory line and called for a boycott of all products its ships handled. At about the same time, Dallas Alliancemen joined their Knights of Labor brethren in a boycott of the Sanger dry goods company, which had run afoul of the Knights in another labor dispute. Lamb wanted the Alliance to formally endorse both boycotts, but Alliance president Andrew Dunlap refused, exposing the fissures within the order. When asked if there were "any political features about your organization," Alliance vice president J. S. Morris declared, "None whatsoever; that was the rock upon which the Grange stranded. Our objects are purely commercial." Perhaps, but by early 1886 the Alliance's increasingly militant position on labor-related issues was placing serious strain on the meaning of "purely commercial." When local Alliancemen in Dallas discussed formal cooperation with the Knights, it "led to a stormy debate" and a resulting decision to let it be "one of individual sympathy and not of organized compulsion."[46]

The Mallory and Sanger boycotts were but the prelude to a more serious development. In March 1886 the Knights' strike against the Gould lines resumed, as Gould had reneged on the agreement reached the previous year. The Great Southwest Strike, as it became known, brought rail traffic to a halt throughout most of Texas and several other states, accompanied by considerable violence as strikers clashed with strikebreakers and with state militia and Texas Rangers dispatched by Democratic governor John Ireland. William Lamb and like-minded Alliancemen called for the Alliance to support the strike, and in many places considerable cooperation developed, with Alliancefolk providing direct aid to strikers in the form of money and agricultural produce. Alliance president Andrew Dunlap and Joseph N. Rogers, the editor of the order's state newspaper, both condemned the strike and repudiated Alliance cooperation, and the war between the two wings of the order grew ever more public and bitter, spurring the publication of a "blistering" public letter from Lamb castigating the state leaders for their lack of sympathy for laborers.[47]

Gould and his government allies soon crushed the strike, dealing a devastating blow to the Knights of Labor. The Alliance, however, emerged stronger than ever, despite the public feuding among its members over the place of the order in political affairs. It soon became apparent that the boycotts and the strike had actually politicized large numbers of the Alliance rank and file. The joint meetings with the Knights and the rhetoric of political Alliance leaders like Lamb spurred a new wave of political organizing on the part of Alliancemen and their allies in the spring of 1886. In Fort Worth a Knights-Alliance "independent party" elected as mayor Dr. Hiram S. Broiles, himself both a Knight and an Allianceman, leading Knights leader Bill Farmer to proclaim that "a revolution . . . has begun" and that "the ballot box is our battlefield." In similar fashion, a "Laboring Men's Convention" composed of Alliancemen and Knights of Labor in neighboring Wise County resulted in the nomination of an independent ticket there. In adjacent Jack County, a "People's Convention" likewise put out a full county ticket. Alliancefolk who viewed their order as strictly a farmer's self-help organization were coming to realize that association and cooperation with the much more militant Knights of Labor was politicizing their Alliance brothers and sisters in ways that the conservatives considered dangerous, if not heretical.[48]

As these developments unfolded, the Alliance moved ever closer to an open rupture over the question of the order's role in politics. Into the breech stepped S. O. Daws, the organizer whose work had enabled the organization to survive during its difficult early years. A cautious man by temperament, Daws understood that "to degrade the alliance to a political machine will subvert its purposes, ruin the order, and fail to accomplish anything in politics." But in May Daws proposed a solution: "There is a way to take part in politics without having it in the order. Call each neighborhood together and organize anti-monopoly leagues . . . and nominate candidates for office." In other words, Alliancefolk should continue to study and debate political questions, and they should translate those debates into independent political action, but they should do so apart from the Alliance and not under the Alliance banner. Of course, this was precisely what was already transpiring in many localities.[49]

That summer, an independent movement in Comanche County, led by newspaperman Thomas Gaines, president of his local suballiance and a protégé of Daws, nominated a full county ticket consisting almost entirely of Alliancemen. Acquiring the moniker "the Human Party," it went on to triumph later that fall. In nearby Erath County, the president of that county's Alliance, Evan Jones, spearheaded an "Independent Party" that likewise swept to victory in the general election. The Daws Formula troubled the conservatives in the order, particularly Joseph N. Rogers, editor of the state organ the *Rural Citizen*, and for good reason. Its tacit sanctioning of political action by individual Alliancemen empowered and encouraged third-party advocates like Lamb, Gaines, and Jones. For their part, the conservatives were determined to keep the political genie in the bottle, if it was not already too late.[50]

The state Alliance convened for its August 1886 annual meeting in the town of Cleburne, thirty miles south of Fort Worth. As the first trainloads of delegates arrived, a procession eventually stretching over a half-mile, led by the Diamond Queen Brass Band, the Cleburne Light Guard, and a local hook-and-ladder company formed to escort them to the Johnson County Courthouse. Over the next two days, deliberating behind closed doors, a "Committee for the Good of the Order" fashioned a set of seventeen legislative resolutions, each of which pointedly began with the phrase "We demand." The demands bore the mark of the political activists in the order, notably James Madison Perdue, a schoolteacher and preacher from Gilmer in East Texas and a committed Greenbacker. Apart from enunciating the orthodox Greenbacker position on fiat money, the Cleburne Demands included a number of prolabor and anti-railroad planks, clearly showing the influence of the Knights of Labor and evidencing the recent collaboration between the two orders. Indeed, the question of some sort of formal Knights-Alliance coalition appears to have been one of the most divisive questions in an already divisive meeting.[51]

The convention narrowly approved the demands by a vote of ninety-two to seventy-five, after many of the delegates had already departed, leaving in question whether they really spoke for a majority of the members. As a sop to the conservatives, the delegates added a statement that the Alliance should work for reform "in a strictly non-partisan spirit," but this failed to mollify the antipolitical wing of the organization. After midnight on the last night of the convention, a group of the conservatives met and took steps to form a rump state alliance dedicated to keeping clear of politics, a dangerous development for the third-partyites not only because it would split the Alliance but also because the conservatives controlled the organization's treasury.[52]

The Alliance seemed on the verge of disintegration, but it had one asset that just might save it. His name was Charles Wesley Macune (plate 3). A native of Wisconsin, Macune had come to Texas at age nineteen, whereupon he studied and practiced both law and medicine, edited a newspaper, and joined his local Alliance in Milam County. Sent as a delegate to the Cleburne convention, the handsome, well-spoken, charismatic Macune, who was identified with neither side in the dispute over politics, so impressed his fellow delegates that they elected him chairman of the executive committee. Realizing the dire danger the order faced, Macune managed to quell the conservative secession movement and hold the Alliance together until a specially called meeting of the feuding leaders could convene in Waco in November. In the meantime, fueled by the Cleburne Demands as well as the ongoing cooperative program, membership in the Alliance exploded. When the November meeting took place, Macune downplayed the political disagreements between the two sides, accepted the resignations of President Dunlap and other conservative leaders (while retaining the treasury), talked about ambitious plans for expanding the Alliance into other states, and then scheduled another state convention for January 1887.[53]

At that meeting Macune proposed a bold solution: the creation of a statewide Alliance Exchange that would collectively market Texas Alliance members' crops, purchase supplies in bulk direct from manufacturers, and perhaps most important, offer low-interest credit to farmers using their collectively pledged crops as collateral. It was the ultimate expression of self-help through cooperation, and it gave the conservatives a new cause around which to rally. Equally thrilling, to all Alliancefolk, was Macune's ambitious plan to spread the Alliance into the Deep South and beyond. Macune was able to report the first major step in that plan: Texas representatives had already negotiated a merger with the Louisiana Farmers' Union and the creation of the new National Farmers' Alliance and Cooperative Union, commonly (and more accurately) referred to as the Southern Alliance. S. O. Daws, the order's original traveling lecturer, would soon be dispatched to organize Mississippi, and J. M. Perdue, the principal author of the Cleburne Demands, to Alabama. Other Texans were soon organizing in other southern states.[54]

On the surface, it looked as if the Alliance would remain the nonpartisan and largely nonpolitical entity that the conservatives desired. A loyal Democrat, Macune was certainly no advocate of third-party action, and to this juncture his main efforts had been directed at expanding the scope of the cooperative crusade. Yet, anyone who had attended the Waco conference surely would have seen indications to the contrary. Lamb and Perdue, whose political proclivities were no secret, had played prominent roles at the meeting. Evan Jones, the capable leader of Erath County's independent political movement, was elected the new president of the state Alliance, replacing Dunlap.

Joining them was a man destined to play a leading role in the People's Revolt. Harrison Sterling Price Ashby was a thirty-nine-year-old Missouri native who had served in the Confederate army, after which he spent three years in Mexico, where he worked as a circus clown and stage actor, among other things. Returning to Texas and settling in Montague County, he drove a herd up the Chisholm Trail and then became a teacher. In 1872 he was licensed as a Methodist preacher, and over the next sixteen years he pastored churches in several Texas towns and served as a missionary to the Kiowa and Comanche Indians in Oklahoma. As a boy he had been given the nickname "Stump" by amused relatives who saw him honing his oratorical skills before an audience of cornstalks. Those skills, practiced mainly from the pulpit, had already made Ashby a well-known figure across Texas when he left the ministry in the mid-1880s and bought a farm a few miles north of Fort Worth, where he planned to raise purebred cattle. His fellow Alliancemen soon recognized his talents and sent the tall, lanky, boyish-faced Ashby as a delegate to the Waco meeting. An unabashed Greenbacker and proponent of third-party action, Ashby also joined the Knights of Labor. He had supported the independent political movement in Tarrant County in 1886, running unsuccessfully for the state Senate. No leader would bring more energy and enthusiasm to the agrarian crusade.[55]

The political Alliancemen and their allies in the Knights and in the various independent political movements seem to have realized that for the moment, at least, Macune should be allowed to pursue his strategy of expanding the Alliance and launching the statewide Exchange. To capitalize the Exchange, all Alliance members were assessed a two-dollar fee. The city of Dallas offered a subsidy and a free city lot, on which the Alliance built a grand four-story building to house the Exchange's headquarters (plate 4). With Macune as its manager, the Exchange opened its doors for business in September 1887, just in time for that year's harvest. If successful, it would liberate farmers from the crop-lien system of financing, provide affordable supplies, and revolutionize the entire cotton marketing system, securing a much larger share of agricultural profits for actual farmers.[56]

Almost immediately, however, it encountered problems. By April 1888 only about $20,000 worth of the assessment fees had been paid, even as the Exchange had authorized loans of $200,000 and had begun to sell equipment and supplies on credit. With the shortfall in capital, Macune was forced to turn to commercial bank loans, but most banks refused to accept members' joint notes (that is, pledges of yet-unharvested crops) as collateral. Alliance leaders soon devised a plan to save the Exchange: on June 9, county Alliances across the state would meet, collect additional assessments from members, and place the Exchange back on a solid footing. Amid much fanfare, the day arrived, but the contributions proved woefully insufficient. In September the Exchange ceased to sell supplies on credit, and by the end of 1889 it was bankrupt. Alliancefolk watched in dismay as the fine building in Dallas was foreclosed on by its creditors. Some blamed Macune personally, but many others cast the bankers and large merchants as the villains. Some surely understood that the poverty of Texas farmers had made the enterprise's vision of large-scale cooperation unlikely to succeed. Almost all, however, sensed that they were caught up in a fundamentally unfair system—an economic system, enabled and abetted by a corrupt political system, that so stacked the deck against the common man and woman that no amount of hard work would ever produce success. It was this realization that fueled the emerging political revolt.[57]

That revolt began to unfold in earnest in the spring of 1888. In February third-party advocates met in Cincinnati, Ohio, and created the Union Labor Party (ULP). William Lamb was named to the national executive committee and chaired the credentials committee. His colleague from Fort Worth, Capt. Sam Evans, was offered the vice presidential nomination but declined. In July the Alliance- and Knights-backed independent mayor of Fort Worth, Hiram S. Broiles, called a "nonpartisan" conference to meet in his city three days in advance of the state Union Labor Party convention. Lamb chaired the meeting, which wrote a platform borrowing liberally from the Cleburne Demands and from the Knights' platforms. When the ULP convention met, it rubber-stamped that platform and nominated Alliance president Evan Jones for governor, Broiles for lieutenant governor, and longtime Dallas Greenbacker Jerome Kearby for chief justice of the state supreme court. Jones subsequently declined the nomination, fearing it would divide the Alliance. Broiles and Kearby also declined their nominations, but Alliancemen and Knights were still well-represented, with Evans running for Congress in the Sixth District, Knights leader Bill Farmer (who had also joined the Alliance) in the Third, and the white superintendent of the Colored Alliance, Richard M. Humphrey, in the Second.

In the meantime, the insurgent movement spread at the local level. Variously calling themselves "independents" or "nonpartisans," third-partyites nominated tickets in many of the usual hotbeds of agrarian discontent such as Erath, Wise, Lampasas, Brown, and Robertson Counties. But the movement also appeared in unexpected places, including Travis County, home to the state capital, and McLennan and Smith Counties, with their commercial hubs of Waco and Tyler. In Navarro County south of Dallas, the independent move-

ment adopted the name "People's Party," with the press reporting that its "platform differs only in phraseology from other labor platforms." North of
Houston, in Waller County, where the Farmers' Alliance counted as members
"nearly every farmer the county," Alliancemen threw off all pretense of nonpartisanship, meeting at the county's Alliance warehouse and nominating
their own "people's ticket" for all county offices. In nearby Walker County, the
local white and colored Alliances met jointly and created a biracial Union Labor
Party organization, with the meeting presided over by Andrew M. Turnbull,
the Alliance state lecturer and minister who later served on the first Populist
state executive committee. The county's Union Laborites would subsequently
hold their monthly meetings in Grant's Colony, an all-black settlement east of
Huntsville, indicating the prominent role that African Americans played in
the local third-party organization. "General surprise is felt," according to a
Democratic correspondent, "at the Alliance admitting negro Republicans in
their meetings and joining in with them." Either unable or unwilling to recognize the mounting threat to its political dominance, the state Democratic
Party in its platform only vaguely denounced monopoly and gave a lukewarm
nod to the regulation of railroad rates, while proffering a "united and enthusiastic" endorsement of conservative presidential nominee Grover Cleveland.[58]

As politics heated up in the summer of 1888, cotton farmers were dealt a
new blow. The eight large firms that manufactured the nation's supply of jute
bagging, needed for wrapping cotton bales after ginning, created a trust to fix
prices, resulting in a near-doubling of the price of the coarse fabric. Taking a
page now from their Knights of Labor comrades, Alliancemen called for a boycott of jute, urging farmers to use cotton bagging instead. Factories scrambled to begin producing the fabric, and the state Alliance made plans to begin
manufacturing it at its proposed textile mill at Marble Falls in the Hill Country. Little could be done in time for the 1888 harvest, but in 1889 the jute boycott became a unifying cause for the Alliance, much as the Exchange had
been the year before. Throughout the state, local Alliancefolk enacted scenes
such as one in the town of Cameron, where they met at the Alliance cotton
yard and in a solemn funeral ceremony, buried with faux-military honors the
last roll of jute from the local Alliance store. "It was somewhat of a ludicrous
proceeding," the local paper reported, "but it has a significance which will not
be lost sight of, and it will be safe to say that 'Old Jute' will be buried in every
section of the cotton raising South between now and the ides of July."[59]

Suddenly awash in unsold jute, the trust opened negotiations with the Alliance, offering to reduce the price in return for an end to the boycott. The

Alliance refused, reasoning that if the trust were left intact it could simply jack up the prices again after the boycott ended. The trust reduced the price anyway, making cotton bagging more expensive than jute. The boycott soon faltered. Alliancemen could claim a partial victory, since prices had been reduced, but the experience also served to underscore the pitfalls inherent in a reliance on private collective action. Many Alliancefolk understood that as long as combinations in restraint of trade like the jute trust were allowed to stand, ordinary Americans would be at their mercy. Each episode like the collapse of the Alliance Exchange or the defeat of the jute boycott served to convince more people that only government action could level the playing field between ordinary people and powerful, wealthy corporations. The political rhetoric of a William Lamb or a Stump Ashby could help Texans understand the forces arrayed against them, but real experiences of injustice and powerlessness were the greatest politicizing factor. J. T. Brooks of the Macedonia Alliance in Grimes County spoke for many when, in the aftermath of these events, he wrote, "In my humble opinion, if we are to have permanent relief, we must enter the legislative halls of both state and nation, before the victory is won."[60]

The cobbled-together Union Labor Party and the patchwork quilt of local independent and nonpartisan movements ultimately posed little threat to the well-entrenched, well-funded Democrats in 1888. The insurgent cause was not helped by a sensational story broken by the *Fort Worth Gazette* in the weeks just before the election. It told of a secret organization known as the National Order of Videttes, which it depicted as an oath-bound, paramilitary arm of the agrarian political movement. The *Gazette* revealed the names of supposed members, and it read like a who's who of Alliance and Knights of Labor third-partyites: Evan Jones, Bill Farmer, Stump Ashby, William Lamb, Hiram Broiles, Jerome Kearby, Sam Evans, and numerous others. The clear implication of the reports was that its adherents were plotting armed revolution. Papers across the state soon picked up the story. Most of the alleged leaders of the group simply ignored the charges, although at least one—Sam Evans—denied membership and threatened to sue his hometown paper, the *Gazette*. The Alliance state newspaper, the *Southern Mercury*, soon felt compelled to distance itself and the Alliance from the Videttes, saying that "the Alliance has no room for 'videttes,' and they may as well seek quarters elsewhere." Nothing more ever came of the Vidette hysteria, although when the Populist movement began in earnest in 1892, political opponents would occasionally characterize it as "a political hash of greenbackers, laborites, videttes and voodettes."[61]

Charles Macune now occupied a curious position in the Alliance. Blamed by many Texans for the Exchange's collapse and distrusted by others who saw him as an obstacle to political action, he retained his position of leadership in the recently created Southern Alliance. In March 1889, armed with a $10,000 loan from Hays County Alliance leader Robert J. Sledge, Macune moved to Washington, D.C., and commenced publication of the *National Economist*, the new official organ of the Southern Alliance. Over the next several months the *Economist* proved true to its title, becoming, in the words on one historian, "a virtual schoolroom of currency theory." Macune also operated the Alliance Publishing Company, which translated much of that theory into tracts for national distribution, along with histories of the Alliance, almanacs, and other publications of interest to farmers. Of course, the currency theory that Macune worked so hard to disseminate was greenbackism in its various forms. And greenbackism, by its very nature, meant politics, since only the federal government could set the nation's monetary policy on a new course.[62]

When the Southern Alliance convened its annual meeting in St. Louis in December 1889, Macune delivered a lengthy address to the delegates. Speaking on the second day of the convention, he explained that farmers had three strategies for relief: scientific farming, cooperative buying and selling, and securing legislative reforms. Macune noted that greater efficiency alone would never solve the farm crisis as long as prices hovered near the break-even point. He also knew, better than anyone, that business cooperatives had been tried and had failed. That left only the third strategy, politics. Macune, however, was still not talking about the creation of a new party. About this he was quite clear: what was now needed was "a united effort . . . brought to bear upon the authorities, that will secure such changes in the regulations that govern the relations between different classes of citizens as are necessary to secure equal rights, equal privileges and equal chances." In short, he was calling for an organized and sustained lobbying effort aimed at Democrats and Republicans in Congress, and he proceeded to lay out a detailed plan for how that lobbying should advance. He followed with an emphatic declaration: "We are a complete opposite to a political party. We dissolve prejudices, neutralize partisanism, and appeal to reason and justice for our rights, and are willing to grant to all other classes the same. Party appeals to prejudice and depends on partisan hatred for power to perpetuate itself." Macune closed his address with what sounded like a thoughtful, even bland, admonishment: "With these thoughts as to the policy to pursue, let us carefully consider which is the most urgent, most important and necessary reform to be dignified as the battle cry of the order temporarily till accomplished."[63]

There was more here than meets the eye. Indeed, Macune knew precisely what this "most urgent, most important and necessary reform" should be. On the fifth day of the convention, the Committee on the Monetary System consisting of Macune, Stump Ashby, W. Scott Morgan of Arkansas, Lon F. Livingston of Georgia, and the newly elected Alliance president Leonidas Lafayette Polk of North Carolina issued a report proposing two major changes in the nation's monetary system. The first demand, comprising but one perfunctory sentence, called for the free and unlimited coinage of silver. The second demand, requiring nearly three pages to introduce, outlined what would soon become known as the Subtreasury Plan. The delegates endorsed the demands by an overwhelming margin. With its sweeping program of abolishing the national banking system, implementing an irredeemable paper currency, regulating commodity supplies to boost farm prices, and extending affordable credit to farmers, the Subtreasury became, in the words of Alliance publicist Nelson A. Dunning, "the rallying cry of the order."[64]

Dunning, an editorial assistant to Macune, perhaps should have qualified his assessment of the plan's reception. While it certainly became the rallying cry of *many* in the order, others were less sure. Because it would entail an unprecedented expansion of federal power, conservative Alliancefolk, especially in the South, viewed it with caution, if not alarm. Those who had always opposed the Alliance "going into politics" believed, with good cause, that it would eventually propel the order into third-party action, which would tear apart the organization. The debate played out on street corners, in local Alliance meetings, and in the pages of the reform press. While a majority of county Alliances seem to have favored it, a vocal minority took the position of the Alliance of Grayson County, one of the banner Alliance counties in the state, which declared the Subtreasury "too paternal to be indorsed by any one who believes in equal justice to all and special favors to none." From Gregg County, an Allianceman reported that he could not join with his brethren in voting for the Subtreasury resolution, complaining that "there was a little too much third party politics for the good of the order." Through the summer of 1890, the editor of the *Southern Mercury*, Sam Dixon, continued to straddle the fence on the plan, reflecting the divided opinions of the Alliance membership. While claiming that some of the most "conservative" men in the country supported the plan, he also stated that "the alliances are not particularly wedded to the sub-treasury bill" and that "if relief will come from some other source, well and good."[65]

William Lamb and J. M. Perdue did not share Dixon's ambivalence about the plan. With the blessing of state president Evan Jones and the assistance of Milton Park, the new editor of the *Southern Mercury*, in the fall and winter of 1890 they reorganized and mobilized the state Alliance's lecturing system, with the explicit goal of educating the membership on the fine points of the Subtreasury. This effort included the appointment of seven special congressional district–level lecturers to work alongside the existing county and state lecturers. By early 1891 hundreds of suballiances had heard presentations on the plan, and Alliancefolk were being asked to stand up and be counted: Did they support the plan or not? If so, then they could not in good conscience continue to support any party that opposed it.[66]

The leadership of the state Democratic Party opposed it, virtually to a man. This is not to say they took the Alliance lightly; the only question was whether they could maintain the allegiance of Alliancemen while opposing what was fast becoming a litmus test of the order's members. One Texas politician thought he knew a way. Born in 1851 on a small plantation in Rusk County in the East Texas Piney Woods, James Stephen Hogg had used his considerable talents and the connections of his father, a Confederate general, to enter local politics, where he earned a reputation as a successful district attorney. Intelligent and personable, the six-foot, three-inch, three-hundred-pound Texas governor was an effective orator who could speak the language of ordinary people (plate 5). In 1886 he had run successfully for attorney general and soon gained a reputation as a reformer. The 1889 legislature passed a weak antitrust law but refused to act on railroad regulation, which gave Hogg the political opening he needed. In 1890 he announced for governor, making the creation of a railroad commission the centerpiece of his campaign—a clever way to co-opt Alliance support without having to endorse the much more controversial Subtreasury. With strong backing from Alliancemen, he won the race. A sizable minority of the new legislators were themselves Alliancemen, a development that boded well for the commission bill.[67]

Almost from the start of his administration, however, Hogg ran afoul of the Alliance. When the legislative session got under way in January 1891 and Hogg's commission bill began winding its way through the legislature, Alliancemen were dismayed to discover that members of the proposed three-man commission would be appointed by the governor, not elected. To lobby the legislature on behalf of the Alliance, President Evan Jones appointed a committee consisting of R. J. Sledge, the well-to-do Allianceman from Hays County who had bankrolled Macune's *National Economist,* and Jesse Harrison "Harry"

Tracy, a successful farmer, reform editor, and deputy national lecturer for the Alliance.[68]

Tracy had already emerged as one of the keenest minds in the nascent People's Revolt (plate 6). Born in Georgia in 1840, he had risen to the rank of lieutenant colonel in the Confederate army before settling down to farm and engage in the mercantile business in Milam County. He made enough money to turn his business over to his younger brother Nat (who later became a prominent Democratic legislator) and moved to the new Dallas suburb of Oak Cliff. Soon he rose through the lecturer ranks of the Alliance and became the publisher of the *Southern Mercury*. A dapper dresser who sported short, dark hair and a neatly trimmed full beard and moustache, the urbane, articulate Tracy became the foremost expositor of the Subtreasury Plan. Arriving in Austin, Tracy and Sledge settled in to their quarters in the opulent new Driskill Hotel, where they hobnobbed with legislators and other lobbyists when they were not buttonholing lawmakers a few blocks up Congress Avenue at the pink-domed capitol. As the session proceeded, it became clear that some of the Alliance legislators owed more allegiance to Governor Hogg than to the Alliance, and they supported his appointive commission while steadfastly opposing any legislative endorsement of the Subtreasury Plan, which Tracy and Sledge surely wanted.[69]

Matters came to a head six weeks into the session, when eight of the thirty-two Alliance members in the House signed a manifesto denouncing Tracy and Sledge and branding pro-Subtreasury Alliancemen traitors to the order. Tracy responded with a letter charging that the signers were disgruntled because they had been ousted from leadership positions at the last state Alliance meeting. Two weeks later Tracy and one of the manifesto's principal authors, Benjamin Franklin Rogers, a former Alliance state lecturer and member of the order's state executive committee, got into an argument that degenerated into a fistfight in the rear of the House chamber. Rogers landed the first punch, a "stunner" on Tracy's prominent Roman nose, but then the fifty-year-old Tracy, said to be "bulky and tough," returned the blow. A "stand up, left and right fisticuff" ensued, with Tracy holding a slight advantage when bystanders finally broke up the fight. These events brought the rupture in the Alliance ranks out into the open as never before, with charges and countercharges of corruption and duplicity exchanged between the two sides.[70]

After the Railroad Commission bill passed, Hogg ignored Alliance requests to name an Allianceman to the three-person agency, disingenuously claiming he had never seen a petition calling for an Alliance appointee. His actions further divided the Alliance, hastening the exodus of Alliance radicals from the Democratic Party. In retrospect, Hogg's tactics probably were purposeful. He was astute enough as a politician to recognize that the appointment of one Allianceman to the new commission would not forestall the third-party movement. The political Alliancefolk had moved well beyond the Railroad Commission in their demands. No Democrat could embrace the Subtreasury Plan and hope to hold a statewide office, so Hogg likely calculated that it was time to force the issue; Hogg's moderately progressive reforms, most notably the commission, would hold enough Alliancemen in the party, and the rest might as well go their own way, sooner rather than later.[71]

Meanwhile, plans at the national level for a new third-party movement had gained momentum. In December 1890 the Alliance's National Council convened in Ocala, Florida, and officially made the Subtreasury part of the order's platform. Daws and Perdue were among the four official Texas members of the council, although Macune, Tracy, Lamb, and other Texans were there, too, in their various capacities as officers of the organization. Prominent Knights of Labor and representatives of the Colored Alliance were also present. The burning question was whether these leaders would commit the Alliance to a new third party. A majority of the delegates, being southern Democrats and reluctant to abandon the Party of the Fathers, opposed the idea. However, the Colored Alliancemen and the Texas radicals, no doubt backed by some of the Knights who were present, pushed for the third party. In his presidential address, President L. L. Polk outlined a political agenda that seemed highly unlikely to ever garner the support of the major parties, and a National Reform Press Association was founded, with William Lamb as one of its three national directors. Macune, still influential as chairman of the executive committee and never a proponent of third-party action, again forged a compromise, proposing that a grand conference of farm and labor organizations be held in February 1892 to decide the third-party question. The radicals acquiesced, probably sensing that the movement still lacked sufficient strength to sustain a new national party.[72]

Now Midwesterners took the lead, calling for a conference of reform organizations to meet in Cincinnati in May 1891 to debate the creation of a new party. The question of whether the Texas Alliance would send delegates immediately arose. As it happened, state Alliance leaders were meeting in Waco in April to further enlarge and perfect the lecturing system, and that meeting soon turned into yet another debate about the order's role in politics. Sentiment ran strong for a declaration of support for a third party, but Macune, fighting his last rearguard action, succeeded in defeating the move, in exchange for acquiescing in sending a delegation to the Cincinnati conference.[73]

Just over fourteen hundred delegates arrived in Cincinnati, with nearly a third of them Kansans (where a state People's Party had already been founded) and another third hailing from four other Midwestern states. Only thirty-six delegates were from southern states, but twenty-seven of these were Texans. When it assembled, the gathering bore all the marks of a major-party national convention. In short order, the delegates brushed aside all opposition and declared the birth of the People's Party. A committee headed by the Minnesota writer Ignatius Donnelly drafted a platform incorporating the Ocala Demands, including the Subtreasury Plan. As Donnelly finished his speech, an "unearthly Indian-like yell" issued forth from the Texas delegation. One reporter jocularly claimed that the voice "gave all the women in Cincinnati and for miles around the hysterics." The source of the yell was James Harvey Davis, an Alliance newspaper editor from Sulphur Springs in northeast Texas. Better known by his moniker "Methodist Jim" (though he was a Disciple of Christ, not a Methodist), bestowed on him because of the preacher-like zeal of his political speeches, he had been a county judge in the early 1880s and a loyal Democrat until the promulgation of the Ocala Platform. Rail-thin and more than six feet tall, with a goatee and dark piercing eyes, he exercised daily, dressed flamboyantly, and had a knack for attracting attention. He was soon called to the podium to reprise the rebel yell, after which he gave an impromptu but impassioned speech declaring his southern heritage, calling for an end to sectional hatred, and a making a full-throated endorsement of the newly written platform. As he finished his speech, an Indiana delegate who was a Union veteran mounted the stage and grasped hands with him, saying "God bless you my brother from Texas." As the delegates cheered them on, a third man— Superintendent Richard Humphrey of the Colored Alliance—mounted the stage and joined them in the embrace, prompting papers to later run the headline "BLUE, GRAY AND BLACK Clasp Hands During a Scene of the Wildest Enthusiasm." It was a memorable scene, despite the fact that Humphrey was white and Davis later had to clarify that he was too young to have actually fought in the late war. Davis would soon be stumping the nation on behalf of the People's Party, and at a debate in Kentucky he gained another nickname: "Cyclone." Sometimes for better and often for worse, the tireless, ambitious, loquacious Davis would become the most famous Texas Populist nationally, a force to be reckoned with on the stump and in party councils but also a loose cannon with more than a hint of the demagogue in him.[74]

At Cincinnati each state's delegation elected three members to serve as their state's representatives on the new party's national executive committee. The twenty-seven Texans chose Davis, Lamb, and Thomas Gaines, the able young leader of the independent movement in Comanche County. In states like Texas with no established People's Party structure, the three-man committee was also empowered to begin the work of creating the state party. Lamb, who had done more than any other man to bring about the People's Revolt in Texas, was chosen by his fellow Texans to chair the effort in the Lone Star State. After returning to Texas, in early June he issued a call for a convention to meet in Dallas in mid-August to inaugurate the new party. During June and July, Lamb, Davis, Knights leader Bill Farmer, and others began attending Alliance encampments, labor rallies, and other events where they openly promoted the new party. When speaking at Alliance gatherings, some, including Stump Ashby and Harry Tracy, continued to maintain the pretense that the Alliance was strictly nonpartisan and avoided openly proselytizing for the new party, but with the Alliance on record with the Subtreasury as its litmus test, such declarations seemed increasingly academic. All seemed to be looking forward with great anticipation to the Dallas convention that would officially give birth to the Texas People's Party.[75]

It had been a long road from those earliest Alliance third-party efforts in the Cross Timbers, through the Greenbacker and Union Labor campaigns, to the point where Texans could now see a viable vehicle for challenging the political status quo at the state and even national level. The Alliance had been the principal vehicle on this road, but it was often a ramshackle vehicle prone to breakdowns and reversals. Without the much more focused efforts of the Knights of Labor, prodding, pushing, and making common cause with Alliancefolk, the Alliance's demands—now the People's Party demands—would lack their punch and specificity. The cooperative experience had also played a crucial role, though ultimately a negative one. The movement had recruited tens of thousands of men and women to the Alliance with the promise of economic empowerment in the face of corporate monopoly. Steeped in the political culture of laissez-faire classical liberalism, Texans had been taught to distrust government, especially a powerful federal government that might interfere with the South's "peculiar" racial arrangements. The cooperative crusade had required no abandonment of these principles. Indeed, the Colored Alliance notwithstanding, it seemed comfortably consistent with both white supremacy and the communal spirit of southern churches and families. But the failure of the cooperatives, and especially of the Alliance Exchange, had produced disappointment and disillusionment, which were all the more acute because of the cooperatives' great promise. If a solution as brilliantly devised as Macune's Exchange—and as fervently supported by thousands of hardworking, God-fearing people—could not succeed in curbing the greed of the monopolists, then what alternative remained other than to seize control of the one institution with the power to rein in the corporations—the government? Industrial workers had been the first to reach this conclusion, for they were not bound by the hoary mythology of the Jeffersonian yeoman that proclaimed the providential sanctity of the individual. Farmers had required more time, more association with the plight of those workers, more education by their lecturers and the reform press, and finally, the searing firsthand experience of the failed cooperative crusade, to bring them into consonance with their brethren in the labor movement.

Out in the hinterlands, people like Sam Johnson had seen and read enough. They were ready for action. As a Confederate veteran, Sam could have reasonably been expected to loyally—some would say blindly—support the Democratic Party. But folks like Sam had also been taught to think for themselves, and the Alliance had been Sam's school of political economy. Once he had grasped the logic of the Subtreasury Plan, other Alliance political demands, such as a progressive income tax or government ownership of the railroads, seemed not nearly as radical as the Democratic mossbacks made them out to be. From his remote Hill Country farm, it was a long buggy ride over bone-jarring roads just to get to a railroad, but Sam would answer William Lamb's call and make his way to Dallas in the sweltering August heat to be there for the birth of the new party.

Sam was not alone in reaching these conclusions. In the months that followed, from across the Lone Star State, men and women who had been schooled in the Alliance called on their fellow Texans to embrace third-party action. In the pages of the *Southern Mercury*, militant pleas began to appear, such as one that asked, "Does It Pay Working Men to Vote the Old Party Ticket?" The anonymous writer then ticked off a list of reasons why the answer was no:

Look at your wife and daughter in the cotton patch!
Look at your 6 cent cotton!
Look at the mortgage on your property!
Look at the old hat you wear!
Look at your old clothes

Look at the old leaky, rickety house you live in!
Look at the food on your table!
Look at the furniture in the place you call house!
Look at the empty schoolhouse and full jail!
Look at the 9,000,000 mortgaged homes!
Look at the millionaire in his palace and the working man in his hovel!
Look at the millionaires' militia shoot down peaceable citizens!
Then feel in your empty pocket and, if you are not thoroughly convinced,
   go and hang yourself for being an egregious fool and you will do one
   sensible thing.[76]

Nor was it just men who were deciding that the time for political action had come. As Alliancefolk debated the wisdom of third-party action, an anonymous woman from Ellis County in the Blackland Prairie south of Dallas wrote to the *Southern Mercury*. Her use of the pen name "Ann Other" revealed two things about her. First, she (or perhaps her husband) did not want to risk the disapproval or ridicule from her neighbors that might well await a woman who spoke out on political issues. Second, the name suggested her firm belief that she spoke for other Texans; she was but "another" of the many who felt this way. In her letter "Ann" called for the Alliance to join with the Knights of Labor and other labor organizations to unite "in the great objective work of elevating labor." She argued that self-help of the type championed by the Alliance "cannot lift the burdens of her people alone, no matter what her enterprises. This must be accomplished by legislation, and legislation demands a majority, and, in these times of corruption, an immense majority." She then painted a dramatic picture of children laboring in fields and factories, illustrating the cost of continuing inaction. The Alliance's cooperative ventures, she explained, have been like ships launched on a stormy sea, "but they have invariably been started with a debt hanging over them, and the result has been broken masts and leaking vessels, and finally the swallowing up of the whole enterprise by our financial system. And still, some are short-sighted enough to think all that is needed is the work of the Alliance, never seeing that she is but as one wave of the mighty ocean of labor, and although some of her local enterprises may go down the principle of labor united against oppression will never die while free government exists."[77]

The key, in Ann's analysis, was "free government." In a democracy, the government was not supposed to be some distant, disembodied power. It was intended to be controlled by the people and conducted in their interest.

To Populists, the very definition of the word "democracy"—from the Greek *demos* (people) and *kratia* (rule)—was something to be taken seriously and literally. When Populists complained about the rule of "elites," "plutocrats," or "the money power," they were identifying a system gone awry, in which democracy had ceased to function properly. The government did not merely belong to the people, it *was* the people. It remained to be seen whether Populists could reclaim the heritage of democracy they believed to be their birthright as Americans.

2 • The Birth of the People's Party and the Election of 1892

There has never been such an upheaval of the people as is being witnessed to-day. He who does not see it is blind; who does not hear it is deaf, and who does not understand it is too stupid to be classed among the intelligent. The great industrial problem, embracing labor, land, finance, transportation, monopoly, taxation, etc., is being discussed more earnestly and thoughtfully than ever before and the people intend to enforce their ideas at the ballot box; in fact there is a complete uprising of the people.
—R. Alford, Milam County, Texas, 1891

Alonzo Bostwick Bristol seemed an unlikely choice to become a Populist. An Ohio-born architect and builder, he had moved to Houston after the Civil War and to North Texas in the 1880s, eventually settling in Dallas. He developed an interest in spiritualism, helping to found the First Spiritualist Society of Dallas, and he also became an ardent supporter of women's rights, serving in a leadership position of the Dallas Equal Rights Club. His unconventional religious and social views did not keep his business from thriving, though, and in 1887 his firm received a plum contract: to design and build a new city hall for the booming city.[1]

When the structure at the corner of Commerce and Sycamore Streets was completed seventeen months later, it was a landmark of which the growing city could be proud. Costing the city the extravagant sum of eighty thousand dollars, the four-floor building was described by the local newspaper as "modern mainly, with a slight leaning toward the gothic," although Bristol probably would have classified it as Renaissance Revival. Its most notable feature was the unusual amount of glass used, leading the *Dallas Morning News* to observe "that there appears more glass on the walls than masonry" (plate 7). The ample windows, which made the structure exceptionally "well ventilated," were particularly welcome at 10:00 a.m. on August 17, 1891, because the temperature outside was already well on its way to a high of ninety-eight degrees when, in the building's second-floor auditorium, forty-year-old William Lamb gaveled to order the founding convention of the Texas People's Party.[2]

There is no record of whether Bristol was present that Monday morning in the building he had designed, but as a man who been among the "old guard of greenbackers" in the 1870s and an organizer of the Union Labor Party in the 1880s, he surely was in sympathy with the goals of this latest third-party movement. (He went on to chair the Dallas County Populist executive committee, serve as president of the Dallas Populist Club, and run for county tax assessor on the Populist ticket.) In truth, the gathering did not really need the capacious auditorium, which seated a thousand people, because only fifty delegates, plus a smattering of interested onlookers and reporters, had arrived in downtown Dallas that day to see the new party born. Stump Ashby was there, of course, having spent the previous few months feverishly traveling the state, giving three-hour speeches and promoting the idea of the third party. Politically knowledgeable attendees would have immediately recognized the venerable, bewhiskered intellectual and longtime political maverick Ebenezer Lafayette Dohoney from Paris, Texas. Other notables included Hiram Broiles, the independent mayor of Fort Worth; James Madison Perdue, the main author of the Cleburne Demands; Thomas Gaines, the energetic young editor from Comanche who was already a Populist national committeeman; Marion Martin, the former Democratic lieutenant governor; Theodore J. McMinn, the loquacious attorney from San Antonio; and up from his remote ranch on the Pedernales River in the Hill Country, the lanky former Confederate cavalryman, trail driver, and Alliance lecturer Sam Ealy Johnson.[3]

The road to Dallas had not been a straight one. The rough-hewn Lamb—if not the father of the Texas People's Party, then certainly its godfather—had faced criticism for scheduling the convention the day before the annual state Alliance meeting in Dallas, because it looked like a transparent effort to merge the Alliance into the new political party. Harry Tracy, the dapper, well-to-do Alliance lecturer and editor who had spent so much time promoting the Subtreasury Plan and who lived just across the Trinity River from downtown Dallas in the affluent new suburb of Oak Cliff, had spent much time and energy that spring in a last-ditch effort to head off a third-party movement by trying to get the state's Democrats to endorse the Subtreasury. When he learned that Lamb had scheduled the Populist convention for Dallas on the day before the Alliance meeting, Tracy was reportedly "considerably hot under the collar about it" because it would create the perception that the two bodies "were meeting together for political purposes." "I want to emphasize the fact," he declared, "that the alliance has nothing on earth to do with the people's party convention, and is in nowise responsible for its being held in Dallas at the time of the meeting of the state alliance." Tracy worried "that the enemies of the alliance will spread the report that the call was made for the purpose of enabling the alliance to affiliate as such with the third party movement." Tracy had not attended the Cincinnati convention that created a structure for the national People's Party, choosing instead to stay home in Texas delivering Alliance speeches and debating Democratic congressman David Culberson. He would be found in the ranks of the Populists soon enough, but his absence at the Dallas convention suggests the probable reason so many others stayed away: giving up on the Democratic Party was not something undertaken lightly, and it was still possible that the plunge into third-party politics was premature. Other future leaders of the party had their own reasons for not attending. Men like Cyclone Davis, Thomas Nugent, and Jerome Kearby, who would likely be candidates for office at the hands of the new party, would not want to appear to be jockeying for position or currying favor with the delegates. Better to see what happened in Dallas and bide one's time. After all, the next elections were still more than a year away.[4]

Of course, Lamb had never been reticent where politics were concerned. From his earliest days as an Alliance organizer he had been pushing the organization in the direction of independent political action, and he had little patience for those like Tracy who took the cautious approach. When a reporter from the *Dallas Morning News* interviewed him in early July, Lamb had minced no words, as the reporter's questions and Lamb's answers reveal:

REPORTER: "While the alliance is not a partisan political organization, is it not true that it has adopted demands that can only be secured through legislative enactments?"

LAMB: "It is."

REPORTER: "Will those demands be granted by either of the old parties?"

LAMB: "They will not."

REPORTER: "Is your party in line with those demands?"

LAMB: "It is, it having adopted them in full."

REPORTER: "That being the case, what remains for the alliance as a non-partisan organization but to vote with your party?"

LAMB: "That's all that is left for it."[5]

With Lamb presiding as temporary chair, he appointed members to the committee on permanent organization and the platform committee. While the committees commenced their work, Lamb gave a short speech recommending the adoption of the Cincinnati platform, supplemented by state platform planks as recently promulgated by the Texas Federation of Labor. When the committees reappeared, the organization committee announced its choice for permanent convention chair, Stump Ashby, with Thomas Gaines as secretary. William Lamb would remain a significant figure in the new party, but he would never again chair a state Populist convention. That job would be left to men like Ashby, whose oratorical abilities and political skills far outstripped those of Lamb.[6]

Once in the chair, Ashby realized that if the new party were to have any real legitimacy in the eyes of the public, a convention with a mere fifty delegates could not commit the party to any significant course of action. After some general speechmaking and a somewhat contentious debate about the role of African Americans in the party—a debate that will be examined in depth in Chapter 5—Ashby wisely adjourned the convention with plans to meet in February 1892 in Fort Worth.

In the months following the Dallas convention, the political divide in Texas grew deeper and wider, with the Subtreasury Plan the principal point of division. In October the chair of the state Democratic executive committee, Newton Webster Finley, issued a public statement barring all pro-Subtreasury Alliancemen from participating in the 1892 Democratic primaries, a move that essentially read Subtreasuryites out of the party. Branding the Subtreasury men "skunk Democrats," Finley seemed determined to test whether Alliancemen and other advocates of the Subtreasury would really abandon the Party of the Fathers.[7]

In response to Finley's proclamation, a group of men identifying themselves as "sub-treasury democrats" issued "a hot manifesto," likely written by Harry Tracy, denouncing Finley and reiterating its signers' support for the Subtreasury Plan. Among those who signed were a number of men destined to become major Populist leaders, including J. K. P. Hanna, Henry E. McCulloch, E. S. Peters, Milton Park, Taylor McRae, E. O. Meitzen, R. W. Coleman, and Tracy himself. Interviewed about the manifesto, Tracy stated, "This is no

Farmers' alliance nor any other organized labor movement, but a plain, blunt, protest. . . . It is a movement on the part of democrats to preserve democratic government in Texas." Throughout the first half of 1892, even as the People's Party became better organized, meetings of so-called Jeffersonian Democrats convened throughout the state to denounce Finley and the Democratic establishment and to endorse various versions of Alliance and Populist demands. William Lamb attended one such conference that Tracy called in February, good-naturedly telling a reporter, "I was merely present as a looker-on. I took no part whatever in the proceedings, I being a people's party man." Establishment Democratic papers were quick to argue that the terms "Jeffersonian Democrats," "Third Party," and "People's Party" were all synonymous, inasmuch as they all endorsed Populist platforms.[8]

In the meantime, the state Populist convention reconvened in a state district courtroom in Fort Worth on February 2. This time, between three and four hundred people were present, although that number included press and onlookers. The main work of the convention was to fill the positions on the state executive committee that had gone unfilled at the sparsely attended Dallas meeting and to select delegates to the upcoming national conference of reform organizations to be held at St. Louis. Significantly, the St. Louis delegation would include two women, Bettie Gay and Ellen Dabbs, and two African Americans, Henry Jennings and R. H. Hayes. Recognizing the need to "aid the colored members of the party in spreading the People's party principles among their race, a general subscription was asked for and was liberally responded to." Before adjourning, the delegates agreed to meet for a state nominating convention sometime prior to July 4, ahead of the state's Democrats and Republicans.[9]

The Congress of Industrial Organizations convened in St. Louis on February 22. Members of the Southern Alliance constituted about one-third of the delegates, but it attracted representatives from a dozen or so reform organizations. Technically, the People's Party was not one of the organizations represented at the congress, although the national Populist organization and the recently established National Reform Press Association both planned to meet in St. Louis that same week. Editor Milton Park of the *Southern Mercury*, who was still trying to maintain the nonpartisan stance of the Alliance, made a show of claiming that the state's Populist contingent and the official Alliance delegation were traveling on different trains and had absolutely nothing to do with one another, but in truth virtually all of the Texans going to St. Louis planned to attend the congress, and most of those who had publicly endorsed the Third Party intended to push the convention toward an endorsement of the People's Party. Certainly no one could doubt where William Lamb, J. M. Perdue, Thomas Gaines, Cyclone Davis, Ellen Dabbs, O. F. Dornblaser, and E. L. Dohoney—all of whom were in St. Louis—stood on the Third-Party question. Indeed, the only Texans still seeming to oppose an endorsement of the People's Party were Charles Macune and his ally, Alliance national lecturer Ben Terrell, and both men still wielded significant influence. Indeed, Terrell had been chosen to open the convention as its temporary chairman. After two days of wrangling, however, the credentials committee certified as delegates almost all who could claim to represent one of the reform organizations comprising the congress, and since virtually all the Texans were also members of the Alliance or the Knights, they were allowed to participate. When Southern Alliance president Leonidas Lafayette Polk of North Carolina, a proponent of third-party action, was chosen as permanent president of the convention, Macune and the conservatives knew they were outnumbered. In the end, the conference adopted a platform based on Alliance and Knights of Labor demands. Finally realizing the near inevitability of a national third party, as the meeting was adjourning Macune leapt to the floor and called for the congress to join with the People's Party in calling for a national nominating convention to be held that summer, after the conventions of the two major parties. Although this sudden quasi-endorsement of the People's Party appeared to be a dramatic reversal on Macune's part, in reality it was his last-gasp effort to give the Democratic Party one final chance to endorse Alliance demands and head off the third-party movement. The nominating convention was set for July 4 in Omaha, Nebraska. Although he may not have known it, Charles Macune, whose fertile mind had done so much to bring about the People's Revolt, had just performed his last major act on a national political stage. The Populist future would belong to other, more politically daring leaders.[10]

~

When Texas Populists gathered for their state nominating convention in Dallas on June 23, 1892, it marked the culmination of ten months of intensive grassroots organizing. A report from Erath County in the Cross Timbers illustrates the nature of that organizing. In late February the local Alliance paper, the *Dublin Progress*, printed the speaking schedule of an organizer from neighboring Jack County. "Brother" Wesley W. Brandenburg was due to speak thirty-nine times in forty-four days in Erath County. It is significant that Brandenburg was making Alliance speeches in February and March but by June he was back in Erath County, and the *Progress*, reporting on a four-hour speech he had made, now noted that "as a missionary Mr. Brandenburg is a success and he generally leaves the people's party a booming."[11]

In the region between San Antonio and Houston, home to many Germans, Czechs, and Poles, Edward Otto Meitzen had been doing similar work. The son of a radical refugee who had fled the Silesian region of Prussia in the aftermath of the Revolutions of 1848, Meitzen had risen to the position of assistant state lecturer of the Alliance. Like many Alliancefolk, he had been reluctant to leave the Democratic Party, and he had even questioned the wisdom of the actions taken at the St. Louis convention, but now he relinquished all reservations. Gathering five hundred Lavaca County citizens before him in front of the courthouse in Hallettsville, he read the St. Louis platform, first in English and then in German. Another speaker then read it again in Bohemian, whereupon the crowd enthusiastically approved the document by a show of hands. As the local paper reported, the people of Lavaca County had "crossed the dead line that separated them from the party of their fathers and of their youth and manhood without regret, and with the enthusiasm of new converts some even administered a parting kick at its intangible corpus." The lines between the Alliance, the People's Party, Jeffersonian Democrats, and other independents were gradually dissolving. The hard work of Lamb, Ashby, Tracy, Perdue, Brandenburg, Meitzen, and many others was finally paying off.[12]

The extent of the party's progress became apparent in Dallas. At the 1891 convention the fifty attendees had seemed lonely in the grand A. B. Bristol–designed city hall auditorium; this time, every chair in the thousand-seat hall was occupied by a credentialed delegate. Bristol himself, having chaired Dallas's county Populist convention the previous week, was now there as a Dallas County delegate, undoubtedly pleased with the scene. As the delegates prepared to nominate candidates, draft a platform, and plan the upcoming campaign, reporters commented on the fact that a large majority of the delegates were gray-headed men over forty, although many of the leaders were younger. The *Southern Mercury* claimed that 90 percent had always belonged to one of the two major parties, but clearly many had been active in the various third-party and independent movements of the previous two decades. The *Mercury* also reported that three-fourths had served in the Confederate army, although the source of that statistic is unclear. The proceedings of the convention provided numerous indications of ways in which the People's Party would both resemble and dramatically depart from the traditions of Texas party politics.[13]

Party leaders arrived in Dallas with several objectives. Although few admitted it, many likely understood the improbability of a new party electing its statewide slate of officials the first time out. Two years later, Thomas L. Nugent allegedly told "intimate friends" that he had viewed the 1892 race as "a forlorn hope otherwise than in its educational effects upon the people." But whether or not the realists among the Populists expected victory, the campaign that was to be inaugurated at the Dallas convention would, as Nugent noted, lay a foundation on which Populism's fate in Texas would depend. The delegates needed not only to nominate a strong slate of candidates—men who would embody Populist ideals of civic virtue and moral rectitude—but also to do so in a manner that would set them apart from the corrupt politicians who controlled the old parties. The platform should strongly express Populist principles but also be broad enough to attract the largest possible number of voters. And the delegates would have to achieve these goals while using the traditional mechanism of the American political convention, which lent itself to the kind of petty arm-twisting and selfish infighting that Populists had denounced in the Democrats and Republicans. It was a tall order.[14]

The day before the convention began, party insiders caucused at the law office of Jerome Kearby, the longtime Greenbacker and champion of independent political causes in Dallas. It was "whispered," according to the Dallas-Galveston *News*, that the purpose of the meeting "was the preparation of a slate upon which all could be harmonious." While this may have been a wise tactic, it risked alienating delegates who wished to avoid the appearance of decisions being made in a smoke-filled room. Leaders soon found themselves denying that any slates of candidates had been formulated in advance of the convention. "If there are," stated W. R. Cole of Dallas, "the delegates will smash them as soon as they are discovered. These people are not here to hand out offices, but to labor for principle." When another delegate tried to "have a consultation for the adoption of a programme merely to expedite business" prior to the convention, he discovered that "even this was opposed because it smacked of caucusing."[15]

Party leaders kept tight-lipped about what transpired in the meeting at Kearby's office, but subsequent events strongly suggest that their aim was to derail the candidacy of Henry E. McCulloch. During the weeks leading up to the state convention, county conventions had met all over Texas to choose delegates and instruct them on whom to support for the gubernatorial nomination. Overwhelmingly, they backed McCulloch. Born in Tennessee in 1816, McCulloch was a well-known figure in Texas, having compiled a celebrated record as an early pioneer, Texas Ranger, and Confederate general. In the 1850s he had served in both houses of the legislature and as US marshal. Since many southerners viewed a military record as a valuable prerequisite for high office, and few Populists boasted widespread name recognition outside Alliance and labor circles, the McCulloch boom in the spring of 1892 was easy to understand.[16]

Populist leaders, however, were wary of the old soldier. At age seventy-five his health was poor, and he likely would not be able to endure the rigors of the upcoming campaign. Worse still, his only significant post–Civil War political service had come as superintendent of the state Deaf and Dumb Asylum, where his mismanagement had led to a legislative investigation and his resignation under a cloud in 1879. Party insiders no doubt shuddered at the thought of such a flawed candidate leading their ticket.[17]

Fortunately for the party, an alternative candidate existed, and the Populist leaders were determined to bring his name to the fore. Thomas Lewis Nugent was a fifty-year-old native of Louisiana who had moved to Texas in 1861 after graduating with highest honors from Centenary College (plate 8). His interests tended toward the intellectual—he loved classical music and philosophy, and as a young man had considered the ministry—but he had served in the Confederate army and distinguished himself at the Battle of Shiloh before returning to Texas, where he taught school and studied law. In 1873 he moved to the frontier town of Stephenville, eighty miles southwest of Fort Worth, where he established a successful legal practice. Nugent entered public life in 1875, when Erath County voters elected him as a delegate to that year's state constitutional convention. There he exhibited his first populistic tendencies, working unsuccessfully to defeat the granting of public lands to railroad corporations. Four years later Democratic governor Oran M. Roberts appointed him to a state district court judgeship, and he went on to win two elected terms on the court, retiring from the bench in 1888 to return to private practice. He supported the 1887 state prohibition campaign and, with backing from the Farmers' Alliance, received the Union Labor Party's nomination for the state supreme court in 1888. By 1891 he had relocated to the rapidly growing city of Fort Worth, where good-paying legal clients were more plentiful and he could find better treatment for his diabetes-related health problems.[18]

Except for the issue of his health, Nugent was in many respects an ideal candidate. Reserved, thoughtful, and scholarly, his private character was beyond reproach. Those familiar with his judicial record held him in the highest regard, and having never held a legislative or executive office, he was untainted by the rough-and-tumble world of partisan politics. Although a lawyer and thus ineligible for membership, he had long supported the Farmers' Alliance and was much respected by the order. As one supporter exclaimed when Nugent's name first began to emerge as a gubernatorial possibility, "The people want such a leader, with the heart of a patriot, the experience of a statesman, the legal acumen of a judge and the bonhomm[i]e of one who loves his fellow man." Few of the Populist rank and file outside of his home region knew him, however, so he could scarcely match McCulloch's name recognition. Indeed, prior to the month of the convention, his name was almost wholly absent from press discussions of Third-Party affairs. On June 6, barely two weeks before the Dallas convention, the Dallas and Galveston papers published a letter from Nugent discussing the situation. He stated that he had given his "half-hearted consent" to let his friends put forward his name, but now he was definitively declining the honor, citing his health and the state of his finances. Far from putting a stop to the mounting speculation that he would be a candidate, though, the letter only seemed to encourage supporters who could claim, in the finest tradition of American politics, that their candidate was the reluctant statesman with no personal ambition for office.[19]

Less than a week later in his former hometown of Stephenville, Nugent delivered a major policy address that was widely published in both the big-city dailies and the reform press, garnering his first real statewide publicity. The sister papers *Galveston Daily News* and *Dallas Morning News* called the speech "the most cogent and most persuasive which has thus far been contributed to the promotion of a people's party campaign in Texas. It has features well calculated to alarm the mechanical unitarians of both the old parties who have been accustomed to rely on straddling, trimming and organized cowardice with regard to great questions of principle as staple expedients for gaining or retaining offices and power." Although the conservative, probusiness *News* was no friend to the active-government liberalism that Nugent enunciated in his speech, the newspaper clearly recognized that if a man like Nugent became the new party's standard-bearer, it would indeed signal the arrival of a new brand of politics in Texas—new both in style and in substance. In the space of a month, the quiet man with the bald head, full gray beard, and placid countenance had gone from being a relatively obscure ex-judge to being the insiders' favorite as the leader for the new party.[20]

At ten o'clock on the morning of June 24, temporary chairman Stump Ashby called the convention to order, wielding a gavel made from a timber taken from the Lampasas farmhouse where the first Alliance supposedly met in 1877. That the Populists recognized the symbolic significance of the founding of the Alliance in this way suggests that they understood the emotional and historical dynamics of their undertaking. Delegates soon elected Ashby permanent chairman, which clothed him with the power of appointing committees, including the all-important rules committee. Ashby, a former Methodist minister, had enjoyed a long association with Nugent, having once served as his preacher in Stephenville, and he planned to use his influence to make sure that the rules favored Nugent's candidacy. When the committee reported rules for consideration by the whole convention, it proposed requiring a three-fourths vote on the first ballot for nominations, followed by a two-thirds vote on the second ballot and a majority on subsequent ballots. Delegates immediately objected, arguing that "they should follow the footsteps of Jefferson" and support majority rule from the outset. The proposed rule, one delegate complained, "was instituted to defeat the will of the majority" and was therefore "anti-people's party." Politically savvy delegates understood what was happening. Since so many county delegations had come to the convention with instructions to support McCulloch on the first ballot, allowing a simple majority vote on the first ballot would almost certainly give him the nomination. If, however, McCulloch could not muster the three-fourths vote on the first ballot, delegates would be released from their pledges and would then be free to support another candidate, presumably Nugent. After some heated wrangling, delegate Thomas King of Erath County, a former law partner of Nugent, called the question and the three-fourths rule won adoption.

On the second day of the convention McCulloch indeed led on the first ballot, 547 votes to Nugent's 412. "It was clearly seen that a great many delegates who were instructed for McCulloch wanted to change to Judge Nugent, who seemed to be a favorite, owing to his personal popularity and his wonderful ability in handling his subject," a Populist editor reported. Nugent's supporters swung into action, "leaving no stone flat on the ground without turning over for a Nugent vote," according to the *News,* which described the opposition to McCulloch as "firm, though gentle and considerate." Following a recess, McCulloch mounted the podium, "and to the astonishment of the convention withdrew his name in the interest of harmony." He gave a magnanimous speech, declaring that if his "name did not meet with perfect unanimity it was best for the cause that I would withdraw," after which the delegates nominated Nugent by acclamation. Interviewed after the convention, Dallas city alderman M. B. Loonie, a Democrat, exclaimed, "I never in my political experience saw such slick work as was done" in the Populist convention. "In the first place McCulloch, with a majority vote, unexpectedly to the outsiders withdrew in the interest of Judge Nugent, the stronger man before the people.

This example was followed by others all through the nominations for state offices, showing a purpose to solidify the following of the leaders."[21]

The McCulloch-Nugent contest revealed the complex mix of idealism and realpolitik that would necessarily characterize the history of the People's Party in Texas. Nugent was clearly the stronger candidate, and his personal qualities and reformist credentials also made him the best possible spokesman for, and exemplar of, Populist principles. But engineering his nomination required the sort of political maneuvering that characterized old-party politics. Strictly political considerations in fact entered into several of the nomination contests. Stump Ashby, for example, was nominated for lieutenant governor but withdrew his name, acknowledging that it would be politically unwise for Fort Worth residents to receive the nominations for the two top spots on the ticket. (Marion Martin, a former Democratic lieutenant governor from Corsicana, received the nomination for his former office.) Delegates nominated C. C. Drake, an executive of the Fort Worth and Denver Railroad, for the office of state comptroller on the grounds that it "would be a concession to the railroad men," suggesting that the Populists were not out to demonize everyone associated with railroads or corporations. Similarly, the convention chose W. E. Clemmons, a school principal from Goliad County, for superintendent of public education in part because "he was of German parentage and potent among the Germans."[22]

Political expediency likewise dictated the party's course on certain controversial issues, including woman suffrage and prohibition. While some prominent Populists such as Eben Dohoney supported both causes, many did not, and party leaders understood the political risks of embracing policies they viewed as divisive or extraneous to the central issues of Populism. "It is my opinion that we should deal with these subjects very carefully and not load ourselves down with a good thing just because it is good," Alliance warhorse William Lamb had written back in February. "Let us put on only a moderate load and not make the cargo so great as to wreck the train by falling through the first little bridge we attempt to cross."[23]

Woman suffrage proved not to be terribly divisive, thanks largely to a strong speech by delegate Dr. Ellen Lawson Dabbs, who, though a suffragist herself, assured her fellow Populists that, for now at least, winning elections took precedence. Prohibition, however, caused a greater clamor at the convention. As a member of the platform committee, the veteran reformer Dohoney, known as the Father of Prohibition in Texas, authored a minority report denouncing the liquor traffic. Dohoney did not seek to outlaw alcohol; rather, he called for an abolition of federal revenue laws concerning liquor, "leaving the question of the manufacture and sale of liquors to the states, where it belongs, and that the deficit occasioned by the repeal of the law be supplied by an annual issue of legal tender treasury notes." He likewise called for a repeal of state liquor licensing, apparently basing both his demands on the belief that as long as state and federal governments were profiting from the liquor trade, prohibition stood little chance of succeeding. Despite this rather incremental approach to the prohibition question, the delegates viewed Dohoney's minority report as a "bombshell," with voices from the floor shouting, "Vote it down." After some heated debate, a motion to table the report carried, and the prohibition genie was coaxed back into its bottle.[24]

Another controversial proposal came to the floor courtesy of Gregg County's John O'Byrne, a member of the state executive committee. O'Byrne offered an amendment to the land plank calling for all unimproved land to be taxed at the same rate as improved land, a measure that would effectively force speculators to sell their land to actual settlers. This proposal embodied a key element of the so-called Single Tax, the radical scheme of New York economic theorist Henry George, who argued that heavily taxing unimproved lands would enable the government to abolish all other existing taxes while greatly spurring investment in productive resources. O'Byrne's plank had been part of the platform passed at the August 1891 convention as well as the February 1892 gathering, and it enjoyed broad support from many Alliancemen and the more radical Populists. The convention adopted the amendment, whereupon several prominent delegates objected, pointing out that "you will have to go before the people and defend this platform." Several voices cried out, "We cannot do it, we cannot do it," and confusion momentarily reigned in the hall. Harry Tracy, now definitely in the Populist camp and ever the hardheaded pragmatist, took the floor and warned, "If you don't look out you'll get in the soup. I tell you, you are wading in to deep water, and the best thing you can do is to look out for it." Tracy's warning prevailed, and the Single-Tax amendment was removed from the platform. Clearly, Texas Populists in 1892 wanted to draft a platform that would preserve the core elements of Populism without unduly alienating a large cross-section of more moderate voters.[25]

The convention likewise signaled the move toward the political center when it altered or eliminated two other planks that had been part of the August 1891 and February 1892 platforms. The earlier documents had called for free textbooks for Texas schoolchildren; the new platform suggested that the state publish textbooks and furnish them to students at cost. The convention also eliminated a proposal that the state use convict labor to build a railroad from the Red River to the Gulf of Mexico in order to create competitive rates and serve as a benchmark for setting commercial rates. Both of these proposals, if enacted, would have entailed great taxpayer expense, and with the state's deepening economic problems, they were deemed both politically and practically inexpedient. Populists might not oppose "big government," but they understood that expensive programs needed to be paid for, if not for strictly economic reasons then for political ones. The casting overboard of the Single Tax and the decisions to ignore or postpone divisive policies like prohibition, woman suffrage, and the state railroad gave the platform a decided liberal tone, as opposed to a radical or agrarian one.[26]

One constituency that the party desperately needed to attract was the urban labor vote. The 1891 platform had endorsed the eight-hour workday, an equitable mechanics' lien law, the removal of convict labor from competition with citizen labor, and the timely payment of workers discharged by the railroads. These planks would be repeated in the 1892 platform, but Cyclone Davis, among others, believed they did not go far enough. On the second day of the convention he introduced a resolution calling for the establishment of a state bureau of labor. His proposal elicited cries of "table it," probably because many Populists, who so often called for economy in government, wanted to avoid being seen as supporting the creation of another expensive state bureaucracy. Davis countered that farmers had a state department of agriculture, and laborers deserved "equal representation." He went on to note that "the laborers of the cities and towns are the most helpless class of workers in this country. To protect them against corporate greed is a crying necessity." Refusing to support this plank, he told his fellow delegates, would be tantamount to saying "you don't recognize the workingman's condition as requiring your attention, and do not recognize him as having a part in our movement." Davis prevailed, and the final platform included not only the establishment of a state labor bureau but also the creation of a state board of arbitration "to adjust all differences between corporations and employes."[27]

If the Dallas convention displayed many examples of Populist liberalism, it also revealed some of the political obstacles, grounded in time-honored southern tradition, that the Populists would struggle to overcome. One such obstacle was the matter of military service, especially Confederate military service. One of the nominating speeches for Henry McCulloch lauded his war record, whereupon another delegate objected, saying, "I thought that the war was over. I thought we had buried the bloody shirt at Ocala and St. Louis. The people's party of Texas are not hero worshipers." These comments elicited "applause and much excitement" from the delegates, and the speaker went on to declare the "idea of nominating generals" as "all bosh." Since Nugent had a respectable Confederate war record himself, the issue apparently had limited effect in this instance, but the question of Civil War service would never entirely disappear, and Populists sometimes found themselves touting their candidates' Confederate records, all the while claiming that there was no place for bloody-shirt politics in Populism.[28]

The one issue that might reasonably have been expected to cause dissension in the convention ended up being the least controversial—the role of African Americans in the party. A number of black delegates attended the convention (how many is not clear), and by all accounts they received a warm welcome. African Americans Henry Jennings of McKinney and R. H. Hayes of Fort Worth, both of whom had been elected to the state executive committee at the 1891 founding convention, won reelection as at-large members of the committee "without discussion." Jennings spoke to the convention on the first afternoon, offering up a glowing report of his success organizing colored Populist clubs, and his speech was met with amens and applause. Later, when delegates were being elected to the national convention slated to meet in Omaha, Nebraska, ten days hence, a white delegate realized that the two African American delegates inadvertently had been made alternates rather than voting delegates. The white delegate yelled, "That is not right," and the mistake was promptly corrected. That Confederate service proved more controversial than including blacks in the ranks of the party's leadership speaks volumes about the extent to which the Populists were seeking to create a new sort of liberal politics at this point in the Third-Party movement.[29]

Of course, the creation of those new politics did not occur in a vacuum. The birth of the People's Party in Texas had depended in large measure on parallel events at the national level, and in the summer of 1892, Texans remained active in shaping those events. At the Dallas state convention, party leaders made preparations for the upcoming Populist National Convention, which convened in Omaha on July 2. Texas's representatives on the national executive committee, William Lamb, Thomas Gaines, and Cyclone Davis, had labored in Dallas to arrange special railroad rates for delegates and make sure the state delegation's credentials were in order, and when party chairman Herman E. Taubeneck of Illinois gaveled the convention to order, the Lone Star State was well represented. Ben Terrell of Seguin, the national lecturer of the Farmers' Alliance, who along with Macune had been a reluctant Populist, delivered the

opening speech on the first day and played a major role in the meeting, ultimately finishing second in the balloting for the vice presidential nomination.
Cyclone Davis, according to the *Dallas Morning News,* displayed "burning eloquence" in his opening-day speech, and was later named to the national executive committee. Harry Tracy served on the platform committee, where he
helped write the finance plank.[30]

American political conventions always offer up sizable doses of pageantry
and political symbolism, along with a fair measure of silliness, and the Omaha
convention featured generous quantities of all three. The first two days were
prologue to the session of July 4, the date having been purposefully chosen to
mark what delegates considered a second American declaration of independence. When the platform was unveiled that afternoon and delegates "realized
that the birth had taken place," according to a Chicago newspaper, "then began a scene which beggers [*sic*] description. Men and women grew hysterical
in their joy." Delegates climbed on their chairs, "shouted and prayed, they sang
and shed tears." An impromptu procession of state delegations paraded around
the hall, flags and banners flying. "The spirit of 1776 was there," the press reported. A competition among delegations ensued to see which state's banner
could be hoisted the highest, and when the Massachusetts banner claimed that
honor, a Texan wearing a hickory shirt, alpaca coat, and cowboy hat "clambered
upon the shoulders of the men who stood next to him until he had the name
of the Lone Star State high above even Massachusetts." In the euphoria, two
white Texans lifted one of the black Texas delegates to their shoulders and carried him in the procession, "determined to make a show of harmony such as
has been predicted for the People's party" and bringing even greater cheers
from the crowd. With a drum and fife band alternating playing "Yankee Doo-
dle" and "Dixie," "the bedlam continued for twenty minutes." The nomination of former Union general James B. Weaver of Iowa for president and
ex-Confederate officer James G. Field for vice president seemed almost anti-
climactic compared to the enthusiasm over the platform.[31]

The platform itself largely restated the document drafted at St. Louis in 1891,
minus a plank on woman suffrage, which the national convention, echoing
the action of the Texas state convention, deemed too divisive. With its three
pillars of reform—finance, land, and transportation—the Omaha Platform
would become the bible of Populism, the standard against which Populist orthodoxy would henceforth be measured. And no Populists would exhibit
greater devotion to it than the Texans. After returning from Omaha, Harry
Tracy, one of the most pragmatic Texas Populists, asserted that the conven-

tion rekindled hope that the country could be saved. "My opinion is that the democratic party will never again meet under its present organization," he remarked. "In the east it will go to the republican party and in the south and west to the people's party." It would now be up to Populists at the state level to make Tracy's bold prediction a reality.[32]

The Texas Democratic Party in the summer of 1892 certainly gave Populists reason for optimism. The incumbent governor, Jim Hogg, owed his office in large measure to Alliancemen, who had supported his reformist agenda, especially the creation of a railroad commission. But Hogg had refused to give the Alliance representation on the three-man commission, and when Alliancefolk called for making the body elective, Hogg opposed that, too. Moreover, by 1892 it was clear that the Democratic Party was never going to endorse the Subtreasury Plan or any of the major Populist financial demands beyond silver coinage, so the Populists could reasonably expect a large harvest of votes from disaffected Alliance members.

Attacks from the left, however, were only part of the Democrats' problems. Equally threatening opposition came from the right. In February 1892 George Clark of Waco, a former secretary of state, attorney general, and appeals-court judge with close ties to railroad interests, entered the governor's race (plate 9). Nicknamed "the Little Giant" because of his short stature and "the Little Warwick" because he had managed the successful campaigns of two previous Texas governors (and thus was regarded as a kingmaker), Clark charged that Hogg's regulatory policies were discouraging economic growth in general and railroad construction in particular. Clark adopted the campaign slogan "Turn Texas Loose," a libertarian theme that resonated with conservative Texans (plate 10). The Clark forces soon published a campaign song bearing the slogan as its title. Although the song never mentioned the Populists or the Hogg Democrats by name, the lyrics left no doubt where Clark stood on the question of government regulation of business:

> From vicious laws turn Texas loose, From visionaries' dreams,
> From patriots whose plots produce, Base mercenary schemes;
> From law makers who know no law, Who err, then make excuse,
> From bosses with rapacious maw, Oh Lord turn Texas loose.
>
> Turn Texas loose from government, Paternal partisan,
> From spoils and spoilsmen fully bent, To capture all they can;
> From office holders who ne'er hold Their berths without abuse,
> From all these ills, we here make bold, To pray turn Texas loose.[33]

Early in his campaign Clark had apparently had some conversations with Harry Tracy about possible cooperation between the Clark forces and the Populists in the upcoming elections. Though it seems incongruous for the right and the left to have seriously considered joining forces against the center, many Populists personally respected Clark, who had spoken kind words about the Populist platform and had opposed the efforts of the Hoggites to read Subtreasury Alliancemen out of the Democratic Party. Moreover, Clark agreed with the Populists about the need to make the Railroad Commission elective, albeit for different reasons. But the main point of agreement between the Populists and George Clark was their mutual dislike of Jim Hogg. In the end, a Populist-Clark alliance fell under the heading of bedfellows who were simply too strange to coexist politically, although rumors that Thomas Nugent would withdraw and endorse Clark persisted down to the very end of the fall campaign.[34]

When a deal was not forthcoming from the Populists, Clark turned to the Republicans, where he found a more sympathetic ear. Led by the African American political boss Norris Wright Cuney, the Republicans in March declined to put out a state ticket, endorsing Clark instead. It remained to be seen how much of his party's vote Cuney could deliver, but the endorsement by the Republicans certainly brightened Clark's outlook for the fall, notwithstanding racist charges from the Hogg camp that its candidate was forced to run against the three C's: "Clark, Cuney, and the Coons."[35]

By itself, Clark's alliance with the Republicans would not win him the Democratic nomination. That would have to happen at the party's state convention, due to meet in Houston in mid-August. It was traditional in Texas Democratic politics that sitting governors receive the nomination for a second two-year term with little fanfare, and nomination was always tantamount to election in the fall. But these were not normal times. Never had an incumbent Democrat faced a challenge from within his own party like Hogg faced from Clark, and there was no guarantee that the loser in Houston would accept the results of the convention. The consequence could be a bolt by the supporters of the losing candidate, and a divided Democratic Party.

Populists followed these developments with intense interest. Conventional wisdom suggested that two Democratic tickets in the field would greatly enhance Nugent's chances of being elected, but such was not necessarily the case. Realistic Populists knew that their party still lacked the strength to win on its own; it needed disgruntled Democrats (and, hopefully, Republicans) to cross party lines and vote for Nugent. If both Hogg and Clark stayed in the race till November, there would be little cause for any Democrat to vote Populist. But

Populists believed that the wounds from the bitter Hogg-Clark contest were "of too recent infection to heal by November," and that Nugent could expect "a large disaffected Democratic vote" from the supporters of the losing candidate.[36]

By August, though, Hogg had more than enough delegates to secure the nomination. Clark's supporters thought their man had been cheated—that Populists had inadvertently handed the nomination to Hogg by voting for him in the spring Democratic primaries—back before it was certain that the Third Party would put out a state ticket. When Democrats finally met in Houston, the cavernous city streetcar shed where the convention was held was said to be "full of knives and pistols," with delegates "thoroughly prepared to engage in the business of making widows and orphans if some fool had started the ball rolling." Violence, though, was averted, thanks in part to the action of Texas Ranger captain Bill McDonald, a Hogg supporter who had his men construct a fence across the one open side of the enclosure during the night to keep non-delegates from gaining access. As widely predicted, the Clark men bolted the convention and nominated their man in a rump convention. There would be two Democratic candidates in the fall election. Populists tried to put the situation in the best possible light. "The picture they draw is Clark on one side, Nugent on the other and Hogg between the two, catching whatever he can from either side," the *Dallas Morning News* reported after interviewing several Populist leaders. But they must have known that they faced an uphill battle.[37]

The party named a campaign committee consisting of Stump Ashby, Thomas Gaines, and J. T. Crawford to oversee the statewide effort, with editor Milton Park of the *Southern Mercury* serving as treasurer. Nugent enlisted Henry Lewis Bentley, a former district attorney, land broker, rancher, and newspaper editor from Abilene, to manage his own campaign. The hostile *Fort Worth Gazette* described the goateed, genteel Bentley as "fertile in resources, quick of perception, cautious, trained in the science of belligerent politics, and himself one of the best stump speakers in the state," deeming him "a foeman worthy of [D]emocratic steel." Bentley established his campaign headquarters at the Powell Building in downtown Fort Worth, just a few blocks from Nugent's home and law office. The Populist campaign would center on four main tactics: the establishment of grassroots Populist clubs, the deployment of speakers, the work of the Third-Party press, and the staging of large rallies and camp meetings. Populists understood that they could not tap into the coffers of railroads and corporations the way the Democrats could, so they would depend on these four elements for fundraising as well as for disseminating the party's message.[38]

As early as April, Milton Park of the *Mercury* had recognized the obstacles that the Third-Party movement faced. "Those who are declaring themselves free and independent voters, or are entering reform clubs, must not forget that the machine manipulators have them at great disadvantage, that they must build from the ground up; that they have no campaign fund, no boodle [money for bribery], no blocks of five [a vote-buying scheme from the 1888 national election], no railroad receiverships, nor Tammany organizations to depend upon for money to pay speakers, buy and distribute literature, no keen wire pullers with plenty of money to spend in fixing up newspapers," he warned. "Reformers have nothing to depend upon but their impoverished pockets, their independent manhood, their efforts and their votes. They must not forget that if they fail to use them solidly, they will be defeated, and if defeated, will have only their own cowardice or stupidity to thank for it."[39]

The basic building block of the party was the Populist club. Typically, a county executive committee would try to identify a capable man in each of the county's voting precincts. That man would then publish a call in the local newspaper for interested persons to meet at a local schoolhouse or other "convenient" place, elect a president, secretary, and treasurer, and formally organize the club. Dues would be meager—perhaps a quarter or fifty cents—with ladies sometimes admitted as honorary members. The club would then meet regularly, discuss the issues, listen to members or invited guests make speeches, pass resolutions to be forwarded to the county party or published in the local reform newspaper, and plan campaign events such as picnics, rallies, and camp meetings. The state campaign committee expected clubs to remit a portion of the money collected at their meetings to the state office, but the poverty of many Populists was so great, and the amounts raised were so small, that the state committee rarely saw any of it. After the election, party leaders bemoaned the fact that the entire amount raised by the state party from all sources was less than $1,800.[40]

But if fundraising proved difficult, reports on the organizational front were nonetheless encouraging. By summertime, Populists were establishing clubs by the hundreds. At the beginning of June, for example, came a report that eighty clubs had been organized in Collin County, in the fertile farming district just north of Dallas. A Democratic editor in Central Texas expressed concern about "the numerous 'third party' clubs" that were being organized in Williamson County near Austin. From Bandera County in southwest Texas came reports that clubs had been organized throughout the county, with new names being added daily. In June the *Galveston Daily News* reported that two

thousand Populist clubs had been established in Texas. By September Bentley claimed 2,800 clubs statewide, with 160,000 members, prompting the
Dallas Morning News to describe him as "simply hilarious in his gleeful pleasure at what he terms a certainty of success in November." Especially heartening were the reports of black Populist clubs being organized in various parts
of the state. By the week of the election, Bentley boasted 3,170 Populist clubs
in the state, with "compact organizations in 213 counties." Even allowing for
considerable exaggeration, it was a remarkable organizational achievement in
such a short time.[41]

While local Populists conducted much of this grassroots organizing in their
own home neighborhoods and counties, the party also depended on a large
corps of more or less professional lecturers and organizers to spread the party
gospel. Through the summer and fall of 1892, the *Southern Mercury* regularly
carried speaking schedules of Harry Tracy, James Madison Perdue, Stump
Ashby, and John Wilson Biard, and as the election drew nearer, their names
frequently appeared alongside those of candidates such as Thomas Nugent,
Jerome Kearby, Charles H. Jenkins, and Ben Terrell. The big-city dailies likewise covered their movements. Sometimes the work was intensive. S. O. Daws,
the original state lecturer for the Farmers' Alliance, labored an entire month
organizing People's Party clubs in heavily populated Fannin County in June
and July. Henry Jennings, the septuagenarian African American minister
from McKinney, spent much of May, June, and July organizing black Populist
clubs in his home county of Collin and several neighboring counties. Reports
of lesser-known lecturers spending a week or ten days in an individual county
were common.[42]

The work of grassroots organizing could be grueling and thankless, but the
Populists approached their task with missionary zeal. In early September 1892,
E. O. Meitzen, the Alliance assistant state lecturer from Lavaca County who
had already established himself as the foremost leader of the state's German
American Populists, recounted a trip he made from his home in Hallettsville
to Galveston. Traveling in his two-wheeled gig, he delivered thirty-nine
speeches along his route. "If I drove by a store and saw five or six or more men
there I would jump out and talk with them and explain the people's party teachings," he reported. "Then I would leave them a lot of circulars and would
drive away, having made several converts. This I did on every occasion. If I
met a man in a crowd of democrats who wanted to discuss the political problems with me I always discussed with him—on the corner or anywhere else—
and so I made converts among the listeners if I did not convert my opponent."

Explaining the reason for his dedication, Meitzen, who was known as "the learned blacksmith," lectured the reporter for the *Galveston Daily News,* saying, "This is a campaign of education, young man."[43]

The organizing effort depended heavily on the Third-Party press. In an era before electronic media, newspapers were the indispensable tool for communicating with the party faithful. Prior to the birth of the People's Party, a handful of Farmers' Alliance papers operated in Texas, with many more offering a weekly Alliance page or column. The leading Alliance journal was the Dallas-based *Southern Mercury,* published weekly by Harry Tracy and edited after mid-1891 by Milton Park. Though it remained officially nonpartisan, the *Mercury* openly supported the People's Party by the fall of 1892. That year, Tracy purchased another newspaper, the *Advance,* and made it the official organ of the party. But the *Advance* proved unprofitable, and in 1894 it ceased publication, and the *Mercury* became the official organ of both the Alliance and the party.[44]

As crucial as the *Mercury* and the *Advance* were to the party's fortunes, in some ways the *Dallas Morning News* and its sister paper, the *Galveston Daily News,* were even more important. Owned by Alfred H. Belo and carrying many of the same articles shared via telegraph, these two papers prided themselves on being the papers of record for the state of Texas, and they carried full coverage of state politics as well as a surprising amount of local reporting from their small army of correspondents scattered across the state. Although the papers took a decidedly conservative editorial stance, including staunch support of the gold standard, they had remarkably objective—and sometimes even sympathetic—coverage of the People's Party, which Populists readily recognized and publicly acknowledged. As Populist and Knights of Labor leader Bill Farmer put it, "We populists like The Dallas News. We read its editorial columns and see that it is a goldbug paper straight out. But we like it because we can be heard in its columns."[45]

Populism, however, heavily depended on the local Populist weeklies to do the work in the trenches. Publishing a rural paper required relatively little capital; in 1892 there were over five hundred weeklies in Texas, the vast majority of them loyally Democratic. Only about twenty papers openly supported Populism in 1892. In reality, most reform papers struggled, suffering from undercapitalization, poorly trained editors, inability of subscribers to pay for their subscriptions, and hostility from the major-party establishment. Circulation usually numbered in the hundreds, and many sheets lasted only for a few weeks or months before quietly ceasing operation. The Populist press operation received a boost from the establishment of the Texas Reform Press

Association, founded by William Lamb and others in April 1891 "to promote the purity of purpose, harmony of action and the reform of the state press." Eventually the state Association, working in conjunction with its national counterpart and with the state party organization, would greatly assist local editors by providing "ready-print" pages and boilerplate editorial material in order to fill the columns of the weeklies with low-cost content and ensure that the party's views were accurately represented in the local press. But in 1892, much of the Third-Party press was still in its infancy, and Populists would have to rely heavily on face-to-face politicking to get their message to the voters.[46]

That meant speechmaking. The nineteenth century was the golden age of American political oratory, and that tradition, established in the antebellum period, was reaching its zenith in the Populist era. The People's Party in Texas could boast more than its share of the state's great orators, as the 1892 election season soon proved. Speaking styles varied. Using his experience as both a stage actor and a Methodist minister, Stump Ashby combined quick wit, a sharp tongue, and plain but emotional language to woo crowds. Thomas Nugent, reflecting his lawyer's training and rather subdued personality, marshaled facts, logic, and understated eloquence to make the case for reform. Cyclone Davis, already nationally famous by the fall of 1892, brought a more theatrical style to the stump. Dressed in his trademark Prince Albert coat with matching vest, "pants the bottom of which struck him somewhere in the neighborhood between the knee and ankle, displaying alligator boots about No. 10 or 11, and a woolen shirt," the six-foot-three, goateed Davis often mounted the podium with ten volumes of the writings of Thomas Jefferson, which he referred to repeatedly throughout his speeches to show that Populism was consistent with the teachings of the Sage of Monticello. Jerome Kearby's charisma, keen intellect, and unmatched skills as a criminal lawyer served him well as an orator, and no Populist could equal him on the attack against a political adversary. The African American labor leader Melvin Wade—brawny, dark-complexioned, with a massive head—mastered the art of self-deprecating humor, keeping audiences in stitches with folksy anecdotes that cleverly exposed the absurdities of southern racial traditions while making pointed political arguments. In contrast, the speaking style of the other great African American leader of the party, John B. Rayner, harkened back to the antebellum oratorical tradition. Employing his polished education and his childhood experiences hearing his white congressman father speak, the light-skinned, stoutly built Rayner deployed his impressive vocabulary and knowledge of the classics in speeches worthy of Edward Everett or Daniel Webster.[47]

These Third-Party luminaries and many lesser lights showcased their talents at party conventions, meetings of Populist clubs, party rallies, joint debates with Democrats, and the great political camp meetings that became the high point of the political season (plate 11). Often speaking to crowds numbering in the thousands, they frequently held forth for two, three, or even four hours, sometimes in the blazing sun, without benefit of microphones or amplifiers. Audiences valued both style and substance, and it was not unusual for speeches to attract large crowds drawn from both parties. Shortly after the 1892 state convention, Populists in Ellis County just south of Dallas held a rally at an isolated crossroads schoolhouse, reachable only by "dirt road conveyance" over seven miles of winding country roads. Between thirty-five hundred and four thousand people attended to hear Thomas Nugent and Jerome Kearby speak. A reporter for the *Dallas Morning News* captured the scene: "The reception of the speeches was refreshing to one who has been nauseated by yelling and howling and the deafening efforts of brass bands. There was no big bass drum to beat or cymbals to clash whenever the drummer thought the speaker made a hit. There was no jumping-up-and-knocking-your-heels-together style of enthusiasm. All the speakers were listened to with intense interest. Men and women bent forward eagerly to catch every word. Every eye spoke the intense thirst of the owner for knowledge, the desire to hear it all. Whenever there was applause it was quiet but deep. During Judge Nugent's speech there were frequent utterances, such as 'Thats so,' 'Now you are hitting them.'" Many campaign events, of course, did partake of the carnival atmosphere that was so markedly missing from this account. This was particularly true of the party's summertime camp meetings (which will be discussed in Chapter 4), but brass bands or no brass bands, Populists clearly understood the importance of effective oratory. Renowned Democratic speakers such as Jim Hogg and Joe Bailey could hold their own with anyone, but taken as a whole, the Populists fielded the abler group of orators.[48]

On August 18, the day after the bolt of the Clarkites from the Democratic state convention, Thomas Nugent officially opened the Populist general election campaign. On the grounds of the state capitol in Austin before a crowd of twenty-five hundred, he commenced his speech by quoting the words of Ulysses S. Grant on accepting the presidential nomination in 1868: "Let us have peace." It is telling that Nugent chose the theme of sectional reconciliation for this occasion. Clearly he believed that Democratic bloody-shirt politics, with their intendant racial demagoguery and appeals to ancient party loyalties, posed the greatest obstacle to Populist success. If not for self-interested politicians' calls for unthinking party devotion, he asserted, Grant's plea for sectional peace would have long since been realized. He then used this theme to segue skillfully into an indictment of major-party corruption. "The 'rule of the ring' has been supreme in this republic of ours for the past thirty years, and he who can manipulate most skillfully the political machine secures the prizes of public life, the offices and spoils," he asserted. "Great men no longer lead the old parties, because great men are men of soul, of humanity, of genius, of inspiration. They never are machine men." In good Populist fashion, Nugent juxtaposed the corrupt machine politician with the plain farmer, who, he avowed, "is a reading and thinking man, rejoicing in a new-found intellectual strength, of which but lately he did not dream." Denouncing both of the major parties, he scored Democrats for having "inherited from Jefferson nothing but a few well worn formulas of speech" and Republicans for turning their backs on "the humanity and unique greatness of Lincoln." While politicians scurried over the country "repeating political platitudes, holding up tariff schedules in one hand and the 'bloody shirt' in the other," he charged, "labor is in chains." The old parties' determination "to head off the moving column of reform" was doomed to failure, he declared. "It will not win."[49]

Nugent's speech focused heavily on national issues, with particular emphasis on the financial question. Buttressing his arguments with detailed statistics on such matters as per capita currency circulation, bankruptcy rates, and the maldistribution of wealth, he built a lawyer's case for the Populist national platform. Only near the end of the speech did he address one state issue, the debate over the railroad commission. He favored a strong commission with the power to fix rates, but he sounded a relatively conservative note in adding that as long as railroads were privately owned, the rights of private property must be respected and railroads must not be regulated so heavily that they could not "produce a reasonable income." Given the constitutional constraints on a commission, he concluded, the commission was a "partial" solution at best, with government ownership of the railroads "the only final and adequate solution of the problem." Likely waiting for Jim Hogg to make his own first campaign speech following his nomination by the Houston convention, Nugent chose to leave discussion of other state-level issues for another day.[50]

Those discussions would not be long in coming. Despite the Populists' enthusiasm and George Clark's corporate support, the election largely became a referendum on the Hogg administration. In addition to endorsing silver coinage and a graduated federal income tax, which put the Texas Democratic Party at odds with its national counterpart but in harmony with the Populists, the Hogg platform repeated three Populist state platform planks: the call for a more liberal mechanic's lien law, a six-month term for free public schools, and reform of the convict lease system. The *Southern Mercury* charged that the Democrats "unblushingly purloined" these planks from the Populist platform, and the notion that the Hoggites were cynically trying to pose as quasi-Populists would become a theme in Third-Party campaign rhetoric. Indeed, selective endorsement of Populist demands by Democrats became a major Democratic strategy at both the state and, eventually, the national levels. To whatever extent the Democratic Party in the early twentieth century contributed to what would eventually become known as modern American liberalism, it was largely because of its adoption of Populist policies.[51]

If Populists found it difficult to deny entirely the reformist bent of the Hogg Democrats, they could always attack on the grounds of competence. During Hogg's first term, a uniform-textbook bill championed by the governor had failed to become law due to a legal technicality, and a measure prohibiting alien land ownership had been overturned by the state supreme court, though it later was revised and passed. Four days after the Democratic conventions, a federal judge in Dallas issued an injunction suspending operation of the Railroad Commission, Hogg's signature reform. Populists argued that the "superior legal learning and profound reach of Judge Nugent will enable him to steer clear of the rocks which gored Hogg's [Commission] law to death, while at the same time affording the people of Texas the full measure of relief hoped for through commission regulation." But mostly, the Populists chose to focus on the limited reach of Hogg's reform agenda in comparison to Populism, his allegedly poor record of fiscal stewardship, and above all, his masterful manipulation of the state Democratic Party organization, which Populists characterized as corrupt, business-as-usual machine politics. J. M. Moore, a former Democratic Texas secretary of state who became a Populist, encapsulated the Populists' disdain for Hogg when he wrote, "A real statesman, my friends, does not devote his energies to building up great personal power; a great reformer does not punish those who differ from him, reward henchmen and multiply his patronage by three. These are the characteristics of ring chiefs and political bosses."[52]

The Populists were certainly correct in noting the advantages that Democrats in general, and Hogg in particular, enjoyed in the race. Every major big-city newspaper in the state, including the Galveston-Dallas *News*, backed Clark, with the exception of the *Houston Post* and *Fort Worth Gazette*, which supported

Hogg. Railroad executives provided lists of their employees for use by the Clark campaign, and black Republican leader Wright Cuney not only engineered the Republican fusion with Clark but also used his organization to help organize African American Clark clubs throughout the state. Hogg, however, shrewdly wielded the power of incumbency to offset any advantages his opponents might have had. Influential US senator Roger Q. Mills, who had preferred Clark, balked at further dividing the party and recognized Hogg as the party nominee. The powerful South Texas political boss James B. Wells, fearful of losing his influence in the state party, also switched to Hogg. The governor made sure that the state's politically appointed officeholders lent active support to his campaign, and at the local level, patronage likewise aided the Hogg forces. (In one example, it was reported that the superintendent of roads in Galveston County allegedly threatened the jobs of two hundred men on the county's road crews if they failed to vote for Hogg.) Hogg benefited greatly from the work of his campaign strategist, the enigmatic Edward M. House, whose Machiavellian control of patronage matters and skillful manipulation of the electoral machinery left nothing to chance.[53]

The gubernatorial race grew increasingly tense as the election drew nearer. The Populists understood that Clark was not their real enemy, and relations between the Nugent and Clark forces remained respectful, if not actually cordial. But the two Democrats hammered away at each other, with the Populists joining the Clarkites in their attacks on Hogg. Neither of the Democratic candidates seemed eager to attack the Populists head-on, for both seemed to think they still had a chance of winning Populist support, and they did not want to risk it by frontal assaults. Two principal questions stood out: How many reformminded white Texans would desert Hogg for Nugent, and where would the black vote go? In early October, apparently worried about the groundswell of support for Nugent, Hogg stepped up his previously muted criticism of the Populists. Speaking at the state fair music hall in Dallas, he criticized Populist leaders as "ex-democrats, poisoned from disappointed ambition, and with the world in general, chimerical in political convictions, shifting in party name, and [unable to] stay on any platform or with any party long." Still hoping, though, to woo Populist-leaning voters by driving a wedge between them and their leaders, he asserted that "the followers of the populists are impatient, restive and honestly misled" by the "false teachings" of the leaders. Seeking to associate the Clarkites with the Populists in the minds of voters and to portray both as corrupt office seekers, he began derisively referring to the Clarkites as "copulists."[54]

The other front in the new Hogg offensive involved the all-important black vote. African Americans still voted in large numbers in Texas, and as a general rule they faithfully supported the Republican Party, which was overwhelmingly African American. With blacks constituting less than a quarter of the electorate, the Republicans stood no chance winning statewide races, but everyone understood that if whites were divided, blacks potentially held the balance of power; they could exact concessions from whatever white party they endorsed. With Clark having won the official endorsement of Cuney and the state Republican organization, and the Populists actively courting the African American vote, Hogg desperately needed some grounds on which to make his own bid for black support.

The Hogg campaign awoke to this reality late in the campaign. Former governor Richard Coke's "Clark, Cuney, and the Coons" slogan had already become part of the season's political vocabulary, and this was followed by a widely publicized complaint by Hogg campaign manager Waller Baker about the Clark campaign's efforts to establish Clark Negro clubs. Such comments had alienated many black voters. The Galveston-Dallas *News* suggested that "the palpable purpose of the remark about Clark negro clubs is to inject race prejudice into the campaign" by insinuating "that negro support is a dishonor to any candidate." Desperate to undo the damage done by these gaffes, Hogg seized on an issue that resonated with African Americans like no other: lynching.[55]

The governor actually had some bona fides on the issue, having publicly urged sheriffs to protect prisoners and offered rewards for the arrest and conviction of lynch-mob members. Campaigning in the black areas of the state, he now reminded African Americans of his record. Events strengthened Hogg's hand in September, when a triple lynching near Paris in northeast Texas afforded him another opportunity to denounce mob violence and offer rewards for the perpetrators, although in this case, like all others, no lyncher was ever brought to justice.[56]

As Hogg's courting of the black vote intensified, the Clark forces wasted no time in pointing out the change in the governor's strategy. "This Hogg campaign has taken a sudden turn in the last two weeks," the *Morning News* reported. "From a proud, high-strung democrat who wanted no negro votes," Hogg had now "gotten sweet on the darkies." The papers noted Hogg's declarations against lynching and ridiculed his oft-repeated stories about being "rocked in the cradle of a black mammy's arms," while pointing out how differently the Hogg campaign conducted itself in heavily white portions of North Texas:

"Up there it is 'Clark, Cooney [sic] and the coons.'" Hogg's organization flooded East Texas with campaign literature stressing the governor's friendship toward Negroes and fought back when the opposition dug up racist quotes he had allegedly uttered. The Clarkites countered by claiming that while Hogg was "weeping the water of the crocodile over his old black mammy at one place his managers are busily engaged mailing to the white settlements only these disgraceful cartoons in which the old black mammy of whom he preaches for political purposes is depicted as a 'coon' without character, and with lips like the lips of a horse." Charges and countercharges about buying the influence of local black leaders flew between the two campaigns.[57]

If Hogg could plausibly appeal for black votes on the basis of his public stance against lynching, he made no pretense about his position on another issue of key importance to both African Americans and Populists. Since the days of Reconstruction, voter fraud and intimidation had been the stock-in-trade of Democratic politics in Texas. In 1891 Congress had defeated a proposed Federal Elections Bill, derided in the South as the "Force Bill," which would have provided for federal supervision of elections. The Hogg campaign steadfastly opposed it; the platform of the Houston convention castigated it as "a violation of the Constitution, corrupt in conception, vicious in sentiment, criminal in detail, the only mission of which is to foment race prejudice," and Hogg himself vigorously denounced the Force Bill from the stump. Campaigning for him, the always-vitriolic Sen. Richard Coke cited the Force Bill and then pronounced anyone who opposed the Hogg Democrats a traitor who "ought not to live." Predictably, the Clarkites again charged that the Hogg forces were using the question to "abuse the negroes and thus pander to race prejudices for campaign purposes," while the Hogg campaign distributed a circular on the eve of the election falsely claiming that Clark supported the measure.[58]

As a party, the Populists scarcely knew how to respond to either the lynching issue or the Force Bill controversy. On lynching they largely remained silent, simply refusing to be drawn into the discussion.[59] Where the Force Bill was concerned, they sent mixed signals. Milton Park of the *Southern Mercury*, who throughout his Populist career would be susceptible to racist thinking, applauded Populist presidential nominee James Weaver for helping to defeat the bill. But other major Texas Populist leaders, while stopping short of endorsing the Force Bill, criticized the Democrats for making it an issue. Nugent disparaged the bill as just another bloody-shirt issue that enabled "the money kings [to] rub their hands gleefully and watch with delight the 'sham battle' whose 'clamor' drowns the cry of distress that comes from the farm, the workshop and the factory." State Alliance president Evan Jones, Populist nominee for Congress in the Eighth District, likewise characterized it as "a scarecrow which originated and died in the republican camps, and nobody but the democratic party was trying to resurrect the old corpse." Most notable, though, was the tack taken by Jerome Kearby. Addressing the Populist state convention, he pointed out that the Force Bill "applies to everybody in Maine as in Texas" and asked, "Are we prepared to confess that here alone the ballot box is corrupted?" In reply, a voice from the floor cried, "Mighty nigh it." "Do you need protection of the ballot?" he implored, and another voice from the crowd responded, "We do." Kearby then declared that "a free ballot and a fair count may be considered the safety valve upon which your and my liberties rest and it should be secured if necessary," a sentiment that evoked applause from the delegates. That fall, as he campaigned for Congress in the Dallas district, he repeatedly ridiculed the Democrats' "force bill talk" as "silly" and argued that "the force bill would not be more direful in its consequences than the continuation of the Hogg crowd in office."[60]

As the campaign rhetoric continued to heat up, the Populists fought to get their message before the voters. "Their plan is to start out a hundred speakers and keep the best ones remorselessly hanging on to the governor's heels," the *Morning News* reported in late August. "They are to follow steadily in the governor's wake and keep the trail redhot." To the best that their severely limited war chest would allow, they did just that. Nugent himself campaigned steadfastly, devoting long, scholarly addresses—from the stump and in the press—to all the major Populist policy issues, including the railroad question, the Subtreasury Plan, political corruption, and the plight of labor. Ever the dignified gentleman, he outlined the failings of the Hogg administration and the inadequacies of Clark's laissez-faire approach while scrupulously avoiding personal attacks. When necessary, he calmly and with gentle humor answered charges that he was a religious crank. Although populism (in the generic use of the small-*p* word) has entered the modern vocabulary as a synonym for demagogic appeals to the masses, Nugent's campaign was just the opposite; in his appeals to the common man he spoke to them as equals but urged them to elevate themselves and the nation's politics to a higher plane. In the Austin speech that formally opened his campaign, he told the audience that "the times demand great men to mould the elements of reform into proper shape and they will come as the inspiration finds them amid the ranks of the common folk. The farmer of today is a reading and thinking man, rejoicing in a new found intellectual strength, of which but lately he did not dream." This was indeed a new politics, and even non-Populists were forced to acknowledge it, as an editorial about Nugent from a small-town East Texas Democratic paper shortly after the election observed: "He has no equal in the true knowledge of political questions that can compare with him in honesty of intentions and fidelity to his deep convictions. . . . A thoughtless press, in general censures Judge Nugent and his followers, but they cannot point out a man that has added more dignity and grandeur to the state than Mr. Nugent—the William Tell of Texas. His conduct during the late campaign was grand. He resorted to no false promises, illusions or fraud. Throughout the struggle he never for a moment forgot that he was a gentleman, and, without the aid of the public purse or moneyed powers, the vote he received from the farmers and laboring classes—the very backbone of the nation—was the grandest achievement ever recorded in the history of the politics of the state. Defeat to such a man is an honor." By the end of the election of 1892, the Nugent legend had been born.[61]

In an era before election polling, nobody knew whether Nugent and the Populists would be able to overcome Hogg's advantages as the incumbent, Clark's personal popularity and deep pockets, and the deep-seated devotion of white Texans to the Democratic Party. All sides in the three-way race predicted victory for their cause, although knowledgeable Populists knew that the odds were against them. The Hogg forces seemed the most worried, judging from one last set of dirty tricks they attempted during the final phase of the race. In mid-October, rumors allegedly originating with "the Hoggite managers" began to circulate purporting that Nugent would withdraw from the race. Oddly, some of the rumors had Nugent withdrawing in favor of Hogg, while others maintained that he would withdraw in favor of Clark. So rampant did the rumors become that Nugent finally had to publish an open letter categorically denying them. "Evidently this has been done to mislead our people and induce them to abandon our ticket," he explained, pledging that "under no circumstances will I withdraw." But with Nugent having laid the rumors to rest, the Hogg campaign apparently had one last trick up its sleeve. Six days before the election the *Dallas Morning News* reported that the Hoggites, in "a campaign of desperation," were planning to "issue a fraudulent statement that Clark will withdraw in favor of Nugent (having failed to convince people that Nugent will withdraw in favor of Clark)." In the end, all three candidates remained in the race, and feverish campaigning before the largest crowds in the state's history continued until election day.[62]

Texans went to the polls on November 8 and reelected James Stephen Hogg governor by a vote of 190,486 to George W. Clark's 133,395 and Thomas L. Nugent's 108,483. More than 70 percent of eligible voters turned out to cast ballots. Statistical analysis of Nugent's vote reveals that approximately 38 percent of those who had voted for Hogg in 1890 defected to Nugent in 1892, accounting for almost all of Nugent's votes. (A handful of Populist votes came from former Prohibition Party voters.) Populists were convinced that "Judge Clark was the scare crow that frightened many Nugent men into voting for Governor Hogg," a proposition that, while likely true, almost certainly did not cost Nugent the victory. Despite the party's overtures toward African Americans and the work of Henry Jennings and others, black support for the People's Party was statistically negligible.[63]

The sheer size of Texas and its racial, ethnic, economic, and topographical diversity make it difficult to generalize about the sources of Populist strength or weakness. A given portion of a heavily Democratic county might poll a Populist majority, or vice versa, for a variety of reasons relating to race, ethnicity, quality of the soil, the presence of a town or a railroad, or the work of a particularly effective Alliance or People's Party organizer. That said, the greatest concentration of Third-Party strength occurred in a north-to-south string of fifteen counties running roughly from Jack County in north-central Texas southward to Frio County southwest of San Antonio. These counties encompassed a variety of topographies, beginning in the Western Cross Timbers, extending through much of the Hill Country and into the South Texas Brush Country. Every one of these counties touched either the ninety-eighth or ninety-ninth meridian or lay between them. The upper counties of this region were the birthplace of the Farmers' Alliance in the 1870s and were heavily populated by small farmers, many of whom owned their own land but some of whom were in the process of being forced into tenancy. The lower counties tended to be the home of small ranchers, many of whom resented the enclosure of the range by large corporate ranching companies, often owned by foreign investors. A second cluster of Populist strength could be found in the Piney Woods of East Texas, from Walker and Houston Counties in the west to San Augustine and Sabine Counties on the Louisiana line, another section where struggling small farmers, eking out a living on marginal land, found Populism appealing. A third tier of counties south of Austin in south-central Texas, ranging from Caldwell County in the north to Live Oak County in the south, proved receptive to the Populist message. Populists did well in many of the densely populated, black-soil cotton-growing counties north and east of

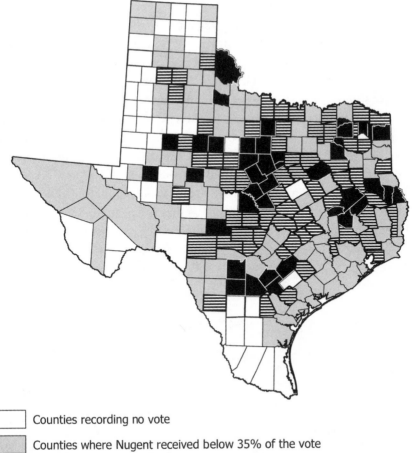

Counties recording no vote

Counties where Nugent received below 35% of the vote

Counties where Nugent received between 35 and 49% of the vote

Counties where Nugent received 50% or more of the vote

Figure 5 Populist electoral strength, 1892. Map by Claire Holland.

Dallas, but only in two of those counties, Delta and Titus, were they able to outvote the opposition.[64]

Populists complained of fraud, a claim that would be repeated—with good reason—in every election throughout the People's Revolt. In the famously rotten borough that was Harrison County on the Louisiana-Texas border, Hogg polled more than the total vote of the county two years earlier, and supposedly captured virtually 100 percent of the African American vote in the heavily black county. In Lampasas County, Democrats perpetrated a rather common

election-fraud trick, printing and distributing Populist ballots that looked legitimate but whose format violated the intricate election laws, thus creating a
pretext for having those ballots thrown out. How widespread such tricks were,
and what impact they had on the election, is impossible to know.[65]

One thing about the election seems clear. Populism, at that juncture of the
People's Revolt, was still overwhelmingly a white farmers' movement. Party
leaders understood that the party would need to broaden its appeal, particularly to African Americans and to urban workers, if it wanted to win statewide
elections. But one other thing was also clear to anyone observing Texas politics in the wake of the 1892 election: the People's Party had now become the
second major party in a two-party system. If Populism continued to grow, and
if the Democrats remained as divided as they had been in 1892, Texas might
become the largest state, and the first southern state, to be governed by Populists.
That reality, despite its relatively poor showing in its first statewide election,
was enough to keep Texas Populists optimistic—indeed, almost giddy—about
their party's future prospects.

3 • Ideology and Policy

We believe that the power of government—in other words, of the
people—should be expanded (as in the case of the postal service) as rapidly
and as far as the good sense of an intelligent people and the teaching of
experience shall justify, to the end that oppression, injustice, and poverty
shall eventually cease in the land.
—Preamble to the Omaha Platform, 1892

We are not fighting corporations. We are fighting monopoly.
—Thomas L. Nugent, 1894

The government is a corporation doing business for you.
—Jerome Kearby, 1894

Cynics have sometimes argued that American political parties are little more
than cobbled-together coalitions of interest groups. It is certainly true that in
a two-party system where power flows to the party that can win 51 percent of
the vote, it is vitally important for any party hopeful of success to champion
particular policies that will bring a variety of such groups into the electoral
fold. Yet, parties also must stand for something. Those that are perceived as
only pandering to interest groups run a real risk of alienating voters who rightly
question the motives of party leaders and the efficacy of the party to govern
once in power. The Democratic Party of Andrew Jackson may have appealed
to the economic interests of southern slaveholders, northern urban workingmen, and subsistence farmers, but it also rallied these groups around the proposition that in America, no white man was the social superior to any other
white man. The Republican Party in the 1850s may have been a coalition of

northern antisecessionists, nativists, and moral reformers, but it also united those groups around the proposition that slavery should be put on a path to extinction and that a free labor system should be spread across the entire nation. In the American system, ideas do matter. The successful political party, then, is the party that unites its followers around a central theme or ideology and then proposes policies consistent with that ideology that will appeal to the constituent parts of its electorate.

An earlier generation of historians viewed the People's Party largely as a pragmatic response on the part of farmers to the hard times of the 1890s, and it was certainly that.[1] But it also had to be more than that. For Populism to become a serious political force in Texas, it had to develop a coherent set of values and beliefs about society and government, an ideological framework that could appeal equally to a struggling white farm owner, a wealthy professional, a black sharecropper, a large cotton planter, a Mexican American ranch hand, a small-town preacher, a unionized Thurber coal miner, and a member of the Dallas Freethinkers' Society. By the time the dust had settled on the epic three-way election battle between Jim Hogg, George Clark, and Thomas Nugent in 1892, the Texas People's Party had built the basic intellectual superstructure for their political movement. Specific policies would continue to evolve throughout the party's existence, but by 1893 or 1894 most Populists had come to share a certain set of beliefs about how America's political economy functioned, how it *should* function, and what changes were needed to make it function properly. It is not too strong a claim to say that Texas Populists had forged an identifiable ideology that shaped, and in some cases was shaped by, the specific policy positions that the party championed. This chapter explores that ideology and those policy positions.

~

Like most political ideologies, that of Texas Populism derived from multiple sources. Historians who have argued for the primacy of one element—say, greenbacker monetary theory or the Farmers' Alliance cooperative experience—have ignored or overlooked the complex genealogy of Populist thought. One important strand in the skein of Populist ideology, and a logical starting point for its analysis, is the received folk culture of the southern plain folk. Texas Populism emerged in large measure from rural communities characterized by well-developed networks of social, economic, and religious institutions that connected kinfolk with kinfolk, neighbors with neighbors, farmers with farmers, parishioners with parishioners, lodge brothers with lodge brothers, veterans with veterans. Although honoring individual enterprise and valuing individual rights and liberties, southern folk culture, drawing as it did from the values of evangelical Protestantism, also heavily emphasized the Christian duty to care for one's fellow man and woman. Particularly in a state like Texas, so recently removed from the frontier, cooperation was at least as much a part of everyday life as competition. Kinfolk, neighbors, or fellow church or fraternal order members had traditionally provided the safety net that helped people survive illness, fire, flood, drought, insects, Indian attacks, and cattle rustlers. When the arrival of the railroads, the penetration of the market economy, the unresponsiveness of the government, and the subsequent onset of hard times rendered these traditional institutions inadequate to ensure a decent standard of living, it is not surprising that people would be attracted to a political movement that seemed to embody these "ancient habits of mutuality" that had been transmitted down through generations of rural southerners.[2]

As certain aspects of traditional southern culture served to animate Populist ideology, so did elements of the country's political history. Like the culture itself, the American political system had been constructed of a complex mix of ideas. Historians have identified three dominant influences: classical liberalism, republicanism, and Protestant Christianity.

Born of the Enlightenment, classical liberalism emphasized individual rights and liberties, including the pursuit of economic self-interest without government interference. In its early years, in the hands of theorists such as Adam Smith and Thomas Jefferson, it was a radical if not heretical doctrine, as these thinkers saw the mercantilist governments of Europe as hopelessly and intentionally designed to benefit the entrenched upper classes. The idea that individuals should be left unfettered by government to pursue their private economic interests promised a meritocratic sort of liberation from the constraints of traditional, hierarchical society, and by the middle of the nineteenth century it had become something of a gospel for many Americans. However, the Americans of Jefferson's generation never envisioned private enterprise on the scale of a Standard Oil, a Carnegie Steel, or a Pennsylvania Railroad. Indeed, the earliest corporations were not really private enterprises at all; they were quasi-public institutions, chartered by government to serve public needs such as the construction of bridges or roads. With the rise of the mammoth industrial corporation, classical liberalism developed a strange sort of dual personality, still embraced by many ordinary citizens but increasingly wielded by the captains of big business to ward off any unwanted interference by the government.[3]

During the century from the American Revolution to the late nineteenth century, classical liberalism had existed in a sometimes uneasy symbiosis alongside a second political ideology, republicanism. Defined here as a particular set of beliefs that warned against the corrupting potential of unchecked power, republicanism sought to keep government in the hands of a virtuous and disinterested citizenry that would legislate for the common good. Although both liberal and republican political thought resonated with Populists, republicanism probably held the most salience. It had provided to their grandparents a language of protest in the revolutionary era, by which they gave voice to their grievances against a tyrannical king and corrupt parliament. Adopted by Americans of all political persuasions after independence, it lent Jacksonian Democrats an antimonopolist vocabulary by which they could oppose the "monster" Bank of the United States, while it simultaneously enabled Whigs to push back against the dictatorial reign of "King Andrew the First." Later, secessionists had used it to justify a revolt against a supposedly power-hungry abolitionist government in Washington, D.C., and antislavery northerners had held up decadent slaveholders as examples of antirepublican corruption and self-interest run amok. Clearly, republicanism could mean very different things to different people, but by the 1890s it had been the dominant language of political protest in America for well over a century.[4]

Neither classical liberalism nor republicanism could have existed in the first place without a third important influence, Protestant Christianity. Protestantism owed its very existence to a rebellion against hierarchy, and with that revolt it proposed a new relationship between the individual and God. The Reformation in fundamental ways set the stage for the liberalism of Locke, Montesquieu, and Rousseau. Enlightenment liberals may have contended that the inalienable rights of individuals were ordained by natural law, but they also believed that natural law was "divinely established." Jefferson, though not religious in any conventional sense of the term, famously declared that people were endowed with certain inalienable rights not by natural law but "by their creator." But Christianity also emphasized virtue, which, as we have seen, was a central idea in *republican* ideology. According to republican theory, only a virtuous citizenry could rule in the public interest; a republic without virtue would inevitably fall, as had the ancient Greek and Roman republics. But republicans were not the only political theorists who emphasized virtue. That avatar of economic liberalism, Adam Smith, had anticipated that the market economy he envisioned would contribute positively to the virtue of the citizenry, an idea he explored in his aptly titled book *The Theory of Moral Sentiments.*[5]

Just as virtue served as a common denominator uniting the liberal, republican, and Christian strands in early American political thought, so did popular sovereignty. The idea that the people are the supreme authority of their government had its roots in Americans' experience with self-government during the colonial era. By the mid-eighteenth century, the idea had become firmly entrenched in American society, manifesting itself in Americans' devotion to self-government in town meetings and colonial assemblies. Popular sovereignty became a fundamental part of republicanism, embodying the ideal of publicly interested citizens legislating for the common good. At the same time, as Americans gradually jettisoned English notions of virtual representation and commonwealth, liberal theorists embraced popular sovereignty as the means by which autonomous individuals exerted their rights as citizens. Much of the story of American political life, then, from the Revolution to the Populist era, was the story of the creative (and sometimes destructive) tension between classical liberal, republican, and Christian thought. All would contribute to Populist ideology in the 1890s.[6]

Republicanism posited that power corrupted, and nineteenth-century Americans translated that belief into the slogan "equal rights to all and special privileges for none." Nevertheless, by the late nineteenth century many Americans were coming to view that phrase as something of a quaint relic of a bygone era. As the *Dallas Morning News* remarked in 1891 (in a squib that infuriated Populists), "It sounds like the silly declaration of the school boy to talk these days about 'equal rights to all and special privileges to none.'" But Populists still held republican ideals dear. "We want a democratic party like that inspired by Jefferson and by Jackson," the *Southern Mercury* inveighed in 1891, "which will align itself on the anti-monopoly side of the branch and stand on the doctrine of 'equal rights to all; exclusive privileges to none,' and will fight the battle of the producing classes against monopoly in all its varied forms." Populists were convinced that the Democratic Party was "not today, what it 'used to be'" and that Democrats had abandoned the fight against special privilege and "repudiated every fundamental principle laid down by the democratic fathers."[7]

In mentioning the struggle of the producing classes against monopoly, the *Mercury* was deploying the two most important ideas in Populist-era republicanism. Populists, like American workers extending back to the Jacksonian era, believed in the so-called labor theory of value: that labor was the ultimate source of all value. Invoking the biblical injunction, they declared that "the labourer is worthy of his hire"—another way of saying that the worker deserved to be paid the full value of his work.[8] The chief transgressor of this injunction, according to Populist ideology, was monopoly. When Populists spoke of monopoly, they meant much more than simply the narrow economic definition of one person or firm controlling an entire industry (although they certainly used it in that sense as well); they employed the term as shorthand for concentrated power in general, power gained or sustained through unfair advantage, or "special privilege," especially special privilege granted by the state. As Eben Dohoney explained at the birth of the Texas People's Party in 1891, "The leading issue in American politics is monopoly against the liberties of the people," and he promised that the party would "defend the producing classes against monopoly in every form." One of the hallmarks of monopoly was its tendency to limit or destroy competition. John D. Rockefeller buying out all his competitors or driving them out of business comes to mind. Another hallmark of monopoly was discrimination. Monopolized railroads, for example, could bestow favorable rates on one customer and punitive ones on another, violating republican notions of equality and justice. The monopoly that Wall Street held over the nation's finances favored one section over others. Almost every Populist policy position had an antimonopoly justification, either on the face of it (as in the case of their campaign against the railroad trusts) or just beneath the surface (as in the case of the Subtreasury Plan, which by democratizing banking and credit and expanding the money supply would break the monopolistic stranglehold of Wall Street and private bankers on the nation's financial system). Antimonopolism, then, much like its cousin republicanism, could be used to justify a wide range of different policies, and deployed along with republicanism, it provided a powerful tool for Americans seeking to critique a political and economic system that their life experiences told them was unjust.[9]

The Populists' religious faith, the "habits of mutuality" inherent in rural folk culture, and the complexly intertwined ideas of classical liberalism, republicanism, and Protestant Christianity attracted them to a wide range of theories and specific reform measures. Relatively few planks in the People's Party's platforms were truly original; indeed, Populists freely borrowed from a disparate body of theoretical writings and from other reform movements. Historians have traced the genealogy of certain specific Populist causes as far back as the workingmen's movements of the Jacksonian era, but more direct antecedents of Populist thought and policy were the various labor conventions of the immediate post–Civil War years. The short-lived National Labor Union (NLU), itself a collection of local unions, was founded in 1866 and worked out a series of demands in conferences over the next few years. These included the abolition of convict leasing, reserving the public lands for actual settlers, collective bargaining rights, the eight-hour workday, a mechanic's lien law, the creation of government bureaus of labor statistics, and—perhaps most significant of all, vis-à-vis Populism—the abolition of the National Banking System and the creation of a system of government-issued legal-tender treasury notes (i.e., fiat money, or greenbacks). All of these would find their way into Populist platforms in the 1890s. The Industrial Brotherhood, a successor to the National Labor Union with some of the same leaders, retained virtually all of the NLU's planks when it was first organized in 1873. One significant addition was a plank calling for the inauguration of "systems of cheap transportation to facilitate the exchange of commodities," at least vaguely foreshadowing the Populists' call for government ownership of the railroads.[10]

Even more important as a direct source of Populist doctrine was the platform adopted by the Knights of Labor at its January 1878 convention in Reading, Pennsylvania. The Reading Platform, almost identical to those of the NLU and Industrial Brotherhood (with the exception of the "cheap transportation" demand), proved significant not for its originality but because of the subsequent success of the Knights, which in the 1880s became the preeminent labor union in the country. The Knights' popularity in Texas, its overlapping membership with the Farmers' Alliance, and the relationship that the two organizations forged during the state's labor strife of 1886 brought the Knights' platforms to a much broader audience than those of the previous groups, whose membership was largely confined to urban laborers in the eastern states.[11]

As the Knights of Labor was slowly growing in the 1870s, reformers mounted the first serious third-party movement of the postwar era, the Greenback Party (variously known as the Independent Party, the National Party, or the Greenback-Labor Party). Early Greenback platforms in 1874 and 1876 had been brief and focused rather narrowly on the monetary issue, but when the party convened in Toledo in 1878, less than two months after the Knights' Reading convention, it drafted a document very similar to the Reading Platform, the principal addition being a call for a graduated income tax—another demand that would be found on Populist platforms in the 1890s. Two years later, in advance of the 1880 presidential campaign, the Greenbackers elaborated on a number of their prior demands and added several more. One called for federal regulation of interstate commerce, declaring, "All lines of communication and transportation should be brought under such legislative control as shall secure moderate, fair, and uniform rates for passenger and freight traffic."

Another denounced "as dangerous the efforts everywhere manifested to re-
strict the right of suffrage," presaging Populist calls for fair elections.[12]

The list of prominent Texas Populists who had once been Greenbackers
includes Eben Dohoney, Stump Ashby, Jerome Kearby, Bill Farmer, Harry
Tracy, Charles Jenkins, Sam Evans, James Madison Perdue, and Henry L.
Bentley. These were men willing to turn their backs on the Party of the
Fathers—the Democratic Party— when the supposed trauma of Radical Reconstruction was still fresh in the public's mind and to do so was to challenge
not only the political but also the racial orthodoxy of the South. Nevertheless,
greenbackism was so popular in Texas that in the 1882 gubernatorial race,
Greenbacker George W. "Wash" Jones, running with the support of both the
Greenback and Republican parties, polled over 100,000 votes out of some
250,000 cast. Maj. C. H. Hanson, a Populist newspaper editor in Gonzales in
1893, left a biographical account of his career that indicates the staying power
of greenbackism: "As a democrat I began to denounce the contraction of the
currency in 1872, and continued to do so up to 1878, when I took up the greenback cause while publishing the Rising Sun in Groesbeck, Limestone county,
and since that time have published papers in eleven towns in the state advocating the financial policy as promulgated by the old greenback party, viz:
Groesbeck, Hope, Hubbard City, Dawson, Cleburne, Joshua, Itaska [sic], Al-
varado, Marlin, Fort Worth and Gonzales." Hanson explained that his frequent
moves were the result of his "aggressive and uncompromising position on the
money question," which invariably had antagonized the local businessmen on
whose good will and patronage an editor depended. Old Greenbackers like
Hanson constituted a sizable core of the left wing of the People's Party, and
greenback monetary theory would become a central component of the Populist agenda.[13]

The proto-Populist platform planks of the National Labor Union, the Industrial Brotherhood, the Knights of Labor, and the Greenback Party appeared
again in the late 1880s with the creation of the Union Labor Party (ULP). By
then the Farmers' Alliance had risen to prominence in Texas and across the
nation, and many Texas Alliancefolk, including most of the aforementioned
Greenbackers, could be counted in the ranks of this latest third-party movement. The 1888 national platform of the ULP reflected all these influences,
repeating most of the demands of past labor organizations and explicitly calling for government ownership of "the means of communication and transportation" as well as the prohibition of alien land ownership and the direct
election of US senators. In its financial plank, the party not only called for

greenbackism but also suggested that the federal government might issue the greenbacks via low-interest loans direct to citizens who pledged land as security. At the ULP's national convention in 1888, future Populist Sam Evans of Fort Worth was offered the vice presidential nomination but declined, and Harry Tracy of Dallas was named to the national executive committee. The Texas ULP convention nominated state Alliance president Evan Jones for governor, Fort Worth mayor Hiram S. Broiles for lieutenant governor, and Dallas attorney Jerome Kearby for chief justice of the state supreme court. Jones later declined the gubernatorial nomination and was replaced by former lieutenant governor Marion Martin. All four men would go on to become influential Populists.[14]

None of this is meant to downplay the importance of the Farmers' Alliance as a leading source of Populist ideology but rather to suggest that the Alliance was only one of several sources, and that most of the ideas found in the Alliance's demands had been worked out in the various labor and third-party movements of the preceding twenty years. A look at the Alliance's 1886 Cleburne Demands, which has been called "the first major document of the agrarian revolt," reveals the influence of those movements. (Of the organizations and parties mentioned above, all but the ULP preceded the Cleburne Demands.) Although several of the seventeen demands were Texas-specific (e.g., calling on the state attorney general to enforce corporate tax collection), and some went into greater detail than in past platforms (e.g., enumerating the several practices by railroads that the Alliance wanted regulated), most of the demands were quite familiar: public lands should be made available for actual settlers at affordable prices; alien speculators should not be allowed to own land; interstate commerce should be regulated; the convict lease system should be abolished; a bureau of labor statistics should be established; a mechanic's lien law should be passed; silver should be remonetized; and of course, the gold standard should be abandoned in favor of greenbacks. The demands made no mention of *how* the new paper money was to enter into circulation; Macune's Subtreasury proposal still lay three years in the future. Significantly, Texas Alliancefolk in 1886 were not yet ready to call for a graduated income tax as the Greenback Party had done, nor to demand government ownership of the railroads and telegraphs or the direct election of senators as the Union Labor Party would do in 1888. The fact that the People's Party would incorporate all of these demands, and then some, into their state and national platforms in the 1890s indicates that Populist policy indeed sprang from multiple sources, and that most of those sources antedated the Farmers' Alliance.[15]

Individual thinkers and theorists also influenced Populist ideology. One of them, the utopian novelist Edward Bellamy, whose 1888 novel *Looking Backward* was a nationwide bestseller in the years leading up to the Populist revolt, received a great deal of attention from Texas Populists and their detractors—especially their detractors. Set in the year 2000, *Looking Backward* depicts a United States where the abolition of private property and technological innovation have led to a sort of collectivist utopia—an odd mixture of positivism, socialism, and communism where social harmony prevailed and ample leisure time led to individual self-fulfillment. By the early 1890s the novel and the system it described (which Bellamy called "nationalism") had entered the mainstream of American culture, to the point that one could attend a church benefit concert in Galveston and hear the "Bellamy Quadrille" performed by the orchestra. Texan devotees of Bellamy even created two Bellamyite colonies in the Lone Star State. The first, the Magnolia Colony, established in San Jacinto County in the southeast Texas Piney Woods in 1895, reportedly admitted "none but the most earnest and thorough socialists" to membership. The other, in Milam County in east-central Texas, was founded in 1897 by a group including the Swedenborgian minister and Populist state education superintendent nominee A. B. Francisco. At least two others were contemplated, though there is no record that they ever materialized.[16]

It is impossible to say how much real impact Bellamy's ideas had on Texas Populists. Speculating on the growth of what it viewed as a growing craze for government "isms" at the very beginning of the Populist era, the *Dallas Morning News* got it about right when it mused, "How largely this paternal mania may be due to such works as the Bellamy book . . . is uncertain." Even before the founding of the People's Party, conservatives in Texas were dismissing Macune's Subtreasury and any related plans as savoring "too much of paternalism and Bellamyism." Bellamy likewise was reported to have "figured largely" in an 1894 speech by Cyclone Davis, and there can be little doubt that *Looking Backward* at least furnished food for thought for many Populists. In any event, "Bellamyism" became a shorthand in public discourse for any sort of socialist or collectivist idea or enterprise, and it became commonplace for Populists, whether or not they had expressed admiration for Bellamy's work, to be tarred with the Bellamyite brush. As one Central Texas editor put it, "Populism, as explained by Edward Bellamy, means the extinguishment of individual property rights and general government ownership of all wealth."[17]

Predictably, the Texas Populist who left the most actual commentary on Bellamy was Thomas L. Nugent. An intellectual who kept abreast of current theological, philosophical, and sociological thought, Nugent often discussed authors such as Bellamy in his speeches and essays. In one widely distributed speech titled "Reformers," Nugent remarked on the way human selfishness hampered reform movements, and he briefly mentioned that if such selfishness could ever be "transcended," then "the dream of Bellamy will be a realized fact in concrete social life." These comments, along with Nugent's ardent defense of many of the more progressive elements of the Populist platform, led critics such as the editor of the *El Paso Times* to declare, "In fact he is a communist of the communists, and looks forward with hopeful eyes to the day when the only government will be that celestial thing painted for his own amusement by Edward Bellamy." After Nugent formally opened his 1894 gubernatorial campaign with a speech at Grandview in which he described "capital" as "organized, arrogant, intrenched in special privileges," conservative East Texas judge George Aldredge responded to the speech by explaining, "Capitalism means private ownership of property and the antidote is collectivism, which means common ownership, Bellamy's idea. All [of the Populists'] demands tend to socialism." Democrat J. D. Rankin made a similar charge after Nugent delivered a speech to a carpenters' union in Fort Worth, leading Nugent to publish another formal response. "The doctrines of the extreme socialists and communists I have no sympathy whatever with," he avowed; "Bellamyism I regard as the loveliest of dreams—a state or condition that might prevail among angels, but totally unfit for selfish human beings." Nugent readily admitted that he had "derived inspiration from 'Looking Backward,'" but whenever he was accused of being some sort of a Christian socialist or democratic socialist (characterizations that historians have also repeated), he made it a point to correct the record and take policy positions that modern liberals would readily recognize. If he found elements of Bellamyism theoretically attractive, he simply turned his critics' charges back at them, declaring, "I am neither ashamed nor afraid to think."[18]

Bellamy's writings may have influenced Texas Populists only in general ways, but Henry George's had a much more concrete impact. One of the Gilded Age's more original political economists, George is best known for his book *Progress and Poverty* (1879), in which he endeavored to explain the persistence of poverty in an age of wealth and technological innovation. At the root of the problem, he argued, lay the monopolization of natural resources, particularly land. His solution was the "Single Tax" on land values, whereby all unimproved land would be taxed at its full improved value, thus incentivizing speculators to either bring the land into productive use (hence providing fuller employment) or sell it to those who *would* use it for productive purposes. The revenues derived from the tax would eliminate the need for tariffs, property taxes, and other taxes that discouraged investment and job creation. Reformers, including many Populists, liked George's plan because it incorporated the widely held labor theory of value, it was avowedly antimonopoly, and it provided tangible benefits to the working poor.[19]

It was also considered very radical. George defended his scheme against charges that it amounted to confiscation of private property. In fact it was *not* socialism in any technical sense of the term, since the goal was the widespread private ownership of land, the exact opposite of socialism. But the redistributive aspects of the Single Tax led critics to class George, along with Bellamy, among the socialists and communists. This did not stop many Texas Populists from endorsing George's theory. The state party's first two organizing conventions in August 1891 and February 1892 adopted a Single Tax plank, but when the time came to write a platform for candidates to actually run on in June 1892, the proposal evoked a heated fight, with Charles Jenkins of Brownwood—a party moderate and one of its cooler heads—warning delegates that this was "the Henry George proposition" and that "you will have to go before the people and defend this proposition." This created an uproar, whereupon Harry Tracy, whose reform credentials were unimpeachable, joined with Jenkins in telling their fellow Populists that they were "wading into deep water, and the best thing you can do is to look out for it." In the end, the convention reconsidered the resolution and dropped it from the platform, leaving a bitter taste in the mouths of Populist Single Taxers. Shortly after the convention, Edmund P. Alsbury, a Houston civil engineer whose successful bridge-building company made him an unlikely radical, complained that elimination of the Single Tax was the "only real cowardice" in the 1892 platform. (Alsbury would later be elected to the party's state executive committee.) "The people's party is full of single taxers," he contended, "but the leaders have brought with them from the democratic fold a modicum of democratic political cowardice and are afraid to announce the whole truth on the land question." Nonetheless, Alsbury and other Single Taxers such as W. E. Brokaw and J. G. H. Buck continued to champion it at every opportunity, as did virtually the entire labor wing of the party. The fact that this wing consistently lost the intraparty debate suggests the relative strength of Populist liberalism versus Populist radicalism, agrarianism, or socialism.[20]

As usual, Thomas Nugent offered the most cogent explication of the party's position on the Single Tax. The Populist leader clearly admired Henry George, whom he said had "shattered the idols of old political economists" and had rendered economics "no longer the dismal science." Nugent believed, like George, that "labor should have the fullest opportunity to produce wealth" and that the "private appropriation" of land "for speculative purposes" prevented that opportunity from being realized, but he supported only a modified version of the Single Tax. "I have no doubt that Mr. George has taught more sound, economic truth than all the writers whose books have been thrown upon the market within the past twenty years," Nugent stated, "and yet, there are many views stated by him in his wonderful and luminous writings that I do not concur in." Nugent believed that George "doubtless expects too much from the single land tax, and too greatly undervalues other remedies," but he tipped his hat "to the fearless thinker" who had "aroused the 'heartsore and footsore' multitudes of earth to shake off the dust of ages and stand for the rights and dignities of labor." In the end, Nugent left it to the Populist *Texas Advance* to sell this pragmatic position to the party's Single Taxers. As the *Advance* argued:

> The single tax theory may be the germ of a future reform destined to revolutionize the economics of the world, and prove a paramount blessing to humanity; but the Advance feels called upon to urge the leaders of the people's party movement to decline to take it on board at this time. . . . Why take on a single other theory, and especially one as yet only imperfectly understood, if actually not so engulfed in theory as to be beyond practacle [sic] application? The people's party is conducting a campaign of education, and its scholars are of the class little accustomed to handling abstruse political problems. . . . This being the case the course of study should be devoid of all bewildering isms and obscure theories. The Omaha platform puts the reform doctrine down in plain A.B.C. style and it should be thus dealt out to the people. Let them get proficient in these rudiments of reform before the higher branches of economics are taken up.[21]

As previously noted, Nugent scolded the Democratic press for saying that he was "more addicted to Bellamyism or Georgeism than to Populism, as set forth in the Omaha platform," and his profession of the Populist faith undoubtedly reflected the sentiments of the vast majority of the party rank and file. The statist solutions of Bellamy and George appealed to many Populists whose life experiences told them that in the industrial age laissez-faire had failed. This same conclusion, however, is also what made the full panoply of Populist demands resonate so strongly with them.[22]

The final necessary condition for the creation of a Populist ideology were the lessons born of bitter experience. A Texan fifty years old in 1890 could look back on his (or her) lifetime and recall how a Democratic Party dedicated to limited government had gotten the South into a catastrophic war to save rich men's slaves, only to see the Republican Party win that war by marshaling the power of the federal government. He had watched, perhaps approvingly at first, as both parties returned to the laissez-faire faith of classical liberalism after the war, and he had marveled at the staggering growth of industry, commerce, and finance in America. Over a quarter-century's time, that marvel had turned to dismay as he watched the captains of industry amass princely fortunes while plain farmers or laborers like himself slipped closer to actual poverty, despite their unremitting hard work. In true American fashion, he had tried self-help through organizations such as the Grange and the Alliance, only to see those private solutions prove wholly inadequate. The America that could bestow millions on an Andrew Carnegie or Jay Gould while it watched him struggle to put food on his table did not seem very fair to him. It did not seem very democratic. It did, however, prepare his mind for a new way of thinking about politics and government.

As outlined above, the raw materials of Populist ideology in Texas included the heritage of southern frontier evangelical Protestantism; the "habits of mutuality" inherent in rural southern culture; the political inheritance of Christian, republican, and classical liberal thought; producerist antimonopolism; the particular ideas pioneered by previous third-party, labor, and agrarian movements; and the statist theories of thinkers like Edward Bellamy and Henry George. If these were the combustible materials of their received political heritage, the economic crisis of the 1890s served as the spark that ignited the People's Revolt. Over the ensuing few years, as that revolt played out, Populists fashioned a coherent, and largely original, ideology. It was an ideology based on particular ideas about power in a democracy, and many of its beliefs resonate down to our own time.

Their background and experiences led hundreds of thousands of Texans to reach some basic conclusions about the nature of modern political economy. The rise of industrial capitalism since the Civil War had resulted in monopolistic combinations of power that impoverished individuals and restricted their freedom. The intractable public problems caused by monopoly had demonstrably defied private solutions. (Populists would be quick to cite contraction of the currency, abuses by the railroads, widespread unemployment, and collapsing commodity prices as but a few examples of such public problems.) Private solutions had been tried and had come up lacking: any member of the Knights of Labor could tell you what chance their union stood against the Gould railroad lines in the 1886 Great Southwest Strike, and any Texas Allianceperson could relate the story of how the banks, merchants, and cotton factors had crushed the Alliance Exchange. Populists had learned that the preservation of freedom required a counterweight to privately wielded monopoly power.

Since the Revolutionary era, Americans had understood that a too-powerful government threatened liberty, and they had designed their government in such a way as to limit its power. It was not power per se, however, that threatened liberty, but rather unchecked power, wielded by corrupt leaders and corrupted institutions. Nineteenth-century Americans could look at their nation's own history and see that a powerful federal government had often been necessary—necessary to stabilize the economy after the failed experiment of the Articles of Confederation, necessary to win wars against Britain and Mexico, necessary to conquer the western frontier, necessary to put down secession. Indeed, necessary to preserve freedom, as they defined it. Power, then, was not inimical to freedom, as long as there were adequate checks on that power. Indeed, a too-weak government could threaten liberty just as much as a too-powerful government could. Ask merchants trying to do business under the Articles of Confederation, frontier folk facing Indian attacks, or slaves yearning for freedom what they thought about weak government. What was really new in the late nineteenth century was not powerful government but an all-powerful private sector. Gilded-Age Americans were discovering that huge corporations posed a threat to liberty at least as great as the monarchy that the Founders had fought against. Private enterprise—even large-scale private enterprise—was not inherently bad, any more than powerful government was inherently bad. As early as 1885, responding to charges that the Alliance opposed "the legal protection of capital," the Wise County Alliance passed a formal resolution denouncing the charge "as false and in fact without foundation, believing it to be the right and to the interest of the people of Texas to protect capital and the establishment of all legitimate enterprises in their midst." In fact, the Wise County Alliancefolk declared that "we favor the construction of railroads through our county and the establishment of factories, and that they shall receive our hearty co-operation and moral support." But just as unchecked governmental power could lead to tyranny, so could unchecked economic power. The Populists had a word for it: monopoly. And ironically, the only means to check monopolistic economic power was to use the power of government as a counterweight. In reaching that conclusion, Populists had taken a major step toward the elaboration of modern liberal ideology.[23]

Although their solutions to problems of private monopoly varied and some-times even conflicted, Populists' faith in democracy, no doubt augmented by their religious faith in many cases, gave them hope that powerless people might use their only available source of power—the ballot—to solve those problems. Private property and free enterprise were to be scrupulously protected, but when these resulted in monopoly, the business in question could and should be controlled by the government in the public interest. For some antimonopo-lists, government regulation was the answer, and they supported measures such as the Interstate Commerce Commission, the Texas Railroad Commis-sion, and antitrust legislation at the state and federal levels. (Texas's 1889 state antitrust law, heavily backed by Alliancemen in the legislature, was one of the first such statutes in the country.) Experience, though, soon led many to ques-tion the efficacy of regulation. If regulation proved unequal to the task of solv-ing problems caused by monopoly power in industries serving an important public function (e.g., railroads, telegraph and telephone systems, electric and gas systems), they concluded that the government should own and operate those monopolies in the public interest, subject to democratic control. Still others harbored doubts about the *constitutionality* of regulation, believing that government ownership (although not nationalization of existing corporations) was the only legitimate solution to the problem of monopoly. Much of the pub-lic debate over transportation, communication, and utilities in the 1880s and 1890s, including debate *among* Populists, would revolve around which of these positions was the correct one. However, government ownership clearly emerged as the predominant position of Texas Populists, a stance that placed them at odds not only with progressive Democrats in the 1890s but also with progres-sives of whatever party in the early twentieth century.

Whatever their particular solution to the problem of monopoly, Populists were clearly willing to cede new powers to the state. This led many critics at the time, and some historians since, to view their new political economy as a sort cobbled-together combination of capitalism and socialism, if not actually the first step down the slippery slope toward communism. For conservatives who embraced the laissez-faire, limited-government position of classical liberalism, any activist-government position was anathema. As we saw in Chapter 2, George Clark led these forces of conservatism in Texas in the 1890s. Clark had deeply imbibed the classical liberal position that government is the great enemy of freedom, and that all problems facing the nation could be solved by free markets and private enterprise. Running for governor as a breakaway Democrat in 1892, his libertarian campaign slogan, "Turn Texas Loose," was directed primarily at the mildly reformist Hogg administration, which had championed a railroad commission and an alien land law, two policies originally pushed by the Farmers' Alliance. Clark, a railroad attorney, claimed that "step by step state socialism has invaded our state and debauched the minds of our people" and that if the citizenry did not awaken to the dangers of activist government, Texans would soon find "the ideas of Bellamy prevailing in our midst, dominating our government and destroying our people." Like politicians of all persuasions, Clark invoked the heritage of Jefferson and Jackson, claiming that "all the evils and all the ills under which our people suffer, come from a departure from the true principles of democratic government as taught by the fathers of the republic." Probusiness supporters of Clark were certain that "in an evil hour the agrarian spirit" had been "aroused by political demagogues," leading to the current distressed economic conditions. If businessmen could only win the fight for "commercial freedom" and regain "control over their own property," Texas would witness "a return of that marvelous progress which the state was making before the evil days of unjust railroad and alien land laws." If Clark and his supporters believed that the mildly antimonopolist Hogg administration had put Texas on the path toward socialism and ruin, one can well imagine what they thought about Populism.[24]

Populists vigorously disputed Clark's assertion that Texas needed only to be turned loose by its intrusive, paternalistic government. At the heart of this conflict lay a fundamental disagreement about the nature of government in a democracy. Anticipating Ronald Reagan's declaration a century later that government was the problem, not the solution, Clark had stated from the stump, "I don't want a rich government and a poor people, but a rich people and a poor government." Such an assertion flew in the face of the Populist belief that in a democracy the people *are* the government. Or at least that they should be. Populist J. B. Cone took issue with Clark's "rich people and poor government" line, asking, "Is this democracy? A government characterized by one condition while the people are otherwise circumstanced? In other words, is a government democratic that is not in and of the people? That is composed of the people?" Cone surmised that Clark must not have known "what a democratic government is" when he made his remarks juxtaposing the people and their government. An anonymous essayist in the *Southern Mercury* elaborated on the idea that government should be the expression of the will of the people and not some distant, adversarial institution to be mistrusted, calling government "the social trustee, the repository in trust of all social powers and duties, to be exercised and administered in the preservation and conservation, of the equal unalienable rights of all men." The basic Populist belief about the relationship between the government and the people was plainly expressed in Ignatius Donnelly's preamble to the Omaha Platform when he referred to "the power of government—in other words, of the people."[25]

Populists believed that conservatives' talk of turning Texas loose was really just another way of asserting that nothing mattered but complete and unfettered freedom for the individual to pursue his own selfish interests, no matter what the cost, or to whom. As Cone observed, "Instead of desiring to 'turn Texas loose' as [George Clark] would fain have us believe, he wants to turn the vampires loose upon Texas, and turn them loose unrestricted!" Cone captured the essence of the difference between conservative Clark-style Democratic ideas and liberal Populist ideology. Democrats, he contended, believed "that legislation should have very little to do with regulating the intercourse of individual citizens one with another, but that it should let them alone, and let the strong oppress the weak." Democrats like Clark might argue that the key to prosperity was to "throw open the doors of Texas, and invite capitalists everywhere to come in and help us develop the resources of this great state," but Cone believed that "everybody who has been watching the drift of things in this country for the past thirty years" knew that the consequence of unregulated free enterprise too often had been abuse and exploitation. "I think I have seen something of Judge Clark's ideas of 'personal liberty,'" Cone concluded, "and it smacked pretty strongly of a license to do that which is inimical to the peace and safety of society."[26]

Populist criticism of corporations, couched as it so often was in the language of Jacksonian antimonopolism, sometimes created the impression, among contemporaries as well as later historians, that Populists longed nostalgically for a bygone era of Jeffersonian self-sufficiency. In this view, the Third Party's ideology comes off as backward-looking or antimodern. This interpretation obviously is difficult to reconcile with the Populists' overarching solution to the country's problems: harnessing the power of a democratic government to fight monopolistic concentrations of power. Populist admiration for what they called "business methods"—large-scale organization, efficiency, and technological innovation—further gives the lie to the notion of Populists as Luddites. Populists understood that such methods were what had made companies like Carnegie Steel and Standard Oil so successful that they had achieved monopoly power. They were the same methods that the Alliance had sought to emulate with the now-defunct Texas Alliance Exchange, that Populists admired in the Post Office Department, and that they envisioned in the Subtreasury Plan. Populists might occasionally rhapsodize about the simple pleasures of life on a bucolic yeoman farm, but most of them had no time for such nonsense. State Populist chairman Stump Ashby, though himself a small farmer, spoke for most Populists when he outlined the realities of modern life to Dallas Populists in 1894. Explaining why George Clark's libertarian vision of limited government was an anachronism, he declared,

> A time there was when it was wisdom to proclaim that the duties and powers of government should not exceed the protection of life and property, for in those days, now gone forever, competition was the life of trade and the race in life was free alike to all. But with the progress of invention, with machinery destroying the trades and transferring labor to congested centers, with the locomotive displacing the oxcart and the electric telegraphy destroying distance in communication, collusion had become the life of trade and in fact of all political economy. Things had so changed that the principles of government which were best adapted a century ago could not possibly be suitable to-day.[27]

Clearly, Populists had embraced modernity, or at least understood its stark realities, despite convenient rhetoric that sometimes harkened back to simpler times. Even the conservative *Dallas Morning News* recognized that Populists were pragmatic innovators. Observing that the People's Party was "thoroughly free from empty sentiment," the *Morning News* correctly noted that Populists "do not hesitate to ignore traditions in seeking remedies for modern ills. Perhaps the better way to put it is to say that they take the ground that democracy is whatever the people will, and that it is part of democracy to solve present problems with present means." Returning home from the Omaha convention in 1892, Harry Tracy professed to be "astonished at the depth of the knowledge of the delegates from the north and west on practical political economy, sociology and the science of life." (Tracy seems to have taken it as a given that Texas delegates possessed knowledge of such things.) In the all-important debate on monetary policy, Populists frequently described greenbacks as "scientific money," differentiating such money from precious metal, the primitive, *un*scientific form of money used since ancient times. *Scientific American* magazine advertised in the *Southern Mercury*, apparently understanding that it would find a receptive audience among Texas Populists. Several individual

Texas Populists displayed a conspicuous scientific bent, including J. G. H. Buck, who secured a US patent on a tamper-proof mechanical voting machine, and Henry Bentley, who likewise patented a device for locating geographic features on maps.[28]

The Populist belief in using the power of a scientifically administered government to counter the power of the corporations led them to share some policy positions in common with socialists, the most obvious being government ownership of railroads. But they did so not because of any philosophical belief in the inherent justice or superiority of collective ownership of the means of production but rather because in certain cases public ownership either provided needed competition in a monopolized industry or replaced a "natural" private monopoly with a publicly owned monopoly responsive to the public good. In other words, public ownership or control of certain industries addressed the market failures that modern capitalism invariably produces, thus allowing capitalism to function properly.

Populists spent a fair amount of time and energy explicating their views on capitalism. As the People's Revolt was taking shape in the 1880s, an Alliance editor declared that "the Farmers' Alliance as an organization does not favor labor against capital nor capital against labor, but it stands with outstretched arms firmly on the broad plane of equality, holding aloft the scales of justice, teaching that each is necessary to the existence and welfare of the other." Populists regularly identified "three distinct and important factors of all government and society; namely land, labor and capital." As state Alliance president Evan Jones explained in 1892, "Land and labor are the creating factors . . . [that] co-operate to create wealth." Populists were fond of saying that "labor is prior to and independent of capital" and, occasionally, that "labor is more important than capital or capitalists," but these were mostly rhetorical flourishes intended to appeal to Populist audiences and to push back against a culture that tended to glorify capitalists as captains of industry and creators of jobs. In their actual analyses of the economy and society, Texas Populists consistently stressed the coequal importance of all three elements. They recognized and accepted the place of capital in the American system, and they virtually never called for the overthrow of the capitalist system of production.[29]

Perhaps because his opponents so often accused him of socialism, communism, paternalism, and Bellamyism, Thomas Nugent went to great lengths to explain Populist beliefs about capital and capitalism. "Capital!," he exclaimed before a San Marcos audience in 1894—"It is the hand maid of labor and the dispenser of blessings to all classes and conditions of humanity." Defining capital as "surplus wealth employed in the production of more wealth," Nugent noted that "without capital, schools and universities would vanish, churches cease to exist and organized charities pass away. Taste, culture and refinement would wither and die as if stricken with a curse; art and science would linger only as dead memories and all the multiplied social agencies which minister to human happiness, comfort and use would disappear forever." Nugent realized that the stark distinction that some Populists drew between producers and nonproducers was artificial. On one hand, Nugent reminded them that "if you were to go out into a desert without any money or without any implements you would not be a great producer of wealth." On the other hand, he asserted that even "the retail merchant is a producer of wealth, for he by his labor and skill and capital makes the final use [of the farmer's products] possible."[30]

Nugent was not the only Populist who sought to refute the charge that the party was anticapitalist. When the Populist state executive committee in 1894 unanimously passed a resolution affirming "that the people's party is not the enemy of any necessary industry or class," Harry Tracy was called on to explain the resolution. He replied that it meant just what it said; Democrats had so frequently "made it a point to endeavor to get merchants and manufacturers to believe that the people's party was their enemy, seeking to destroy their business," that the committee felt the need "to call the attention of the capitalistic interests of the country to the fact that the people's party is the friend and not the enemy of legitimately invested capital." In an 1892 joint statement by Stump Ashby, Henry Bentley, and Thomas Nugent, the three leaders envisioned a time when "labor and capital shall dwell together, not as warring enemies, but as kindly friends, joining willing hands in the beneficent work of production." An Erath County Populist wrote to his local newspaper to say, "There is, and should be, no necessitation of antagonism between capital and labor. They are intended to be, and should be, mutual help. Each has a mission to fulfill and it should be honestly done."[31]

Their belief in science and their dedication to a modernized, socially responsible capitalism shed needed light on Populists' conception of the term "progress." No doubt there were some Populists who, as the New Dealer Ray Moley once put it, nostalgically yearned to live in a "nation of small proprietors, of corner grocers and smithies under spreading chestnut trees." Likewise, there were Populists who fit the description of the "harassed little country businessman," a frustrated man on the make who "gambled with his land" and blamed a rigged system when he didn't get ahead financially. Neither stereotype captures the mainstream of Texas Populist thought. Certainly, most Populists wanted to succeed, to prosper, and to enjoy the benefits of modern life. Too many of them knew firsthand what poverty was like, especially poverty in the land of plenty. While they might reflect positively on the seemingly more democratic politics of the Jacksonian era, few evinced a desire to live in houses lit by candles, draw their water from wells, travel long distances by horseback, or cook over an open fire. Like many modern people who choose their professions or places of residence based on "quality of life" considerations rather than strictly financial ones, Populists sought balance. To observe that they aspired to a comfortable living, a better life for their children, and some savings for a dignified old age is not the same thing as saying that they had become slaves to a culture of consumption, driven by a soulless ethos of insatiable materialism. Populists believed that family, church, and community were important—indeed, sometimes more important than great wealth—but also that in a rich country, those who worked hard and led virtuous lives should reap financial and material rewards commensurate with their abilities. This was the mainstream Populist conception of progress, and one shared by many modern liberals.[32]

In the minds of Populists, then, the nation's problem was not capitalism itself but rather conditions that had thrown that system out of kilter. As Nugent succinctly phrased it, "We are not fighting corporations. We are fighting monopoly." Populists believed that if society would balance private power with public power, ensuring that there are proper checks on each, then corporations and individuals alike would be free to pursue their own interests on a level playing field. This idea was the great genius of Populism, and it directly presaged the liberalism of the twentieth century. No body of Populists anywhere in America understood it as thoroughly and accepted it as widely as did the Populists of Texas; it was their signal contribution to modernity and the legacy that they bequeathed to later generations.[33]

~

The Populists' plan for government ownership of the nation's railroad, telegraph, and telephone systems offers the best, and most important, example of their conception of the relation between government and society. Strangely, historians have usually given it short shrift in comparison to the Subtreasury Plan and monetary reform, even though many Texas Populists considered it to be the single most important Populist demand. Jerome Kearby, the party's standard-bearer after Nugent's death, was unequivocal on this point, saying in 1896 that "I consider the financial plank of our platform and the ownership by the government of railroads and telegraph lines the most popular and strongest planks in our platform." A Populist from the small Cross Timbers town of Dublin urged his "brethren" in 1893 to "educate the people upon the whole of our demands, especially upon the railroad and telegraph plank," because he believed that "the country will go into the hands of the railroads sooner or later if the railroads are not placed in the hands of the government." He also noted perceptively that the Democratic Party "hurled its strongest argument at this plank of our platform and succeeded in turning thousands of good men from us who was with us heart and soul" on other issues. Milton Park of the *Mercury* admitted in 1896 that "government ownership of railroads is one of the most popular issues before the country." As usual, however, it was Thomas Nugent who provided the most thoughtful and thorough explanation of the issue. "The inter-communication of intelligence and the exchange of wealth products by the railroad and telegraph," he argued, "certainly lie at the very foundation of our industrial, and thus of our social, well-being, since our complex social life finds expression (evolution) in our complex industrial system." This was no nineteenth-century rustic longing for a simpler agrarian past. Nugent clearly understood that complex, capital-intensive systems like the railroad and telegraph were here to stay and indeed made necessary and positive contributions to modern life. He argued, therefore, that they should be regarded as essential public utilities, and "their maintenance must be seen to be rather a function of government than of the individual."[34]

The Populists knew of what they spoke. In the late nineteenth century, railroads epitomized the modern corporation. As the leading historian of the railroads notes, "Railroads dwarfed textile mills and iron foundries, the other large enterprises of the United States, both in the capital they required and in the complexity of their management. . . . And in the number of people they employed and in the elaborateness of their bureaucracies, these corporations had more in common with governments than with other business enterprises." Some may view the railroads and the men who made staggering fortunes off them as examples, whether admired or despised, of the free enterprise system in full flower. Nothing could be further from the truth. The railroads— especially in western states like Texas—were creatures of the state. Of course, the very act of incorporation conveyed the special privilege of limited liability on the roads, as it did all corporations. The government used its power of eminent domain to help the railroads secure rights-of-way. But beginning with the Pacific Railway Acts of 1862 and 1864, the federal government became *the* major player in the development of the railroads west of the Mississippi River.

For the transcontinental lines alone, government loans and subsidies eventually exceeded the staggering sum of a billion nineteenth-century dollars. On top of this, the companies were granted 12,800 acres of public land, along with any coal or iron they contained, for each mile of track built, totaling some 113 million acres. Since the state of Texas owned all its public lands, the legislature in Austin did the granting, bestowing 33 million acres on the roads there. If all the public lands granted to railroads were combined into one state, it would rank third in size, behind Alaska and Texas. The government turned a blind eye to all calls for minimum wages, working hours, or regulations on working conditions, and when workers went on strike, the government used its police powers to crush the strikes, often violently. The roads were shoddily built, poorly maintained, and dangerous for railroad workers and passengers alike. Railroad lobbyists exercised such influence in Washington that critics referred to them as the "Third House of Congress." An 1887 congressional commission charged with investigating the Central Pacific concluded that this one road alone had likely spent $4.8 billion buying legislators and influencing legislation. All the while, the principal financiers of the railroads—men like Tom Scott, Jay Gould, Collis P. Huntington, and Leland Stanford, who knew little about running railroads but who knew a great deal about selling securities—pocketed kingly fortunes, even as the roads they built collapsed financially. By the beginning of the People's Revolt, the Northern Pacific, the Atchison, Topeka and Santa Fe, and the Texas and Pacific, to name but a few, had declared bankruptcy and been placed by the federal courts into receivership, where they became even more directly wards of the state. No less an authority than Charles Francis Adams Jr., grandson and great-grandson of presidents and himself the president of the Union Pacific, lamented in 1888, "I do not believe that there is any power on earth,—and certainly I am sure there is none in the heavens over the earth—which can save from destruction a system which is managed on such vicious principles and is so devoid of all that basis of good faith by which only the business of civilized communities can be successfully conducted, as the railroad system of this country now is. It is plunging to destruction just as fast as it can go. The contempt I feel for the railroad men of this country as a whole I make no effort to express as language is wholly inadequate for the purpose." Still, railroad executives and their family and friends profited handsomely off construction contracts, townsite speculation, and other insider opportunities. When a central figure in the development of both the Central Pacific and the Southern Pacific (two railroads that owed their existence to the federal government), Collis Huntington, died in 1900, he left an estate of $50 million.[35]

Most importantly to Populists, the railroads constituted the most obvious example of monopoly. Where only one railroad existed, it could dictate rates in true monopoly fashion: pay our rates, or carry your cotton to market in an oxcart. When parallel-built railroads competed for the same customers, competition quickly became ruinous, leading to bankruptcy for both. Railroads sought relief by forming pools—essentially agreements not to compete—but the agreements quickly fell apart when the parties cheated on the agreement, and the pools proved unworkable. But whether the problem was too little competition or too much, it was the actual practices of the railroads that enraged Populists. The roads charged more for short hauls than long hauls. Rates overall remained high even as commodity prices tumbled through the 1880s and into the 1890s. The rates were also capricious; nobody really understood how they were determined, and since the railroads themselves actually had no idea what the cost of service was, there was no rationality in their rate structures. To curry political favor, they granted free passes by the thousands to politicians, thus raising the rates for everyone else. The service was poor and often dangerous, and as previously noted, employees were abused and exploited.[36]

The Omaha Platform of 1892 called for the railroads, the telegraph, and the telephone systems to "be owned and operated by the government in the interest of the people." The state party platforms of 1892 and 1894 concurred, although the delegates added that until state ownership was accomplished, the state railroad commission should "be elected by the people" and "be administered in the spirit of fairness to all." The 1896 document elaborated on the party's position vis-à-vis the railroads, noting, "We are not the enemy of railroads, and we here declare that, while we favor government ownership of railroads, yet, so long as such property is owned and operated by corporations, it is entitled to fair and impartial treatment at the hands of the government and the people and to the same protection that is accorded to private property." Texas Populists demanded that lands granted to railroads wherein the roads "have not complied with the conditions of the grant, should be forfeited to the State for homestead purposes," and they called for an end to various labor abuses and a prohibition of free passes.[37]

The Populists' demand for government ownership was based on a sophisticated understanding of the railroad problem. Even the US government had recognized the railroads as common carriers under common law, giving them a quasi-public character and making them subject to government regulation. As we have seen, Thomas Nugent regarded the railroad as one of the "prime essentials" of "our highly organized industrial and social systems," and as such, he considered it to be "public in its character." "Our social and industrial systems are organized upon railroad and telegraph systems," he argued, and therefore as "public utilities which affect the interests of all alike," they "should not be the subject of private ownership or appropriation." Indeed, the railroad industry itself performed "the functions of government, including a delegated right of eminent domain," and because the "exactions levied in the form of railroad and telegraph tariffs" amounted to a tax on production, the proceeds of that tax "should not be lodged in the hands of individuals" for their own "private gain." Writing in the *Mercury*, B. W. Williams asked, what right did the government have to "take possession of the railroads for the benefit of the people?" He answered his own question: "the same right it had in the first place to take for the railroads the land on which they were built."[38]

The word "nationalization" is often bandied about when discussing the Populists' plans for government ownership, bringing to mind images of the government simply confiscating the roads. But no serious Populist ever considered outright expropriation of the railroads. All envisioned either a gradual purchase of the roads, the building by the government of competing roads, or some combination of the two. As with so many of their reforms, Populists actually engaged in a vigorous debate about the details of government ownership. Speaking to his fellow Third Partyites, the Dallas architect and Populist A. B. Bristol opined, "We should study and discuss the best methods of becoming railroad owners." He claimed to have taken an informal poll of party members, and he concluded that "about 50 per cent say 'buy them'; about 30 per cent, 'condemn and take them at a fair valuation,' and the remaining 20 percent, 'I don't know.'" Bristol, though, had his own solution; he suggested that rather than nationalizing the railroads, the government should just build its own. Competition with cheaper government railroads would whip the private lines into line. A writer identified only as "Advance Thought" in the *Mineola Alliance Courier* added yet another wrinkle to the Populist build-their-own railroad plan: "Let us build new roads," he or she urged, "pay for them in greenbacks, operate them at cost, and let the railroad-kings keep their roads." Paying for the new lines in greenbacks creatively married government ownership with the Populists' greenback monetary policy, a sort of two-for-the-price-of-one reform package.[39]

Populists like Bristol probably overestimated the efficacy of competition, especially since cutthroat competition among parallel-built railroads had been the source of much of the chaos in the nation's roads. Few if any Populists advocated ownership of *all* the nation's railroads. Nugent took a characteristic approach, suggesting that the federal government would never need to acquire "strictly state lines," and that "in entering upon the policy of acquiring the ownership of interstate railways it ought doubtless to proceed cautiously." Nugent suggested that an appropriate "test of the policy might be made in the case of the Pacific [transcontinental] roads, which might be acquired both for this purpose as well as to protect the government against fraudulent practices of those great corporations in the future," a proposal that made sense inasmuch as most of the transcontinentals were already in government-directed bankruptcy receiverships due to the gross mismanagement and malfeasance of their leaders.[40]

Attorney Charles H. Jenkins of Brownwood, one of the best educated and most intellectually rigorous of the party's major leaders, spoke extensively on the issue during his 1892 congressional campaign. He admitted that "our position on this question is in advance of the times," and as such, he thought it probably "adds no strength to our platform." Therefore, he argued, "It is a proposition that demands thought, and our best thought." But Jenkins quickly put to rest any suggestion that he was hesitant on the issue. "Railroads are necessary monopolies," he declared, "and we cannot shave them of their monopolistic powers while others own them." Regulation by a commission, which had already been tried, was actually the more radical, if ineffective, approach. It was "repugnant to American common sense that one set of men . . . should control the properties of another set of men." His conclusion: "To control these roads completely in the interest of the people the people must own the roads."[41]

Jenkins put forward what was probably the most mainstream Populist strategy for achieving the goals of government ownership. While the government could try the Bristol approach and, if the owners would not sell at a fair price, build competing government lines, Jenkins thought this would not be necessary. Rather, he contended that Congress could move toward government ownership starting with the nearly bankrupt Union Pacific. Since the government held a mortgage on that line "which it seems will never be paid," as a first "experiment" the government could simply foreclose on the railroad and begin operating it. "If this proves a success let the government buy another through line and run it, and gradually let the government own them all." The *Mercury* echoed Jenkins's ideas, endorsing the gradual and partial purchase of the railroads. "The Pacific roads which the government practically owns now, might be taken in first, and then the other trunk lines," the paper editorialized.

The *Mercury* believed that with control of major trunk lines, "the control of the traffic rates will be secured, and the other roads can be taken in hand as necessity demands." In other words, the mere threat of government ownership would likely be enough to make many roads act in a socially responsible way. The party's 1896 national platform specifically mandated the foreclosure option in the case of the Pacific railroads.[42]

Those Populists who favored government construction of new, competing railroads had another important goal in addition to securing reasonable rates and service. With the country in the depths of what was quickly becoming the worst depression the nation had ever seen, building new government lines would help address the unemployment crisis. As an advocate of this strategy, A. B. Bristol in 1892 spelled out the benefits with great clarity: "From the day the work began multitudes of men employed would begin to enjoy blessings that would spread to all the people. . . . Those in greatest need will be benefitted first, instead of last of all." That same year, Alliance leader-turned-Populist William Lamb took an even more expansive view of the benefits of government-built railroads: "If I could have what I would think the best method of putting money into immediate circulation I would have the government build trunk lines of railroads, public buildings for postal and other uses, for which the government needs such buildings, and make levees, etc., and issue a full legal tender paper money and pay for same. This plan would at once employ the idle labor of the country and stimulate industry and business, and I believe that the time is not far in the distant future when our government will conceive the idea that it is better to build up than tear down." Lamb made these comments in the context of an interview about what should be in the next party platform, acknowledging that the party was not yet ready for such advanced thinking in its platforms, just as it was not ready to commit to woman suffrage. But by 1898 the construction of a "Relief Railroad" from the Red River to the Gulf of Mexico by the state government had become the leading plank in the Populist state platform. Populist steps toward the modern welfare state were few and halting, but the idea of government railroads as a public jobs program for the unemployed indicates that Populists were willing to think creatively about an enlarged role for government in assisting its neediest citizens.[43]

Being what today we would call policy wonks, Populists spent a great deal of time and energy explaining how the government's purchase (or construction) of the railroads would and could take place. Democrats naturally seized on the enormous cost involved to paint their opponents as visionaries whose plans were practically impossible. Ex-senator John H. Reagan, from his perch as chairman of the Texas Railroad Commission, led the charge, and in the ensuing highly partisan battle of statistics it is likely that neither side won many converts from the other. In that battle, though, the various Populists displayed a remarkable grasp of the complex but monumental financial frauds that the railroads had perpetrated on the nation, including watered stock issues, inflated interest on bonds, insider contracts, and bloated salaries for corporate officers. The *Mercury* observed that "nearly one-half of the reported railroad indebtedness is fictitious," which modern scholarship has shown was almost certainly true. Populists pointed out the economies of scale to be realized by consolidating the management of railroads under government control. "Each system of roads has all the officers necessary to run it at enormous salaries," James Armstrong noted in the *Mercury*, "and all the roads under government management could be run by the one set of officers for one system of roads, thereby dispensing with many officers and many big salaries, among which might be enumerated the many commissioners, both State and Federal." Armstrong also provided a stinging answer to Reagan's charge that private enterprise can always run a business cheaper and more efficiently than the government. Armstrong wondered why Reagan, former postmaster general of the Confederacy, "did not recommend to the Congress of the Confederate States the letting out by contract to private corporations the business of carrying the mails of the Southern Confederacy. It was certainly his duty as postmaster general to have the mails carried as cheaply as possible. But it is a notorious fact that the mail service of the United States, vast and complicated as it is, is the best and cheapest managed business in the country, and from its inception the tendency has been to cheapen rates."[44]

In all this, the Democrats and Republicans naturally charged the Populists with socialism and communism, but they most often deployed the then-damning word "paternalism" to describe the party's plan. Writing in 1894 to explicate the Subtreasury Plan, Harry Tracy vented his frustration at the charge. "If there has been any one word in the English language used more than another to stampede the people, side-track them, so as to prevent the investigation and discussion of great vital questions of National importance, it has been the word 'paternalism,'" he complained. Best known as the leading champion of the Subtreasury Plan, Tracy addressed the paternalism charge in an 1896 speech to the Dallas Populist Club. Echoing Charles Jenkins's point that regulation of the railroads was actually more radical than government ownership, he compared the state Railroad Commission's setting of rates to a father controlling the property of his minor child. "The people's party is opposed to that kind of paternalism," Tracy stated, "because it is un-American, it is unfair, un-just, and it is absolutely unconstitutional." Populists repeatedly answered the paternalism charge, arguing, as did an essayist in the *Southern Mercury*, that government ownership of the railroads "is no more paternal than management of the postal service, the granting of patents or the construction of a national road from Washington to St. Louis." Paternalism may have been socialism's kissing cousin, but the word carried a more culturally charged meaning, sug-gesting that those who would submit to such a government somehow lacked independence or, worse, manliness. Another reader of the *Mercury*, contend-ing that "it is no more paternalistic to own and operate a public highway made of steel rails than it is to own and operate a public highway (such as a county road) made of dirt, plank, gravel, or broken stone," explained that "paternal-ism implies the abandonment of self-government and the surrender of that right to some other source of power. The people would no more abandon self-government in operating the railroads than they have already done in owning and operating the postal service, the police force, the judiciary system, or the public school." Populist congressional candidate Isaac Newton Barber agreed, noting that "the people [look] upon the word 'paternal' as a great 'bugbear.' It mearly [*sic*] means 'fatherly.' The free school system and homestead laws were paternal so far as that was concerned, yet no public man had courage to denounce the free school system as such, although many thought even [it] paternal." Running for Congress in 1892, Evan Jones told audiences that the Populists intended "to buy the [rail]roads outright and let the government operate them just as the postal system is operated."[45]

Invoking the example of the Postal Service to defend government owner-ship of the railroads became one of the keenest weapons in the Populist arse-nal. In terms of personnel, in 1891 the Post Office Department was the largest branch of the federal government, with 95,440 employees, more than double the size of the armed forces. Indeed, in the private sector only the mammoth Pennsylvania Railroad, with 110,000 workers, was larger. With the growth of the nation and the spread of railroads and other technological advances, the mail system expanded dramatically after the Civil War, transforming life in rural areas. For two cents, a letter could be mailed to anywhere in the country. The commercial bulk rate of one cent for newspapers and related items kept people connected to events in the broader world in ways that had never been possible before, and a special provision for free delivery within county limits placed newspapers within reach of millions who might not otherwise be able to afford them. Although it violated many of the precepts of the free-enterprise system, the postal service was widely hailed as a triumph of the modern age. Most Americans loved it.[46]

Populists in Texas and elsewhere were quick to grasp the lessons of the Post Office. Here was a government agency performing an essentially public task, which all citizens utilized and from which all benefited, and doing it in a way that seemed efficient, fair, and democratic. In one sense it was anomalous, since it had been one of the few federally owned and operated enterprises present since the nation's founding, and relatively few people questioned its legitimacy. But the very fact that it was so successful and so widely accepted is what rendered it so useful to Populists. Although it operated at a loss in many parts of the country, essentially forcing urbanites to subsidize service in rural regions, it offered valuable competition to private carriers, keeping any of them from exercising monopoly power. In that regard it served as a model for what government-owned and -operated railroads would do for the railroad industry. Indeed, Populists needed only to look at the nation's telegraph system for an illustration of how *not* to run a nationwide communication network. Western Union, with 90 percent of the national market share, was America's first true industrial monopoly. Year after year its lobbyists in Washington blocked virtually all efforts at congressional regulation, and the company earned thirty to forty cents net profit for every dollar of revenue it brought in. If you wanted to send a telegram, you sent it via Western Union and paid whatever rates Western Union chose to charge. Populists therefore most often invoked the Post Office to defend not only their planks calling for government ownership of the railroads but also the planks advocating nationalization of the telegraph and telephone systems. All should be considered public utilities, they argued, indispensable for modern life.[47]

In the Post Office Department (and to a lesser extent, public schools), Populists had identified a precedent and a model for activist government and had found it much to their liking. They knew that the postal service was popular, even among those who otherwise professed to abhor paternalism and socialism, and they believed that they could use that popularity as a tool to educate the public on the party's other statist policies. Still, some Texans were not even prepared to grant legitimacy to the postal service. "In demanding government ownership of railroads the populists refer often to the postal service as an indication of the government's success as a business manager," one conservative East Texas editor argued. "If the populists will sit down and reason a little while and compare the earnings of the mail service with that of the express companies they will be bound to admit that private enterprises are far more successful than those owned and controlled by the government." The editor was factually correct—the Post Office Department operated at a deficit overall, whereas a private enterprise like Western Union made handsome profits. But as Populists, often in vain, tried to explain, that was precisely the point: if the postal service operated like a private company and only served profitable routes, then large portions of the population living in isolated areas or in difficult terrain would have no mail service. Those citizens would remain cut off from the rest of the nation, potentially alienated and, at the very least, not participating fully in the new national economy. The Post Office Department existed because affordable communication among *all* Americans was deemed vital to the national interest, and it was a service that for-profit private enterprise could not or would not provide. Political parties, including the Populists, relied on the mail to carry partisan newspapers and political tracts. Retailers such as Montgomery Ward and Sears, Roebuck and Company depended on cheap postage for their nationwide mail-order businesses. (Indeed, mail-order houses and political parties were the greatest champions of one-cent bulk mail, which was responsible for the greater part of the Post Office Department's annual deficits.) Thus, except in the minds of a relatively few doctrinaire apostles of the free market, the public interest justified the existence of the quasi-socialistic institution of the postal service. The arguments that Populists deployed in favor of the postal service would become staples of twentieth-century liberal rhetoric.[48]

Many Populists employed the concept of public utilities in their arguments for government ownership and in drawing the distinction between Populism and socialism. Populists defined a public utility as any "industry of a public character, exercising the functions of government" and which was "itself necessarily a monopoly." It was an enterprise that affects "the interest of all alike," and therefore "should be performed, owned and controlled by the government for the benefit of the people." The telegraph and telephone systems, Charles Jenkins explained, were public utilities because they were "necessary for the transmission of general news and the diffusion of general intelligence." In the case of the railroads, H. F. Clark contended, "transportation becomes a public utility, because the products of one section cannot be exchanged for the products of other sections without the means of transportation." Indeed, Clark, who had clearly thought long and hard about matters of political economy despite hailing from the isolated Hill Country community of Baby Head, Texas, creatively extended the public utility argument to the monetary debate, contending that "as the exchange of commodities cannot be effected without a circulating medium that is safe, sound and flexible and free to all alike, and that in sufficient quantities to transact the business of the country, . . . it becomes a public utility that should be controlled by the government." But Clark, clearly an advocate of an activist government, drew the crucial distinction between these legitimate functions of government and socialism: "I for one cannot accept the theory that the community can farm gardens or raise stock for me better than I can for myself, but I do believe that the government or community should operate all utilities that are essentially public in their nature, thereby insuring to every American citizen an equal chance in the race of life to produce all its blessings." This distinction Populists drew between Populism and socialism would persist as the principal divide between liberalism and socialism in the twentieth century and beyond.[49]

Virtually all of the arguments and justifications that Populists used in explaining and defending their plans for the railroads proved equally useful in the debate over the Subtreasury Plan. Most modern historians studying Populist ideology have focused on the Subtreasury as the linchpin of Populist antimonopolism. It is more accurate to say that it was *one* of the party's most significant demands, but only one. It was certainly the most controversial in its day, and the word "radical"—a relative term if ever there was one—is commonly applied to it. However one cares to characterize it, though, the Subtreasury Plan vividly illustrates the basic Populist doctrine that certain public problems born of monopoly require public solutions, and that in a democracy, private concentrations of power sometimes must be checked by the public exercise of power.[50]

First introduced by Farmers' Alliance president Charles Macune in 1889, the Subtreasury Plan proposed that the federal government build warehousing and elevator facilities for nonperishable crops like cotton and wheat throughout the nation's farming regions. These "subtreasuries" would accept farmers' crops at harvest time, store and insure them for a modest fee, and then extend loans of up to 80 percent of the value of the crops for up to one year at 1 percent interest. As an adjunct to the Subtreasury proper, Populists called for a land-loan system in which farmers or urban homeowners could borrow from the government up to 80 percent of the value of their farms or homes, using that property as security for loans at 2 percent interest. Whether secured by crops or by real estate, the loans were to be payable in legal tender treasury notes, or greenbacks. The Subtreasury Plan had multiple benefits. It would boost crop prices by storing crops and releasing them onto world markets in an orderly fashion. The loan provision would address the immediate credit shortage faced by farmers, and the greenback feature would effectively take the nation off the gold standard, reversing the deflationary contraction of the currency and making the country's money supply more flexible and adapted to a modern economy.[51]

As we have seen, most elements of the plan were not entirely new. In the 1880s the Greenback Party had championed fiat money. The Union Labor Party called for low-interest government loans secured by land. Programs in France and Russia provided imperfect analogues. About the same time that Macune was formulating the Subtreasury Plan, Kansas Alliance leader and future US senator William A. Peffer was devising a plan for low-interest loans based on private warehouse or elevator receipts. Macune's short-lived Texas Alliance Exchange had planned to issue its own "exchange treasury notes" as loans to farmers who pledged to market their crops with the Exchange, and the Subtreasury Plan's commodity-loan component was essentially a public version of that. But therein lay the true significance of the plan—it was a *public* solution, controlled by the people through their elected representatives. Harry Tracy, described by one Populist reporter as "the sub-treasury giant" and probably the plan's most thorough expositor, estimated that it would cost $17 million to build the necessary facilities in the thousand or more counties that qualified for a subtreasury. A federal bureau would have to be created to gather crop statistics and set price standards, and personnel would have to be hired and trained.[52]

But it was not its unprecedented size and scope alone that made the plan seem radical to many observers. As Populists were wont to point out, the postal service was a sizable federal operation, but relatively few Americans thought of it as radical. What made the Subtreasury Plan seem radical was the way it democratized the country's monetary system. By taking the issuance of money out of private hands (that is, abolishing the National Banking System, or NBS) and placing it in the hands of the people (as expressed through their elected representatives), the plan struck a blow at what many Populists considered the nation's most insidious monopoly, the so-called money power. Their criticism of the system was well founded. A relatively small number of powerful national bankers determined how much money entered circulation. Wall Street's stranglehold on the nation's money supply was made possible in large measure by the pyramid reserve structure of the NBS, whereby small banks were required to maintain reserves in larger urban banks, which in return had to deposit their reserves in Wall Street banks. Modern scholars agree that the system greatly promoted the economic development of the industrial Northeast at the expense of the agricultural South and West.[53]

Along with the National Banking System, the country's continuing adherence to a currency backed by gold virtually guaranteed Wall Street's power over the economy. During the Civil War the Union government had been forced to abandon the gold standard in favor of a nonredeemable paper currency, the greenbacks. That currency had played a large part in providing the money needed to fund the massive war effort. Backed only by the good faith and credit of the US government, the greenbacks, as critics had warned, depreciated to a point, but then, as the Union war effort proved successful, they stabilized in value. Wall Street bankers snatched them up at a deep discount after the war, then urged the government to redeem them at face value in gold. The fact that gold was the standard for international trade seemingly gave credence to the bankers' arguments in favor of returning to the gold standard. In 1873 Congress quietly demonetized silver, an opening volley in the postwar battles over monetary policy. (Antimonopolists would later brand this the "Crime of '73.") Two years later Congress passed the Specie Resumption Act, which phased out the greenbacks over a four-year period. The result of these two measures was a sustained per capita contraction of the nation's money supply that would last until the end of the century. To placate westerners who wanted inflation—and a market for the product of their mines—Congress partially remonetized silver with the 1878 Bland-Allison Act and again with the 1890 Sherman Silver Purchase Act (repealed three years later), but these were piecemeal and largely ineffectual measures that had only limited effect on the overall money supply. The collective result of all these actions was that prices for commodities fell into a deflationary spiral that continued for two decades, while interest rates soared.[54]

Farmers, especially in the South and West, who needed credit to finance the coming year's crop, particularly felt the pinch of scarce money and falling crop prices. In rural areas, the few banks that did exist were unwilling or unable to meet the need for agricultural credit, so most farmers turned to furnishing merchants, local storekeepers who advanced supplies at astronomical interest rates, often securing the loans with a lien on that year's crop. Populists may have sounded paranoid when they railed against the "money power" and suspected that the nation's monetary policy was a devious conspiracy on the part of Wall Street bankers and their bought-and-paid-for politicians in Washington, but their suspicions were largely borne out by the facts. Money, credit, prices, and government policy were all inextricably connected, and the Subtreasury Plan offered the best solution to the crisis.

As with the railroad debate, Democrats and Republicans rolled out the usual cries of socialism, communism, and paternalism. One critic derided both policies as "hock shop pumpkin schemes," while another labeled them "abstractions" that were "preposterous," "absurd," and "impractical." John Reagan spoke for most of the Populists' opponents, saying that both the railroad-ownership plan and the Subtreasury would "be unconstitutional, dangerously paternalistic, destructive of the best interests of the country" and would "augment the power and patronage of the federal government to dwarf the rights of the states and to revolutionize the character of the federal government."[55]

The Subtreasury Plan was controversial from the very start. Even the 1892 Omaha Platform had hedged its bets, recommending "the sub-treasury plan of the Farmers' Alliance, or a better system" as a way of introducing fiat money into the economy. Nugent did not endorse the plan until mid-1891, six months after its inclusion in the Ocala Demands had made it something of a litmus test for Populist principles. A reporter for the Alliance paper the *Dublin Progress* found it "strange . . . that a gentleman of such intelligence as the Judge" had for so long been unable to endorse the Ocala Demands. As late as 1896, Jerome Kearby worried that the plan constituted "class legislation"; that is, it catered to a special interest group—farmers. He then admitted, however, that "the parties and the country have indulged in class legislation, and if this is to be done, I want to see it extend to the impoverished farmer, just as it has extended to the money classes. If a man can put up a bond and get money issued to him on it, I do not see why a farmer should not put up something of value and of an imperishable nature and get money on that." Even Charles Macune, who had opposed the creation of a third party, came home to Texas in 1893 to campaign for the People's Party, arguing on the stump that "nothing will revive and build up the trade but the sub-treasury plan."[56]

Because of its sophistication and the way it addressed multiple structural problems in the American economy, the Subtreasury Plan functions as something of a Rorschach test—one can find in it whatever one is ideologically predisposed to see. Its status as a service offered to individual farmers makes it possible to portray it as an effort to maintain the small producer on his land in republican independence. Its currency-related features enable it to be seen as the essence of greenbackist monetary policy reform. Its regulation of agricultural supply and demand make it possible to see it as a harbinger of New

Deal–style centralized state economic planning. But several key realities of the plan render it intelligible as a protoliberal project. First, its sheer scope and scale were truly unprecedented in the annals of peacetime America. That alone suggests its kinship with many of the government-sponsored initiatives of the twentieth century. The plan was not in any meaningful way anticapitalistic; its defenders intended it as a means of making the new global markets more rational, more predictable, less prone to ruinous fluctuations, booms, and crashes—in short, an expression of the new business methods of the era. Harry Tracy, its most able explicator, hastened to emphasize how the local subtreasury facilities would be of the most modern design and utilize the latest technology, how the system's central bureau in Washington would scientifically use crop statistics to determine price standards, and how the nation's new telegraph and telephone networks would facilitate rapid movement of commodities and money throughout the system. The scheme recognized farmers as businesspeople who, because of their relative disadvantages in the market, required government action to level the playing field between individual producers and the much larger, often-monopolized wholesalers, processors, shippers, and buyers. In short, the Subtreasury Plan was a forward-thinking, statist solution designed to distribute the benefits of the capitalist system more equitably to its participants, a hallmark of modern, liberal political economy.

By 1893 party members were waging a vigorous debate over whether to retain the plan. Arriving in Waco for the 1894 state convention, Col. W. K. Street of Montague County predicted that the convention "in its wisdom will probably abandon the subtreasury idea for something better," adding that the party "was never wedded to the subtreasury plank." He believed "it was regarded as the nucleus of the plan to be built upon by blended thought and matured plans after deliberation." Indeed, the 1894 state platform did *not* mention the plan by name, although it endorsed the Omaha Platform, with its "or a better system" hedge words. Instead, the state platform simply called for "the issuance by the government of full legal tender paper money upon some system or plan, which, while securing all flexibility, shall so regulate the volume of currency as to limit it to the actual needs of business." The fact that the *Southern Mercury* felt the need to editorialize for retention of the Subtreasury Plan suggests that many Populists harbored reservations, and editor Milton Park continued to publish articles supporting it. Ultimately the plan was removed from both the national and state platforms of 1896. The national platform simply demanded "a national money, safe and sound, issued by the General Government only, without the intervention of banks of issue, to be a full legal tender

for all debts, public and private; a just, equitable, and efficient means of distribution direct to the people and through the lawful disbursements of the Government."[57]

Some Texas Populists may have had reservations about the specifics of the
Subtreasury Plan, but most never wavered on the larger question of fiat money,
or greenbacks. As they repeatedly pointed out, the Subtreasury was simply one
means of taking the nation off the gold standard and getting greenbacks into
the economy, although to farmers it had the added virtue of the commodity-
loan feature. Most Populists, though, were always amenable to "something better," should it be devised. Every Populist national and state platform demanded
the creation of an irredeemable national currency, that it be issued not by private banks but by the federal government itself, and that it be legal tender for
all debts public or private. Most of the Populists' efforts to educate voters centered
on this monetary theory. "Money is not a material thing, as many believe it,"
the *Mercury* editorialized in a typical article. "It is a function, or arbitrary
term, the same as a yard, a pound, a bushel, or a mile. It is wholly a creature
of law. The law makes, and the law unmakes, money." Populists were fond of
describing their monetary theory as "scientific money," contrasting it with
the ancient and decidedly unscientific notion that precious metal was the only
"real" money. "A specie basis is the same old hobby through which the aris-
tocracy have been robbing the people for lo, these many years," the *Mercury*
explained on another occasion. "A greater humbug was never palmed off on
an intelligent people. We have too many evidences that it is the stamp of the
government that makes money, to be fooled any longer by the money mon-
gers." Bill Farmer, the influential East Texas Knights of Labor and Alliance
leader, contended that the goldbugs believed "in the intrinsic value of gold,"
whereas Populists "do not believe in the intrinsic value of gold, but in a law
made value for money." Silverites, he reasoned, in maintaining that "the government's stamp will make 50 cents worth of silver a dollar," wanted to have
it both ways: they seemed to want a monetary system based on intrinsic value,
but they admitted that it took a government fiat to make it so. "If the theory of
intrinsic value is right, then the goldbug is right," Farmer noted. "If the theory of law made money is right, then the populist is right and there is no place
for the free silver democrat." In all of this, the Populists were decidedly modern, not to mention correct. John Maynard Keynes, regarded by many as the
twentieth century's most influential economist, famously called the gold
standard "a barbarous relic" of the past, and even the free-market economist
Milton Friedman argued that a redeemable metallic standard was "neither a

feasible nor a desirable solution to the problem of establishing monetary arrangements for a free society." The Populists' basic ideas about fiat money would find partial expression in the creation of the Federal Reserve two decades later, although they almost certainly would have seen that banker-dominated, quasi-public institution as being too close to Wall Street and too unanswerable to the popular will.[58]

The Populists' devotion to fiatism explains their divided and inconsistent attitude toward silver. Many Populists simply thought that the full remonetization of silver, thus placing the nation on a bimetallic standard, would be little more than a stopgap measure that would only modestly and temporarily reverse the deflationary trend that had impoverished so many. Jerome Kearby voiced the sentiments of these silver skeptics when he estimated that with every one of the nation's mines and mints running at top speed for a year, the increase in the per capita money supply would only be seventy-five cents, whereas the goal of the party's fiat money plank was to raise the per capita supply from its current value somewhere under ten dollars all the way to fifty. Others objected not so much on the merits of silver as currency but rather because they saw silver as the political Trojan horse that it eventually proved to be.[59]

But still other Populists enthusiastically supported silver, which by the mid-1890s had taken on a sort of mythic quality in the American imagination. It is perplexing to modern Americans—as indeed it was to the mainstream of Texas Populists—how silver suddenly became the leading issue in American politics. Until 1893 the free and unlimited coinage of silver (meaning that the US Treasury would mint into coins all silver bullion presented to it, free of charge) had been pushed primarily by the political representatives of silver-producing states like Colorado and Nevada. Understanding that it would be a small part of an overall program to counter deflation, and no doubt wanting the votes of western states, Populists had embraced it rather matter-of-factly. In the 1892 Omaha Platform, for instance, it was only one of five planks in the document's section on finance. As a nationwide phenomenon, however, the silver craze was a consequence of the events of 1893. In the spring of that year the hard times that had beset the nation for several years (and the rural South for two decades) suddenly descended into a full-blown financial panic. In May the stock market crashed, banks and businesses began to fail in unprecedented numbers, and unemployment soared. The country was soon plunged into the worst depression yet in the nation's history. Seeking some explanation, which in turn might suggest a course of action, Democratic president Grover Cleveland blamed the Sherman Silver Purchase Act of 1890, a compromise measure that had been passed by the preceding Republican administration to placate the silver interests. Certainly, the act had contributed to the run on the nation's gold supplies that triggered the 1893 banking crisis, but the depression that followed, like all depressions, was the result of many complicated factors. Cleveland decided to make repeal of the act his top priority, and in an acrimonious special session of Congress that fall he finally succeeded. The president's stubborn focus on silver as the culprit had the unintended consequence of galvanizing opponents both within his own party and in the other parties in its favor. As one leading historian of the subject noted, "Cleveland anointed silver in trying to kill it."[60]

When repeal did nothing to ease the deepening depression, free silver rapidly became more than just an arcane political and economic topic. Helped along by countless pamphlets, editorials, speeches, and didactic books like William H. Harvey's *Coin's Financial School* (1894), it soon blossomed into a full-fledged social movement, taking on a symbolic and even moral quality in the minds of many Americans looking for an answer to the grinding hard times of the depression. In the popular imagination, silver seemed to represent rural rather than urban values, the common people over the elites. It even spilled over into popular culture, as children's writer L. Frank Baum in *The Wonderful Wizard of Oz* made Dorothy's silver (not ruby) slippers the possessors of "wonderful powers," although the little people of Oz—the Munchkins—"never knew" how to harness it. The politics of silver and the so-called Battle of the Standards in 1896 will be dealt with extensively in Chapter 10, but the point here is that in the wake of the Panic of 1893 free silver suddenly and unexpectedly became a sort of force unto itself, a political and cultural tiger that the Populists would find themselves riding. Many Populists nationwide, seduced by the popularity of the issue and persuaded by all the pro-silver propaganda, mounted that tiger willingly, but large numbers of Texas Populists, including almost all the party's leadership, rode it largely against their will and to their own intense distress. Their worst fears would be realized in 1896.[61]

Meanwhile, one additional reform assumed a much larger place in the firmament of Populist demands: the graduated income tax. Americans had experience with a federal income tax, much as they had with greenbacks, because one had been enacted as a wartime measure in 1861. As with the greenbacks, the income tax was done away with in the 1870s, and the country had returned to its traditional means of raising revenue, the tariff on imported goods. For decades tariffs had been a source of sectional and class resentment, as they helped the Northeast-based industrial sector while penalizing the rural and agricultural South and West. Populists resented the heavily regressive indirect tax the tariff levied on them and wanted to replace it with a more equitable means of raising revenue.[62]

It would be disingenuous to suggest that a resentment of the great fortunes piled up by the great Gilded-Age captains of industry did not play a sizable role in the Populists' call for an income tax. A writer identifying himself as "Farmer Dean" outlined a standard Populist complaint in the pages of the *Mercury*: "Twenty-five years ago a rich man or corporation was compelled to pay some of the burdens of government through an income tax. Now they pay no tax of any kind that they do not unload on the shoulders of the farmer, through the formation of combinations by which they arbitrarily fix prices in buying the products of the farm, or in selling the farmer the necessary supplies for his farm." The *Mercury* itself observed sarcastically, "It is such a pleasant proceeding to the rich to compel the poor or middle classes to bear the burden of contributing the money to support government, that they dislike to yield the pleasure." This same writer charged that "during his life Jay Gould succeeded in evading taxes on his personal property to the extent of millions of dollars," suggesting that "when men with $80,000,000 in personal property swear and keep on swearing year after year that they only have a few hundred thousand subject to assessment, as Jay Gould did, it is time that there was a reform in our methods of taxation."[63]

But the arguments Populists developed in favor of a radical revision of the country's tax system went well beyond mere resentment of the rich; they actually demonstrated a sophisticated and nuanced understanding of the issue. It was not just that men like Gould, Carnegie, and Rockefeller had grown unimaginably wealthy; Populists rarely begrudged the success of those who had prospered by their own hard work or ingenuity. Rather, it was that these men had gotten rich specifically *because* of their ability to manipulate a corrupt government, utilizing unjust incorporation laws, generous state subsidies, government help in suppressing labor discontent, and all manner of favorable legislation, including the tax system. Those who had amassed such fortunes, Populists charged, had "used government, i.e. society, to accomplish their aim, and consequently they should contribute to society in proportion to benefits received." Just as the Civil War–era income tax had been a "result of the conditions created by the war," Populists acknowledged that "legislation incident to the war period and since" had "been the direct means of affording opportunities to capitalists to make enormous fortunes and corresponding incomes, and also to build up a race of millionaires whose numbers are legion."

Populists believed it "peculiarly appropriate that a tax of some kind should be imposed upon that wealth, that property, that income so created." Piece by piece, they built a convincing case for their central argument in favor of the income tax: that "the colossal private and corporate fortunes accumulated in this country are a menace to our democratic institutions."[64]

Apart from these philosophical justifications, the proponents of an income tax also marshaled some pragmatic arguments. If the rich had to pay a larger share of the taxes, it would "interest" them "in securing economic government." ("Rich men get particular when they know they must foot the bills," one writer noted.) It would allow for a great reduction or even an elimination of the unjust and discriminatory tariff. And as a bonus, it would help to "substitute the love of country for the love of gold." The *Mercury* closed one of its pro–income tax pieces with a rather striking declaration: "Let us hail it as our 'shibboleth' of a coming salvation, greater in a political sense than can be conferred upon the people of this land by any other act of legislation." Even allowing for some hyperbole, this was a striking indication of the importance Populists placed on a reform that was destined to become a mainstay of liberal reform in the twentieth century.[65]

With the income tax, Populists for once seemed to gain the ear of politicians in the major parties. The Cleveland administration had been returned to power in the 1890 elections, hoping to effect a traditional Democratic goal, tariff reform. Tariffs were at an all-time high, thanks to the McKinley Tariff of 1890. But the only way Cleveland could get a significant reduction in tariffs was to replace the lost revenue with proceeds of an income tax. Repeal of the sugar tariff alone would cost the Treasury $70 million the first year. After much wrangling, a bipartisan coalition in Congress passed the Tariff Act of 1894 (also known as the Wilson-Gorman Tariff Act), which lowered tariffs, although not nearly as much as many Democrats wanted. To offset the lost revenue and to placate southerners and westerners, the act included a 2 percent income tax on incomes over four thousand dollars. Both Democrats and Republicans supported this modest income tax, at least in part, to stave off potentially more radical demands from Populists. It was a classic case of what political scientists call "selective issue endorsement," a way of co-opting the opposition by embracing some minor portion of its platform. As one House Democrat warned his colleagues, failure to do so "eventually will sweep back and curse this country, as it did in France in the days of the French Revolution." If the major parties were viewing the Populist threat as a potential French Revolution, then the Populists must have been making some progress.[66]

Populists hailed the enactment of the income tax, although they would have preferred a more progressively "graduated" rate schedule. But their joy proved premature; in 1895 the US Supreme Court ruled the income tax portion of the 1894 act unconstitutional. Dallas Populist Barnett Gibbs expressed the general sentiments of his fellow Third Partyites. "When the populist platform demand for an income tax was put into a law to make the other fellow pay even a small part of it," Gibbs stated, "the supreme court by the vote of a democratic judge decided that it was unconstitutional for anybody but a mudsiller to pay the fiddler and that it was a free dance for the other fellow." Thanks to the Court, then, the income tax was back in play as a political issue in time for the critical 1896 elections—in play as a Populist demand, but also in play as potential fodder for selective issue endorsement by Democrats who might see it as easy bait for luring Populists back into the party fold.[67]

Alongside the income tax plank in the 1892 and 1896 financial sections of the Populist national platforms was one final demand, the call for postal savings banks. Historians have almost entirely ignored the plank, but as with the income tax, actual Populists keenly desired its enactment. A brief examination of the plan further reinforces several of the basic elements of Populist financial thought.

Like many Populist policies, postal savings banks had been tried with considerable success in several foreign countries, including Great Britain, Austria, Canada, Italy, Belgium, Sweden, and the Netherlands. The basic idea as put forward by the Populists was that the federal government, using postal service infrastructure, would assume a banking function whereby citizens could make deposits up to some modest account limit (something under $500), have those deposits guaranteed by the government, and receive 2 percent interest. Populists were quick to tout the benefits. First, the deposits would be safe. After the Panic of 1893, countless Americans had seen their uninsured deposits vanish as banks failed by the hundreds. In an era before the federal deposit insurance, this feature alone made the plan highly desirable. Deposits could be made in very small sums, even by children—the sort of customers that commercial banks were reluctant to serve. Many rural areas and small towns, especially in Populist strongholds like Texas, simply had no banks, period. Yet, all but the tiniest hamlets had a post office. And finally, as the *Southern Mercury* argued, there were social benefits: "The inculcation of habits of saving promotes thrift, industry and independence. It lessens extravagance and the chances of want and poverty in old age and sickness." Children would learn "the value and management of money." The plan would help people "feel a direct personal interest in the stability of government." It would provide "needed security to millions striving to be provident, and millions more thoughtlessly improvident," all of which made it "worthy of the loftiest statesmanship."[68]

As with virtually all platform items, the postal savings plank gave scant details about its operation. Populists debated how the system would actually work, particularly what the government would do with the deposits and how the system's solvency would be assured. One possibility—probably the safest—was for the Post Office Department simply to invest the deposits in government bonds, using the interest from those bonds to pay the interest to depositors. But most Populists thought that the postal banks should loan the money directly to the people, who would use real estate as collateral, thus helping to alleviate the terrible credit crunch brought on by the depression. Some took the loan feature to its Populistic logical conclusion, arguing that loans should be made in greenbacks, making the system a means of taking the country off the gold standard. One reform journal explicitly referred to the Omaha Platform's Subtreasury plank, which called for the Subtreasury Plan or a "better system," arguing that the postal savings bank was the "better system" the convention had in mind. But whether or not these more ambitious plans for loans direct to the people came to fruition, the scheme would still be an economic boon to the nation, because as one proponent pointed out, "In the United States the chimney corner, the trunk, the bed ticking, the old stocking, hid amounts of money which, though small individually, collectively make a grand total now practically withdrawn from circulation and non-productive." No matter how the government invested the deposits, it would contribute positively to the economy. As the plank in both the Omaha and St. Louis platforms had made clear, the purpose of the postal banks was to provide "for the safe deposit of the earnings of the people" and "to facilitate exchange."[69]

Postal savings banks, the income tax, free silver, fiat money, and the Subtreasury constituted the heart of the financial portion of the People's Party's national platforms, but Populists commonly depicted their platform as a three-legged stool, with finance, land, and transportation each comprising a necessary leg. The transportation leg, of course, principally involved the railroad issue, which we have already examined. The land plank in the Omaha Platform was two sentences long: "The land, including all the natural sources of wealth, is the heritage of the people, and should not be monopolized for speculative purposes, and alien ownership of land should be prohibited. All land now held by railroads and other corporations in excess of their actual needs, and all lands now owned by aliens should be reclaimed by the government and held for actual settlers only." (The 1896 platform went into somewhat more detail but retained the essential elements of the 1892 document.) As we have seen, a small minority of Populists favored Henry George's Single Tax scheme, but neither the national nor the state party would touch such a radical plan. Instead, the Populist land plank simply echoed ideas that were widely popular, even among adherents of the major parties. Answering charges that the Populists favored the "confiscation" of private property, Jerome Kearby correctly noted that the party's land plank was nearly identical to that of the Democrats in 1884. That platform plank had read, "We believe that the public lands ought, as far as possible, to be kept as homesteads for actual settlers; that all unearned lands heretofore improvidently granted to railroad corporations by the action of the Republican party should be restored to the public domain; and that no more grants of land shall be made to corporations, or be allowed to fall into the ownership of alien absentees." Having established that Populists were no more radical on this than the Democrats of a few years earlier, Kearby declared, "There is not a man in the people's party that would not defend with his life the sacred right of private ownership of land." The railroad lands in question were only those "wrongfully obtained or held," and the prohibition against foreign ownership was clearly aimed at the great British land syndicates that had acquired millions of acres of land in Texas and elsewhere for speculative purposes. Kearby specifically noted that the Populists wanted land to be available for "Americans native born or naturalized," and indeed the party's 1896 national platform, which Kearby helped to write, specified that the federal homestead law be applied to lands that the Pacific railroads had acquired through "frauds." In their 1896 state platform, the Texans broadened their position on the land issue to include a general statement of policy: "The People's party favors all State legislation that tends to increase the number of homeowners and that will assist in the settling of our unoccupied land." And seeking to deflect charges of nativism once and for all, the state platform only prohibited "non-resident alien ownership of land." As with all Populist policies, the land plank would require significant action on the part of the government, but those hoping to find radicalism in Populist platforms would better look elsewhere.[70]

The Populists' three-legged policy became, for most of them, something of a holy trinity. One North Texas Third-Party editor named his paper the *Texas Triangle,* with the masthead reading, "Finance, Land, and Transportation." This emphasis, however, disregards what properly should be understood as fourth and fifth legs: reforms affecting organized labor and reforms to the political system. As noted earlier in this chapter, Populists held an expansive definition of "labor," using the term to include all "producers," whether they were farmers, farm hands, or urban workers. A Third-Party editor from Erath County reminded his readers that "this People's Party is not a movement of the farmer and common laborer exclusively. It is a movement of the people against the parasites." To be successful, the party needed to "unite all legitimate interests, labor, business and professional." In the aftermath of the 1892 elections, party leaders Stump Ashby, Henry Bentley, and Thomas Nugent issued an address in which they looked forward to the day when "merchant and farmer, lawyer and artisan, each in his own sphere of active usefulness without the disturbance of a single right, shall find self-interest consistent with the interest of all, as each partakes of the all-pervading prosperity." Only then would capital and labor "dwell together, not as warring enemies, but as kindly friends, joining willing hands in the beneficent work of production."[71]

These were hardly militant positions. The Omaha Platform celebrated "the union of the labor forces of the United States," and even as it enunciated the labor theory of value ("Wealth belongs to him who creates it"), it stressed that "the interests of rural and civic labor are the same; their enemies are identical." Such pronouncements created a somewhat ambiguous attitude toward *organized* labor, and the labor-specific planks of the platform reflected this ambiguity. Ignatius Donnelly's preamble to the platform strongly supported the right of "urban workmen . . . to organize for self-protection," and it castigated the "hireling standing army, unrecognized by our laws," which had been "established to shoot them down." But the platform itself was largely silent on specific prolabor policies until the "Expression of Sentiments" section, which technically was not part of the official platform. There the platform committee denounced the use of imported "pauper" labor, expressed sympathy with organized labor's efforts to shorten working hours, demanded abolition of the Pinkerton strike-breaking organization, and voiced solidarity with the Knights of Labor in its ongoing conflict with Rochester clothing manufacturers.[72]

Texas Populists certainly hoped to win the votes of urban workingmen in general and organized labor in particular, but the party's hesitance on the issue of strikes worked against them. During the 1894 campaign, as the Pullman Strike was making national headlines, the *Mercury* approvingly reprinted an essay whose basic contention was that "strikes are not the methods of populists. They believe neither in their efficiency nor their policy." The piece declined to "quarrel" with the unions "nor lecture them as to their plans"—

"certainly not in these trying and critical times when all are on a strain and the blood at white heat." But the author believed that strikes "do not reach the root of the disease nor remove the cause" and that there was surely "a better and an effective remedy." In that same issue of the *Mercury*, North Texas Populist congressional candidate and Disciples of Christ minister S. J. Brownson opined that while the People's Party was likely to reap political gains from the strike, "it will teach the trades unionists all over the country that the proper place to strike, if they would remedy the evils that beset them, is at the ballot box." Most observers believed that the great bulk of union members in Texas voted Populist—and they probably were right—but union support for the party was not always enthusiastic. As the *Dallas Morning News* reported from a convention of the State Labor Union in the summer of 1896, "there are a number of the delegates who insist that on many of the questions affecting the welfare of the laboring people, the party is not radical enough."[73]

Nevertheless, the Texas People's Party went far beyond its national counterpart in making specific policy overtures toward labor. Its state platform called for the eight-hour workday, an effective mechanic's lien law, and reform of the convict lease system. Although not endorsing the right to strike, the party called for the creation of a state bureau of labor to collect statistics and protect the rights of workers. Reflecting the views of many Populists regarding strikes, the platform also called for "a State board of arbitration to adjust all differences between corporations and employes." In his opening speech of the governor's race in 1894, Thomas Nugent expounded at length on the party's position vis-à-vis organized labor. Castigating Grover Cleveland's use of "arbitrary military power" in using the army to suppress the recent Pullman Strike, he observed that "the power with which the corporations are now armed cannot be overcome by strikes, which at best are unwise and oftentimes unjustifiable." He strongly endorsed the state party's arbitration plank, acknowledging that for it to be "effective," enforceable, and "productive of any practical good," an amendment to the state constitution would be required. "Whatever can be done on this line," he declared, "we stand to do."[74]

In the state legislature Populists supported a bill providing heavy fines "for any person who shall by means of threats of discharge of an employe from his own or the service of any one else, prevent, or attempt to prevent him from joining any labor organization." Populist representatives sponsored legislation limiting the length of workdays for railroad employees and prohibiting employers from paying workers in company scrip, and of course the party's various planks in support of public education surely appealed to workers from all walks of life who hoped to educate their children. As so often was the case, Thomas Nugent eloquently summarized what he believed Populism promised for the laborer: "When the work of reform is done, brother populists, let us hope that it may be rounded and complete. Let us resolve that when reform shall bring good prices for the products of labor, it shall also, by god's blessing, make homes cheap for the laborer. . . . If sordid and foolish men call this socialism, let us not be disturbed. Such socialism is so near akin to genuine Christianity that we can well afford to welcome it."[75]

Populists like Nugent sincerely believed that the full range of Populist demands would transform life for ordinary Americans. But after the first few heady years of their crusade, many of them came to realize that as long as government at all levels was both inefficient and corrupt, policy reforms in finance, transportation, land, or labor would stand little chance of being implemented and even less of being implemented effectively. As the *Mercury* noted in 1893, "The last few years of practical researches for the cause of our troubles" had revealed that the problem did not "exist with our merchants or business men . . . but we find that they exist in the legislative halls, in the halls of congress, where laws are made that will enable the rich to grow richer."[76]

Since government was the one large-scale institution that could be democratically controlled and used to counterbalance the modern corporation, Populists extended their oft-professed affinity for business methods to that government. Campaigning for Congress in 1894, Jerome Kearby pronounced that "politics was business, not sentiment." He told a mixed crowd of Populists and Democrats that "the government is a corporation doing business for you," and he used a bank to illustrate his point: "Here is a corporation in which men are employed by stockholders. At certain times they are called on to give an account of the way they have conducted business. No sentiment is tolerated here." Likewise, he argued, "in the government, a much more important affair, business principles should prevail. No sentiment should be tolerated. If a party is faithless, condemn it." Kearby returned to this theme the following year, telling a Bell County audience that "government is a science. Politics is the method by which government is administered. There should be as much business and intelligence in your politics as there is learning and philosophy in your government. Combine all sciences, business methods and intelligence and you have the nearest approach to perfected government." The prominent Dallas architect and Populist A. B. Bristol agreed, saying that "the government is only the machinery to do our business with, and is owned by its superiors, the people." The problem was that the people had "imagined themselves too busy to operate it," so they had "loaned it out" to corrupt politicians and monopolistic corporations. "We must go after it, repair it and use it," he avowed, to conduct the public's business.[77]

Populists had no difficulty citing the many laws that had led to the disproportionate power of corporations in modern America. Incorporation itself, by granting limited liability to companies, constituted an unrepublican special privilege not envisaged by the Founders.[78] The structure of the national banking system that concentrated capital in the hands of Wall Street bankers, laws that favored management over labor, and policies that benefited northern industrial interests at the expense of southern and western agricultural ones likewise constituted "class legislation" that unfairly privileged capital. Weak or nonexistent labor laws prevented labor from effectively organizing to bargain collectively with corporate employers, tilting the economic playing field in favor of the corporations. Massive grants of the public lands to railroads had made the railroads the most powerful organizations of their era while preventing would-be settlers from acquiring farms of their own. Nugent believed that "capital could never have attained such ascendancy, but for the legislation which has given it unjust advantages and enabled it to monopolize both natural resources and public functions and utilities."[79]

But to Populists, the unjust or unwise laws that had led to such disparities in wealth and opportunity would never be rectified unless the people could gain an effective voice in their own government. Ignatius Donnelly's famous preamble to the Omaha Platform began with the need for political reforms, even before it laid out the problems of monopoly. "Corruption dominates the ballot-box, the Legislatures, the Congress, and touches even the ermine of the bench," he wrote. The preamble went on to cite the "universal intimidation and bribery" that voters faced at the polls, and it denounced "the struggles of the two great political parties for power and plunder." Although the platform proper did not mention any specific political reforms, an "Expression of Sentiments" appended by the platform committee and approved by the convention did call for sweeping changes: the Australian or secret ballot, the initiative and referendum, term limits for the president and vice president, and the direct election of US senators.[80]

Texas Populists knew, however, that much of the corruption that afflicted their state's politics lay beyond federal control. In its 1896 state platform, the party denounced "the present administration of this State as being purely personal and dominated by ring rule," adding that "a long lease of power tends to corruption, and is subversive of economy and efficient government, and we believe that the best interests of Texas demand a change of administration and an inspection of the books." Reiterating the national platform's charge of widespread voter fraud, the state document called for "a free vote by every qualified elector without reference to nationality, and an honest count," even though its authors knew that by doing so they left themselves exposed to the time-tested charges of racial treason from the Democrats, who seemingly never tired of exhuming the corpse of Reconstruction. As Kearby explained in an 1894 stump speech, "When the people have remonstrated they have cajoled them with promises, coerced them with the party lash, intimidated them with the cry of 'negro rule,' 'force bill,' 'Edmund J. Davis and his policies.'" Two years later Barnett Gibbs concurred, telling readers of the *Dallas Morning News* that "when the people become restless" the Democrats cry, "look out for the nigger and the force bill," reminding voters that this is "the politics of our fathers." Concerns about fraud at the polls grew so great that Populists in the 1895 legislature proposed a comprehensive overhaul of the way elections were conducted in Texas, complete with harsh penalties for violators. The bill, of course, went nowhere.[81]

Even if votes were freely cast and fairly counted, Populists struggled against a political system they believed to be rigged in the Democrats' favor. Democrats, they charged, had egregiously gerrymandered the state following the 1890 census, resulting in "a great hardship" for the People's Party in the 1894 elections. Concern over gerrymandered districts and a general frustration with the Democrats' stranglehold on Texas politics led Populists to embrace the idea of proportional representation in Congress and the legislature, whereby representation is apportioned according to the percentage of the vote each party receives. Populists devoured pamphlets and articles by social scientists touting the scheme, which grew in favor among the party faithful following the 1894 congressional races wherein Democrats won narrow pluralities in a half-dozen districts yet retained every seat. "There is something wrong with a system that allows this," a frustrated Charles Jenkins wrote, and the party included a proportional representation plank in both its 1894 and 1896 state platforms. Efforts by Texas Populists to curtail the influence of money in politics led them to support a ban on the practice of railroads granting free passes to politicians, and a major push to reform the notoriously corrupt fee system of county government met with defeat in the 1895 legislature, although it remained a rallying cry for Populists (and some Reform Democrats) throughout the 1890s and beyond. At the state level, Texas Populists embraced not only the national party's call for the initiative and referendum but also the

"imperative mandate," another name for the recall. By 1896 the various political reforms had grown in importance to the point where many Populists
now placed them ahead of all the party's other demands. Without sweeping
repairs to the machinery of politics—particularly the electoral machinery—
no other reforms, no matter how worthy or appealing, seemed possible.[82]

~

There has never been a mass political party in the United States that could
boast ideological purity, and the Texas People's Party was no exception. The
party had what we today would call its left and right wings, and something in
between that might be termed centrist. No two Populists were likely to agree
on every specific policy. Yet, certain core beliefs united almost all Texas Populists. They shared a sense that the modern corporate order had grown disproportionately and dangerously powerful, to the point where it jeopardized the
ideals of American democracy. Having witnessed personally the failure of private self-help to rein in the corporations, they became convinced that the only
institution that the "people" could control—the government—must act as the
counterbalance to the monopoly power of the corporations. But to achieve that
balance, they believed that the people must first take control of their own government, which had been captured by the special interests. It was a tall order—
maybe an impossible one—but the Populist movement had built an esprit de
corps, a movement culture, which made such things seem possible. Despite
initial setbacks at the polls, they moved forward with hope and optimism, convinced that with enough effort and perseverance on their part, other Texans
and Americans would soon embrace the Populist gospel.

In his opening speech of the 1894 governor's race, Thomas Nugent called
labor "the great, vital, controlling question of the times," a challenge that lay
"at the center of the social difficulties into which our country has been led."
He exhorted his fellow Texans,

Solve this question, so that the man who produces wealth shall own a
just proportion of it, and those difficulties will vanish as mists before
the rising sun. Labor, slowly rising from the dust of ages, stands at last
erect upon its feet. Already it confronts capital, not to provoke strife, but
for reconciliation and peace. It does not ask charity, it demands justice.
It does not ask that capital be enslaved, but that it, the age-old burden-
bearer be made free. It demands for itself, not superiority, but equality;
and it knows by a wise instinct that, in the coming epoch now dawning
upon the world, equality is coming to it in the sure unfoldings of God's

providence. This it knows; and it rejoices that in that day of deliverance the doom of "special privileges" shall be pronounced, and "equal rights" shall come to all alike.[83]

Two years later, a Johnson County Populist, identified in his county paper only by the initials "S. J. M.," provided his own summation of Populist doctrine, simpler than Nugent's but no less eloquent and compelling: "The common people," he wrote, "are not anarchists, neither are they socialists nor nihilists as some of the 'sored-headed' democratic brethren have branded them, but they are big hearted, liberty loving people who claim that law should be enacted for their protection as well as for the protection of the national banker, whisky manufacturers etc. They demand this protection in order that they may reach a nobler and higher plane of civilization, may educate their children and enjoy a greater freedom than some of them are not permitted to enjoy."[84]

4 • The Religious World of Texas Populists

I 'spose I got my share of brains when nature fixed my route,
But I never used them very much to think these matters out.
I kept on chopping cotton, plowing corn from six to six,
With my preacher made religion and my lawyer politics.

I'm going to turn a leaf or two and try to have a change,
I'll join the people's party club, the Alliance and the grange,
And read and think and study hard, put in my hardest licks,
To get my own religion and reform my politics.
         —Unidentified poet, *Texas Advance,* reprinted
                  in *Southern Mercury,* 1894

While we don't want any politics in our religion, we want all
    the religion of our heads, hearts and souls in our politics.

    —Populist Rev. Marshall McIlhaney, president,
            Centenary College, Lampasas, Texas

When Texas Populists met in Dallas in June 1892 to write a state platform and nominate candidates for its first statewide campaign, the *Dallas Morning News* editorialized about the character of the delegates: "Their earnestness, bordering on religious fanaticism, has a touch of the kind of metal [*sic*] that made Cromwell's round heads so terrible a force in the revolution that ended with bringing the head of Charles I to the block. It would be supreme folly to despise and belittle a movement that is leavened with such moral stuff as this."[1]
    Although the analogy between Texas Populists and Cromwell's seventeenth-century revolutionary Puritans may have been imperfect in many respects,

the writer correctly sensed the presence of strong moral and religious strains within Populism. Indeed, any effort to understand Populism without considering its religious dimension is bound to fail, for religion not only shaped the Populist worldview but also gave the movement much of its language, its popular appeal, and its approach to organizing. When Populists addressed each other as "brothers" and "sisters" and spoke of the Populist "gospel" or the Populist "faith," it was with full realization that their religious beliefs were part and parcel of their political crusade, and vice versa.

Modern Americans may associate religion—and particularly the mixing of religion with politics—more as hallmarks of conservatism than of liberalism, but that would amount to a presentist misreading of history. John Locke, the classical liberal whose thought probably influenced Americans more than any other figure of the European Enlightenment, was a devout Christian whose religious beliefs informed his political philosophy, but he was also a zealous defender of religious toleration. He held the view that since true faith required a personal and sincere commitment on the part of the individual, any attempt by a powerful state to *coerce* belief was fruitless, if not actually blasphemous. The first widespread political usage of the term "liberal" was in the early nineteenth century, to describe anticlerical politics in Europe. But as with the case of Locke and toleration in the seventeenth century, anticlericalism in the eighteenth or nineteenth century did not necessarily mean irreligion; for many it simply meant an opposition to coerced religion. The Populists were heirs to this brand of religious liberalism. Their religious world, then, differed in dramatic ways from that of the so-called religious right of today. Intellectual curiosity, a surprising degree of tolerance for those with opposing views, and an emphasis on the spirit of Christianity rather than a narrow, legalistic reading of scripture mark the Populists as the intellectual forebears of today's Christian *left* more than of the fundamentalists who have composed such an important component of the Republican Party's base since the Reagan era.[2]

Texans in the late nineteenth century were certainly a religious people, although exactly how religious they were defies easy generalization. According to the 1890 census, just over 30 percent of Texans were "communicants," meaning that they enjoyed full church membership privileges, including (in Christian congregations) the taking of Communion. Since evangelical Protestant denominations heavily dominated, this figure excludes not only those who held to Christian belief without formally joining a church, but also those who attended church but had not been baptized, including many children who would later join. Of the state's communicants, 70 percent were Baptists or Methodists. Nearly 15 percent were Catholics, reflecting the large Hispanic population of South Texas and the lesser number of European immigrant Catholics. Protestant denominations such as the Disciples of Christ and Presbyterians (each with 6 percent) and smaller numbers of Episcopalians, Lutherans, Congregationalists, and others rounded out the total. Texas no doubt had its share of nonbelievers, freethinkers, and backsliders, but on the whole, traditional southern Christianity reigned supreme and greatly shaped the social and political culture of the state.[3]

Evangelicalism in America was born in the eighteenth century as a countercultural movement, aiming to overturn the established church, tear down Old World–style hierarchies, and embody the new democratic ethos of the emerging American republic. American evangelicals developed what has been termed "'patriotic millennialism'—the notion that God had special designs for America as the beacon of democracy to the world." By the late nineteenth century, most evangelicals saw their religious beliefs and the American political system as two sides of the same coin, each reinforcing the other. Evangelicalism, with its emphasis on congregational autonomy, democratic church governance, and the ability of the individual to interpret the scriptures and affect his or her own salvation through the gift of God's grace, melded seamlessly with Jeffersonian, Jacksonian, and Lincolnian precepts of democratic republicanism.[4]

Within the ranks of the evangelicals, however, theological and doctrinal differences had the potential to shape conflicting political beliefs and actions. Evangelicalism may have sprung from a tradition of dissent and confrontation with authority, but by the 1890s in Texas, evangelicals, by the sheer weight of their numbers if nothing else, had *become* the establishment. Wealthy planters, urban businessmen, struggling white farmers, African Americans—worshipping in large urban churches, tiny backwoods meetinghouses, and every sort of church in between—were part of the evangelical community. So it comes as no surprise that the political orientation of Texas evangelicals could range from archconservative to progressive to radical. This fact renders it almost impossible to discern any clear denominational lines of demarcation between those who became Populists and those who did not. Still, certain religious patterns emerge that tell us a great deal about the impact of religion on the People's Revolt.

First, the conservative orientation. If evangelical Protestantism could be subversive of the established order, it also could staunchly support it. Alongside the liberalizing tendencies of evangelicalism there was a strong emphasis on discipline. In its obvious manifestation, Christians were expected to exercise self-discipline in matters such as family obligations, sexual morality, and other forms of personal conduct such as drinking, dancing, and gambling. But there was also the matter of congregational discipline—submitting to the rules of the church and preserving the social order. "Discipline," as one scholar has explained, "involved adherence to fixed codes of belief and action. . . . Conformity to such divine ordinances ultimately meant adherence to cultural, racial, and political norms; such conformity was summarized by the command to submit to the 'powers that be.'" With the close connection in the minds of white Texans between good government and Christianity, and with good government having been synonymous with the "redemption" of Texas from the "evils" of Radical Republican rule in the aftermath of Reconstruction, religion could exercise a strongly conservative influence over the political proclivities of Texans. Moreover, the emphasis on individualism that was so deeply rooted in both evangelical doctrine and Jeffersonian-Jacksonian political ideology further discouraged political innovation, especially if that innovation involved a dramatic expansion of the role of government at the expense of the individual. All too often, from their perspective, Populists found themselves stymied by these conservative tendencies within the evangelical community.[5]

As the nexus of economic and political power shifted away from rural planters toward urban business and professional elites in the late nineteenth century, an additional strain of conservatism entered Texas Protestantism. Known as "premillennial dispensationalism," it was popularized in America by evangelists such as the Englishman John Nelson Darby, Massachusetts-born Dwight L. Moody, and the Dallas preacher Cyrus Scofield. Dispensationalists taught that God had divided history into distinct periods, or dispensations, which will culminate in the Rapture, when the saved will be removed to heaven to escape the impending Tribulation, a period of great suffering and devastation, to be followed by Christ's return for a thousand-year reign, ultimately followed by the final Judgment Day. The present era, known as the "Church Era," was the final dispensation prior to the Rapture, which could come at any time. While dispensationalists often agreed with Populists and other reformers about the wretched conditions facing the country, they saw little use in trying to improve society. What was prophesied was prophesied, and any efforts at social uplift were at best futile and at worst blasphemous. On the other hand, classically liberal ideas of limited government and laissez-faire economics seemed quite compatible with dispensationalist thought.[6]

Dwight L. Moody conducted a revival tour of North Texas in 1895, speaking to large crowds. Not surprisingly, the Populist press harshly criticized him, charging that "he took as much money out of Texas as would Barnum's circus." "How much more in accordance with the principles of Christianity," the *Southern Mercury* editorialized, "it would have been to have given this money to the poor and needy, instead of to this plutocratic preacher!" The *Mercury* even provided Moody a list of Bible verses from which it was suggested that Moody take his sermons, saying that "if Rev. Moody is following in the footsteps of the Master he will attack the devil in every form, and especially the devil of greed and usury that is grinding the millions of poor of this land to dust." In Dallas, Moody shared the podium with Texas's best-known dispensationalist, Cyrus Scofield, who did much to popularize this strain of evangelical thought. Born in Michigan, Scofield had moved to Tennessee as a young man. He served in the Confederate army and the Kansas legislature before moving to Dallas in 1882 to take the pastorship of the First Congregationalist Church, which he built into one of the city's most prominent and prosperous congregations. "The true mission of the church is not the reformation of society," Scofield contended in a characteristic statement. "What Christ did not do, the Apostles did not do. Not one of them was a reformer." In the twentieth century, Scofield's *Reference Bible,* first published in 1907, sold more than twelve million copies and became arguably the single most important work in American fundamentalism.[7]

Perhaps even more influential than Moody or Scofield in Populist-era Texas was the Georgia evangelist Sam Jones. The fiery, folksy Jones repeatedly crisscrossed the Lone Star State in the 1890s, preaching to huge crowds. His revivals inspired the kind of popular adulation and press coverage reserved for rock stars a century later. Unlike Moody or Scofield, Jones was no systematic theologian, but his message also worked against Populism. Preaching a revival in the old Alliance stronghold of Cleburne a month before the 1894 elections, Jones upbraided his listeners for being so preoccupied with politics. "Here I am trying to save Texas souls and you going around in politics, trying to keep Texas from going populist and the whole business from going to hell," he declared. "You bet your Uncle Jones is just a little too decent to run with your political gang and if you don't quit it you'll be sorry for it some day." After castigating the Democrats for their fondness for "drinking red licker," he turned his guns on the Populists: "And these populists? Oh, my! But I'm sorry for them. They are more honest than the democrats, but haven't got as much sense. I'd rather trust the government to a lot of rascals than a lot of fools. We might reform the rascals, but what on earth can we do with the fools?" Noting the personal fortune that Jones had amassed, the Populist *Southern*

Mercury declared him "a fraud—a pious humbug." But Populists would need more than simple denunciations of conservative evangelists such as Jones, Moody, and Scofield; they would have to construct powerful counterarguments if they were to employ the religious culture of Texas in the service of reform.[8]

Fortunately for them, Populists had a ready source of such arguments: the long evangelical countercultural tradition, stretching back a century or more into the southern past. This tradition to which Texas Populists were heir emphasized, above all, the freedom and ability of the individual to discern the will of God, to live morally, and to receive the gift of salvation through belief and atonement. Long before there was "large-*p*" Populism, southern evangelicals had fashioned a "small-*p*" populist version of Christianity in which the common man was the equal of a king, a millionaire, or an educated clergyman in the eyes of God. In its most populist forms, this tradition could even posit the equality of women and blacks with white men. Self-consciously antielitist, this strain of southern evangelicalism welcomed plainspoken, even uneducated, clergy who freely exalted the virtues of the common folk and who felt no compunction at denouncing decadent planters, money-grubbing urbanites, and venal politicians.[9]

The African American evangelical churches particularly embraced religion as a countercultural force. Indeed, because the churches had often been the first institutions that the ex-slaves could truly call their own in the years after emancipation, black congregations were, as one leading scholar puts it, "by definition political institutions" that "drew no clear distinction between the sacred and the secular, the spiritual and the political." In the churches, newspapers were read, issues debated, speakers listened to. Ministers were expected to be political, and there were no pretenses of nonpartisanship or bipartisanship. The prominent role of black women in their churches meant that these women probably became far more politicized than their counterparts in white churches. The eagerness with which African American churches engaged in partisan politics, however, could be a double-edged sword for Populists; the ties to the Republican Party were strong and often buttressed by ministerial authority. For the Third Party's organizers, breaking the bonds between the black churches and the GOP would be a daunting challenge, but if it could be done, those churches could be a major force in bringing African Americans into the party fold.[10]

As the *Dallas Morning News* reporter noted in his comparison of Populists with Cromwell's Roundheads, the Populists brought a religious fervor to their cause. But it was more than merely religious fervor; they brought their religious beliefs, too, and taking a lead in bringing religion to politics were many Populist ministers. A list of prominent Populists who were, or had been, preachers includes H. S. P. "Stump" Ashby, a former Methodist circuit rider, People's Party state chairman, and lieutenant governor nominee; James Madison Perdue, a Methodist minister, Alliance state lecturer, state executive committeeman, and congressional nominee; S. O. Daws, a Baptist preacher, state lecturer for the Farmers' Alliance, and nominee for state treasurer; Reddin Andrews Jr., a Baptist preacher, former president of Baylor University, and congressional nominee; Uriah M. Browder, a Disciples of Christ minister and congressional nominee; Willis Lyman Harrison, a Populist state senator and Disciples of Christ minister; Henry Jennings, a minister in the Colored Methodist Episcopal Church and the first major African American Populist organizer; and John B. Rayner, a Baptist preacher, state executive committeeman, and the best-known of the state's black Populists. The list of lesser lights in the party who were also clergymen would be much lengthier. During the 1894 campaign the *Dallas Morning News* asked rhetorically, "How many preachers are there in the populist party? Who knows?" The *News,* however, went on to cite the "popular belief that more than two-thirds of the populist orators have at some time or other been connected with the ministry." While there is no way to verify this estimate, it is clear that the presence of clergymen among the party's leadership, as well as within the rank and file, gave Texas Populism a distinctly religious cast.[11]

The prominence of preachers naturally led to questions about the meaning and appropriateness of their role in the party. In the same story quoted above, the *Morning News* avoided making judgments on the subject, choosing instead to simply repeat the explanations offered by the Populist clergy, who "all say that their action is based solely on a desire to do the greatest good to the greatest number. . . . They all say that they can accomplish more for the moral welfare of the people by going to the people in their conventions and primaries on week days than by waiting for the people to come to them on Sundays. They claim that the populist party is the greatest moral political organization in earth and made so largely through the influence of the preachers."[12]

Democrats rarely took such a charitable view, and the issue of Populist preachers inevitably led to questions about the role of religion in politics and government. Few adherents of any party advocated an elimination of the constitutional prohibition on an established church; Populists and Democrats alike endorsed the legal separation of church and state, and there was no late nineteenth-century version of today's claim by the religious right that the

United States is a "Christian nation." Indeed, more than one Texas pastor in the 1890s favored the withdrawal of the tax-exempt status of churches, suggesting that they could not be truly independent if they accepted special privileges from the government. But Populists and Democrats argued vigorously about ministers addressing political subjects from the pulpit and even more contentiously about ministers campaigning and running for office. Robert Lewis Dabney, a prominent Presbyterian theologian who taught at the University of Texas, voiced the conservative position in 1894 when he inveighed against "political preachers," stating that "political questions are not decided by any recognized standards of truth, but by the competitions of interest and passion." According to Dabney, it was "inevitable that he who embarks publicly in the discussion of these questions must become the object of party animosities and obnoxious to those whom he opposes," thus making it impossible to "approach them as the messenger of redemption." Dabney concluded that "by transcending his proper functions," the political preacher "criminally prejudices his appointed work with half the community, for the whole of which he should affectionately labor."[13]

Populists saw it differently. Since the early days of the Farmers' Alliance, ministers had played an active role in the agrarian protest movement. Their activism in the highly political but avowedly nonpartisan Alliance probably helped pave the way for them to embrace party politics once the People's Party was founded. In any case, the scores of clergymen who advocated Populism from the pulpit, made stump speeches, wrote pro-Populist tracts, and even ran for office developed an elaborate defense of their own political activism.

The issue arose conspicuously in the 1894 elections, when Uriah M. Browder, pastor of a Disciples of Christ congregation in Gainesville, resigned his pulpit to run for Congress as a Populist against Democratic firebrand Joseph Weldon Bailey. A Democratic editor, referring to Browder, opined that "when a preacher quits preaching the gospel and goes to dabbling in politics, he is entirely out of his place," whereupon a Populist editor responded with the standard defense: "One of the highest duties of a citizen of the American union is to take a lively interest in politics, study the condition and needs of the people, denounce wrong not only in the pulpit but from the hustings. We submit that because Dr. Browder is not a demagogue, a gambler [or] libertine, but is a high-toned, intelligent, honest gentleman, [we] should not bar him from entering the political arena." After his defeat, Browder moved to Indiana and returned to preaching, but he continued to defend the mixing of religion and politics, asking, in a published sermon, "What is the pulpit for? What is the church for? If my pulpit is not for the uplifting of poor, distressed and suffering humanity, it's good for nothing." Browder's resumption of the ministry was short-lived, as he accepted the Populist nomination for Congress in Indiana's Fourth District in 1896, making him perhaps the only Populist to run for Congress in two different states.[14]

For Reddin Andrews, the Baptist preacher and former Baylor University president, the need to defend the political activism of ministers took a personal turn when his name was mentioned in 1894 as a possible congressional candidate in Central Texas's Ninth District (plate 12). Although Andrews was unusual due to his high profile in the state's Baptist circles, his path into Populist politics was one that likely would have been reflected in the biographies of many Populist preachers. In a published interview, Andrews traced his interest in agrarian affairs to 1874, when, while serving as pastor of the Navasota Baptist Church, he joined the Grange, the "principles" of which "attracted my attention." As the years passed, he explained, and "political corruption, class legislation and the oppressions of the organized money powers appeared to me to be threatening the stability and perpetuity of our government, I predicted that the principles of the grange and Farmers' alliance movements would develop into the only forces that could possibly check or destroy the evils that were fast becoming formidable. Bad legislation, bribery in high places, extravagance in the conduct of the government, drifting away from the fundamental principles of our political safety and the failures of parties to fulfill their platform promises and vows, were all telling awfully upon our body politic." Andrews stuck with the Democrats until 1890, when he voted for the Prohibition Party in state races but abstained from voting in presidential contests. Thereafter he supported the Populists. "I need not give my reasons further than to say that I will not wear a [party] collar and feel compelled to vote for a man in whom I have no confidence," he said. "If my party should nominate such a man I shall not vote for him. I always vote as I pray." Andrews's response regarding the reaction of his religious friends to his conversion to Populism is worth quoting at length, both for its gentle rebuke of those who insisted on a separation of preachers and politicians, and for its clarity in linking political and religious corruption:

It is various. Some Christian friends, men and women, and some preachers, are writing to me to go ahead, and they ask God's blessing upon me. Some [D]emocratic friends write me that my course shocks them. Two or three Christian friends have written to me and begged me not to go into politics . . . . As to my denomination at large, I can not tell what the members of it think about my speaking in the interest of populism or good government. They are "mightily" mixed themselves in the matter of politics and theology. I doubt whether the majority of them, preachers included, know what they do believe, either in politics or religion; or why they believe it, even if they do believe anything. I am a Baptist after the Pauline type, and my faith is precious to me. I do not worship my denomination, with a big D. I wear no political color nor ecclesiastical collar. Ecclesiastical corruptions, corners, cliques, combines and machines curse the world to-day. My opposition to these things, political and ecclesiastical, has cost me dearly. Many of my church friends . . . are doing everything that they can by letters, by word of mouth, misrepresentations, charitably called such, to destroy me and prevent my being called to the pastorate of churches. I owe them nothing but prayers and good wishes. I preach to two country churches, one of which at least is full of populists. Of course, what I have already done in the way of speaking on the issues that are matters of life and death to our country has given pain to some of the best Christian brethren in my denomination. I am sorry of that, for their love, interest and advice I cherish dearly. But for denomination bosses and leaders, so called, I have less respect than for political bosses and leaders.

Andrews eventually withdrew his name from consideration in 1894, but two years later he accepted the nomination and ran a hard-fought though ultimately unsuccessful race. His account of the sacrifices required by clergymen who took up the Populist mantle undoubtedly rang true for the many lesser-known ministers who likewise answered the call of reform.[15]

As Andrews could attest, Populist preachers certainly were not immune to political attack, sometimes of the most scurrilous sort. Uriah Browder, for example, had to defend himself against Joseph Weldon Bailey's charge that Browder's Gainesville church had forced him first from the pulpit and then from the parsonage, leading church members to "come to the front and [prove] Bailey guilty of a willful and malicious falsehood." Democrats leveled a similar charge against W. L. Thurman, another Christian Church minister from North Texas, forcing a Democratic editor to print a rare retraction after it was conclusively proven false. When a Collin County Democratic leader accused Populist Henry Jennings, the first African American named to the party's state executive committee, of being a chicken thief, a local white Populist came to

Jennings's defense, saying that Jennings was "a sober and honest old colored preacher of McKinney, he having helped to build the first colored church in the city." Not content to single out individual Populist ministers for criticism, the editor of the *Texas Farmer,* a Democratic paper published in Dallas, issued something of a blanket condemnation when he surveyed the delegates at the 1892 Populist state convention and remarked on "the number of expelled preachers who took prominent parts." A Democratic editor from the Populist stronghold of Comanche referred to Populist preachers as "pious galoots [who] are really too trifling to hold any sort of a job in the vineyard of the Lord, and they naturally gravitate toward the third party, where all kinds of human trash is destined sooner or later." The editor proposed that "credulous church members ought to cut off their supply of corn bread and buttermilk and tell them to go and work just for a change."[16]

But whether they were ministers in good standing, preaching Populism from their pulpits on Sunday, or men who had quit the ministry to follow a political calling, or preachers who had been expelled for becoming too political, Populist clergymen as well as religious laypeople frequently employed biblical language and imagery in their political discourse, and they directly used the scriptures to make the case for Populism. In doing so, they were dealing in the cultural currency of southern evangelicalism, speaking a language that their listeners understood and appealing to widely held moral values.

As previously noted, evangelical Protestantism, like southern society and politics, had its more conservative and its more liberal strains, each rooted in its own theological and doctrinal conventions. The liberal or progressive strain, of which Populists partook, could trace its origins to the eighteenth-century tradition of countercultural evangelicalism, when Baptists, Methodists, and other sects broke away from the established churches and sought to create a more democratic and personal faith. Early evangelicals explicitly rejected the notion of rigid hierarchical relationships of power in favor of an emphasis on individual liberty and conscience. This orientation led them to associate political democracy with religious belief, as expressed in the common Latin proverb "vox populi vox Dei"—the voice of the people is the voice of God. In the nineteenth century, southern evangelicals usually found the political expression of these beliefs in Jeffersonian and Jacksonian democracy. The Jacksonian slogan "Equal rights for all, special privileges for none," and its accompanying antimonopoly position, resonated with evangelicals.[17]

But even as early as the Jacksonian period, some evangelicals worried that their churches were losing sight of the benchmarks laid down by the scriptures and the first-century church. As a consequence, the first half of the 1800s saw the spread of restorationist groups intent on restoring the ancient purity and simplicity of early Christianity (later these groups would evolve into denominations, although they fought against the denominational label). Often calling themselves simply "Christians" or "Disciples," they eventually seceded from more established denominations—often the Baptists—which they believed had become too worldly and hierarchical. By the late nineteenth century, the Christian Church (which itself would later divide into the more liberal Disciples of Christ and the more conservative Churches of Christ) was the major restorationist denomination in Texas, although there were a number of smaller ones, such as the Landmark Baptists, Primitive Baptists, and Christadelphians. Restorationist thought, though, was not the exclusive domain of the avowedly restorationist denominations; to varying degrees, adherents of mainline evangelical denominations like the Baptists and Methodists also often held restorationist views. These divisions within the mainline denominations, which often were most obvious between poorer or rural congregations and their wealthier or urban counterparts (the so-called first churches—the local First Baptist and First Methodist Churches), would figure large in the story of Populism in Texas. Whether they belonged to restorationist groups or were dissenting voices in the mainline denominations, restorationists found it natural to extend their penchant for reforming and purifying their churches into a parallel desire to reform and purify politics and society.[18]

In Texas, restorationist evangelicals rejected the pessimistic premillennialism of a Dwight Moody or a Cyrus Scofield and adopted a reformist mindset in some ways mirroring that of the northern Social Gospel movement, which held that Christian ethics should be applied to solving social problems. As Austin minister Edwin M. Wheelock explained in an 1894 sermon published in the *Advance,* the state Populist paper:

> Jesus meant His religion to be carried into practice. The law of the sermon [on] the mount—the law of good will and fraternal co-operation, was announced to govern men in their industrial, social, and political relations here and now. Christ did not come, as our theological quacks are so fond of saying, to prepare men for another world, but to teach them how to rightly live in this. He who lives rightly in this world will be prepared for the next when his time comes to enter it. Religion is the doctrine of human relations. Every question that involves the welfare of man is a religious question. The social problem is a sacred problem, and the

minister of the church that avoids its discussion on Sunday, denies his
Lord and Master as much as Peter did. If we do not christianize human
relations in business, trade and industry, substituting the law of associated and fraternal justice for the infernal principle of competition, our
civilization will go down to ruin, we will go down with it and we will
deserve our fate.

While our preachers are talking about "the everlasting bliss of heaven,"
the hell of injustice, of social inequality, of trampled, outraged labor is
opening right under their feet.[19]

Wheelock, a northern-born Unitarian, had commanded black troops in the
Union army, served as state superintendent of the Freedmen's Bureau schools
in Texas during Reconstruction, and held various offices as a Republican before joining the People's Party in the 1890s, so he was by no means a typical
Texas Populist. But his explication of the social role of Christianity was published in the Populist press and echoed by countless Third-Party men. In an
article titled "The Church and Reform" in the *Southern Mercury* in 1896, an
unidentified Populist argued that while "church and state should be separate;
still I do believe as individuals we are morally bound to take an interest in political matters. Christians should be the leaders in all reforms as they are supposed to represent everything for the uplifting and elevation of humanity." The
writer, who claimed to have belonged to "an orthodox church" for two decades,
contended that Christians "should be the leaders in every reform because
Christ was the great reformer of the church. . . . We are 'our brother's keeper,'
in more than one way." As he and many other religious Populists saw it, the
problem was not too much engagement by preachers in worldly affairs, but
too little: "Would to god," he exclaimed, "every minister were a political economist and would take a stand as a leader of reform."[20]

Criticism of ministers who ignored social ills and of churches that were too
worldly became a standard feature of Populist politico-religious discourse.
Milam County Populist leader J. D. Shelton, a grizzled veteran of the Texas
Indian wars and Baptist preacher, made a speech in Rockdale "criticising
the recreancy of certain so-called preachers; certain ones the devil called, soft
place hunting, high salary grabbing, contemptible, modern priesthood, 'who
knew not Joseph,' and cared less for him than they knew." For this unflattering portrayal of his fellow clergymen, he explained, "they kicked me out of
the [denominational] association." When a Populist poet referred to the poor
farmer's "preacher made religion," he was making an implicit jab at people

who blindly followed the directives of their ministers rather than thinking for themselves. In an unsigned 1895 editorial titled "Plutocracy and the Churches," the *Southern Mercury* argued that "plutocracy not only controls the governments of earth, but it controls the pulpits and the avenues to heaven!" A few months later, one J. F. Perritte asked, "Did Christ teach the building of the many thousand and million dollar church edifices, while human beings were starving in the shadow of these same structures? . . . Did Christ, in broadcloth and diamonds, from costly pulpits, denounce the oppressed as anarchists and traitors because they asked for justice?" Another Populist writer, Walter Roper, declared, "I am going to take our clergy to task, for a neglect of duty. Christ was a reformer, but can this be said of many of those who profess to represent his teaching?" Admitting that "a few brave, bold preachers have made a stand against the modern flood of corruption," he nonetheless contended that "the great mass of mediocrity continues to bemoan the sin and wickedness of the world, without making any rational or philosophical effort to discover or remove the cause." Roper concluded that "unless the clergy awake to full realization of their responsibilities and duties and use their immense power in an effort to reform physical as well as moral conditions, the last vestige of christianity will disappear in the cataclysm which awaits the continuance of our present system." S. J. Brownson, editor of the Fort Worth *Industrial Educator,* suggested that the church "was on the wrong side of the slave question a generation ago . . . and is today on the wrong side of the greatest question of the age," which he identified as "the industrial reform movement." Brownson, a former Methodist minister who apparently had suffered his own crisis of faith, believed that the People's Party, not "so-called orthodox church[es], is leading the industrial millions out of slavery into freedom. The church that professes to be the light of the world under Christ is not doing it."[21]

So popular were such themes among the Populist faithful that in September 1894, just weeks before the momentous elections of that year, the *Southern Mercury* devoted two full columns of its front page to a sermon by a Populist minister from Colorado, Florida F. Passmore. Denouncing, among other things, lynching, "the oppression of the poor, political corruption," and "the outraging of womanhood and girlhood," Passmore excoriated his fellow Methodist ministers for being "the most worldly, unfaithful and cowardly that has ever been." He professed to be "no longer surprised at the inefficiency of the ministry, the corruption in politics, the deadness of the church, the development of trusts, and growth of monopolies, the wealth of the few and the poverty of the many," and general immorality. He spoke of seeing women and children scavenging pieces of coal in the streets of Denver to keep themselves from freezing, while the Methodist church several blocks away boasted a $250,000 building and a $30,000 organ. "Our bishops and editors and secretaries, and the pastors of our large churches, are pandering to the rich and corrupt elements for the sake of high salaries, and are living in splendor and affluence, while millions of men, women and children are in distress, hundreds are starving." Clearly the *Mercury*'s editors were not worried that the sermon's condemnation of establishment religion would offend Populist readers; the piece was accompanied by an editorial note urging that it "Should be Read by Everyone."[22]

Populist condemnation of mainstream churches and preachers was not limited to white Populists, either. The irrepressible Melvin Wade explained that "he didn't want to be understood as being against the churches, but negro preachers . . . were ruining the negroes. Instead of telling them how to get along in the world they were talking them out of all their money." Wade complained of preachers enjoying high salaries while their parishioners lived in poverty. "The poor negroes, he said, would go to church and after giving their money to the preachers, who eat ham and eggs and all such good things, would go home and sit down to corn bread and bacon. Yes, and they would ask the Lord to bless it when they didn't have enough on the table for the good Lord to take notice of." One another occasion, Wade told a black audience, "I love the church and believe in Jesus Christ, but the darkies run too much to church. We're allus singin' 'Give me Jesus,' and the other fellers can have all the rest. Well, the white man owns the world and the niggers own Jesus. Let us sing, 'Give me Jesus and a share of everything else.'" Speaking before a crowd of four thousand delegates at the 1894 Populist state convention, John B. Rayner advised his fellow Populists that if they meant to help the Negro, they should "let the dude school teachers and long-tailed preachers alone." Some years later Rayner, whose background as a Baptist preacher belied his fierce animosity to most organized religion, proposed that "religious conservatism is made up of an army of bigots and fanatics" who were "so vigilant in watching and guarding their creeds and traditions that they have no time to do good to any one."[23]

The Populists' rough treatment of decadent preachers and worldly churches sprang from their beliefs that modern Christianity had strayed too far from the ancient verities taught in the scriptures. If they turned to the Bible as their authority on how to live and worship, it stands to reason that they might also believe it could provide guidance on politics. Not surprisingly, they believed they found plenty of guidance in both the Old and New Testaments. What was perhaps the most frequently cited Old Testament passage came from the fifth chapter of Nehemiah. In this story, set during a time of hardship when the Hebrew people were suffering under mortgages and high interest rates, the wise ruler Nehemiah outlawed usury. Populists were quick to note the parallels with modern times. Former Methodist minister S. J. Brownson called the scripture "gospel for the masses" and noted, "You may call me a calamity howler if you will, but if I am one so was old Nehemiah." Other Populists cited injunctions against usury from Exodus, Leviticus, and Deuteronomy.[24]

Populists often examined Old Testament scriptures and, employing some literary license, found sanction for specific Populist policies. A. W. Dumas, a Presbyterian minister who quit his Montague County pulpit to spread the Third-Party gospel, gained a unique place in the Populist ranks for his political lectures that were based exclusively on the Bible. Dumas had compiled a list of chapters and verses from no fewer than sixteen Old Testament books and five New Testament gospels as sources for his series of lectures, "Bible Indorsement of Populism." For example, Dumas referenced the story from Genesis in which Joseph, as administrator in Egypt, stockpiled food in storehouses during good times, to be distributed in the coming time of famine. "The chapter is one of the grandest pictures of a subtreasury ever written by the hand of man," Dumas contended. "Go home and tell your plug hat preacher to preach you a sermon on the subtreasury. No man was made a millionaire and his brother a pauper under Joseph's administration." In a similar vein, Uriah Browder preached an entire sermon based on the book of Daniel and reprinted in the Populist press, titled "The Gold God, or, Babylon on a Gold Basis," drawing dubious parallels between the great golden idol built by Nebuchadnezzar and the return of the United States to the gold standard.[25]

But if Old Testament examples of biblical Populism could seem a bit strained at times, Populists had no such trouble invoking the New Testament. The Third-Party press bristled with references to Jesus being a Populist. "The Savior was the greatest Populist of any of the Bible characters," declared an unidentified writer in the *Southern Mercury*. Populists particularly emphasized Jesus' working-class birth and upbringing, and his identification with the poor and downtrodden. Cyclone Davis's paper, the *Alliance Vindicator*, editorialized that "the greatest and most successful reformer the world ever saw was of humble parentage and born in a stable. He never attained riches or social eminence. His associates were the lowly and humble. He never wore a plug hat, patent leather shoes, a b[o]iled shirt, a pompous mien and an air of insolent superiority. His financial rating did not appear in the financial reports of his time." Another editorialist noted that Christ "associated with the common people, and if he was on earth to-day he would not be admitted into Washington society, and the high-toned people would not recognize him on the street." Commenting on Jacob Coxey's "army" of the unemployed that was then marching on Washington, Stump Ashby asked, "What if some people did say they were bums? They should be careful about speaking about bums, especially people who belonged to the church, because Jesus Christ himself was a homeless wanderer here—a bum as now called—and the propagandists of his religion were homeless bums." A Collin County Populist claimed to be "a people's party man because Christ was one" and "a labor party man because Christ was a carpenter. Rich men crowned him with thorns and he died poor." S. J. Brownson likewise characterized Jesus as "the poor man's friend. He defended the rights of the people, beat back their oppressions, showed up their tricky priests and politicians; even pointed some of them, like Herod, out by name, and warned his followers against them."[26]

As Brownson's mention of Jesus showing up tricky priests and politicians suggests, Populists went beyond simply noting Christ's identification with the downtrodden; they often placed him in a specifically political context. For restorationist evangelicals who had left the established denominations to create purer churches, leaving the old parties to create purer politics did not seem particularly heretical. "The good book teaches us that Christ was a third party man," wrote Denton Populist leader C. A. McMeans. "When he came on earth there were two parties, the Pharisees and the Sadducees, and he made the third party." Stump Ashby similarly contended that "Christ could not reform the religious organizations of his time—the Saducees, the Pharisees and the Essenes—so he founded a new one." Another Populist writer claimed that "the political leaders of to-day stand in the same relation to the people that the pharisees did to the Jews 1,800 years ago," and yet another noted that "Christ was too much of a reformer, a crank, a calamity howler, and was not in sympathy with either the Pharisees or the Sadduces." The idea of Jesus as a working-class dissenter also drew support from Thomas L. Nugent. "It is not written that he drew to him those in authority, the wealthy or the elite of society," Nugent argued. "How could he do so, seeing that he was but a humble man and was clothed in the coarse garb of a mechanic?"[27]

Other New Testament references occasionally were employed in Populist discourse. In his extensive study of the biblical foundations of Populism, A. W. Dumas, for example, suggested that "party prejudice existing between the Jews and Samaritans" furnished the context for the parable of the Good Samaritan.

Nugent invoked the Sermon on the Mount in his stump speeches, noting that "the author earned by its utterance the crown of thorns and death on the cross. Social and industrial justice has since that time been denied to the toiling and suffering classes, because truth has been on the cross wearing the crown of thorns." But by far the most commonly cited Populist New Testament lesson was the story of Jesus driving the money changers from the temple. "Christ plainly taught that the money changers and the banking institutions of that day were the same outfit," wrote a Dublin, Texas Populist. "They changed and exchanged money with usury, and our American banks could be no better described." Castigating bankers as "money changers (the same class that Jesus Christ drove from the temple)" with their "soulless hands of monopoly on the throats of the people" and "their hands in the pockets of the people," J. W. T. Loe asked his fellow members of the Dallas Populist Club, "Is it not time to lay down prejudices and the hollow names of democrat and republican and return to the principles of our fathers?" Noah Allen, the Galveston Populist leader, similarly identified Wall Street with the biblical money changers: "If Christ came to Wall street to-day and put the robbers out Grover Cleveland would call out the militia and Christ himself would be indicted for contempt of court in not obeying omnibus injunctions."[28]

As previously noted, the appeal of Populism was not confined to any specific denomination, although the avowedly restorationist denominations certainly attracted a disproportionate number of Third-Party Texans. Their desire to reform the organized religion of the day by replacing it with a purer, more moral, more democratic practice of faith informed and reinforced their desire to reform the politics of the day by replacing *them* with something purer, more moral, and more democratic. A reformer in religion needed to be a reformer in politics, and vice versa. In 1895 an anonymous writer in the Populist *McKinney Democrat* voiced this argument about the relationship between religion and politics. "Whether politics and religion will mix or not," he wrote, "it is very plain that civil policies and governments are the outgrowth and expression of the religion of the people who adopt them. . . . Without doubt a man's politics is an infallible rule to judge his religion." Religion, in other words, was the very basis of politics, so if politics were ever to be reformed, religion would also have to be purified. While such views could potentially discourage political activism in the service of reform, they nonetheless illustrate the commonly held Populist belief that religion and politics were inextricably linked.[29]

The association of religion with politics and the central role of restorationist thinking in Texas Populism has led some observers to conflate Populist religion with the Protestant fundamentalism of the early twentieth century, and thus to equate Populists with the religious right of American politics a century later. As this line of reasoning goes, unsophisticated rural hayseeds ("pious galoots," as the previously quoted Democrat termed them) were backward-looking innocents, nostalgically longing for the good old days of a bygone world and proposing solutions that were out of step with modern realities. But as we have seen, Texas Populists actually were at odds with the leading evangelists of the day, harshly denouncing preachers like Dwight L. Moody and Sam Jones, who were the true forerunners of twentieth-century fundamentalism. One major factor in the confusion of Populists with fundamentalists in the memory of modern Americans is the widely held popular identification of William Jennings Bryan—the Bryan of Scopes Monkey Trial fame—as a Populist, which he certainly was not. Among other things, it is worth noting that it was Bryan's *adversary* in the 1925 Scopes trial, atheist Clarence Darrow, who supported the People's Party in the 1890s.[30]

In their religious thought, Texas Populists, while seeking a restoration of biblical principles of Christianity both in their churches and in their politics, were actually seeking to break away from institutions and ways of thinking that had become rigid and unresponsive to modern needs—hence their harsh criticism of mainstream preachers and churches and the established political parties. In addition to citing the words and deeds of Jesus-the-counterculture-figure, they also approvingly invoked the early Protestant Reformation. In justifying the Populist break from the established parties, Jerome Kearby asked, "How long think you that it would have taken Martin Luther to establish the Protestant religion within the Catholic church?" Clearly, Populists saw their movement as a sort of political Reformation, tearing down outmoded political structures and practices. When they defended themselves as the heirs of first-century Christianity, the Reformation, and Jeffersonian-Jacksonian-Lincolnian democracy, they were invoking the past in the service of modernization.[31]

Certainly Stump Ashby, perhaps the most iconoclastic of all the major Populist leaders, saw no conflict between the Bible and political reform. Ashby, a former Methodist preacher, ridiculed those who "hug the blessed book to their bosoms and repeat a verse of that grand old hymn: 'Holy Bible, book divine'" without knowing what was in it. Though he breezily claimed he "believed in the Bible all of it, the story about Jonah and the whale and all," he had no problem departing from a literal interpretation to claim that "when Christ was on earth the people were organized," and though he admitted lacking "evidence of the fact, he believed that Jesus Christ himself when on earth was a member of a carpenter's union."[32]

One of the most striking examples of modernist religious thought, however, came from the pen of the Presbyterian Populist preacher A. W. Dumas, who, in a lecture about "God's idea of civil government," contemplated the role of God in "the evolution of progress." "God's thoughts," Dumas mused, "are expressed in the spider's web": man observes the web and decides to build a bridge across a river. "He accordingly throws a wire across the river and he works and weaves with wires until the bridge is finished." Likewise, he noted, "God's thoughts are expressed in the stratification of the earth's crust," inspiring man to build "from rocks in the earth's crust beautiful palaces and with coal and fire and water driving the machinery of the globe." Such, Dumas explained, "is the evolution of progress," and "for this evolution the race in life should be left free to all." Dumas was quite willing that man should use his abilities to make money, but lest he sound like a social Darwinist, preaching survival of the fittest as nature's immutable law, he added, "he should not make it by methods [oppressive of] his fellow man, such as have been made possible by class legislation." In short, Dumas, like many religious Populists and American liberals in a later era, was reconciling religion with material progress but arguing that government should be restrained from creating conditions that artificially advantage one class of people over another.[33]

If the rhetoric of Populist Baptists, Methodists, Presbyterians, Disciples of Christ, and other evangelicals suggests a decidedly modernist outlook, the trend is even more striking when one considers the views of Populists outside the ranks of the established evangelical denominations. Populism attracted a small but disproportionate number of freethinkers, spiritualists, and those who held vaguely Christian but nonsectarian beliefs. Into this last category fell John B. Rayner. "Suppose I declare that the life and character of a Christian is God's only church on earth," Rayner wrote a few years after the end of the Populist revolt. Though he was ordained as a Baptist preacher, Rayner had long since grown disillusioned with organized religion. "A Christian can not be a sectarian," he wrote, "because a sectarian is a devotee to some ecclesiastical concoction boiled in the crucible of religious intolerance by high caste hierarchs. God's church is a personal character who believes in the great Jehovah, and who knows it to be his duty and highest privilege to be Christ like in his life and works, and who continues to speak out against every species of sin, and injustice." While Rayner expressed "the utmost contempt for religious creeds and religious rites" and admitted that he had "no reverence for denominationalism," he embraced his own brand of Christianity that combined personal striving for perfection and service to others. "The time has come for the people to know the great difference between Christianity and religion," he argued. "Religion is the counterfeit of Christianity." He defended Thomas Paine and Voltaire against charges that they were infidels, stating (with some poetic license) that "these men were not deists, nor atheists nor agnostics; but were true believers in god . . . and did more for Christian liberty than all the powers of hierarchy found in temples, synagogues, mosques, and cathedrals."[34]

Several prominent Populists found their version of social Christianity in the teachings of the eighteenth-century Swedish scientist-turned-theologian Emanuel Swedenborg. Swedenborgians believed that salvation came not through faith alone, but rather through faith joined with charitable works, guided and enlightened by reason. Not an evangelical denomination as such, the Church of the New Jerusalem, or New Church (as the Swedenborgian denomination popularly came to be known), adopted the Chautauqua, with its emphasis on education and speaker-audience discussion, as its model for spreading their faith. In Texas, Galveston became the center of Swedenborgianism, with a congregation drawn heavily from the faculty of the state medical college. Smaller concentrations of the faithful existed in Dallas, San Antonio, Stephenville, and in rural Milam County.

One leading Populist Swedenborgian was Thomas Benton King, the county judge of Erath County. King had come to Texas after the Civil War as a Methodist preacher, but as he grew interested in Swedenborgianism, he drifted away from the Methodist church. He became a successful lawyer in Stephenville, where he was Thomas L. Nugent's close friend and law partner. Like Nugent, he left the Democratic Party and embraced Populism in the 1890s. Though he never sought office beyond his local county judgeship, he played a high-profile role at Populist state conventions and was considered a leader of the state party. Despite his status as a small-town lawyer and politician, King was an intellectual, contributing occasional religious-themed essays to the *Dallas Morning News,* and in 1903 he published an autobiographical novel based on his own personal spiritual odyssey. Like so many other religious Populists, King's faith led him to embrace political reform. Swedenborgianism taught the perfectibility of man: "The only concern a man has is to receive the light and to 'walk in the light,'" King wrote in 1895. "Now a man having light, he is not to use it merely of a Sunday, or in praying, or howling long and loud praise to God, but in all of the relations of life in the world, such as arise from being a citizen, a seller or buyer, a father or mother, or son or daughter, or husband or wife, or neighbor, or legislator, leader or follower." King believed that mate-rial progress went hand in hand with spiritual and political progress, suggest-ing that in the "wonderful inventions" of the modern age one could see "the coming of the life of God on earth." The Bible, he noted, was "written after a science more perfect than mathematics," and man need only to "open his eye to receive the light and keep his eye in health that he may receive it."[35]

Closely allied with King was Rev. Albert B. Francisco, who came to Texas in 1895 to fill the New Church pulpit in Galveston. A native of Missouri who at-tended the state normal school and worked as a teacher before being called to the ministry, Francisco had been the Populist nominee in Missouri's Sixth Congressional District in 1894. He apparently made a very favorable impres-sion on Texas Populists in a relatively short time, because in 1896 the Popu-list state convention nominated the handsome, mustachioed, dark-haired thirty-five-year-old for state superintendent of public instruction. In a biograph-ical sketch, a reporter for the Galveston Daily News characterized Francisco as "a man of deep religious convictions, entertaining at the same time broad and liberal views." The reporter commented on Francisco's "strong, manly char-acter, his remarkable insight into the true spirit and life of the age, together with his lovable social qualities," which "have endeared him to all with whom he has come in contact."[36]

Significantly, Francisco's chief rival for the education superintendent's nom-ination in 1896 was another Populist with unconventional religious beliefs, Ebenezer Lafayette "Eben" Dohoney (plate 13). The Kentucky-born Dohoney came to Texas in 1859, settling in the northeast Texas city of Paris to practice law. Raised a Cumberland Presbyterian, he joined the Disciples of Christ in 1889 and was soon made an elder. Though he remained a nominal Disciple, Dohoney, who served as district attorney and state senator in the 1870s and was Populist nominee for an appeals-court judgeship in 1894, had little pa-tience for denominationalism. In his 1907 autobiography he discussed the re-cent schism between "Progressives" and "Old Liners" in the Christian Church, noting that he was "more progressive than either wing" and was there-fore "regarded as a heretic by both factions." Dohoney went on to explain that he believed "in accepting truth wherever it is found; whether in Spiritualism, Christian Science, Mental Science, Swedenborgianism, Holiness, or the Sal-vation Army." Like so many religious Populists, he found no conflict between science and religion, but he was more explicit than most in contending that all religious teaching "which is in conflict with Natural Law, is man-made and of course error." Accordingly, he claimed he did "not believe the world was created in six literal days; nor that Joshua made the sun stand still until he fought a battle." He was particularly intrigued by spiritualism, which mirrored Swedenborgianism in its appeals to natural law and science. Over a long lifetime of intellectual inquiry, he authored no fewer than six books, including *Man: His Origin, Nature and Destiny* (1884) and *The Constitution of Man* (1903).[37]

Dohoney was known as the Father of Prohibition in Texas because of his successful efforts in the 1875 state constitutional convention to secure a local-option provision, and he remained an ardent prohibitionist all his life. But his opposition to liquor stemmed not from religious objections but rather from purely public-policy considerations. In his autobiography (which is written in the third person), he explained that he "is a great stickler for individual liberty; and does not propose to prescribe what anybody shall drink. His whole fight against the liquor traffic is from the legal standpoint." He argued that liquor was responsible for three-quarters of the crime and pauperism in society, and he offered a detailed scientific analysis of the chemical makeup of alcohol and its deleterious health effects. But while he came to be known in Texas politics primarily for his prohibitionist fervor (he lost the 1896 nomination for education superintendent to Albert Francisco because delegates feared his prohibitionist stand would cost the party the German vote), Eben Dohoney was no one-issue politician. He had opposed secession in 1861, fought for public education in the legislature, and was a prominent Greenbacker in the 1880s before helping to found the Prohibition Party in Texas. He was an outspoken champion of woman suffrage, prison reform, and gun control. He opposed capital punishment and supported the creation of a "Congress of nations" to promote disarmament and "arbitration for the settlement of all international difficulties." In short, Dohoney, like so many other Populists, rejected religious orthodoxy in favor of an expansive worldview that attempted to reconcile religious faith with science and progressive public policy—an outlook that would be eminently recognizable to many twenty-first-century liberals.[38]

Dallas turned out to be something of a hotbed of Populist heterodoxy. The prominent architect and People's Party county chairman A. B. Bristol was one of the founders of the First Spiritualist Society of that city. Dr. Geno Scott Lincoln, a New York–born physician, and Ormond Paget, a Louisiana-born print shop proprietor, were active Populists who both served terms as presidents of the Dallas Freethinkers' Society. Bristol and Lincoln, not surprisingly, could also be found in the ranks of the woman-suffragists, which in the eyes of many Texans also placed them among the infidels.[39]

Heterodox beliefs were not limited to well-known or well-educated Populists. Even in the rural hinterlands, Populists often held unorthodox religious views. In the People's Party stronghold of Grimes County, in the Central Texas Black Belt, John W. H. Davis, a poor cotton farmer with a rudimentary education who served as secretary of his county's Populist organization, rejected conventional religion and entered into a lifelong search for truth. Although he acknowledged a supreme being, he rejected the idea of heaven and hell. God could be found in nature, he posited, and there was divinity within each person, but "religion as practiced was 'dead.'" Like Sam Johnson, the Populist grandfather of Lyndon Johnson, Davis sought answers to life's mysteries by reading journals devoted to the study of "mental science," a metaphysical system defined as "the belief in the regenerative and healing powers of the human mind." Davis appears to have largely kept his nonconformist religious views to himself, and it is unclear precisely what relationship they bore to his politics, but his example further reinforces the image of the Populist as freethinker.[40]

Whereas Davis confined his spiritual quest to his private writings, such was not the case in nearby Milam County, where the editor of the local Populist newspaper published an extraordinary exchange over several weeks between various freethinkers and their critics. The exchange began when the editor, W. M. Ferguson, printed a letter titled "The Passing of the Modern Church," signed by "A Thinker." In it, the writer claimed the Bible was a forgery and questioned Jesus' divinity and the virgin birth. "The church as a whole would be a comedy if it was not of so serious a nature," he stated. Two weeks later another reader identifying himself as "Thinker No. 2" weighed in, taking to task Moses in the Old Testament book of Numbers for waging brutal war on the Midianites and then ordering the slaughter of captive women and children. "I think Moses must have been worshipping the same God then that the people who are directing the affairs of this country are worshipping today," he wrote, "the commercial god—the gold god—the self-interest god." This sparked a running debate over several weeks, in which some readers defended the paper for being "brave enough to publish both sides of the question" while other outraged citizens mounted a boycott of the paper. Editor Ferguson defended his paper in an editorial titled "Why Suppress Thought," noting that he wished to "be liberal" with his readers and inviting critics to respond. J. E. Longmoor, a local Democrat, was willing to admit the intelligence of the Populist freethinkers, but he suggested that "in propagating their ideas, it seems remarkable that they have overlooked one fact, and that is, that disregard of a pure religion always has and always must be destructive of law and order. . . . You never saw or heard of a red-handed anarchist who was not a rebel to religion." At one point a reader named M. Cotten—apparently a member of the local Swedenborgian congregation—attempted to introduce a tone of optimism into the increasingly acrimonious debate. "A majority of the religion of today is a mixture of dogma, ignorance, superstition, selfishness," he complained. "But men are drifting out of the apostate church and are drifting into the new church—the true church—which will leave men free to think, free to speak and act; when the scientist, the poet, the man of activity will be encouraged to give his thoughts free range. The church of the future will count creeds of less value than deeds." Ferguson finally tired of the controversy (and probably of the boycott) and put an end to the debate, explaining that he did not want his paper "to be placed in the light as some would place it, of being the champion of infidelity." But the fact that such an extraordinary public debate took place at all speaks volumes about the Populists' receptiveness to new ideas, even if they knew those ideas might spark backlash and controversy. Very few, if any, Democratic editors would have sponsored such a debate or allowed it to go on as long as it did.[41]

The brouhaha in Milam County underscores the complex interaction of religion and politics in the Populist era. While most Populists were neither atheists, agnostics, Swedenborgians, spiritualists, mental-science practitioners, nor other varieties of freethinkers, large numbers of them did hold what would have been termed "liberal" religious beliefs—not in today's sense of political liberalism but in the more generic nineteenth-century meaning of the word: broad-minded, flexible, tolerant of dissent, and interested in reconciling religion with science. As in Milam County, their conservative opponents were quick to brand them as cranks, socialists, or anarchists, destructive of law and order and a threat to the social fabric. And nowhere was this phenomenon more evident than in the Democratic response to the most revered Populist of them all, Thomas L. Nugent.

Nugent's religious beliefs became an issue as soon as he received the Populist nomination for governor in 1892, and they remained so until his death in 1895. Raised a Methodist in a Louisiana slaveholding family, from an early age he had shown an intense interest in matters of faith. Avid reading in theology and philosophy became a lifelong habit. As a teenager he seemed to be headed for a career in the ministry, but his love for playing the violin apparently was frowned on by his fellow Methodists, and after a stint in the Confederate army he settled in Texas, taught school, and finally decided on a legal career. For a while, the Methodist minister and future Populist leader Stump Ashby was his pastor, but by the early 1870s his spiritual pilgrimage had led him away from Methodism, and indeed from denominationalism itself, though he remained a devout Christian. "The fault of Methodism," he explained, "consists in the fact that it makes salvation to depend on an *experience*, and by logical implication remands ninety-nine hundredths of the human beings on this globe to the uncovenanted mercies of God." Having rejected the Methodist conversion experience, he argued instead that "regeneration is not an act of instantaneous mercy" but rather "the slow growth of years." By 1873 Swedenborgianism had captured his interest. That year, when asked by his brother what church he was attending, he answered, "all churches alike. Swedenborg has taught me to see more clearly than ever how scriptural is the doctrine which my parents taught me, that no church was exclusively the key to Heaven, and that all must finally enter the Lord's kingdom who live in the love and practice of truth. I, therefore, am pretty much at home with all the denominations, since I am fully instructed in the blessed truths which enable me to sift the 'chaff from the wheat.'" Nugent freely admitted that different people found their spiritual truths in different religious traditions, and he was loath to judge them too harshly. "Thus in the present day," he wrote in 1884, "some believe Swedenborg, some Wesley, some Campbell, some Calvin, etc. Each occupies his own plane and cannot by any long stride reach another. He must slowly thread his way, through perilous quicksands, it may be, but his true place will be reached just as he is pressed forward by God's Divine law of evolution, operating in strict harmony with his free agency." Nugent stopped attending church, readily admitting his preference for private reading and study.[42]

His private character, intellectual attainments, and public record as a judge were so spotless that Democrats could find little ammunition for attacks on him other than his supposed religious infidelity. In the 1892 campaign, the *Southern Mercury* answered charges "that Judge Nugent is a 'spirit[u]alistic crank'; that he is a disciple of Emanuel Swedenborg." The *Mercury* claimed to "have it from his own lips that the charge is false in toto," although the editor added that even if it were true, "what does a man's view upon religion have to do with his eligibility to civil position?" It is unclear whether Nugent actually denied being a Swedenborgian, as the *Mercury* claimed, but he soon set the record straight, denying that he was a spiritualist but admitting that he was indeed a Swedenborgian and had been one for twenty-five years. "It never would have made any difference so long as I remained in the democratic

THE RELIGIOUS WORLD OF TEXAS POPULISTS 175

ranks," he wryly observed. Responding to a rumor that he once "emerged from a room and declared I had had an interview with St. Paul," he replied that he preferred communicating with the living rather than the dead, "but I am free to say that if I had had an interview with the spirit of St. Paul I would have derived very much more wisdom than I ever find in Jim Hogg or Dick Coke."[43]

Despite his 1892 admission, Nugent was a Swedenborgian only in the sense that he found the Swedish mystic's teachings instructive. His was a very personal belief system, derived from his long years of study, and from numerous sources. For example, having rejected the conversion experience as preached by the Methodists and Baptists, he replaced it with the notion "that all may reach that stage in the ascending religious life where peace and joy are the settled habitudes of the spirit, and where all fear is dissolved in love." The New Church's "failure to teach this clearly as a present and possible privilege for all," he declared, "is the cardinal defect of Swedenborgian preaching. Hence I do not regard the so-called New Church very highly. It is a small ecclesiasticism centered around a high system of spiritual philosophy, but possessing little of the genuine inspiration of an unselfish, vital religion." To the extent, then, that there was such a thing as Swedenborgian orthodoxy, Nugent would have nothing to do with it: "I am, in other words, in *no sense* orthodox, and I am devoutly thankful that it is so. Orthodoxy throws a blight over the whole intellectual man, and precludes a normal, free evolution of the faculties."[44]

It is impossible to say how much Nugent's free-religionist views affected his candidacy, but the attacks certainly continued. During the 1894 governor's race, he constantly received letters from Populists who reported that he was "charged with being a Catholic by some, a free-thinker by others and a Bellamyite by others still." He finally felt compelled to issue a forceful clarification, though he omitted any mention of Swedenborgianism:

> Let me say, therefore, once [and] for all, that I am a Protestant of the most pronounced type, and believe most faithfully in the fundamental teachings of the Christian religion—particularly in the vital doctrine of Christ's divinity and that of the saving efficacy of the divine truth— divine truth applied to the life, that is accepted, believed and obeyed. I am no enemy of church organizations, but believe that the concentration of all ecclesiastical power in the hands of any one religious body would result in the destruction of political and religious freedom. I regard it as a singular manifestation of the divine good will, that protestantism has led to the development of so many forms of religious belief

and to the organization of so many churches. . . . But I believe, that any effort to thrust religious controversies into the arena of party politics must be attended with evil consequences. . . . Let the theologians quarrel as much as they please; the People's party will have its hands full if it devotes itself with full and complete abandonment to its great mission, which contemplates nothing less than the elimination of monopoly, both in spirit and fact, from our entire industrial scheme.[45]

Religious controversies dogged the Populists throughout the party's history in Texas. Nugent was not the only major leader charged with infidelity, or at least with lax morals. Jerome Kearby was a Congregationalist, though it is unclear whether it was his denominational affiliation, his reputation for drinking, or some other factors that led opponents to accuse him of nonbelief. Everyone knew of Stump Ashby's background as a Methodist circuit rider, but his equally well-known alleged penchant for alcohol called his religious sincerity into question. Barnett Gibbs, the former Democratic lieutenant governor who converted to Populism in 1896, likewise found his piety challenged for the first time when he ran for Congress in that year. Religion became an issue in the race when his Democratic opponent, Judge Robert E. Burke, touted his own credentials as a teetotaling lifelong Baptist. When Gibbs discovered that Burke had been baptized only after the start of the campaign, he ridiculed Burke as a "dryland Baptist." Gibbs, a wealthy Dallas lawyer and businessman, may not have been a particularly devout Methodist, but he vehemently denied being an infidel. "I haven't got religion enough to go to heaven on," he stated, "but enough for an average congressman, and too much respect for it to [bring] mine or anybody else's into politics." Two years later, when he was the Populist gubernatorial nominee, Gibbs again faced charges of infidelity. "For your information I will state that I was born and raised a Methodist," he responded to a fellow Populist who reported the accusations. Claiming to be "a good enough Methodist to be governor, if not to go to heaven," he declared, "My religion is between me and my God and is not a matter of vox populi. . . . I am a better Christian than the slanderers referred to, for they are liars."[46]

As the preceding account has shown, with relatively few exceptions, Texas Populist leaders held what today might be termed liberal or progressive views on religious questions. Though they often spoke the language of restorationism, seeking to recapture the spirit of "pure" Christianity, many were of a decidedly modernist bent, eager to reconcile religion with science, all in the service of progress and reform. Whether remaining within the ranks of the traditional Protestant denominations or standing outside them, they frowned on creeds and hierarchy. Given these proclivities, one of the most revealing tests of Populists' open-mindedness would come with their response to two religious groups outside the American Protestant mainstream: Catholics and Jews.

Anti-Catholicism was resurgent in Gilded-Age America, as millions of European immigrants—many from Eastern and Southern Europe—poured into northeastern cities. While prejudice against Catholics had never been as virulent in the South as in the North, southerners were not immune to it. Galveston, Houston, Dallas, and San Antonio all had attracted enough foreign immigrants to create breeding grounds for nativist sentiment. To many native Texans, Catholics were as objectionable—maybe more so—than "freethinkers" or atheists, for they were suspected of harboring anarchist or communist sympathies. Politicians of all parties, however, had to be careful how they approached the Catholic question, because in addition to the small but growing number of recent Catholic immigrants in the growing cities of Texas, there were much larger concentrations of German and Czech Catholics, especially in Central Texas and the Hill Country, who had been in Texas for decades and whose votes could not be ignored.

As previously noted, apart from fending off questions about his Swedenborgianism, Thomas L. Nugent was somewhat absurdly accused of being a Catholic during the 1894 governor's race, prompting him to proclaim, "I am a protestant. I was born a Methodist, reared and educated in that belief and have never taken a step towards Roman Catholicism." But he was quick to add, "It is not Catholicism we are fighting, but organized capital." On another occasion during that same campaign, he reiterated that he was "a protestant in every fiber of my nature for the simple reason that I am in favor of absolute intellectual freedom," but then went on to defend Catholicism. "In my judgment," he wrote, "the Roman Catholic church is just as much entitled to freedom in religious matters as any protestant organization. The liberal tendencies of the Roman Catholic church during the last few years have been very marked." He then presented a spirited defense of Catholic education and the patriotism of Texas Catholics.[47]

Nugent's defense of Catholics had come in the midst of Democratic accusations that the Populists sympathized with the American Protective Association (APA), a national nativist organization. Though Populists were quick to deny the charge, they did not necessarily approve of Catholicism in general. A writer to the *Advance* applauded Nugent's stance against the APA, calling it evidence of "a broad and liberal mind," but added, "With the dogmas of Catholicism I have no sympathy, but they are rapidly succumbing to education and civilization. Priestcraft thrives on ignorance and superstition. It could not bear the light of political discussion and will never force itself into it unless it is where it has an overwhelming majority and the masses are ignorant." The *Mercury* itself had taken a dip into nativist waters the year before, when it published a collection of propagandistic quotes from Catholic sources, intending to show "the radical position held by the leaders of Romish theology in America." Given the sensationalistic nature of the quotes, however, the *Mercury*'s editorial position was rather mild, as the editor was content simply to pose the question, "Will it not be well to watch encroachments upon our liberties from this direction also?" On balance, there is little evidence of any systematic or widespread anti-Catholicism in Texas Populism, which is somewhat surprising given the overwhelmingly Protestant nature of the party's membership and Populists' avowed disdain for all things hierarchical.[48]

Populists' attitudes toward Jews in some ways mirrored those toward Catholics. Populists were not insulated against the racial and ethnic stereotypes that abounded in Anglo-American culture, and like Americans of all political persuasions and walks of life, they occasionally resorted to those stereotypes, sometimes consciously, sometimes unthinkingly. Little evidence exists of social discrimination against Jews by Texas Populists, just as there is little evidence of social discrimination against individual Catholics. Most Texas cities and larger towns in the 1890s contained Jewish families, often respected merchants and community members, and if Populists objected to them any more than they resented the Protestant furnishing merchants, landlords, and bankers whom they so often believed were fleecing them, they left no record of it. Indeed, charges of anti-Semitism against Texas Populists made by some historians would not exist at all but for two stereotypical Jewish figures commonly found in Populist rhetoric, Shylock and Rothschild.[49]

The Populist press abounded with references to Shylock, the fictional Jewish moneylender in Shakespeare's *The Merchant of Venice*. Texas Populists frequently used the term "Shylock" (often not capitalized) as a sort of shorthand for greedy bankers, but these references only occasionally mentioned, or made much to-do over, the bankers' Jewishness. Most often it was a throwaway term, as when Hunt County Populists called on voters "to save our country and her institutions from the grasp of gold shylocks" by casting People's Party ballots.[50]

A more specific negative reference involved the frequent Populist discussions of the Rothschilds, the European Jewish financial dynasty, and especially the London branch of the family headed by Alfred de Rothschild, who played a major role in guiding British (and, to the extent that the United States followed the lead of Britain, Anglo-American) monetary policy in the late nineteenth century. Texas Populists were harshly critical of the Rothschilds and European Jewish bankers in general, frequently citing the sizable body of conspiratorial literature, including the so-called Hazard Circular that posited an international conspiracy to demonetize silver. Twentieth-century charges of anti-Semitism against the Populists have relied heavily on these financial conspiracy theories, without recognizing that while many of them identified bankers as Jews, the Jewishness of the bankers per se was virtually never the issue. Most often, as in their use of the Shylock trope, Populists invoked the name of Rothschild simply as a way of identifying British banking interests, as one East Texas Populist paper did when it printed a satirical version of the Lord's Prayer for plutocrats, beginning with the line "Our father which art in England, Rothschild be thy name."[51]

Even more damning in the eyes of some modern scholars who have investigated alleged Populist anti-Semitism is the occasional political cartoon in which Rothschild is caricatured as the stereotypical large-nosed Jew, fat with his ill-gotten wealth and invariably wearing the banker's fancy suit and silk top hat. While offensive to modern sensibilities (and probably to Texas Jews who saw them), such caricatures were the stock-in-trade of the era's political cartoons. The Populists, after all, often caricatured themselves as ragged, wild-haired, barefoot hayseeds—a stereotype that belied the sizable number of prosperous, well-educated, urban sophisticates among their ranks but also provided an instant visual cue that readers readily recognized. The Populists may have been "politically incorrect," to employ a modern term, in their graphic representations, but they practiced equal opportunity in their insensitivity.[52]

More instructive is what Texas Populists actually wrote about Jews. Milton Park of the *Southern Mercury*, not the most enlightened of the state's Populist leaders in matters of race, ethnicity, and gender, provided perhaps the closest thing to a truly anti-Semitic statement in discussing the 1896 Republican National Convention. When the Republicans chose a rabbi to deliver the opening invocation at the convention, Park wrote that "it was fit and proper that Rabbi Saale, a Jewish minister and a distant relative of the Rothschilds, should open the Republican national convention with a prayer. He was doubtless appointed to perform that duty by Rothschild himself by cable from London." Park, of course, was sarcastically making a larger, if conspiratorial, point about Rothschild's influence over the Republican Party's monetary policies, saying that "as the Rothschilds will supply the bulk of the campaign funds to elect the republican nominees, it is but reasonable to expect that they should dominate the convention. Down the Rothschild ticket!"[53]

Missing from Park's screed, and from virtually all Populist condemnations of the Rothschilds and Jewish bankers, were any blanket aspersions against Jews, Judaism, or the Jewish character in general. And occasionally Populists explicitly came to the defense of Jews. In the summer of 1892 a West Texas Alliance editor sympathetic to Populism led page 1 of his paper with a story pulled from the *New York Herald*, with the headline "ANTI-JUDAISM UNAMERICAN. The Jew Compares Favorably with the Christian if They be Weighed Fairly." In the midst of the 1894 campaign, the *Advance*—then the official state organ of the Texas People's Party—published a letter from a Jefferson County reader who addressed the issue of nascent Populist anti-Semitism head-on. "Another very common error that our people have fallen into is that of holding the whole of the Jewish race responsible for what the Rothchilds [sic] only have said or done," he asserted. "There are a great many Jews in this country, and I think they will compare quite favorably with any other class of citizens in point of patriotism and citizenship, yet all have been wantonly antagonized by our papers and speakers, when only the Rothchilds and perhaps a few others of that race were meant. We cannot afford to antagonize the whole of the Jewish race because of the Rothchilds. What would you think if the Jews were to attempt to hold you responsible for the conduct of John Sherman and Grover Cleveland? We certainly have opposition enough without wantonly antagonizing any section or race." It is significant that this writer, while calling his fellow Populists to task, emphasized that those who were guilty of stereotyping Jews *meant* "only the Rothschilds and perhaps a few others of that race." The evidence strongly suggests that he was correct in his analysis.[54]

~

As the preceding discussion has demonstrated, the religious beliefs of Texas Populists encompassed a wide range of theological and doctrinal traditions and orientations. But the vast majority of the party's adherents remained evangelical Protestants, and they brought to their political crusade the cultural institutions of southern Protestantism. Chief among these was the camp meeting.

The camp meeting was one of several organizing techniques bequeathed to the Populists by the Farmers' Alliance, which for years had held encampments in the summertime, when crops were laid by and there was a lull in the agricultural season prior to the harvest. After the birth of the People's Party in 1891, the Alliance continued to hold camp meetings, but apart from some

Alliance-specific activities, they were largely indistinguishable from the Populist meetings, featuring Third-Party speakers giving the same political speeches they gave at the party's gatherings. Populist encampments served much the same purpose for the People's Party that the religious camp meetings served for evangelicalism: an opportunity for folks to socialize, be educated and inspired, convert the unconverted, and return to their daily lives rededicated to the cause. For rural Texans who lived with the backbreaking toil and monotony of life on isolated cotton farms, the summer camp meeting might well be the highlight of their entire year.[55]

Camp meetings were usually planned by the county party organization, which appointed a committee to oversee local arrangements. At the larger, better-planned meetings, committees of men from each of the surrounding counties would be chosen to canvass the crowd and collect names to be forwarded to the central Populist clubs of their respective counties, to be used later in get-out-the-vote efforts. Some camp meetings were held in truly rural areas, requiring attendees to travel miles by foot, horseback, or wagon, but more often they were held on the outskirts of a town with nearby rail connections for those coming from a distance. In the larger cities, campers sometimes gathered in a city park. Still, it was not unusual for the press to report that people had come from as far as a hundred miles away by wagon, often hung with handmade banners, such as one seen at an 1892 Fannin County meeting reading, "A third party drive, by jacks." The urban press marveled at the crowd of four thousand that converged on Fort Worth that same year, noting that "the horny handed sons of toil arrived in vehicles of every description, including the old-time canvas-covered wagons which wound their way over the broad prairies of Texas before the advent of the railway corporations."[56]

Organizers placed a premium on locating a spot with ample shade, abundant potable water, and pasturage for horses and mules. Good food and drink were deemed essential. Meals were usually prepared by "the good wives of the sovereigns present," and reports from encampments often boasted of the quality and quantity of beef, pork, and mutton barbecued for the occasion, along with "the less substantial luxuries of ice cream, peaches, melons and such." At the 1892 Fannin County camp meeting, it was reported that "the merry-go-round men are here in full force, and also the man with the dolls and the fat boy." Games were organized on the grounds for the children, and dance platforms were sometimes set up at a safe distance from the speakers' stand for "the pleasure loving element." An 1896 gathering in Collin County featured an exhibit by the Texas Disc Plow Company, described as "by far the grandest display ever made by any plow company in this country," attracting "great crowds of men, women and children out to see the plow work at each exhibition." Vendors peddling lemonade and soda water also saw opportunities for profit, and a hostile Democratic paper reported that at an 1893 Delta County encampment "ice water was sold at 5 cents a glass and a pool was fenced in and 10 cents per head was charged for watering stock." The editor snidely commented, "No wonder encampments are so numerous. They are certainly profitable when water is sold so high."[57]

Given the Populists' religious inclinations and their reputation for moral rectitude, the sale and consumption of alcohol was generally forbidden, but beer and whiskey could often be discreetly purchased just off the premises. The question of liquor at Third-Party camp meetings fed into the larger issue of prohibition, where Populists always had to juggle their advocacy of personal liberty with the religious convictions of many Texans, all the while guarding against alienating important constituencies such as beer-loving Germans and Mexican Americans. In covering a large 1894 encampment at the fairgrounds in Paris, the *Dallas Morning News* reported, with some evident amusement, that "there was beer right under the grand stand, where the vendor could vie with Col. E. L. Dohoney, the original Texas prohibitionist, who opened exercises this afternoon in a speech of two hours, in which he animadverted upon the liquor traffic and stated that the democrats now had nothing left but the bunghole." About the time Dohoney began his speech, the *Morning News* observed that "crowds of democrats and populists surged about the beer counter and affiliated like brothers." Still, good order nearly always prevailed, especially since large numbers of women and children were in attendance.[58]

Music was an indispensable element in a successful camp meeting. Organizers usually provided a raised platform that served as bandstand and speakers' platform. In McKinney in 1896, the local Christian Church provided much-needed relief from the broiling August sun by furnishing a large canvas awning for the stage, which "added much to the attractiveness and comfort of the stand." String or brass bands played hymns and rousing campaign songs. At Proctor in Comanche County, the crowd was entertained by "very sweet violin music rendered by a blind man." But no camp meeting was complete without the singing of Populist anthems by the audience. "The tunes to nearly all their songs are familiar to all Sunday school attendants and church goers," the *Galveston Daily News* reported, with old gospel hymns such as "All Hail the Power of Jesus' Name" transformed into "All Hail the Power of Working Men." Others took their melodies from popular songs of the day, the most ubiquitous being "Goodbye, Old Party, Goodbye," an adaptation of the song, "Goodbye, My Lover, Goodbye." The *Daily News* provided an astute commentary on the importance of music to the Third-Party faithful: "Undoubtedly these songs, sung to lively and familiar airs, are in themselves a strong lever for this movement. They savor strongly of political revolution, though not a revolution of blood."[59]

Of course, the main attraction of the camp meetings was the speeches. Organizers vied for the services of party heavyweights, and no encampment was considered a success unless it featured appearances by at least several of the party's stars, a list that included Thomas Nugent, Jerome Kearby, Stump Ashby, Cyclone Davis, Harry Tracy, John Rayner, and others. Prominent out-of-state Populists were also in high demand, and most of the larger encampments managed to secure the services of at least one imported speaker such as Sen. William A. Peffer or Mary Elizabeth Lease, both of Kansas; "General" Jacob S. Coxey of Ohio, leader of the famous 1894 march on Washington; James B. Weaver, the 1892 Populist presidential nominee; or Thomas P. Gore, renowned among Populists as the "Blind Boy Orator of Mississippi."[60]

Nowhere was the Populist melding of politics and religion more evident than at the camp meetings. Coming at a time when religious revivals had largely abandoned the traditional outdoor meeting grounds for more genteel settings such as auditoriums, the camp meetings harkened back to purer times, providing an emotional link between the restoration theology held dear by many Populists and the reformist politics that they came to hear preached by their orators. Populist campaign songs set to the tunes of old gospel hymns contributed to this linkage, as did the common practice of calling each other "brother" and "sister" at their gatherings. The numerous ministers and ex-ministers among the ranks of the Populist orators naturally were in their element in such settings, and many of the biblically based political speeches discussed earlier in this chapter were delivered at the camp meetings, but the atmosphere at the encampments encouraged even the lay speakers to invoke biblical imagery. Typical was the speech of J. B. Rhodes, a Lamar County Populist party organizer and lecturer, delivered at the 1892 encampment near his hometown of Paris. Described as "a plain, unassuming farmer and one of that numerous class whom the war deprived of educational advantages," Rhodes addressed the gathering of several thousand, announcing as his text, "Blessed is the man who walketh not in the way of the ungodly nor standeth in the way of the people's party." What followed was a thoroughly political speech sounding many common Third-Party themes, but near the end of his oration he touched on the issue of political persecution of Populists by landlords threat-ening to withhold tenants' rations and employers coercing would-be Populist employees. "All reform movements have been persecuted from the days of Christ to the present time," he thundered, closing his speech by declaring that "the hand of God" was in the Populist movement, "as it was in the deliverance of the children of Israel from Egyptian bondage. The people's party is the Mo-ses that shall lead the Americans to political freedom." Little wonder, then, that in the minds of the Populist rank and file, the regeneration of the soul and the regeneration of the body politic were so inextricably linked.[61]

In the summer of 1896 a reporter for the *Galveston Daily News* editorialized perceptively about the Populists of Texas. "The Populists are like no other party," he wrote. "Their earnestness may approach the fanatical . . . but call-ing them fanatics doesn't move them one iota from their preconceived notions of what is right." The only thing that could move them to a new position, he noted, was an "argument from a brother populist, and not always that." But even more than their stubborn adherence to principle, there was another as-pect to the Populists that struck the reporter: "Did you ever hear a populist speaker who did not, during some part of his speech, bring in Scriptural quotations or allusions? That's an indication of their earnestness. A party that mixes its religion and its politics may become revolutionary very quickly once they get to going in that direction, for there's no man on earth more earnest than the man who takes his religion into his politics."[62]

The reporter had stumbled upon one of the keys to understanding the Pop-ulists. Their religious ideals imbued their politics with a sense of purpose that set them apart from Democrats and Republicans. That sense of purpose helped make the People's Party not just a political party but also a movement, with its own movement culture. Over time this would prove to be both the greatest strength and the greatest weakness of Populism in Texas, for while the idealism and esprit de corps of the movement would create great devotion and dedica-tion among Populists, it would also expose them to the dangers of disillusion and alienation if they ever perceived that the party had surrendered its purity or compromised its ideals. That danger, however, lay in the future.

But what of those Populists who were not particularly religious? The *News* reporter had that one figured out, too. "Of course, there are many of them who are not Christians and who do not talk of their religion and politics. They are none the less earnest," he declared, "for populism is their religion."[63]

5 · Black Texans and the People's Party

We want to do good to every citizen of the country, and [the Negro] is a
citizen just as much as we are, and the party that acts on that fact will gain
the colored vote of the south.
—H. S. P. "Stump" Ashby, 1891

Young feller says he's a Democrat because his father was one. According to
him I ought to want to be a slave because my father was one.
—Melvin Wade, 1894

Armed with a new ideological outlook that embraced the notion of a democratically controlled activist state protecting individual liberty, Populists confronted an issue that has perplexed, frustrated, and sometimes nearly destroyed
the liberal project ever since: the vexing problem of race. White Populists who
held relatively enlightened views on race, or who simply recognized the political reality that electoral success required cooperation across racial lines, faced
a fundamental problem. They had to fashion policies that would genuinely appeal to African American voters, but they had to do so in ways that would not
alienate large swaths of the white electorate. Accomplishing this feat demanded
that they examine their own racial attitudes and consider, in practical political terms, what it meant to be a citizen. Like their modern-day counterparts
on the American left, they struggled to reconcile their belief in individualism
with the realities of white privilege.

African American Populists, or those black Texans who might become Populists, faced very different challenges. The appeal of the Populist economic
program to black farmers seems obvious, because they were in even direr

straits than their white counterparts. But African Americans had other, often even more pressing concerns: education, the criminal justice system, lynching and other forms of racialized violence, and the countless other injustices and indignities that all people of color were forced to endure on a daily basis. No party that turned a blind eye to these issues could expect much black support, no matter how progressive its economic policies might be. African Americans had good reason not to trust white Populists, whose own political base of marginalized white farmers had often numbered among the most racist of whites. Black Texans had a much better understanding than whites of the problems that historical white privilege created, and it took clear-eyed realism on their part to see how Populism could, in time, advance African Americans further down the road toward full citizenship.

The electoral realities were not so hard to grasp. Despite the overthrow of Radical Reconstruction fifteen years earlier, African Americans still voted in large numbers and took a keen interest in politics. Comprising 22 percent of the state's population, they still potentially held the balance of power if whites were divided. Most blacks were nominal Republicans; the GOP, after all, was the party of Lincoln, of emancipation, and of the Fourteenth and Fifteenth Amendments, which had conferred citizenship and voting rights on the newly freed slaves. Fifteen counties had black majorities, and in fourteen more African Americans constituted between 40 and 50 percent of the population. In these counties Republican organizations often remained strong, electing local officials and the occasional state legislator. But African Americans had also learned to be pragmatic in their politics. When coalitions with independent or third-party movements had held the promise of furthering their interests, black Texans had often signaled willingness to participate in such arrangements. Likewise, when supporting a white Democrat in a specific race seemed to offer some tangible benefit, that Democrat often succeeded in attracting black votes. While it is certainly true that Democrats often corruptly manipulated the black vote, this was by no means always the case. Overall, black Texans retained a surprising degree of political independence at the beginning of the 1890s. Parties and politicians ignored them at their own risk.

At the same time, race relations were very much in a state of flux. Most of the legal structures of Jim Crow had yet to be erected in Texas in 1890. De facto segregation was widespread, as blacks had created their own churches, clubs, businesses, and professional organizations in the years since emancipation. But with the important exception of public schools (relatively few of which existed) and a controversial railroad-car segregation law enacted just that

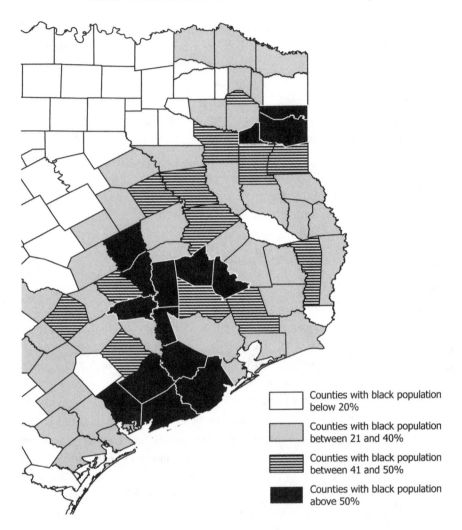

Counties with black population below 20%

Counties with black population between 21 and 40%

Counties with black population between 41 and 50%

Counties with black population above 50%

Figure 6 African American population, 1890. For county names, see Figure 2. Map by Claire Holland.

spring, the races were not legally separated in most aspects of life, and the "color line" was drawn only with great imprecision and inconsistency. Despite the political setbacks that had come with the defeat of Reconstruction, and the continuing violence and bigotry on the part of many whites, African Americans took pride in their remarkable economic and educational achievements. Many remained optimistic that political progress would follow.

For their part, white Texans failed to think with one mind or speak with one voice when it came to the "negro question," as it was often termed. Although racialist thinking positing the inherent inferiority of nonwhite races was on the rise, many whites continued to hold "environmentalist" views about race that suggested that over time, with the proper social conditioning, the possibility of black uplift, if not full equality, was real. Whites who held such views often lauded cooperation between the "better elements" of the black and white races, signaling that class sometimes might trump race.

It was against the backdrop of this fluid racial environment that Populists met in Dallas in August 1891 to organize the state People's Party. As discussed in Chapter 2, only about fifty delegates were present when William Lamb gaveled the meeting to order in the auditorium of the Dallas city hall. Within the first few minutes, as committee assignments were still being made, Lamb spotted Melvin Wade at the back of the room. For those familiar with Dallas politics, or Republican politics at the state level, Wade needed no introduction. Born a slave in Tennessee in 1842, he had been a fixture in Dallas political and labor circles since the Civil War. He may have acquired his political proclivities from his master, James K. P. Record, who brought him to Dallas sometime before the war and who later served as Dallas district attorney and state senator in the first postwar legislature. When African Americans were enfranchised in 1868, Union military authorities named Wade to the board of voter registrars in Dallas, launching his career in Republican politics. Over the next two decades he represented Dallas at state GOP conventions, twice serving on the platform committee. A skilled carpenter by trade, he helped found the Texas Federation of Labor and also served on its platform and state executive committees. Although Wade carefully crafted a public persona as plainspoken workingman, he was literate and deeply involved in the affairs of Dallas's rapidly growing black community, exercising leadership in such diverse organizations as the Colored Men's Educational Club and the local black cemetery association. His children Ida and George participated actively in the Colored Literary Society, and another daughter, Mary Ann, later worked for the black newspaper, the *Dallas Express*. Wade's oratorical skills, in which he masterfully used humor to make serious points, placed him in high demand as the featured speaker for Emancipation Day festivities and labor gatherings as well as political rallies and conventions. His influence in the black community was such that politicians of all races and political leanings felt obliged to treat him with a certain respect, whatever they personally thought of him or his politics.[1]

On sighting Wade in the back of the hall at that first Populist convention, Lamb interrupted the proceedings to ask him "if he was in sympathy with the

People's Party." Wade replied that he did not know there *was* such a party yet, "but he had read what that body was there for and he was in sympathy with the objects of the meeting." Still, he noted, "I want to see a thing before I go into it." Lamb must have taken this as an encouraging sign, but Wade, a life-long Republican who had resisted cooperation with other parties, was far from being sold on the new movement. If Lamb and the other white delegates thought they were going to be able to ignore the race issue, or gain black support with a few platitudes, the proceedings that lay ahead would disabuse them of these notions. The convention would also bring the basic racial dynamics of Texas Populism into sharp relief.[2]

Lamb made an opening speech in which he sketched out the broad outlines of the policies he believed the party should pursue, along with some tactical suggestions for organizing the party. He offered the opinion that "it would be a very great mistake to put in men [on the party's district and state executive committees] who have recently affiliated with the republican party, not that they would not do good service, but we have to refute the charge that our movement is the work of the republican party to break up the democratic party." Lamb understood that memories of Reconstruction ran deep in the minds of white Texans and that any third-party movement that put ex-Republicans in positions of leadership would conjure up images of the alleged "dark days" of "Negro-carpetbagger rule." The People's Party of Texas was scarcely an hour old, and already its leaders were engaging in the delicate racial balancing act needed to challenge the Democrats. Accordingly, Lamb concluded his speech by noting that "the colored people are asking admission [to the party], promising that they will put their speakers in the field and battle for the cause," and he asked the white delegates to "give their claims consideration."

This set off Melvin Wade, who demanded, "I would like to know what you mean by considering the colored man's claims in contradistinction to the claims of any other citizen of the United States?" Lamb replied that he "disclaimed drawing distinctions," whereupon Capt. Sam Evans of Fort Worth, a sixty-year-old Confederate veteran, ex-state senator, and prominent leader of both the Greenback and Union Labor parties, rose to put words in Lamb's mouth: "Every colored citizen in these United States has the same privileges that any white citizen has and that is what is meant." Wade was having none of this. "When it comes down to practice such is not the fact," he pointedly noted. "If we are equal why does not the sheriff summon negroes on juries? And why hang up that sign, 'Negro,' in passenger cars? I want to tell my people what the people's party is going to do. I want to tell them if it is going to work a black and a white horse in the same field." Lamb defended himself, saying that this was why he raised the issue—so that the convention would openly address the status of blacks in the party. Evans then went on the counterattack: "I would suggest to the colored gentleman that he has been serving a plutarchy [i.e., a plutocracy—the Republican Party]; . . . that he has been acting with those who make the [Fourteenth and Fifteenth] amendments a pretense to free him while enslaving the American working people." The convention then moved on to other business, and Wade apparently left the hall, unconvinced by what he had seen.[3]

Melvin Wade was not the only African American present at the birth of the party. A sprinkling of black delegates remained, including R. H. Hayes and Henry Jennings. Hayes, a member of the Colored Alliance who was active in Fort Worth independent politics, rose during the afternoon session and pressed the Populists on the question of Negroes' role in the party. Hayes declared that "in electing members of the executive committee the colored brother would have to be taken hand in hand, otherwise the streams would be poisoned." Stump Ashby, now in the chair, assured Hayes that "the colored people should have representation in the committee." It was only a question of how it was to be done. Another unnamed white delegate concurred, stating that blacks "are in the ditch just like we are." Ashby, the former preacher and stage actor, then voiced in dramatic language what he believed should be the overarching policy of the People's Party in regard to African Americans. "You are approaching a battlefield in which many errors have been made in the past," he warned the white delegates. "The democrats have never given those people representation; they have said they would buy enough of their votes with liquor and money. The republicans have left the negro without a party. If he has a friend it is we, and he can be our friend. If the committee is large, we do not propose to be governed by party regulations in the past. I am in favor of giving the colored men full representation." This elicited applause from the convention, whereupon Ashby added, "We want to do good to every citizen of the country, and he is a citizen just as much as we are, and the party that acts on that fact will gain the colored vote of the south."[4]

In their debates that day, Ashby, Evans, Wade, and Jennings had actually been wrestling with the central question of the Populist revolt, at least where race was concerned: What did it mean to be a citizen? Ashby could pronounce the Negro "a citizen just as much as we are" and Evans could claim that "every colored citizen in these United States has the same privileges that any white citizen has," but Melvin Wade and every black Texan knew these were lies. In the Gilded-Age South, as in George Orwell's *Animal Farm,* everyone may have been equal, but some were more equal than others.

Political theorists have distinguished between different types or categories of citizenship, and reality in the South reflected these categories. Political citizenship involves the right to participate in the political system as voters, delegates, and elected officials. Civil citizenship includes rights such as freedom of speech and religion, the right to own property and make contracts, equal access to public spaces, the right to an education, and effective access to the justice system. Social citizenship is harder to define, but it suggests rights such as freedom of association (including sexual and marital freedom), a certain degree of economic and occupational freedom, and one's general acceptance by others as a full and legitimate member of society. For racial minority groups in the Populist era, all three categories of citizenship were contested ground. But Texas Populists championed civil and political citizenship rights for nonwhites (and often for women) to a much greater extent than did their Democratic opponents. The Populists' great failure came in the area of social citizenship. It was not just that white Populists balked at intimate personal associations across the color line; their critical blind spot was their erroneous belief that social citizenship could be separated from civil and political citizenship. Over and over, Populists tried to embrace civil and political citizenship for blacks while denying them social citizenship. Indeed, so taboo were certain aspects of social citizenship (mainly those relating to sex) that even black Populists hastened to deny any interest in seeking what people at the time called "social equality." Melvin Wade, when asked in 1896 if he believed in social equality, had to turn it into a joke, saying, "'No; I don't believe in it and the fust white scountrl that comes foolin' around my folks is goin' to be got after with a shotgun.'"[5]

Wade's joke may have elicited laughter from his audience, but it was likely nervous laughter, because the joke came with a sharp and telling edge. Any white person who heard Wade's line (or later read it in the newspaper) could, with some reflection, understand that he was addressing one of the most volatile issues in American life: the color line. African Americans knew that the color line was crossed all the time—by white men raping or otherwise sexually exploiting black women. Wade certainly understood that he could not have given a serious talk to whites, looking them in the eye and threatening violence against them if they violated the black household. Joking about it was a way not so much to veil the threat as to seize an opportunity to remind whites of the brutal absurdity of the South's racial mores. That he could do so at all demonstrates the relative fluidity of race relations at the height of the People's Revolt. No black man who valued his life would have uttered such a statement, even in jest, in Texas in the half-century following the Populist era.

Intellectually, the Populists' racial Achilles heel was what one historian has called "the Othello problem: once the black man has been admitted to the republic, is there any way to limit his rights in private?" Serving on juries, for example, would fall under the rubric of civil citizenship, but if blacks sat on juries, might one of these juries refuse to punish consensual sex between a black man and a white woman? Voting is a basic characteristic of political citizenship, but once African Americans are guaranteed the right to vote, at some point might they use their political power to decriminalize interracial marriage? White conservatives in the 1890s understood such lines of reasoning all too well and were quick to charge that civil and political rights for African Americans would unavoidably lead to social equality and the supposed horrors of miscegenation, or racial mixing. As one Texas Democrat succinctly argued in 1892, it was "the intention of the Third party to place the Negro in the South on a political equality, and then next step to place him on an equal footing socially." Another Democrat was more explicit in his prediction of what would occur if the Populists kept pushing for black civil and political rights: "The negro will soon think himself as respectable as the white man. He will insist that his children attend the same school, board at the same house, eat at the same table, sleep in the same bed and enjoy social equality with the whites." When Democrats made such arguments to Populists, the Populists had to either deny the arguments' obvious logic, make light of the charges as Melvin Wade did, try to change the subject, or capitulate to the racist position and give up on the entire project of civil and political rights for nonwhites. Moreover, the Othello problem actually worked both ways: not only was it impossible to limit the black man's rights in private once he had truly gained civil and political rights, but it was also true that without granting blacks a certain measure of social equality, it was nearly impossible to guarantee civil and political rights. In capsule form, the question boiled down to this: How could a black man serve on a jury without sitting next to a white juror? At some visceral level, whites and blacks alike understood that the personal is political, that power is always wrapped up in private interactions. Neither race dared to acknowledge this, for practical political reasons that both sides understood, and for personal reasons that neither would admit.[6]

The Othello problem emerged from the very beginning of the Populist revolt, as a further examination of the 1891 founding convention in Dallas

reveals. At that convention, after Ashby and others called for black representation on the party's state executive committee, a vigorous debate immediately
ensued. Sam Ealy Johnson proposed a scheme whereby each congressional
district chairman would "appoint one colored man to co-operate" with the
white committee. R. H. Hayes, who had first demanded recognition of African
Americans by the convention, again objected. "We do not propose to be appointed by chairmen," he emphasized, demanding that the convention itself
must *elect* blacks to full membership on the executive committee. He warned
that the Populists would lose "in spite of the devil and high water" if they failed
to treat Negroes fairly. At this juncture Sam Evans again spoke up, proposing
that blacks be elected by the convention to at-large seats on the state executive
committee. This satisfied the black delegates, and Hayes and Jennings received the nominations and were elected to the party's seventeen-man governing body.[7]

What had really transpired that day in Dallas? Certainly the proceedings reveal the unsettled nature of 1890s-era race relations; not only were there black
and white delegates present, but the black delegates felt free to confront the
white leaders and demand concessions. The whites treated the black men re-
spectfully, and at the very least, the placing of two African Americans in the
ranks of the party leadership was an important symbolic step. (No African
American had ever sat on the Democratic state committee.) If their presence
pushed the party to adopt more favorable policy stances on "black" issues, then
it would be more than symbolic.

But the events of that day also underscore the limitations of the initial Populist approach to the issue of African Americans in the party. Clearly this was
a white man's movement, and though some of the leaders—men such as
Stump Ashby—harbored some fairly well-developed ideas regarding the role
of blacks in the party, it appears that others had essentially given it no thought.
Many of the whites at the convention, like Sam Johnson, came from the Alliance strongholds of the Hill Country and Cross Timbers regions, where few
blacks lived, and they were focused primarily on getting the party established
with a platform embodying core Farmers' Alliance principles. So, when confronted by two urban blacks—Melvin Wade and R. H. Hayes—their response
was to welcome African American votes but otherwise ignore black interests.
Only when Ashby and Evans spoke of blacks being citizens "just like we are"
and called for a new approach to the race issue did their fellow white delegates
begin to realize that the old ways needed to change. Still, their halting suggestions about having local white leaders appoint blacks to "cooperate" with

the party indicates the distance Populists would have to travel in winning their trust and support.

Even the election of two African Americans to the state executive committee fell short of creating the building blocks of a truly biracial coalition, and the details of their election underscore the complex interaction between political and social citizenship. The fact that the white delegates elected Hayes and Jennings to at-large seats rather than to seats from their own congressional districts enabled the white Populists to maintain the fiction that Hayes and Jennings were representing only African Americans statewide in the party's councils. No white man was put in the position of casting a vote that would make him the direct constituent of a black representative. Moreover, in the platform adopted at the meeting, the Populists ignored Melvin Wade's question about what the party intended to do about issues such as black jury service and the recently passed segregated railroad car law. The white Populists were determined to appeal to blacks primarily on the basis of shared economic grievance and on other non–racially specific issues, and to avoid those issues that might cross the boundary into social citizenship. For whites, this seemed like a correct and honorable approach, for it would mean that any African American votes they gained would be won honestly, rather than having the party appear to be pandering to blacks, a charge that carried real political risks in Texas politics.

Inevitably, questions of race intersected with those of gender. White Populists believed that honesty, forthrightness, and independence were the marks of "political manhood" and that African Americans could and should exhibit these qualities by resisting demagogic race-based appeals and voting for real political and economic reforms. Allowing one's vote to be purchased or manipulated or pandered to rendered one a dependent, something less than a man. Hence, when R. H. Hayes demanded that black state committeemen be elected rather than appointed, he explicitly argued that doing so would "make us feel that we are men." In the dominant culture of the South, participation in the public worlds of commerce and politics was in itself a marker of manhood, while the private sphere of the home was the proper place for women. This, then, raised the question: If blacks achieved political rights, if political rights (as Hayes suggested) equate with manhood, and if men are supposed to exercise dominance over dependent women, then what is to keep black men from gaining dominance over white women?[8]

For African American men considering allying themselves with the new political movement, gender in some ways united them with their white counterparts, but in other ways it functioned quite differently. Black male Populists, as Hayes expressed it, wanted their political participation to "make us feel that we are men." For whites, political participation had long been one of their society's major markers of masculinity, and black men wanted to share in that male privilege. But as Melvin Wade indicated in his joke about taking a shotgun to any white man who approached his women, African Americans lacked the same masculine control over their own households that white men enjoyed; they knew how often in southern history black men had been forced to watch helplessly as white men violated their wives or daughters. Would Populism someday make real what Wade had joked about—black men being able to guarantee the safety of their dependent women? Would Populism someday enable black women to enjoy the idealized perquisites of middle-class (white) femininity—that is, the freedom from being forced to toil in the fields or to perform demeaning domestic work for whites? And would Populism someday break the fever among whites that led to the hanging, burning, and torture of black men suspected, on the flimsiest of pretenses, of violating white women? For the black men who became Populists, the answer seemed to be yes, or at least there was the hope that it would be so.

Black and white Populists thus arrived at something of a modus vivendi: although each race had its own long-term objectives, which were poorly, if at all, understood by the other, they would attempt to separate the public sphere, where white and black men could have something resembling civil and political equality, from the private sphere, where white men and black men could arrange their individual households as they saw fit but where black men could still be excluded from any sort of social interaction with white women. Blacks and whites alike struggled to articulate this complicated position, which allowed civil and political citizenship for blacks in the public sphere while remaining largely silent on questions relating to social citizenship. But it was particularly challenging for African American Populists to explain it in terms that would be acceptable to voters of both races. As one "Colored Voter" explained in a letter to the editor of a Third-Party newspaper: "We don't want to rule the government; we don't want to come into your family; we don't want to enter your schoolhouses or your churches. But I tell you what we do want: We want equal rights at the ballot box and equal justice before the law; we want better wages for our labor and better prices for our produce; . . . we want to school our children, and we want a chance to earn a home."[9]

What *did* the party really offer African Americans, then, apart from the standard Populist economic planks on finance, transportation, and land?

Populists could point to the education planks in the 1891 state platform, in which the party demanded "an effective system of public free schools for six months in each year" along with free textbooks furnished by the state. But the platform was silent on the funding or governance of the segregated black schools, and African Americans could legitimately question whether the benefits promised under the proposed reforms would trickle down to the historically underfunded and neglected black schools. Another plank that Populists believed would especially interest African Americans was the reform of the convict lease system. The 1891 platform called for convict labor to be "taken out of competition with citizen labor; that convicts be given intellectual and moral instructions, and that the earnings of the convict, above the expense of his keeping, shall go to his family." Everyone knew that blacks were vastly overrepresented in the state's prison population and that the system of leasing out convicts to private industry in some respects exceeded slavery in its brutality. Nevertheless, the 1891 plank was vague in its wording, and the platform did nothing to address the larger problem of racial injustice in the state's judicial system. Finally, the platform called for "fair elections and an honest count of the votes," a plank that surely would appeal to African Americans who for a generation had seen their votes stolen, miscounted, or otherwise fraudulently manipulated. But the platform's proposed solution was use of the Australian, or secret, ballot, in which voters had to mark the names of candidates for whom they wished to vote, in the privacy of a voting booth. People who could not read—and blacks were disproportionately represented in the ranks of the illiterate—could find voting under the Australian system difficult or impossible.[10]

At this point, whether one viewed the Populists' racial glass as half-full or half-empty depended on one's perspective. For a black leader like Melvin Wade, who knew just how hard it was to separate social equality from questions of political rights (and whose loyalty to the Republican Party ran deep), it was half-empty. But party leaders could have pointed to the response of the hostile Democratic press to show how daring their actions had been. Barely a week after the Dallas meeting, referring to Sam Evans's statement that blacks "should have an equal show with other men in the party," the Fort Worth Gazette lambasted the convention for capitulating to the demands of "Melvin Wade, a notorious negro politician of Dallas." The paper also highlighted R. H. Hayes's demand that the party "take the negro hand in hand," a phrase sure to resonate negatively with the Gazette's white readers. The editor spelled out what this all meant: "Of course an equal show means a fair division of the spoils. What else could it mean?" He cynically demanded that the People's Party make good on its "promises" by equally distributing the nominations for public offices in the 1892 elections. A few days later, the *Gazette* returned to this theme, claiming that the Populist gathering had "outdone the Republicans in its offers to the negroes," an assertion that indulged in considerable hyperbole. The effort to paint the Populists as a party of Negrophiles was under way.[11]

Over the next few months the party did relatively little to fashion a coherent racial strategy. When the party convention reconvened at Fort Worth in February 1892, delegates reelected Jennings and Hayes to their at-large seats on the state executive committee. Jennings won a seat on the platform committee, where he may have been instrumental in amending the convict-lease plank to call for abolishing the leasing of prisoners altogether and instead employing convicts in building a state-owned and -operated railroad from the Red River to the Gulf of Mexico. The convention also elected Jennings and Hayes to represent Texas at the upcoming convention of industrial organizations in St. Louis, which would give birth to the national People's Party. Texas Populists could only hope these relatively modest gestures would spur interest in the African American community and motivate disenchanted black Republicans to take to the stump on the party's behalf. The Democratic *Fort Worth Gazette* caricatured Henry Jennings's speech before the Fort Worth convention by publishing it in Negro dialect, but Populists must have found the sentiments heartening: "I'm a People's party advocate smack to de bone, and I believe in de sub-treasury plan. When I go on de stump in behalf ob de party, if de Lord lets me live, I'll sweep de kitchen clean among my race; I'll go down whar de darkeys are as thick as stubbles in a wheat field, and I'll sing de song. 'Come ye sinners to de feast.'"[12]

The *Gazette* may have made light of Jennings's zeal for the cause, but in fact his conversion to Populism worried North Texas Democrats. Whereas R. H. Hayes was apparently a relatively minor figure in his hometown of Fort Worth, the seventy-year-old Jennings was arguably the most respected black leader in heavily populated Collin County, just north of Dallas. Born a slave, he became a minister after emancipation and in 1879 founded the McKinney CME Church, the town's first black congregation. As his successor in that pulpit later related the story, Jennings's church started without "a foot of land, or stick of timber or a dollar," but trusting in God and with "the aid of some of the best white citizens," the church prospered, and Jennings "gained the confidence of all the good people of McKinney, white and black." In the spring of 1892, Jennings took the stump for the People's Party, and by late May he had organized four black Populist clubs with 182 members in Collin and Rock-wall Counties. As a local white Populist noted, "His work shows, that the colored people see and know that something is wrong, and are abandoning the republican party and organizing separately in clubs, to help the reform movement." By summer he was keeping a grueling schedule, traveling as far as Houston County (150 miles to the south) and making up to twenty speeches in a one-month period. When called to speak before his home county's Popu-list convention in June, Jennings was "loudly applauded" by white and black delegates when he declared, "I tell you, we will no longer become the tool of political trickery—whiskey, old shoes and clothes will not buy us again." En-joying, as the white newspaper reporter phrased it, "the respect of all fair minded people of both races," he was unanimously elected as a delegate to the June state convention, the third such meeting he attended.[13]

Jennings soon became the focus of local Democrats' attacks. At Democratic rallies, speakers charged that he was elected to represent the *white* Populists of Collin County at the upcoming state convention, and that whites even took up a collection to defray his expenses to the convention. For good measure, the Democrats also leveled the scurrilous charge that Jennings was a chicken thief. The response of the county's white Populists is instructive. On one hand, they defended him as "a sober and honest old colored preacher," and they sought to condemn the Democrats' race-baiting. White Populist J. W. Chappell wrote facetiously to the Populist *McKinney Democrat*, putting words in the mouths of fictitious Democrats: "Don't go into 'this er' third party.' It is engi-neered by fools and idiots—it's delusive, it sends 'niggers' as delegates to its conventions, and it's leading to 'nigger supremacy' . . . Oh, horrible!" The lo-cal Populist editor likewise condemned the Democrats for calling the Popu-lists "a negro party" when so many Democratic officials "hold their places by virtue of the votes of bribed and intimidated negroes." He also pointed out, correctly, that "this late whining about 'negro representation' is simply born of fear and is used with the hope of creating prejudice." The Populist editor believed that "the people of this country are too well informed to swallow such stuff, knowing that it is simply insincerity.[14]

On the other hand, however, the local Populists took pains to correct the Democrats' charge that whites had elected Jennings as *their* representative to the state convention, insisting explicitly that he represented only the *black* Pop-ulists of the county. The money collected from whites, they added, was to de-fray his expenses in organizing black Populist clubs, not to pay his way to the state convention. Once more, white Populists found themselves conducting a delicate balancing act, one that pitted their desire for political coalition with blacks against their need to demonstrate that they opposed social equality. Here the difference between Populists and Democrats becomes significant. In the honor-based hierarchical worldview shared by most white Democrats, white men exercised domination over all other groups, be they racial minorities or women. Hence, blacks did not belong as delegates to political conventions or officeholders, where they would be accorded equal status with whites. By contrast, most Populists, who were prepared to accord civil and political citizenship to African Americans while withholding the rights of social citizenship, could countenance blacks in positions of political leadership as long as they were elevated to those positions by their fellow blacks, and their positions did not place them in direct authority over whites. So, Henry Jennings could be elected by the *black* Populists of Collin County as *their* representative to the state convention, where he could then deliberate on an equal basis with white delegates. But as we have seen, he could only be elected to the state executive committee as an at-large member, because electing him to one of the district seats would mean that he was representing white Populists from his home congressional district. Similarly, the white Populists of Jennings's home county could pass the hat to pay his expenses in organizing black Populist clubs, but paying his expenses as a Collin County delegate to the state convention left open the suggestion that he was *their* (that is, the white Populists') representative. When white Populists, then, spoke of the "political equality" of whites and blacks, they still had a specific meaning in mind; they meant honorable cooperation, but on something resembling a "separate but equal" basis rather than color-blindness, a balancing act aimed at maintaining the distinction between political and social equality.[15]

At the June 1892 state nominating convention in Dallas, which attracted over a thousand delegates, attendees heard encouraging reports about the party's progress in attracting African American support. After lunch on the first day of the meeting, Jennings mounted the podium and addressed the enthusiastic gathering. He acknowledged the difficulty in persuading black Americans to forsake the Party of Lincoln. Jennings "said he had been born a slave, and there was a time when he would rather have his head screwed into an auger hole, than meet this party, which he now recognized as destined to be the savior of the country." Jennings recounted his experiences over the past weeks organizing black Populist clubs, and he predicted that "if I can only get among the niggers, I'll whale them to the tune of 40,000. (Applause.) The democrats will cry 'Hark from the tomb' with a doleful sound. (Applause.)" Later in the convention, the delegates elected Jennings and Hayes for the third time to at-large seats on the executive committee. One of the last organizational matters to be dealt with involved the selection of at-large delegates to the upcoming national convention in Omaha. Hayes and another African American, Jasper Crenshaw, were prepared to go, along with a number of white aspirants. It tran-spired, however, that there were twice as many candidates as there were avail-able seats, so someone suggested that the odd-numbered names on the list be elected delegates by acclamation, with the even-numbered men becoming al-ternates. This seemed acceptable until a delegate yelled, "this will make the two colored men alternates and that is not right." Realizing the problem, the decision was made to vote on the delegates one by one, and when that was done, the two black candidates were elected.[16]

If all seemed positive and harmonious on the final day of the convention, another black delegate injected a bit of realism. In the course of making nom-inating speeches, a white delegate touted the Confederate war record of gu-bernatorial candidate Henry McCulloch, whereupon an ex-slave named Watson from Grayson County gained the floor and told the audience, "You look over this large assembly and find very few of my people represented in this great movement." He reminded his fellow delegates that blacks would hold the bal-ance of power in the upcoming election, and then he warned that every time the Populists trumpet the war records of their candidates, "you are putting tools into democratic and republican hands to help them keep the negro out of your movement." Other, white speakers agreed with Watson, whose senti-ments elicited applause, and even though most of the candidates for statewide office did have Confederate records, the party generally sought to downplay sectional issues and the racial baggage that went along with them.[17]

As the 1892 election season progressed, one development seemed to play into the Populists' hands—the actions of Texas Republicans. African Ameri-cans had always constituted a heavy majority of the Republican vote in Texas, but blacks and whites had shared in the party's leadership and in whatever federal patronage came its way. In the 1880s whites had shown signs of chaf-ing under this arrangement, especially with the rise to power of African Amer-ican Norris Wright Cuney of Galveston as the state party's leader in 1885. By 1890 the party was increasingly divided into feuding "black-and-tan" and "lily-white" factions, with the lily-whites wanting to purge blacks from the party. Finally, in June 1892, just two weeks before the Populists met, the lily-whites held their own convention in Dallas and nominated their own state ticket. Their actions greatly alienated longtime black Republicans and presented a major opportunity for the Populists. Among those disaffected Republicans was Melvin Wade.[18]

The reason for Wade's defection from the Republicans cannot be stated with precision, but it was apparently a combination of the rise of the lily-whites, Cuney's decision in 1892 to endorse the conservative Democrat George Clark for governor, the rapid growth of Populism into a viable movement, and the nearly wholesale transference of the labor movement into the Third Party ranks. In his own inimitable style, Wade simply explained, "If my wife was to quit me I'd quit her, and that is the reason why I quit the republican party—it quit me." Whatever the circumstances, by August 1892 Wade had given up on the GOP and cast his lot with the People's Party. He campaigned hard for the Populist ticket throughout the fall, and for the remainder of the Populist revolt he would rank as one of the party's two most influential black leaders.[19]

The other of those leaders seemed to come out of nowhere. In late August 1892 a brief item in the *Dallas Morning News* reported on a Populist rally in Milam County, in the Brazos Valley cotton-growing region, at which "white and colored people's party folks, democrats, republicans and prohibitionists" had heard an hour-and-a-half-long speech by one "Professor Raynor [sic], a colored orator from Robertson county." The reporter described the speech as "conservative, sensible and logical, and . . . well received by all present." Two weeks later he appeared again in the county, speaking before a crowd of "colored brothers" as well as "white third party sympathizers." This "Professor Raynor" was in fact John Baptis Rayner, who rose from obscurity to become the preeminent leader of Texas's black Populists (plate 14).[20]

Rayner had little in common with Melvin Wade, except for being a gifted orator and having been the slave of a white politician. In Rayner's case, however, the slave owner—Kenneth Rayner of North Carolina—was also his father. John Rayner, born in 1850, grew up in the Raleigh household of his wealthy planter father, who served in Congress as a Whig and later became one of the major national leaders of the American (or Know-Nothing) Party. Kenneth Rayner apparently openly acknowledged the boy as his son and saw to it that he received a college education after the Civil War. After the war, while Kenneth Rayner served as a federal claims-court judge and solicitor of the US Treasury, John entered politics in Edgecombe County, where he held a succession of local offices during Reconstruction. In 1880, with Reconstruction having been overthrown, he led a migration of black North Carolinians to Robertson County, Texas, settling in the bustling cotton town of Calvert. There he preached, taught school, and charted an increasingly independent political course. During the 1887 statewide prohibition campaign, he had briefly gained notoriety for his work on the prohibitionist cause, a stance that on at least one occasion pitted him in debate against Melvin Wade, who campaigned for the "wets." But apart from his brief role in the 1887 campaign, Rayner was a virtual unknown outside black Republican circles in Robertson County.[21]

He nonetheless brought exceptional talents to the Populist crusade. One was his speaking ability. Short and stocky, the fair-skinned Rayner (he was probably no more than one-eighth "black," by the racial calculations of the era) possessed a strong, clear, surprisingly high speaking voice capable of reaching, and mesmerizing, large crowds in an era before electronic amplification. He had grown up hearing his white father—widely regarded as the finest public speaker in antebellum North Carolina—make political speeches, and he used that experience, along with his polished liberal education, to craft orations in the grand nineteenth-century tradition, replete with flowery diction and frequent allusions to American and world history and ancient mythology. But when the occasion called for it, he could also shift rhetorical gears and speak the unadorned vernacular of rural Texans, black and white. By all accounts, he possessed a keen sense of humor and a rapier wit, which he directed at everyone from hecklers at his speeches to sitting governors, though he also knew how to ingratiate himself with white audiences by appealing to sentimental memories of the antebellum South and the "Lost Cause." Only a handful of his contemporaries could match him on the stump, and none surpassed him.

Rayner's other invaluable asset was his ability as an organizer. As Stump Ashby and others had recognized at the party's founding in 1891, a party so strongly identified with the white Farmers' Alliance, born in the midst of a depression with a largely impoverished constituency, faced nearly insurmountable obstacles in attracting, keeping, and motivating black voters. The election results in 1892, despite some encouraging anecdotal evidence, revealed that the People's Party had failed miserably in its efforts to woo African Americans. Despite the work of men like Hayes, Jennings, and Wade, the party polled a statistically negligible black vote. The Populists needed more than just an attractive platform and good speechmakers at election time; they needed men who could do the hard work of grassroots organizing and education in the scores of counties and hundreds of rural communities where blacks comprised a significant proportion of the electorate. With his intelligence, his tireless store of energy, his ability to move comfortably in both black and white circles, and his understanding of the mechanics of local southern politics,

Rayner filled the bill admirably. Between the 1892 and 1894 elections, white party leaders gradually came to realize this.

In the immediate aftermath of the 1892 defeat, party chairman Stump Ashby, gubernatorial candidate Thomas Nugent, and state campaign manager Henry Bentley issued a joint address analyzing the state of the party. They correctly acknowledged that the Populist electorate had been "composed almost entirely of white men," but they also lauded "the fidelity and devotion of that comparatively small number of colored men, who, with rare courage, stood with us in the fight for principle," noting that "some of them, even at the risk of their lives, hesitated not to unfurl the banner of reform and boldly champion the cause it represents in the presence of the enemy." The following summer, in the state convention held in Waco, party leaders continued to wrestle with the racial question. If money is the mother's milk of politics, the Populists recognized that this was never truer than in the quest for black votes in 1890s Texas. Meeting in executive session, the state committeemen grimly noted: "Orators can't eat railroad passes. They must have money for grub, or the party will disband. Men of the right sort to organize and protect the colored populist lodges are scarce and come high, but they are necessary to keep the Hogg people from rounding up 'my dear colored fellow-citizens' to the utter defeat of the party. Unless these particular workers are kept in the field it is all up with the people's party. Postage and stationery require money, and there are other and more expensive demands for purposes which it might be unparliamentary to mention in open session."[22]

Here in their most naked form lay the hard realities for the Populists. Even the black intelligentsia—men like John B. Rayner—often lived a step or two away from poverty, dependent on the meager salaries paid by black schools or the nickels and dimes from black church offering plates. The Populists needed the full-time services of dozens of such men, who would have no means of support apart from whatever the party could furnish. And if, as the election drew nearer, voters were to be "treated" by the party to barbecue and, often, whiskey, the price tag rose exponentially. With no patronage to help grease the wheels and no corporate support, the Populists had no ready answers beyond simply calling on supporters to make contributions. The executive committee concluded that it would "try and rake $50,000 together to do the work of propagation and hold the colored brother firmly in line," but it never raised even a fraction of that amount. In the end, Populism would demand a degree of dedication from its black organizers that would exceed even that of its white activists, and it would require interracial cooperation of an unusual order.[23]

Since 1893 was not an election year, the newspapers did not provide exhaustive coverage of that year's state Populist convention, but the press accounts gave no indication of the presence of any black delegates at the meeting. Jennings, who was in his seventies, had retired and was likely in declining health; he died in 1894. Hayes's whereabouts were unknown, and Melvin Wade had to support his large family and fulfill his demanding obligations as a community leader in Dallas. Rayner was apparently just coming to the attention of party leaders. Given the paucity of records, we have only bare glimpses into the challenges these men must have faced. In addition to character assassination by hostile white Democrats, the preacher Jennings faced censure shortly after the 1892 election from the Colored Methodist Episcopal Church's state conference, which complained of him "going about making political speeches" and "dabbling in political matters." When Populist leaders in 1892 noted that black workers sometimes campaigned "even at the risk of their lives," they were not engaging in hyperbole. The *Dallas Morning News* reported the week before the election that Melvin Wade had been assaulted by a "hired bully" at Mineola in East Texas; other black Populists, including Rayner, would face repeated threats of violence on the campaign trail. Black Populism was not for the faint of heart.[24]

Some degree of white patronage was vital. Evidence is sketchy, but it seems likely that Rayner first came to the attention of statewide Populist leaders through the auspices of Eber Seth Peters. The forty-year-old Peters was another on the long list of prominent Third-Party men who defied all the stereotypes of Populists as eccentric hicks. Born in Detroit, Michigan, he came to Texas for his health at age twenty-one, learning the hardware and newspaper businesses in Dallas and Corsicana. In 1879 he married the daughter of James Scott Hanna, a wealthy Robertson County cotton planter, and soon entered the ranks of the planters himself. By the early 1890s he owned nearly two thousand acres in the Brazos Bottoms, some of it in partnership with his brother-in-law, James K. P. Hanna, who would also become a prominent Populist. Peters displayed the sort of restless energy that characterized so many Populist leaders. Not content with the life of gentleman planter, he continued to operate a hardware business in Calvert and acquired shares in two area newspapers. He was also an inveterate joiner, and once he joined an organization, he invariably ended up as one of its leaders. In the 1880s, Peters, an enthusiastic supporter of Charles Macune's Subtreasury Plan, joined the local Robertson County Farmers' Alliance and soon became "a leading and influential alliance man" in the statewide organization. He served as president of both the Texas and the Southern Cotton Growers Associations, as well as chief of the agricultural department for Texas at the 1892 Chicago World's Fair. Founding a Populist newspaper, the *Calvert Citizen-Democrat,* in 1892, he was soon elected to the state executive committee of the Texas Press Association and to the executive committee of the National Reform Press Association. Publicly resigning from the Democratic Party in 1892 over its refusal to endorse the Subtreasury Plan, he joined the Populists and was elected first to the new party's state executive committee and eventually to the Populist National Committee. He also was named a delegate to the Omaha convention and received the Populist nomination for state senator in 1892. If ever there were a Populist who embraced Charles Macune's vision of "business methods" in agriculture and who believed in an active role for government in rationalizing the nation's economic affairs, it was E. S. Peters. He even looked the part of the modern businessman, with his hair cut short and face clean-shaven except for a neatly trimmed moustache.[25]

Perhaps Peters's Michigan upbringing gave him a different perspective on race than most other southern cotton planters, but he was certainly no carpetbagger. He had been a lifelong Democrat until 1892, and his marriage and business alliances with the Hannas, who had been slaveholders and secessionists, suggests a certain level of comfort with southern culture and institutions. Indeed, his brother-in-law, business partner, and fellow Populist leader, James K. P. Hanna, was a veteran of Hood's Texas Brigade and studied at Washington University when Robert E. Lee was president there after the war. Rather than being inspired by northern-bred racial liberalism, it seems more likely that Peters saw in Rayner a sort of kindred spirit. Peters may have recognized that but for the South's peculiar racial order that rendered the olive-skinned Rayner a "Negro," it might well have been Rayner rather than himself who, by dint of enterprise and fortuitous marriage, owned a magnificent estate and moved in elite business and social circles. Whatever the case, Peters became Rayner's ally and patron in the People's Party. When Rayner ran low on campaign funds, he knew he could turn to Peters. When political fieldwork kept Rayner from attending a state executive committee meeting, it was Peters to whom he entrusted his proxy vote. Moreover, in a county and region of the state where political violence against African Americans was the rule rather than the exception, Rayner surely knew that his alliance with the Peters-Hanna family provided a degree of protection that no amount of money could purchase. A grateful Rayner described Peters as "a rich farmer and a true populist, and always a friend to the poor."[26]

Rayner fairly burst onto the Texas political scene in the spring of 1894, working virtually full-time for the party for the eight months leading up to the November elections. In his public addresses, he almost always drew enthusiastic, racially mixed audiences. Typical was a speech he delivered in early March at the opera house in the Central Texas town of Taylor, where, as the press reported it, "A large crowd of both whites and blacks turned out to hear him, and from the applause The News correspondent could hear from a neighboring window, the address was well received and heartily enjoyed." By the end of March he was being identified by the *Texas Advance*, now the state party's official organ, as "Rev. J. B. Rayner, colored, our populist orator." Throughout the spring he maintained a relentless schedule, repeatedly crisscrossing the eastern half of Texas, an area as large as Alabama and Mississippi combined. In letters to the *Advance* and the *Mercury* he would keep the party faithful apprised of his progress. "'I have fought a good fight and have kept the faith,' and by telling the truth converted to our political ideas every colored man and woman in Jasper and Newton counties," he reported in typical dispatch. "I have converted at least fifty per cent of my white auditors." Rayner took pride in his debating prowess. "When I first came to these two counties," he related in this same letter, "the Democrats tried to hire a little pride-intoxicated colored school teacher to follow and reply to me, and so when I spoke at Jasper he came to reply and commenced to take notes of my argument, and when I had finished my talk, I found that he was nailed to his seat, and from now on he is out of politics." On another swing throughout deep East Texas Piney Woods, Rayner gave a two-hour speech at the courthouse in San Augustine, again to a "crowded house of both white and black," after which a local white Populist reported that "a great many of them declared that they would never vote the old ticket any more, but would stick to the people's party." The white Populist declared, "Wherever J. B. Rayner speaks the populist party booms." Another white Populist from Waller County concurred, saying, "He is one of the hardest hitters I ever heard."[27]

State party leaders were quickly learning what they had in Rayner. Calling on "all patriotic Populists who can reasonably do so" to send a small donation to help defray the black committeeman's expenses, Stump Ashby frankly admitted, "The work I want Rayner to do, no white man can do." White Populists who saw Rayner in action were stunned by what they witnessed. As a Populist from coastal Jackson County, W. P. Laughler, explained to a fellow white Populist in a rare private letter discussing Rayner, "I have heard him speak twice in this county, and he is the ablest speaker for the service I have ever heard. He carries such conviction by his appeals and arguments, that few colored men can resist. I am willing to pledge my reputation for a man of judgement upon what I say with regard to him. I am too old a man to allow any temporary enthusiasm to overcome my cooler judgement, and I tell you I have seen and heard him destroy all the effect of a strong Republican [or] Democratic speech in a single sentence, and turn over not only colored Republicans but white Democrats, nor were they slow to acknowledge it. You hear him first, and judge for yourself." Whether this experience made Laughler stop and ponder the logic of the South's racial system—a system that deemed Rayner inferior on the basis of his admixture of Negro "blood"—is not recorded.[28]

~

As the Populist challenge to the Democrats grew more formidable in 1894, the risks of violence grew greater. On an August night in Omaha in the northeast corner of the state, Rayner spoke before an audience of 450 black and white listeners. After the speech, he reported that "some of the Democrats that worship at the shrine of Bacchus tried to frighten me and make me leave town. One poor little fellow wanted to know who would pay him to run 'that nigger' out of town." Rayner continued undeterred, noting simply that "the colored people of Morris county are doing their own thinking and will vote with the Populists. . . . Our party is growing daily and I am cheerful, hopeful and feel that victory is waiting to crown our efforts. My people are . . . developing an individuality that will command the respect of all men."[29]

A potentially more serious situation developed that summer in heavily black Waller County near Houston. Populists were strongly courting the black vote, even placing an African American on the county ticket, and they had summoned Rayner to the county to deliver a series of speeches. In this atmosphere, Democrats spread the rumor of a "race war" or "negro rising" in the Brazos Bottoms. A posse of sixty or seventy armed white men subsequently rode into the Bottoms, sending black families fleeing in terror, and for several days all work in the fields halted. Rayner postponed his speaking engagements, and the local Populist county chairman charged the Democrats with creating the incident to frighten blacks and then blame it on the People's Party. Rayner rescheduled his trip, amid reports that local Democrats had sent him a telegram threatening his life if he showed up. Rayner and the editors of the *Hempstead News* dismissed the reports as unfounded, and Rayner ultimately gave several speeches in the county, including an address at the county courthouse in Hempstead before a large, racially mixed audience. Candidates from all the parties attended the speech, and despite the tense racial climate, Rayner reportedly pulled no punches "in abusing the Democratic party." As a result of the speech, the Populist county chair reported, "I have heard 100 persons say they was done with the old parties."[30]

By the time of the 1894 state nominating convention, party leaders believed they had finally solved the riddle of how to deal with the race issue. It is unclear how many African Americans were among the twelve hundred delegates arriving in Waco on June 19, but the *Waco Evening News* noted that "the colored brother was a conspicuous figure and . . . a hearty welcome was accorded him." The correspondent from the Dallas-Galveston *News* took special notice of "the absence of the bigotry and intolerance which usually characterizes the movements of new political organizations." Wade and Rayner both addressed the convention on the first day. The text of Rayner's speech was not recorded, but Wade delivered one of his characteristic addresses in which he used humor to make serious points. Arraigning both of the old parties, he contended that the Republicans had "been treating the nigger just like the hunter treats his dogs. Snaps its finger and they jump and bark, then does this way (motioning down with his hand) and they lay down for four years." But he saved his best line for the Democrats: "Young feller says he's a Democrat because his father was one. According to him I ought to want to be a slave because my father was one."[31]

Rayner's moment in the spotlight came on the second day, at the high point of the convention. His speech was met with "loud applause," and the convention went on to nominate Nugent by acclamation. Rayner subsequently won a place on the platform committee and an at-large seat on the state executive committee. Although we know relatively little about the platform committee's deliberations, circumstantial evidence suggests that Rayner wielded influence there. Some delegates simply wanted to adopt the 1892 state and national platforms. Rayner's white planter ally from Robertson County, J. K. P. Hanna, spoke out against the plan, saying, "This is a party of progress, and changes in the platform may be necessary to make the document up to date." Rayner surely knew—and perhaps had already impressed the idea on Hanna—that the 1892 platform had not offered enough to African Americans. After a six-hour meeting, the committee indeed produced a platform that retained the progressive features of the 1892 document but added two new planks specifically aimed at blacks. One called on the state to provide "sufficient accommodation for all its insane, without discrimination in color." The other, which clearly seemed to bear the imprimatur of Rayner, involved the funding and governance of black public schools.[32]

The plank called for a six-month school term (the current term was only four months) and demanded that each race was "to have its own trustees and control its own schools." As the *News* observed, "This declaration appeals irresistibly to the colored brother. He fairly dotes on schools and the colored delegates enthusiastically declared that 50,000 republican votes would land in the populist camp next November. They meant it, too. It remains to be seen whether or not they can deliver the goods, but there is no doubt about their sincerity. They will do their best." The *News* then made a condescending but revealing observation. Blacks, the reporter noted, "have found a party in which they can occupy front seats and talk as much as they please, and if there is anything the dusky sovereign loves it is a chance to make speeches." Ignoring the many white men to whom this description also applied, the reporter ridiculed blacks for their supposed affinity for speechmaking, but he also hit upon an important point: African Americans *did* "occupy front seats" at the convention and make speeches that white delegates cheered. In short, they were treated with respect, which never happened in Democratic conventions and was becoming rarer in Republican gatherings. The *News* concluded its analysis by speculating that "if a large number of colored votes do not roll up for the populist ticket it will prove a great disappointment for the reformers, and especially the colored members of the late convention." Summarizing the racial dynamics of the convention, the *News* reporter declared, "In the nomination speeches negro and white man, ex-slave and ex-master, from the same chairs gave thanks that the barriers of race prejudice have been smashed and that hereafter, at least in Texas, all men, of whatever political conviction can vote according to their judgment and not according to color, race or previous condition of servitude."[33]

When the fall elections arrived, the People's Party had made inroads into the black vote, but the result fell far short of what they had anticipated. From a statistically negligible level of African American support in 1892, the Populists now polled about 17 percent of all eligible black voters (and 22 percent of those who actually voted). That was the good news. But 33 percent of eligible black voters continued to support the Republican Party, and 29 percent landed in the Democratic column, a figure probably significantly inflated by fraud. Milton Park of the *Southern Mercury* certainly thought so, noting that the largest Democratic majorities "came from the counties containing the greatest negro population," prompting him to ask, quite plausibly, "Does anyone believe for a moment that the negroes deliberately voted the democratic ticket in these counties?" But Park also displayed a blame-the-victim attitude that in subsequent years would lend itself to racist scapegoating: "The colored people of Texas need to start a campaign of education among their race. As long as they permit such men as [Republican leader Norris Wright] Cuney to sell their suffrage they are slaves."[34]

Whoever deserved the blame, fraud would remain a chronic problem for the duration of the Populist revolt, and it is likely that no party had a monopoly on clean electoral practices. In any case, the 1894 elections had demonstrated that Populists could win black votes, and the party was determined to keep trying. Doing so would depend in part on concrete demonstrations of its sincerity. Although it had not carried the state, the People's Party did manage to send twenty-four Populists to the state legislature, and while very few of them hailed from areas with large black populations, their presence in the legislature nonetheless presented an opportunity to see how Populists would handle racial issues once they actually confronted the challenges of governing.

When the newly elected Populist legislators arrived at the massive pink granite capitol building in Austin for the January 1895 session, race, as usual, was very much on the mind of lawmakers of all parties. As the Populists had recognized during the campaign, one source of complaint from African Americans was a law enacted two years earlier involving the governance and funding of public schools. That law, while nominally providing black school trustees for the segregated black schools, actually placed them "under the direction" of the white trustees, with results that infuriated black Texans. One of them, L. M. Sublett of Waco, a politically active Republican who had supported Jim Hogg in 1892, became a Populist because of the law. Sublett declared that the Democrats had "ruined the schools as far as the colored people are concerned." A school trustee himself, he observed that under the law he had "no power to hire a teacher, fix a salary or participate in any respect in the administration of school affairs." African American trustees only had "the right to make suggestions, which are usually ignored." Another black Wacoan, Rufus Evans, asked why, given that black people pay the same taxes as whites, "the superintendent of the free schools does not provide for the white and colored schools alike." As an example of discriminatory treatment, he mentioned the fact that every white school had a janitor, whereas at the black schools the children did the cleaning.[35]

Populists had made a campaign issue of the 1893 law, promising in their platform to give African American trustees real control over their schools and to provide equal per-capita funding. Early in the session two Populists in the House, Van Buren Ritter of Falls County and Thomas R. Watkins of Navarro

County, introduced bills doing just that. In their bills, separate but equal was truly intended to be equal; neither bill made it out of committee. Meanwhile, Democrats (and the one lone black Republican) in the House introduced a variety of bills amending the unpopular 1893 law in various ways. The bill that finally emerged from committee was a combination of two Democratic bills, and it greatly watered down the Populists' efforts at fairness. Under the new bill, there *would* be elected white and colored boards of trustees, and the colored boards would "be the trustees for all purposes in reference to the management or control of the colored schools and the funds apportioned for their support." This language echoed that of the Populist bills. The devil, however, was in the details. Under the Democratic plan, the white and colored boards were ordered, "if possible, [to] agree upon a division of the funds of the district between the white and colored schools" and upon the length of the school term. If they failed to agree, however, the bill empowered the county superintendent, invariably a white man, to distribute the funds and set the length of the school term as he saw fit. Since the likelihood of white trustees voluntarily agreeing to treat the black and white schools equally was remote, the result in most cases would be a perpetuation of grossly unequal schools. With no hope of getting their own version of the bill enacted, the Populists reluctantly voted to support the Democratic version, which became law. To do otherwise would have provided campaign fodder to the Democrats, who would have charged Populists with opposing their own platform promise of black trustees for black schools. Upon final passage of the bill, and realizing the untenable position he and his fellow Populists found themselves in, Populist Tom Watkins took the unusual step of inserting into the House *Journal* his own personal explanation of his vote in favor of the bill: "I vote 'yea,'" he tersely noted, "because it is the best I can get."[36]

The debate over schools illustrates the complex dynamics of the Populist racial agenda. Schools were always a combustible issue, because they were a space where the line between the masculine public sphere and the feminine private sphere was blurred. The presence of white women and children as teachers and pupils in schools, and the general absence of white men, meant that the presence of African Americans, either as pupils or teachers, immediately raised the specter of social equality in ways that the commingling of blacks and whites on public streets, in the workplace, or in political settings did not. The prospect of black trustees in charge of hiring, firing, or supervising white female teachers likewise posed unacceptable challenges to white racial orthodoxy. Having determined, then, that their pursuit of civil and political rights for African Americans required them to display a strict commitment against social equality, white Populists supported segregation in the public schools as staunchly as Democrats did. Unlike most Democrats, however, Populists' willingness to accord blacks the rights of civil and political citizenship meant that Populists did not need to subordinate blacks to whites in the more public aspects of education by denying black schools equal funding or by placing them under the direction of white trustees. This was a distinction not lost on African Americans, many of whom would abide segregation if it were separate but, in terms of funding and governance, truly equal.[37]

White Populists may have striven to establish their bona fides as opponents of social equality, but they never took the lead in championing segregationist bills in the 1895 legislature.[38] The most controversial of these measures was a bill calling for separate waiting rooms at railroad depots, introduced by Democrat J. L. Greer of Collin County, a former Confederate officer who had served under Stonewall Jackson and Robert E. Lee. The *Dallas Morning News* called the measure "one from which no beneficial result would have accrued" and speculated that "an overwhelming majority of the intelligent people of the state" would applaud its defeat, but in fact the bill enjoyed considerable support among Democrats. The *Southern Mercury* editorialized rather snidely that "Democrats don't want to mix up with the colored people in any capacity save as voters," but as long as Democrats from the heavily black counties could use African Americans' votes to maintain power, they were loath to antagonize them needlessly. Moreover, railroad companies opposed the bill because of the added expense of building and maintaining hundreds of new waiting rooms across the state, and they undoubtedly lobbied to defeat it. When this strange-bedfellows coalition of Black-Belt planters, pro-railroad conservatives, and Populists finally succeeded in bringing to the floor a motion that would kill the bill, Democrats divided evenly, but a bloc of fourteen Populists (out of seventeen voting) provided the margin by which the bill was defeated, fifty-five to forty-two. Certainly the Populists who voted against the bill must have wanted to avoid alienating black constituents, just as some Black-Belt Democrats did, but they also may have concluded that a railway waiting room was not like a schoolroom; white men would presumably always be close at hand in the waiting room, making it a space sufficiently public so as not to violate the taboo barring private social interaction between white women and black men.[39]

An even more striking example of the contrasting Populist and Democratic views concerning African Americans' public rights arose midway through the 1895 legislative session when Robert Lloyd Smith of Colorado County, one of two black Republicans in the House, introduced a resolution tendering the use of the House chamber for local African American citizens to hold a memorial service for the famed black leader Frederick Douglass, who had recently died. Not surprisingly, some Democrats opposed the idea from the start, but on a voice vote the House approved the resolution. This would have been the end of the matter, but three Populists, John A. O'Connor, T. J. Floyd, and W. B. Whitacre, demanded a roll-call vote, obviously wanting the printed record to reveal who had supported and who had opposed the measure. When the yeas and nays were taken, sixteen of eighteen Populists present had voted to allow the service. One of the two who opposed it, J. W. Carson of Lavaca County, fearing that his negative vote would be misconstrued, explained, "I vote 'no' because I voted no allowing the use of the hall for [evangelist Dwight] Moody's meetings, and because I voted no allowing the use of the hall for an inaugural ball, and as I wish to go on record as always voting for equal rights to all and special privileges to none." Evidently the Populists viewed use of the House chamber—a quintessentially public space—as a right of civil citizenship to which African Americans were entitled, much as they were entitled to equal use of a railway waiting room.[40]

We do not know if any white lawmakers attended the memorial service for Frederick Douglass in Austin, but as the preceding examples demonstrate, Populist support for racial segregation clearly did not constitute a knee-jerk desire to see African Americans discriminated against and humiliated in ways that would publicly underscore their subordination to whites. If traditional southern conceptions of white supremacy required black subordination to whites, the Populist determination that African Americans should be accorded the rights of civil citizenship meant that they should share an equal right to a public space like the capitol, even if they were to be consigned to a separate-but-equal status in the private sphere. As we have seen, the gray areas where the lines between public and private were unclear always complicated matters, as when they led Populists to support segregated schools but oppose segregated waiting rooms.

Thomas Nugent seems to have enunciated the standard Populist position on segregation. Nugent declared his support for segregation of the state prison system and other state-run institutions such as asylums, with the proviso that they be staffed and managed by Negroes. "Anything which helps to remove this controversy about so-called and impossible social equality is wise," he argued. But the Populist leader was always quick to note that he was "in favor of giving the negroes recognition in such positions under the state government

as they are able to fill, and in favor of their advancement." Other Populists followed Nugent's lead and took the same position. Nugent enjoyed a well-
deserved reputation as a humanitarian and a progressive thinker, and his
support for blacks holding responsible positions in the state bureaucracy certainly reinforced that reputation. But his clear support for segregated institutions and his comments about the "impossible social equality" of the races
underscore the Populists' dilemma over how to reconcile civil and political citizenship with social citizenship. It was easy to conclude, as one African American from San Antonio did, that Nugent was simply a hypocrite whose belief in
segregation appealed to "race prejudice" while his support for Negroes as officers of the government was "a bait for the unwary negro voter—it is a straddle."[41]

Few issues exposed the fault lines between civil and political citizenship on
one hand, and social citizenship on the other, as did the question of blacks
serving on juries. Few issues also evoked such strong emotions, and with
good reason. True, the courthouse was a public space, but within that space
juries mediated not just public disputes but also private ones; they decided
everything from business litigation to cases of rape and adultery. Furthermore, jury service, though a public act, placed jurors in fairly intimate physical contact with one another and necessitated debate and voting among
supposed equals. Because jury trials necessarily involved the promiscuous
mixing of the public and private spheres, it took particular courage for any
politician to advocate seating African Americans.

Yet in 1894, as Texas Populism neared its zenith, a few Populists did just
that. In a county convention in Houston, Harris County Populists narrowly
passed a resolution reading, "Whereas, We believe that all qualified citizens,
regardless of race or color, should have representation upon the juries of the
county, therefore be it resolved, that it is the sense of this convention that we
will support men for the various offices who will favor both white and colored
to serve on juries under their jurisdiction." In the Piney Woods town of Crockett that same year, a local Populist judge was said to have "stated openly in all
of his speeches that the jury commission should be constituted on political
lines and that the colored citizens should be put on the juries of the country."
Speaking at the People's Party county convention in Cherokee County, Populist editor and congressional nominee C. C. Bearden reportedly "advocated allowing negroes to sit on juries, a right which had been denied by the
democratic and republican parties alike."[42]

African Americans were usually the ones pressing local Populist organizations to move positively on the jury issue. Only once, though, did any Populist

official ever actually take action on the jury issue, and the episode speaks volumes about the racial environment in Texas in the 1890s and the limits of Populist racial liberalism. The episode began in October 1894 when the widely admired Populist sheriff of Nacogdoches County, Andrew Jackson Spradley, summoned five "intelligent and prominent" African Americans as potential jurors for the local state district court (plate 15). This act caused, in the words of the *Galveston Daily News*, "a profound sensation," because blacks had not served on Texas juries since Reconstruction. Spradley's precise motivations are difficult to divine. The press noted that "there had been a breeze of complaint from the colored voters as to their rights in this connection, and they had even tried to get the two leading political parties to declare themselves, but the question was dodged till Spradley precipitated it." It is probably no coincidence that John Rayner had just completed "a most glorious and successful canvass" of the county, reporting that he "broke up the democracy" and "painted despair on the cheeks of the county candidates." Rayner knew that he could count on Spradley's protection, and he proudly reported that "not an unkind word was said" to him during his time there. Rayner pronounced Spradley "the best sheriff in Texas" and declared him "brave as a lion." Whether or not Rayner had stirred up black voters to the point where they were demanding the right to serve on juries, Spradley's action soon put the county "in a political broil."[43]

Spradley later explained his motives in an open letter to the Galveston-Dallas *News*. He said that the whole affair had begun with a whispering campaign by local Democrats, who spread the false rumor in the black community that the Democratic Party had passed a law allowing African Americans to serve on juries, but that the Populist officials who controlled the government had refused to enforce the law. (In point of fact, no laws specifically barred blacks from juries.) According to Spradley, the Democratic dirty-tricks campaign went on to suggest to black voters that if they returned the Democrats to power in the county, black jurors would indeed be called. Spradley insisted that he then called the five black jurors because he wanted to see "if the democrats were sincere or fooling the negroes, and to test the practicability of them serving on the juries."[44]

Spradley's gambit placed the Democrats on the defensive. The jurors would be summoned, but they could be kept from actually being impaneled by the district attorney, a Democrat, who could simply strike them from the pool. Spradley may have assumed that this would happen, thus cementing the Populists' hold on the black vote while sparing the Populists the political fallout from whites for actually having impaneled blacks. However, the district attorney, W. M. Imboden, had a trick of his own up his sleeve: he planned to actually seat the black jurors. He knew that some of the whites in the jury pool were Populists, and he calculated that their presence would turn the tables on Spradley. "If they served with the negroes they would lose the vote of every respectable white man in their party," a Democratic editor later explained. "If they refused to sit, as they said they would, they would lose the negro vote." Either way, the tactic would "force the Populists in the most public way possible to declare their true position." If Spradley and the Populists were going to play a game of chicken with Democrats over the issue, it was a game the Democrats were prepared to play.[45]

Imboden's plan came to naught when defense lawyers apparently exercised *their* right to strike the five men from the jury pool. But with the issue now out in the open, local African Americans soon presented the Democratic district judge, in whose court future black jurors might serve, with a petition calling for blacks to "be recognized equally with the whites as to jury service in general." The judge responded, publishing an open letter in the local press denying their request and saying "in substance . . . that the colored man is not mentally and legally competent." The county chairman of the Democratic Party next weighed in with a public letter affirming "that we, as a party and as individuals, are utterly and unqualifiedly opposed to negroes serving as jurors in the courts of this county" and calling on the Populists to state their party's official position on the matter.[46]

At this juncture the African American leaders of Nacogdoches called an extraordinary public meeting to determine their community's course in the election, which was less than two weeks away. After calling the meeting to order, the chairman of the gathering lauded Spradley's actions as well as District Attorney Imboden's in being prepared to seat black jurors. Imboden immediately stepped forward and set the record straight, vowing that he had never supported the idea and that he did not want anyone to vote for him on the basis of a misunderstanding. "This is a white man's country," the Democrat reminded the crowd, "and the white man will always rule it." Jury service was "not a right, but a duty, a burden imposed on free citizens," he added, "a burden the colored man will never be called on to bear." Calls for the Populist county chair to definitively state the Third Party's position on the issue went unanswered, and in the election two weeks later every Populist in Nacogdoches County was replaced by a Democrat, including Sheriff Spradley, who lost by thirty-six votes—to his own brother. As far as we know, no other Populist official in Texas ever sought to seat a black juror, and whatever Spradley's true motives may have been, he got to spend the next two years as a private citizen. It seems clear, though, that the African American citizens of Nacogdoches County believed that Spradley had dealt fairly with them, if not in the jury controversy then in his day-to-day administration of justice in the county. With their support he was returned to office in 1896.[47]

If the African American citizens of Nacogdoches and other Texas locales exhibited a keen interest in the issue of jury service, it was for good reason: the justice system brutally discriminated against nonwhites. Blacks constituted less than 22 percent of the state's population, but they accounted for nearly half of the inmates in the state penitentiary. Because they were rarely able to afford a lawyer and often faced an assumption of guilt from white jurors, blacks' experiences with the judicial process were rarely satisfying and frequently devastating. Theft of a hog carried a prison term of two to four years, and once in the system, convicts could expect to be leased out to work on plantations, railroads, and other private enterprises where the conditions lacked even the minimal safeguards that had been present under slavery. Early on, Populists recognized the injustices inherent in the system and wrote planks into all of their state platforms calling for an end to convict leasing. Still, this was another issue where actions spoke louder than words, and in the 1895 legislature Populist representative John A. O'Connor of San Antonio introduced a bill that would thoroughly overhaul the system.[48]

O'Connor's proposed bill made it illegal for the penitentiary "to hire any convict to any person, firm, or corporation if suitable and profitable occupation can be found for such convict within the walls of the penitentiaries or on farms owned or leased by the state." It further provided that any profits derived from a prisoner's labor after paying for the expenses of his incarceration be equally divided between the inmate and his family, after his release. The bill was sent to the committee on penitentiaries, which subsequently tinkered with the wording, added a clause that prohibited the penitentiary from selling any of the goods it produced for less than a 10 percent profit, and then reported the bill back to the House with a favorable recommendation. But if O'Connor and his allies expected to finally be able to show a legislative victory to the voters, they were mistaken. The bill died on the Democratic speaker's desk, and meaningful prison reform would have to wait until the twentieth century.[49]

As badly as African Americans wanted to serve on juries and see the prison system reformed, these concerns paled in comparison with an even more urgent problem with the justice system—lynching. Mob violence against blacks, usually in retaliation for alleged assaults on white women, had been rampant since the 1880s. Although the frequency of lynching varied from year to year, a relatively new phenomenon, the so-called spectacle lynching in which crowds numbering in the thousands often hideously tortured and burned their victims, became alarmingly common in the 1890s. One of the most widely publicized of the era's spectacle lynchings, the execution of Henry Smith on the town square of Paris in northeast Texas before a crowd estimated at ten thousand, took place in early 1893, just weeks after the election. Governor James S. Hogg had spoken out against lynching during the campaign and offered a reward for the capture of lynchers, earning him the gratitude and votes of many black Texans. After the gruesome Paris lynching, in which relatives of the three-year-old girl allegedly murdered Smith by sadistically torturing him with a hot poker for fifty minutes before burning him alive, Hogg proposed antilynching legislation, a call that the legislature subsequently ignored. But Hogg's outspokenness on the issue placed pressure on politicians of all parties to respond to the atrocity. Most Democrats, including many Hogg allies, bitterly denounced the governor and defended the lynchers. Former US senator Samuel Bell Maxey, in whose hometown the lynching took place, defended the mob's actions, calling Smith's executioners men "who morally, socially, intellectually, are lovers of law and order," and speculated that "ninety-nine out of every hundred men in Texas will say of the execution of Smith, 'Served him right.'" In Washington a few weeks later to seek an appointment as United States attorney, prominent Democrat Jake Hodges, also from Paris and a childhood friend of Hogg, joked with Democratic president Grover Cleveland about the Smith lynching. As reported by the *Dallas Morning News,* Cleveland, on meeting Hodges, said, "'Now, I believe I have heard of you as the man who divided time [i.e., debated] with the negro who was burned at Paris, and then Mr. Hodges went on to state how he happened to be the chief orator of that occasion." The president then "laughed till his sides shook" as Hodges made the case for his federal appointment.[50]

People naturally wondered where Populists stood on the subject of lynching in general and the Paris outrage specifically. Although some prominent white Populists did denounce lynching, Thomas Nugent voiced what became, more or less by default, the party's position. It should be remembered that Nugent was no Negrophobe. Born to a Louisiana slaveholding family, as a young man he developed doubts about the institution of slavery, and in his later years he even suggested that in the immediate aftermath of the war "justice rather demanded that the slaves . . . ought to have been paid at least enough to start them in life." He mixed easily with his black neighbors and, as one observer claimed, never hesitated to shake hands with them "as if they were princes of royal blood." When he died in 1895, some two hundred African Americans attended his funeral in Stephenville. Commenting on the Paris lynching, Nugent, like every white politician, acknowledged the horrific nature of the initial crime, arguing that the people of Paris and the relatives of the murdered child were "scarcely to be regarded as responsible for their acts." Indeed, he theorized that the child's father must have been "bereft of reason" when he applied "the implements of torture to Smith's quivering flesh." But Nugent asked, "Does this justify the torturing of a human creature as an expiation for crime? Christianity can only make one reply to this question. No crime possible to human depravity can warrant a resort to refined cruelty in the infliction of punishment." If human passions were thus to be left unbridled, he argued, "it is easy to see that the foundation of our social and political system must soon give way." Nugent, perhaps in keeping with his Swedenborgian religious beliefs, seemed prepared to extend forgiveness and understanding to those responsible for the lynching. He expressed his "unaffected sorrow for the conditions that made both crime and execution possible." He felt less sympathy, though, for those who "at a distance from the place of execution and who witnessed none of its sickening details even now justify all that was done." Nugent wondered how ex-senator Samuel Bell Maxey could defend the lynching. He was sure that Maxey was "a member of a respectable Christian church," but he pointedly reminded his readers: "Christian people do not always remember the scriptural saying: 'Vengeance is mine, I will repay, saith the Lord.'"[51]

Nugent had kinder words for the man who had just defeated him for the governorship. "Gov. Hogg's message [in support of an antilynching law] was creditable to his humanity," he wrote. "It shows that he is an earnest, honest and courageous man." But Nugent also believed that Hogg was "strangely incautious and very often unwise." In the end, Nugent could not go along with Hogg's legislative proposal to arrest and punish lynchers, which in the case of the Paris lynching would have included the dead child's father. He branded the governor's bill as "extreme, born of the hot impulse of the moment, and essentially unwise and unjust," and he predicted—wrongly—that Hogg himself would later change his mind. (Hogg in fact laid the same proposal before the 1895 legislature, again with no success.) Nugent, who had now squandered an opportunity to stake out a bold position on human rights, ended his statement on a strangely vague note, saying, "Still, [Hogg's] recommendations will bear fruit and the final remedy will, I think, be found not in fierce legal retributions but in wholesome methods of prevention."[52]

What those methods of prevention might be, Nugent failed to say explicitly, but clearly he saw black uplift as a long-term project best enabled by improved education, the development of an African American leadership class in separate-but-equal black institutions, and above all, enactment of the Populist economic program, a rising tide that would lift all boats. His failure to join Hogg in supporting antilynching legislation may have sprung in part from political expediency; the Populist political outreach to African Americans had already rendered the party vulnerable to Democratic charges that Populists were too friendly toward blacks. Nugent was also pragmatic enough to know that a state antilynching law of the sort Hogg proposed would be impossible to enforce. (The rewards Hogg had already offered for the arrest of lynchers had always gone unclaimed, even when, as in Paris, the identities of lynchers were widely known.) But like almost all white Populists in the Lone Star State, Nugent also clung to the mistaken belief that the rights inherent in civil and political citizenship could be separated from those of social citizenship. The Populist concept of a public sphere where blacks could exercise political and civil rights required the strict maintenance of a private sphere where white supremacy would be guaranteed. When the two came into conflict, as they did when a black person allegedly committed the ultimate breach of the private sphere by raping, assaulting, or murdering a white person, there could be only one outcome: maintaining white supremacy in the private sphere trumped civil rights for blacks in the public sphere, even if the civil right in question was something as fundamental to the American system as the right of an accused criminal to due process. Nugent's equivocation on the issue starkly exposed the limits of Populist racial liberalism.

～

Viewed with the benefit of hindsight, the Populist vision of a society where African Americans would exercise political and civil rights in public but be denied equality in private was fatally flawed. The Populists' opponents understood the Othello problem all too well; every time Populists denied or made light of the Democrats' charges that black political power would invite social equality, some real-world event proved the Populists wrong—they found themselves defending segregated schools or refusing to seat blacks on a jury or excusing a lynching, because to do otherwise would be to invite the very social equality that they claimed to abhor. Such acts ultimately made a mockery of their well-intentioned, even noble, efforts to forge an honorable political coalition across racial lines.

But to say that Populists' liberalism was flawed or incomplete—which it indisputably was—or that they were "products of their time," unable and unwilling to rise above the white privilege that undergirded daily life in their society, is to miss an important historical point. Trying to do the right thing mattered, even when it was grossly inadequate. Putting into office men who would treat African Americans with dignity, listen to their problems, and contend for their votes did make a difference. African Americans learned this in places like Nacogdoches and Grimes Counties, where Populist sheriffs with a sense of decency and fair play, backed by Populist county administrations and a strong biracial coalition in the rank and file, affected the lives of black citizens in materially important, positive ways.

That Populists, black and white, had reason for optimism about their future together as citizens is borne out by a curious scene that unfolded at the regular monthly meeting of the Dallas Populist Club in January 1894. The night was cold, and those members of the club, black and white, who had braved the weather to come hear Third-Party speechmaking "were concentrated in the immediate vicinity of the stove" at Labor Hall in the Deep Ellum neighborhood just east of downtown Dallas. One of the speakers that night was Charles Shelley Hughes, a young Virginian who had recently moved to the city and had just launched a new Populist newspaper, the *Argus*. As Hughes, who fancied himself a poet as well as a journalist, began to warm up the crowd with his oration, applause broke out, whereupon Melvin Wade caught the spirit and yelled, "Talk, boy" to Hughes. If a black man addressing a white man as "boy" raised any eyebrows among the assembled Populists, the newspaper account of the incident gave no indication of it. Instead, as the *Morning News* reported it, Hughes turned to Wade and remarked that "he could shake the hand of that grand representative of his race, the Fred Douglass of the populist club—Melvin Wade—and he meant it." Hughes's expression of racial solidarity brought "loud applause," especially from Melvin Wade, and the white editor finished his remarks by exhorting his fellow Populists to "stand together like men and brothers."[53]

The men (and as far as we know, the attendees *were* all men) gathered around the stove that night in Dallas were not representative Texas Populists; they all were urban dwellers, much more likely to be exposed to different experiences and new ideas than their rural counterparts. Their long association with one another in the Populist Club seems to have bred an easy familiarity among the participants, something likely rare for a mixed-race gathering. Meeting in a union hall, the club had always had a strong organized-labor flavor to it, and Populists who came to the movement from the labor side had always stood a better chance of overcoming racial barriers because of their understanding of class and the need for solidarity it bred. (In the decades after the People's Revolt, union shops would be one of the principal seedbeds in which the twentieth-century civil rights movement would germinate.) But with all of these caveats, the anecdote nevertheless underscores that Populism held the potential to point the way down a road different than the one that was ultimately taken. With no crystal ball to reveal the grim realities of the Jim Crow, one-party future that lay a few years ahead, the Populists in Dallas that night could, with some justification, look forward to a better, more tolerant day where race was concerned.

6 · The Election of 1894

I see more in this movement than the mere organization of a party. . . . I see
more in it than mere reforms in policy. . . . Greater than all party platforms,
greater than all mere party movements, greater than all mere success or
defeat . . . is this concourse that is gathered together in a spirit of brotherhood for the restoration of liberty and for the protection of life and property.
—Thomas L. Nugent, 1894

Judge T. L. Nugent is speaking in the opera house to a large number of his
deluded followers, who ought to be picking cotton instead of listening to his
harangue.
—*McKinney Examiner*, 1894

The 1892 elections did not bring victory to the People's Party statewide, but
Texas Populists could point to several noteworthy achievements resulting from
the contest. Thomas Nugent's 108,483 votes for governor, though only a quarter of all ballots cast, constituted a highly respectable showing for a party in
its first election, and it provided a solid base from which to build for 1894.
Nugent had carried 61 of Texas's 248 counties. In most of those counties, and in
some where Nugent did not win, Populist county officials had been swept into
office as well. The newly elected sheriffs, county judges, commissioners, clerks,
constables, and other officials could begin to show citizens how Populist government at the grass roots would differ from the corrupt Democratic "rings"
and "bosses." Having Populists in positions of political power also meant that
the party would possess some patronage to dispense, a factor vital to its continuing growth. Citizens could now see that the People's Party truly might offer a viable alternative to the old parties.

Much depended on what the old parties—particularly the Democrats—did in the coming election cycle. Although some had predicted in 1892 that the split in the state Democratic Party would lead to a Populist victory that year, that had not been the case. Populists comforted themselves by claiming that the exact opposite had happened: they believed that voters who otherwise voted Populist "scratched" Nugent's name from the top of their tickets and voted for Hogg, either because they truly believed in his brand of moderate reform or because they feared that a vote for Nugent would result in the election of the conservative Clark. To support such claims, observers repeatedly cited instances where, despite Nugent's personal popularity, Populist candidates for local office ran far ahead of Nugent in their counties. Accordingly, many Populists and Democrats alike believed that the Populists would fare much better against a reunified Democratic Party in 1894. In that scenario, Hogg would have served his two terms as governor and would not be on the ticket to attract wavering Populists. A reunified Democratic Party would have to be conservative enough to bring the Clarkites back into the fold, further alienating reform-minded voters. In short, Populists—and many worried Democrats—predicted that the Democrats would return to their conservative roots, and that with the pretender Hogg gone from the scene, Texans desirous of true reform would flock to the People's Party banner.

Yet, the idea that reformers ultimately would become Populists by default carried with it troubling implications for the party's success. If a voter cast a Populist ballot merely because it was the only alternative to the reactionary policies of the Democrats, then that voter might be quick to desert the party if the Democrats could convince him that it had again embraced reform. One writer to the *Southern Mercury* said as much when he explained, "The way is clear for the democrats to bring the ship of state back to its moorings. If it is done we can console ourselves with the fact that we have forced them to do right." Even the *Mercury*'s editor, Milton Park, presumably speaking for his Alliance readership, continued to maintain that "the Farmers Alliance doesn't care a fig which political party engrafts its demands into law. It was organized to secure needed reforms, not to build up political parties, nor to put certain men in office." At the end of 1892, as Park wrote those words, he was convinced that the People's Party was the best vehicle for securing Alliance demands. But he hastened to add that if the party "should, in the future, refuse to indorse the demands of the order, the membership will be in a position to support any party that does." Such utterances were hardly ringing pronouncements of party loyalty.

Nevertheless, by the end of 1892 the party had achieved the critically important goal of creating its own political identity and culture. Populism inherited
some of this culture from the Alliance, the Knights of Labor, and previous independent political movements, but it coalesced into something new during
the 1892 campaign and flowered in the years thereafter. The rallies and camp
meetings and party newspapers certainly played instrumental roles in the creation of the Populist movement culture, as did the grassroots organizing of
Populist clubs. The party's success at creating an us-against-them mentality
likewise contributed to the party's esprit de corps. Populist editors and speakers rarely failed to remind the party faithful that Populism was "a movement
of the people against the parasites," which led some contemporaries to view
them as cranks and some latter-day observers to highlight Populist paranoia
and conspiracy theories. But whatever animated the movement culture of Texas
Populism, its adherents knew they had created something special—something
that went beyond mere anger over their poverty or resentment of elites. Thomas
Nugent captured its essence in his acceptance speech before the 1894 state
convention, when he said, "I see more in this movement than the mere organization of a party. I see vastly more than a mere organization to capture certain offices from the dominant party. I see more in it than mere reforms in
policy that have grown upon this country through the mal-administration of
officers of the old parties. . . . . Greater than all party platforms, greater than
all mere party movements, greater than all mere success or defeat, if I may use
that term, is this concourse that is gathered together in a spirit of brotherhood
for the restoration of liberty and for the protection of life and property. Personally, I have but little respect for mere partyism. It is not because we want office
that we make a fight, but because of the questions involved." Despite their frequent declarations that Populism was based on reason and dispassionate analysis of the issues, for the true believers who made up the party's base, Populism
became an emotional as well as an intellectual and political undertaking. Populists' political identity carried over into their everyday lives, sometimes in unexpected ways. One day in 1893 a Populist fruit-tree salesman strolled into a
sheriff's office in the Central Texas town of Cameron to see if he could make a
sale. Asked by the Democratic sheriff if he was peddling Third Party or Democratic trees, the salesman "replied that if the quality of the fruit was affected by
the agent that it was third party to the core," an answer that led to a "cursing
and shoving match" and the man being thrown out of the sheriff's office.[1]

Populism divided families, literally pitting brother against brother, sometimes cordially, often not. The list of prominent tandems of Democratic and

Populist brothers includes longtime Democratic leader and US ambassador Alexander Watkins Terrell and his brother Joe, nominated for Tarrant County judge on the Third Party ticket; Populist stalwart Harry Tracy and his brother Nat, a Democratic state representative; William H. Lockett of Abilene, who ran for attorney general as a Populist, and his brother Osburn, who "failed to show up" for a scheduled debate with his brother during the 1894 campaign. But perhaps the most dramatic case of a divided political family involved the Cain brothers, Robert and Andrew, from the East Texas hamlet of Alba in Wood County. In 1892 the brothers ran against each other for a seat in the legislature, and when the votes were counted, Populist Robert had vanquished Democrat Andrew by a total of seven votes.[2] Robert Cain took his seat in the legislature, only to have his brother officially contest the results. It fell to the House Committee on Elections to hear the case, which revolved around the typical charges of fraud and voting irregularities; in this instance, testimony revealed that men who had not resided in the county for the required length of time illegally voted, and that the superintendent of the county poor farm had forced its residents to vote against their will. As the proceedings unfolded, the press reported that "the brothers are in earnest and hardly speak to each other." Ultimately the legislature's investigation resulted in a sixteen-vote increase in Robert's vote, and after much partisan wrangling, the Populist was permitted to keep his seat. When news of Robert's triumph reached his home district, jubilant Populists in the brothers' hometown of Alba celebrated with "an anvil shooting and grand to do," a scene that was repeated in Emory, Golden, Mineola, and other towns in the district.[3]

Meanwhile, during that same 1892 election, out in the Hill Country Sam Ealy Johnson received the nomination for the legislature, only to find that local Democrats had nominated his son-in-law Clarence W. Martin. Interviewed about the race seventy years later, Sam's grandson Lyndon told a journalist about the stories he had heard when he was growing up: "Sam and Clarence would ride together to a speaking, Sam would cuss his daughter's husband as 'a reactionary so-and-so' and Clarence would cuss Sam as a wild radical, but then they would happily 'get back on the double buggy on the front seat and ride to the next speaking.'" LBJ's memory notwithstanding, the extant newspapers call into question just how "happy" the contest actually was. Clarence Martin was reported in the Democratic press to be "a hot debater" who "bears down heavy in telling the truth." The *San Antonio Express* noted that "his father-in-law is one of his opponents, and it has been said that he [Martin] generally burns him [Johnson] hard." Two weeks before the election, at a speech in a dance hall at a place called Twin Sisters in Blanco County, Martin delivered a stump speech to what was said to be a mostly Populist crowd. After being hooted down by hecklers, he got in a shoving match with some bystanders, whereupon a sixteen-year-old boy pulled a knife and stabbed him. Martin "was carried out in an insensible condition," but the wound proved relatively superficial. When Martin resumed campaigning five days before the election, he could not resist getting in one last dig at Johnson. "My father-in-law has gone home," he told the press. "He is a slim man and one good lick might finish him." Martin went on to win the race, and Johnson retired from electoral politics. In the case of Sam Johnson and Clarence Martin, however, time apparently healed all wounds, whether inflicted by knife or by words, for in their old age, Sam and his wife Eliza moved in with the Martins, spending their last years in the house that their grandson would someday transform into the Texas White House.[4]

Populism had become a part of the fabric of people's lives, and in some cases their devotion to the cause also followed them to the grave. Witness the case of William McEwin, a "well known farmer" from Lamar County in northeast Texas who had seen military service in both the Republic of Texas army and the US Army during the Mexican War. When McEwin died at age seventy-five at the end of 1893, "it was his dying request that he be buried by the Farmers' alliance and the people's party and it was complied with." We know nothing about the actual funeral service or burial rites, but if the eulogies included mention of the Subtreasury Plan or the Omaha Platform, it seems safe to assume that farmer McEwin's spirit was looking on with approval.[5]

As Populism in Texas attracted ever-greater numbers of adherents, events on the national stage simultaneously strengthened the party's appeal and contributed to the growing disillusionment with the old parties. Economic conditions in Texas and the nation, especially for farmers, had been deteriorating steadily for twenty years as cotton and other commodity prices fell and credit grew ever tighter. Voters restored Democrat Grover Cleveland to the White House in 1892 and elected Democratic majorities in both houses of Congress, but by the time the new administration took office the economy was already teetering on the brink of collapse. The stock market crashed in May, resulting in widespread financial panic. By mid-August unemployment stood at perhaps two million people, almost 15 percent of the labor force. The bankruptcy of the Northern Pacific Railroad in May was followed by those of the Erie, the Union Pacific, and the Atchison, Topeka and Santa Fe by year's end. Some five hundred banks and sixteen hundred other businesses joined the railroads in bankruptcy.[6]

President Cleveland blamed the country's economic woes on the Sherman Silver Purchase Act of 1890, which, in an effort by the Republican Harrison administration to placate the western wing of his party, had required the government to purchase 4.5 million ounces of silver bullion each month. The government purchased the bullion with Treasury notes redeemable in either gold or silver, and most investors who bought the notes redeemed them in gold, which led to a rapid and catastrophic depletion of the government's gold reserves. This run on the nation's gold, Cleveland believed, had triggered the depression, and during the summer and fall of 1893 he fought a long and difficult battle to have the law repealed. On the first of November Cleveland signed the repeal, and the US government effectively, if not formally, returned to the gold standard.[7]

Repeal of the Sherman Act, however, failed to bring economic recovery, and by 1894 the president and his policies were nearly universally discredited, even in the eyes of dyed-in-the-wool Democrats. In New York, Pennsylvania, Massachusetts, Iowa, Ohio, Rhode Island, Michigan, and Connecticut, Republicans scored sweeping victories in off-year state and local elections. In Texas, where the Republicans were weak and Cleveland's hard-money policies found support only among a minority of white Democrats, the depression held the promise of sending tens of thousands of new recruits into the ranks of the People's Party.[8]

Populists were quick to associate the depression with the old parties. In a newspaper interview, San Antonio Populist Theodore J. McMinn noted that "the country is fairly a-tremble with the tramp of the unemployed; thousands are gathering into hungry and unmanageable groups; want and starvation is driving them into the absurdity of a march upon the capital; the cities are swarming with the destitute, who feed at the soup houses, and helpless women are driven to barter their souls for bread to feed their little children." Meanwhile, he complained, Democrats in Washington, "like old Nero . . . fiddle away while the conflagration spreads." Evan Jones, the former president of both the state and national Farmers' Alliances and a Populist congressional candidate in 1892, wrote a poignant letter to the *Texas Advance* telling of his encounter with two hundred homeless men in a Houston soup kitchen. "As sure as there is a God in Heaven today, unless relief is secured for the poor of our land speedily, riot and revolution will surely result," a shaken Jones declared. "Human nature cannot and will not stand it."[9]

Talk of vigilante action or armed revolt began to make its way into the press. Following the 1892 elections, a Greenville Populist vowed, "We are going to get out of bondage. How will we get out? We must vote out or shoot out—which shall we do? Let every man go to the polls and cast his vote, and if we are de-frauded then let the shout be 'To arms! Strike for your altars and your fires! For God and native land.'" A few weeks later the *Dallas Morning News* reported from "an entirely reliable source" that an "industrial league" was being orga-nized throughout the south and west "for the purpose of enforcing a free bal-lot and a fair count vi et armis [with force and arms] if necessary." The league allegedly originated in districts of Alabama and Georgia where the Democrats had stolen elections from the Populists, and now there were said to be fifty lodges of the organization in Texas. "Of one thing be assured: There will be fair elections or bloodshed two years from now," the story darkly warned.[10]

An unsigned editorial in the *Texas Advance*, likely penned by its editor-publisher Harry Tracy, captured the grim mood of many Populists at the be-ginning of 1894:

> Probably no darker prospect has dawned upon the American people since the republic was established. Certainly there has never been more squa-lor, want, and misery among those who have created the wealth of the republic and fought its battles.
>
> Plutocracy is enthroned, and the voice of the people is no longer heard in the councils of the nation. Avarice and greed hold full sway, and many of the weak and helpless have about lost their right to "life, liberty, and the pursuit of happiness." Strong men, who are willing to earn an hon-est living, are becoming beggars and tramps, and the outraged and dis-inherited millions are losing hope in our political institutions. Discontent is rampant, while the darkness of the future is blinding many to the phi-losophy of reason.[11]

As economic conditions grew more dire and Democratic administrations in Washington and Austin seemed either oblivious to the crisis or impotent to do anything about it, defections from the Democrats accelerated. In 1894 Maj. William M. "Buck" Walton, a former slaveholder, Confederate officer, and state attorney general who had been a member of the 1892 Clark campaign execu-tive committee, publicly announced he was joining the People's Party. Al-though Populists certainly cheered Walton's conversion, they could not have taken too much satisfaction from the published explanation he gave. For twenty years, he noted, Democrats at the national level had advocated silver coinage and low tariffs, while Republicans stood for the gold standard and high tar-iffs. But now both of the old parties supported tariffs, and neither favored sil-ver: "They stand in all substantial and important particulars in principles and policies of government on well nigh the same plane." Walton's lengthy statement focused almost entirely on silver, and he declared that it was "time for men who think alike on the silver question to act together." Speaking only briefly of Populism, he said, "I know there are some vagaries advocated by the party, but they can be in due time eliminated." Of course, what Walton considered "vagaries"—demands such as the Subtreasury Plan and government ownership of the railroads—most dedicated Populists viewed as the heart and soul of the party's platform. The People's Party could win over disillusioned Democrats like Walton on the strength of the free silver issue, but such men clearly lacked a strong ideological commitment to Populism. Walton spoke more frankly than most recent converts, making it clear that his allegiance to the People's Party was provisional and possibly temporary: "Until [the Democratic Party] returns to its old landmarks, low tariff[s] and free silver, I shall vote on all political questions with the populist party," he stated.[12]

Other defecting Democrats echoed Walton's sentiments. Denton County newspaper editor R. M. Collins, also a former Clark executive committeeman, though admitting that "it was a very trying thing for me to abandon the party in whose service I have spent the greater years of my young manhood," now asserted "that the difference that once existed between the two old parties had vanished—they are two only in name." Collins hoped that "the better element of the old parties"—a list that included Nebraska Democratic congressman William Jennings Bryan—would "come together on common ground where all can find a sure footing." Such people could "form a party under some other name. . . . It may be 'silver democrats,' 'Jeffersonian democrats,' 'reform democrats,' 'constitutional democrats,' 'populists,' 'peoples party' or any other name, just so there is a clean-cut platform that means what it says and says what it means." Like Walton and Collins, Joe Terrell, a former mayor of Fort Worth and brother of a prominent Democrat, justified his conversion to Populism simply on his belief that if the "free and unlimited coinage of silver . . . is ever to be consummated it will be only by reason of the triumph of the third party." Such pronouncements constituted a slender reed on which to rest the party's prospects, but Populists could hardly afford to impose tests for ideological purity when they needed every vote they could get.[13]

At the same time, though, the party also continued to recruit new supporters from outside the political mainstream. And those with politically heterodox views tended to become more reliable and committed Populists than did those who came to Populism strictly because of the silver issue. One such convert was fifty-seven-year-old James Garland Hardwick Buck of Hill County.

A Mississippian who had fought in the Confederate army, Buck attended the University of Alabama and had taught school for over twenty years when he was appointed postmaster of Hillsboro by Grover Cleveland. In 1892 he ran successfully for tax assessor of Hill County on the Democratic ticket, only to announce his conversion to Populism in the spring of 1894. A biographical sketch published in 1892 noted that Buck, a Baptist, was "exceedingly liberal in his opinions relative to the subjects of science and religion." He maintained "varied and voluminous" reading habits, and it was said that "he is perhaps more frequently appealed to for information on doubtful points than any citizen of the community." His intellectual curiosity apparently brought the writings of Henry George to his attention, and when Buck announced his conversion to Populism, he proudly proclaimed, "I am in all its lengths and breadths and depths a single taxer." Other Populists, including Thomas Nugent, privately admired elements of George's radical land-reform theory, but few advocated it as passionately or as publicly as Buck, and the party carefully sidestepped the issue in its platforms. Nevertheless, Buck's admiration for the Single Tax led him to embrace the many other progressive elements of the Populist platform, and after casting his lot with the People's Party, he never turned back. Populists might not embrace the Single Tax now, Buck explained, "but the populists, the prohibitionists, the Knights of Labor, the homeless man, the landless and the laboring man are alike, the victims of the bond-holding plutocrat, the protectionist republican and the silver demonetizing democrat. For purpose of common defense against a common foe they should unite on grounds common to them all." When one Democratic newspaper editor sarcastically complained that the Populist movement had "developed many scribbling professors who write after very imperfect copies," he probably had men like Buck in mind. But while the opposition might make light of the way that Populism was attracting freethinkers like Buck, no committed Democrat could deny that the ranks of the Populists were expanding, and that the Third Party was likely to be much more competitive in 1894.[14]

Planning for the 1894 campaign had begun as soon as the results from the 1892 contest were known. In December 1892, Stump Ashby, Henry Bentley, and Thomas Nugent issued a public call for county chairmen to hold mass meetings in every county in January to begin the long process of organizing for the coming campaign. They publicly emphasized the paramount importance of two tasks: first, "carrying on the educational work," which encompassed the full range of activities from holding camp meetings to distributing campaign literature to sponsoring lecturers to publishing newspapers, and second, translating Populist support into an electoral victory by preventing fraud on election day.

Crucial to the first of these tasks—the party's ongoing "educational work"— was the growth and success of the reform press. In 1892 Populist newspapers in Texas had numbered approximately twenty, but by May 1893 the *Mercury* reported that there were fifty-three Populist weeklies in operation. By the time of the 1894 elections the party claimed more than 125 papers statewide, boasting that most were "doing tolerably well and spreading the gospel in large gobs every week." The appetite for Populist journalism was so great in the party stronghold of Weatherford in Parker County that the town actually sup- ported two Populist papers for a while in 1894, the *Appeal* and the *Leader*. The ranks of the Populist papers would eventually include a Spanish-language paper, *El Regidor* in San Antonio, and two German-language sheets, the *Forschritt* in San Antonio and *Der Deutsche Anzeiger,* published by E. O. Meitzen in Hallettsville.[15]

As for the second priority outlined in their letter to the party faithful— preventing fraud— the party's leaders urged Populists to petition their county commissioners "to appoint a fair proportion of the presiding judges of elec- tions from our ranks, or at least to appoint judges whose fairness and sense of justice will not permit them to refuse us participation in the management of elections hereafter." It was a telling measure of the voter-fraud problem that it received such prominent mention in the initial organizing effort a full two years before the next election.[16]

Having identified voter education and fair elections as the party's top stra- tegic priorities, Ashby, Bentley, and Nugent candidly went on to note the two greatest tactical failures in the party's ongoing efforts to forge a winning elec- toral coalition. The first was the fact that the Populist coalition in 1892 was "composed almost entirely of white men," although the leaders gave "full rec- ognition of the fidelity and devotion of that comparatively small number of col- ored men, who, with rare courage, stood with us in the fight for principle." The other area that the party leaders singled out for attention was the party's failure to attract urban laborers in sufficient numbers. "Our people crowded up to the front in the late campaign, upbearing the banner of labor's cause," the open letter asserted, "but, alas! they did not always find the city laborer where the shadow of that banner fell upon the onrushing host." Nevertheless, the leaders struck a hopeful note, predicting that the urban workingman "will be there when the next battle is joined; and then farmer and artisan linked together in the ties of true fraternity will stand side by side in the perilous places, to deliver the last shot and wield the last blow in defense of the common cause." It would remain for Populists to devise plans for winning both the labor and African American vote, but at least they recognized the need to reach out to these groups.[17]

Populist efforts to court the labor vote suffered a setback in early 1894 when the *Mercury* and the *Advance,* the state organs of the Farmers' Alliance and the People's Party, respectively, became embroiled in a bitter dispute with the Dallas chapter of the American Typographical Union. The two papers, both managed and edited by Milton Park, always struggled to remain solvent, and in April, citing an inability to pay the union wage scale to his printers, Park fired the printers and replaced them with nonunion workers. What followed was an unsavory public battle, with each side claiming that the other had failed to bargain in good faith. The union called for a boycott of the papers, declaring them "rat offices" and filing protests with the local Trades Council, the state Federation of Labor, the Knights of Labor, the Dallas Populist Club, and other bodies. The state press reported that Park was "having coals of fire heaped upon his head" over the issue, and the public-relations nightmare persisted when the Populist state convention met in June. At that gathering, a committee appointed by the party disclaimed having jurisdiction over the matter and passed the buck to the state Reform Press Association, one member of which speculated that "the People's party will be forced to wash its hands of official organs" because it could "not afford to fight labor organizations." When the party punted on the question, the union complained that the party's leadership had given "organized labor the grand 'razzle dazzle,'" and union officials vowed to keep fighting. Meanwhile, the Farmers' Alliance had a member of its state executive committee, C. A. McMeans, conduct an official investigation, which resulted in an exoneration of Park. Needless to say, the union viewed this as a whitewash, and the controversy continued. The Dallas Populist Club weighed in on the issue, passing resolutions "regretting the condition of affairs" at the papers and calling on the two sides to "submit all differences to arbitration." Finally, in mid-July, the *Mercury* and *Advance* reached a settlement with the printers and agreed to rehire union workers, although the terms were not disclosed.[18]

How much the dispute damaged Populist efforts to gain the support of organized labor cannot be stated with any precision, but it could not have been helpful. In September the *Advance* bought out the *Mercury,* merging the two papers under the older and better-known *Mercury* nameplate. The merger was a cost-saving measure that also signaled a final abandonment of any pretense that the Alliance and the People's Party were independent entities, as the *Mercury* would now be the official state organ of both the Alliance and the party. Populists continued to discuss the need for a new daily paper, and in early 1895 all of the Populist members of the legislature joined with Nugent, Bentley, and other party leaders in calling for the establishment of such a paper. Nothing ever came of the plan, though the instigators went as far as to explore the possible purchase of the *Austin Statesman* or the *Waco News*. Certainly, a statewide daily would have been a valuable political asset if the party could have afforded it, but the persistent talk about a new state organ—talk that always seemed to originate with Populist political leaders—was likely a sign of dissatisfaction with Milton Park's leadership at the *Mercury*. The brouhaha with the printers' union was only the latest in a series of impolitic actions that the irascible Georgian had taken over the years, and it would not be the last.[19]

Coming as it did in the spring and summer before the fall elections of 1894, the timing of the flap with the typographical union was unfortunate, but much larger strategic questions faced the party leadership as the campaign got under way in earnest. Chief among these was the question of fusion. A common strategy in nineteenth-century American politics, fusion involved the forging of coalitions across party lines. The term encompassed a wide range of practices. Sometimes it involved two parties agreeing on a joint slate of candidates, some drawn from one party and some from another, and having that slate of candidates run as a formal fusion ticket. Sometimes the same basic tactic took place under the name of the dominant party but with the second party still being allowed to name certain candidates. Such arrangements were prevalent in an era before primary elections were commonplace and when conventions, with their famous smoke-filled rooms, still determined parties' nominees. In yet another form of fusion, one party might refrain entirely from placing a candidate or even an entire ticket in the field, with an implicit understanding that that party's voters would support the other party's ticket, or sometimes with the first party explicitly instructing its voters to do so. This is what had happened in 1892, when the Texas Republican Party, under the leadership of Norris Wright Cuney, had thrown its support behind conservative Democrat George Clark for governor. In Gilded-Age Texas, where the Republican party was consigned to more or less permanent minority-party status, and where various independent and third-party movements proliferated, fusion was almost always a possibility, but it carried with it a certain odor of disrespectability if not outright dishonor. One might always invite adherents of another party to unilaterally support one's own party without a sacrifice of principle, but promising to support another party's candidates in some sort of quid pro quo strictly to win an election smacked of corruption, a charge that self-described reformers were particularly loath to invite. When politicians did support fusion, they usually tried to frame it as something like "an honorable union of reform forces" arrayed against "a common enemy," but even then it carried sizable political risks. The *Mercury* explained the problem succinctly in an 1893 editorial: "The word fusion, when used in a partisan political sense, implies that the fusionists have made mutual sacrifices of principles to secure office, which they realize they are unable to secure otherwise, and thus admitting by their action that offices are more important than the support of principles. Fusion in itself may be harmless, but the effect upon the minds of the voters is quite different. . . . Just as soon as they [the rank and file] see the leaders fusing with outside organizations, they take in the situation and become disgusted at the betrayal of principle for office, not only quit the ranks of the party themselves, but become its most active enemies. We fail to note a reform movement that has not split upon this 'fusion' rock. . . . To go into a fusion is to invite disaster, swift and certain."[20]

Speaking on behalf of Texas Populists in 1894, party chairman Stump Ashby unequivocally opposed any sort of fusion at the statewide level. In his New Year's message to the party faithful, Ashby grandiloquently proclaimed that "our ranks are being rapidly filled with the conservative, justice-loving people of our State," and he exhorted "the editor in his sanctum, the speaker on the rostrum, the farmer at his plow, the workman at his bench, and all those noble men and women who have espoused the cause of reform" to "press onward . . . in the cause of justice." But he ended his address with a pointed message on fusion, suggesting "to the populists of Texas that they entertain not for a moment a proposition to fuse with any political party."[21]

Things were different, though, at the local level. Many Populists could see no harm in cutting deals with Republicans, disaffected Democratic factions, or other third parties or interest groups to elect county officials or, in some cases, legislative or judicial officers. As the *Mercury* explained, "Populists, independent democrats and republicans can get together on a good county ticket without any sacrifice of principle, and should do it, as those offices and their fees are being used to perpetuate the power of the tax-raising Austin syndicate and the do-nothing Washington delegation."[22]

Accordingly, the state party largely left local leaders alone to decide for themselves whether to pursue fusion deals. In Black-Belt Montgomery County north of Houston, cooperation between Populists and Republicans proceeded smoothly, and the two parties "completed the nomination of a fusion ticket for county officers, about equally dividing the offices between the said parties." Sometimes, though, they either saw no need to fuse, or opted not to. In nearby Robertson County, where Rayner, Peters, and Hanna had done so much organizing for the Populists, the Republicans simply endorsed the entire Populist county ticket, an action that was undoubtedly repeated in other counties. Just to the north in Grimes County, where a vibrant biracial Populist coalition led by sheriff candidate Garrett Scott was taking shape, party members likewise believed they could win the county outright; therefore, when they met in the spring of 1894 to choose delegates to the state convention, they "refused to entertain the ideal of fusion with the republicans or any other party." Their resoluteness paid off, and in August when local parties nominated candidates for county offices, the Republicans unilaterally endorsed half of the Populist ticket. But the Populist determination to avoid fusion proved incomplete; as it turned out, both the Republicans *and* the Populists agreed to support William H. Taylor, "a Cleveland democrat," for the office of magistrate in Precinct One. How much flak they caught for this partial surrender of principles is unknown, but it demonstrates that even in the highly partisan atmosphere of Populist-era Texas, local politics was still often more about the man than the party.[23]

Fusion always involved difficult and delicate negotiations, often behind closed doors. In Hopkins County in northeast Texas, the home county of Cyclone Davis, the Populists held their county convention and nominated candidates for district clerk, county clerk, tax assessor, tax collector, treasurer, and state representative. But they balked at making nominations for the important offices of county judge and county attorney. The press could only speculate as to what was afoot: "The supposition is that a fusion has been arranged between the republicans and populists on these offices." Downstate in Fayette County where German, Czech, and African American Republicans were numerous, Republican and Populist leaders held "a quiet conference" to discuss a fusion deal in the Tenth Congressional District race, but the press could only report that "nothing was accomplished" because "some of the populists insist on making a straight fight."[24]

When it came to fusion, rumors alone could be damaging. In Freestone County in the spring of 1894, John B. Rayner had been "circulating among the colored people" in the two weeks prior to the Populist county nominating convention. The Democratic press reported that he had offered to let the local black Republicans name the candidates for state representative and two of the county's commissioner seats in exchange for Republican support for the balance of the Populist ticket, a rumor the Populist editor indignantly declared "emphatically false." Rayner himself had to backpedal, and the Democrats then charged that the Populists had offered to pass a resolution favoring black jury service to "smooth things over" with the Republicans. Ultimately the main thing the Populists gained from the affair was a fair amount of bad press and ill will from some of the local Republicans.[25]

If fusion was a tricky maneuver, by the fall of 1894 the *Dallas Morning News* could nevertheless report that "in many counties and legislative districts there have been fusions with the republicans, and through these the populists expect to win counties that would ordinarily go democratic." Moreover, although the fusion arrangements would almost certainly not result in Populist control of the state legislature, Populists did expect to claim enough seats in Austin "to wield a strong influence upon legislation." They intended to "labor industriously to that end."[26]

It remained to be seen what issues and themes the party would emphasize in the upcoming election. The *Dallas Morning News,* which usually had good sources, reported in April 1894 that "the main fight of the populists this year will be on members of the legislature." But the goal was not strictly to influence state-level policy. Instead, "the silver question will be injected into these local contests and the administration will be bitterly assailed," with the goal of electing "a sufficient number of members of the legislature to dictate the election of a demo-populist if not a straight populist to the United States senate." Because the legislative races held such importance in the Populist strategy, "local leaders all over the state have been advised to lay aside personal preferences, nominate the biggest and strongest man in the party for the legislature and lend all of their energies to the election of the nominees. If necessary, county offices will be sacrificed wherever the success of legislative nominees can be assured by such action."[27]

Obviously, candidates for local, statewide, or congressional offices would have disagreed that the legislative races were the linchpin of the party's strategy in Texas, and in some locales these other races undoubtedly took center stage. But to the extent that the *Morning News's* reporting was correct, it sent the unmistakable message that many Populists, including many prominent leaders, were prepared to emphasize the financial issue—and specifically silver—over all others. Doctrinaire Populists continued to stress that the Omaha Platform's three broad reform categories of finance, transportation, and land were like the legs of a three-legged stool; take away one and the stool could not stand. Moreover, many who did assign primacy to the financial issue continually reminded everyone who would listen that silver was but one minor element of the broader Populist financial program, with greenbackism the only real solution to the money question. But even as early as 1893, with the major parties having made silver such a point of contention, Populists found themselves drawn into the debate, and many either earnestly came to believe in its importance or saw it as the issue by which the People's Party would win elections, thus opening the door to the enactment of other Populist demands. The siren song of silver, then, was being heard long before the so-called Battle of the Standards reached its climax in the presidential election of 1896.

Even those with deep roots in the Alliance and a thorough knowledge of Populist demands found it easy to overemphasize silver. Thomas B. King, Thomas Nugent's former law partner and the Populist chairman of Erath County, told local party members in 1893 that the Populists were "making the financial issue the one paramount to all others" in the upcoming canvass, inviting all "who are opposed to Cleveland's policy, of a single gold standard . . . and who favor free and unlimited coinage of silver" to join the Populists. King added that Populists also favored "the issue of a national currency so that the ratio of labor and property to money shall be equalized," but his nod to greenbacks came almost as an afterthought. If silver could be so heavily emphasized by a Populist as well-versed and prominent as King, who was soon to run for (and win) the office of county judge in his home county, it comes as no surprise that the rank and file tended to raise the issue to an unwarranted level of importance.[28]

By 1893 silver occupied a place of prominence in the popular culture of Populism, despite the best efforts of many party leaders to downplay the issue. At conventions, rallies, and club meetings, supporters carried banners bearing slogans such as "Silver Is the Money for the People" and "Silver Was Stabled in the House of Its Friends" (a reference to the recent repeal of the Sherman Silver Purchase Act), and they enthusiastically sang campaign songs with titles like "Silver 16 to 1." So concerned were Populist hard-liners that they frequently used the reform press to warn readers about the dangers of becoming overly preoccupied with silver. As early as the spring of 1893 the *Southern Mercury* was editorializing against "making the discussion of the silver question paramount to everything else," warning, "This is wrong." Although changing the nation's monetary policy to allow the free coinage of silver would help, the *Mercury* declared—correctly—that "if every ounce of bullion, both silver and gold, in the United States was coined into money, it would not afford a

tithe of the circulating medium required by the toilers of this country." The
agitation of the silver issue was "intended to divert the mind of the people from
the main issues," which were "more money—less taxes—government ownership of railroads, telegraphs, and telephones; [and] a graduated income tax."
But the editorial reminded readers that "most of all, we want the sub-treasury
plan, or 'something better,' and the men or party who think we can be silenced
by free silver alone, are doomed to disappointment. Don't forget that free silver is not a cure for the ills that now afflict us."[29]

At the opposite end of the spectrum from federal monetary policy were
strictly local concerns, which might sound mundane but could sometimes resonate with voters in ways that federal issues could not. The two major parties
were what one scholar has called "machines within machines, elaborate interlocking combinations of local, state, county, and national organizations." While
national leaders formulated their parties' positions on issues such as tariffs
and monetary policy, and state leaders concerned themselves with matters
such as who would run for governor or senator, much of the real action took
place at the county level. It was there that most of the patronage of southern
politics was dispensed: jobs for supporters from whence most real political
power flowed. Orchestrating all this was a small group of party elites, disproportionately composed of lawyers, bankers, and merchants in the county seats
and railroad junctions, men whose affluence, business connections, available
leisure time, and proximity to the courthouse enabled them to exercise influence far beyond their numbers. By the 1890s these "rings," "machines,"
"gangs," or "courthouse cliques" had become a major grievance of farmers and
others who found the local political system essentially closed to them. Populists were quick to tap into this disgruntlement and offer to open up local politics to "the people."[30]

The *Mercury* succinctly laid out the problem in 1891 at the very start of the
Populist revolt: "It has been the rule, by common consent, that the tillers of
the soil, the industrialist, the artisan and the mechanic should attend strictly
to these respective callings, and leave matters of law and state to courthouse
cliques, party rings and plutocratic bosses." This had been the case for so long
now that "the hand of a relentless fate" had dug "an almost impassable gulf"
between ordinary citizens and the heritage of democracy "bequeathed them
by the fathers of our constitution." A year later, in his first campaign for governor, Thomas Nugent returned to this theme. "The 'rule of the ring' has been
supreme in this republic of ours for the past thirty years," he asserted, "and
he who can manipulate most skillfully the political machine secures the prizes

of public life, the offices and spoils." Nugent lamented that "great men no longer lead the old parties, because great men are men of soul, of humanity, of
genius, of inspiration. They never are machine men."[31]

Condemnation of bossism became a central element in Populist rhetoric.
In 1893 the *Mercury* elaborated on how the county "rings" traditionally operated: "Not more that [than] five years ago the politics, the reading, the thinking, the legislation of the country was entrusted to the 'Kunnels,' 'Majahs,'
'Jedges,' and that class of social and political parasites known now as 'bosses'
and 'ward bummers.' Like birds of the air they made their annual migration.
Just before the election they sweep down upon the 'dear people' and exhibit
the greatest of solicitude for their welfare. The babies are praised, the mothers
complimented for their skill in the culinary art, and the old man treated with
'nickle' cigars or four-bit whisky. All done for the sole purpose of getting support. After the election these same vampires, whether successful or not, seek
other fields for their talents."[32]

But Populism promised to change all that, and that promise appealed tremendously to voters who had so long felt disfranchised by the system. When
Harry Tracy opened the 1892 campaign in Ellis County south of Dallas, the
Populist press trumpeted that the speech "gave birth to a new party which
threatens the overthrow of bossism in Ellis county." The exuberant correspondent crowed that "if an earthquake had struck this county the bosses would
have felt no worse." Likewise, when Huntsville Populists planned "a grand barbecue" to kick off the campaign there, the Alliancefolk hosting the event
claimed that the celebration would mark the date when "'bossism' [was] forever killed in Walker county." In the small Central Texas town of Rockdale,
the local Populist editor waged what he called "the fight against the court house
official syndicate." Even in Dallas, the state's largest city, Populists complained
that "the city government in all its departments is run and ruled by rings,"
prompting members of the local Populist club to support the nomination of a
nonpartisan "citizens' ticket" in upcoming municipal elections.[33]

The local "ring" had its counterpart at the state level, and Populists found
plenty to criticize there as well. The Populist *McKinney Democrat* charged that
"less than one dozen men in this state make the democratic platforms, nominate its candidates for office, shape the party's policies, administer the affairs
of state and dispense the state patronage." Barnett Gibbs, a former Democratic
lieutenant governor who became a late convert to Populism, spelled out how
the "bossism of the Austin ring" rigged the primaries (in the counties that
had them) to ensure the nomination of its preferred candidates. "In nearly

every county in Texas these democratic fixers have forced the candidates for county offices to go into a primary and carry certain men for delegates and state nomination or not be nominated themselves, no matter how great their merits as county officers," he explained. Gibbs, who possessed an insider's knowledge of the system, complained that it did not "let the sovereign democratic voter have anything but Hobson's choice in this primary. Every state officer will owe his nomination to the ring of delegates, and not to the democrats who are expected to vote the ticket in November." Another prominent politician who declared his independence from the Democratic Party, Frank W. Ball of Fort Worth, complained of how the Democrats in the legislature "allowed themselves to be led off by a gang of paid lobbyists who were backed up and furnished with finances by cliques and rings of office holders who were then and are now making a moderate fortune out of each year's salary," thus failing to enact much-needed reforms of county government. For those Texans who might not appreciate all of the finer points of the Omaha Platform, returning some semblance of democracy and public accountability to state and local government by ousting the corrupt "rings" might be reason enough to vote Populist. The twentieth-century adage that "all politics is local" was never entirely true in the 1890s or today, but Populists counted on the widespread disgust with local and state politics to motivate voters.[34]

Traditionally in Texas some campaigning for a fall election began informally in the late spring but did not commence in earnest until the summertime party state conventions nominated state tickets. Those traditions did not hold true for the Populists in the crucial year of 1894. When Charles Macune, the controversial former national president of the Farmers' Alliance, arrived home in Texas from Washington, D.C., in December 1893 to make a series of political speeches, the *Dallas Morning News* asked an unnamed informant whether this signaled the opening of the 1894 Populist campaign. The informant was not sure (and Texas Populists hastened to distance themselves from Macune), but he tellingly remarked that Populists "campaign all the time." A few weeks later state committeeman E. S. Peters confirmed this assessment. "We have been steadily at work since the [1892] election," he noted. "Our speakers have been always in the field. The work has never lagged. In season and out of season, through seed time and harvest we have carried on an unremitting campaign of education." The *Morning News* explained that the party's "plan for an early and aggressive campaign is based on the experience in the campaign of 1892 when they conducted an intermittent attack on the enemy till the last few weeks and then commenced to heat things up in good style." Populist leaders were said to believe "that this hot and cold method weakened the confidence of their following and accounts mainly for the large defections to the Hogg democracy. So this year they propose to go in early and stay late and keep firing away all the time."[35]

Indeed, work at the grassroots level had never ceased. The summer of 1893 had seen Populist camp meetings held throughout the state, and even during the following winter the work had continued. A precinct organizer in Fannin County reported in January 1894 that he had recently organized four Populist clubs in his precinct, and he explained his modus operandi: "The way I manage the matter is to go to the school houses and with the permission of the teachers I make a short talk to the children and get up a meeting through them at night." When asked what sort of "talk" he made to the children, he replied that he gave "a good moral talk" about "the evils of drinking, then talk the use of tobacco and the evils thereof, and wind up with a few wholesome stories in which I always succeed in leaving the youngsters in a good humor and full of laughter. Then I tell them I will speak at night and to tell their parents all to come out as I had something good to tell them." The organizer claimed that this method "beat all the advertising you could do so far as getting a crowd out to hear you speak," and that in using it he had "never failed to have a good crowd and organize a club." He swore that he "never saw such enthusiasm in my life" and that the Populists had the Democrats "badly licked in this county."[36]

Enthusiasm ran high when party chairman Stump Ashby gaveled the state nominating convention to order on the morning of June 20 in Waco. With more than twelve hundred credentialed delegates in attendance, it was said to be the largest political convention ever held in Texas. The gathering took place in Padgitt's Park under a mammoth tent with seating for four thousand people, provided by the Waco Commercial Club. Surveying the throng, one observer noted that "most of the delegates were old men, many of them being up in the seventies, with frosty hair and snowy beard." Not surprisingly, as in previous conventions "a great majority" of them were said to be "farmers, laborers, and mechanics." The irrepressible Melvin Wade also commented on the composition of the convention, quipping, "I notice here an absence of 'representative citizens'—the tight breeches lawyer, the banker and the other 'leading men' usually seen in conventions. But I see lots of what I call the boardin' bosses— the farmers, the men who furnish what feeds the world." But as the convention got under way one correspondent noted that they also had "among them professional men and dealers in merchandise, and taken as a whole they are dressed well and appear to be in good circumstances." Moreover, by the second day of the convention the reporter acknowledged that "some kids have come in, and they are progressive and wide-awake, as prosperous a lot of young-sters as you will find in a day's ride." "The truth," he admitted, "is the dele-gates in this convention compose a fine body of men. They come from every section of Texas—from the panhandle to the Gulf—and they are representa-tives of the sections from whence they hail. Many of them are above the aver-age intelligence, too." For two full days and one very late night, the delegates sat on "hard, rough benches without backs," enduring "boiling hot" summer temperatures and perspiring "until their cotton shirts were wet about the col-lar and of a decidedly brownish hue." The veteran reporter was struck by the difference between this convention and those of the Democrats and Republi-cans. "They got down to their knitting and stuck to it to the finish," he noted. "They were not to be found in the hotel corridors and on the street corners. They boasted in their speeches that they were on a business bent and did not have to preserve their party harmony in alcohol. When out of their seats in the tent the majority of them were at their dollar-per-day boarding houses."[37]

The convention opened with party chairman and former Methodist minis-ter Stump Ashby leading the delegates in singing the old Protestant hymn "Nearer My God to Thee," followed by a prayer. As was tradition at political conventions, most of the first day was spent with speeches from party heavy-weights, while credentials were vetted and committees met behind closed doors. The old agrarian warhorse, seventy-six-year-old John "Rutabaga" John-son, who had served in the 1875 state constitutional convention with Thomas Nugent, opened the oratory with a strong speech in which, among other things, he "especially implored them to do what they can for the emancipation of woman," reminding delegates that "woman bore the greatest burdens of pov-erty and distress and they were the ones who most needed a government where all could have an equal chance in the race of life." He was followed by such luminaries as William Lamb, John Wilson Biard, Cyclone Davis, Marion Mar-tin, and Melvin Wade.[38]

The high point of the convention came on the second day, when Biard placed Thomas L. Nugent's name in nomination for governor. Among those taking the podium to second the nomination was John Rayner. Invoking a theme that resonated with the white delegates, Rayner, who was now the acknowledged leader of black Populists in Texas, declared that "the white man of the south is the negroes' first, best, and firmest friend." He urged the delegates, "Nom-inate Nugent and the negro will be as faithful to your flag as he was to your wives and children when you were fighting the battles of your country." This allusion to faithful slaves during the Civil War, while of highly dubious historical accuracy, nonetheless brought down a hail of "loud applause," and after several other seconding speeches Nugent was "nominated by a rising vote amid a perfect storm of applause." Former lieutenant governor Marion Martin likewise received unanimous support for his old office, and although several of the lesser statewide offices required balloting to choose between more than one potential nominee, overall the nominations proceeded "almost if not entirely without incident."[39]

Much of the harmony and good feelings can be traced to the leadership of Stump Ashby. The *Morning News,* though unsympathetic to Populism, unabashedly characterized the party chairman as "a wonderful man" who, "untiring and diligent . . . held those 1200 men under his absolute control." Whatever he might have lacked as a parliamentarian, he possessed "the patience of Job," never losing his temper: "While ruling the boys with a rod of iron, so to speak, he does it in such a kindly manner that they have no desire to incur his slightest displeasure. He is the head and front of the populist party, and it would be hard to find a third party man who would not support him for anything he wanted."[40]

Ashby's skills were put to the test in debate over the platform. Some delegates had wanted simply to re-adopt the Omaha Platform and the 1892 state platform, but others wanted to make various additions or deletions. New planks designed to appeal to African Americans—most notably one calling for black schools to be placed under the direction of black trustees—and others intended to strengthen the party's position vis-à-vis organized labor were relatively uncontroversial. Such, however, was not the case with a proposed plank declaring the party in favor of "local self government and the enjoyment by the individual of his natural rights to the greatest extent compatible with good society." Everyone know what this innocuous-sounding plank referred to; as the *Morning News* pithily put it, "personal liberty is a more refined name for Sunday beer." Along with women's rights, prohibition was the great social issue with which Populists struggled throughout the party's existence. Twenty-first-century liberals tend to look on the banning of alcohol as illiberal moralizing by religious prudes, not to mention an unenforceable public policy that promotes organized crime. But those liberals' counterparts of the 1890s could support prohibition because they saw the liquor trade as an amoral industry that exploited people's weaknesses and contributed to all manner of social ills: crime, unemployment, domestic abuse, and poor public health, to name but a few. Moreover, it contributed signally to the violent and predatory masculinity that Populists generally rejected. Lacking the benefit of the hindsight provided by the nation's failed experiment with Prohibition between 1920 and 1933, reformers who supported prohibition in the 1890s had many sound arguments on their side. At the same time, however, other Populists took the libertarian position shared by most modern liberals, contending that one part of society should not coercively impose its religious or moral standards on another part, and that the decision to imbibe was a matter of personal freedom. Populists disagreed over prohibition in much the same way that today's liberals can be found on both sides of various drug-legalization debates; liberalism has always been a tradition rich and capacious enough to be divided against itself.[41]

Sure enough, the debate over prohibition proved to be "the biggest fight of the convention," and the adoption of the "local self government" plank, which committed the party to the existing local-option solution rather than a state-wide ban on alcohol, was said to have marked "an era in the history of populism in Texas." There was no question that many Populists, including many leaders of the party, were prohibitionists. They also knew that their failure to take a firmer stand *against* prohibition had "cost them thousands of votes among the Germans and other citizens of foreign extraction." But with the explosive growth of Populism beyond its old-guard Alliance core, prohibition was now "not nearly so dear to the heart of the populists as a party as it was two years ago." Younger members in particular, realizing "that it takes votes to win," struggled to secure the anti-prohibition plank, and though it was a hard fight, the *Morning News* noted that its supporters were "young and full of vigor and can last longer than the old fellows." Whatever the role of realpolitik may have been in the formulation of the liquor plank, in the end, the convention's official commitment to "the enjoyment by the individual of his natural rights to the greatest extent compatible with good society" stands as a prime example of very modern-sounding Populist liberalism.[42]

No aspect of the convention invited more comment than the role played by African Americans and the party's handling of the race question. Rayner served on the platform committee and was elected to the state executive committee, and Melvin Wade brought down the house with one of his characteristic humorous speeches. An unspecified number of African Americans attended as delegates, and the press reported that they were "intelligent representatives of their race" who manifested "deep interest" in the proceedings and "were well equipped with argument and leaders among their people." Repeatedly throughout the conclave black speakers took the podium to give speeches. "It was noted, too," according to the *Morning News*, "that they were extended every courtesy by their Anglo-Saxon brethren and encouraged to take a prominent part in the deliberations." Remarking on "the absence of the bigotry and intolerance which usually characterizes the movements of new political organizations," the press marveled at how "negro and white man, ex-slave and ex-master, from the same chairs gave thanks that the barriers of race prejudice have been smashed and that hereafter at least in Texas all men of whatever political conviction can vote according to their judgment and not according to color, race or previous condition of servitude." It came as little wonder that the *Morning News* pronounced the convention "one of the most remarkable political gatherings ever witnessed in the state."[43]

Populists had watched the Democrats with intense interest for the past several months. In March the state executive committees of the two warring Democratic factions had met in Dallas and negotiated a "harmony" agreement that officially reunited the party, using the 1892 national platform as a basis for that unity. On the all-important financial issue, that platform had adopted a conservative silver position, agreeing in principle with a bimetallic monetary system but supporting silver coinage only on a limited basis—essentially the system that had been in place for most of the previous two decades. Of course, as president since 1893 Grover Cleveland had abandoned silver altogether, but the 1892 platform seemed to offer a middle ground that could provide worried Texas Democrats the fig leaf they needed to heal the rift in the state party. A Third-Party editor in Bryan voiced a common Populist understanding of the "harmony" meeting when he wrote that "the farce was finally consummated at Dallas last month, by which the people were to be handed over to the expected candidates of this present year for state offices, just as the Roman crown was put up to the highest bidder by the soldiery in the last days of the empire."[44]

As expected, Populists for the most part welcomed Democratic "harmony." In 1892 they had thought that the division of the Democrats into the Hogg and Clark factions would spell victory for Nugent and the Populists, but this had not been the case. The two tickets instead had given both conservative and progressive Democrats a choice on the ballot that allowed them to stay in the party. Now the Populists' reasoning seemed to be that disaffected progressive Democrats would abandon a state party that had sold out to its conservative wing, sending thousands of free-silver Democrats into the arms of the People's Party. As Milton Park of the *Southern Mercury* spun it, "Harmony don't scare us. . . . We will get 65,000 republicans and 40,000 Hogg men who believe in our platform and have belonged to us all the time."[45]

By the time the Democratic state convention met in July, three viable candidates had emerged: senior statesman John H. Reagan, who championed free silver; Congressman S. W. T. Lanham, the conservative gold-standard candidate; and state attorney general Charles Culberson, who, under the clever management of his campaign manager Edward House, had essentially taken the middle ground on silver. The fact that national monetary policy—an issue over which a state governor has virtually no influence—continued to define gubernatorial candidates says much about the power of the monetary issue in American politics in the 1890s. But it is also generally true that Democrats who took the most conservative position on monetary policy also tended to oppose most other reform measures, so candidates' stances on the money question often served as a sort of proxy for their positions on the many other reform issues of the day.

The enigmatic "Colonel" House's wily management played out masterfully at the Democratic state convention. First, Culberson's forces joined with Reagan's to repeal the traditional two-thirds rule for nominations. Next the platform committee wrote the conservative silver plank that echoed that of the 1892 national platform, forcing the free-silverite Reagan to withdraw. Culberson then defeated the conservative Lanham on the first ballot to gain the nomination. The *Southern Mercury* gave an unflattering account of how the Culberson campaign engineered its victory by manipulating the rules, saying that "Mr. Culberson's gang of criminal lawyers, village pettifoggers, damage suit attorneys and eviction barristers ran the convention to suit themselves." Clearly Populists would have preferred to run against the goldbug Lanham, but they also believed that the straddling, uncharismatic Culberson would prove beatable. As the campaign heated up in the fall and Culberson began to speak glowingly about free silver despite his party's conservative platform, the *Mercury* asked, "How can Culberson look a democrat in the face, while deliberately repudiating their platform; or even [look at] a populist, when he knows that every populist in the state realizes that he and the Hogg contingent are basely false to every principle set forth by their party?" It was a fair question, but Culberson and House knew that their chances of defeating the Populists might well hinge on their ability to be all things to all Democrats.[46]

With a seemingly vulnerable candidate at the top of the opposing state ticket, an economy at rock bottom, a thoroughly discredited national Democratic administration to run against, and a far clearer and more comprehensive campaign strategy than two years earlier, the Populist campaign commenced in earnest. Populists knew that they could probably count on the support of a majority of the state's white farmers. At the state convention the party had committed itself to serious pursuit of the African American and German vote. The other significant bloc that needed courting was the urban labor vote. After the 1892 defeat, the Populist central campaign committee had acknowledged the party's failure to forge a coalition of rural and urban laborers. As a consequence, in 1892 the Populists had polled "a very small per cent" of that vote, and recognizing their "mistake in not missionizing the towns," they now vowed "to do all they can to rectify past errors by a strong invasion of the cities from now till the end of the campaign." In September Milton Park of the *Mercury* announced that Thomas Nugent would soon speak in Dallas, Fort Worth, San Antonio, Galveston, "and other labor centers." The People's Party, he declared, was "going before the laboring men of the cities. We are going to show them who are their friends. We are going to show them who represents the wage worker and the common field hand in this fight and we are going to get their votes." Populists believed that workingmen were "profoundly dissatisfied with the ninth and tenth planks" of the Democratic state platform, which forbade union shops and called for "the suppression of lawlessness"—a veiled reference to putting down strikes. "Wherever laboring organizations are strong," the *Morning News* reported, "the populists are going to send their speakers." By Stump Ashby's calculation, if Populists could poll half the vote in the labor strongholds of Dallas, Fort Worth, and Galveston, and if Houston, where organized labor and Populism were both weak, "would give anything," the Populists could win. (San Antonio, Ashby dismissively quipped, might as well "go and join Mexico.")[47]

The Populist platform adopted in Waco had retained the liberal, prolabor planks from previous platforms, with the only minor change being wording that exempted agricultural and domestic labor from the operation of the party's proposed eight-hour-workday law. Farmers argued that the seasonal nature of farm work made such a law impractical, a position that was not entirely without merit, but of course there was also a strongly racialized component to the argument: a large proportion of agricultural and domestic workers were people of color. Not surprisingly, Democrats charged the Populists with hypocrisy on the issue, and some Populists agreed with them. The party, however, counted on its editors and speakers to counteract such charges, and they made special efforts during the campaign to enlist and utilize men with ties to organized labor, who emphasized the liberality of the party's labor planks. The debate over whether to include farm and domestic labor in workday-length laws reappeared at the national level in virtually identical form during the New Deal, when Congress debated the Fair Labor Standards Act. The outcome, to the misery of farm and domestic workers, was the same. Populists in the 1890s, like their liberal successors in the 1930s, understood that compromise, even on issues that cut against progressive principle, was sometimes necessary to keep progress moving forward.[48]

The labor agenda continued to be pushed, primarily by the Knights of Labor. Although on the decline in many states, the Knights was still the preeminent labor organization in the Lone Star State. Never exclusively an urban working-man's union, the Knights allowed farmers to join, and in Texas there was considerable overlap in membership between the Knights and the Farmers' Alliance. The two groups had cooperated during the Great Southwest Strike of 1886, and indeed the Alliance could trace many of its demands back to the Knights' platforms of the 1870s. Numerous high-profile Populists were, or had been, members of the Knights, including state party secretary Thomas Gaines of Comanche, whose sudden death in 1894 robbed the party of one of its ablest leaders. Others, such as Stump Ashby and Jerome Kearby, had been outspoken supporters of the Knights during the tense days of the Great Southwest Strike. Barnett Gibbs, though a late convert to Populism, gained the lasting thanks of Knights for his pro bono defense of strikers in federal court in the aftermath of that strike.[49]

Despite their connections with the Knights and their support of organized labor, none of the aforementioned leaders really came to Populism directly from the labor movement. Three leading Texas Populists, however, did: Melvin Wade of Dallas, William E. "Bill" Farmer of Mineola, and John "Johnnie" Dwyer of Galveston. In 1894 the party was hoping that these union men and others like them would enable the People's Party to achieve its long-cherished goal of creating a true coalition of rural and urban "producers." Wade, of course, was the well-known leader of the black community in Dallas, and his conversion to Populism made him important not just as an African American but also as a veteran trade unionist and prominent Knight of Labor in the party's ranks. In 1886 the *Dallas Morning News* described Farmer, who held the office of master workman for Knights District Assembly 78, as "radical to the root in his opinions" but also "above the average in intelligence and prudence." He ran for Congress as a Greenbacker in 1888 and was an early and vocal advocate of Populism, serving as one of Texas's delegates to the 1892 St. Louis convention that officially created the People's Party. A fixture at Texas Populist conventions and meetings, he received the party's nomination for the Third Congressional District in 1896 and after the defeat of Populism went on to become a leading Texas socialist.[50]

But perhaps the most intriguing of the state's labor-Populists was Johnnie Dwyer of Galveston. Born and educated in Dublin, Ireland, he immigrated to Galveston in 1880 at the age of thirty and took a job as a laborer on the Mallory steamship line's wharf. By 1886 he had risen to the post of secretary of the Knights' sprawling District Assembly 78, serving under Bill Farmer. He emerged as a spokesman for Galveston Knights when longshoremen went on strike to protest pay cuts by the Mallory line, a strike and subsequent boycott that helped to set the stage for the massive Great Southwest Strike against the Jay Gould railroad network. Possessing "a combination of native wit, personal magnetism, and considerable learning," Johnnie Dwyer had a knack for politics. In 1893 he was serving on the legislative committee of the Texas Federation of Labor and rising rapidly through the ranks of the People's Party. The following year the Populist convention at Waco appointed him to one of the two at-large seats on the state executive committee, alongside African American leader John B. Rayner. Galveston Populists soon nominated him for the state legislature, and in September he shared the speaker's podium with Governor Hogg at Galveston's Labor Day festivities. When a state labor convention met in Fort Worth in late September, Dwyer played a leading role in making it for "all intents and purposes a populist convention"—a task made easier by the Cleveland administration's recent violent suppression of the celebrated Pullman Strike in Illinois. After the convention the *Morning News* groused that "the action of the state labor convention of Monday last in practically indorsing the various demands and reforms advocated by the populists has given the leaders great confidence in their success and the claim is now freely made that Judge Nugent will poll 200,000 votes in the pending campaign."[51]

The city of Fort Worth was a logical place to hold a labor convention, because along with Dwyer's Galveston, it boasted probably the most active organized labor movement of any Texas city. And in 1894, Fort Worth stood as a model for Populists who might want to forge a viable coalition with urban laborers. In early July, Tarrant County Populists held their county convention and invited representatives of all the local labor organizations. As a price for their active support, the Populists agreed to let the unions select a portion of the ticket, whereupon the Federation of Labor put forward a member of the Brotherhood of Locomotive Firemen for district clerk; a member of the typographical union for state representative; a member of the machinists' union for constable; a member of the American Railway Union for justice of the peace; and several others, including the candidate for sheriff, who were said to belong to the Farmers' Alliance, the Knights of Labor, or other labor organizations. "The populists granted the organized labor of the city all they requested," the press reported, "and the result is a harmonious and brotherly feeling between the man at the plow and the boy on the train, at the case and in the shop, that augurs no good for the [Democratic Party]."[52]

Despite official Democratic "harmony," developments such as the budding coalition between Populism and organized labor created intense anxiety among Democrats, as evidenced by the measures they resorted to in the last weeks of the campaign. Of course, demagoguery and ridicule were nothing new to Texas politics, and Democrats held no monopoly on them. But in 1894 the Democrats seemingly raised these practices to a fine art. "The populists claim that it is their mission to save the country," wrote one editor from the Lamar County hamlet of Blossom. "They have doubtless heard that Rome was once saved by the cackling of geese, and concluded that by a parity of reasoning this country may be saved by the braying of the paternal ancestor of a mule." This sort of comment was standard fare, but sometimes editors and politicians crossed the line and evoked true outrage. For example, when Thomas Nugent spoke at the McKinney opera house a week before the election to "a large number of his deluded followers" (as the local Democratic paper put it), the editor opined that the Populists in attendance "ought to be picking cotton instead of listening to his harangue." The local Populist editor responded with a large headline that read "AN INSULT" and accused his Democratic counterpart of being "void of every principle of manhood, of human feeling and christian charity": "How would the gentleman . . . like to see his own dear wife and little ones bending their backs by HIS side, picking cotton from early morn until darkness comes to relieve their tired frames! How would he like to sit at a meagre meal with a family half clad, gazing into the sunburnt wrinkled features of a wife, whose health is impaired, whose hopes are dimmed by the ravages of avarice and greed! How would he like to gaze upon a number of his own offspring who ought to be in the school room, but are kept in the 'cotton patch,' the victims of ignorance! These conditions are in existence and the *Examiner* is heartless enough to deny it."[53]

Not surprisingly, the Democrats' hardball tactics went well beyond rhetoric; they were also prepared to use their actual authority as the party in power to suppress Populism. One Populist congressional candidate complained of "the blacklisting of railroad men and other employes, whereby, in many instances, useful and deserving men are kept out of employment and their innocent families plunged into want and distress" because of their political opinions. From Huntsville a Populist reported that state penitentiary officials had "discharged all guards and employes who assert their fealty to the people's party" and "that all guards are required to sign a pledge to support the democratic ticket or be removed" from their posts.[54]

As in 1892, the Populists' relative poverty placed them at a serious disadvantage. With a month to go before the election, party chairman Stump Ashby was reported to be "badly in need of the necessary funds with which to manage a state campaign, and it is said that $250 will cover the sum total of all contributions in this direction to date. Thus far the expense incurred has been largely borne by a few citizens in this county, including Mr. Ashby." But what they lacked in financial resources, the Populists made up for in enthusiasm. Crowds at party rallies in the waning days of the campaign were massive. In late September Thomas Nugent published a letter in the *Mercury* stating that he could not physically fill all of the invitations that he had received to speak at Populist gatherings. In hotly contested elections, such as the congressional race in northeast Texas between Democrat Joe Bailey and Populist Uriah Browder, a typical crowd for a joint debate drew an audience of four to six thousand spectators. An election-week rally in Paris featuring Cyclone Davis and several prominent Democrats drew a crowd "estimated conservatively at 10,000."[55]

Populist optimism ran high, as it had done all year. "The populist who is not sanguine at all times and under all circumstances is yet to be found," one rural Democratic editor observed a month before the election. The week of the election, Thomas Nugent, who had steadfastly refused to make predictions, was said to be wearing an "air of confidence" and claiming that "if the populists stand firm and vote solidly on Tuesday he will in no wise be surprised at his election." Stump Ashby was even less circumspect, telling a reporter, "Boy, you little dream how much strength we have gained within the last two years. There has almost been a landslide to the populist party."[56]

~

Election day, November 6, dawned with clear skies and pleasant temperatures across the entire vast extent of the Lone Star State. Turnout shattered all previous records for a nonpresidential year and nearly equaled the all-time record from 1892, when there was not only a presidential election but also the hotly contested Hogg-Clark-Nugent race for governor. As the returns trickled in, Populists maintained their optimism, despite early indications that their party had fallen well short in statewide races. The November 8 *Southern Mercury* led with the headline "Well Done, Texans! The Populist Flag Waves Proudly Over the Wreck," boasting that the party's vote had almost doubled since 1892, "despite the stupendous frauds and the campaign of falsehood and deception" conducted by the Democrats. Congressional races in eight districts were too close to call, and the *Mercury* claimed that the gubernatorial race was still "in doubt." When all the votes were finally counted, though, Populist hopes at the statewide and congressional levels were dashed. Nugent lost to Democrat Culberson by a vote of 207,167 to 152,731. Nugent's vote had not doubled as the *Mercury* predicted, but it *had* grown by nearly 50,000 votes over 1892. Culberson won the governor's office with 49 percent of the overall vote, a sobering tally for a supposedly unified Democratic Party. (The Republican nominee polled 54,520 votes, and the balance went to minor-party candidates.)[57]

For many Populists, the outcome of congressional races was even more disappointing, if only because so many of the races were so close. The party's greatest hope had rested with the popular and charismatic attorney Jerome Kearby, running for Congress in the Sixth District, which included Dallas and surrounding counties. Running with heavy labor and African American support in his home city of Dallas, Kearby lost to Democratic incumbent Jo Abbot by fewer than four hundred votes out of more than 40,000 cast. In the Eighth District of west-central Texas—a district that ran from Fort Worth southwestward through the old Alliance strongholds of the Cross Timbers region—Populist Charles H. Jenkins lost to incumbent C. K. Bell, 16,480 to 16,104. In the sprawling Thirteenth District (popularly known as the "Jumbo District"), which reached from just west of Fort Worth to El Paso in the west and included the entire Texas Panhandle, Populist D. B. Gilliland lost to Democrat J. V. Cockrell by a vote of 13,697 to 13,321. In the Fourth District of northeast Texas, Cyclone Davis lost by a margin of 15,873 to 14,515. In four other districts, Populists ran races nearly as competitive as these.[58]

In the state legislative races, which had been a major focus of the Populist campaign strategy, the party elected twenty-two members of the lower house and two state senators. These were not enough to pass any legislation on their own, but with a Democratic Party so factionalized, they were sufficient to give the Third Party the balance of power on many votes. In the new legislature that would convene in January 1895, the Populists would so often join forces with progressive Democrats that conservatives derisively began to refer to the progressive Democrats in the legislature as "assistant Populists." Throughout the state, Populists won local races, with the Third Party sweeping dozens of counties.[59]

Despite the lack of victories at the statewide and congressional levels, the Populists could take considerable satisfaction in their progress. In 1892 the party had appealed primarily to small farmers who had been thrust into the market economy but who found their economic independence either threatened or actually vanishing. Statistical analysis reveals that in 1894 the People's Party significantly broadened its appeal, attracting not only many Alliancemen who had previously stood by Jim Hogg on the Railroad Commission issue but also sizable numbers of silver Democrats disgusted with the conservatism of both the state and national Democratic parties on the monetary issue. Almost exclusively rural in 1892, the People's Party also now displayed strength in railhead towns and even in some of the larger cities, recording gains in all the major urban occupation groups and especially among railroad workers. The party's heavy emphasis on the urban labor vote had clearly paid off.[60]

Efforts to win African American votes, while not entirely a failure, nonetheless fell short of what the Populists had hoped. In 1892 the black vote for Nugent had been statistically insignificant; in 1894 an estimated 17 percent of eligible African Americans voted for the Populist state ticket. Most Populists saw this as a promising start, but they also despaired over the widespread reports of Democratic voter fraud targeting African Americans. As will be discussed in Chapter 9, Populist efforts to overcome fraud in the Mexican American–majority counties of South Texas met with even less success than in the heavily black counties, and with the exception of a few individual counties with strong local Third-Party organizations, the party essentially gave up on that region. Combating fraud would become a major focus of the upcoming 1896 campaign.[61]

Despite the mixed results of 1894, Texas Populists could point with pride to a party that had grown dramatically in the three short years since its founding. Optimism for the future ran high. But that optimism also masked serious potential problems. Populism was both a social movement *and* a political party, and movements and parties operate with very different dynamics. Movements create an ideology and then set concrete goals that their adherents believe can and must be achieved. The movement's opposition helps to define those goals by placing obstacles in the movement's path, which further adds to the unity and esprit de corps of the movement. If the movement fails to achieve its goal and members of the movement believe that the goal is no longer attainable—especially if the failure is attributed to a surrender of ideological principle by the movement itself—then the movement becomes susceptible to disillusionment and rapid demobilization. The near-religious fervor of Populists, then, was a double-edged sword: it created great devotion to the cause, but it also could lead to self-destruction.[62]

By contrast, parties, or at least successful ones, create more or less stable bureaucratic structures that address the needs of individuals and of the various interest groups that comprise the electorate. As long as these individuals and interest groups believe that their party is championing their interests and stands a realistic chance of someday succeeding, the party can survive, even in the face of repeated defeats. In the American winner-take-all two-party system, however, third parties always fight an uphill battle, because the major parties can either use their superior resources to attack the proposed reforms of the third party, or they can selectively endorse certain demands of the third party and thus co-opt enough of the program of the third party to ensure its defeat. This had been the successful strategy of the Hogg Democrats at the state level, where they created the Railroad Commission and paid enough lip service to silver and other Populist demands to keep the Third Party at bay. Since its founding in 1891, the Texas People's Party had done much to create a party structure and to forge a diverse coalition of interest groups. But it remained a third party, subject to the vulnerabilities encountered by all American third parties. In the end, the only truly successful third parties are those that replace one of the existing major parties in the two-party system, as the Republicans did to the Whigs in the 1850s. This was the ultimate goal of Populist true believers, and 1896 was the year they believed it would happen.[63]

Thus, as the People's Party looked ahead, it faced challenges both as a party and as a social movement. The growing emphasis on silver made the party vulnerable to selective endorsement and co-optation if the Democrats should embrace silver. Such an eventuality alone might not destroy the party immediately, but as participants in a social movement, Texas Populists had also committed themselves to the belief that the salvation of the country depended on victory in 1896, raising expectations to a point where that election became something close to a do-or-die proposition for the movement. The lead editorial in first issue of the *Southern Mercury* after the 1894 election captured that sentiment, proclaiming that "the people of Texas have marched steadily forward, and the reform banner is floating from every village and hamlet in the state. The results are highly encouraging." But the editorial made the stakes for Populists very clear: "One more reform battle and Texas will be carried for the party of the people." What if victory did not come with that "one more" battle? Could both party and movement hold together in the face of defeat, when Populists were staking so much on it?[64]

Populists thought they could hold both together, and one reason they thought so was because they believed they had revolutionized politics. That revolution went beyond a new conception of the relationship between the individual and the state, or even a more egalitarian ethos when it came to race. It also encompassed a new *style* of politics. When twenty-first-century Americans invoke the concept of "populism," they think of a political style in which politicians make direct appeals to the "people," with rhetoric that pits the common man against special interests, government corruption, and monopolistic corporations. The 1890s Populists certainly did all of that. But these elements of Populist political culture were not entirely new; their roots stretched back at least to the Jacksonian and Jeffersonian eras. By 1894, however, Texas Populists were in the process of doing something else revolutionary, something that finds no analogue in modern-day iterations of "populism." At the same time they were embracing the modern liberal idea of a democratically controlled activist state, they were also redefining gender roles—what it meant to be manly and womanly. Those new meanings gave a new tone to the public sphere, and in doing so they also affected private relationships between men and women in subtle and not so subtle ways. Only occasionally were Populists able to articulate how Populism was ushering in a new—and more modern—system of gender relations, but they knew that the new style of politics that it ushered in set the People's Party apart from its rivals. As the next chapter demonstrates, that new style proved to be one of the key elements of the Populists' political identity. It also proved to be one of their greatest sources of strength and unity.

Plate 1 Sam Ealy Johnson and family on his Hill Country farm, ca. 1893–1897. Johnson ran for the legislature against his own son-in-law in 1892 and later tutored his grandson Lyndon on the common man's need for an activist government. Courtesy of the Johnson Family Collection, LBJ Library, B10144.

Plate 2 S. O. Daws. He guided the Farmers' Alliance in its first major expansion in the mid-1880s. From the *Galveston Daily News* (Galveston, TX), vol. 55, no. 137, ed. 1, Saturday, August 8, 1896, newspaper, August 8, 1896; Galveston, Texas (texashistory.unt.edu /ark:/67531/metapth465546/m1/1/?q=daws, accessed January 30, 2019), University of North Texas Libraries, The Portal to Texas History, texashistory.unt.edu; crediting Abilene Library Consortium.

Plate 3 Charles W. Macune. His creative mind was responsible for both the Alliance Exchange and the Subtreasury Plan, but Macune was never enthusiastic about third-party action. From N. A. Dunning, *Farmers Alliance History and Agricultural Digest*, 1891.

Plate 4 Farmers' Alliance Exchange Building, Dallas. Alliancefolk took great pride in their state Exchange, an ambitious cooperative venture that promised affordable credit, better crop prices, and discounted farm implements. Its failure pushed many Texans toward third-party political action. From *Art Work of Dallas, Tex.*, 1895, in the collections of the History and Archives Division, Dallas Public Library.

Plate 5 James Stephen Hogg. As governor of Texas from 1889 to 1895, Hogg's reformist policies were too cautious for Populists. Courtesy of Marks, Austin, Texas, James Stephen Hogg Papers, di_11290, The Dolph Briscoe Center for American History, The University of Texas at Austin.

Plate 6 Harry Tracy. The prosperous Dallas editor and Alliance lecturer sat on the Populist National Executive Committee and was the ablest proponent of the Subtreasury Plan. From N. A. Dunning, *Farmers Alliance History and Agricultural Digest*, 1891.

Plate 7 Dallas city hall, built in 1889. Designed by Dallas architect and
Populist A. B. Bristol, it was the site of the founding convention of the
Texas People's Party in August 1891 and the party's first nominating
convention in June 1892. From *Art Work of Dallas, Tex.*, 1895, in the collections of the History and Archives Division, Dallas Public Library.

Plate 8 Thomas L. Nugent. An intellectual
and religious nonconformist, he was the
most revered of Texas Populists and was
twice the party's nominee for governor.
Courtesy of the Prints and Photographs Collection, di_11286, The Dolph Briscoe Center
for American History, The University of
Texas at Austin.

Plate 9 George Clark. The leader of the conservative Democrats of Texas, he ran for governor on the libertarian slogan "Turn Texas Loose" in 1892. From John Henry Brown, *Indian Wars and Pioneers of Texas*, 1896.

Plate 10 Street scene during the 1892 governor's race. A buggy bearing a banner reading "Turn Texas Loose" awaits the arrival of candidate George Clark in an unidentified Texas town. Courtesy of the Texas State Historical Association Photo Collection.

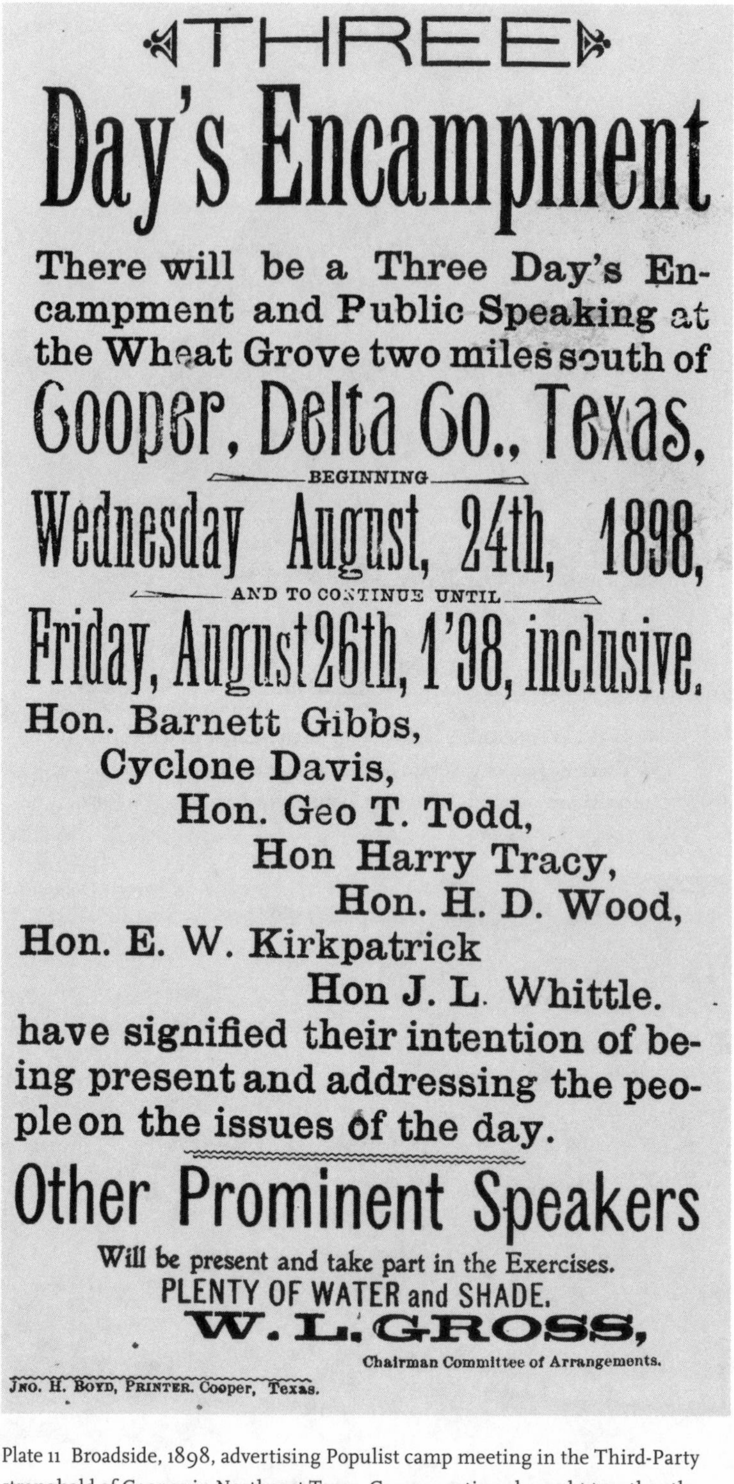

THREE

Day's Encampment

There will be a Three Day's Encampment and Public Speaking at the Wheat Grove two miles south of

Cooper, Delta Co., Texas,

BEGINNING

Wednesday August, 24th, 1898,

AND TO CONTINUE UNTIL

Friday, August 26th, 1'98, inclusive.

Hon. Barnett Gibbs,
Cyclone Davis,
Hon. Geo T. Todd,
Hon Harry Tracy,
Hon. H. D. Wood,
Hon. E. W. Kirkpatrick
Hon J. L. Whittle.

have signified their intention of being present and addressing the people on the issues of the day.

Other Prominent Speakers

Will be present and take part in the Exercises.

PLENTY OF WATER and SHADE.

W. L. GROSS,

Chairman Committee of Arrangements.

Jno. H. Boyd, Printer. Cooper, Texas.

Plate 11 Broadside, 1898, advertising Populist camp meeting in the Third-Party stronghold of Cooper in Northeast Texas. Camp meetings brought together the party faithful and contributed to the making of the movement culture of Populism. Courtesy of the Beinecke Library, Yale University.

Plate 12 Reddin Andrews. The former president of Baylor University ran for Congress as a Populist and became a prominent socialist in the twentieth century. Courtesy of the Texas Collection, Baylor University, Waco, TX.

Plate 13 Ebenezer Lafayette Dohoney. An intellectual and author of six books, he was a prominent Greenbacker and prohibitionist before joining the Populists. From E. L. Dohoney, *An Average American*, 1907.

Plate 14 John B. Rayner. The son of a white congressman and a slave woman, he became the foremost leader of the African American Populists of Texas. Courtesy of the late A. A. Rayner Jr.

Plate 15 Andrew Jackson Spradley. The legendary sheriff of Nacogdoches County, Spradley earned a reputation as a friend to African Americans in his East Texas Piney Woods county. Courtesy of the East Texas Research Center, Stephen F. Austin State University, Nacogdoches, TX.

Plate 16 Milton Park. As the irascible editor of the Dallas *Southern Mercury*, Park's less than progressive stands on many issues and scorched-earth political style often alienated his fellow Populists. From the *Southern Mercury* (Dallas, TX), vol. 13, no. 44, ed. 1, Thursday, November 1, 1894, newspaper, November 1, 1894 (texashistory.unt.edu/ark: /67531/metapth185585/m1/6/?q=milton, accessed January 30, 2019), University of North Texas Libraries, The Portal to Texas History, texashistory.unt.edu.

Plate 17 Bettie Munn Gay. The most prominent female leader of the Texas Farmers'
Alliance and People's Party, she ran a large
plantation in Colorado County and championed women's rights. From N. A. Dunning,
*Farmers Alliance History and Agricultural
Digest*, 1891.

Plate 18 Willis Lyman Harrison. A
Confederate surgeon turned Disciples of
Christ minister, as a Populist state senator
Harrison led the effort to reform the state's
statutory rape law. Courtesy of the Texas
State Preservation Board, Austin, TX.

Plate 19 John A. O'Connor of San Antonio.
The only big-city Populist to serve in the state
legislature, O'Connor championed progressive causes and opposed efforts to limit the
voting rights of Mexican immigrants. From
Frank W. Johnson, *A History of Texas and
Texans*, vol. 5, 1914.

Plate 20 James Harvey "Cyclone" Davis. Pictured here during his one term in Congress in the 1910s, the erratic Davis earned national fame as an orator but frequently found himself at cross-purposes with his fellow Texas Populists. Courtesy of the Library of Congress, Prints & Photographs Division, photograph by Harris & Ewing, LC-DIG-hec-06600.

Plate 21 Theodore J. McMinn. The mercurial San Antonian twice was a candidate for
statewide office, but his reputation suffered
damage when he tried to combat election
fraud in South Texas by limiting the voting
rights of Mexican immigrants. Redrawn
by Devon Nowlin from the *Galveston Daily
News*, August 9, 1896.

Plate 22 Selig Deutschmann. A prominent
German Jewish immigrant, Populist, and
successful businessman, he fought to preserve Mexican voting rights in San Antonio. Courtesy of the Congregation Agunas
Achim, San Antonio.

Plate 23 Barnett Gibbs of Dallas. The affluent former lieutenant governor converted to
Populism in 1895, was a floor manager at the
1896 Populist National Convention, and ran
for Congress and governor on the Third-
Party ticket. Courtesy of the Texas State
Preservation Board, Austin, TX.

Plate 24 Jerome C. Kearby. A veteran of independent politics, the charismatic Dallas attorney became the face of the Texas People's
Party after the death of Thomas Nugent,
receiving the party's nomination for governor
in 1896. Courtesy of Church, Dallas, Texas,
Prints and Photographs Collection, di_01583,
The Dolph Briscoe Center for American History, The University of Texas at Austin.

Plate 25 Convention hall, St. Louis, 1896. Known as the "Wigwam," this temporary structure hosted the Populist National Convention, where Texas Populists fought a losing battle to deny the nomination to Democrat William Jennings Bryan. Courtesy of the Swekosky Notre Dame College Collection, Series 3, Missouri Historical Society, P0245-S03-00031-6G.

WHEN PARTY LEADERS BETRAY THE PEOPLE, IT IS TIME FOR THE VOTING MASSES TO GET IN THE MIDDLE OF THE ROAD.

SOUTHERN MERCURY.

VOL. XV., NO. 32.   DALLAS, TEXAS, THURSDAY, AUG. 6, 1896. $1 PER ANNUM

Men on the Donkey—Say, Mister! Won't you please endorse us?
Pop—Not jest yet! You fellows have deceived us too often! We can't afford to trust you; especially that feller on thar behin'. I prefer to keep in the middle of the road.—Adapted from the Cleveland Press.

Plate 26 Cartoon, Dallas *Southern Mercury*, 1896 (adapted from the *Cleveland Press*). Published after the Populist National Convention nominated Democrat William Jennings Bryan for president, this cartoon shows a Populist refusing to support Bryan and his conservative running mate, Arthur Sewall. From the *Southern Mercury* (Dallas, TX), vol. 15, no. 32, ed. 1, Thursday, August 6, 1896, newspaper, August 6, 1896; Dallas, Texas (texashistory.unt.edu /ark:/67531/metapth185671/m1/1/?q=southern%20mercury%2C%20august%208%2C%20 1896, accessed February 20, 2019), University of North Texas Libraries, The Portal to Texas History, texashistory.unt.edu.

Plate 27 Harrison Sterling Price "Stump" Ashby. One of Texas Populism's most effective leaders, the former Confederate soldier, circus clown, stage actor, trail rider, and Methodist preacher was a spellbinding orator who refused a Democratic bribe to abandon his race for lieutenant governor in 1895. Courtesy of Harry Watton, H. S. P. "Stump" Ashby, photograph, 1889 (gateway.okhistory.org/ark:/67531/metadc962899/, accessed January 26, 2019), The Gateway to Oklahoma History, gateway.okhistory.org; crediting Oklahoma Historical Society.

Plate 28 Charles H. Jenkins. One of Texas Populism's most respected leaders, the Brownwood lawyer ran for Congress twice as a Populist before becoming an appeals-court judge and serving three terms as a progressive Democratic state legislator. Courtesy of Susan Orton.

Plate 29 Joe Henry Eagle. After running two unsuccessful races for Congress as a Populist, Eagle served in Congress as a Democrat from 1913 to 1921 and again from 1933 to 1937, supporting progressive and liberal causes. Courtesy of the Library of Congress, Prints & Photographs Division, photograph by Harris & Ewing, LC-DIG-hec-05554.

Plate 30 Henry Lewis Bentley. Lawyer, journalist, farmer, scientist, and agricultural reformer, the multitalented Bentley managed Thomas Nugent's 1892 gubernatorial campaign, ran for Congress and state land commissioner, chaired the state party, and served on the national executive committee. From the *Galveston Daily News* (Galveston, TX), vol. 55, no. 113, ed. 1, Wednesday, July 15, 1896, newspaper, July 15, 1896; Galveston, Texas (texashistory.unt.edu/ark:/67531 /metapth465294/m1/6/?q=%22Henry%20 Lewis%20Bentley%22, accessed February 20, 2019), University of North Texas Libraries, The Portal to Texas History, texashistory.unt.edu; crediting Abilene Library Consortium.

7 · Women, Gender, and Populism

His presence at the front is certainly calculated to impart peculiar features
of controversial dignity and moral elevation to the campaign.
—*Dallas Morning News,* commenting on the entry of Populist
Thomas L. Nugent into the governor's race, 1892

It might have been wrong for me to threaten to cut his throat,
but what was a man to do?
—Democratic congressman Joseph Weldon Bailey, explaining his actions
in a debate with Populist opponent Uriah M. Browder, 1894

At noon on the first day of August 1894, ninety-one men assembled at the
Navarro County Courthouse, an ornate French Second Empire–style structure
in downtown Corsicana, in the Blackland Prairie region fifty miles south of
Dallas. They were all Democrats of local or statewide prominence, and they
had come from Navarro and six neighboring counties as elected delegates to
their party's nominating convention for the Sixth Congressional District. Such
gatherings were a standard feature of late nineteenth-century politics in Texas,
where primaries had generally not yet supplanted conventions as the means
of selecting party nominees.[1]

This particular convention attracted extraordinary press coverage only
because it was an exceptionally contentious gathering. Four major candidates,
each with favorite-son backing from his home delegation and each occupying
slightly different positions on the policy issues of the day, vied for the right to
face Populist nominee Jerome Kearby in the general election. It soon became
clear that no faction would cede ground to the others, and the voting continued

for 842 ballots before adjourning for the night. The next morning brought more of the same, and as the August heat in the courtroom rose, so did tempers. After the thousandth ballot, delegates exchanged "cutting" remarks, which led Johnson County delegate H. P. Brown to charge that the Dallas delegation had violated its instructions—a transgression of the political honor code governing such proceedings. Dallas mayor Bryan Barry indignantly denied the charge, whereupon Brown hurled a chair at him. The chair missed, and "while held by friends, the men, with pale faces, stood eyeing each other and seemingly anxious for a tilt." "The convention was immediately in a big uproar," but friends of the two men intervened, the sergeants at arms soon restored order, and the balloting continued. After three days and over twelve hundred rounds of balloting, the convention adjourned with plans to meet again three weeks later in Dallas. When that session remained deadlocked after another thousand ballots, someone proposed another adjournment, this time to the town of Hillsboro, sixty miles to the southwest.[2]

This proposal provoked vehement protests, not just because it would necessitate yet another time-consuming trip for the delegates but because prohibition was in effect in Hillsboro. The idea that Texas Democrats could conduct the manly business of nominating a congressional candidate without the ready availability of whiskey was, to many, unthinkable. "It was urged that a town that had voted strong drink out was thereby forever barred from entering the lists as a candidate for a Democratic convention," delegates argued when the new venue was proposed. Only after being personally assured by Hill County men that Hillsboro had "excellent jug connections with both Dallas and Waco" and that delegates would be allowed to "nip it on the sly" did the motion carry.[3]

Five days later in supposedly dry Hillsboro, the balloting resumed. More late hours of wrangling ensued, followed by a long day of interminable balloting and rising tempers. A turning point finally came when the Dallas delegation's favorite son, Judge Robert Burke, rose to deliver what the *Johnson County Review* termed "a manly speech." "I pitched my lines of battle upon the planes of democratic truth and honesty," he declared in a decidedly martial tone. "I would esteem it a great honor to be entrusted with the flag of democracy of this, the sixth congressional district, and I would fearlessly and loyally defend it against every foe, upon every hill top and in every valley in this district." But recognizing that his continued candidacy would "open old wounds afresh," he announced his withdrawal from the race. "I shall continue to fight the battle of democracy and to meet her foes upon every field," he concluded, whereupon the delegates finally renominated the incumbent, Congressman Jo Abbott, on the 3,389th ballot. With the deadlock broken, supporters of Abbott threw their hats in the air and climbed on chairs and tables, shouting victoriously as if their side had just triumphed in battle.[4]

Scenes like this were played out endlessly in the dominant political culture of late nineteenth-century Texas. Although it would not have occurred to them, the men meeting in Corsicana and Hillsboro were participants in one of their society's most heavily gendered rituals. The all-male political convention, with its (literally) smoke-filled caucus rooms, readily flowing whiskey, possibilities of violence, and speeches rife with masculine metaphors of war and battle, was an arena where white men demonstrated and proved their "manliness"—their fitness to rule over a society in which women and nonwhite men occupied subordinate and dependent positions. The campaigns that followed such conventions likewise served as rituals in which men left their homes and families to confirm and celebrate their identities as men, as Democrats, and as wielders of power. This masculine political culture reached its apex on election day, when men congregated at polling places with other men to very publicly cast their ballots, often in a highly charged atmosphere where liquor flowed freely, intense partisan and peer pressures were brought to bear on voters, and the possibility of violence was real.[5]

To have championed a politics that challenged all this would have been to call into question the very foundations of the social and political order. But this, in large measure, is what Texas Populists did. If gender, as modern historiographical understanding has posited, "is a primary way of signifying relationships of power," and if Populists formulated constructions of gender fundamentally at odds with those of Democrats, then the fact that they did so suggests that much more separated Populists from their opponents than mere policy disagreements or even conceptions about the proper role of government. In proposing what (to Texans) were radically new answers to the question of what it meant to be "manly," Populists were proposing nothing less than a radical redefinition of who would exercise power and authority, and on what terms.[6]

In the Populist era, American ideas about gender were in flux, particularly where politics was concerned. In the North in the mid-nineteenth century, the notion of "separate spheres" for women and men had given women the mantle of moral superiority within the home, and women had used this new role to exert influence in ways that increasingly, and paradoxically, brought them into the public arena. Women played leading roles in the panoply of antebellum reform movements, including temperance and abolitionism, and when the Civil War came, northern Republicans justified their expansion of federal authority in part on the moral superiority expressed by the northern maternal ideal. Union generals and Republican politicians readily portrayed themselves as acting under the influence of pious, morally superior mothers and wives, in opposition to southern slaveholding Democrats who were said to rule their women—white and black—with a violent disregard for, and rejection of, moral and religious values and the sanctity of the home.[7]

For their part, southern Democrats developed a defensive ideology of gender relations that linked patriarchal control of the household to the broader political environment. In a slaveholding society that necessitated total control of slaves by their owners, there could be no questioning of white male authority by the white women in the household. Granting wives moral authority over their husbands would threaten the slaveholder's authority over his slaves, as wives could potentially overrule their husbands in matters relating to his bondspeople. Southern white men thus developed a notion of manliness that carried over into their political beliefs; allowing a distant government to control them (and to interfere with their patriarchal authority at home) constituted an unthinkable surrender of their rights as free men and citizens. It comes as no surprise that Democrats ridiculed Republicans like John C. Frémont and Abraham Lincoln as weak, effeminate men under the control of domineering, masculine wives. A generation later, in the 1890s, when Populists championed programs such as the Subtreasury Plan, which would have entailed the greatest expansion of federal power since the Civil War, the most damning charge that Democrats would level at them was the accusation that the plan was "paternalistic," meaning that Populists were ready to surrender to the government their manly prerogatives as masters over their dependent inferiors.[8]

These gendered understandings of household relations, race, and politics received jolting reinforcement during Reconstruction. With the South defeated and occupied, and with slaves emancipated and white men stripped, at least temporarily, of political power, the linkage of gender and politics took on a new urgency. Northern "paternalism" was suddenly an everyday reality, as ex-slaves began exercising the right to vote and hold office, abetted by those same "effete" Republicans whom southern Democrats had once ridiculed. Democrats in states such as Texas mounted their political counterattacks by accusing black and white Republicans of corrupting the South's once-pure government with regimes that robbed white men of their independence and thus of their sacred honor. Democrats carried this theme over into the household, raising the specter of black rapists violating white women, further cementing the connection between political dominance, domestic mastery, and honor. Any political threat to the Democratic Party became a threat to white manhood and the honor that went with it. For the generation following the end of Reconstruction, then, gender, race, honor, and politics would be linked at least as overtly as they had been in the prewar era. Just as Populists would have to overcome deeply ingrained prejudices associated with race and the role of government, so they would have to construct a new and viable prototype of gender.[9]

The South, of course, had never been a monolith in politics or anything else. The southern "plain folk" who had owned few or no slaves had never entirely subscribed to the political, racial, religious, or gender orthodoxy of the dominant slaveholders. In Texas these were the people who had supported the unionist hero Sam Houston before the war, opposed or at least halfheartedly supported secession, demanded agrarian concessions in the Redeemer state constitution of 1876, and enthusiastically joined the Grange, Alliance, and Knights of Labor in the 1870s and 1880s. Although many of them had fought for the Confederacy, some had at least given the Republicans a fair hearing during Reconstruction. Most, however, either remained Democrats or returned to the party after Redemption, though many of them strayed into the various Greenbacker or independent movements of the period. Just as they were receptive to different political thinking, so were they willing to challenge the gender orthodoxy of the dominant culture.

As we saw in Chapter 4, southern churches, especially those of the restorationist bent, aided in this. It was in the evangelical churches of the antebellum era that southern notions of manly honor came under the most sustained attack. Evangelicals identified the southern code of honor, with its explicitly hierarchical assumptions (gentlemen vs. rabble), its hedonism (drinking, dancing, horse racing), its emphasis on display and ostentation, and its readiness to resort to duels and other forms of violence to avenge alleged insult, as a barbaric relic of medieval Europe that had no place in a modern, Christian, democratic republic. Baptists, Methodists, Disciples of Christ, and other evangelicals also posited the spiritual equality of men and women, even if women were barred from the ministry and other positions of church leadership. Although evangelicalism expected women to nurture the piety of their children and husbands within the domestic "sphere" of the home, it nonetheless vested them with an autonomy rarely experienced in the honor-based society, where women gained identity and prestige only through association with a protecting male relative. New conceptions of gender—in many ways echoing those being heard in the North—thus lay at the heart of the evangelical assault on the southern code of honor.[10]

If honor was the organizing principle of elite southern culture through much of the nineteenth century, the evangelical counterculture needed a principle of its own, and it found it in the concept of dignity. In the code of honor, insults were to be settled through violence; in the code of dignity, insults were to be ignored, or countered with logic and reasoned debate. Restraint and self-control were the hallmarks of dignity. Unlike honor, dignity knew no economic class, occupation, race, or gender; it was the property of all people, however humble, who lived lives of virtue and propriety. The new code of dignity, then, grew out of the evangelical churches and, after the Civil War, found secular expression in the Grange, the Knights of Labor, and the Farmers' Alliance. In the 1890s, these groups bequeathed that code to the politics of Populism. We find evidence of it in the gendered language that Populists used in their political discourse, in their behavior on the campaign trail, and in their actions as elected officials.[11]

A society's gender consciousness necessarily derives from the gendered rhetoric available in the received culture. Therefore Populists, like Democrats, frequently invoked notions of "manhood" and "manliness," but they rarely did so in the physical or martial sense employed by Democrats. In Populist rhetoric, "manliness" indicated not an imposing physical presence, bravery in combat, or the ability to dominate others (be they men or women), but rather several different qualities: honesty, forthrightness, restraint, magnanimity, and independence, all of which fall under the rubric of dignity.[12]

Populists contrasted their manly honesty and forthrightness with Democratic deception and obfuscation. Addressing the state Reform Press Association in 1895, the group's president Owen F. Dornblaser advised his fellow editors to "do your very best; be truthful and at all times, when you find yourself in error or make a mistake own up; take it back; that is manly." When he announced his conversion to Populism, Hill County's J. G. H. Buck drew a stark comparison between the Democratic and People's Parties: "In the people's party I find what I look for in vain in the national democracy so-called—a manly, honest defense of popular rights, a clear cut expression of principles, a bold demand for the restoration of that of which they have been despoiled under the deceitful forms and names of law." At the very end of the Populist revolt, Houston Populist Joe Eagle explained that he preferred, "right or wrong, to fight in the open," and he declared, "I am not ashamed of the part I have played—it has, I hope, been open and manly."[13]

Populists viewed dignity, with its emphasis on restraint and self-control, as key elements in defining manliness. A female contributor to the *Southern Mer-*

cury criticized "labor slaves" who, in refusing to stand up against the "lash of oppression," lacked "the dignity of full-grown manhood." A *Dallas Morning News* correspondent tellingly commented that Thomas L. Nugent's entry into the 1892 governor's race was "calculated to impart peculiar features of controversial dignity" to the campaign. The idea that dignity would be seen as peculiar and controversial suggests just how unusual dignity was in Texas politics, but Populists saw it as the manly way to conduct a campaign. In dispensing campaign advice, the *Mercury* in 1892 recommended that Populists "be ready at all times to give a calm, dignified plain but pointed answer to all inquiries."[14]

This emphasis on dignity likewise extended to the way one handled defeat, where magnanimity was seen as a hallmark of self-control. When Nugent received the 1892 gubernatorial nomination over the popular and better-known Henry McCulloch, McCulloch magnanimously proclaimed that if his "name did not meet with perfect unanimity it was best for the cause that I would withdraw," which he proceeded to do. This prompted even the hostile *Fort Worth Gazette* to admit that "the new movement has passed from the stage of firebrand agitation to the stage of definite principle and tolerant discussion." In a similar vein, when Populists in the 1895 legislature found themselves divided over whether to nominate Nugent or House Populist leader John A. O'Connor for the symbolic honor of being the party's nominee for US senator, the press reported that "O'Connor's magnanimity then asserted itself and in a manly way he withdrew in favor of the defeated man for governor."[15]

Of all the elements constituting Populist manly dignity, though, perhaps the most important was independence—economic independence as well as independence of thought and action. The ability to earn a living sufficient to support one's family in a dignified manner was certainly one aspect of this independence. Populist discourse teems with discussions of how the economic crisis of the 1890s had made it impossible for hardworking men to fulfill their obligations to their wives and children. An 1898 editorial described an economic system that "leads your toil-worn, care-driven wife and helpless little children into a deeper, darker, more degrading industrial and intellectual bondage, and possibly, ignominious shame." Another mentioned "sunburnt wrinkled features of a wife, whose health is impaired, whose hopes are dimmed by the ravages of avarice and greed." An African American Populist listed the ability to educate his children and "the chance to earn a home" as the principal aspirations of black Texans. The solution, according to Populists, was for men to rise up and exercise the manly independence that came from standing up against the political system responsible for these hardships. Cataloging the many indignities endured by farmers who could not support their families on five-cent cotton but who continued to vote Democratic, a Populist farmer in 1894 urged Texans, "Why not assert your manhood, shake off the shackles of industrial slavery and cast one honest vote in behalf of your home, your God, your wife and your loved ones?" Noting that Populists had no corporate campaign funds or corrupt political machines to back their cause, the *Southern Mercury* in 1892 remarked, "Reformers have nothing to depend upon but their impoverished pockets, their independent manhood, their efforts and their votes." On another occasion, the *Mercury* spoke of black voters, saying that "they should adopt an honorable and manly course, and refuse to be a political commodity for the old parties. Let the colored voters take a stand for honest politics and political independence." Scoring his fellow Populists who failed to go to the polls and cast votes against the "political cunning" of corrupt machine Democrats, Milam County Populist J. D. Shelton asserted, "You owe it to your manhood, self-respect and common decency to rebuke this brazen effrontery and corruption by defeating the whole gang of perpetrators." In her ringing call for a third party in 1891, Alliance leader Bettie Gay echoed this conception of masculinity, which no doubt had a greater impact, coming as it did from a woman. "It is only a lack of political manhood," Gay avowed, "which causes 80 per cent of the people to submit to the political dictation of a few lawyers, bankers, politicians and speculators, who control the party machinery of the old parties and continue a reign of plunder and legalized robbery."[16]

None of this is to suggest that Populists failed to appreciate the more traditional forms of southern masculine courage. Confederate service records were frequently acknowledged, though in the interest of burying the bloody shirt of sectionalism, Populists often noted that they did not consider military service a prerequisite for holding office. But Populists seemed to admire most a type of masculinity leavened with a more civilized quality that could even contain feminine elements. Black Populist John B. Rayner, who in preaching the Populist gospel before hostile white audiences clearly knew something about physical bravery, once lauded the legendary Populist sheriff of Nacogdoches County, A. J. Spradley, saying that Spradley was "brave as a lion and kind hearted as a woman"—a description that would have resonated with the readers of the *Southern Mercury*, which published his comments.[17]

The Populist conception of gender that led them to define manliness in ways at odds with the dominant political culture carried over into their actions on the campaign trail. Here Populist candidates and speakers frequently found themselves directly confronting the long-established notions of southern honor that sanctioned the use of violence—either in language or in deed—to defend oneself against insult. And again, Populists believed that restraint, rather than passion, was the manly way to conduct a campaign. In 1896, in one of the most remarkable moments of the entire Populist revolt in Texas, John B. Rayner, making a speech before a mixed-race audience in Market Square in downtown Houston, found himself being shouted down by white hecklers. Although Rayner, with his rapier-sharp tongue, differed strikingly in his oratorical style from the more restrained Thomas Nugent, he too had imbibed the Populists' gendered understanding of civility on the stump. According to the *Houston Post*, he quieted the hecklers—and in doing so "aroused the crowd to numerous applauses"—by aiming some "quick-witted thrusts" at them and denouncing them as "unmanly in their persistence in interrupting him while exercising his privilege of free speech."[18]

Rayner's oratorical skills, and possibly the presence of white Populist defenders in the crowd, may have saved him from physical harm that day, but Populists frequently faced the threat of violence at the hands of Democrats. At various times Populist heavyweights Ralph Beaumont, Evan Jones, Joseph S. Bradley, and John Wilson Biard all endured barrages of rotten eggs from hostile Democratic audiences. In the isolated East Texas settlement of Daley's in Houston County during the heated campaign of 1896, A. F. Nash, a Populist candidate for justice of the peace, had a close brush with violence at the hands of the "rotten ring democracy" of the village: "There was a mob of 75 or 100 of the toughs and hoodlums of the town who were backed by their leaders, and who would surround me every time I appeared on the streets, and, fearing I would be killed, I stopped making any efforts to solicit votes about 12 o'clock on election day. They surrounded me several times, and would have done me up had not the officers come to my rescue. I intended staying in town all night, but some 35 or 40 of my friends came to me and told me to leave town before night or I would be killed, and, believing my life was in danger, I left town before night, and as I rode out of town the mob yelled and hissed at me until I was out of sight." Nash did not overtly refer to his assailants as being "unmanly" on this occasion, as Rayner and many other Populists might have done, but by this stage in the agrarian revolt, readers of his account in the *Southern Mercury* certainly would have cited it as yet another example of the Democrats' lack of restraint and their corrupted idea of manhood. Nash simply pronounced his own plain but eloquent judgment on the episode: "People may talk of a free country and a free ballot but this does not look like it."[19]

266 THE PEOPLE'S REVOLT

At first glance, the conduct of disruptive hecklers, rotten-egg throwers, and threatening mobs seems to bear little relation to the "chivalrous" code of honor to which the Populist code of dignity stood in opposition, and respectable Democratic politicians would have been quick to say so. But Populists saw such forms of political violence as the inevitable result of a culture that valued force over restraint and tolerated corruption at the expense of morality. If elite Democrats could drink good bourbon and hurl chairs at one another in a district congressional convention, was it particularly surprising when the party's rank and file got fired up on cheap rotgut and hurled eggs at Populists? In either case, the behavior signaled a lack of the manly dignity that Populists valued—a dignity which, unlike the traditional southern code of honor, was achievable by men of all economic and social statuses, and not just reserved for elite gentlemen.

At no point in the history of Texas Populism did the violence-prone manliness of Democratic political culture come into sharper contrast with the Populist ideal of dignified manhood than in the 1894 congressional contest between Joseph Weldon Bailey and Uriah M. Browder. The thirty-two-year-old Bailey had already earned a reputation as a hothead before moving to North Texas from Mississippi in 1885. The previous year he had been called before a US Senate committee investigating violence in local Mississippi politics in the 1883 election, in which he presumably played a part. Elected to the House of Representatives as soon as he was old enough in 1890, he was running for his third term in Congress when Disciples of Christ minister Browder ran against him on the Populist ticket. A newspaper article described Browder, an Indiana native and former drummer boy in the Union army, as "a middle aged man of pleasing address" with "a fine voice for public speaking," whose speech in the small town of Honey Grove "was argumentative and clothed in choice language devoid of abuse except when he referred to contemptible 2×4 lawyers and 1×2 editors of county newspapers"—relatively mild stuff for an 1890s stump speech. A local Populist paper concurred, stating that Browder "has a state wide reputation as a strong debater, an upright, honorable gentleman with undoubted ability." As the race progressed, Populists extolled the manly dignity of Browder, claiming to be "highly elated over the dignified canvass made by their candidate" in the campaign.[20]

But this was a Joe Bailey political race, and even a mild-mannered minister could scarcely be expected to avoid calling attention to Bailey's abundant ethical lapses. A month before the election, the *Dallas Morning News* reported that the campaign had grown "quite warm, and the joint debates at times reached the

danger line, and trouble was expected." Sure enough, in a debate in Denison, as
Browder prepared to read some affidavits charging Bailey with having failed to
pay certain debts he owed, Bailey leapt to his feet, brandished a knife, and
threatened to cut Browder's throat. Bloodshed was barely averted, when bystanders intervened. Bailey later defended his actions, saying, "It might have
been wrong for me to threaten to cut his throat, but what was a man to do? I had
borne with that man until patience had ceased to be a virtue." Bailey went on to
win the race, rise to become House minority leader and US senator, and on one
occasion, assault fellow senator Albert Beveridge following a debate. In the
twentieth century "Baileyism" became synonymous with political corruption
in Texas when it became known that he was in the pay of the Standard Oil
Company, and in a supreme irony, his exploits eventually contributed to the
enactment of an old Populist platform plank, the direct election of senators.[21]

Differing partisan notions of gender obviously surfaced in the question of
woman suffrage. When it was considered as a policy matter, Populists were divided, including Populist women. Texans had debated female voting as far back
as 1868, when the Republican-dominated constitutional convention considered
a suffrage measure, only to defeat it. The issue met the same fate in the 1875
Redeemer convention. But the admission of women to membership in the Alliance and Knights provided a forum for women to discuss politics, and they
kept the issue alive. By the late 1880s, the "Ladies' Department" section of the
Southern Mercury was carrying on a vigorous debate on suffrage by Alliancewomen who wrote to express their views. They laid out all the major arguments
that would inform the suffrage debate throughout the Populist revolt.[22]

The main question facing those who supported suffrage involved the impact
of female voting on the traditional domestic role of women. Some prosuffrage
Alliancewomen took a defensive position, arguing that voting would not necessitate an abandonment of separate spheres but rather that it would actually
protect and enhance female domesticity. "Mary M." voiced this "home protection" argument in an 1888 letter to the *Southern Mercury*, maintaining that if
women voted, "there would not have been a drop of whisky now in existence."
To the argument that women would neglect their children in order to vote,
she retorted, "I have got a house full of children who will be left sometime, in
this troublesome world, to work for themselves and I know that [if] by me casting a vote that would make the laws of this country better, I would surely vote."
A writer styling herself "Ann Too" agreed, observing that "I don't believe I
would forget to wash the children on election day, or forget that I was a woman
either."[23]

Alliancewomen also sought to answer the frequently heard claim that going to the polls would either corrupt or endanger women. Responding to a fellow *Mercury* letter writer who had contended that "it would be a downfall to the female sex to go there among so many grades of people," Mary M. asked, "Well, have we not got all kinds of people in our country and do we have to stop and shake hands with them and tell them we are on their side?" Ann Too concurred, noting that she would hardly join the men drinking in a bar on election day. "Speaking for my neighborhood," she added, "I don't think we have many women who could be bought for a drink of whiskey but can't say about the men." If anything, allowing women to vote would actually make the polling places safer for women and men alike, according to "Poor Gal," who recounted the scene—all too common in Texas politics—of women having their menfolk on election day, "after spending all day in town, being treated by so many friends seeking office, coming home totally unbalanced, reeling, staggering, swearing, thinking the wife and mother a robber, while she tries to get their clothes off and put them into a nice warm bed before any one outside should suspect the disgrace." It would be far less a disgrace, she argued, when the woman, "by the side of her husband, brother or son, . . . goes to town and puts in her vote."[24]

The most persistent prosuffrage voice among pre-1891 Texas Alliancewomen was an Ennis woman who wrote frequently under the pseudonym "Ann Other." Ann took the suffrage argument beyond the defensive "home protection" arguments that suggested that voting would carry women beyond their proper sphere. "Now will someone kindly tell me what is her proper sphere?" she asked. She catalogued the many occupations that women had held in bygone days, from bakers and brewers to weavers and midwives. In the modern era, she explained, man's "intrusion and invention" had displaced woman from these fields, leaving them to "either accept a life of idleness, and be satisfied with such as her brothers see proper to give her, or she must demand a more useful and energetic life." The consequence was that "woman in idleness naturally loses the bright vigor of her mind," leaving her with nothing to do but marry. Ann looked forward to the day "when society becomes enough advanced in marking the bounds of woman's sphere to give her the untrammeled right to write her name as high on the book of fame in any sphere her tastes dictate," freeing women to marry according to "the dictates of their own lofty sentiments." In making a prosuffrage argument based on the tenets of individualism without defending it on the grounds of domesticity, Ann was anticipating the calls for female equality that would characterize many Populist suffragists' rhetoric once the agrarian revolt entered its political phase in the 1890s: she was arguing that full political rights would liberate women, unlocking the unrealized human potential in half the population. In supporting the People's Party, women such as Ann recognized that Populism held the promise for change that was not merely incremental but truly radical.[25]

In politics, however, reality has a way of intruding on idealism, and this is what happened with regard to woman suffrage. While some Texas suffragists like Ann Other eagerly anticipated the creation of the Third Party in 1891, believing that it would adopt a suffrage plank as part of its state and national platforms, others recognized that endorsing suffrage might jeopardize the party's chances of victory. Better to win elections that would place sympathetic men in office, they argued, and then press for suffrage once the party had consolidated its power. In the party's first state nominating convention in Dallas in 1892, Ellen Lawson Dabbs made just this argument. A medical school graduate and mother of five children and four stepchildren, the thirty-nine-year-old Dabbs was truly a Renaissance woman. In addition to her duties as a practicing physician, wife, and mother, she helped organize the state's first woman suffrage society, actively worked for the Woman's Christian Temperance Union, and founded the Texas Woman's Council, an umbrella organization for women's groups statewide. In 1891, after separating from an abusive husband, she moved to Sulphur Springs, where she became a co-owner and -editor of the *Alliance Vindicator,* Cyclone Davis's old paper. That position lasted only a few months, and later that year she relocated to Fort Worth, where she balanced her medical practice with her job as editor of William Lamb's Alliance-labor newspaper, the *Industrial Educator.* Encouraged in her work by Thomas Nugent, she served as a delegate to the national organizing convention of the People's Party in St. Louis, and now she was called to address the Dallas assemblage. Taking the podium on the convention's first night, she lauded the Populists, saying, probably without exaggeration, that "it was the first time in Texas that a woman had been received in the councils of a political convention." Though a staunch suffragist herself, she came out strongly against the party adopting a suffrage plank. This was "no time to be adding new planks," she asserted, adding that she "preferred success to the people's party above all things." The delegates "heartily applauded" Dabbs's remarks, and the suffrage issue was laid to rest for the time being. She remained a dedicated Populist for the duration of the movement. A tireless advocate of suffrage, she continued to champion a broad range of women's and children's causes until her death from tuberculosis in 1908.[26]

Despite their party's official reticence on the issue, Populist women played a prominent part in the creation of the state's first suffrage organization, the Texas Equal Rights Association (TERA). Founded in 1893, the initial public call for an organizing meeting was signed by eleven women, including not only Ellen Dabbs but also Alliancewoman Grace Danforth, who, like Dabbs, was a medical doctor, and Bettie Gay, a successful plantation owner prominent in both Alliance and People's Party affairs. When the first meeting was held, Dabbs, Danforth, and Gay were among the charter members, and they were joined by Alice McFadin McAnulty, an Alliancewoman and state organizer for the Knights of Labor who later described herself as "a Populist of the deepest dye." Dabbs, Danforth, and McAnulty would all eventually serve as officers in the TERA. Representatives of the Association were frequently featured speakers at Populist and Alliance gatherings throughout the 1890s.[27]

Given the prevailing gender roles and expectations of the era, it required considerable courage for women to organize for suffrage and especially to speak in its behalf at political rallies and conventions, traditionally considered to be masculine affairs. Female suffragists could expect to face ridicule, to have their meetings written off as "hen conventions," and to be portrayed as desexed, masculine women. (Ellen Dabbs once joked that antisuffrage men viewed female suffragists as members of "the shrieking sisterhood.") Men needed a similar, if slightly different, sort of courage to actively champion women's rights. If prosuffrage women ran the risk of appearing unwomanly, male suffragists who publicly assisted them were almost certain to be considered not only unmanly but downright kooky. Describing the first Dallas TERA meeting, the Democratic *Brenham Herald* sneered that "with beating heart and bated breath men slunk around the streets cowed into sullen fear by the gallant array of war-like amazons, who had marched thither from every part of the state. They spoke. In ringing tones mankind was denounced."[28]

It was one thing for a man to admit, as some rather sheepishly did, that they supported suffrage as a means of cleaning up corrupt politics. Such support could be couched in terms that did not violate the separate-spheres ideology— that women's superior moral sensibilities would have a salutary effect on politics by making men behave themselves better at the polls and in the legislative chamber, and that allowing women a voice in government would ensure better legislation on matters such as education and public health, which fell within the bounds of the female sphere. But it was another thing for a man to participate in a suffrage organization and champion women's rights using the liberal arguments of justice, equality, and civil rights. The presence of male

Populists doing just that in the Texas woman suffrage movement demonstrates just how different and forward-looking the political culture of Populism had become.

When the TERA was founded, its list of forty-eight charter members included the names of nine men. Of these, several were prominent Populists. Leading the list was the indefatigable reformer and Populist leader Eben Dohoney of Paris, best known as a prohibitionist but an ardent champion of the full range of Populist causes. One of the original founders of the People's Party in Texas, he sat on the platform committee in 1891 and 1892 and the state executive committee in 1894, served as delegate to the St. Louis and Omaha conventions, and received the nomination for chief justice of the Court of Criminal Appeals in 1894. Joining him as a charter member was Tom J. Russell, one of the leading Populists of Beaumont. A well-known lawyer and Confederate veteran, Russell received the party's nomination for chief justice of the Texas Supreme Court in 1894. Only slightly less prominent in Populist circles was A. B. Bristol, the respected architect who designed the 1889 Dallas city hall and who served as chairman of the Dallas County Populist executive committee, president of the Dallas Populist Club, and delegate to the 1896 Populist National Convention. Bristol's brother-in-law W. A. Jones was another TERA charter member, and while his political affiliation is not known, it seems likely that he was also a Populist. As we saw in Chapter 4, both Bristol and Jones and their wives were also active members of the Dallas Freethinkers' Society, whose membership included at least one other well-known Populist and suffragist, Dr. G. S. Lincoln. L. B. Roebuck, a physician from rural Ellis County who would later run for the state legislature on the Populist ticket, was yet another TERA charter member. It is also safe to assume that C. W. McAnulty shared the enthusiasm of his wife Alice for the People's Party. In all, then, it appears that at least six of the nine male charter members of the TERA were Populists, with four of them prominent enough to have run for office on the Third-Party ticket.[29]

Other Populists soon became actively involved in the suffrage movement. At the TERA's 1894 state convention in Fort Worth, John Wilson Biard, a Populist of statewide renown, appeared as a delegate. Even before the creation of the People's Party he was already well-known in reform circles, having held the post of district lecturer and secretary of the state executive committee of the Farmers' Alliance. The sixty-three-year-old Biard hailed from Jones County in west-central Texas, where he supported his family as a farmer when he was not on the lecture circuit. Enthusiastically embracing Populism from the start, he ran for the state Senate in 1892 and Congress in 1896 and served on the party's state executive committee from 1894 to 1896. A newspaper sketch described him as "a rather quaint character, with a fund of droll wit and an inimitable delivery" whose "diction resembled the uncut diamond." Biard embodied the stereotype of the Populist hayseed; the *Southern Mercury* characterized him as "an old, shabby looking farmer" but acknowledged that "he can talk. His pants are too short, but his tongue is not. There are holes in his elbows, but none in his brains. His humor is keen, and his language, while very rough, is forcible." He even acquired an appropriate nickname, perhaps intended to compare his oratorical skills to those of Cyclone Davis: "Earthquake."[30]

To say that "Earthquake" Biard stood out among the refined women at the 1894 TERA state convention would be an understatement. As a local newspaper reported the scene, "J. W. Baird [sic], whose abundant shaggy grey whiskers looked oddly enough surrounded by his feminine co-laborers, sat in solitary grandeur, the only masculine representative." Biard caused a momentary uproar in the convention when he sided with some other delegates in opposition to a proposed visit to Texas by famed suffragist Susan B. Anthony. Although he called woman suffrage "the cause so dear to our hearts," he worried that a northern woman speaking on suffrage might meet with rough treatment from hostile male audiences. (Biard's specific concern was that she might get pelted with rotten eggs, a fate that he himself met from a Democratic audience just a few months later.) But his presence at the convention signaled that Populist support for suffrage was not limited to the urban sophisticates of the Dallas Freethinkers' Society, and he must have taken pride when, two years later at the People's Party state convention, his niece Minnie Biard officially placed E. L. Dohoney's name in nomination for superintendent of public instruction, giving her "the distinction of being the only lady in Texas who has appeared before a state political convention to nominate a man for office."[31]

More important than the presence of Biard, Dohoney, and other male Populists in the ranks of the suffragists was that of Thomas L. Nugent. Publicly Nugent remained circumspect in his support for suffrage, reflecting his status as the standard-bearer for a party that had not endorsed the measure. "If the reform movement fails," he once wrote, "it will only be because misguided and deluded people insist on packing upon it issues it cannot safely carry." But while he left little commentary on suffrage, his Swedenborgian religious beliefs and well-documented "liberality of nature" put him in sympathy with the movement. His own relationship with his wife Catharine embodied his beliefs about the equality of men and women. Alice King, daughter of Nugent's closest friend Thomas B. King, boarded with the Nugent family in 1888 to 1889, and she recalled that "he shared everything with his wife. He had no thought too high or too low to share with her." Nugent himself believed that "marriage is something more than a mere civil institution." In an age when most men viewed their wives as helpmeets at best, he claimed to need "a wife who can enter by sympathy and purposes into my spiritual life" and who would "labor in the same sphere" as himself. Consequently, he delighted in reading works of literature and philosophy with Catharine, noting that while they did not attend church, they enjoyed their joint studies "more highly than preaching."[32]

Little wonder, then, that when Fort Worth suffragists met to discuss plans for a local suffrage club in 1894, Catharine was there and presided over the meeting. Later, when they met to actually establish their TERA chapter, they elected her as vice president. Moreover, when the TERA met in Fort Worth for its second annual convention, Thomas attended along with Catharine, despite the certainty that he would be the Populists' nominee for governor when the party's state convention met just two weeks later. In a significant moment at that meeting, Catharine rose to tell the delegates that her husband had informed her "that there is no serious obstacle at present existing to prevent the exercise of the right of suffrage by woman," echoing a tactic Susan B. Anthony and others had used to challenge the constitutionality of laws barring their vote in an earlier era. Although Nugent was wrong about the law—the word "male" was indeed in the state constitution's suffrage article—the fact that he was present at the meeting and advising his wife on suffrage in an encouraging way suggests where his sympathies lay. The press noted that Nugent, along with fellow Populists Biard and Dohoney, "encouraged the meeting by their presence." Less charitable Democratic papers identified him as one of the "male cranks" at the convention, and during the fall campaign, his opponent, Democrat Charles Culberson, would attempt to link him with suffrage. Commenting on the establishment of the Dallas suffrage group, the press noted that "the club has recently waxed strong from the receipt of new members and has found encouragement in having on their side Judge Thomas L. Nugent, who has a following of 160,000 voters in Texas."[33]

The party's official silence on suffrage at the state level certainly did not prevent the issue from being discussed—and often championed—at the grassroots level. In early 1892, several months before the first state nominating convention, William Lamb acknowledged that several Populist county conventions had endorsed female voting. He cautioned that "we should deal with these subjects very carefully and not load ourselves down with a good thing just because it is good. . . . Let us put on only a moderate load and not make the cargo so great as to wreck the train by falling through the first little bridge we attempt to cross." But local Alliance and Populist groups continued to pass resolutions favoring suffrage, and the issue never entirely went away. Preparing to introduce a suffrage plank at an upcoming Populist congressional convention in 1894, Major William Flournoy of Waco exclaimed, "Ours is essentially a reform party and great reform is impossible without the direct co-operation of the ladies. They were the first in promoting Christianity and they will be first as heralds of pure politics, which are only impure because of continuous and exclusive masculine control." Flournoy believed he would have "hearty support from prominent delegates whom I have converted." At an 1894 meeting of the Dallas TERA chapter, architect A. B. Bristol, then chairman of the Dallas County Populist executive committee, spoke in favor of suffrage. He said he was a member of a committee (appointed by whom, we are not told) that was planning to attend the upcoming Populist state convention and work to secure a suffrage plank. He was not sure if it would succeed, because the People's Party "was a new party and was cautious about the subject," but he thought that a majority of the delegates favored suffrage. In any event, he expressed certainty that when the Populists controlled the legislature they would enact a suffrage law immediately.[34]

No record exists to indicate whether Flournoy or Bristol acted on their intentions to push for a suffrage plank in the state platform, but prosuffrage speakers received invitations—and often warm welcomes—in Populist gatherings great and small. In 1893 Williamson County Populists held a Fourth of July picnic that attracted between two and three thousand. One of the featured speakers was Sarah L. Trumbull of Dallas, first vice president of TERA. "Mrs. Trumbull was listened to with much interest and her views were presented with much force," the Dallas Morning News reported. "She is a pleasant speaker, and as the populists are friendly to woman suffrage she found her audience in sympathy with her." Even at their state conventions, the Populists always went out of their way to seat women prominently on the speaker's platform, a rarity at Democratic conventions. The TERA sent two representatives to the 1894 Populist state convention to lobby for suffrage, including Alice McAnulty, the Knights of Labor organizer and secretary of TERA. In 1896 she was one of twenty women seated on the platform, although the press reported that "she is not present in an official capacity and made no effort to secure a plank on equal suffrage."[35]

Clearly women's inability to vote did not disqualify them from active participation in party affairs. During the 1892 elections, the state executive committee issued explicit instructions that local Populist clubs, the most basic building block of the party's organization, were to admit women as "honorary members." That designation might sound condescending—and in some ways it was, echoing as it did the "woman-on-a-pedestal" mentality of the era—but there was a very practical reason to admit women as only honorary rather than regular members: by being admitted to membership on that basis, they were excused from having to pay dues. If the party had wanted to discourage female participation, the surest way to do it would be to tell a male Populist that he had to pay double dues if he wanted to bring his wife.[36]

That women played more than merely an ornamental role in local party affairs is evidenced by events in at least two Texas counties where women actually ran for office. In 1894, McLennan County Populists nominated Hallie Milburn Dunklin of Waco for the office of county superintendent of public instruction. Dunklin was another example of a multitalented professional woman who was drawn to Populism. Educated at the Salem (N.C.) Female College, she married a prominent medical doctor and landowner from Galveston, moved to Waco with her husband around 1880, and after his death in 1882 managed his estate and worked as a schoolteacher. Sometime in the 1890s she went to work on a Waco newspaper, the *Telephone,* which she later bought. In addition to working on her newspaper and participating in Populist politics, she was a member of the Texas Women's Press Association and a wide range of civic clubs and philanthropic causes. Her entry into the race, according to the *Morning News,* was sure to "add much interest to the county campaign."[37]

Two years later, in like fashion, the *Morning News* reported that Miss Narnie Harrison of Hunt County, a faculty member at Burleson College in Greenville, was a Populist candidate for county school superintendent. "The populists are enthusiastic in her support and claim a certainty of her election," the paper noted. The story acknowledged the potential problem with a female candidate, since Texas law required that any officeholder be a qualified voter. Harrison's supporters, however, argued that this provision dated to an earlier era when the superintendent's office was appointive, and that when the office was made elective no mention was made of the requirement. In both Harrison's and Dunklin's cases they were advised that if they won there would certainly be legal challenges, but their supporters believed that an act of the legislature could remove their disabilities, and they both seemed confident that this would happen. Neither won, so the issue was never tested. The Dunklin and

Harrison candidacies were isolated occurrences, and their nominations were for the one local office—school superintendent—that could most easily be reconciled with woman's sphere of expertise. Nevertheless, the fact that these women received nominations at the male-dominated county conventions and presumably campaigned actively against male Democratic opponents in the highly masculine political culture of 1890s Texas meant that the Populist men of those two counties—both of which were among the most heavily populated counties in the state—underscores the distance that male Texas Populists had traveled on the road to a new understanding of gender relations. If they could enthusiastically back female candidates, they clearly were open to woman suffrage and other forms of equality.[38]

The fact remains that the People's Party at the state level dodged the suffrage issue; however, they sounded like staunch feminists when compared to Texas Democrats. In March 1894, a few weeks before the three-day TERA convention in Fort Worth, the *Dallas Morning News* conducted an extraordinary set of interviews with thirty leading Democrats to see where they stood on the question. Their answers reveal the extent of their resistance to the idea of women voting, in stark contrast with the progressive positions of many Populists.[39]

The politicians polled included the governor, lieutenant governor, other statewide officials, state legislators, judges, railroad commissioners, ex-congressmen, and various candidates. Of the thirty Democrats, only three voiced unqualified support for suffrage, with three others willing to consider female voting on school-related matters and four others not prepared to say. The reporter, who asked quite probing questions, perceptively prefaced his story by observing that "to the large majority the possibility of woman's comradeship at the polls had never occurred; they could scarcely imagine such a condition of affairs, and were hardly ready to meet the exigencies of the question." This alone indicates how radical most Democrats considered the proposition. Nevertheless, those who answered managed to serve up virtually all of the standard objections.[40]

Most simply fell back on the separate-spheres argument. Former state senator J. W. Crayton of Rockwall spoke for several others when he argued that "it would tend to degrade her to mix and mingle in political convention and at the polls with men." Former Confederate cabinet member and US senator, and present Railroad Commission chairman John H. Reagan agreed, saying, "I wouldn't approve of women making political speeches and particularly in canvasses and campaigns." Judge Beauregard Bryan contended that he held "such a high regard for women that he intends doing all in his power to prevent women from the degradation of voting." Another judge, E. W. Terhune, feared that "her fine mental and moral senses would become degraded in politics." Congressional candidate Jake Hodges opined that women "were altogether too near being angels to be allowed to vote," and that "politicians were too bad and the ballot too impure for lovely woman to come in contact with, and he hoped that there would always be enough good men to see that they were kept far, far away." L. L. Foster, former speaker of the Texas House and current railroad commissioner, snidely claimed to be "an ardent advocate of woman's suffrage for at least fifty yards around the house," adding that he had seven children, "and if every woman was as busy as his wife they had enough to contend with without going into politics. The latter would tend to destroy the home, break up family life and overturn the status that men and women occupied in reference to natural laws."[41]

Many of the respondents argued either that existing laws or the votes of husbands satisfactorily protected women's interests, so there was no need for them to vote. John Reagan took this view, stating, "I believe the laws of Texas already sufficiently protect their rights, and that they already have all the rights they can reasonably expect." J. M. Carlisle, the state superintendent of public instruction, concurred, claiming that "the laws of Texas do her ample justice and grant her full protection, all that she can ask, and that she would lose more than she would gain by going into politics." Lieutenant Governor Martin M. Crane "was so positive that every woman made her husband do as she pleased that there was no necessity for her to vote." Queried by the reporter if it was "possible that men have no political individuality," Crane facetiously explained that "no married man has any individuality of his own whatever." State senator George Jester, who would soon replace Crane as lieutenant governor, believed, "It is absolutely necessary for one sex or the other to be the home-keepers and remain within the precincts of home, instead of seeking political precincts. Women are amply represented by men." When the reporter asked who would represent widows and single women, Jester replied, "Well, I never saw a woman yet that couldn't be represented if she wanted to. If she isn't, you may put it down that it is her own fault."[42]

The Democrats held mixed opinions on women's mental capacities for exercising the franchise, though almost all condescendingly acknowledged their "moral superiority." E. G. Senter, the editor of the *Fort Worth Gazette,* stated that he "regretted the lack of opportunity to consult with his wife before giving a full opinion" but then went on to say that women's "sympathies were too easily worked upon, they were too impulsive, and apt to be governed by what the heart dictates rather than reason." Charles Morse, clerk of the state supreme court, voiced "a doubtful 'perhaps' to the question of their mental ability." Congressional candidate James S. Wood vowed that he favored "electing every good woman to an office—the office of queen of the household," but he stated, "with mild sarcasm," that "she is about as well qualified to vote as the nigger." And of course, no Democratic discussion of suffrage would be complete unless someone raised the specter of black women gaining the franchise. Judge Norman Kittrell voiced this concern, and when the reporter pointed out that black men voted, the judge replied that "the white woman wouldn't vote if she could, and the negro woman would vote early and often."[43]

Of particular interest, naturally, were the comments of the sitting governor. "Gov. Hogg was opposed to women taking a hand in politics, carrying six-shooters and going to war," the reporter noted, adding that "the group of robust statesmen that hung on his words instinctively drew a long breath and felt relieved." Hogg could not have been unaware of the growing ferment over suffrage in Texas—a local TERA chapter had just been founded in Dallas, the following week one was slated to be established in Fort Worth, and the state meeting would take place in May—but he revealed his casual attitude toward the movement later that summer on a trip to the North. Asked about suffrage by a reporter there, he replied inaccurately that the movement had not yet reached Texas. When word of his comments reached the TERA, its members decided to "kindly put his honor right on this question by sending him the following resolution: Resolved, that it is the sense of every member of this association that Gov. James Stephen Hogg owes to the Equal Rights association of Texas, and especially to the forty-five lady members of this club, an apology for his conduct, and a further apology to the citizens of Texas for denying the existence of one of the most necessary of her institutions." Hogg subsequently thanked them for their "courteous letter of the 1st, notifying me of the organization of the Equal Rights association of Texas, and to express my appreciation of the good ladies of Texas under all circumstances." Needless to say, no endorsement of their cause accompanied the governor's perfunctory statement.[44]

None of this is meant to suggest that all Populists supported woman suffrage, or that all suffragists were Populists. But overall, the contrasts between Populists and Democrats on the subject could scarcely have been more striking. So rare was a Democrat openly endorsing suffrage that when Perry Hawkins, a Baptist minister who also edited the *Taylor Journal*, joined that city's suffrage club, local suffragists found it remarkable enough to note that "he is a democrat and advocates 'justice to women' editorially." What the Democrats were revealing here was their traditional understanding of what really entitled men to vote. It was a sensibility rooted in antebellum conceptions of masculinity and race—the independent white man protects his dependents (which before the Civil War included white women and slaves) and speaks for them politically through the ballot. The white woman lost her legal independence when she married; her status became essentially that of the slave, dependent entirely on her husband. Marriage was a *contract*, but once that contract was consummated, women had only *status*—the status of a dependent. Emancipation made the relationship of ex-slaves to their former masters a contractual one, but married women remained the dependents of their husbands, nonpersons in the eyes of the law. Indeed, with the loss of their mastery over slaves, white men in the postbellum era may have guarded their mastery over their wives even more jealously, as suggested by the paternalistic comments of leading Texas Democrats. When E. L. Godkin, the editor of the *Nation*, wrote in 1867 that the growing tendency in modern America was "to submit our social relations more and more to the dominion of contract simply," he was anticipating what Populists would be doing in the 1890s. The Populists, in entertaining the notion that women should vote, had clearly left the paternalist sensibility behind and moved toward something more similar to the modern liberal notion of individual rights, a notion embodied in the principle of "one person, one vote."[45]

One searches in vain for any Populist leader of any prominence who took the sort of positions that the aforementioned Democratic politicians did—with one exception, and the responses to his statement by friend and foe alike reveal him to have been the proverbial exception that proves the rule. In November 1894, just after the fall elections, *Southern Mercury* editor Milton Park editorialized about the recent elections in Colorado, in which the Populist governor Davis Waite met defeat. The previous year, voters had approved a suffrage referendum with Waite's active support and with relatively little controversy, making Colorado the second state in the union (after Wyoming) to give women the right to vote. Populists naturally claimed credit for the measure and used that claim to woo female voters in the 1894 elections, but in reality suffrage had come about as a consequence of a well-organized campaign by suffrage groups not necessarily friendly to Populism. In any event, after the election Waite bitterly, though probably incorrectly, blamed women for his defeat. Now Milton Park seized on these events to warn Texas Populists about the dangers of woman suffrage. The results in Colorado, he wrote, stood as "incontrovertible evidence that women are not sufficiently educated in the duties of citizenship to exercise the functions conferred on them, by the ballot, safely and considerately." Park qualified his statement, saying, "Let the right to vote on minor offices, such as school commissioners and other non-political offices, begin them first, and they will gradually grow into a knowledge of the responsibilities and duties devolving upon the voter and sovereign." But he ended his editorial by warning that if Texas enacted full suffrage, "there is little doubt but that they would repeat the mistakes made by their sisters in Colorado. Woman suffrage has now been tried, and it develops that women have a very important lesson to learn before they can pass examination."[46]

It is difficult to say what motivated Park (plate 16). Georgia-born and Alabama-raised, he had served in the Confederate army before moving to Texas in 1876. After returning in the 1880s to Alabama, where, ironically, he served as president of a women's college, in 1886 he again moved to Texas and resumed his career as an educator. In 1891 he became editor of the *Mercury*, replacing Samuel Dixon, who had refused to support the Subtreasury Plan and the Alliance's move toward third-party politics. Perceptive readers (particularly women) might have noted that Park's ascent to the editorship had coincided with a drastic curtailment of women's content in the pages of the *Mercury*, although this may have been a result of the decline of the Alliance and the rise of the Third Party more than any conscious bias on the part of Park. More likely is that Park was simply very committed to achieving victory on the standard Populist economic platform, and anything that might stand in the way of that goal was not to be tolerated. He would later number among those Populists who would tend to blame African Americans for the party's defeat, another indication that he lacked the liberal mindset that characterized so many other Populist leaders.[47]

Whatever his motives, he was probably unprepared for the reaction from readers—especially prosuffrage women who had come to expect better things from the party's leadership. A month after the initial antisuffrage editorial ran, Park told readers of a letter he had received from Grace Danforth, an Austin medical doctor, Alliancewoman, and one of the officers of the TERA, asking him to publish an article answering the editorial. Park explained that he would not publish Danforth's letter, saying, "It is 'just like a woman' to assert that we declared that women ought not to receive the right of suffrage until they were educated to vote the populist ticket." He claimed his editorial was simply "a statement of facts relative to the Colorado election" and asserted that the

Mercury favored equal rights, "but everything cannot be accomplished in a day. The motto, 'Hasten slowly,' is quite appropriate in this connection." This might have helped to mollify prosuffrage readers, but then he made the mistake of repeating the old chestnut about the polling place not being a suitable environment for women, and advised women to "continue knitting a while longer, and the populists will have the power, and they will make the voting places fit to be visited by the women. See?"[48]

Indeed, they saw. It did not help that Park finished his comments by calling suffrage "a good cause" and wished Danforth success in convincing the two old parties to support it. It was clear at this point that the editor of the party's state organ held little sympathy for suffrage. There followed another exchange of letters and editorials between Park and Danforth that degenerated into a petty argument in which Danforth contended that men had been blaming their problems on women ever since Adam and Eve, and Park, in turn, branded Eve a suffragist. Finally Park declared that if women want to vote in Texas, they "should define the measures they propose to champion when they secure equal rights." Then, as if to punctuate his argument, he published an antisuffrage letter from one Mary Raborn, who declared it was "time to stop howling for woman's suffrage when not one woman in five hundred has ever read the Declaration of Independence and would not know the Constitution of the United States from a patent office report."[49]

This war of words finally drew a response from the senior stateswoman of Texas Populism, Bettie Munn Gay (plate 17). The fifty-eight-year-old Gay was one of the extraordinary figures in the People's Revolt. She was born in Alabama but moved to Texas with her parents as a small child. Her father died when she was young, and her mother then married Reddin Andrews Sr., whose son and namesake went on to become president of Baylor University and a prominent Populist himself. As a young woman Bettie married a well-to-do planter from Colorado County, Rufus King Gay, and applied herself studying philosophy and natural science. The war and Reconstruction took its toll on her husband's fortune, and when he died in 1880, he left her with a burden of heavy debt and daunting economic prospects. By dint of hard work, economy, and exceptional ability, she managed to pay off the mortgage on her 1,776-acre plantation. In the 1880s she became an ardent Alliancewoman, contributing frequent letters to the *Southern Mercury*. When the Democratic Party balked at the Alliance's demand for the Subtreasury system in early 1891, she announced that she could "see no hope of reform in either of the old parties." Writing in the *Mercury*, she called for "a new political party whose platform is based upon the principles of the reform movement" and urged her fellow Al-liancefolk to "go to battle and contend for our principles instead of compro-mising with the party politicians." Several months later, an open letter she wrote to Democratic congressman William H. Crain displayed such a mas-terful knowledge of Populist economic policy that it commanded the entire front page of the *Mercury*. By early 1892 her stature in the party was such that she was elected to represent Texas at the founding convention of the national People's Party in St. Louis, where she made such an impression that one East Coast newspaper questioned why she was not named to the national execu-tive committee. Although she never held another official position in the party, she spoke at Populist rallies and was seated on the speakers' platform at the 1896 state convention. Her son James Jehu Bates Gay served on the state ex-ecutive committee.[50]

Milton Park must have felt he could ill afford to refuse the columns of his paper to a Populist of Gay's stature, so he published her letter, which sounded a ringing call for suffrage: "John the Baptist lived in the wilderness till he came forth to herald the time of the coming of the Saviour. The women have been in the wilderness for one hundred years. According to the prophecy of John it is time for them to come out of the wilderness, for he (John) says: 'And all flesh shall see the salvation of God.' There may be those in the people's party who, like Herod, would be willing to behead them, but the wise women of Texas will yet lead the men out of darkness, as they (the men) have been a failure in their management of governmental affairs." Significantly, Gay did not make the case for woman suffrage using the common "home protection" argument, that women should have the right to vote because, as the guardians of domes-ticity, they had a duty to protect their children. And while she did invoke the "civic housekeeping" argument, which proposed that women's votes were needed to clean up the mess that men had made, she ultimately invoked the liberal argument for suffrage on the grounds of individual rights: "We pro-pose to have a say in the laws that govern us, as intelligent beings. . . . No party will give woman her rights till she demands them. The time is not distant when she will demand, and not ask, any party to recognize her. All that is needed is the proper education, and that is going on faster than any party is aware of."[51]

She also leveled a stinging rebuke at Park, expressing surprise that "an in-telligent editor" would blame women for the Colorado Populists' defeat, and she went on to give a surprisingly accurate account of how the Democrats and Republicans "spent piles of money" there to win the election. "All the fraud that is perpetrated hereafter in Colorado will be laid upon the women," she bitterly complained. To Park's ungenerous offer to publish Grace Danforth's defense of suffrage if she would boil it down to one column, Gay angrily responded, "To fully define our position would take too long an article for a newspaper. If all the women were like myself they would not ask man for any rights. What more rights have they than we? Ignorance on the part of woman has kept her in slavery."[52]

The Democratic press rather gleefully seized on the Populists' brouhaha over suffrage, praising Park for his un-Populist-like opposition to women's rights. Although the Democrats rarely missed an opportunity to exploit any division in the Populist ranks, their effusive praise of Park's position only underscores how thoroughly Populists had become identified with woman suffrage in the public's mind; it was the sheer novelty of an important party spokesman going against that trend that made Park's comments so newsworthy.[53]

~

If campaign styles and rhetoric, and the debate over suffrage, suggest a major ideological fault line dividing Democrats from Populists—a fault line defined by gender—then we would expect to see these differences reflected in actual policy once Populists were elected to office. The election of twenty-four Populists to the state legislature in 1894 provided the opportunity to test whether this fault line was mere style or actual substance. When the legislature convened for its biennial session in January 1895, a major petition campaign by women's groups was already in full swing. The object of the campaign was to raise the "age of consent"—that is, the minimum age at which females could legally consent to sex outside of marriage, so their male partners were not guilty of statutory rape—from twelve to eighteen. Not surprisingly, Populist women numbered prominently among the leaders of the campaign. Spearheading the effort was the state Woman's Christian Temperance Union (WCTU), along with the Texas Woman's Council, an umbrella organization for various women's civic, religious, and literary groups, led by its founder and president, Dr. Ellen Lawson Dabbs, one of the foremost female Texas Populists. Before long, petitions even from groups of local women unaffiliated with any particular organization were flooding the mailboxes of state legislators. One count put the total number of signatures at fifty thousand, an astonishing achievement.[54]

The women based their case on two main points. First was a variety of the "home protection" argument—that young girls simply lacked the maturity to resist the wiles of predatory adult men. As "A Mother of Girls" asked in the

Dallas-Galveston *News,* "What knowledge did you possess at 12 years of age to help you to decide upon any course of life? What does your daughter know? Our habit has always been to shield our baby girls from the knowledge of the wickedness in the world. Perhaps we should not, but we all do it. We keep them as innocent as babes, yet our law says they should be as wise as mature women." The second argument was a legalistic one—that according to the law women were not mature enough to make contracts or control their property until twenty-one, and that they could not even marry without their parents' consent until eighteen: "Only when it comes to consenting to a dishonorable act that forever shuts her from an hour's happiness or the possibility of regaining her lost estate, dooming her until death—to such an act she may legally consent at 12 years of age!"[55]

Leading the charge for the bill in the legislature was sixty-three-year-old Populist senator Willis Lyman Harrison of Bell County in Central Texas (plate 18). The Alabama-born Harrison was a medical doctor who had served as a surgeon in the Confederate army before moving to Texas in 1869. Sometime after 1877 he received ordination as a Disciples of Christ minister. Little more is known about him, but the fact that he was one of only two Populists to win a state Senate seat—and that from a five-county district—suggests the regard in which he must have been held. In the House, Populist representative William E. Cureton also introduced an age-of-consent bill, though his bill proposed raising the age only to sixteen. Cureton, born in 1848, had grown up on the Texas frontier, where his father Jack gained renown as a ranger and Indian-fighter. As a young man William worked as a cowboy in a region still contested by the Comanche Indians, and in his later years he prospered as a cattleman and farmer, amassing seven hundred acres in northern Bosque County. His two sons also became Populist leaders, with one of them, Calvin, later becoming state attorney general and chief justice of the state supreme court. Although a sizable number of Democrats also supported the idea of raising the age of consent, Harrison's version of the bill eventually became the main focus of the debate, and it was soon substituted for Cureton's and other members' bills in the House. Texas legislative rules only rarely required recorded roll-call votes on legislation, so we have limited information on how individual members voted, but in every case where votes or the sentiments of Populists were recorded, they supported raising the age, if not to eighteen, then at least to sixteen or seventeen. This placed them at odds with lawmakers— invariably Democrats—who opposed the measure on a variety of grounds.[56]

The debates over Harrison's age-of-consent bill starkly reveal the conflicting ideologies of gender and honor between Populists and the Democrats who opposed them. At first, many supporters of the measure assumed that it would meet little opposition; one writer to the *Galveston Daily News*, hearing that funds were being raised by women's groups to employ a lobbyist to promote their cause, expressed disbelief that such a tactic was necessary. He asked, "Do we have to pay a man to lobby for this purpose? Is all honor dead? Have our representatives forgotten their wives, mothers, daughters and sisters? No; I will not believe it of them. Texas men have too correct an idea of right. . . . When this is brought to their notice they will as one man demand that the 'age of consent' be raised."[57]

But in asking whether honor was dead, the writer had unwittingly touched the raw nerve that the debate had exposed among Texans; the two sides in the debate, perhaps without fully realizing it, held very different conceptions of what manly honor meant. The Populists and their allies who supported the bill had long since abandoned the traditional southern ethic of honor that vested honor solely in the individual white gentleman, a head of household who personally defended his dependent women and children—with violence, if necessary—against any and all threats. In the culture of honor, assigning the protection of young women to the state constituted a direct affront to manly honor. As one Democratic editor succinctly put it, "The best law on the age of consent is proper training, followed by the shotgun when veered from right by a miserable scoundrel." Sen. William J. Bailey of Tarrant County, a Democratic opponent of the bill, asked, "Shall it go out to the world that the chivalry of our southern men is not sufficient to protect the virtue of our southern women? . . . Has southern manhood become so degraded that it is necessary for us to protect our daughters by the enactment of a law originally intended for infants?"[58]

In place of the culture of honor, Populists—and some like-minded Democrats—had embraced the concept of manly dignity, wherein men governed their passions, exercised self-control, sought to avoid violence, and relied on the rule of law to treat all people equally and enforce community values. The editor of the *Austin Statesman*, though not a Populist, strongly supported the Populist position on the age-of-consent bill, and he expressed that position through language that reflected the code of dignity over that of honor. Addressing lawmakers, he asked, "Are you like men, brave men, ready to rise to the dignity and strength of the occasion and throw around the innocence and purity of this state the sacred harness of the law to protect it from disgrace and infamy?"[59]

The debate on age of consent, centered as it was on the question of individual male prerogative, inevitably involved not just men's exclusive control over women but also their control over government. The issue of suffrage thus entered the debate. When the consent bill was being debated in mid-February, women who supported the measure packed the Senate gallery, prompting the Democrats who opposed the bill to cry "intimidation." A correspondent for the *San Antonio Light* reported that "50 grim visaged and determined women, all of them members of the women's Christian Temperance Union and most of them from Kansas and other states, loomed up in the Senate chamber." The description of these women as "grim visaged" suggested that they lacked womanliness—womanly women were always smiling—and the reporter added that "many of the Senators expressed themselves as being grateful that the faces of very few southern women could be seen in the line." The reference to Kansas women, of course, needed no explanation to the paper's readers: Kansas was the Populist state that had given the vote to women, thus unsexing them and, in the process, rendering Kansas men unmanly. As Senator Bailey noted, it was "all well enough for the women to appeal in writing for their bill, but to come into the lobby of either House and openly assert their right is very unladylike to say the least," and he criticized the "easy affront with which some of these female lobbyists have discussed the matter with the Senators," a breach of gender etiquette that had caused male senators "to blush." Defenders of the bill were quick to point out that the charge was false and demanded that Bailey withdraw "his offensive allusion to them as Kansas women." Populist-feminist Ellen Dabbs drew perhaps the clearest parallel between the age-of-consent issue and women's lack of a voice in government. Answering a critic who had claimed that women indirectly "originate every law" through their moral influence over men, Dabbs referenced laws that set the age of consent at twelve or thirteen: "Woman never made these laws; her stamp is not on them."[60]

It soon became clear that the bill would not secure easy passage. In the Senate, Willis Harrison's original bill was referred to the all-Democratic judiciary committee, and when it emerged, the committee had lowered the proposed new age of consent to fourteen and added a provision that allowed the jury to consider whether the victim was "a female of bad character for chastity." (The committee later amended this phrase to read "a common prostitute.") What followed was a contentious month-long debate, with attempts to amend the bill up to sixteen, then to eighteen, then back down to thirteen, then seventeen, and finally, in an obvious attempt by Senator Bailey to kill the bill entirely, to twenty-five. Realizing the hopelessness of the bill's original age of eighteen, the two Senate Populists finally supported the compromise age of sixteen, at which point opponents began filibustering the bill by demanding several calls of the Senate, a time-consuming maneuver technically intended to ascertain the presence of a quorum, although everyone knew that a quorum was present; this was merely a stalling tactic. At one point in the debate, Willis Harrison took the floor and made a speech reiterating his support for his original bill. Summoning his training as a minister, he excoriated those who opposed raising the age to eighteen as "certain lewd fellows of the baser sort," a phrase from the New Testament book of Acts which the apostle Paul uses to describe a violent mob. Harrison asked, "Is not this legislation sought in response to a constantly growing desire to raise the standard of our civilization and to the demands of progress?" In likening the anti–age-of-consent Democrats to Paul's "lewd fellows of the baser sort," Harrison was clearly invoking the Populist conception of dignified manhood, which subordinated passion to reason and individualistic honor to the more "civilized" idea of the rule of law. He noted that "the very best element of society of both sexes" supported the age-eighteen standard, and he closed by adding, "Should there be an old bachelor here who opposes the protection herein guaranteed to the girls of Texas, I only wish he may live and die an old bachelor." The bill eventually passed the Senate with the age set at fifteen, with the Populist senators supporting it, no doubt reluctantly. In the House, where Populists were outnumbered 109 to 22, events played out in similar fashion, and Gov. Charles Culberson signed Harrison's watered-down bill into law.[61]

The age of consent, like so many other gendered issues, could not avoid being linked with race. Just as white men derived much of their identity and power from contrasting (and exaggerating) their differences with women, so did they derive identity and power by contrasting (and exaggerating) their differences with African Americans. In doing both, gender was racialized and race was gendered. Opponents of the age-of-consent law repeatedly raised the specter of supposedly licentious black and Mexican girls luring unsuspecting white boys or men into sexual liaisons, where, if the age of consent were raised, the males would become the victims of blackmail or face rape charges. And any world in which a white male might be victimized by a nonwhite female was truly a world turned upside down. Democratic senator Walter Tips observed that he had "seen Mexican girls marry at 12 and have a child at 13 years.

I have often seen negro girls of 14 almost developed into womanhood." In such cases, he said, a girl might commit "sexual cohabitation of her own free will" and it "will never be rape no matter how often you may declare by law that it is rape." Tips and other Democrats were open to amending the state's seduction laws to accommodate such cases, but that was as far as they were willing to go. (Seduction laws carried relatively mild penalties.) In the House, when the judiciary committee reported favorably on such a law, the two Populists on the committee were joined by three Democrats in issuing a dissenting minority report deeming it "inexpedient and unwise to consider or pass a measure calculated to lessen the crime and lower the punishment" in such cases.[62]

Helen Stoddard of the WCTU, Ellen Dabbs's partner in leading the age-of-consent campaign, appeared before the Senate Judiciary Committee after it had reduced the age in Harrison's bill from eighteen to fourteen. She addressed the contention of some Democrats that the bill would wrongly protect African American girls. "As I pass along the streets of our city and see the mulatto children, I think the colored girl needs protection," she noted, "and more than that, the Anglo-savage man needs the restraints of this law to help him realize the dignity and sacred heritage he possesses by being born into the dominant race of the world." She also touched on the argument that the bill would result in the blackmail "by debased colored girls against innocent white men." She told legislators what they undoubtedly already knew, that in a state where all judges and juries were white, "no conviction could be made against an innocent man." Moreover, it was not the daughters and sisters of elite whites who were really endangered by the current law: "The defenseless, the orphaned, or worse than orphaned, these are the children of the state, and it is surely for the state's interest that these should grow into virtuous womanhood."[63]

Stoddard was echoing the case that Melvin Wade made when, in response to a question about social equality of the races, he joked about taking a shotgun to "the fust white scountrl that comes foolin' around my folks." Stoddard and Wade both knew that for all the Democrats' talk of white men being entrapped or blackmailed by women of color, the reality was that many white men could not imagine not having sexual access to such women, access that reinforced their patriarchal dominance. With slavery and the unfettered access it afforded white men to black women a thing of the past, white men in the 1890s were all that more determined not to lose this marker of masculine privilege. No white male Populist ever came out and said this in so many words, but their advocacy of the age-of-consent cause gave breathing room to those, like Stoddard and Wade, who did.[64]

In the midst of the Senate debate over the age-of-consent law, Democratic senator Oscar B. Colquitt suddenly introduced a bill expanding the possible penalties for a rape conviction to include death, castration, or life in prison. Another measure introduced by Sen. Joseph B. Dibrell would allow juries to impose life imprisonment for *attempted* rape. A House Democrat later unsuccessfully sought to add a castration clause to this bill as well. (The *Morning News* explained that "the temper of the house was decidedly in favor of its adoption," but that concerns that the castration clause would "vitiate the bill" led to the amendment's withdrawal.) At first glance, it might seem counterintuitive that Democrats who had fought so hard against raising the age of consent in statutory rape cases would support such draconian punishments for rape convictions under the existing laws. But when the overlay of race is added—which always must be done when considering rape in the late nineteenth-century South—the Democrats' purposes come into sharp focus. These expanded-punishment bills all had one thing in common—they applied only to *sentences*, so in effect they granted all-white judges and juries power to selectively apply the punishments—that is, to mete them out only to nonwhite defendants. The Populist age-of-consent laws, by contrast, expanded the *definition* of rape, which would apply to perpetrators regardless of race and thus place white men in jeopardy of punishment, exposing them at least to the minimum penalties prescribed under the law. In other words, Democrats who adhered to the southern culture of honor, which vested all meaningful power in the hands of white men, had no difficulty using the power of the law in ways that bolstered their authority over women and nonwhites. But when confronted by laws that might limit their control over these groups, they stood their ground.[65]

One final, little-noticed bill further confirms this interpretation. Near the end of the 1895 session, Populist representative T. R. Watkins of Corsicana introduced a bill amending a provision in the state criminal code that placed a one-year statute of limitation on the time in which rape indictments could be brought. Watkins's bill would remove that limit in age-of-consent cases, or when the rape was committed "upon a woman of unsound mind, or upon a prisoner by a keeper or custodian, or upon a ward by a guardian, or when the offense of rape and incest are combined." These types of rape cases were precisely the sort most likely to be brought against abusive family members or acquaintances, where the consequence of the rape—an unwanted child whose presence was concealed for a time, or mental anguish that delayed the victim's report—might require a year or more to result in an indictment. Accusations against alleged black rapists, by contrast, were almost always virtually instantaneous following the incident (or in the case of consensual black-white relationships, following its exposure). Once again, here was a Populist-backed sex-reform law that might operate against whites as readily as it would against nonwhites. The House *Journal* left a terse testimony to the bill's fate: "Died on speaker's table."[66]

~

It would be easy to view Populist support for more equitable sex-crime laws, for suffrage, and for an expanded role for women in public life as phenomena springing mainly from the party's leadership and educated class, but such a reading of the evidence would be in error. When ordinary farm women joined local Populist clubs and participated in those clubs' deliberations, when they stood for hours in the hot sun at a party camp meeting to hear a speech by Ellen Dabbs or Alice McAnulty or Bettie Gay, when they wrote letters and essays and saw them published in the Populist press, or when they signed petitions to reform the age-of-consent law and sent them to Populist legislators for action, they were challenging the very foundations of power in a society organized around a system of patriarchy. When Populist men encouraged female participation in party affairs, listened to women's opinions and desires, and acted on those wishes in their meetings and in the halls of government, they likewise challenged that system. Texas Populists' reformulation of gender, far from being a peripheral aspect of their story, lay at the heart of what it meant to be a Populist. It meant more than just championing a fairer economic system (although some Populists such as Milton Park could not see past that); it meant rethinking how society itself should operate—whether white men would continue to determine what was best for themselves and everyone else, or if something more closely resembling actual democracy would come to pass. That most male Populists were not yet committed suffragists, or that they still saw women's principal duties as being in the home, should not obscure the fact that they had participated in a quiet revolution in what it meant to be "manly" and "womanly." Their rejection of the patriarchal system of southern honor and their substitution of the code of dignity in its place, along with their efforts to think and act more liberally when it came to race, offered a path to a future very different from the one offered by the Democrats who controlled Texas.[67]

Very few of the voices of ordinary Populists—especially Populist women—survive to give form to this path not taken. But in 1892, Mrs. M. E. Forbes (we do not know whether the initials were hers or her husband's), from the small farming community of Allen in Collin County, took time from her day to write a letter to the editor of the local Populist paper. Addressing her fellow women, she proposed to "tell what I think of the politics of today": "Sisters, who ever heard of the like, a woman thinking about such things [as politics]? Why, that is perfectly 'rediculous' so the democrats say, but I can't think that way, and I think I have a few on my side. I think that any one that has to abide by the laws of the country, ought to have a perfect right to help make them, but the democrats of my neighborhood, and I suppose it is the same all over the country, seem to think that the place for a woman is at home rocking the cradle and cooking what little they get to cook, and say nothing about it." She went on to put words into the mouths of those Democratic men: "We men don't want any of your help. I guess we have been running things for the centuries past and I guess we can still run them." She then recited all the ways men had mismanaged the affairs of the nation, from the brutal crushing of the Homestead Strike to the government's mishandling of monetary policy, and offered some advice to her "sisters": "Ladies, Listen! We have no right to vote, but we have a right to talk, thank God, and as we have tongues to talk with let us use them to the best of our ability. Young ladies when your sweet-heart comes next Sunday, ask him to vote for the peoples party, and if he says he can't, tell him he c-a-n'-t tie his mule at your gate again until he gets his eyes open."[68]

As far as we know, Mrs. Forbes never joined a suffrage association or went to Austin to lobby the state legislature for the reform of rape laws. But in writing her letter in a public forum, expressing her political opinions, and urging other women to join her, she was challenging patriarchy just as much as Ellen Dabbs or Bettie Gay, if not more so. After all, she lived in a rural community where her words would potentially brand her as "unwomanly" and expose her husband to ridicule. Populism made such actions possible, and if Mrs. Forbes passed her ideas down to her daughters and sons, those ideas shaped the world of the twentieth century in ways that we are only beginning to understand.[69]

8 · Legislating Populism

If the present Texas legislature does not kill what little life there
is left in the democratic party in the state, then there are no frogs
in Ireland nor horned toads in Texas.
—*Southern Mercury,* 1895

We endorse the noble stand taken by the populist members of . . . our state
legislature in opposing all vicious class legislation and boldly advocating
all measures for the relief of the people.
—McCulloch County Farmers' Alliance, 1895

I put morals above money.
—Populist state senator Willis Lyman Harrison, 1895

The 1894 elections failed to bring the People's Party to power at the state
level in Texas, but the Populists made major gains over 1892, putting the scare
into their Democratic opponents. Although their loss in statewide races disappointed the party faithful, they were heartened by the fact that the People's
ticket polled pluralities in 59 of the state's 246 counties. It is unknown how
many Populist county-level officials were elected, although clearly the party
swept some counties and elected at least some individuals in dozens of others.
At the county level, being a Populist officeholder meant efficiently assessing
and collecting taxes, maintaining public roads, and administering the local
justice system, but apart from curbing corruption and perhaps giving minority citizens a fairer shake, these local officers had relatively limited opportunities to display what it meant to be a Populist in ideological or policy
terms.

That was not necessarily the case, however, with those Populists elected to the state legislature. Certainly, much of the business of state lawmaking, like that of local governance, revolved around what might best be termed "good-government" measures, which might be expected to be relatively nonpartisan. But Populist ideas about the role of the state in social and economic policy would also potentially find opportunities for expression, and in that regard Populist lawmakers would give voters (and historians) their first real taste of what Populist rule might actually look like.

When the votes were counted in November 1894, Texans learned that 22 Populists would be taking their seats in the 108-member state House of Representatives and 2 in the 31-member state Senate.[1] Although their numbers were not sufficient to pass any legislation on their own, the Populists were numerous enough to influence the course of legislation significantly, especially when the dominant Democrats were so faction-ridden. As the newly elected Democratic speaker of the House, Thomas Slater Smith, announced to the Populist members on the first day of the session, "I intend you shall have opportunity to make a record. If you can make a better record than the [Democrats] you shall have opportunity to show from the record the credit you deserve."[2]

These twenty-four Populists were a surprisingly diverse lot. With an average age of forty-nine, they may have been older than their Democratic colleagues, but they certainly did not fit the often remarked-on image of the People's Party as a party of graybeards. Almost all were southerners, and at least ten of them were either born in Texas or brought there as children. Only three were born outside the South, and two of those had at least one southern-born parent. Politically, four are known to have been members of the Greenback or Union Labor parties, although it is likely that a number of others had been involved in pre-Populist third-party movements. Nearly half (eleven) could boast Confederate records, but nine were too young to have fought in the war. In an age when college educations were rare, only one, Jesse Burney, had earned a college degree, although another, Thomas L. Edwards, was a medical school graduate.

Occupation is where they differed most markedly from their Democratic counterparts. Whereas about half of the Democrats in the legislatures of this era were attorneys,[3] only one of the twenty-four Populists was a lawyer, and he had been admitted to the bar only eight months earlier. Twenty of the twenty-four Populists could have listed farmer or rancher as their occupation at some point in their lives, but fifteen of these could also legitimately claim multiple occupations. Four had been schoolteachers, three were merchants, four were editors. Two were ordained ministers, and a surprising three were—or someday would be—bankers. The full list of verifiable occupations that these men pursued at some point in their lives also includes: surveyor, cowboy, minister, physician, mill owner, ginner, carpenter, merchant, policeman, postmaster, railroad laborer, and blacksmith. At least twelve had been members of the Farmers' Alliance, and several of them were prominent in that organization.[4]

That the Populist lawmakers differed demographically from their Democratic counterparts is important. For example, the fact that so few of the Populists were lawyers is strong evidence that they had not aspired to a profession in politics; then, as now, law was considered the surest pathway to a political career. Instead, most grassroots Populist officeholders ended up in politics unexpectedly, a consequence of their activism as reformers or the result of constituents who pushed them to the fore. But to really understand what fueled the Populist surge of 1894, and to get a better sense of how Populist liberalism manifested itself in public policy, a closer examination of their individual lives and backgrounds is warranted.

~

The twenty-four newly elected Populist legislators began arriving in Austin the first week in January 1895. Not surprisingly, the Cross Timbers region of west-central Texas sent the most Populists to Austin, seven in all. This was the birthplace of the Farmers' Alliance, and several of these members fit the classic profile of the Populist farmer who had come to third-party politics through the Alliance. One, James Madison Townsen, hailed from Lampasas, where the first Alliance had been founded in the 1870s. Another, Samuel T. Foster of Alvord in Wise County, had been both an Allianceman and a Union Labor Party presidential elector in 1888. Townsen and Foster might fairly be said to have fit the expected profile of the grassroots Populist. Yet when examined more closely, many of these representatives from the Populist heartland had elements in their biographies that set them apart from the rank and file of struggling Texas farmers, and even from their fellow Alliancemen.[5]

The Illinois-born, Ohio-raised William Bye Whitacre of Erath County had been a justice of the peace and district clerk as a young man. Like so many Populists, he joined the reform-minded Disciples of Christ Church and the Farmers' Alliance in his hometown of Lingleville, where Alliancemen built and operated their own Alliance high school. In what was intended as a compliment, his local Populist newspaper described him as "a man of vindictiveness and force of character excelled by few."[6]

Tillman Kimsey Seago of Comanche County was an old Greenbacker and president of his county's Alliance, but he had also been a merchant and town promoter, having founded and served as the first postmaster of Seagoville (now a Dallas suburb) before moving out to the Cross Timbers. Similarly, James Francis Barron of Strawn in Palo Pinto County had started out as a schoolteacher, later acquiring his own ranch. Like Seago, he also became a town promoter, helping to found the Panhandle town of Lamesa, where he eventually became a gin director and president of the First National Bank.[7]

William Euphrates Cureton of Walnut Springs, elected to represent Bosque and Hamilton Counties, started out as a cowboy but became a legendary cattleman, making what may have been the longest successful cattle drive in history, an epic, two-year trek all the way to California. An Allianceman and a director of the American Live Stock Association, he became friends with William Sidney Porter, better known as O. Henry, often inviting the Austin writer to join him at his desk on the floor of the House during the 1895 session. Cureton's son Calvin served as secretary of the state Populist Party and years later became chief justice of the Texas Supreme Court.[8]

Rounding out the Cross Timbers contingent was Peter Radford of Whitt in Parker County. Although a farmer, Radford was a scholarly and surprisingly cosmopolitan man referred to in one press account as a "farmer-philosopher." After the Populist era he went on to become president of the Texas Farmers' Union, lecturer for the national Farmers' Union, and a member of both the State Warehouse Commission and the Texas State Normal School board of regents. In 1913 he was spoken of as a potential candidate for governor.[9]

Moving eastward, northeast Texas sent three new legislators to the 1895 session. Two came from Delta County, the tiny Populist stronghold nestled between the north and south forks of the Sulphur River. The "boys from the forks of the creek" was already a widely used label for Populists generally, but Delta's Populist lawmakers were anything but rural rustics. James Lewis Darwin of Lake Creek was a highly successful teacher, farmer, and gin operator who had been an Alliance leader in his county. The only Populist legislator known to have been a Republican prior to Populism, he was described by his biographer as a "philanthropist," and like the aforementioned James Barron, he eventually became a bank president. Delta County also sent a Populist member to the lower house—Dr. Thomas L. Edwards, a graduate of the Nashville Medical University and a practicing physician. Like several other Populist members, he moonlighted as a newspaper editor, in this case overseeing the *People's Cause* in Cooper, the county seat. Rounding out the northeast Texas delegation was a third representative, Dr. J. M. Nix of Detroit, representing neighboring Red River County. The Georgia-born Nix, a dentist by profession, had been active in the Greenback movement in Louisiana before emigrating to Texas. The northeast Texans, then, would give a decidedly professional tint to the Populist delegation in Austin.[10]

Moving south, the Piney Woods region of deep East Texas also sent three members to the House. Zachary Bartholomew Stokes, a farmer from Wells in Cherokee County, doubled as an agricultural scientist, working in later years to develop and test a boll weevil insecticide. Martin Luther Huddleston, a saw-mill operator and part-time preacher from Palestine in Anderson County, was something of a backwoods intellectual who labored, as he confided to his diary, to prove that his spiritualism-tinged Christian faith was "in perfect harmony with true scientific reason."[11] The final Piney Woods representative was Lee Lightfoot Rhodes from Providence in eastern Van Zandt County. One of Texas Populism's most outspoken politicians, Rhodes had been active in the Knights of Labor and the Union Labor Party before becoming a Populist, and he would enjoy a long career as a socialist leader in the twentieth century, often partnering with his brother Jake, who in mid-1895 started his own town (Rhodesburg) and his own "populist institute," a high school specifically designed, as the press put it, to inculcate "the populistic faith" in its students. If the three northeast Texans, with their business and professional backgrounds, defied the stereotype of Populists as unlettered farmers, the three Piney Woods representatives did the same as independent thinkers who were clearly unafraid to chart their own intellectual paths.[12]

The rich Blackland Prairie region of east-central Texas sent six members to the Twenty-Fourth Legislature. Here cotton was king as in no other part of the state, and the prolonged agricultural depression of the past decade had made it fertile recruiting ground for the Farmers' Alliance, which was reflected in the election of Populists from the region. John Mordecai McWilliams of Corsicana had been assistant state lecturer and secretary of the state Alliance. Thomas R. Watkins, also of Corsicana, raised blooded horses and edited the local Alliance and Populist newspaper. In neighboring Limestone County, Allen Drinkard of Kosse likewise edited his local Alliance and Populist paper, leading a biographer to describe him as "a red-hot champion" of the party's measures. One county to the south, Van Buren Ritter of McClanahan presided over the Falls County Alliance, and further south in Elgin, Thomas J. Floyd did the same for the Bastrop County Alliance. Floyd, who had been active in planning the famous Alliance jute bagging boycott of 1889, was a clever writer and a forceful enough speaker to be elected district lecturer for the Ninth District Alliance and secretary of the state Alliance Lecturers' Council.[13]

Populism was strong enough in the Blackland Prairie to furnish one of the party's two state senators. The Populists of the state Senate's Twenty-Seventh District sent sixty-four-year-old Dr. Willis Lyman Harrison of Troy in Bell County to the legislature's upper chamber. The only nonagriculturalist Populist lawmaker from this region, Harrison was a medical doctor who had served the Confederacy as a surgeon in a Texas cavalry regiment. Having seen enough blood, after the war he traded his bone saw for a Bible, becoming a prominent Disciples of Christ minister. However, even he had been an active Allianceman in the 1880s, as rural doctors and ministers were among the few professionals allowed to become members. Looking very much like the Old Testament patriarchs of whom he preached, he was described by the Democratic *Fort Worth Gazette* as "an affable gentleman and liberal in his views, unlike the majority of preacher politicians." The dignified, gray-bearded Harrison was a man of few words, and when pressed he said simply that he expected Populism to bring about "the amelioration of the people." His personal motto, he explained, was "Morals above money."[14]

Rounding out the Populist delegation were the five members from south-central Texas. The Tennessee-born farmer James Rogers Cocke from Rancho in Gonzales County hailed from a prominent political family. His father Frederick Bird Smith Cocke had served in both the Ninth and Sixteenth Legislatures, and the younger Cocke raised three sons who all went on to become prominent lawyers. Cocke was in his second term in the legislature, making him one of the few veteran Populist lawmakers. He was perhaps the nearest thing the Populists in the Twenty-Fourth Legislature had to a professional politician.[15]

Cocke's colleague James W. Carson from Hackberry in neighboring Lavaca County was perhaps best-known for his distinguished war record, having fought at Glorieta Pass and in the Battle of Galveston, where he was among the first Confederates to board the USS *Harriet Lane* and capture her captain and crew, which garnered him a battlefield promotion from sergeant to captain. Carson's adventurous life continued after the war, as he spent several years in Peru, Bolivia, and Brazil working as a surveyor for those countries' governments.[16]

From the South Texas ranching country of Live Oak County came Thomas Peyton "Peyt" McNeill of Lagarto, one of his section's most prominent and well-to-do citizens. McNeill was an Allianceman and civic leader, and by the

1890s he was bringing a thousand head of cattle to market annually. Like several other Populist lawmakers, he fancied himself something of an agricultural innovator, experimenting with the commercial cultivation of Mexican frijoles on his 12,000-acre ranch along the Nueces River.[17]

Equally prominent was Jesse Green Burney from Kerr County in the heart of the Hill Country. Like McNeill, Burney came from a well-known family. His father Hance McCain Burney had been county judge, and his brother Robert Hance Burney was Democratic state senator in the Twentieth, Twenty-First, and Twenty-Second Legislatures, and later a state district judge. Jesse Burney graduated from both Southwestern University in Georgetown and the Waco Business College, and at the time of his legislative service was listed as a farmer, stockraiser, and merchant. Later he moved to Austin, went into the grocery business, and then became vice president and a member of the board of directors of the Capitol Bank and Trust Company. The civic-minded Burney also later served as secretary of the Austin Business League and was one of the incorporators of the Travis County Fair. His education, experience, and prominence suggested that he would be one of the leaders of the Populist caucus in the House.[18]

The final member of the Populist delegation, John A. O'Connor, also came from South Texas, but almost everything about him set him apart from the other Third-Party legislators (plate 19). He was orphaned at a young age, spent his youth and early adulthood as a farmhand in Kerr County, and finally moved to San Antonio in the 1880s, working first on a street-paving crew and then for four years as a policeman. From that start he went into the furniture business, all the while reading law at night. O'Connor passed the bar exam just a year before being elected to the legislature in an unusual fusion arrangement with local Democrats, making him the only Populist to represent a major urban area. Strikingly handsome with a broad forehead, full head of dark hair, and neatly trimmed moustache, his biographer described him as "a man of brilliant mentality and a speaker of force and magnetism." He became one of the most active and outspoken Populists in the Twenty-Fourth Legislature and probably its highest-profile member. Despite being a political newcomer and only thirty-six years old, his fellow Populists held him in such high esteem that he was their choice in January 1895 to be the party's nominee for US senator, an honor he graciously declined in favor of Thomas L. Nugent.[19]

~

Most of the twenty-four newly elected Populists came by train to Austin that first week of 1895, as Texas roads were primitive and distances for most lawmakers were great. Stepping off the train at the Union Depot at the intersection of Third and Congress, they would have looked up Congress Avenue to the magnificent pink-granite capitol dome nine blocks away, where they would be spending most of their days over the next four months. Congress Avenue was still unpaved, but members eager to see their new offices could have taken the city's new electric streetcar up to the 311-foot-tall, seven-year-old structure, modeled after the US Capitol but purposely built, in typical Texas fashion, to be twenty-three feet taller than the national dome. For those coming to Austin for the first time, it was likely the largest and grandest building they had ever seen. Not only was it the tallest building in Texas, it was said to be the seventh-largest building in the world at the time of its completion. Populist lawmakers making the trip from their homes in Dingler, Grundyville, Lingleville, or Whitt could only stare in amazement at the massive edifice.[20]

But the Third-Party legislators would also have had ample cause to view the new capitol building with mixed feelings, if not outright hostility, because it embodied many of the things Populists despised about the Democrats who had controlled Texas politics since Reconstruction. First there was the sheer extravagance of the building—its construction had cost $3.7 million (nearly $100 million in today's currency)—when the average unskilled worker might expect to make a dollar a day. Then there was the way the state had paid for the building, raising the money by selling three million acres of the public domain, a tract nearly the size of Connecticut, to a Chicago-based syndicate. And finally, there was the way the building had been constructed: the state used convict labor to quarry the granite and imported nonunion stonecutters from Scotland to work on the building itself, incurring the wrath of organized labor groups who mounted an unsuccessful boycott against the job. The Texas state capitol building, then, stood as a spectacular reminder of many of the things that Populists deemed wrong with Texas politics.[21]

By the terms of the 1876 Redeemer constitution, the Texas legislature was required to meet only once every two years for a four-month session. The constitution required a balanced budget, and any deficits due to an unexpected shortfall in revenues over the previous biennium had to be made up for in the current budget. It was the duty of the state comptroller to certify to the legislature the amount of cash on hand and to project the revenue anticipated at current levels of taxation and economic conditions. As the national recession had just bottomed out over the previous year, the Twenty-Fourth Legislature found itself facing a current deficit of over $700,000, with the shortfall for the next two years projected to balloon to a massive $1.4 million. By the comptroller's estimate, even if the state property tax (which was the main source of state revenue) was increased from its present rate of 12.5 cents per $100 valuation to the constitutional limit of 20 cents, it would only be enough to deal with the existing deficit. To close the projected deficit looming ahead, further cuts or additional types of taxes or fees, or both, would be necessary. To illustrate the severity of the situation, the new Democratic governor, Charles A. Culberson, pointed out that in the absence of new revenue, the state would be able to provide an annual public-school term of only 2.91 months (the constitution required a six-month term). The state faced a grim financial situation.[22]

While Populists believed in the positive use of government to achieve a more equitable society, most of them had campaigned on a platform of "retrenchment and reform," and they were joined in this sentiment by many Democrats, including Governor Culberson. Indeed, the *Dallas Morning News,* no friend to Populists or to progressive-minded Democrats, editorialized that "the populists, in spite of their visionary vagaries, have learned the Texas democracy something." With the Populists' electoral success in 1894, progressive Democrats had "about decided to take the populist cudgel and swing it on their own hook for a while. Three out of five of them have sharp pruning knives in their sleeves and they are laying [sic] awake at night trying to discover something to carve." For Populists, then, the challenge—and it would be a stiff one—would be to reconcile these two seemingly contradictory impulses. They were committed to *retrenchment* (and with the balanced-budget requirement, they really had no other choice), but they also wanted to *reform* the way the state's government operated. Most Populists believed that both could be done—that an activist government, working in the public interest, did not necessarily mean a vastly more expensive government. The upcoming session would put that belief to a severe test.[23]

But first came the traditional beginning-of-the-session housekeeping rituals. Newly elected members had to present their certificates of election and be sworn in. One Populist, dentist J. M. Nix of Red River County, immediately faced a problem because his election certificate was in the pocket of the overcoat he had lost on the train to Austin. (He somehow managed to get sworn in anyway.) Three House members faced official contests of their election, although only one of these cases involved a Populist, and he was the contestant, not the contestee. Contested cases would have to be heard in committee and settled by a vote of the full House. Finally, a new House Speaker and one of the state's US senators would be elected.[24]

In the senatorial race, a difference of opinion arose within the Populist ranks, as some wanted to nominate Thomas L. Nugent while others supported John A.

O'Connor, the newly elected state representative from San Antonio. Of course, the nomination was only a symbolic honor; with Populists outnumbered five to one, the Democrats easily had the votes to elect their own nominee. A vote in the party caucus soon revealed that eighteen of the twenty-two Populists preferred O'Connor, upon which "O'Connor's magnanimity then asserted itself and in a manly way he withdrew in favor of the defeated man for governor." Then, in a further show of solidarity, the Third-Party men lined up solidly behind the revered Nugent, whom Lee Rhodes characterized in his nominating speech as "the sage of Texas and one of the greatest political philosophers of modern times."[25]

In the case of the Speaker's race, the Populists sought to chart a pragmatic course. Apparently they approached Democrat Seth Phineas Mills of Waco, tendering Populist support for him if he would agree to certain favorable committee assignments for Populists. But when Mills indicated that as Speaker he would scatter Populists "among the committees where they would do the least harm to the democratic party," the Populists gave up and nominated one of their own, T. J. Floyd, the former Alliance lecturer from Bastrop. After the initial vote, however, in which the Democrats' candidate, Thomas Slater Smith of Hillsboro, received 102 votes to Floyd's 22, Floyd moved to make the vote unanimous, which was done. Speaker Smith responded by inviting all members to suggest to him their committee preferences, with the understanding, of course, that Populists would chair or control no committee. Party lines, it appeared, were to be clearly drawn, but in a collegial and respectful manner.[26]

That collegiality, however, was almost immediately tested. The legislature had barely gotten down to business in earnest when a sensational rumor began to circulate in the halls of the capitol. It seems that in the one case where a defeated Populist was contesting the election of his Democratic opponent, "a certain attorney" had allegedly boasted "that he could command the Populist vote of the legislature" and indeed that he had solicited payment for his pledge to deliver the party's twenty-two House votes in favor of the Populist contestant. On January 23 a Democratic representative introduced a resolution calling for an investigation. As the *San Antonio Light* reported on the story, "It is generally conceded that the thing is loaded with dynamite." The story, however, would have been far less sensational but for the name of the "certain attorney," which soon became known: it was none other than James Harvey Davis, the inimitable Texas "Cyclone" (plate 20).[27]

The initial reporting on the story proved inaccurate. Davis *was* the attorney for the defeated Populist House candidate, J. H. Frost of Cass County, who had hired Davis to represent him before the House Committee on Privileges and Elections, which would initially adjudicate his case. But the votes that Davis had supposedly promised to deliver were for an unrelated judicial bill. It turned out that the citizens of Texarkana, in Bowie County, were supporting a bill to create a new state district court in their city. The nearest court was in the county seat at Boston, twenty-one miles away. The citizens of Boston opposed the new court, fearing that it would be the first step in an effort by Texarkana to move the county seat there. Since Davis was planning to go to Austin to represent Frost anyway, he had proposed to the supporters of the bill, one of whom was Texarkana's Democratic state representative, that if local Democrats could somehow get two unfriendly members removed from the committee on elections, and that if local lawmakers would give a written pledge promising not to move the county seat, then for $100—$20 down and $80 when the bill passed—Davis would secure the votes of the Populist legislators for the court bill. Davis had even put the proposal in a written note to the Texarkana representative, and it was the exposure of the note that led to the controversy.[28]

From Davis's perspective, this was a legitimate, win-win proposition for himself, his client Frost, and the supporters of the Texarkana court bill. In his written proposal, Davis had made it a point to say, "This money I want for Frost, as he is paying my expenses in the case while here." There was no guarantee that the objectionable members of the elections committee could or would be removed from the Frost contest case, but if they were, it would enhance Frost's chances of unseating his Democratic opponent. Moreover, the supporters of the Texarkana bill would gain the solid support of the Populist bloc. Davis viewed the scheme as appropriate lobbyist behavior, but his high profile in the People's Party made him an irresistible target of the Democrats, who saw his statement—"I think I can pledge twenty-two votes in the house and two in the senate for the bill"—as evidence of corruption. Davis's claim (or boast) that he could influence the Populist lawmakers likewise upset some of *them*, who wanted it to be known that nobody controlled their votes. Delta County Populist senator James Darwin, for example, publicly asserted that "no attorney has a cinch on him."[29]

Soon various resolutions of censure against Davis were being debated. The speaker appointed a special committee to investigate, and Populists succeeded in getting three of their members appointed to the nine-man committee. The "tempestuous debate" over the investigation tied the House up for parts of several days. In the end, the investigating committee issued majority and minority reports, divided strictly on party lines, with the Democrats' majority report censuring Davis and calling his behavior "reprehensible in the extreme." The Populists' minority report, by contrast, failed "to see any moral turpitude or censurable culpability, or any willful wrong or corrupt motive," although it did characterize Davis's proposal for the removal of the two members of the elections committee as "imprudent." During the final debate over the resolutions, Populist representative Tom Watkins of Corsicana introduced a resolution to allow Davis to speak in his own defense before the full House. The resolution passed by a wide margin; apparently many Democratic politicians could not resist the oratorical performance that would ensue.

Taking the floor, the Cyclone did not disappoint. As one journalist reported, "At times he grew pathetic and his voice shook with emotion. He asked his hearers to look into his blue eyes and see if there was any guilt reflected from those portals of his soul." Of course, Davis's histrionics did not affect the final vote; the majority report easily passed. But he had accomplished the one thing that Cyclone Davis relished the most: a big moment in the spotlight.[30]

The *Dallas Morning News* astutely summarized the political impact of the episode:

> If it has accomplished more than to manufacture political history by the bucketful for the populists in their next campaign the fact is not apparent here at this time. . . . . If the populists are shrewd enough to make their democratic opponents waste several days in senseless discussion at the expense of the state and in the face of the democratic solemn pledge to retrench and reform, nobody can blame them for doing it. . . . Every dollar they can make a democratic house throw away in a silly expenditure of valuable time adds that many sinews of war to the populist army when the campaign opens next year. . . . In other words, the populists accomplished exactly what they sought to do. . . . By the martyrdom of one of their number they have made themselves an issue and succeeded in getting enough campaign thunder to last them for a season.[31]

With the Davis sideshow concluded, lawmakers finally were able to get down to the people's business. Most of the Populist Party's major platform planks—the Subtreasury Plan, government ownership of the railroads, abolition of the national banking system, and others—were federal policy positions and beyond the reach of state legislatures. For those legislators hoping to craft laws embodying Populist political causes, the potential field of operations was relatively circumscribed. But one area where they could prove their Populist bona fides was in labor legislation, or more broadly stated, legislation benefiting workingmen, be they wage laborers, farmers, mechanics, or other small producers.

Not surprisingly, Lee Rhodes, the Knights of Labor member and former Union Labor Party candidate from Van Zandt County, led the way in introducing prolabor bills. One such bill, House Bill 484, undoubtedly dear to the hearts of farmers, would lower the maximum rates that the Railroad Commission would allow railroads to charge for the transportation of freight. Another, House Bill 515, protected "certain employes and laborers against extortion and forced rebates of their wages through the medium of checks, coupons, etc.," a clear attempt to reform the exploitative system of paying mine and mill workers with scrip and requiring them to patronize company stores, a practice that led to a system resembling debt peonage. Jesse Burney introduced a measure, House Bill 204, regulating charges levied by public grain mills, limiting their charges to one-sixth of the value of the grain at steam-powered mills and one-eighth at water-powered mills. This bill, like Rhodes's railroad-rate bill, was a classic expression of Populist resentment against middlemen in the agricultural economy whom farmers deemed to have monopolistic power.

The railroads, of course, offered the most egregious examples of monopoly in the Populists' worldview. Not only would Populists seek to regulate freight rates, but they also hoped to rein in the roads' worst labor abuses. Accordingly, John O'Connor introduced House Bill 402, which set the workday for railway workers at ten hours, after which they were to receive overtime pay. The bill also mandated eight hours of rest for any conductor, engineer, fireman, or brakeman who had worked for twenty-four consecutive hours.[32]

O'Connor's railroad bill was actually more conservative than the various Populist platforms, which had consistently called for the establishment of an eight-hour workday in all but agricultural and domestic occupations, but he must have viewed it as a necessary first step toward fulfilling the party's platform. Similarly, he introduced another bill, House Bill 398, in an effort to fulfill the plank in the state platform calling for "an efficient lien law, that will protect the artisan, mechanic, laborer, and material men." Organized labor had criticized the existing 1889 law, saying that it encouraged "collusion between dishonest contractors and homestead owners." O'Connor's highly technical bill would remedy that problem, giving laborers, material suppliers, and subcontractors additional legal recourse against unscrupulous builders while also providing greater transparency for all parties, including homeowners. In what proved to be an unusual experience for Populist-authored legislation, the bill was quickly reported out of committee with a favorable recommendation and no changes. Like many such bills, it would compete with similar measures introduced by Reform Democrats.[33]

Two different Populist legislators sought to reform the state's notorious convict lease system, a scandalous institution that organized labor had long criticized for the way it placed convict labor in competition with free labor, thus driving down wages. The fact that the system also brutalized and exploited penitentiary inmates for the profit of private employers was not lost on reform-minded Populists. Jesse Burney, the Kerrville farmer and merchant, authored House Bill 613, which would apportion inmate labor to the various counties to work on the public roads, under the supervision of the commissioners' court. The bill instituted certain safeguards such as requiring that convicts be photographed and have their weight and physical description recorded, that they be fed, housed, clothed, and treated "humanely," and that "for good work and proper behavior each convict shall have a commutation of six (6) days per month." To Burney's thinking, keeping convicts under government supervision, rather than placing them in the hands of private lessors, would remove the most exploitative aspect of the system, while the people of Texas would benefit from better public roads.[34]

The newly licensed lawyer John O'Connor of San Antonio went further with his convict lease bill. House Bill 507 specified up front that "convict labor shall be employed in a manner not to conflict with free and honest labor," and it sought to abolish the leasing of inmates to "any person, firm, or corporation" altogether. The act instead provided that convicts be employed within the walls of the penitentiary or in state-owned prison farms. At the end of each year an audit of prison labor was to be conducted, and if the state had derived a net profit from a convict's labor, the surplus was to be paid to the convict's spouse or dependent children, or, in the case of a convict with no dependents, to the convict himself upon his release. Although different in their particulars, both O'Connor's and Burney's bills exemplified the liberal Populist belief that government, wielded as an instrument of the people's will, could help to create a more humane society, and that society's most vulnerable members deserved some measure of public protection. Lawmakers also would have been aware that African Americans were disproportionately represented in the inmate population, which surely figured into the political calculus of members whose party was actively courting black votes.[35]

Populists rarely differentiated between wage laborers and small landowners, viewing both groups as representatives of the producing classes. As the depression of the 1890s bottomed out, the rate of foreclosures and the resulting forced sales of homes and farms had reached epidemic proportions. Creditors, sometimes in collusion with corrupt sheriffs, were often able to turn around and purchase a foreclosed property at the sheriff's auction for a fraction of its true worth, as the prior owner watched on helplessly. Seeking to remedy this problem, the Gonzales County Populist J. R. Cocke introduced House Bill 475, which provided for an honest appraisal of any property being put up for forced sale, and then stopped the sale if the property failed to sell for at least two-thirds of its appraised value. Cocke took the step of declaring his bill an emergency measure, which would suspend the constitutional requirement that it be read and passed three separate times and allow the law to go into effect immediately after passage. In doing so, Cocke gave a very Populist-sounding justification for the emergency: "The lands of the people are being sacrificed at forced sales during the great money famine and it is imperatively necessary for the protection of the citizens."[36]

Cocke's bill was only the opening salvo in the Populist effort against foreclosures. His colleague J. M. McWilliams proposed a bill that picked up where Cocke's left off. This bill provided that "when any real estate shall be sold under a mortgage, deed of trust, or execution issued by any court in this State," the debtor had two years in which to redeem the lost property if he paid back the buyer's purchase price, along with all costs and 10 percent annual interest. That the two Populist lawmakers may have collaborated is borne out by the language McWilliams used to justify emergency action on the bill, which echoed Cocke's expression: "Owing to the existing money famine . . . the real property of debtors is being daily sacrificed at nominal prices given at forced sales and there [is] no law to protect debtors from such ruinous sacrifices."[37]

Another measure championed by Populists would have made it easier and safer for working people to save for and purchase a home. Senate Bill 194, introduced by the Populist surgeon-turned-preacher Willis Lyman Harrison, sought "to define building and loan associations and their powers, and to prescribe the conditions on which they may do business in this State, and to define and fix the rights and liabilities of their stockholders." The bill, however, was apparently the brainchild of none other than Thomas L. Nugent, who came to Austin during the session to personally lobby for it. The presence in the capital of the party's most respected leader guaranteed that it would receive a great deal of public scrutiny and commentary.[38]

Building and loan associations (B&Ls), the forerunner of modern savings and loans, had come into being a half-century before the Populist era. Intended to help working people become homeowners, the early, member-owned thrifts embodied much of the same cooperative spirit as the Alliance and the Knights of Labor, as members purchased shares and then could safely deposit their savings and apply for loans at reasonable rates of interest. Indeed, promoters described the B&L industry not as a "business" at all but rather as a "movement," and they viewed it as an instrument of social reform, a way to make the lives of ordinary people in the nation's industrializing cities more humane. Women comprised a sizable minority of shareholders, and officers were usually local community leaders, elected by the members.[39]

Until the 1890s, most B&Ls were small, averaging less than $90,000 in assets. In 1893 Texas was home to only forty-one of the institutions, and of these, thirty-one had total real estate loans of $50,000 or less. Half were newer than five years old, and only two had been in business more than a decade. They were entirely unregulated.[40]

The problem by the 1890s was that what had started as a working people's self-help movement was rapidly being transformed into a part of the new corporate order. In the 1880s the "national" B&Ls appeared on the scene. Established by bankers or industrialists and often having influential politicians on their boards, the "nationals" were for-profit businesses. They paid their officers handsomely and attracted investors by offering dividends three or four times higher than other financial institutions. They quickly became some of the nation's largest financial institutions, with assets in the millions. It was a recipe for a financial bubble. When the depression of the 1890s struck, some of the nationals, unable to maintain their high expenses and high dividends, began to fail, taking with them their members' life savings. Harrison's bill was aimed at creating a commonsense regulatory structure that would provide stability to the industry and protection for B&L members. Nugent, himself a founding director and attorney for a fledgling B&L in his home city of Fort Worth, understood firsthand the need for such safeguards.[41]

Apparently written by Nugent, Harrison's bill followed, almost verbatim, the so-called Dayton Plan, a set of procedures pioneered in Ohio over the previous decade. The US Bureau of Labor reported that "very many consider it a model plan," and the Fort Worth thrift that Nugent helped to found had voluntarily embraced most of its tenets, announcing that "there is no plan so scientific and perfect in its details." The plan incorporated many features familiar to American banking today. Perhaps most important among these was the modern amortizing mortgage in which interest comprises a declining proportion of the loan payment as the loan matures, resulting in overall lower interest rates. But the bill also mandated certain financial safeguards. All B&L

officers had to be bonded to insure against malfeasance. A reserve fund for contingent losses was required. Expenses such as salaries had to be paid out of earnings, not from deposits. The state insurance commissioner was to periodically inspect each B&L, and the bill included several provisions requiring stringent transparency in reporting on an institution's financial condition.[42]

Nugent managed to enlist the support of a Tarrant County Democrat, Robert E. L. Roy, to sponsor the House version of the bill, and like many Populist measures, the bill clearly garnered some support from a fair number of progressive, or Reform, Democrats. But it came as no surprise to political observers when the bill met stiff opposition. The bill would regulate *all* B&Ls doing business in Texas, including the growing number of freewheeling national thrifts. "The foreign building and loan associations [the nationals] have a great deal of money invested in Texas, and their agents are very greatly exercised over the strength developed by the friends of these bills," the *Fort Worth Gazette* reported. The conservative, probusiness *Dallas Morning News* attacked the measure in a manner unusually harsh for that paper, saying that the bill was "fraught with paternalistic provisions and covertly seeks to make all contracts for building and loan associations subject to governmental control, treating them as public corporations." The *Morning News* called the provision of the bill requiring inspections by the state insurance commissioner "positively inquisitorial," and it characterized other aspects of the bill as "vicious," "undemocratic," and "obnoxious to patriotic and thinking people." But recognizing the potential public appeal of the bill, the paper also cynically tried to play a small-*p* populist card, attacking Nugent's motives and charging that the bill would favor the large national B&Ls at the expense of the small locals: "As the leader of the party of visionary vagaries and wild schemes, Mr. Nugent is presumed to be the sworn enemy of corporate cannibals, but there must be a mistake about this, judging from the fact that he is known to be here trying to get a corporation measure enacted into law." According to the *Morning News*, the bill would be "squarely in the interest of those 'venal corporations' which the pops are constantly denouncing from every pine stump in Texas." The paper failed to explain why Nugent would champion a measure that would hurt the locally owned thrift that he represented; instead, it distorted Nugent's ties to the Fort Worth thrift, saying simply that "he himself is a director in a Fort Worth corporation and attorney for the same." So blatantly did the state's leading newspaper distort Nugent's motives and the nature of the bill that J. V. Bergen, the state manager of the nation's largest national, the giant Southern Building and Loan of Knoxville, Tennessee, publicly came to Nugent's defense.

Although he was a genuine corporate executive who opposed the bill specifically and Populism generally, Bergen declared, "I do not like to see unfair advantage taken and motives ascribed which were far from his thoughts." No
"fair minded man," he added, "will censure Judge Nugent for being a director
in and attorney for such an association."[43]

Nugent himself finally felt compelled to weigh in on the bill and his role in
promoting it. "It was approved by a number of business men in Fort Worth
who have had large experience in connection with building and loan associations," he wrote. "All of these gentlemen, I believe, without exception, are
[D]emocrats, and they believed that legislation was necessary on this subject."
The *Dallas Morning News* notwithstanding, Nugent was right in touting his
bill as a measure that would reconcile business interests with the needs of the
people. Within a few years, because most states had failed to enact the sort of
legislation that Nugent was promoting, the rate of failure for the national thrifts
escalated. When Southern Building and Loan—the mammoth national whose
Texas manager Bergen had publicly defended Nugent—collapsed in 1897, it
sparked a national financial scare. Over the next few years every one of the
nationals went broke, leaving only the well-managed locals like Nugent's Mutual Home and Savings Association of Fort Worth, whose prudent operating
rules he had sought to impose on thrifts statewide. Few Populist policies better exemplified the liberal belief that there were times when the state should
act in the public interest to temper the excesses of laissez-faire corporate capitalism. Few were more strikingly modern.[44]

These bills suggest that Populist lawmakers came to Austin intent on legislating in the immediate interest of the farmers and laborers who comprised
their core constituency. A larger body of Populist-sponsored bills, however,
might be termed "good-government" legislation; that is, bills aiming to mod-
ernize government agencies, increase efficiency, lower costs, or curb corruption. Populists actually saw little conflict between the producerist legislation
described above and the modernizing "business methods" that they so consistently championed. Populist platforms frequently demanded such good-
government reforms, and the legislators who arrived in Austin in January 1895
came determined to fight for them.

As noted, economic realities had put the phrase "retrenchment and reform"
on the lips of many legislators, Populists and Democrats alike. Before the session had even begun, Texans knew that there would be a push for a major reform in the way that county and local government operated. At the center of
these efforts would be a movement to end or reform the "fee system." In Texas,

many local officials, including sheriffs, judges, tax collectors and assessors, county and district clerks, and other officeholders, were paid according to the fees they collected for doing their jobs. The system was scandalous in many ways. At the lowest levels, ordinary individuals, including many poorer people, black and white, who might vote Populist, experienced the system's injustices on a regular basis. Texans were all too familiar with the phrase "one dollar and costs," because it was common in petty cases like disturbing the peace or public intoxication for law enforcement officials to levy a minor fine, which went into the public treasury, but then for the fees to amount to "anywhere from a dozen to forty dollars of swag for the diligent officers." As one critic explained some years later, "This system means that men are punished not to avenge the outraged law, but to fatten the pockets of thrifty officials."[45] The system remained largely intact for decades after Populism, and calls for its reform or abolition can be found in Texas newspapers over many years. Black Texans undoubtedly suffered disproportionately from the system, since it was standard practice for them to plead guilty to minor offenses, knowing that to fight an unjust charge was futile with all-white juries and judges. One national magazine, publishing an exposé of the system some years later, counted eighteen different fees that a Texas justice court could levy.[46] As a consequence, in the 1890s county officials in the state's large urban counties sometimes earned the astronomical sum of $10,000 a year or more. One unnamed county official was said to have earned more than the state's governor, attorney general, treasurer, and three supreme court judges combined.[47] Calling it "the odious fee system," the *San Antonio Light* editorialized that "the people of Texas, including men of all shades of political opinion," as well as "every newspaper in Texas," had "declared loudly and almost unanimously for the abolition of the fee system."[48]

The Populists felt so strongly about abolishing the system that they wrote it into their 1892 and 1894 platforms. The Democrats' platforms were silent on the subject. It might have remained exclusively a Populist cause, but the problems with the system did not stop with its unfairness to common people. For although defendants and litigants paid fees when using the courts, the state treasury did, too. Under Texas law, for example, sheriffs billed the state for executing warrants, for summoning juries, for feeding prisoners and transporting them to trial, and for testifying as witnesses. Judges, district and county attorneys, and district and county clerks collected standard fees from the state for performing a wide range of official duties, as did tax assessors and collectors and county treasurers. The cost to the state for the 1893 to 1895 biennium for sheriffs', clerks', and prosecuting attorneys' fees alone totaled $1.1 million, making it one of the largest items in the entire state budget and a major contributor to the huge budget deficit.[49] In his opening address to the legislature, the newly elected governor Culberson joined with the Populists in calling for reform, referring to the "unconscionable charges" submitted by county officeholders and citing the "gross abuses" perpetrated under the system.[50]

Populists had long complained of the Democratic "rings" that controlled many Texas county governments. The fee system was a big part of what kept the rings' wheels greased. Although many Reform Democrats joined the Populists and Governor Culberson in calling the system "a fruitful source of political corruption," the county Democratic rings and the officeholders who profited from the system could be counted on to fiercely oppose reform. The 1892 Populist platform had called for a ceiling of two thousand dollars on any individual county salary and a requirement that any fees in excess of expenses would go into the county's public-school fund. In 1894 the party altered the plank to suggest that excess fees go into the state's general fund, in recognition of the need to address the deficit. Either plan would curb the worst abuses of citizens by removing the lucrative incentives for county officials to make arrests and manipulate the system for their own gain.[51]

A week into the session the Populist newspaperman Allen Drinkard of Limestone County introduced a bill setting fixed salaries for all county officials, with the top salary being the two thousand dollars recommended by Culberson. In Drinkard's version, any surplus was to be allotted "to the various county funds" on a pro rata basis, meaning that the surplus was to stay in the county to defray the costs of local government, not to line the pockets of officeholders. In the meantime, Reform Democrats filed three other fee-system bills, all seeking to reform the system and lessen the burden on the state treasury. As the *Dallas Morning News* editorialized, "The big deficit now on hand has made the reformers as wild as a rabbit, and they are prepared to remedy it if such a thing is possible." The committee on state affairs subsequently wrote its own bill, incorporating various elements from the four bills, and reported it back to the full House as a substitute for the four competing bills. On this issue, as in so many others in this legislative session, legislators would divide not exclusively along party lines but along an axis that pitted Populists and Reform Democrats against conservative Democrats opposed to reform. The politically savvy *Austin Statesman* correctly noted at the start of the session that the bill would encounter "one of the heaviest lobbies known on any one measure," and indeed the battle over the fee system raged for the next three months

and became the most contentious issue of the entire session. That such a reform met with such fierce opposition, even when the need for it was widely
recognized by the public and by politicians of all parties, was stark evidence
of the corrupt state of Texas politics.[52]

Almost as controversial as the fee-system bill was another Populist-sponsored
governmental-reform bill from the prolific pen of John O'Connor. Midway
through the session O'Connor, the lone Populist lawmaker from a major urban area, introduced House Bill 707, an act that would establish a civil service
system for police and fire departments in cities with populations greater than
thirty-five thousand, namely Dallas, Galveston, Houston, and O'Connor's own
San Antonio. The bill, modeled on similar laws in Missouri and elsewhere,
would place urban police and fire departments under the control of boards of
local commissioners appointed by the governor. The three-person boards could
have no more than two members from the same political party. A detailed and
well-crafted piece of legislation reflecting O'Connor's recent training as an attorney, the three thousand–word bill prohibited the removal of any employee
for his political opinions or affiliations. It specified pay grades and qualifications for employment and created a merit-based system of internal promotion.[53]

Initially, O'Connor naively predicted that the bill would "go through with a
whoop" because "it meets no objection from any source." He was soon dis-
abused of that notion. As in the case of the fee bill, Populists learned how
impervious the Texas legislature was to reform. Sitting mayors and city coun-
cilmen frowned on the notion of having rich sources of patronage taken away
from them. From O'Connor's home city of San Antonio, Mayor Henry Elmendorf, a Republican who had just won office in a nominally nonpartisan election, was reported to have said that the bill was "a scheme of his local enemies
to get control of the patronage after being defeated at the polls." Elmendorf
lobbied the other cities' mayors to oppose the bill, and the San Antonio city
council joined in the opposition, passing a resolution condemning the bill as
"a covert attack on our liberties." O'Connor was able to counter with a petition
from two thousand citizens of Bexar County supporting the measure, along
with an endorsement from the Chiefs of Police Association of Texas. He was
also cheered by the fact that the respected, long-serving police chief of Dallas
endorsed the bill, as did a former Austin fire chief. Before long, "a big lobby"
for each side had descended on Austin, and observers were predicting "a hot
contest" over the bill. But apart from patronage considerations, the supporters of O'Connor's bill still had to contend with the conservative ideological position, so strong in Texas, which viewed an activist government as anathema.

The *Galveston Daily News,* long a bastion of antigovernment libertarianism, concisely stated that ideological position: "Let the people, as a matter of self-defense, call a sudden bull on politicians who are eager and diligent to enlarge the functions and expenses of government. No more boards. No more bureaus. No more commissions."[54]

The Populist battle against political corruption found further expression in a bill introduced by the Bastrop Allianceman T. J. Floyd. House Bill 378 would prohibit any elected or appointed official from serving "as an attorney for, or to act as agent for, or in any manner or capacity to represent any private corporation, Association, Joint Stock company or other Corporate body." Floyd and the Populists were aware that some politicians served two masters—their constituents in the legislature and corporations who retained them as legal counsel—and Texas law did little to prohibit the practice. In the 1895 legislature, for example, when Democratic representative Robert H. Ward introduced a bill to override the state's antitrust law and allow the consolidation of railroad companies, Ward was forced to swear "by the memory of the great departed that he is not representing corporations." Ward may well have been telling the truth, but with a majority of the Democrats in the legislature working as lawyers in private practice, the potential opportunities for conflicts of interest were plentiful and apparent.[55]

Floyd's bill addressed the problem of corrupt government officials, but a measure introduced by Tom Watkins of Corsicana set its sights on corrupt elections themselves. From the beginning of the Populist revolt, Third-Party members had bemoaned the blatant fraud that so often took place at voting places and in the official handling, counting, and reporting of election results. Ignatius Donnelly's famous preamble to the 1892 Omaha Platform had declared that "corruption dominates the ballot-box," and Texas Populists knew it was true. In its 1891 founding convention in Dallas the Texas People's Party castigated Democrats for refusing to reform the election laws, despite the fact, as it noted, that "the people have long felt the corrupting influence of the ward politician, bummer, and striker, as well as the more baleful effects of bribery and intimidation." The first state platform, therefore, had demanded "fair elections and an honest count of the votes," a call that was repeated on all subsequent platforms.[56]

In a bill that ran twelve handwritten pages, Watkins crafted a comprehensive law that would fulfill the party's pledge. The bill mandated that election judges, clerks, and special election constables be appointed from all major political parties, and it instituted various safeguards for counting and reporting the ballots, which were to be standardized and printed and distributed by the election officials, not by party workers as was currently done. But the legislation went much further. Much of the chicanery so common on election days in Texas took place in the immediate vicinity of the polls, and Watkins's bill proposed sweeping changes there. In an article foreshadowing modern election procedures, it empowered the multiparty constables to "prevent and suppress any political discussion, debate, electioneering, controversies or other obstruction, or annoyance to the voters" within fifty feet of the polls and prescribed stiff fines for a first offense and jail time for repeat offenders. Sheriffs and any other regular law enforcement officers—the long arm of the county "rings" about which Populists so complained—were barred from exercising their "official duties" in the vicinity of the polls. Finally, the bill made it a felony for anyone to offer or receive anything of value in return for a vote, with penalties of two to five years at hard labor in the penitentiary and a fine of between five hundred and a thousand dollars. Addressing the problem of voter coercion and intimidation, the legislation imposed these same stiff penalties on "any one who by threats to discharge from service or deprive of home or supplies upon which to live, or to make a crop, or shall by any unlawful means intimidate or frighten any citizen away from the polls, or attempt to control the vote of another person, cause a citizen to vote contrary to his wishes." If this were not enough, Watkins included a final article in the bill extending its draconian penalties to any official at any level of government who in any way participated in fraud, including failure to report it. Populists clearly were serious about cleaning up Texas elections, but in a fashion that latter-day liberals would have applauded—by safeguarding the *right* to vote, not by making it *harder* to vote.[57]

Populist lawmakers may have devoted much of their effort to passage of the prolabor and good-government bills outlined above, but they still displayed a keen interest in what might be termed social legislation; that is, bills aimed at protecting or enhancing the health, safety, or morality of Texans, or in other ways promoting their social welfare. A number of these bills have been discussed in previous chapters. The surgeon-turned-minister Willis Lyman Harrison and the cattleman and former trail driver William E. Cureton spearheaded the Populist efforts in their respective legislative chambers to raise the age of consent for statutory rape cases. In related legislation, Tom Watkins sought to remove the one-year statute of limitations in rape cases involving underage victims or in cases of incest or instances where the victim was mentally handicapped.[58] Populists steadfastly opposed Democratic efforts to segregate railroad waiting rooms and to impose a poll tax as a requirement for voting.[59]

John O'Connor introduced three additional pieces of health and safety–related legislation. The first made it a misdemeanor to sell cigarettes and other tobacco products to minors. The second sought to limit the speed of trains approaching railroad intersections to six miles per hour when the intersection was equipped with modern interlocking switch and signal mechanisms, amending an existing 1893 amendment that had allowed trains not to come to a full stop but had failed to impose a speed limit at said intersections. The third provided that in cities of ten thousand or greater population, telegraph companies had to bury their wires underground, presumably as a safety measure. In other social legislation, the East Texas agitator Lee Rhodes introduced a bill—endorsed two years earlier by the state Farmers' Alliance—calling for the state to "provide for one or more competent female physicians" to assist male doctors in the state's insane asylums. Tom Watkins likewise sought to improve conditions at the state orphans' home by sponsoring legislation to grant the home fifty thousand acres of land out of the unappropriated public domain.[60]

Much of the Populists' social legislation revolved around efforts to improve the state's deplorable system of public education. As noted in Chapter 5, Watkins and Van Buren Ritter both introduced bills seeking to give African Americans meaningful control over black schools and to equalize funding for black and white schools. But much of the Populists' legislative agenda dealt with public education in general, and the Third-Party lawmakers mounted a multipronged reform effort. From the pen of Zachary Bartholomew Stokes came a bill requiring a six-hour day, and a five-day week, in the public schools, a major improvement over the current sporadic rules. Jesse Burney addressed the issue of textbooks, proposing a bill that would empower a three-person commission consisting of the state superintendent of higher education and the presidents of the University of Texas and Texas A&M to select "a uniform series of text books" for the subjects of "Spelling, reading, English grammar, geography, arithmetic, the elements of physiology and hygiene, history of the United States, and a graded series of writing books, provided that nothing of a sectional, partisan, or sectarian character shall be contained in said books." The commission was to be provided with the funds for commissioning the writing of the books, and they were to be printed by the state printer and provided to parents at cost. The proposal that textbooks for the state's schoolchildren would be produced and vetted by a board with a majority of academicians reinforces the notion of Populists as rationalists and modernizers, prepared to marshal the power of the state to enhance the public welfare.[61]

Two bills authored by the wealthy South Texas rancher Peyt McNeill addressed teacher qualifications. The first would cancel teachers' teaching certificates if they failed to attend their annual county teachers' institutes (an important form of continuing education for teachers in an era when formal educational requirements were so lax). This bill also provided for the dismissal of county superintendents who failed to perform their duties. McNeill's second bill prescribed the actual "requisites for obtaining teachers' certificates" and the procedures by which these certificates were to be granted by county boards of examiners. A bill by Z. B. Stokes further sought to improve teacher qualifications, setting forth a more stringent procedure for the granting of county teaching certificates.[62]

The scientifically minded Stokes also championed another bill that would have enacted sweeping reforms of the state's entire system of public education. The East Texas representative's bill would abolish the state's traditional countywide school districts altogether, ordering county commissioners' courts to subdivide them into "convenient school districts" as dictated by population and geography. It furthermore provided a method by which parents of school-age children could petition for further subdivision when a district got too large *or* for consolidation of two or more adjacent districts if they were too small. In short, the bill added much-needed flexibility to the unwieldy traditional system of county-based school districts, allowing something like the modern system of independent school districts to take shape. At the same time, the bill stayed true to Populist principles by giving parents at the grassroots level a large say-so in the crafting of districts. In this case, as in so many others, Populists found ways to reconcile their belief in modernization with their faith in government by the people.[63]

Holding only 22 of 108 seats in the House and 2 of 31 in the Senate, the Populists had scant hopes of passing legislation without significant Democratic help. But matters were not as hopeless as they might have seemed. The Democratic Party, as we have seen, was deeply divided, principally along conservative versus progressive lines, although those lines could be very fluid and inconsistent. Best estimates place the number of progressive, or Reform, Democrats in the House at about forty, leaving conservatives barely in the majority of their party's caucus, with forty-two votes. Strictly political considerations, however, dictated that even if the Reform Democrats might support a Populist measure, they were loath to vote for it, lest they give the Populists a public victory. Instead, what often happened was that the Reform Democrats ended up promoting their own versions of bills very similar to the Populists', and it then became a matter of the Democrats seeking enough Populist support to get the bills passed.[64]

Conservative Democrats bitterly decried the frequent common ground between Reform Democrats and Populists. Reporting on the heated battle over reforming the fee system, the conservative *Dallas Morning News* observed that "a well organized obstructive coterie of populists, ably assisted by the populist faction of the democracy, have delayed legislation and prevented the adoption of real retrenchments by incessant clamors and time destroying harangues against the county officers, porters and clerks of the departments." The *Morning News*, which opposed reform on the grounds of expense, complained that "the well organized populist minority holds the balance of power in the house and that so-called democrats deluded into their support have shared legislation so that it will be condemned by the people." Reform Democrats came under withering criticism from the conservative press, which began calling them "assistant democrats because of their bulging populistic proclivities." Other critics referred to them as "supplemental democrats," "alleged Democrats," "populistic democrats," "would-be Populists," and "disguised Populists." Conservative Democrat Frank Burmeister summarized his faction's attitude toward the Reform Democrats, declaring that "there were 22 Populists with backbone enough to say that they were Populists, but there were a whole batch of Populists in the house who were afraid to acknowledge their allegiance to the party, whose standard they . . . rallied to whenever opportunity offered."[65]

Conservatives pointed in particular to the session-long battle over the fee bill as evidence of the cooperation between Populists and Reform Democrats. "The fact is the fee bill is a populist platform demand and was never asked for by the democracy," the *Morning News* editorialized. "In spite of this fact the supplemental democratic contingent is fighting for it tooth and nail, thus presenting the spectacle of alleged democrats warring against the real democrats in behalf of a populist demand."[66] Such criticism had its intended effect, making it politically more difficult for Populists and Democrats to cooperate with one another. In the end, the Populists remained the distrusted junior partners in the uneasy reformist coalition.

Two major Democratic bills, considered by their sponsors to be reforms, demonstrated the limits to Populist-Democratic cooperation. The first of these bills was Senate Bill 1, introduced on the fourth day of the session by Democrat Oliver P. Bowser of Dallas. Bowser's bill sought to change the state's libel law, limiting the damages that plaintiffs could collect from newspapers in libel suits. Specifically, unless a plaintiff could prove that the libelous statements were knowingly made with "express malice," and if the paper subsequently printed a retraction, the paper was required to pay only actual but not exemplary or punitive damages. In practice, the legislation would have made it exceedingly difficult to collect meaningful damages in a libel suit. Honest people could, and did, disagree as to the merits of the bill. Some saw it as protecting freedom of the press, while others charged that the bill was the work "of a few men interested in the publication of one or two large newspapers." Unsurprisingly, newspapers across the state lined up in support of the measure. When the bill came before the full Senate, both Populist senators voted against it.[67]

The bill then went to the House, where it met stiffer opposition. After much debate, the measure's opponents managed to kill it by a vote of fifty-eight to forty-two. A large majority of the Populist representatives opposed the bill, but five—O'Connor, Rhodes, Floyd, Cureton, and Radford—voted for it, demonstrating that the Populists did not always march in lockstep.[68] The recriminations began immediately, with Democrats laying the blame for the bill's defeat squarely at the feet of the seventeen Populists who had voted against it, even though forty-one Democrats had also opposed it. The Populists, according to the *Dallas Morning News*, "can not tolerate a free, untrammeled and independent newspaper which dares to print the news with fairness to all and malice toward none." The Democratic press soon made an even more specific charge: the bill's defeat was the work of Thomas Nugent, who had appeared at the capitol during the final debate and lobbied against it. Nugent had recently lent his support to a movement on the part of prominent Populists to start a Populist daily paper in Austin, and the *Morning News* now editorialized that "Judge Nugent is sighing for a populist paper, a partisan organ," and that might account for his opposition to the bill.[69]

Nugent finally felt compelled to answer the charges. He had been in Austin on unrelated business, he explained, and had gone to the capitol to meet with Rep. Lee Rhodes. During the course of the debate on the libel bill, Rhodes and a handful of other legislators asked him his opinion of the measure, and he replied that with some amending he could support it. Nugent claimed that his discussions of the bill were done "in a casual and incidental way," and he had "long favored a just and fair libel law."[70] The Austin correspondent for the Populist *Southern Mercury* characterized efforts to blame the Populist legislators and Nugent for the bill's defeat "supremely ridiculous and puerile . . . excuses."[71]

The libel bill was not the only legislation that exposed the ragged edges of the reform coalition. A second bill, involving a subject of intense concern to Populists, brought even worse divisions to the fore. In 1889 the state had passed a landmark antitrust law. It was one of the nation's first such laws and it pre-dated the federal Sherman Antitrust Act by a year. The legislation had enjoyed strong agrarian support, made possible by the inclusion of an amendment exempting agricultural organizations from the law's provisions. Without such an exemption, it was believed that the law would prevent organizations like the Farmers' Alliance from cooperatively marketing farmers' crops and from mounting boycotts like the famous one that had defeated the jute bagging trust in 1889. The much-heralded 1889 law, however, had run into difficulties almost as soon as it was passed. Although it appeared to be effective in reining in the railroad pools, the law had failed to include insurance companies in its provisions, and furthermore it lacked any means of prosecuting violators who lived beyond the borders of Texas. When the 1895 legislature convened, Governor Culberson called on legislators to remedy these deficiencies.[72]

Populist lawmakers, for whom monopoly was a central concern, could have been expected to support Culberson's call for a stronger antitrust law, but one problem loomed large: because the agricultural exemption protected one class of people (farmers) at the expense of other classes (corporations and their employees), the exemption was widely suspected of being unconstitutional, based on the equal protection clause of the Fourteenth Amendment, and thus it might render the entire law unconstitutional. Many Democrats, then, believed that if the deficiencies in the law were to be fixed, the agricultural exemption would have to be thrown overboard. In calling for a revised antitrust bill, Governor Culberson himself noted that the exemption "may be omitted in the new law without injustice," saying rather disingenuously that if the exemption were truly unconstitutional, "patriotic farmers and stockmen do not want it." Other Democrats *wanted* to throw the exemption overboard, reasoning that it gave them a chance to strike a blow at the Alliance and other such organizations from whence Populism had sprung. Populists thus found themselves in the position of either having to oppose antimonopoly legislation or risk banning the Alliance and possibly even labor unions.[73]

The new antitrust bill, as introduced in the House by Democrat William T. Armistead, lacked the agricultural exemption. When it came to the floor, all the Populists but two voted against it. Fourteen Third-Party lawmakers took the unusual step of recording the reasons for their vote in the Senate *Journal:*

"We vote no . . . because the bill is directly antagonistic to all labor organizations and individual and collective industrial effort."[74]

The bill eventually passed the House and was sent to the Senate. There the battle over the bill was repeated, with the two Populist senators opposing it as long as the exemption was omitted. At one point the Delta County Populist senator James Darwin justified his opposition to the bill on the grounds that "it will dissolve all farmers and labor organizations in Texas." Just as it appeared that the bill might stall, the state supreme court upheld the constitutionality of the agricultural exemption. A special Senate committee restored the exemption, and the bill passed both houses and was eventually signed by the governor. In the end, Populists had joined with Reform Democrats to enact a measure both supported, but only after a great deal of acrimony that sowed new seeds of distrust between the two groups.[75]

~

Few Texans of any political persuasions pointed with much pride to the achievements of the Twenty-Fourth Texas Legislature. Forced by the Texas Constitution to balance the budget, and unable to agree on new sources of revenue, lawmakers slashed spending and still had to raise the state ad valorem tax from 15 cents to 22.5 cents per $100 valuation and the state school tax from 12.5 cents to 20 cents in order to close the yawning deficit.[76] The revised antitrust law was one of the few positive pieces of legislation enacted. After several marathon sessions, including one lasting forty-plus continuous hours, the bill reforming the corrupt fee system went down to defeat. More than one newspaper, in describing the total breakdown in parliamentary decorum, characterized the House of Representatives as a "howling mob." In a rare show of agreement across partisan lines, the Republican *San Antonio Light* endorsed the Democratic *Austin Statesman*'s pronouncement "that the unlamented Twenty-Fourth legislature was the greatest abortion in that line that Texas has ever produced." Even the Populist *Southern Mercury*, though not critical of the Populist minority in the legislature, concluded that "the adjournment day of the present legislature should be one of general rejoicing."[77]

The *Dallas Morning News*, which had been unstinting in its criticism of the legislature throughout the session, pronounced a slightly more analytical postmortem on the legislative body. The legislature, it declared, had "wasted barrels of time making political history and warring with a handful of populists whose mission here has been to place the democratic party in a hole from which it can not escape until after the next election. And they have succeeded beyond their wildest expectations. With rare exceptions the little bunch of pop-

ulists has got the best of the big democratic house when it comes to manufacturing campaign thunder. To-day the populists of the house are far better
satisfied with several results than their democratic friends."[78]

For Populists who had gone to Austin to attempt to pass legislation, such
strictly political benefits would have provided little comfort. Of the ten thousand bills introduced in the 1895 legislature, only 141 became law. Populists
had introduced a total of sixty-six bills. Only four became law, with the rest
killed in committee, dying on the Speaker's desk, or suffering some similar
parliamentary fate. Of the four bills that became law, three were minor matters
of strictly local concern. The only Populist bill of statewide importance to become law was Willis Harrison's age-of-consent bill, but the Democrats had
agreed to raise the statutory rape age from twelve only to fifteen, rather than
to eighteen as Harrison's original bill had proposed, thus watering the bill
down so much that Populists took little pride in its passage.[79]

The chief importance of the 1895 legislature lies not in the laws it passed or
even in the fleeting political capital that its Populist members may have
amassed. Its only lasting significance lies in what it demonstrates about the
nature of Populism, about what real-world Populism might have looked like if
the People's Party had ever become a governing party. In pursuing economic
reforms that would level the playing field for ordinary people and monopolistic corporations, in seeking good-government measures that would curb corruption and make government more responsive to the public's interests, and
in seeking social legislation that would safeguard the health, safety, and moral
welfare of the people, Populists displayed a surprisingly keen grasp of the modern idea that in a democratic capitalist system certain public problems require public solutions. To the modern American mind, treating convicts more
humanely, abolishing the corrupt fee system of county government, removing police and fire departments from the control of urban bosses, enacting
commonsense regulations for financial institutions, improving public education for children of all races, safeguarding the integrity of the ballot, making
railroad crossings and telegraph wires safer, and preventing the sale of tobacco
to children scarcely qualify as "radical." Some of these measures presaged the
technocratic reforms of early twentieth-century progressivism. Others gained
widespread support in the New Deal, and still others went mainstream in the
decades after World War II. While some of the Populists' most ambitious
reforms—most notably the Subtreasury Plan and government ownership of
transportation and communication systems—were primarily national in nature
and anticipated the pursuit of collective economic rights that would characterize

the New Deal in its most ambitious moments, there was little in the Texas Populists' legislative record that suggested a socialist rejection of capitalism or some unique attempt to construct a centrally planned economy. Texas Populists were not seeking to construct a "cooperative commonwealth" or a system of "regional republicanism"—terms that historians have sometimes used to describe the political economy of Populism. Instead, the reforms pursued by the Populists in the Twenty-Fourth Texas Legislature bear most of the hallmarks of what Americans in the twentieth century would call liberalism. Few of those Populist lawmakers would have objected to that label, but they probably would have also wondered why future generations would prefer it over "populism," which undoubtedly sounded just fine to them.[80]

9 • The Problem of the Border

Sooner or later the matter of suffrage will have to be better
regulated on the border.
—Theodore J. McMinn, 1897

I feel sure, that the characteristic liberality that has heretofore prevailed in
all our platforms will sustain us in our very pronounced theory of equal
rights to all native and naturalized citizens.
—Jerome C. Kearby, 1896

As the People's Revolt unfolded in the Lone Star State, Populists worried
about South Texas, with good reason.[1] This region, lying below an east-west
line stretching roughly from the Gulf of Mexico westward through San Antonio and then to the Rio Grande, was the only part of the state with sizable numbers of Mexicanos, a population composed of both Texas-born Tejanos and
more recent immigrants from south of the Rio Grande.[2] In South Texas neither the Alliance, the Knights of Labor, nor the various independence political movements of the 1880s had ever been particularly strong, so Populism
there got off to a slow start and faced formidable opposition. In the northern-
most parts of the region, especially in Bexar County (home to San Antonio)
and neighboring counties, a sizable population of Germans and other ethnic
Europeans had often supported the Republican Party, so there was a certain
degree of political competition there. But as one moved southward from San
Antonio, the Democrats reigned supreme, usually through the instrumentality of machine bosses who effectively controlled the Mexican vote, often by blatantly fraudulent means. Following a bloody election riot between contending

factions in Laredo in 1886, the *Galveston Daily News* opined that along the border "a fair election is hardly possible" and that even in the interior cities "votes are purchased, illegal voting practiced, and the people of Texas cheated of their choice by election frauds." The *News* noted that it was "only in the last two or three years that the extent of these frauds has been suspected," and it called for reforms at the state level. In the Populist era, virtually every informed contemporary analysis of the People's Party's prospects began with a glum, if not apocalyptic, prognosis for the party's political success there.[3]

Despite these obstacles, Populists in South Texas courted Mexicanos, much as their counterparts in the eastern parts of the state sought African American support, largely by stressing the shared economic interests of downtrodden minorities and poor whites. By 1894 they were sometimes finding a receptive audience. Writing that year from the town of Yoakum, ninety miles east of San Antonio, J. R. Rice reported organizing "a populist club entirely of Mexicans" and bragged that Populism "was growing down here." From Uvalde, an equal distance to the west of San Antonio, the Populist county chairman in 1894 reported that "the Mexican voters here had formed themselves into a club (90 in all) for the purpose of all voting together and that they were wanting to support the Populas tickett." South Texas Populists, certain that Tejanos were "becoming restive" under Democratic rule and were "ready for revolt," pleaded with the party to send Spanish-language speakers and campaign literature to the region.[4]

In Wilson County, midway between Yoakum and Uvalde, the People's Party received a boost when Vicente F. Carvajal, a prominent Tejano businessman who had been active in Democratic politics, converted to Populism. The *Galveston Daily News* noted the Third Party's efforts among Wilson County's Mexicans, commenting that the Populists were "making great efforts to 'corral' the Mexicans," but the paper predicted failure because "Mexicans are democrats by nature, and have always voted that ticket and probably always will." Matters came to a head when local party leaders met in the spring of 1894 to nominate a county ticket. It was generally understood that "if the populists wished to elect county officers it would be necessary to place some influential Mexican on the ticket," but this idea met resistance from one Anglo member who walked out of the meeting rather than support Carvajal or any Mexican. At this juncture Dr. R. F. Johnson, "a leading Populist," rose to defend Carvajal's candidacy for county clerk, reminding the gathering that Carvajal "was an American citizen by birth" whose "father had fought with the heroes of San Jacinto." Carvajal was "well qualified for the office" and acknowledged to wield "considerable influence among his people," but the newspaper reported that "still many present would not consent" to his nomination and "they did not feel under obligations to vote for him." Clearly the Populists of Wilson County faced a conundrum: Carvajal's Democratic opponent for the office was "one of the most popular men in the county," and with Mexicans constituting a quarter of the voting population, all of the white Populist nominees were "anxious for Caravahal [sic] to secure the nomination, as it gives them a better chance." In the end, the white Populists overcame whatever prejudice they felt toward Carvajal and nominated him for county clerk. That fall, "Mexican orators" campaigned for the People's Party in the county, challenging Democrats to debates. Two weeks before the election one observer was reporting from Wilson County that "the Mexicans here are all Populists" and that Carvajal could muster five hundred Mexicano votes. Carvajal went on to win in November, along with the rest of the county Populist ticket, and the Populists forged a viable coalition across racial and ethnic lines in Wilson County.[5]

Local Populist organizations garnered support sufficient to carry Wilson, Atascosa, Frio, Dimmit, and San Patricio Counties—all counties with sizable Mexicano minorities—for the People's Party gubernatorial candidate Thomas L. Nugent in 1892. Two years later they won fewer outright victories at the gubernatorial level because the Republicans once again fielded a candidate, dividing the anti-Democratic vote, but the Populists still carried Wilson, Lavaca, and Dimmit, and deprived the Democrats of majorities in Atascosa, Frio, DeWitt, Maverick, and Medina Counties. That same year in San Antonio, after fighting many losing battles, the local Populist organization finally scored a major victory when it elected attorney and former policeman John A. O'Connor to one of Bexar County's two seats in the state House of Representatives. O'Connor's election was something of an anomaly; after the Populists nominated him, the Bexar County "machine" placed him on its ticket in "a bid for populist votes for that ticket." Although he won with the backing of the "courthouse combination" and its reliable Mexicano votes, in the legislature O'Connor proved to be a dependable Populist and indeed became a leader of that party's caucus in Austin. Only in the turbulent, complex, faction-ridden world of San Antonio politics could a John O'Connor be possible, but his election nonetheless bolstered Populism in the South Texas city and gave its adherents cause for optimism.[6]

Encouraging victories like these, however, never occurred in the Rio Grande Valley counties of far-south Texas, as Populists repeatedly learned. An 1894 congressional race vividly illustrated the problem and left a lasting impression on

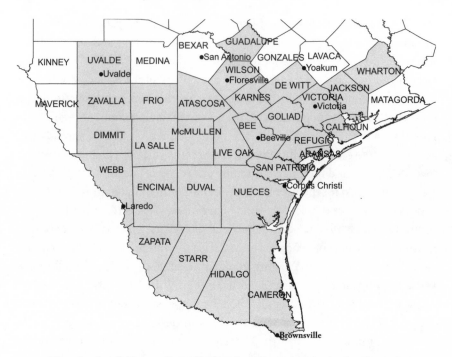

Figure 7 South Texas, 1894. Shading indicates counties in the Eleventh
Congressional District. Map by Claire Holland.

Populists. And because it is the only such race in which the private papers of
the opposition candidate survive, it offers an intriguing glimpse into the byz-
antine world of border politics in the Populist era.

The Eleventh Congressional District consisted of twenty-four counties, en-
compassing most of South Texas below San Antonio and then stretching northward along the Gulf Coast as far as heavily black Wharton County southwest
of Houston. Populist and Republican leaders in the region reading the results
of the 1892 election, in which the Democratic candidate William H. Crain
polled half the vote while the Populists and Republicans each took about a
quarter, could see that clearly this was a vulnerable district. Recognizing the
impossibility of victory on their own, in 1894 the Populists and Republicans
"suspended purely partisan considerations" and reached an agreement to unite
behind an independent candidate, Vachel Weldon, despite the bitter complaints
of some Populists that fusion was a surrender of principle. Fusionist leaders
knew, however, that Weldon sympathized with many Populist policy positions,
and they felt confident that they could get out the vote. One of the first things

they did was to summon the charismatic biracial orator and state Populist executive committeeman John B. Rayner to organize the black vote in the upper counties. He soon arrived in the district and began working his oratorical magic.[7]

The Weldon camp also knew what to expect at the other end of the district in the Rio Grande Valley—the usual lopsided voter turnout by the Democratic machines in those majority-Mexicano counties. It was not just that Texas-born Tejanos could be persuaded, cajoled, intimidated, manipulated, or paid to vote Democratic; one did not have to be a US citizen *at all* in order to vote. Under Texas law a Mexican immigrant needed only to sign a simple form before a county clerk, swearing his "intention" to become a citizen, in order to be granted suffrage. Actually going through the process of taking out final citizenship papers could wait indefinitely. It was the reality of alien suffrage more than any other single factor that led one of Weldon's allies to warn him, "You must look out for the lower Riogrande [*sic*] there is where they will knife [you] if they can."[8]

Prominent Republican attorney R. B. Rentfro of Brownsville knew what the Democrats' strategy would be: "We understand here that these counties are to be colonized by Mexicans in Crains interest," he explained, but he believed that $1,000 properly spent could "counteract" the Democrats' plans. Vicente Carvajal elaborated on precisely what was required: besides the preprinted party ballots to hand to voters at the polls, "we need about five influencial [*sic*] men at every box, on the river, where they are all Mexicans, these men have to have about 4 gall of whiskey at each box and each man has to have about five dollars for eating purposes . . . and if we are not helped with money we will be powerless, we have left, cash on hand $33.05." The money never materialized, whereas the Crain campaign was flush with funds from numerous sources including the Democratic National Committee. Weldon's campaign strategists made an effort to place their own election judges and poll watchers across the district to counteract fraud, but they pinned their hopes mainly on winning with such big majorities in the northern and central counties that they could offset the massive Democratic majorities in the south.[9]

It was not to be. Days before the election Vicente Carvajal wrote to Weldon's campaign manager that "money is flying," as the Democrats marshaled their considerable resources to buy votes in the border precincts. On election day the extent of the fraud in the Rio Grande counties shocked even longtime observers of the region's politics. Numerous witnesses reported seeing Democratic election officials opening ballot boxes, discarding fusionist ballots, and allowing illegal Democratic ballots to stand. On an unprecedented scale the border bosses executed their time-honored practice of having Mexican nationals vote Democratic, either with or without the documents that would have made such votes legal. Hundreds or even thousands of Mexican residents were brought across the river on, or immediately preceding, election day for the purpose of casting fraudulent ballots. Some precincts polled more votes than their entire populations. From Brownsville an outraged R. B. Rentfro estimated that two thousand fraudulent votes had been cast in three counties alone, and he declared that "the fact can be easily demonstrated." He complained that "all concealment was thrown aside and Democratic politicians here return [New York boss William] Tweed's answer to all remonstrances, 'What in hell are you going to do about it?'" If the district's five counties along the Rio Grande are excluded, Weldon won the election with 55 percent of the vote. But in those five counties the incumbent Democrat won by a three-to-one margin, and in Cameron County alone, at the southernmost tip of Texas, the Democratic margin was large enough to cost Weldon the victory.[10]

In the aftermath of the contest, an Atascosa County Populist leader elaborated on the methods that had been used to defeat Vachel Weldon. "Not less than 100 Mexicans appeared (cotton pickers from Mexico or elsewhere) at our county clerk's office and declared their intentions to become citizens the last 10 days before the elections & were rounded up like cattle and voted by their leaders on election day," he explained. "Very many of them Mexicans in a drunken state appeared at the polls, and were voted by the leaders in the voting precinct. Democratic money flowed freely as well as Democratic whisky." Reporting on the election in Starr County on the Rio Grande, R. B. Rentfro claimed to have "abundant evidence" that nearly four hundred Mexicans had been illegally furnished with intention papers. "Their names could be gathered, and brought in to the county clerk who would issue the documents without ever having seen the 'applicant,'" he declared. Moreover, he claimed that the records of the Mexican customhouses at Mier and Camargo would reveal "the passing of more than five hundred Mexicans to Texas, (of course to vote)." Even at Beeville, two hundred miles north of the river, a Populist leader reported that "there was a large number of Mexicans naturalized at this place the day (Nov. 5) before the election and voted against us."[11]

Writing two years later, Texas's commissioner to Mexico, Henry Ryder Taylor, provided a detailed account that further elucidated the methods used by South Texas Democrats. Taylor, an Englishman who had begun his journalism career on the London Telegraph before moving to San Antonio in 1881, had worked intermittently as a reporter for the *San Antonio Light* for much of the previous two decades. The cosmopolitan Taylor had also lived in St. Louis, New York, and Mexico City, and he counted literary figures like the writer O. Henry among his circle of friends. Citing his fifteen years as a journalist in San Antonio, Taylor noted that he "had an inside track in local politics" and that he could "fairly pretend to have acquired some personal and practical knowledge upon which to base a reliable opinion." Taylor gave eyewitness testimony "to the fact that thousands of Mexicans have been imported across the Rio Grande for the mere sake of voting in accordance with the instructions of the importers." He explained that there was "always considerable activity in public improvements just before election[s] and the imported voter is given work on the county roads, on the bridges, on the streets in various places and even on railroads that are interested in getting certain officers elected." On these jobs, he claimed, the Mexicans earned between $1.00 and $1.75 in gold per day, "besides their bribes." The workers, of course, had to be furnished with their intention papers, which Taylor said cost the importer $2.50 unless "friendly officers" issued the papers free of charge. He claimed to have witnessed two hundred such voters "manufactured in a day just before elections." In a city like San Antonio where voter registration existed, "the registrar is appointed by the influence of those that get the voters and issue the papers, and is generally their partisan, [and] he does not scrutinize these papers too closely." Taylor then described the final step in the process: "On election days these imported voters are given their registration certificates, that are retained by the bribers in trust, given a ticket already marked as desired, and are led in squads to polling places to deposit their ballots." Taylor was describing the process in San Antonio, where the state's new urban election law at least mandated voter registration and the secret ballot; in the Rio Grande counties where that system did not exist, the fraud was much more blatant and required less of the legal window dressing detailed in this account. Still, as one knowledgeable critic noted, "There is no law that does not admit of evasion, especially backed by the authorities."[12]

As previously noted, Texas law allowed immigrants to vote; they needed only to file citizenship intention papers (also known as "first papers") to vote in Texas elections. The *San Antonio Light* charged that of twelve thousand intention papers issued in Bexar County since 1871, "not one Mexican" had taken out his final papers (that is, actually petitioned for citizenship), nor did any intend to; for them, voting was "a commercial affair, involving no risk or outlay of money with a certainty of reward." A San Antonio Populist agreed that "there exists a laboring element, non-union, chiefly made up of Mexicans, whose vote can only be had by purchase," but he insisted that the Populists did not "intend to follow the tricks of the two old parties. . . . We must use persuasion wherever we can, but nothing more."[13]

Immigration records substantiate allegations of widespread voter fraud. Two Rio Grande counties, Hidalgo and Starr, saw 2,239 Mexicans file intention papers between 1880 and 1899. Of these, fewer than ten individuals ever petitioned for final citizenship, and a staggering 85 percent (1,914) of the declarations were filed in election years between October 1 and November 7, roughly the last month before general elections. In Hidalgo and Starr Counties in 1894, the year of the Vachel Weldon–William Crain race, 389 intention papers were filed in the month before the election; 133 were filed in the final week, and thirty-seven were filed on the day before the election. And these were the numbers for just two of twenty-nine counties in the district. These, then, were the obstacles Populist leaders confronted as they contemplated waging and winning elections in the region.[14]

~

Prominent among those leaders was Theodore J. McMinn of San Antonio (plate 21). Born the son of a millwright in Logansport, Indiana, in 1845, McMinn worked his way up from blacksmithing to clerking and finally to law school. He chose a career in journalism over law, however, and worked for the *St. Louis Globe-Democrat* and the *Springfield Herald* from the late 1870s to the late 1880s. During that time he also served as agent of the St. Louis Live Stock Exchange, in which capacity he traveled the western states promoting the creation of the National Cattle and Horse Growers' Association. Moving to San Antonio in 1887, he managed the literary bureau of the San Antonio and Aransas Pass Railroad, worked as an agent for the Southwestern Immigration Association, and finally returned to journalism as editor of the *San Antonio Times*. McMinn was always drawn to reform causes, and as a muckraking journalist he could be found publishing exposés of everything from gambling dens to political corruption. Fired from his newspaper position for "political reasons" unrelated to the naturalization controversy, he turned to the practice of law, where he rose to prominence as an attorney and even argued a case before the US Supreme Court. In 1891 he joined the new Populist movement, serving on the platform committee at the party's founding convention in Dallas. Stoutly built, with a square jaw, closely trimmed hair, and handlebar moustache, he was an accomplished operatic tenor, always in demand for public performances. One newspaper account characterized him as possessing "an air of great energy, firm resolution and tremendous reserve power." Throughout a long and varied career, the outspoken, idealistic, mercurial McMinn seemed to easily win friends and admirers in whatever circles he moved. He also gained a reputation as a man unafraid to champion unpopular causes.[15]

McMinn, who himself had lost a congressional race to Thomas M. Paschal in the district including Bexar County in 1892 and a state legislative race in 1894, understandably felt despair over his party's prospects in the region. As early as 1888, as a member of San Antonio's Young Men's Reform Club, he had raised the issue of Mexican naturalization. Citing federal immigration law that prohibited the naturalization of all but whites and blacks, he suggested that dark-skinned Mexican immigrants (as opposed to native-born Tejanos) might be ineligible for American citizenship because of their Indian racial heritage, and he proposed that the Reform Club pass a resolution calling for a legal test case of the proposition. The Reform Club refused to act on his proposal, and McMinn faced a minor tempest in the press from opponents of his ideas.[16]

Whatever else T. J. McMinn may have been, he was no quitter. In the wake of the Weldon race, and coming after his own defeats in contests for Congress in 1892 and the state legislature in 1894, he again raised the issue. As Weldon weighed the question of contesting his election before Congress in late 1894, McMinn wrote him, saying, "I have this suggestion to make in case you contest: that Mexicans are wholly ineligible to citizenship." He repeated his belief that US law admitted only whites and blacks to citizenship, barring "the yellow man the red man and the brown man." With the exception of individuals of pure Spanish blood and those "who supported the Texas republic" (and their children), the Mexican, he declared, "is a red man." He claimed to "have gone *all over* this matter: I speak *advisedly*. If congress should take this position it would cure the river disease with which our politics is suffering." Weldon chose not to pursue the contest, so McMinn's idea that Congress might rule against the naturalization of Mexicans came to naught.[17]

If the 1894 elections had driven home McMinn's belief that fraudulent Mexican voting was costing Populists victories, those same elections now gave him a new hope. With twenty-four Populists in the state legislature, the "river disease" might be addressed at the state level. The Populist lawmakers potentially had allies in the pink-domed capitol; many reform-minded Democrats also found the corruption in South Texas distasteful or, more likely, they resented the power that the bosses in the border region wielded in state Democratic politics. When the legislature convened in January 1895, one such Democrat, Samuel McBride of Hays County, introduced a joint resolution to amend the state constitution in order to restrict voting to American citizens. By ending alien suffrage in the state, McBride's measure would do away altogether with the practice of immigrants taking out their intention papers and then immediately voting. The *Dallas Morning News* speculated that its supporters did so because "its passage would result in the suppression of ballot prostitution on the Rio Grande border and prevent the voting of imported Mexicans in droves." Significantly, the *Morning News* also believed that all of the Populists in the House, "with the exception of Mr. O'Connor of Bexar," supported the measure. When the resolution came to a vote, the Populists voted as a bloc in favor of it, joining more than sixty Democrats in supporting the measure. Even O'Connor, who owed his seat in part to Mexicano voters in San Antonio, fell into line and supported it. Although the yeas outnumbered the nays 83 to 28, the measure narrowly failed because enough members were absent to deprive it of the required two-thirds majority. Three Democrats who opposed the resolution explained that "we believe that it is calculated and intended to deprive a large and industrious class of people who have come among us with the intention of remaining permanently, from any voice in the affairs of the state"—which sounded noble enough until they added a second, more candid, reason for their votes: "and because we believe that it is a blow aimed at the best interests of the Democratic party."[18]

The legislature, however, was not finished with efforts to limit alien suffrage. Ultimately a constitutional amendment requiring foreigners to file their intention papers six months before voting garnered enough support to pass both chambers, again with unanimous Populist support. Gov. Charles Culberson allowed it to become law without his signature, and the following fall the voters approved the amendment by an 84 percent margin. This watered-down effort to curb fraud on the border apparently had little real impact—there were still plenty of ways to circumvent even the six-month requirement—but the narrow failure of the legislature to pass McBride's citizens-only suffrage amendment set the stage for what was about to transpire.[19]

On May 11, 1896, a "copper-colored" man with "dark eyes, straight black hair, and high cheek bones" walked into the federal courthouse for the Western District of Texas in San Antonio and filed papers to become an American citizen. He was Ricardo Rodriguez, an illiterate laborer who spoke no English. The thirty-seven-year-old Rodriguez, a native of Guanajuato, Mexico, had lived in Texas since 1883 and by all accounts was a hardworking, law-abiding man. His only stated reason for desiring citizenship was "because he lived here."[20]

Standing at the ready to contest Rodriguez's application were T. J. McMinn and a fellow lawyer, Republican Andrew Jackson Evans. Filing a preliminary brief as amici curiae (friends of the court), the attorneys challenged Rodriguez's application, based on the proposition that Rodriguez was not a white man and therefore was ineligible for citizenship under the nation's immigration laws. This was the test case that McMinn had long advocated, and the Populist lawyer had clearly orchestrated it. The case, styled *In re Rodriguez*, potentially carried enormous implications for the People's Party and for the thousands of ethnic Mexicans in Texas and the Southwest. It soon ignited a political firestorm that would cause many observers, then and now, to question Populist liberalism.[21]

McMinn and Evans had good reason to believe that their arguments were sound. On the matter of his race, Rodriguez claimed simply that he was "a pure-blooded Mexican" and professed to know nothing about any indigenous Mexican Indian groups. But whereas modern experts would have argued that race has no fixed basis in biology, all of the lawyers involved in the case, as well as the judge, Democrat Thomas Maxey, agreed that the dark-skinned Rodriguez was indeed an Indian or at least of mixed Indian-Caucasian racial heritage, and not "white" by any scientific *or* common understanding of the term. Nobody seemed prepared to argue for his whiteness.[22]

The foundational federal statute on naturalization, in effect since 1802, specified that "any alien, being a free white person," could become a citizen. When the Fourteenth Amendment granted African Americans citizenship after the Civil War, the law was amended to include Africans and persons of African descent, but Congress specifically reiterated that naturalization was still restricted to whites and blacks. In the several decades that followed, several court decisions confirmed and elaborated on this principle, consistently ruling against non-European immigrants seeking citizenship. Significantly, the attorney for Rodriguez in the case, McMinn's former Democratic congressional opponent Thomas Paschal, made blatantly racist arguments against Asians and in favor of "Anglo-Saxon" superiority in his own legal brief in the case.[23]

Although political opponents at the time and historians a century later charged McMinn (and by extension, his party) with anti-immigrant bigotry, there is no evidence that McMinn sought to have Mexican "Indians" like Ricardo Rodriguez declared ineligible for naturalization for any reason other than the sort of political corruption that was such common knowledge. If the legislature had enacted McBride's 1895 bill barring noncitizens from voting, McMinn likely would never have brought his court action. None of this entirely exonerates McMinn on charges of racism; he was, after all, a privileged white man who benefited from his society's racial hierarchy on a daily basis. In his brief before Judge Maxey's court, he had listed those categories of Mexicans whom he deemed legally qualified for citizenship; the list included Tejano veterans of the Texas Revolution and their descendants; all ethnic Mexicans who resided in Texas as of Independence Day in 1836 and their descendants; and all "Spanish, Caucasian Mexican citizens." He then quoted historical figures including John C. Calhoun and Sam Houston in a rather gratuitous attempt to demonstrate that these statesmen had considered Mexicans racially unfit. But though he deployed race here as a tactical matter, it is significant that McMinn never offered a personal opinion on the question of Mexican racial fitness or inferiority. Instead, he and Evans simply offered their interpretation of existing law. As they later summarized their legal position in the *San Antonio Light,* "There are millions of 'white persons' in Mexico today who, if they choose, can become citizens of the United States, but her original Indians and [their] descendants cannot."[24]

McMinn vehemently argued that he did not harbor racial prejudice toward Mexicans. In 1888, when he had first raised the question of the legality of their naturalization and had come under intense criticism for it, he responded by declaring that "our worth and intellect are not fixed by color" and that "history is full of instances of genius and virtue within dusky skins." But his *legal* case rested entirely on the contention that Rodriguez and other dark-skinned Mexicans were not white and thus their naturalization would violate the letter of the nation's citizenship laws. If they were ineligible for citizenship, they could not swear the oath that they "intended" to become American citizens without committing perjury, thus disqualifying them from voting under the state's alien suffrage law. McMinn, then, apparently acted not out of bigotry toward Mexicans or a belief in white supremacy per se, but rather to render the state's alien suffrage law a dead letter. Perhaps the worst that can be said of McMinn's political actions is that if preventing voter fraud came at the high price of barring an entire class of immigrants from becoming citizens, it appeared not to bother him. He defended his action by pointing out that few others who took out intention papers ever did as Ricardo Rodriguez and sought to take out final citizenship papers—a contention that apparently nobody disputed and that indeed was accurate.[25]

As the lawyers developed their arguments, word of the case reached the streets of San Antonio and soon was eliciting comment in the press. "Whatever the outcome of the matter may be it promises to stir up an interesting commotion in local and state politics," the *San Antonio Express* inveighed, adding that "the decision will be looked for with unusual interest." The competing *San Antonio Light,* a Republican paper often sympathetic to Populists, remarked that there was a "great deal of excitement on the streets today" over the action. Even this, as it turned out, was putting it mildly. Unsurprisingly, the public's reading of the case lacked the nuance that McMinn and Evans would have desired. Despite the two lawyers' claims that "the purpose of the proceeding is solely to prevent the newly arrived Mexicans from voting," most thought that a ruling against Rodriguez would result in the disfranchisement of *all* Mexicanos no matter how long they or their families had lived in the United States. Some observers assumed that the two lawyers were directly in the pay of "some political party" that had not been getting its share of the Mexican vote. A *Dallas Morning News* reporter opined that "a decision favorable to McMinn would deprive the democratic party of 20,000 votes" and potentially "turn the two southwestern [congressional] districts over to populism."[26]

Predictably, some of the fiercest denunciations came from the Mexican American community in San Antonio. Leading the attack was Pablo Cruz, editor of the Spanish-language newspaper *El Regidor.* Cruz sympathized with Populism, and his paper frequently endorsed People's Party candidates. Indeed, he would back gubernatorial candidate Jerome Kearby in 1896, despite McMinn's actions. But Cruz lambasted McMinn and Evans, referring to them in his initial report on the *Rodriguez* case as *"dos adoloridos"* (two soreheads) who were disappointed office seekers. Soon Cruz was calling McMinn a "sworn enemy of the Mexicans" and urging his fellow Mexicans to "scratch [out] his name wherever you find it on the ballot." Ominously, in July Cruz reported on an *"anarquistica"* letter that the chief of police had recently obtained, "illustrated with sinister figures such as skulls and other figures representing death," threatening to kill "gringos" and "sour krouts" (Germans) in the city for oppressing Mexicans and other minority groups. Cruz hinted that McMinn was a particular target of the threat, noting that the Populist leader was so alarmed by the letter that he could neither eat nor sleep.[27]

If McMinn did not expect the backlash from Spanish-speaking South Texans, he certainly did not anticipate the reaction of his fellow Populists. Local Populist leader Selig Deutschmann (plate 22) quickly moved to distance himself and the local party from McMinn, saying, "We are not responsible for what a member of our party does, any more than the Republicans can be charged with instigating this because Judge Evans is a Republican." Deutschmann, who with his walrus moustache and pince-nez glasses bore more than a passing resemblance to Theodore Roosevelt, was a German-born Jew who probably knew a thing or two about bigotry. He declared, "Individually, I have always been opposed to anything that is calculated to arouse prejudice between the different races, as well as the different religions. It is a question that ought not to enter in any political discussion." He went on to explain that he had spent several years of his life living among the Mexicans, and he counted some of them as his best friends. The majority of them "make good citizens and are certainly entitled to citizenship," he declared, noting that they "enjoyed in their own country the highest civilization when New York City was a little Dutch village. . . . To classify the Mexicans with the Indian seems to me to be rot." Deutschmann then voiced what he believed to be basic Populist doctrine and suggested where the party really stood on the issue of Mexican suffrage: "Populists believe in doing to others as they would be done by and while everyone is opposed to the methods adopted on the Rio Grande on election day, we favor regulating it by a law making a five year residence necessary before a person can vote, but not by a wholesale disfranchising of good citizens." The party never went on record favoring Deutschmann's five-year proposal, but Pablo Cruz later spoke glowingly of Deutschmann in the pages of *El Regidor,* describing the German American Populist as a "learned lawyer" and "one of the members of said party who has most distinguished himself defending, on the rostrum and in the press, the right of Mexicans not to be denied US citizenship."[28]

Deutschmann's denunciation of McMinn might be ascribed to his own status as an immigrant, but the same could not be said of State Representative John A. O'Connor, San Antonio's most prominent Populist officeholder and a native Texan. When O'Connor learned of the action in federal court, he professed to be "very much surprised, even astonished" at the proceedings—so much so, in fact, that he had "not been able to take the matter seriously, it seems so absurd." At first he thought it was "paying it too great a compliment to dignify it by giving it a political significance," but he then proceeded to unload on McMinn: "As a Populist I desire to denounce this effort to disfranchise the Mexicans with all the fire and vigor [of which] an Irishman is capable [O'Connor was of distant Irish ancestry]. It not only has no support, but has no sympathy among the Populists. Why, some of the best and oldest citizens of this city and section are Mexicans. They have aided in building up this city and country, and were paying taxes to our government before some of those who would now disfranchise them were born. . . . And to say that these people have no right to become citizens here in the home of the free and the

land of the brave, this asylum for the oppressed, is simply absurd." O'Connor
believed that if McMinn were correct, "the good Mexican who has come here
and taken up his abode, been naturalized, bought property, reared his family,
paid his obligations to the State and Federal government, is not a citizen. You
can see where the argument leads to." The Populist legislator finally resorted
to ridicule to express his displeasure with his fellow Populist: "To say it is not
good law is to put it mildly—too mildly for me. It is not good nonsense." Even
the German-language press in San Antonio took notice of the brouhaha; the
Freie Presse für Texas noted that "Representative O'Connor and various other
local leaders of the Populist Party issued a resolute denial that their party is
responsible for the attempt to rob the Mexicans of their right to vote."[29]

It did not take McMinn long to respond to these attacks. The day after
O'Connor's diatribe appeared in the *Express,* he published a response stating
"that no one—certainly no Populist—is in any way responsible in the remot-
est degree for my doings but my individual self." He repeated his contention
that he was not seeking to disfranchise any "recognized citizen," but then he
lambasted O'Connor and Deutschmann as "uninformed persons" who were
"spouting irrelevant rot." McMinn went on to sarcastically suggest that "it
would be quite right for them to appear and champion the cause of the applicant if they feel so deeply on the subject."[30]

By this point, just days after Ricardo Rodriguez's appearance in federal
court, the *San Antonio Light* could accurately declare that "the question has
assumed large proportions." A week later unidentified parties began circulating a "manifesto in the Mexican language signed by 'Mexicano-Texanos'" featuring a translation of the newspaper accounts of the *Rodriguez* case along with
"an appeal to all Mexicans to vote the Democratic ticket, for the reason "'that
both the Populist and Republican parties have combined to disfranchise the
Mexican race.'" Just to the south of San Antonio in Wilson County, where Vicente Carvajal had worked so hard to build up a viable multiethnic Populist
coalition, the party's county convention passed resolutions "denouncing the
move made by McMinn and Evans in the federal court to disfranchise the Mexicans." Two weeks later, in the Bexar County Populist convention in San Antonio, Selig Deutschmann proposed a similar resolution:

Whereas, the democrats are circulating a report to the effect that the populist
party is endeavoring to disfranchise the Mexican citizens; therefore, be it
Resolved, By the people's party in mass meeting assembled, that the
above report is wholly untrue.

Resolved, Further, that the people's party is opposed to disfranchisement of anyone by reason of their race, color or religion.

The convention, however, voted not to bring the resolution to the floor for a
vote, probably deciding that to do so would only throw gasoline on an already
raging fire. In an effort most likely intended to soothe passions, the convention did pass a resolution calling for "fair and honest" elections, a sentiment
upon which everyone could presumably agree.[31]

The county convention's failure to act on Deutschmann's resolution did not
please everyone. John O'Connor had missed the convention, where he surely
would have joined with Deutschmann in pushing the antidisfranchisement
resolution. A week after the convention O'Connor and Deutschmann both
seized on a chance to right the wrong they believed had been perpetrated. At
a June 20 joint meeting of the Independent American Labor Club and the San
Pedro International Club—a gathering at which apparently everyone was a
Populist—they introduced the resolution again, this time with an additional
clause condemning "in the most emphatic terms the method by which an expression on this question was choked off at the late county convention." At this
juncture a leading Tejano Populist, Andrés López Montalbo, gained the floor
and said that while he supported the resolution he believed that this particular
meeting was "no place for it." Apparently Montalbo was so disillusioned by the
entire affair that he now believed that only action by the upcoming state Populist convention could make things right. Deutschmann moved that the members at the meeting adopt the resolution anyway, which they promptly did.[32]

Montalbo had already decided to take his grievance to the highest authority, soon-to-be gubernatorial nominee Jerome Kearby, who in many ways had
become the public face of the party since Thomas Nugent's death in early 1895.
We do not know precisely what Montalbo's June 18 letter to the Dallas Populist said, but he clearly wanted the issue addressed at the state convention, due
to be held in Galveston in August. Kearby responded in a letter that was widely
published in South Texas. He noted that he was scheduled to be in San Antonio on July 13, at which time he hoped to meet personally with Montalbo and
other local leaders. For the present, he was "prepared to say to you now that
the People's party has always favored free suffrage, free ballot, honest count,
subject only to constitutional limitations." Kearby, a famed trial lawyer who,
like McMinn, had personally argued a case before the US Supreme Court,
claimed to "know nothing of Mr. McMinn's contentions before the Federal
Court," but he assured Montalbo that the People's Party had "never been con-

sulted nor has it ever authorized any judicial movement" that might abridge the rights of Mexican Americans, and he promised to "favor in our State convention an unqualified expression of our party on the subjects mentioned in your letter." "I feel sure," Kearby asserted, "that the characteristic liberality that has heretofore prevailed in all our platforms will sustain us in our very pronounced theory of equal rights to all native and naturalized citizens."[33]

At about this point Pablo Cruz used the pages of *El Regidor* in an effort to exercise some damage control. The editor discussed the Kearby letter favorably, and even though Cruz continued to condemn McMinn personally, he also repeated McMinn's contention that the lawyer's purpose in the *Rodriguez* action was only to curtail voter fraud and not to disfranchise any native-born Tejanos. He quoted McMinn as saying that vote buying keeps the Democrats in power and that Democratic leaders "do not dare to condemn such acts because it would be political suicide to do so." Cruz repeatedly reminded his readers that McMinn did not speak for the People's Party.[34]

A few weeks later Andrés López Montalbo addressed a Populist meeting in San Antonio's Central Park. His speech was delivered in Spanish, and no text of it survives, but Cruz reported in *El Regidor* that Montalbo repeated that McMinn did not speak for the People's Party, nor Evans for the Republicans. Nevertheless, it is certain that Kearby's assurances had not satisfied him. The county convention had elected Montalbo as a delegate to the upcoming Galveston convention, and he apparently planned to hold the state party's feet to the fire on the question of Mexican suffrage. In the meantime, from down in Wilson County, where three-fourths of the Mexican voters were thought to have voted the Populist ticket in 1894, came a report from local Democrats who now believed that three-fourths of them would vote the Democratic ticket in the upcoming elections. "Mr. McMinn's action in the federal court at San Antonio had no little to do with it," the newspaper story claimed.[35]

When the Populist state convention met that fall, despite extensive press coverage by all the state's major daily newspapers, no hint of a debate on the issue ever emerged. The *San Antonio Express* did comment tellingly on Bexar County's role in the convention, saying, "The fact is the Bexar delegation has been at outs with itself ever since it arrived. Rivalrous ambitions, loaded with petty jealousies, have frequently collided, and the whole delegation has not been able to exert the slightest influence in the convention and it has been unceremoniously shoved aside every time it got in the road." Although the reporter failed to elaborate on the nature of these "rivalrous ambitions" and "petty jealousies," the infighting over the *Rodriguez* case and the role of Mexicans in the party surely had done little to soothe them. Neither Andrés López Montalbo nor any other Tejano delegate was mentioned in the press accounts of the convention, and if delegates attempted to introduce or debate a resolution specifically concerning Mexican disfranchisement, no record of it survives. The convention did, however, partially address the issues raised by *Rodriguez* by passing a plank demanding "a free vote by every qualified elector without reference to nationality, and an honest count" and another plank calling for "equal justice and protection under the law to all citizens, without reference to race, color, or nationality."[36]

And what of T. J. McMinn? He had been the Populist nominee for Congress in 1892 and state representative in 1894, but his role in the *Rodriguez* case had not only badly damaged the People's Party but also effectively ended his career in San Antonio and South Texas politics. Barely two weeks after the case had been filed, the *San Antonio Express* bluntly asserted that McMinn had "rendered himself unavailable [as a congressional nominee] through his attempt in the Federal court to disfranchise the Mexicans . . . , having aroused the bitter enmity of all that race and its political friends."[37]

Ironically, outside of San Antonio and South Texas, McMinn was still viewed as a rising star in the party. Those who were aware of the *Rodriguez* case may have viewed it as McMinn himself did—as a progressive measure intended only to prevent fraud. Given the nationwide trend to end alien suffrage, many Texans would not have looked askance at McMinn's efforts. At the People's Party convention, no less a personage than longtime state party chairman Stump Ashby himself placed McMinn's name in nomination for a seat on the Texas Supreme Court, and McMinn received the nomination over two other candidates.[38]

McMinn's nomination for the state's highest court was the tipping point for Andrés López Montalbo. In early October Montalbo called a general meeting of San Antonio Mexicans. Two hundred people attended the meeting, which was held at a cockfighting arena, "and there was a picture of determination on every face, which showed plainly that they strongly objected to their rights of citizenship in their adopted country being interfered with." With a distressed Selig Deutschmann looking on from the rear of the amphitheater, Montalbo read a lengthy manifesto in Spanish castigating the Populists and Republicans. McMinn, he pointed out, was nominated for the supreme court "by Stump Ashby, the high priest of the Texas Populists," and it was "clear that the Populist party . . . approved the views of McMinn, and the McMinn views are that the Texas Mexicans should be reduced to the category of pack animals." Referring to rumored cooperation between Populists and Republicans at the state level, and noting that Evans was the Republican nominee for district attorney, Montalbo asked, "Is it not plain that both parties are anti-Mexican?" He concluded by telling his fellow Tejanos that McMinn's election "will mean that the Texas Mexicans will be deprived of their civil rights, and as the law provides that aliens shall not hold possessions, it will also mean that they will lose with their civil rights their possessions also." The unsympathetic *Light,* condemning Montalbo's manifesto as "a piece of low down demagoguery," charged that the meeting's purpose was "to denounce the movement to test the right of the Mexican Indian tramp to vote under our laws," but the damage was done. Obviously the state Populist convention's vaguely worded resolutions had not satisfied Montalbo and his constituents, nor had the strong denunciations of McMinn by white Populists such as O'Connor and Deutschmann.[39]

Perhaps worse still, the People's Party was on the verge of losing the support of the influential Pablo Cruz. Cruz's Populism had always been of the conditional sort, sympathetic to much of the Populist political agenda but wary of the party's stance toward Mexicanos. After the Populist state convention gave McMinn the state supreme court nomination, Cruz's attitude, like Montalbo's, hardened. On August 27, reporting on the repudiation of McMinn by Wilson County's Populists, Cruz editorialized in favor of their actions. "Although McMinn is a member of the Populist Party," Cruz wrote, "he is an idiot, because with his heavy-handed and clumsy acts he is on the verge of destroying the work that we Mexico-Texans have done over the past four years. This is how stupid people act: they do not know how to build but they do know how to destroy."[40]

By October Cruz was calling McMinn and Evans "sworn enemies of the Mexican race." Interestingly, he claimed to support the exclusion of "ignorant and venal" people from voting, but he objected to "the total exclusion of any race." When the time came to endorse candidates, Cruz's defection was seemingly complete: he endorsed Democrat James L. Slayden for the congressional seat that McMinn and Paschal had both sought back in 1892, despite the fact that the Populist nominee was the respected chairman of the Bexar County People's Party, Taylor McRae. Any hopes Populists may have had for a viable coalition with Tejanos in San Antonio lay in ashes, and the relationship was badly damaged elsewhere in the region, too. Pablo Cruz reported with no small measure of glee in *El Regidor* that "McMinn is in the soup, *donde siempre estará* (where he will always be)." The performance of McMinn and his party in the 1896 elections, to be related in the next chapter, would put that prediction to the test.[41]

~

Judge Thomas Maxey delayed most of another year before finally handing down his ruling in the *Rodriguez* case. The judge seemed to accept the contentions of McMinn and the others that, according to both prevailing ethnological theory and ordinary usage, Ricardo Rodriguez probably was not "white." By the strict letter of the law, then, the ruling in the case should have gone McMinn and Evans's way. Maxey, however, concluded that the Rodriguez matter was "embraced within the spirit and intent of our laws upon naturalization." Consequently, the judge wrote, "his application should be granted, notwithstanding the letter of the statute may be against him."[42]

In the aftermath of the decision, the Democratic press in South Texas gloated that McMinn's "ridiculous scheme" had failed. Asked two years later about his long crusade to end the fraudulent voting of Mexicans in South Texas, McMinn admitted, "I have heretofore discussed that subject till I am weary of the whole business. . . . If the residents and the State at large can stand it I presume I ought not to complain. Sooner or later the matter of suffrage will have to be better regulated on the border." In San Antonio, the once Populist-friendly Pablo Cruz again used the pages of *El Regidor* to remind Mexican American readers of McMinn and Evans's roles in the *Rodriguez* case and to praise Democratic congressman James Slayden for allegedly using his influence in Washington to "put an end to such humiliating trials for Mexicans."[43]

The unfortunate McMinn, it seems, was doubly damned: in trying to curb corruption he had alienated legitimate Mexican American and Anglo Populist voters, but the lack of action on the case meant a continuation of voter fraud in the border region and the certain electoral defeats that followed. The Populist vision of color-blind political citizenship—what Jerome Kearby called "our very pronounced theory of equal rights to all native and naturalized citizens"—had run headlong into the party's need and desire to clean up politics, guarantee a free ballot and fair count, and win elections. In short, McMinn's political dilemma was that of southern Populism itself, even if it spoke with a particularly southwestern accent.

McMinn in many ways personified the liberal mindset of Populism, which held that an activist government controlled by the people could tame the abuses of unbridled capitalism, protect the rights and liberties of individuals, and create a more just and humane society. In 1898, when the country went to war against Spain, he warned against war profiteering conducted under "the cry of patriotism." In 1900, he railed against "the sorrow and hunger and nakedness in factories and sweatshops," and even when it came to race—wherein history has cast him as a villain—he believed that "our worth and intellect are not fixed by color" and that "history is full of instances of genius and virtue within dusky skins," attitudes that scarcely comport with his image as a white supremacist. Although he may have cynically sought to prevent Mexican *alien* voting by invoking the legal technicality of their nonwhiteness, McMinn never sought to crudely lump all Mexicans into a nonwhite category, nor did he ever argue that their race per se rendered them unfit for citizenship.[44]

Like other Americans, the Populists lacked a nuanced understanding of race that would have better enabled them to fight the sort of battles that T. J. McMinn undertook when he sought to clean up South Texas politics. At the dawn of a Jim Crow era when even what it meant to be "white" was being renegotiated, achieving reform might require using whatever racial vocabulary was available; hence the tendency of some reformers to equate Mexicans' Indianness with ignorance or venality, and their desire to remove "the Mexican Indian tramp" from the political equation. McMinn had not invented the notion that Mexicans might not be white, nor was he the author of the large body of American jurisprudence that placed racial restrictions on immigration and citizenship. These were part of the received social and legal culture of turn-of-the-century America, and they partook abundantly from the bitter cup of racism. The racialized laws and customs on the border and elsewhere permitted corrupt political bosses to manipulate the votes of Mexicans and other marginalized groups, and reformers like McMinn too often saw no choice but to use race to fight back, sometimes with weapons that even their fellow reformers found repugnant. Indeed, the inherent instability of race as an ideology and a vocabulary led many of his fellow Populists to repudiate his actions, accounting, at least in part, for the avalanche of criticism that he received from his own party. Most Texas Populists were profoundly uncomfortable with any proposal to abridge the political rights of anyone, even while recognizing that wholesale voter fraud threatened their entire reform project.[45]

The story of the People's Party in South Texas nonetheless reinforces certain general interpretive points about Populism. The genuine efforts of Populists like Selig Deutschmann, Vicente Carvajal, John O'Connor, and Andres López Montalbo to reach across racial, ethnic, religious, and class lines to build grassroots reform coalitions bolster the notion that Populist "liberality," to use Jerome Kearby's term, in some ways foreshadowed twentieth-century racial liberalism. As we have seen, even T. J. McMinn's infamous role in the Rodriguez affair, when understood in proper context, scarcely casts him as a racist villain, and the backlash against him by his own party further underscores the Populist opposition to racial bigotry.

The sheer magnitude of corruption and electoral chicanery in the region lends further credence to the key role that voter fraud played in the politics of the era. In the eastern half of Texas and most of the South, it was the African American vote that Democrats so successfully manipulated and stole in order to maintain power. In Texas, observers commonly referred to the "Rio Grande and Harrison County vote" in the same breath (Harrison was the heavily black county in East Texas famous for Democratic voter fraud), recognizing that the combination of stolen African American votes in East Texas and Mexican votes in South Texas kept the Democrats in power. Despite all of this, however, most Texas Populists still kept the faith as the 1896 election cycle began. Even as the McMinn-Rodriguez drama played out in the streets of San Antonio, in the ranching country to the south, and in the Rio Grande towns along the international border, the People's Party prepared to make one final push in the rest of the state, a push that Populists believed would determine the fate of their party, state, and nation.[46]

10 • The Election of 1896

Shall 1896 witness the complete enslavement of labor,
or prove to be its year of jubilee?
—Thomas L. Nugent, 1894

The defeat of 1894 and the continuing problems with Democratic voter fraud did little to dampen the spirits of Texas Populists as the 1896 election season commenced. As a social movement, Populism had grown by creating an us-against-them mentality, a mindset that kept adherents motivated as long as there were concrete signs of progress in spreading the political message. As a political movement, losses in 1892 and 1894 could be accepted as long as vote totals grew and there were realistic chances for an eventual electoral triumph. For those Populists who professed the Protestant faith, the idea that God would test the fortitude of his people and eventually reward the faithful seemed immediately applicable to the political situation at hand. These factors led Populists to see the 1896 elections in rather apocalyptic terms. As early as 1892 Harry Tracy had asked, "The great question, in my opinion, to be decided in 1896 will be, which shall rule this country the citizen or the dollar? This idea has taken root in the minds of the people. It gained such momentum in this election as to convince every thinking man that it cannot be sidetracked. The battle has to be fought." In a similar vein, a Cass County Populist in 1892 had forecast "a four years war" that would "terminate in a great battle that shall turn the government over to the people or the plutocrats in 1896." A Populist newspaper correspondent from Erath County had predicted in 1893 that if Populists would "press the battle forward, educate and investigate, to show up the rascality of those now in power, in 1896 a revolution will take place that will

345

shake the continent of America from center to circumference; there will be changing of seats in the halls of congress like the shaking of dry bones in the valley, and our children can sing 'Babylon has Fallen to Rise no More.'" Even the normally circumspect Thomas Nugent, following his defeat in 1894, asked dramatically, "Shall 1896 witness the complete enslavement of labor, or prove to be its year of jubilee?"[1]

Nugent and other leaders of the party understood that the path to "jubilee" was strewn with obstacles, at both the state and national levels. In both cases, they believed, fusion posed the greatest danger. As we have seen, fusion—the forming of coalitions of minority parties to compete against a majority party— was a recurrent fixture in American politics in the nineteenth century. Texas Populists had used it extensively in local races, although it always invited controversy. By definition, any fusion deal entailed a certain sacrifice of principle in order to win office, and it carried the risk of alienating the party faithful. The costs, therefore, could potentially exceed the benefits. Texas Populists confronted the specter of fusion at state and national levels, although in each case it manifested itself in very different ways.

For Populists in 1895 and 1896, the prospect of fusion mostly revolved around the one issue that had risen to dominance in American politics: the question of silver coinage. Although monetary policy was a federal matter, the debate over currency nonetheless affected state-level politics, and some Texans wondered whether a deal might be cut between the Populists and the prosilver wing of the Democratic Party. The Democrats had run a terrible risk in 1892, when the party had split in half with two competing candidates defined largely by their positions on silver versus gold. In the face of continuing accessions to the Populists, the Democrats had forged a "harmony" agreement between its two wings in 1894, but it was a fragile truce that could come undone at any time. Although a bare majority of Texas Democrats favored silver, regulation of the railroads, and other modestly progressive measures, the conservative gold-standard Democrats remained strong, bolstered by the fact that the national party and its standard-bearer, President Grover Cleveland, favored gold. When John H. Reagan, the senior statesman of the Texas Democratic Party and a leader of its silver wing, mounted an effort to rally the silver Democrats in the spring of 1895, he was roundly denounced by the so-called goldbugs, prompting him to excoriate his fellow Democrats. "'The miserable wretches,' said he, 'call me a populist when I attended the first democratic convention ever held in Texas.'" The press referred to Reagan as "the godfather of the free silver movement in Texas" and predicted that if the party split in two, as it had done in 1892, he would be that faction's nominee. Reagan continued his efforts to woo Populists back into the old party, contending that "the populist party advocates some wise and just political policies which are in accord with the policies of the democratic party" but drawing the line at the Populists' two most radical demands, the Subtreasury Plan and government ownership of the railroads.[2]

His pleas inspired responses from Jerome Kearby, Marion Martin, and other Populists, who turned Reagan's overtures around and argued that it was the silver Democrats who should join the People's Party. One such Populist, William M. "Buck" Walton, spoke for many others when he said, "Judge Reagan, your place and the place of every honest silver democrat, and every honest silver man, is shoulder to shoulder with the populists. They are the heroes of silver, its champions and defenders. Come. The latch string hangs outside. Pull it, and come in with the hosts of silver soldiers who are brave and true." Nugent also believed that the party should reach out to the silverites. "It is the silver element in the democratic party we must work among," he contended. "There is already a strong tendency among this element which is the more liberal, toward populism, and with proper effort on our part they can be induced to join us."[3]

Populists, of course, welcomed another split in the Democrats and hoped to recruit the disaffected, but in September 1895 a bombshell exploded in the form of a public letter from Cyclone Davis proposing that Thomas Nugent and sitting Democratic governor Charles Culberson be elected to the state supreme court, with Reagan becoming the joint nominee of the Populists and silver Democrats. This sort of fusion, which would require the Populists to surrender their independent identity as a party, infuriated the leadership, which scrambled to repudiate Davis's suggestion. Jerome Kearby, the influential Dallas Populist, declared that "Davis has no authority to speak for the populist party" and that he "is not doing the thinking for the populists." The *Southern Mercury*'s Milton Park, unalterably opposed to fusion in any form, ripped Davis, suggesting that if Davis were not joking, he should resign his position on the Populist National Committee. State executive committee chairman Stump Asbhy apparently called Davis "an enemy of reform" and threatened to read him out of the party. The firestorm was such that Davis, who had spent much of the previous four years traveling throughout the nation making Populist speeches and who had clearly been influenced by national chairman Herman Taubeneck and other pro-fusion leaders, finally felt the need to defend himself. Writing in the *Mercury*, Davis denied that there was even "one sentence of fusion doctrine in the letter," claiming that he was calling for "consolidation, not fusion." The Populists themselves, he noted, were a consolidation of other parties and movements, including the Union Labor Party, the Alliance, and the Knights of Labor, and he claimed that he merely wanted silver Democrats and Populists to "consolidate and form one grand line of battle for reform in 1896." Davis lashed out at the "philharmonic unction" of Ashby, sarcastically saying, "Around him there is a halo of wisdom and patriotism that common men like me cannot even approach, except as Moses approached the burning bush." The dustup between the nationally best-known Texas Populist and the state leadership of his party engendered distrust and ill will that never entirely went away. It also foreshadowed the bitter debate over fusion that would dominate Populist politics in the months to come.[4]

If silver was an issue on which Populists and progressive Democrats could potentially agree and perhaps form a basis for cooperation, it also proved tremendously divisive, even destructive, within the Populist camp. As a theoretical matter, most Populists thought that the free and unlimited coinage of silver was desirable as an inflationary adjunct to nonredeemable greenbacks. Silver was a plank in the state and national platforms, and Populists frequently reminded voters that the Populists were the first (and until mid-1896, the only) national party committed to it. When Thomas B. King, an old friend of Thomas Nugent and chair of the party in Erath County, published a call for his county's Populist convention, he invited all "who are opposed to Cleveland's policy, of a single gold standard . . . and who favor free and unlimited coinage of silver at the present, or less, ratio of 16 to 1, as well as the issue of a national currency so that the ratio of labor and property to money shall be equalized." Even the *Mercury*, whose editor Milton Park so staunchly urged Populists to stay "in the middle of the road" and avoid fusion with the silverites, could on one page print a story warning against selling out the party on the issue of silver and on the very next page publish a stirring poem titled "Sixteen to One" exalting silver.[5]

Some high-profile defections from the Democrats came explicitly as a result of the Populists' commitment to silver. Joe C. Terrell of Fort Worth, brother of Democratic stalwart and US minister to Turkey Alexander W. Terrell, became a Populist simply because he gave up on the other parties ever embracing silver. Similarly, Buck Walton forthrightly declared that "until [the Democratic Party] returns to its old landmarks, low tariff[s] and free silver, I shall vote on all political questions with the populist party, it to-day being the only party that has the candor and honesty to plainly declare what it wants and to boldly uphold and sustain its declarations." Walton, a former Democratic attorney general and chairman of the Democratic state executive committee, was able to overlook the bulk of the Populist platform, explaining, "I know there are some vagaries advocated by the party, but they can be in due time eliminated."[6]

At the same time, some Populists were skeptical about whether silver coinage would bring even the modest benefits others had promised. Jerome Kearby rhetorically posed this question to John Reagan: "If you had free, unlimited coinage of silver at the ratio of 16 to 1 go into operation to-morrow, how much would that increase the volume of money, with every silver mine and every mint in full operation for the next twelve months? Judge Reagan knows that the increase would be less than 75 cents per capita." A Hill Country Populist astutely pointed out that "the coinage of silver by itself amounts to nothing. The monopolist under our present system can monopolize silver just as easy as he can gold, iron, coal, etc." And some Populists agreed with the goldbugs (and with many modern economists) that the monetization of silver at the proposed sixteen-to-one ratio would trigger Gresham's Law, the tendency of undervalued money to drive overvalued money out of circulation. As the Populist editor (and Disciples of Christ minister) W. L. Thurman explained, "The gold bugs tell one truth when they say free coinage of silver will make gold hide out. To put in silver and take out gold will not increase the circulation. Hence we must have an issue of greenbacks to increase the money supply." Harry Tracy was very specific in his prediction of how Gresham's Law would operate, forecasting that "the free and unlimited coinage of silver at the ratio of 16 to 1 would drive all the gold out of the county in three months." Clearly Populists were not of one mind on the silver question, even as it gained greater prominence as an issue in state and national politics with each passing month.[7]

But whether they thought silver a modestly beneficial reform or, as Thurman and Tracy did, a delusion, most Populist leaders understood the dangers inherent in focusing exclusively on it. The Ashby-led state executive committee in June 1895 issued a characteristic warning. "Free silver is good as far as it goes," the statement declared, "but it will leave undisturbed all of the conditions which give rise to the undue concentration of wealth." Dropping the full range of the Omaha Demands in favor of silver, or uniting with another party over the silver issue, "may prove to us a veritable Trojan horse if we are not careful." State committeeman Edmund Plummer Alsbury likewise warned his Houston-area constituents that "many unwary reformers in our party are in danger of being misled, to waste their energies and influence, and to substitute for the calm determination to advance along the lines of true reform, a fruitless entanglement in the silver movement as the all-sufficient remedy for existing evils." Silver, he maintained, was "merely a part of the froth and foam of politics" and would "be a relief, but by no means a remedy."[8]

In the aftermath of the 1894 elections, Texas Populists felt confident enough in their prospects that talk of any sort of formal fusion deal with the state's silver Democrats was confined to only a few politicians of the Cyclone Davis ilk. But national politics was another matter altogether. The vast majority of Texas Populists wanted the party to stay "in the middle of the road," which was Populist terminology for maintaining the People's Party as an independent organization and waging its battles on the full Omaha Platform. However, many Populists in other states, and many national leaders, did not share the Texans' commitment to the Midroad position.

Back in January 1895, national chairman Herman Taubeneck, an Illinois ex-legislator, had called a conference in St. Louis to plan strategy for the upcoming campaign. Taubeneck, who had been chairman since the party's creation in 1891, had made no secret of his desire to abandon the sweeping reforms of the Omaha Platform in favor of silver alone, a position held by many Populists in the plains and mountain states. At the conference Taubeneck, along with 1892 Populist presidential nominee James B. Weaver and Davis, openly consorted with leaders of the Silver League and the Bimetallic League (two groups seeking to create a broad prosilver coalition). Milton Park of the *Mercury*—like Davis, a member of the Populist National Committee—was there and reported that the silverites "endeavored to capture the meeting" and absorb the People's Party but that the Populist Midroaders defeated the effort.[9]

The tug-of-war between Taubeneck, Weaver, Davis, and other pro-fusion national leaders on one hand, and the Texas leadership and other Midroaders on the other hand, attained a new urgency as 1896 dawned. In January of that year Taubeneck called another meeting of the national executive committee, again in St. Louis. Milton Park later charged—and it appears to be substantiated—that through the assiduous arrangement of pro-fusion proxies for members who could not attend, Taubeneck, who openly took pride in his skills as a political tactician, succeeded in stacking the meeting in favor of the fusionist position. Taubeneck's efforts produced two crucial consequences, although just how crucial they would be was not widely recognized at the time.[10]

The first consequence involved the way delegates would be apportioned among the various states. It was traditional in American politics to base national convention representation on the number of seats in each state's congressional delegation, regardless of how many votes the party received in prior elections. Such a formula would have the effect of greatly magnifying the influence of heavily populated states, regardless of the party's strength in such states. When the executive committee met, it engaged in a two-day-long wrangle over the basis of representation, with states with large numbers of Populist voters, like Texas, demanding that they be given greater representation. The committee finally decided to give each state one delegate for each senator and congressman, and another delegate for every two thousand votes cast for the Populist ticket in 1892, 1894, or 1895, whichever year's total was highest. It is important to understand exactly what this rule accomplished. While it did give the largest delegation to Texas, the largest state in terms of actual Populist voters, it also gave weak Populist states representation disproportionate to their parties' strength. For example, New York, with its mere eight thousand Populist voters, received 40 delegates. Texas, with 178,000 Populist voters, got 103 delegates. One major effect of this was to create a large bloc of delegates from the northeastern states. Nobody could know for sure how these states' delegates might vote in the convention, but it likely would not set the Midroaders' minds at ease.[11]

This geographical bias was compounded by another crucial detail of the formula as it was eventually implemented. In the part of the formula that awarded delegates for past Populist voting strength, Taubeneck's committee included all votes cast for fusion tickets. North Carolina is an instructive example. There, in 1894, a combined Republican-Populist fusion ticket polled nearly 150,000 votes, but of these, only about 50,000 were from Populists; the rest were Republican votes. If the rules had allowed North Carolina Populists to count only their own 50,000 votes for purposes of determining its delegation size, the state would have gotten to send only 35 delegates to the national convention, but with the inclusion of nearly 100,000 GOP votes cast for Populists in the fusion deal, the state was awarded 95 delegates. The effect was to reward fusion at the state level, and states that had practiced fusion at home were presumably more likely to favor it at the national level. Combined with the decision to give large blocs of delegates to the populous northeastern states, the committee's decision on how to apportion delegates meant that the coming national convention would likely have heavy majorities in favor of dropping all demands but silver, and of using fusion to accomplish it. The deck was stacked against the Midroaders before the convention even began.[12]

With the basis of representation finally determined, the national committee turned its attention to the crucial issue of *when* to hold the national convention. For months Midroaders had been calling for an early convention. As the *Mercury* explained in October 1895, "An early convention will sooner set

at rest fears entertained by many that our party machinery is being manipulated in the interests of the enemy." But Taubeneck and his allies were determined to hold the Populist convention *after* those of the major parties. There
were some arguments in favor of this strategy. Many Populists, Midroaders
and fusionists alike, had long assumed that both the Republicans and Democrats would draft platforms endorsing the gold standard and that holding the
Populist convention after they did so would cause a major realignment of
American politics, as silver Republicans and silver Democrats flocked into the
Populist camp. But the strategy also carried a dire risk: if one of the major parties did the unexpected and declared for silver, the urge for Populists to fuse
with that party and surrender the People's Party's independent identity would
be great. For the pro-fusion delegations from states like North Carolina and
Kansas, it would be nearly irresistible. With his committee well under control,
Taubeneck succeeded in getting his late convention.[13]

Back in Texas, Populists smelled a rat. Rumors abounded that Taubeneck
intended to abandon all Populist planks except silver and deliver the People's
Party into the hands of a new silver party. Taubeneck himself stated after the
January meeting that "the cardinal principles of the people's party would not
be abandoned," but he refused to positively affirm that the Omaha Platform
would be retained. In this atmosphere of suspicion, he traveled to Dallas to
attend a conference of the National Reform Press Association, which was meeting simultaneously with the Texas Populist state executive committee on February 24. In a closed-door session at the St. James Hotel, the committee called
on Taubeneck "to make a statement," after which the committee adopted a surprising resolution: "Resolved, that we favor an honorable union of all the reform forces of the United States along those lines that will best promote the
welfare of all our people and that we reaffirm our expression of confidence in
the integrity and patriotism of our national chairman, Hon. H. E. Taubeneck,
and the national committee." The members then retired to a park in the suburb of Oak Cliff to join the Populist editors in a "Bohemian lunch" featuring
barrels of roast oysters, kegs of beer, tamales, wienerwurst, chili con carne,
beer, and "beautiful women (for there were lots of them there . . .)."[14]

The feast might not have set so well on the state executive committeemen's
stomachs if they had known how their morning's work would be received. As
soon as word of the committee's actions reached the hardcore Midroaders of
the Dallas Populist Club, its members demanded to know "why did the committee indorse Mr. Taubeneck when it was evident to the committee that nine-
tenths of the people of this state do not indorse many of the actions of the

national chairman." John B. Rayner, whose abilities as an orator and organizer had earned him the respect of all the party's white leadership, angrily questioned the endorsement. Rayner had not been able to attend the meeting, and now he speculated that "if you look deep into this resolution you will see the finger of the silver league or the finger of the bimetal[l]ic league trying to erase the best part of the Omaha platform by the endorsement of Hon. H. E. Taubeneck." Finding himself on the defensive, state committee chairman Stump Ashby explained that inasmuch as Taubeneck had "declared his indorsement of the principles of the Omaha platform, the committee thought it just to give him their indorsement."[15]

Such explanations by Ashby and other committeemen did little to calm Populists' fears over what was unfolding at the national level. After the festivities in Dallas, Taubeneck traveled with a contingent of the reform editors to Galveston, where he was quoted as saying that he personally believed the "financial question" should be paramount, along with "the discontinuance of those bond issues, then the income tax, then for direct legislation and some other planks I do not just now recall." The *Mercury* lambasted him, saying, "The attraction of the ladies or the beautiful lay of the Texas landscape had so fascinated the chairman that he had forgotten that there were two other very important planks in the platform, namely land and transportation." A week later the *Mercury* printed a letter from W. Scott Morgan, the Arkansas Midroad Populist leader, in which Morgan speculated that "Mr. Taubeneck is either a very foolish man or he is playing a double game. While he holds up his hand and declares allegiance to the Omaha platform, as he did before the populist executive committee in Texas, he is doing everything in his power to have the transportation and land planks dropped from the next national platform."[16]

Despite these troubling aspects of national Populist politics, Texas Populists still had a state campaign to prepare for, and there was much that they found heartening in their prospects. As the nationwide depression wore on, and the two major parties seemed remarkably unresponsive, the Populists continued to win new converts, with the Democratic press acknowledging the "numerous accessions from the ranks of the free silver democrats." In October 1895 former state senator George W. Glasscock joined the aforementioned Joe Terrell and Buck Walton on the list of Democratic converts. In his announcement, Glasscock denounced the Cleveland administration for abandoning "the common people" and charged the Democrats with being "under the absolute control of the money power." Several months later Joe Eagle, an up-and-coming young lawyer from Houston, likewise accused the Democrats of having "sold their birthright for a mess of potage" and joined the Populists. In 1896 both Glasscock and Eagle would be rewarded with nominations for Congress at the hands of the Populists.[17]

But the most spectacular defection came in early 1896 when Barnett "Barney" Gibbs (plate 23) of Dallas, a former state senator and lieutenant governor, left the Democrats. Gibbs was a wealthy Dallas lawyer and a recognized leader of the progressive wing of the state Democratic Party. A handsome and talented politician, the University of Virginia graduate had long championed farmers' causes, supporting a greenback scheme that shared some common elements with the Alliance's Subtreasury Plan.[18] Gibbs had also endeared himself to organized labor by providing pro bono legal representation to railroad workers accused of crimes during the 1886 Great Southwest Strike, but he had remained within the Democratic Party, even as his views had grown increasingly out of step with it. Beginning in January 1896, he published an extraordinary eight-part manifesto in the Sunday *Dallas Morning News* in which he addressed all the major political issues of the day. Although he took Populist positions throughout, Gibbs initially held back from an outright endorsement of the People's Party. After the first installment, Harry Tracy smugly speculated that "Barney is very near the kingdom," and a week later, as the series continued, Jerome Kearby was quoted as saying, "When Mr. Gibbs comes into the populist house we will not only kill a calf, but we will kill a whole herd of cattle." Soon the public was hanging on in suspense to see if Gibbs's next "shot" (as the *Morning News* called the "breezy and catchy" installments) would culminate in a full-fledged conversion to Populism. At last, in his eighth and final "shot," Gibbs announced his full support for the Populist ticket and platform. Admitting that he had "told much truth" about the sins of the major parties, the conservative *Morning News* editorialized that Gibbs's conversion marked "a culmination of years of folly" on the part of Democrats, folly that now threatened a "general disaster" to the country if the Populists won.[19]

The party's long-running efforts to woo African American Republicans also showed new signs of succeeding. In Dallas, the same week that Gibbs announced his defection, Rev. Alfred Stokes, a seventy-seven-year-old preacher, community leader, and political activist, cast his lot with the Third Party. Local Populists celebrated Stokes's conversion at the weekly meeting of the Dallas Populist Club, where he arrived at the head of the Excelsior Band, an all–African American brass ensemble. Following an introduction by Melvin Wade, Stokes came forward and was "lustfully cheered" by the white and black members of the club, after which he "gave his hearers a red-hot populist speech." When he took his seat, the band struck up a spirited rendition of "Dixie," which produced still more hilarity and applause. When interviewed by a *Dallas Morning News* reporter a few days later, Stokes gave his reasons for becoming a Populist. First, he singled out the Democrats' "making the Jim Crow separate coach law," which he condemned as "a slam on the colored people." And then he suggested that the Populists, "being a new organization never have been corrupt," and he expressed his belief "that they would administer the government honestly and in the interest of the poor and the weak and give the orphan children bread to eat." As with Melvin Wade before him, Stokes's decision did not come without costs; his own son, Prof. David R. Stokes, remained active in the Republican Party, and the conservative press poked fun at the divided African American family.[20]

With very few exceptions, though, Texas Populists remained remarkably unified as the 1896 election season approached. The *Dallas Morning News* commented on "the wonderful unanimity of purpose which seems to prevail in populist circles," noting that there were "no serious quarrels, personal or political, among them, and every day they are growing confident that they will get into the picture in 1896." With two statewide campaigns under their belt, the Populists were said to be "superb" in "the minor details of party organization." They were preparing to make a strong bid to host the party's national convention in Dallas, which would "have an invigorating effect in their ranks."[21]

One potential source of friction disappeared on December 14, 1895, when Thomas Nugent died from complications of diabetes at his home in Fort Worth. Shortly before his death he had published a message announcing that his health and business affairs would not permit him to participate actively in the upcoming campaign. Although Nugent had achieved something resembling sainthood among Texas Populists and would have undoubtedly received the gubernatorial nomination a third time had he sought it, it was no great secret that many insiders really preferred Jerome Kearby (plate 24). Unlike the reserved, scholarly Nugent, the charismatic Kearby was known as "a fighter and a speaker." Although he was a trial lawyer by profession, he had earned a reputation as a champion of the common man. Telling the story of a poor man who was murdered by a wealthy "capitalist," the Populist press related how "Kearby went to the widow and offered to assist in the prosecution for free," spending "a bundle of his own money" and securing a conviction and prison sentence for the rich man. He had compiled a record in independent politics dating back to the Greenbacker days and beyond, and Populists were convinced that he was cheated out of a congressional seat in 1894, when he lost the Dallas district by only two hundred disputed votes. "Kearby's ability as a campaigner needs no description," the *Morning News* reminded its readers. "His strong personal magnetism and ability as a speaker are well known in Texas." An Austin-based reporter called Kearby "a campaigner and fighter from alpha to omega, and an abler man than Judge Nugent," and predicted that "if he goes into the fight he will go in strong and to win." On hearing of Nugent's retirement, Harry Tracy said of Kearby, "His brilliant attainments, his sterling honesty and well-known conservatism will bring thousands of wavering democrats to us, and his personal following will add thousands more." The Populist *McKinney Democrat* pronounced him "a great lawyer, a great man, a great humanitarian and a great patriot." And if this were not hyperbole enough, a North Texas judge, introducing Kearby at a campaign event, characterized the Dallasite as "a Caesar without his cruelty, a Napoleon without his ambition, a Washington without his reward, and a Lee and Nugent without their timidity. A patriot, soldier, statesman and profound lawyer will add to these great virtues that of governor of his native state, ere the ides of November roll by." After Nugent's death, virtually no other name was ever mentioned in connection with the governor's race. When the time came to nominate candidates, it would be tantamount to a coronation.[22]

Populists began holding county conventions in March, with legislative, judicial, and congressional conventions to come later in the spring. A typical report came from the McLennan County convention in Waco, a regional commercial hub situated in the middle of the state's most productive cotton-growing region. When the convention gathered on a Friday morning, the press noted that "its personnel is improved and its delegations stronger than ever before." Every voting precinct was represented, and in a party where observers had frequently commented on the number of older men, it was deemed significant that the local party had "gained in active, enthusiastic young men" even while "it has retained its entire roll of early members." Democratic spectators seated in the rear of the hall observed "with dismay" that "gray-haired veterans who voted the democratic ticket from the age of maturity until the previous election" sat alongside "several colored men of influence" who "were cordially treated."[23]

After organizing itself, the convention heard a series of speeches. One came from "a young man whose hands are in daily acquaintance with plow handles," exhorting his listeners to adhere to "party principles" and avoid fusion. John B. Rayner next spoke to the gathering, telling the delegates that if the party could gain the Negro vote "it will be invincible." A third orator "spoke on the false and pernicious system of finance prevalent which kept the people poor and enriched a preferred class," while another addressed the sins of the Pullman Company and of "courts refusing to sustain tax levys on railroad property." A recent address of party chairman Stump Ashby was read to the appreciative delegates, and after a break for dinner, the committees on resolutions and nominations met, during which more speechmaking took place, including a speech by "Perry Ross, a colored man, . . . giving original views of the Omaha platform." Before nominations were made, a member was asked to recite a poem, part of which went as follows:

> I can't see how to save my life,
>   Why it is I am so poor.
> I work from morn till night,
>   And yet I can not secure
> Enough to get our food and clothes
>   And shelter over head.
> It makes me feel so queer sometimes
>   I wish that I was dead.
> When I look at Nancy Jane,
>   Who rises with the sun,
> Who cooks and cleans and mends the clothes,
>   Her Work is never done.
> And yet with all our work,
>   And saving all we can,
> When rent day comes it finds us short,
>   No matter how we plan.
> 'Tis gold that rules the church and state;
>   In fact, it rules the world.
> And will until the people rise,
>   With freedom's flag unfurled.
> And let the flag the motto bear
>   In letters all can read,
> "'Tis labor that produces all,
>   Let it be first to feed."

After nominations for county offices were made, the convention adjourned to attend a rally estimated to be "the largest populist gathering ever seen in Waco," headlined by twenty-five-year-old Thomas P. Gore, the celebrated blind Populist orator from Corsicana who later served three terms as a US senator from Oklahoma.[24]

Scenes like this played out all over the state, as the grassroots machinery of the party chugged to life in the spring of 1896. By June the all-important nominating conventions for Congress were being held, and most ran relatively smoothly. Dallas-area Populists enthusiastically nominated Barney Gibbs for the Sixth District seat that Kearby had narrowly lost in 1894. In the west-central Texas Eighth District, the highly respected lawyer and judge Charles H. Jenkins, who had also lost a razor-thin race in 1894, was again the nominee. To challenge Democratic firebrand Joseph Weldon Bailey in the Fifth District of North Texas, Populists nominated the young attorney and former Latin professor W. D. Gordon, who had studied law under Charles Jenkins. In the "Jumbo District" of West Texas, the nomination went to state executive committeeman Henry Lewis Bentley, the multitalented lawyer, businessman, editor, and agricultural researcher who had managed Nugent's 1892 campaign and who would preside over the 1896 state convention. Populists in the East Texas Piney Woods Second District united around the candidacy of former state representative Benjamin A. Calhoun of Nacogdoches. In Houston's First District, where Populists had always struggled to gain a foothold, the party chose the young lawyer and recent Democratic convert Joe Eagle. In Central Texas, Seventh District Populists united around the veteran Populist editor and state committeeman William F. Douthit. And in the coastal Tenth District, Populists nominated Noah Allen, a railroad attorney who as former Populist assistant attorney general of Kansas had been a delegate to the Omaha convention in 1892. In the two South Texas districts, Populists made little or no effort in the congressional races, but in the half-dozen races that had been close in 1894, they believed that their candidates stood good chances of victory.[25]

Although the process of choosing candidates generally proceeded harmoniously, there were notable exceptions, and they were revealing. In the Third District, northeast of Dallas, three Populists—James Madison Perdue, William E. "Bill" Farmer, and Henry Dillard Wood—all sought the nomination. Perdue, a farmer, schoolteacher, newspaper editor, and Methodist minister, was an old Allianceman, having served as vice president and state lecturer of the state Alliance in the 1880s and helped to write the order's famous Cleburne Demands. He had been the nominee in both 1892 and 1894, running respectable but unsuccessful races. Bill Farmer had come to Populism from the labor side of the equation, having been master workman for a Knights of Labor district assembly. He had run for Congress on the Greenback ticket in 1888. Both he and Perdue had been delegates to the 1892 St. Louis convention that gave birth to the People's Party, and both could legitimately claim to be die-hard, day-one Populists. The third candidate, thirty-four-year-old attorney H. D. Wood of Hunt County, had been an Alabama Populist before moving to Texas in 1892. He had twice since run for district attorney on the Populist ticket but did not have the long record of his rivals.[26]

All three men began their campaigns early in the year and ran hard, but as the convention drew near, the Perdue and Wood forces got into a petty war of words in the press. It started when the *Dallas Morning News* described the youthful Wood as "the best campaigner of the three" and suggested that Perdue had underperformed in his 1894 race. This provoked a response from the Populist chairman of the district, a Perdue supporter, to defend his man's record and complain of "the evident intention of injuring Mr. J. M. Perdue in particular and the populist cause in general." The chairman also got in a backhanded slap at the lawyer Wood by noting that "although a plain, unassuming farmer, [Perdue] claims to be not a whit behind most of the lawyers on economic questions." Wood quickly fired back, suggesting that Perdue himself had somehow written the offending *Morning News* article and calling the district chair's defense of Perdue "boss methods" unbefitting of the People's Party. The animosity continued all the way down to the district convention in July. Not surprisingly, Farmer, who had managed to stay above the fray, emerged as the winner. Now it was the Perdue forces' turn to cry foul, declaring "that Perdue was defeated by unfairness and that they will not support the nominee." In the end, all this backbiting and petulance succeeded only in dividing the district's Populists and making them look very much like the Democrats and Republicans, putting the desire for office over party unity. Moreover, the spat could not be attributed entirely to opportunistic politicians infiltrating the reform ranks; one could not have found two men with more impeccable Populist pedigrees than Perdue and Farmer, and even the youthful Wood claimed that he had never voted a Democratic or Republican ticket.[27]

A different sort of problem emerged in the Ninth Congressional District. There Populists nominated George W. Glasscock, the former state senator from Georgetown who had just joined the party in the fall of 1895. Now the silver problem reared its head in a concrete way. When he joined the party, Glasscock clearly stated that his main reason for doing so was that "the People's Party is the only party that favors the free and unlimited coinage of silver," and that was good enough for the Populists of the Central Texas district. But when Glasscock delivered his acceptance speech, he voiced his approval of "a paper currency 'bottomed' on gold and silver." This, of course, directly contradicted Populist orthodoxy, which called for, in addition to gold and silver, fiat money—paper currency, or greenbacks, specifically *not* redeemable in precious metal. A firestorm erupted over his statements, and even though Glasscock quickly "repudiated his utterances on the question," he soon offered his resignation, "seeing that his candidacy might create some dissension in our ranks." The controversy divided Populists in the district, with some rising to Glasscock's defense and others demanding that his resignation be accepted. Ultimately it was accepted, and the outspoken Baptist preacher and former president of Baylor University, Reddin Andrews, took his place on the ticket. Populists tried to put the best face on this embarrassing and divisive episode, claiming that "we made a reputation for our district by pulling down Hon. George Glasscock." But the affair not only exposed fissures within the Populist ranks but also showed how the emphasis on silver could attract adherents whose understanding of, or attachment to, the greater Populist agenda was tenuous at best.[28]

These controversies, though troubling, were relatively straightforward compared to the complex situation in the Fourth District, which encompassed eleven counties in the northeast corner of the state. There, in 1894, Cyclone Davis had lost narrowly to the incumbent Democrat David Culberson (father of the sitting governor), prompting a bitter Davis to charge fraud and threaten to contest the results. It was widely assumed that the nationally famous Davis would again be the Populist nominee in 1896, but Eben Dohoney and Pat Clark, two prominent Populist leaders from the district, opposed his candidacy, presumably because of Davis's well-publicized dalliances with fusion. Many rank-and-file Populists in the district no doubt agreed with Dohoney and Clark, but others, like the party faithful across the nation, idolized the flamboyant Davis. Defeating him for the nomination would not be easy. The nominating convention was set for May 1, but when the meeting convened in Texarkana, delegates made the unusual decision to postpone a congressional nomination until August 1, after the national convention. Accounts of the May convention are sketchy; the postponement may have constituted a tactical retreat on the part of Davis's partisans in the face of possible defeat, or skeptical delegates may have forced the postponement as the price for not repudiating Davis. In any event, the convention did elect Davis and seven others as delegates to the St. Louis national meeting, pointedly instructing them "to stand squarely on the Omaha platform." But Davis knew that the Populists of the Fourth District were going to be watching his actions in St. Louis. As one Marion County man bluntly warned him, "If you favor the indorsement of the Democratic nominee for President, you will not receive the Populist nomination for Congress. I feel confident of this. So, for once, stop and think." As we shall see, Davis did stop and think. He knew that his congressional aspirations would hinge on his actions at the national convention. Although he supported cooperation with silverites, he could not appear to be working for fusion.[29]

As a summer of speeches, debates, rallies, and massive camp meetings got under way in Texas, the national convention season arrived. The Republicans went first, meeting at St. Louis in mid-June. There they nominated Ohio governor William McKinley and reaffirmed their allegiance to the gold standard. Populist national chairman Taubeneck was waiting outside the convention hall, literally with open arms, to welcome the small group of silver Republicans, led by Sen. Henry M. Teller of Colorado, who bolted the meeting. Taubeneck made no pretense of his desire to unite silver Republicans, silver Democrats, and Populists into a new coalition that would run on a strictly silver platform, with the Republican Teller at the top of the ticket.[30]

Populists next awaited the Democrats' gathering in Chicago. Convening on July 7 in the Chicago Coliseum, at the time the largest exhibition hall in the world, the party whose hard-money policies, many believed, had caused the current depression made a dramatic reversal of course. Repudiating Grover Cleveland and the gold standard, the Democrats did what many Texas Populists thought they would never live to see—they officially embraced silver. In one of the most famous moments in the history of American political conventions, the young Nebraska congressman William Jennings Bryan, who in the prior year had become the darling of the silverites in the party, mounted the podium and in ringing terms made the case for the free and unlimited coinage of silver. His magnificent speaking voice reaching every corner of the twenty-thousand-seat hall, he arrived at the climactic moment of his well-rehearsed speech with an admonishment to those who supported the gold standard: "You shall not press down upon the brow of labor this crown of thorns, you shall not crucify mankind upon a cross of gold." A delirious forty-minute demonstration ensued, and his nomination for president on the convention's fifth ballot followed the next day. To balance the ticket, the Democrats nominated a conservative Maine shipbuilding and banking magnate, Arthur Sewall, to be Bryan's running mate.[31]

Now the actions of Chairman Taubeneck and the Populist National Committee back in January assumed ominous proportions, as their scheduling of the Populist convention for two weeks after that of the Democrats meant that Populists would have to decide between nominating their own candidate or endorsing Bryan and free silver. That Bryan was popular with Populists is beyond question. Many agreed with the Johnson County delegate to the national convention who stated, flat out, "He is a good Populist. He is right with us." For many it was not so much Bryan's political beliefs but his status as a Democrat that poisoned the well. As editor Frank C. Thompson of the Populist *McKinney Democrat* noted, "Personally, we admire Mr. Bryan. We believe him to be a friend of the masses. Yet if we were to endorse and elect him the election would be heralded as a democratic victory, and immediately the political pie eaters would set to work to belittle the populists and to destroy their organization."[32]

Pie eaters. Therein lay the problem, or at least one of the problems. The term, commonplace in American political jargon in the 1890s, connoted corrupt career politicians who valued lucrative public offices over political principle. Texas Populists might like Bryan and even think him something of a Populist in the abstract, but the pie-eating Democratic Party could not be trusted, even if it embraced Populist causes and nominated a man with some Populist proclivities. To many Texans, throwing away all that they had built up in Texas on the *hope* that a Bryanized national Democratic Party would bring real reform seemed to be a fool's errand. For many, it smacked of treason to the People's Party.

Texas's 103 delegates arrived by train in St. Louis on July 21, the day before the official start of the convention. A correspondent for a San Francisco newspaper recorded a colorful account of their arrival. Undoubtedly employing considerable literary license with an eye toward selling papers, his description nonetheless captured something of the spirit of the state's delegation: "Magnificent specimens of manhood are the Texans—tall, sinewy, sunburned, without an ounce of superfluous flesh, vigorous and as wiry and as hardy as the ponies which they ride in their own country. If they don't like a man or a thing they blurt out their dislike with the candor of an Indian in his native wilds. A Texan will share with his comrade his last dollar, will divide his coat in two to keep the cold blasts from the shoulder of a needy friend. He fights like an Indian, he loves like an Indian, and he hates with the intensity of a savage." The Texans, according to the reporter, "came here whooping from the cars to the aristocratic Southern Hotel into their quarters, a large parlor on the ground floor, to the great surprise of the slow-going St. Louisans and to the great joy of the middle of the roadsters who saw these strange wild men troop. Each man wore a white badge bearing as its prominent emblem a single star—the lone star of Texas."[33]

The comparison of Texas Populists to Indians was but one manifestation of the manner in which journalists—especially those from cities outside the

South—and political opponents—no matter where they hailed from—satirized and ridiculed Populists, who disproportionately came from backward places like Kansas and Texas. On the opening day of the St. Louis convention, a correspondent for the *New York Sun* reported on interviews he had supposedly had, describing the Populists' lack of hygiene:

> "It's a funny thing," said a hotel clerk to-day. "Usually the first rooms taken in our hotel are those with baths in them; but we can not drive these populists into one of those rooms. We usually charge extra price for the baths; now we can't let these rooms for even a reduction from the regular price of the ordinary room without bath."
>
> Inquiries at various hotels showed that the easiest thing to get in St. Louis to-day is a room with a bath.

The clear implication of the story is that Populists were so uncultured that they preferred a room with no bath over a cheaper one with a bath. Such stories, multiplied over time, constructed a stereotype of Populists that persists. Significantly, the New York correspondent's story was reprinted in the *Galveston Daily News* and the *Dallas Morning News,* the two most influential papers in Texas.[34]

The Texas delegation's headquarters, the elegant Southern Hotel at the corner of Walnut and Fourth Streets, which undoubtedly had excellent bathroom facilities, was easy walking distance from the convention hall. As delegates gathered, the national executive committee met. Not surprisingly, a majority of the committee's members were sympathetic toward Bryan, but beyond that, deep divisions soon became apparent, and they would be mirrored in the full convention. One faction supported the endorsement or outright nomination of the Democratic ticket of William Jennings Bryan and Arthur Sewall, even though this would mean the effective end of Populism as an independent entity. A second group was agreeable with regard to Bryan but found the wealthy and conservative Sewall unacceptable. This group hoped to find some way to commit the party to Bryan while still maintaining the separate identity and organization of the People's Party. A third group insisted on staying in the "middle of the road" and nominating a straight Populist ticket on a Populist platform, even though with Bryan in the field the Third Party had virtually no chance of winning.[35]

It soon became clear that the Bryan-Sewall faction, led by Taubeneck, Nebraska senator William V. Allen, James B. Weaver, and others, could control neither the executive committee nor, presumably, the full convention. Neither, however, could the Midroaders. Those favoring some middle course clearly held the balance of power. The executive committee's job was to listen to a few appeals regarding the composition of delegations and, more important, to make a recommendation to the full convention for the important post of temporary chair. After awarding Texas eight additional delegates (probably after Texas members made a case that the committee had shorted them in January), the committee decided to recommend North Carolina senator Marion Butler for temporary chair. The Bryan-Sewall men objected; they "maintained that the opportunity was one which would probably never again be presented to secure the success of populist principles. They contended that it was a patriotic duty to accept the democratic nominees; that wise party policy demanded this course." But Butler had maintained decent relations with all factions, he seemed friendly toward Bryan, and both the Bryanites and the Midroaders reluctantly deemed him acceptable.[36]

Cyclone Davis, who represented Texas on the national committee and whose long record of support for fusion already had placed him under intense pressure from his fellow Texans, supported the nomination of Butler, a position that soon put the lanky Texan on the hot seat. The night before the beginning of the convention, the Midroaders caucused, with Jerome Kearby presiding. When called on to make a speech, Davis assured them that Butler supported the Midroad position, and urged them to support the committee's choice of the North Carolinian when the full convention voted on a temporary chair. But his fellow Texans understandably distrusted Davis. They surely remembered the warning that Milton Park had issued about Davis that very week: "This man Davis has been talking fusion right straight along." Accordingly, the Midroaders appointed a committee to call on Butler and get his personal assurances that he was indeed in the Middle of the Road, as Davis had claimed. When the committee located Butler, they learned that he actually had come out in favor of nominating Bryan on a ticket with a Populist running mate. This was the elusive "compromise" that a large group of centrist delegates seemed to support. There were serious questions about what this would accomplish, or even how the mechanics of it would work, but Butler believed it would preserve the identity of the People's Party. When the committee returned to the Midroad caucus and announced Butler's position, the news landed "like a bombshell upon the caucus." Davis "seemed to be stricken dumb," something that rarely happened to the loquacious Texan. "Cries of 'traitor,' 'turn him down,' were heard on every side." When he recovered his composure, he feigned surprise at Butler's position and pleaded with his colleagues to support the actions of the national committee anyway. "We must be patriots," he argued.

"We must not make a fight on the action of the committee. It will aggravate the northwest section of the country. We shall be antagonized in many sections." He then went on to try to convince the Midroaders that he was indeed one of them, claiming that he would rather "be torn limb from limb before he would do anything to injure the Populist party." He exclaimed that in his own household he taught his children "to hate the Democratic party for all time . . . like Hannibal teaching his sons to hate the Romans." Speaking of his fellow Populists, he "cried excitedly," "Their God shall be my God. . . . Their grave shall be my grave." Many no doubt thought Davis protested too much, but he was about to say even more when an angry delegate shouted him down. "He's a Bryan man," the delegate yelled. "Take him down," shouted another. "He sold us out," cried yet another. Davis, "perspiring freely," finally decided to take a seat.[37]

Having deemed Butler unacceptable, the Midroaders then debated various alternatives. Some delegates had already floated the name of Jerome Kearby for temporary chair, but his fellow Texans believed that it would "injure his chances for the governorship of Texas, and insisted upon his withdrawal." Various other candidates were discussed and then rejected, and Kearby finally adjourned the session for the evening.[38]

At some point during the evening, the Texans seem to have correctly realized that the Midroaders were badly outnumbered by those who favored Bryan in some form. Davis, with his long tenure on the national committee and his extensive experience campaigning across the nation, likely succeeded in convincing the Midroaders of this. Although Davis supported Butler, he realized how damaged his reputation now was with the Midroaders. A St. Louis newspaper reported that some of the Texas delegates accused him of "carrying water on both shoulders." "At times open charges of treachery have been made against the 'Cyclone,'" the story explained. "Threats to roll him were freely heard." Thus embattled, Davis now joined with several of his fellow Texans in hatching a new plan. The idea was for the convention to nominate a Middle-of-the-Road Populist ticket, with genuine Populists for president and vice president, but with the proviso that the Populists and Democrats would name joint slates of electors in each state. In the 1890s, voters voted for actual individual electors who were pledged to their party's candidates. So, under this plan in Texas, a state with fifteen electoral votes, both the Populists and the Democrats would name the same fifteen men as electors, with the electors' partisan affiliations being determined by each party's strength in 1894. Then when the election was held, if the People's Party garnered the most votes, all fifteen electors would cast their electoral votes for the Populist presidential nominee, with the agreement that its fifteen votes would also be cast for the Democratic vice presidential candidate. If the Democrats got the most votes in the state, then Bryan would receive the state's fifteen electoral votes, with the Populists' vice presidential candidate being elected in the Electoral College. On the first day of the convention, Davis released a signed statement to the *St. Louis Republic* detailing the plan, with this explicit explanation: "By the passage of this resolution we lend our aid to insure the defeat of McKinley, if the combined vote of both parties will do this. If this combination controlled a majority of the electors of the United States it would mean, of course, Bryan for President, for a majority of the electors in the Northwest, whether Populist or Democrats, would be for Bryan, as to proportion the electors according to the votes in the other States would still give Mr. Bryan a majority of those electors. We believe that this kind of a plan will carry over fifty more electoral votes than we could carry by indorsing or nominating Bryan." Jerome Kearby, Barney Gibbs, Harry Tracy, and Davis himself were supposed to "take its management on the floor." Davis could now claim his bona fides as a genuine Midroader, while having set in motion a plan that, if successful, would still have the ultimate effect of delivering the Populist vote to Bryan.[39]

With this convoluted plan in hand, the next morning, just before the start of the actual convention, the Texans hastily caucused again and decided not to oppose Butler's nomination, fearing that "it was unwise to show their strength." Nevertheless, the Texans "were not harmonious" over the decision, "and there were many bitter expressions heard against Butler." Delegates began straggling into the convention hall around 10 a.m. The convention was held in the same structure that had accommodated the Republican National Convention just one month earlier. Dubbed "the Wigwam" by locals, it was a temporary wooden building constructed by the St. Louis Business Men's League strictly for the purpose of housing the two conventions (plate 25). Thrown up in a mere sixty days at the cost of $60,000 utilizing a system of fast, temporary construction developed for the 1892 world's fair, its acoustic, ventilation, and lighting systems left much to be desired. Surveying the gathering crowd, one reporter believed that "one glance would show that they represented the 'common people;' they came from the farm, the mine, the workshop and the factory." The reporter observed "many picturesque personalities—men who have been agitators and reformers for many years were there, but there were also many whose ability and force of character have given them rank in high station. As a body they were men of strong and earnest convictions." As the summer air heated up, coats were shed, followed by collars and cravats. When the Mississippi delegation paraded through the hall with a banner reading "No Compromise," the Texas delegation responded with "an answering yell of joy." Party chairman Taubeneck finally gaveled the convention to order at 12:40. After a few preliminaries, Marion Butler was elected temporary chair without a challenge. He delivered a speech short on specifics, and the convention then got down to the customary first-day business of appointing a credentials committee to vet delegates' credentials and resolve contests. At 2:19 the delegates recessed till evening, and when they assembled for the night session, the Midroaders planned to launch a major anti-Bryan demonstration. But when they reassembled at 8:00 p.m., the hall was dark; the electric lights had mysteriously failed. Some attempts were made at speech-making by candlelight, but Chairman Butler finally was forced to adjourn till morning. The Midroaders were convinced that the power outage was a dirty trick by the Bryan men, reminiscent of a similar stunt pulled at the 1876 Republican convention. Others blamed a storm that had passed through that evening; the hall, after all, was a hastily thrown-up, temporary structure with wiring that was likely inadequate. Later the sergeant at arms would state that someone had contacted the electric company claiming to be him and ordering that the lights be extinguished. In any case, Midroaders believed that they had been deprived of an opportunity to show their strength while the supposedly moderate Butler was still in the chair. Conditions might change for the worse the next day, when a permanent chairman was elected.[40]

The next day the weather turned even hotter. Delegates began arriving around 9:00, and the towering form of Davis was seen moving about on the floor, trying to raise support for the Midroaders' complicated plan. Almost everyone in the hall had a palm-leaf fan, leading one reporter to observe that "the thousand or more fans waved convulsively in the pit like the wings or myriads of yellow butterflies hovering above a clover patch." When the dapper Marion Butler took the platform at 10:06, the band struck up "Dixie," but the festive atmosphere soon gave way to frustration, at least on the part of the Texans. The Committee on Permanent Organization was not ready to give its report, and delays mounted. The Midroaders attempted to stage the demonstration that had been aborted the previous night, but it fell rather flat, and as a local paper reported, "it only served to demonstrate the hopeless minority of the straight-outs." The most important business of the convention that morning was to elect a permanent chairman to preside for the remainder of the meeting. To nobody's surprise, the Committee on Permanent Organization recommended Sen. William Vincent Allen of Nebraska, a Bryan partisan. The minority report put forward the name of James Campion of Maine, a relatively obscure Midroader. When Campion's name was called, the Texas and Georgia delegates "climbed on their chairs and yelled like Comanche Indians." They then paraded several large Middle-of-the-Road banners around the hall, which nearly led to several fistfights. From the galleries above the convention floor, someone hurled a shower of green cards with the full 1892 Populist greenback financial plank printed on them, creating a minor sensation. But when the vote was taken, the Midroaders finally had their best indication yet of where they stood: Allen won 758 to 564. Now firmly in control of the convention and its committees, the Bryan men were "jubilant." The Midroaders had to face the reality that their plan for nominating a full Midroad ticket with the promised division of electors—the Davis plan that had seemed so promising the day before—now seemed impossible. The only question was whether the convention would endorse the full Democratic ticket and platform, or nominate Bryan alongside a Populist running mate.[41]

In the afternoon session, a chastened Cyclone Davis was chosen to introduce the newly elected chairman to the convention. In doing so, the Texan insisted that he had been working for the Midroad cause for the past four days, and he made it a point to explain that he had been selected without his knowledge to introduce Allen. Once Davis had issued his awkward disclaimers, the newly elected chairman Allen made a strong speech, urging the nomination of Bryan even if it meant sacrificing the People's Party organization. Allen, Taubeneck, and their allies had always wanted to nominate the full Democratic ticket of Bryan and Sewall, but if Sewall's nomination seemed likely to fail, they were prepared to adjourn the convention without naming a vice presidential nominee. They still desperately wanted to avoid the vast complications that would arise if the Butler plan of pairing Bryan with a Populist running mate succeeded.[42]

That evening, after Allen's address, the Midroaders gathered at the Texas headquarters at the Southern Hotel, with Austin's Marion Williams presiding. "Some of the bitterest invective ever employed at a political gathering" was directed at the Democratic Party and its Populist accomplices, according to one newspaper account. Not surprisingly, Cyclone Davis counseled accepting defeat and securing the best terms they could, a position that further sustains the theory that he had really wanted fusion all along. Several of the Texans, however, including Stump Ashby, supported the radical tactic of a Midroader bolt from the convention if Bryan received the nomination, a move that would

leave the convention entirely in the hands of the Bryanites. But others counseled against it, including Barney Gibbs, who said that in his twenty-five years
in politics he had never seen a bolt in which the bolters did not later regret their
action. As a former Democratic lieutenant governor of Texas, Gibbs had more
high-level experience with political conventions than virtually any of his fellow
delegates, and unbeknownst to most of them, he had come up with a desperate
but ingenious plan to salvage the Midroad cause. He laid out his conditions for
revealing the plan, explaining that "he would not divulge it unless they would
bind themselves to absolute secrecy and agree to stand by him," which they said
they promised to do. Then the doors to the meeting room were locked, and
every man was sworn to secrecy. Gibbs then proceeded to explain the plan.[43]

He proposed that the convention reverse the usual order of nominations,
nominating the vice presidential candidate first, to be followed later by the presidential nomination. He believed that if the convention nominated a doctrinaire Populist running mate, a running mate utterly obnoxious to Democrats,
running on a Middle-of-the-Road Populist platform, Bryan might be forced to
decline the nomination before it ever happened. With Bryan thus out of the
picture, a real Middle-of-the-Road Populist could then be nominated for president. For the plan to succeed, however, its true intent had to be kept from the
pro-Bryan majority in the convention. It had to be sold with the argument that
it would prevent delegates from nominating Sewall on Bryan's coattails, or that
it would prevent the convention from adjourning without naming a running
mate at all. And since Marion Butler's pro-Bryan faction had already committed to the idea of pairing Bryan with a Populist running mate, Gibbs believed
that he could count on the support of the Butler men, including North Carolina's crucial ninety-five votes, as long as the Butlerites, who still favored the
nomination of Bryan at the top of the ticket, failed to realize the true intention of the plan. Gibbs himself would be the Midroaders' floor manager for
the remainder of the convention, assisted by his handpicked lieutenant, Alabama congressman Milford W. Allen. Gibbs was to make every motion, and
no speeches were to be made without his approval. There is no record that Cyclone Davis was included in these proceedings, which stretched well beyond
2:00 a.m. By that time a rumor had spread among the Texas delegates that
Davis had been promised a job in a Bryan administration. He clearly was not
to be trusted.[44]

The following day, the sleep-deprived Texans assembled for what most
thought would be the third and final day of the convention. At 10:30 a.m., Allen
opened the floor for nominations for president, and Gen. James B. Weaver

370 THE PEOPLE'S REVOLT

placed William Jennings Bryan's name in nomination. At the conclusion of
Weaver's speech, banners featuring crowns of thorns, crosses of gold, and Bryan's picture were paraded around the hall, while the Texas delegation and
their Midroad allies looked on sullenly. When a Nebraska man tried to seize
the Texas delegation's guidon and bring it into the parade of state banners celebrating Bryan, several Texans reached into their hip pockets for pistols, and
the Nebraskan retreated. Nominating and seconding speeches continued into
the afternoon. At one point, when it appeared that Chairman Allen might approve a motion to suspend the rules and nominate Bryan by acclamation, the
Texans charged the platform and forced the withdrawal of the motion. With
nominations finally completed, the next order of business was the adoption of
rules to govern the remainder of the convention. Gibbs and his followers now
launched their plan, in the form of a minority report recommending the reversal of the order of nominations. Gibbs managed to speak twice under the
guise of parliamentary inquiries, and he kept up the fiction of supporting the
nomination of Bryan with a Populist running mate and a proposed division
of electors.[45]

At 2:00 p.m. Cyclone Davis gained the floor and, intentionally or not, nearly
sabotaged the Midroaders' plan. He claimed to have pledges from the Kansas,
Nebraska, and Illinois delegations to support a southern Populist for vice president if the Midroaders would allow the regular order of nominations to proceed. Gibbs of course opposed this idea, which would have assured Bryan of the
nomination and probably would have foiled the plan to force Bryan's declination. After a hard fight, the roll call on the question of reversing the order of
nominations was finally taken, and the Midroaders, with support from Butler's
North Carolinians, won one of their few victories of the convention, 785 to 615.

Behind the scenes, and as if on cue, the chair of the Democratic National
Committee, James K. Jones, who had been attending the convention, wired
Bryan with the news and asked Bryan what should be done if Sewall were defeated. Bryan responded immediately: "If Sewall is not nominated have my
name withdrawn." Rumors of the telegram's existence soon leaked to the delegates, but the Midroaders could not afford to have it read to the convention
before a Populist had received the vice presidential nomination, because it
likely would have stampeded the convention into going ahead and nominating Sewall in order to assure the nomination of Bryan. It was all a matter of
timing.[46]

In the tense evening session, nominations for vice president proceeded. The
Texans at first supported Mississippi's John Burkett, but as support coalesced

around ex-congressman Tom Watson of Georgia, the Texans deemed him acceptable and threw their support to him. At midnight, before the final vote was taken, the Bryanites decided it was time to spring Bryan's telegram on the convention. Sen. William M. Stewart of Nevada stepped to the podium to read the message, but the Texas-led Midroaders, still fearing that the convention would accept Sewall rather than risk losing Bryan, raised such an uproar that Stewart backed down. The senator feared that reading the telegram might precipitate a bolt from the convention, and he was probably right. As the final votes were tallied, the lights suddenly failed for a second time, prompting more suspicions of dirty tricks. But the chair ruled Watson the nominee, and the lights soon flickered back on.[47]

Gibbs's assistant Milford Howard immediately moved to recess till the next morning. The Midroad plotters knew that they needed to give Bryan time to withdraw his name from consideration; otherwise, if the convention went ahead and nominated Bryan now, there was the possibility that Bryan might simply ignore the Populists' action, neither accepting nor declining the nomination and taking whatever Populist votes he could get in the various states (which is exactly what eventually happened). Marion Butler moved that the convention proceed immediately to the nomination of president, but Howard's motion carried.[48]

As the night's session ended, a gleeful Milton Park, who claimed personally to have seen Bryan's telegram of declination, announced to the Texas delegation, "We've got 'em beat. Bryan won't accept unless we give him Sewall!" And a short while later, some of the Texans joined other Midroaders at a nearby hotel "shouting for Eugene V. Debs for president." Debs had already positively refused to accept a nomination, having himself come out for Bryan, but this did not stop the most radical Midroaders from thinking his mind might be changed. Summarizing the day's events, a wire-service reporter opined that "to-day, for the first time, the middle-of-the-road element displayed generalship worthy of the name." The weary Texans went to bed fully expecting to read in the morning papers that Bryan had officially declined the nomination.[49]

As it turned out, the morning papers did publish Bryan's telegram instructing that his name be withdrawn (as well as one sent by the Texas delegation to Bryan the previous day asking him outright if he would stand on the full Populist platform, including government ownership of the railroads). But when the convention itself was called to order at 9:30 a.m., with nominating a presidential candidate the first order of business, no formal withdrawal from Bryan was forthcoming. Having been outmaneuvered by the Midroaders in the matter of reversing the nominations, the Bryanites were now determined to squelch any telegram from Bryan himself declining the nomination. From beneath a Middle-of-the-Road banner planted squarely in the Texas delegation, Stump Ashby demanded to know if such a telegram existed, and Chairman Allen flatly denied it. The roll call proceeded, and Bryan proceeded to win the nomination over Midroader Seymour F. Norton of Illinois by a lopsided vote of 1,042 to 340, with the Texans providing 103 of Norton's votes. A pro-Bryan delegate moved to give the national executive committee plenary powers, which would free it to help arrange fusion deals in the states, and Allen declared the motion passed, then hurriedly adjourned the convention.[50]

The embittered Texas delegates, now dubbed the "Immortal 103" by the party faithful, prepared to make their way home, all the while trying to make sense of the convention's work. A St. Louis newspaper had reported that every poor Texan delegate had secured a roll of Republican boss Marc Hanna's money to pay for his trip home, but the Texans laughed off the idea, saying that they would have loved to get Hanna's money, but "after a vigorous search they failed to find a Hanna man and were compelled to draw on every man in Texas thought to be willing or able to stand a draft." Kearby, the rich lawyer, "growled," "Yes . . . and you thought Gibbs and I were the only ones who could and would, for you sent all the drafts to us." Democratic charges—never proven—that Hanna's money was being used to pay off Texas Populists would dog the Third Party for the remainder of the campaign.[51]

Even after arriving home, it was difficult for anyone to explain clearly what had happened at St. Louis and what its implications might be. Stump Ashby bluntly described the convention's work as "the worst conglomeration I ever saw." Evan Jones, the venerable Alliance leader who had been a delegate to St. Louis, believed that the Texans had saved the party by insisting on Watson. Like many other Texas Populists, Jones believed that the Democrats would pull down Sewall, and that if they did not, the Populists would replace Bryan with a real Populist. Charles Jenkins believed that Sewall would withdraw in favor of Watson, in which case the Populists and Democrats presumably would easily be able to agree on a joint slate of electors. Delegate J. J. Burroughs agreed that the convention "beat anything I ever saw," and although he thought that Bryan would either decline or be pulled down by the People's Party, he confessed that "the chaotic condition of things makes it hard to say right now what Texas will do." He did, however, express confidence that "the thing will be cleared up at the state convention Aug. 5."[52]

From Maine, Arthur Sewall privately wrote to Bryan offering to step down if Bryan and the party thought it best, but Democratic bosses were not about to place Populist Tom Watson on their ticket. Nor would Bryan be repudiating the Populist nomination, at least not officially. A private letter from none other than Texas's own ex-governor Jim Hogg to Bryan no doubt reflected the thinking of many party leaders. *"Take time,"* Hogg urged Bryan. *"Do not let any one rush you.* As the Populist nomination has been unconditionally tendered to you it now remains for you to accept it at *your own pleasure* and on such reasonable conditions as you may wish to impose." Hogg craftily advised Bryan to accept only those parts of the Populist platform not in conflict with the Democratic platform, and ignore the rest. "This is better, safer, than to *decline* the nomination. Discuss *nothing* but the money question. . . . *Take time.* Use your friends to heal the differences."[53]

With each passing day after the convention, it became clearer that Bryan would follow Hogg's advice and simply stand pat, neither accepting nor declining the Populist nomination and making no move toward removing Sewall or even acknowledging the Watson nomination. Disturbing reports came from Kansas and Colorado, where those states' Populist organizations moved to simply ignore the Watson nomination and place Bryan-Sewall electors on the People's Party tickets. The newly elected national chairman, Marion Butler, who had first conceived of the plan to nominate Bryan with a Populist running mate, sought to arrange joint slates of electors in the various states, with the aim of securing electoral votes for both Bryan and Watson, but he made little headway with the impossibly complex plan. Southern Populists found themselves hopelessly divided over what course to pursue. The slogan "No Watson, no Bryan" became increasingly common among Texas Populists (plate 26), who felt that if Bryan refused to accept Watson as his running mate, Populists would be under no obligation to support Bryan.[54]

Two thousand Populists descended on Galveston on August 4 for the state People's Party convention, a mere ten days after the close of the national convention. In contrast to the 1894 Waco meeting, where the carnival-like atmosphere had been gleeful to the point of giddiness, the mood at this meeting can best be described as one of grim determination. Prior to the start of the convention, most party leaders hoped to keep all mention of national affairs out of the convention, simply vesting power to decide what to do about the entire Bryan-Sewall-Watson imbroglio in the hands of a committee invested with plenary powers to act in the party's behalf after the convention. The idea was "to give Bryan a chance to declare his position before Texas took a stand which it might be difficult to withdraw from." But lurking in the back of many Populists' minds was another possibility that only a few dared broach at the time: if Bryan never formally accepted the Populist nomination, or if the Democrats refused to replace Sewall with Watson or otherwise acknowledge a formal partnership with the People's Party, then the Populists might fuse instead with the *Republicans* on the state level, offering Populist support for McKinley in return for Republican votes for the Populist state ticket. This was the possibility whose name essentially could not be spoken, at least not yet. Everyone knew, however, that it would be difficult to avoid addressing the national situation, as there were delegates eager to endorse the quixotic actions of the Immortal 103 at St. Louis and declare outright for a repudiation of Bryan, as well as others who were determined to champion an endorsement of the Bryan-Watson ticket, plus an indeterminate number who would vote the Bryan-Sewall ticket if they thought it was the only way to elect Bryan. Ashby, Tracy, "and one or two other radicals" were said to favor issuing an ultimatum to the national Democratic Party: replace Sewall with Watson and endorse the Populist platform, or Populists would not be bound to support Bryan. But Kearby, Charles Jenkins, Henry Bentley, and other pragmatists thought the plan unnecessarily divisive, pointing out that it would likely stampede from the party free-silver Populists like Buck Walton who were predisposed to favor Bryan. Nobody knew what would really happen when the convention began in earnest.[55]

Stump Ashby gaveled the meeting to order in Galveston's Convention Hall on the morning of August 5, with many delegates sporting badges that read, "Kearby's Yarn Gallus Brigade." Unlike at the national convention, there would be no controversy over whose name would head the state ticket. But if the leaders had hoped to keep national affairs quiet, they could not have liked the first thing that happened. Hill County's Owen F. Dornblaser, the excitable president of the Texas Reform Press Association, paraded through the hall with a banner reading

July 22, 1896.
St. Louis.
Middle-of the Road Populist
Ticket.
1896.

When Dornblaser's display elicited cheers from the crowd, an embarrassed Ashby tried to move along quickly, simply noting that he was glad the delegates approved of the Immortal 103's actions in St. Louis "if the grounds had to be gone over again." Ashby soon introduced Galveston's Populist leader Noah Allen, who was supposed to only welcome the delegates to the city, but even Allen, who himself had been one of the 103, could not resist revisiting the St. Louis convention and criticizing both Bryan and McKinley, whereupon Ashby had to call him down, "saying such questions could not be discussed at that time." Later in the evening, undoubtedly with the approval of Ashby and his cohorts, the newly installed temporary chair, State Representative Jesse Burney, read a telegram to the delegates from the Louisiana Populist state convention announcing that the Louisianans had named a full slate of Bryan-Watson electors but had also named a plenary committee "to make changes necessitated by action of national convention." Clearly the Texan leaders hoped that their convention would do the same, leaving them the fullest possible latitude to cut whatever deals they might deem most advantageous down the road.[56]

The group most committed to a cautious course won a victory when Henry Bentley of Abilene, a staunch Midroader but also a thoughtful pragmatist, was elected permanent chair of the convention. His parliamentary skills were tested the next afternoon when a Smith County delegate named D. M. Reedy introduced a resolution providing that if the Democrats refused to substitute Watson for Sewall within ten days, the executive committee would be empowered to name a new presidential candidate in place of Bryan. This instantly threw the convention into an uproar, and Bentley finally referred it to the resolutions committee, a maneuver that displeased the losing side but successfully postponed the issue once more.[57]

On the third day of the convention, a committee consisting of Ashby, Tracy, and Gibbs, which had been appointed to respond to the telegrams sent by Louisiana and several other state conventions, reported with its own version of a "no Watson, no Bryan" message which, if sent, would commit the Texas convention to pulling Bryan off the ticket in Texas if the Democrats refused to accept Watson. Charles Jenkins, one of the levelest heads among the party leadership, gained the floor to oppose the telegrams, saying "they are firebrands and will cause the defeat of the Populist party." Jenkins's speech was cut short by a point of order, but the wisdom of his objection was soon driven home by Buck Walton, a staunch Bryan supporter, who threatened to decline his nomination for state attorney general if the telegrams were sent. The telegrams were placed on hold, and later Tracy's committee withdrew them on the grounds that the other state conventions had adjourned and there was now no point in sending them.[58]

During one of the numerous long recesses, the thirty or so African American delegates to the convention caucused to see where they stood on the difficult issues related to national politics. John B. Rayner opened the session with a stern statement: "The Democratic party can not be trusted with the finances of the country and they can not be trusted with the rights of the negroes." With that, he turned the meeting over to another delegate, and one by one the participants stated their positions. It soon became clear that they were as divided as their white brethren. One man declared that "even if Bryan is a stanch Democrat and I can get a part of what I want I will do it and wait for the rest." Others pushed back, with one delegate explaining, "I canvassed by county before I came here, and if the Populists stick to the Democratic nominee, there are many there who are not going to vote for him. I don't say, mind you, that I'm going to vote for McKinley, but never will I vote for Bryan." This went on for some time, and finally Rayner intervened with a set of resolutions he had written in advance. Endorsing the Omaha Demands, dismissing free silver as a "panacea," and castigating both of the major parties, the document stated that since Bryan had refused to accept the Populist nomination, the Populist National Committee should replace Bryan with a Middle-of-the-Road candidate, and if the committee refused, then Texas Populists should "lead our state with the name of William McKinley and the Republican state electors and we will give the state to McKinley if the Texas Republicans will vote for J. C. Kearby." By a vote of eighteen to thirteen, the black delegates approved the resolution. They made no attempt to force it on the convention, which was a wise choice considering its explosive content. But it outlined a policy that many white leaders privately had been contemplating ever since St. Louis.[59]

As the convention neared conclusion, the leaders who wanted no action taken on the national situation had to exert heroic efforts to continue suppressing those who wanted a commitment to an arch-Midroad position. At the behest of Kearby and others, Tracy, Jenkins, and Bentley waited till many of the delegates had left for home, then took to the floor to buttonhole delegates in an effort to explain to them why matters should be left in the hands of a plenary committee. Kearby, Tracy, and Gibbs finally called delegate Reedy, who had introduced the convention's original "no Watson, no Bryan" resolution, into a back room. There is no record of precisely what they said to him, but few Texas Populists could have withstood the pressure from three of Populism's most persuasive personalities. When the discussion was over, Reedy dropped his resolution. He later glumly told his friends "that possibly he was mistaken after all in his views."[60]

Nominations went more or less smoothly, with Kearby, as expected, being chosen for governor by acclamation. Delegates rewarded Stump Ashby's long service as party chairman with the lieutenant governor's nomination. Recent convert Buck Walton, who had threatened to decline if a "no Watson, no Bryan" resolution was adopted, received the attorney general nomination. The old Alliance constituency gained recognition with the nomination of S. O. Daws for state treasurer. (Daws, the original Alliance "traveling lecturer," is sometimes described as "the first Populist.") E. O. Meitzen, who had done yeoman work among the Germans of Central Texas, was nominated for comptroller. Albert B. Francisco, the Swedenborgian educator from Galveston, got the nod for state school superintendent. Stephen C. Granberry, who had run a strong race for land commissioner in 1894, was renominated for that office, and three of the party's most influential insiders, Evan Jones, W. W. Nelms, and Edmund P. Alsbury, were chosen to run for the Railroad Commission. The most controversial choice was Theodore J. McMinn for the state supreme court—controversial because of his recent attempt in federal court to have Mexican immigrants barred from becoming citizens. (Within days the rumor spread that McMinn would be removed from the ticket, "so unpopular is he in certain districts.") With longtime party chairman Stump Ashby now on the ticket, the delegates chose Abilene editor Joseph S. Bradley, a close associate of Henry L. Bentley, as the new chair of the state executive committee.[61]

Most significantly, the leadership won its battle to prevent the convention from committing itself to a strict Middle-of-the-Road policy. Not that anyone really knew what constituted such a policy, although the most common version of it had the state party naming its own national ticket in the now virtually certain likelihood that the Democrats would not replace Sewall with Watson. The thinking of Kearby, Ashby, Gibbs, Tracy, Bentley, Jenkins, and others was fairly straightforward: putting out such a Midroad ticket would be only a symbolic gesture, since no presidential candidate nominated only by Texas Populists would ever stand a chance of victory. Moreover, such a move would alienate Populists who were inclined to favor Bryan. It was a lose-lose proposition. But some sort of fusion with the Texas Republican Party—the very course endorsed by the African American Populists at Galveston—held almost irresistible appeal for those who bitterly resented Bryan and who were desperate to win state offices. A fusion wherein Populists would support McKinley in return for Republican support of the Populist state candidates was likely the *only* chance the Populists had of electing Kearby and the rest of the state ticket. One of the Galveston convention's final acts was to authorize the appointment of a three-man campaign committee with plenary power to make whatever deals it deemed in the party's best interests. That committee, composed of Harry Tracy, Marion Williams, and J. M. Mallett, now became the de facto ruling body of the Texas People's Party for the remainder of the campaign. Within an hour of the adjournment of the convention, Tracy was reportedly seen "confabing with one of the republican leaders whose mission is well known."

But the Populists could not be seen as rushing into the arms of the despised Republicans, the party of "plutocracy" and the "horrors" of Reconstruction. First, they had to appear to be sincere in wanting to cooperate with Democrats on behalf of Bryan. Two weeks after the Populist convention, Texas Democrats met in Fort Worth for their own state convention. The Populist campaign committee tendered a written proposal to the Democrats, stating, disingenuously, that "we have every reason to believe that Mr. Bryan will accept our nomination . . . and in order to produce harmony among the members of our respective parties in this matter, we ask your party to give us a division of presidential electors of Texas upon the following basis—seven populist electors and eight democratic electors." Bill Shaw, a prominent Democratic editor from Dallas and acerbic critic of the People's Party, moved that the Populists' requests be referred to the state lunatic asylum, but after some debate, the Democrats simply declined the offer, as Tracy and his colleagues surely knew they would. Four things were now crystal clear: Bryan would neither formally accept nor decline the Populist nomination; the Democratic National Committee would not replace Sewall with Watson; the Populist National Committee would not replace Bryan with a Midroad candidate; and the Texas Democrats would not agree to a division of electors. The path seemed clear for the Texas Populists to strike a bargain with the Republicans. After the Democrats' rejection of the Populists' offer, even Milton Park of the *Mercury*, arguably the most extreme Midroader of them all and a confirmed Republican-hater, reluctantly embraced the new reality. "The Republicans are at least decent enough to offer to help the Populists redeem the State," he observed. "Populists are not hunting any fusion, but if they have to take old Sewall and insults, or McKinley and State redemption and an escape of their wives and daughters from the cotton patch, they will choose each one for himself."[62]

When the state Republican convention met in September, the Populists achieved the next step in their strategy. The Republicans declined to put out a state ticket. The Republican chairman explained the decision, saying that while he disagreed with the Populists on the currency issue, "I am in favor of an honest and fair administration of the State government, which we cannot get with the present parties in power; so for that reason I am for Jerome Kearby for Governor of Texas. I have known him a long time, and I believe him to be prompted by impulses of honesty and sincerity." Of course, what he did not mention was the possibility that with the help of Populist votes William McKinley might carry Texas, an outcome that would mean enormous rewards for the state's GOP in terms of federal patronage and prestige and influence in national Republican affairs.[63]

The Galveston convention had vested the Populist campaign committee with plenary powers to act on behalf of the party, and the temptation was great to take the next step and consummate a formal fusion arrangement with the Republicans. Such an agreement would have involved some sort of division of electors with the Republicans, or even pulling down the Bryan-Watson ticket altogether and replacing their electors with the Republicans' McKinley electors. To help cement such a deal, some of the weaker Populist congressional candidates and statewide candidates (such as the controversial McMinn in the state supreme court race) might be pulled down in favor of Republican candidates. But to fuse in such a formal way was to play with dynamite. After consultation, the parties' committees concluded that it was simply too risky. "They feared that if open fusion on an electoral ticket was proclaimed before election day a large percentage of populist voters would be inclined to rebel," the *Galveston Daily News* reported. Instead, the leaders agreed on a less public strategy: "Republican party workers at every voting box will be instructed to say to populists when they go to the polls, substantially, 'Republicans are supporting Kearby and the populist state ticket; you have no chance to elect Watson, and we want you to support McKinley electors.'" Party leaders optimistically estimated that such a strategy could deliver between 55 and 75 percent of the Populist vote for McKinley.[64]

But even this watered-down, informal fusion with Republicans proved too much for many Populists. As newspaper reports of consultation between the Populist committee and Republican leaders spread, Populists began to denounce the rumored fusion. Some objected because they admired Bryan, others because they loathed Republicans. For many it was both. The Democratic press gleefully published each new announcement by a Populist who was abandoning the People's Party and returning to the Democrats. Populists' denunciations were exceedingly bitter: "The populist who will vote for the republican gold standard ticket is at once an object of contempt and pity," one wrote. A Central Texas Populist who had been one of the Immortal 103 avowed,

"I now protest against this unseemly, dishonorable attempt to secure power and office by political prostitution." Such declarations, however, were minor compared to the bombshell that exploded on October 6, when Buck Walton announced his resignation as the Populist nominee for attorney general and his intention to vote for the Democratic ticket of Bryan and Sewall. The party leadership had known all along that Walton, a Bryan devotee and a late convert to Populism, would brook no move that might damage Bryan. At Galveston he had threatened to decline the nomination if the "no Watson, no Bryan" telegrams were sent to other state conventions. His decision may have been influenced by a rumor that the Populist committee intended to pull him off the ticket and, as a show of good faith to the Republicans, replace him with a Republican, but in any case, his apostasy was front-page news across Texas. It prompted a bitter exchange of open letters between himself and new Populist chairman J. S. Bradley, which ended with Bradley stating, "You take the side of the oppressor against the helpless and the oppressed, and in leaving attempt to shove a poisoned knife under the fifth rib of those who trusted you." Walton's action was soon followed by another spate of denunciations and resignations from the party.[65]

Populist leaders certainly anticipated trouble over their dealings with the Republicans, or they would not have gone to such pains to conceal them. But they did not expect the extent of the hue and cry from Populists who felt betrayed. The Populist campaign committee issued a message addressed to "Fellow Citizens" stating that the "wild rumors" about fusion were "without any foundation whatever." By mid-October the Democratic press was describing leading Populists as "panic stricken," even as those leaders continued to deny any agreement with the Republicans.[66]

In this state of affairs, it became harder and harder for individual Populist candidates to agree on the proper course. The official party line, of course, was that there was no fusion, a claim that was technically true enough in terms of an official division of electors. But as the fall campaign proceeded, more and more Populists deemed it in their interest to openly espouse the trade of Populist votes for McKinley in return for Republican votes for the Populist state ticket. In the Houston congressional district, for example, Populist congressional candidate Joe Eagle pronounced publicly for McKinley. Stump Ashby admitted that he would not vote the Bryan-Watson ticket. Barney Gibbs was quoted as saying, "When you vote for McKinley . . . you know what you are voting for, but when you vote for . . . Bryan and Sewall, you don't know what you vote for." H. D. Wood and Marion Williams, both of whom were Populist Bryan-

Watson presidential electors, declared that they would not support Bryan. When Chairman Bradley was asked specifically whether the Populist Bryan-Watson electors would actually cast electoral votes for Bryan and Watson if elected, he refused to answer. Naturally the Democratic press made much hay of all such statements.[67]

But the earliest, most consistent, and most unapologetic Populist espousal of Populist-Republican fusion came from a most unlikely quarter. A mere two weeks after the Galveston convention, Cyclone Davis publicly declared that if the Texas Democrats would not divide electors with the Populists, the Populists would fuse with the Republicans and he would stump the state for McKinley. The next day, in an open letter to the Dallas-Galveston *News,* he exhibited slightly more circumspection, simply saying that there was "nothing dishonorable" about fusion as a general proposition, but he urged the Populist campaign committee, "whatever you do, do it openly, so our people and the world can see and understand." These developments, however, were enough to bring down a torrent of criticism on him from fellow Populists. The old labor warhorse Bill Farmer, running for Congress in East Texas, refused to believe Davis really said it. S. O. Daws, the nominee for state treasurer, said that "Davis should not have made such a talk." Reform Press chief Owen Dornblaser remarked that Davis could do what he wished, "but he'll not be a populist when he begins supporting McKinley." In the Central Texas congressional district, Populist candidate W. F. Douthit wrote a desperate letter to Davis pleading with him to cease his dalliance with the Republicans. Running in a district where the black vote was relatively small but where Populists would suffer if associated with the Republicans, Douthit told Davis that if the voters became convinced that a deal was on with the Republicans, "there will be the most terrible stampede to the free silver democrats ever witnessed." He explained that he had "denied it so vehemently" on the stump that if the "fusion racket" continues, it would make him out to be "a liar unworthy of any one's confidence." Then, if things were not bad enough, Douthit's opponent somehow obtained a copy of Douthit's letter and made it public, making the dissension and disarray in the Populist ranks even worse. Davis, as usual, was uncowed by this criticism and continued "making spread eagle speeches" advocating fusion with the Republicans.[68]

Davis's erratic course can be explained only by his ambition. For at least a year before the 1896 national convention he had worked closely with Herman Taubeneck to effect a fusion of all the nation's free silver forces, a course that required ignoring most of the Populist platform and ultimately supporting the movement to nominate Bryan, a strategy that he mistakenly believed could be pursued while still keeping the People's Party intact. In his memoir written many years later, Davis confirmed his pro-Bryan sentiments, writing, "when the Populist convention met in St. Louis, I worked seriously for two days to have our convention endorse Bryan and Sewall as Democratic nominees and meet the Republican party with a united opposition." But his own constituents had called his bluff prior to St. Louis, withholding the congressional nomination that he so coveted until they could see how he behaved at the convention. As a consequence, he had arrived in St. Louis spouting Middle-of-the-Road rhetoric for all who would listen. A St. Louis reporter astutely observed that "for a Middle-of-the-Road man, he was very friendly to Bryan, although in his speeches he carefully avoided committing himself." A Texas delegate to the convention confided to that same reporter "his belief that 'Cyclone' has been promised a job under President Bryan," and that in suddenly championing the Midroad position he was "trimming his sails to get into the other harbor." There is no actual evidence of such a quid pro quo between Davis and the Democrats, but his sail trimming at the convention—supporting the nomination of a Midroad ticket but advocating a division of electors with the Democrats—did barely manage to keep Davis close enough to the Middle of the Road to salvage his standing at home and secure him the congressional nomination.[69]

Aware of Davis's inconsistencies, Populists in the most staunchly Midroad county in the district, Delta, had convened five days after the St. Louis convention and "denounced and censured Cyclone Davis for his action at St. Louis and elsewhere in advocating fusion with other silver forces and parties." When the district nominating convention met two days later in Texarkana, Davis was nominated, but not before the delegation from another county, Red River, bolted the meeting in protest over the convention's refusal to repudiate the fusion effort at St. Louis, which Davis was seen as having abetted. Davis, in other words, had entered the fall campaign as damaged goods, distrusted by many rank-and-file Populists because of his long flirtation with free silver and Bryan, and by the leaders of the party who had witnessed his seemingly duplicitous course in St. Louis. Davis now surveyed the situation in the Fourth Congressional District, and he seems to have made two calculations. First, he had to show his skeptical Populist constituents that he was truly cleansed of all taint of Bryanism; what better way to do that than to suddenly embrace McKinley? Second, Davis badly needed to attract black Republican votes, which comprised a little over a quarter of his district's electorate. Cooperating *with*

Republicans and *against* Democrats was one way to do this. His calculations made, the Texas Cyclone turned his back on Bryan, whom he later described as "one of the most remarkable and gifted men of the age," and campaigned cynically for William McKinley.[70]

Davis's torturous course of action only underscores the impossible situation in which Texas Populists found themselves in the fall of 1896. Those who admired Bryan or who could not stomach cooperation with Republicans saw the actions of the fusionist leaders as treasonous to Populism. Those who had spent years fighting the Democrats, men who resented the Democrats' sudden embrace of silver or who saw it as a trick to destroy the People's Party, thought it made sense to hold their noses and vote for McKinley if it meant electing Kearby and the Populist state ticket. Individual Populist candidates, like Cyclone Davis and many others, made their own personal calculations about what constituted a sacrifice of principle and whether conditions justified such a sacrifice. What most would not admit at the time, although they all admitted it afterward, was that the Middle of the Road no longer existed. It had been built on a faulty silver foundation in too many states; it had been set on a path to destruction when Taubeneck and his allies gained control of the party apparatus; it had been dealt a mortal blow when the Democrats embraced silver and nominated Bryan; and it had been obliterated when Barney Gibbs's desperate plan to defeat Bryan's nomination in St. Louis failed. Even in the unlikely event that the combined Populist-Republican vote could eke out a narrow win for Kearby and the Texas party in November, it would be a pyrrhic victory, for Populism as a national phenomenon was done, and in the American system, state parties cannot exist for long without a national counterpart.

Still, Texas Democrats were taking no chances. They were no strangers to winning elections through fraudulent means, and most Democrats had come of age believing that in southern politics, where Democratic defeat conjured up the specter of "negro domination" and all its attendant "horrors," the ends justified the means. As the election approached, the Populist leadership publicly raised the question of whether the Democrats would make promises of fair play. Democratic manipulation of the African American vote was so common that it went by the universally understood shorthand label "Harrison County Methods," after the black-majority East Texas county where Democrats openly boasted about their creative methods of suppressing the black vote. Equally well known was the mass manipulation of Mexican immigrant and Mexican American votes in South Texas, a tradition that delivered such huge Democratic majorities, virtually on demand, that it had come to be viewed as an indispensable insurance policy for the Democrats any time their dominance might be threatened. In September Populist chairman Bradley wrote to his Democratic counterpart J. Walter Blake of Mexia, reviewing the Democrats' history of voter fraud and asking that specific state laws designed to curb fraud be scrupulously enforced. After some stonewalling, Blake finally responded by saying that "after a careful examination of our laws relating to the holding of elections . . . I think such an agreement as you suggest is entirely unnecessary because our statutes afford ample safeguards to fully protect the ballot against fraud and to guarantee an honest count and a fair election." Not content to stop with this transparently false statement, Blake went on to lecture Bradley, saying, "You should remember that it is quite a common habit for defeated candidates to charge fraud and unfairness." The message to Populists was clear: be prepared for the worst.[71]

As it turned out, the dirty tricks actually commenced before election day. In a campaign that had featured more than its share of unlikely twists, one final drama remained to be played out. On October 29, four days before the election, the Populist press broke a sensational news story detailing an attempt by the Democrats to bribe lieutenant governor nominee Stump Ashby (plate 27) to resign his candidacy. According to the Populists, Democratic state chairman Blake enlisted the services of a disaffected Alabama Populist named J. R. McMullen to approach Ashby with the offer of $500 to be paid immediately, with another $500 to come, in return for Ashby signing a letter similar to Buck Walton's letter quitting the race and repudiating the People's Party. McMullen brought the $500 in cash to Ashby's hotel room in San Antonio, where the Populist leader was campaigning. Finding Ashby out, McMullen left the cash for him, along with the draft letter he was to sign. Ashby refused to sign the letter and turned the cash over to Populist Party chair Joseph Bradley. Ashby and McMullen both subsequently furnished sworn affidavits to the press testifying to the truth of this version of events, and the Populists deposited the money in a safe-deposit box in Blake's name in the National Exchange Bank of Dallas, along with the letter Ashby was to have signed and McMullen's receipt for the money. Chairman Bradley hastily printed thousands of circulars to be distributed throughout the state, giving details of the plan.[72]

Democratic chairman Blake immediately went to the management of A. H. Belo and Company, the publisher of the Galveston and Dallas *News*, and threatened the papers with a libel suit if they published the story; the Belo papers heeded the warning until several other newspapers had already broken the story. Blake next issued a circular of his own, branding the Populist circular "a falsehood and slander" and warning "all persons whomsoever against circulating said document." But despite Blake's actions, the Democrats struggled to refute the charge. First they sought to discredit the alleged bagman McMullen, claiming that he was a convicted criminal and fugitive from justice in his home state of Alabama. Then they put out a different story, suggesting that McMullen was "a hired tool of Populist leaders," and produced affidavits attesting to conversations in a Dallas hotel bar in which certain Populists had allegedly admitted that it was all part of an elaborate scheme by the Populists to frame the Democrats. The truth of what happened cannot be proven definitively, but the Democrats' shifting explanations, the improbability of such an elaborate frame-up, and the cash and accompanying documentation in the bank all point toward the veracity of the Populists' story. The money remained in the Dallas bank a year later, awaiting Blake's withdrawal, and the Democrats never followed through with their threats of libel suits against the press. In 1898 editor Bill Shaw of the influential Democratic paper the *Texas Farmer* gave yet another version of events, claiming that Blake had indeed offered the $500 to Ashby but explaining that Blake had *believed* Ashby was about to withdraw voluntarily from the race and renounce Populism, and the money was simply a legitimate payment of Ashby's expenses for the remainder of the campaign, a common practice of state committees for high-profile speakers. Not surprisingly, the Populists failed to see the distinction between such a payment and a bribe, and they seized on Shaw's explanation as the final conclusive evidence of attempted bribery. The hostile *Houston Post,* however, probably put it best in an election-eve headline aimed at the Populists but which aptly summarized the entire affair, regardless of party: "Fitting End to a Disreputable Campaign."[73]

On the eve of the election, the anxiety was palpable throughout the vast extent of the Lone Star State. Among Populists there were the usual predictions that the Democrats would try to steal the election. From Cooper, the party's rural stronghold between the forks of the Sulphur River in Delta County, the local Populist editor warned voters: "Pay no attention to lies on the day of the election. You will hear all sorts of stories concerning your candidates, put no faith whatever in them they are all made up and told for the purpose of deluding the voter. Your candidates are all in the field and will all be on the ticket until elected or defeated by the people themselves. Old party methods are and always have been to delude or debauch the voter. Keep a stiff upper lip, vote your self, vote a straight ticket and keep fully in the middle of the road."[74]

Despite such concerns, all sides made the usual predictions of victory, and in an era before polling, the Populists, with Republican help, may well have believed that they would carry Texas. Dallas had been the nerve center of Texas Populism since the party's birth in 1891, and events there on the night before the momentous election revealed the extent of the tension. As night fell, competing rallies attracted huge throngs of people to the downtown streets. Ostensibly the two rallies were devoted to national politics—a free silver Bryan gathering and a "sound money" McKinley event. The Bryan supporters gathered at the imposing red sandstone Romanesque county courthouse, built just four years before, to hear a reading of Bryan's already famous "Cross of Gold" speech. Three thousand McKinley partisans staged an impressive parade up Main and back down Commerce Street, featuring bands, floats, transparencies, and twenty-five hundred torches whose lights created "a phantasmagoria of burning jets that lighted up the whole street and caused huge shadows to dance on the walls of the business blocks." But the McKinley parade and rally also revealed the extent to which the often denied fusion between Republicans and Populists had been accomplished, at least in Dallas. Among the one hundred transparencies in the parade were ones that read "Kearby is for Dallas. Dallas is for Kearby," and "All Dallas for Gibbs independent of politics." The *Dallas Morning News* estimated that twenty thousand spectators—fully half the city's population—witnessed the parade, and noted that "men of all parties were well represented. A populist jostled a sound money democrat and a republican touched both."[75]

Arriving at a speakers' stand, the crowd heard several pro-McKinley speeches, after which "a thousand yells" went up for Populist congressional nominee Barnett Gibbs, who "was received with great applause." Gibbs delivered his speech, largely bypassing the obvious ideological differences between Populists and Republicans, but as he finished a mob from the Bryan rally arrived and raised such a din that nothing from the speakers' stand could be heard. One of the rally's organizers hastily assembled a band of men who charged the mob, cracking a few heads and driving the miscreants from the scene. Calls for Jerome Kearby mounted, and after some delay, he appeared on the stage to the sound of "terrific cheering and yells of welcome."[76]

Populist liberalism was on its fullest display in Kearby's impromptu speech. Referring to members of the mob that had disrupted the rally, Kearby branded them as unpatriotic for their "attempts to repress or suppress free speech." He then turned to the assembled throng and declared, "The men that I see before me here to-night—white and black—are patriots." And lest anyone think

that his reference to the biracial crowd was gratuitous, he castigated the Democratic mob by saying, "That gang of men out there are on a par with that class
of men that burn negroes at the stake," a declaration that was met with "great
cheering." "They constitute the ku klux and the lawless bands of Texas."[77]

Needless to say, Kearby's opponent, incumbent governor Charles Culberson,
did not stand before a throng of Democrats that night and declare black Texans "men" and "patriots," nor did he denounce lynchers as "ku klux and the
lawless bands of Texas." Whatever else Populism may have stood for, whatever
its shortcomings—and there were many—at its best it at least recognized the
fundamental right of all citizens to life and a measure of common respect. On
what would prove to be the party's final night as a political force in America,
Jerome Kearby represented Populism's best.

~

The next morning, November 3, dawned fair and pleasant across the state,
with temperatures climbing into the mid-seventies in most locales, a good sign
for Populists who needed their rural supporters to have dry roads for wagon,
buggy, or horseback trips to the polls. It was the last good sign they would have
that day, as it soon became clear that the Democrats were taking no chances.
Fraud is difficult to document and nearly impossible to prove, especially given
the paucity of surviving Populist newspapers and manuscripts, but the few
extant sources suggest that it was widespread. The experience of A. F. Nash,
Populist nominee for justice of the peace in his southeast Texas precinct, probably was not unique. Nash told of appearing on the streets of Crockett in Houston County to solicit votes and being surrounded by "a mob of 75 or 100 of the
toughs and hoodlums," incited by the local "rotten ring democracy." Rescued
by the town marshal, he narrowly escaped being ridden out of town on a rail or
worse, choosing instead to flee the town. "People may talk of a free country
and a free ballot," he later bitterly complained, "but this does not look like it."[78]

Not surprisingly, African American Populists faced the most concerted—
and the most deadly—efforts to deprive them of their votes. Nowhere in Texas
were they better organized than in Robertson County, the home of John B.
Rayner, in the rich cotton-growing district of the Brazos Valley. There a coalition of Populists and Republicans had for years elected their candidates, including numerous blacks. On election morning armed men began to arrive
in the county seat at Franklin, where they "quietly deposed" the black town
marshal before the polls opened. Forty men armed with Winchester rifles then
stationed themselves around the courthouse, allowing only Democrats to enter to vote. A few miles to the west, a company of black voters had assembled

in the Brazos Bottoms with the intention of marching to Hearne to cast their votes. Accompanied by a brass band, they were accosted on the Little Brazos River bridge by an armed posse of Democrats, who threw the musical instruments into the river and dispersed the marchers. Meanwhile in Hearne "a great number of pistol shots were fired in front of the polls when the negroes from the bottom came in to vote," and as a consequence that box polled six hundred fewer votes than in 1894. Elsewhere in the county, at one heavily Populist box, the election judge reported that "a masked man" took the box and the returns, presumably at gunpoint. In another precinct the Democratic candidates for sheriff and tax collector held off black voters with a gun and a club. At mid-afternoon Democratic county judge O. D. Cannon arrived at the polls in his home precinct with his pistol in his hand. "I went down to the polls and took my six-shooter," he proudly recalled years later. "I stayed there until the polls closed. Not a negro voted. After that they didn't any more in Robertson County." The details of episodes like this virtually never made it into the press. The *Galveston Daily News*'s one line of coverage was typical: "Robertson county seems to have out-Harrisoned Harrison county this year." Texans who followed politics knew precisely what that meant.[79]

More subtle tricks probably accounted for most of the fraud. Among the most common was the manipulation of ballots. Populists alleged that in Fort Bend and other black-majority counties, ballots handed to voters listed the names of the Republican presidential electors and all of the Populist state candidates, with the exception of the line on the ticket where the governor's name went. There Democrat Charles Culberson's name was inserted in place of Kearby's. Only the most careful voter was apt to notice the deception, and illiterate voters stood little chance at all. Jerome Kearby did as good a job as anyone at summarizing the Democrats' methods: "The moment the ring discovered that there was danger they inaugurated a campaign of slander, defamation, intimidation and fraud. The negro vote in many sections was manipulated by fraud, intimidation and open bribery; the ignorant were preyed upon by slander and falsehood; the vicious and purchasable were hired by campaign funds raised to debauch the elector. All manner of devices to deceive, mislead and impose upon the voter were resorted to on election day to compass the defeat of the people's party."[80]

When the votes were counted, Kearby lost to Culberson by a vote of 298,528 to 238,692, and the Democrats swept all statewide offices. We will never know whether fraud was a decisive factor in the outcome. The Bryan-Sewall presidential ticket carried the state with 54 percent of all votes cast, and no Populist congressional candidate won, despite strong showings in five districts. One modern statistical study estimated that forty thousand of those who had supported the Populists in 1894 returned to the Democrats in 1896. Had those forty thousand votes gone to Kearby and *not* to Culberson, it would have been enough to swing the election to the Populist. Despite appeals to African American voters and Populist cooperation with the state Republican leadership, estimates reveal that the official black vote was almost evenly divided between the Democrats and Populists. How many of those black votes were stolen will never be known.[81]

In the weeks and months to come Texas Populists struggled to come to terms with their loss. Many urged a renewed effort to reorganize and reinvigorate the party, arguing that Populists had learned a valuable lesson about the evils of fusion, on both the national and state levels. With Bryan decisively defeated, they believed that the People's Party could return to the "middle of the road" and resume its crusade to bring a new vision of government to America. But many others were not so sure. They knew that the thousands who had followed Buck Walton back into the ranks of the Democrats would never vote Populist again, and the feeling that the People's Revolt was over was palpable. Jerome Kearby no doubt expressed the feelings of many when, six weeks after the election, he wrote, "The opportunity was lost. I trust it may appear again; I fear not. I can afford to speak freely, for I am done with politics."[82]

11 • The Collapse of Texas Populism

Many populists were led to support a democratic ticket one time
but they can never be again.
—Stephen Collier Granberry, 1897

I shall support [Democrat Thomas M.] Campbell . . . because I think he is
the nearest approach to old-time Populism that is now before the country.
—Cyclone Davis, 1906

On March 7, 1897, four days after William McKinley was inaugurated president, forty-nine-year-old Henry Lewis Bentley sat down in his rambling, two-story Victorian house in Abilene, Texas, and composed a letter to the Populist national chairman, Sen. Marion Butler of North Carolina. A university-trained attorney with neatly trimmed dark hair and a dignified goatee, Bentley was the consummate party insider, having managed the party's 1892 state campaign, served on the state executive committee, run for Congress in his home district, and chaired the 1896 state convention. A day-one Texas Populist with Greenbacker and Alliance roots, he had always supported the full Populist agenda. As a delegate to the ill-fated St. Louis convention, he was one of the "Immortal 103" who had opposed fusion with Bryan and the Democrats. A thoughtful, calm, studious family man who would later publish four scientific treatises on native grasses and the restoration of depleted grazing lands, Bentley seemed an unlikely candidate to be fighting for lost causes, notwithstanding his status as a Confederate veteran who had fought under Robert E. Lee. Yet he remained a true believer in Populism, and unlike Jerome Kearby and the thousands of other disillusioned Texas Populists, he thought that if the party would reestablish itself as an independent political entity, standing on the Omaha Platform and repudiating fusion, it could still triumph. "In spite of the complications incident to the campaign of '96," he understatedly explained to Butler, "populism is much stronger in Texas than ever before. If the party shall now show to the voters of the US that it is going to maintain its organization & keep up the fight for its declared principles, we can [win] the fight in 1900. But a half-hearted, wishy-washy policy will disgust self-respecting men who sincerely desire reform. By all means let us get together, *back* in the middle of the road, *& stay there.*"[1]

At the same time that Bentley was beseeching Butler to steer the party back into the middle of the road, another prominent Texas Populist, Cyclone Davis, was actively working with Butler to promote future cooperation with other parties. Butler, of course, had been a leader of the fusionist forces, a man who himself owed his US Senate seat to a statewide fusion between Populists and Republicans in North Carolina. Davis wrote to Butler less than three weeks after Bentley, championing an improbable scheme wherein "the Bryan folks" and the silver Republicans could be persuaded to join the Populists on a pared-down platform featuring the Populist financial plank plus GOP-style protectionism. In this suggestion, Davis again displayed the problems that arise when a lack of fixed political principles meet with self-serving ambition.[2]

Davis stood virtually alone among major Texas Populist leaders in advocating any sort of fusion in 1897, but even *he* publicly had to pay lip service to Midroad principles. Most other Populists who had supported the Bryan fusion in 1896 had already abandoned the People's Party and returned to the Democrats, believing that Bryan had remade the party in a progressive image. Davis would have to push back against other Texans who took the same position as Bentley, including Bentley's two fellow Texans on the Populist National Committee, Harry Tracy and Stephen Collier Granberry. Unlike Davis, these men had never been in favor of fusion with the Democrats. Nor had state chair Joseph Bradley or almost any other major Texas Populist. Yet they believed, as did Davis, that a Populist house divided against itself could not stand.

Tracy, whose capital had maintained the *Southern Mercury* publishing enterprise and whose pen had ably explained and defended the Subtreasury Plan, starkly laid out the party's options in his own letter to Butler. Which was it to be, he asked, "Fuse with the democrats, as we did in the election of 1896, or assent to autonomy and independent existence of our party?" He went on to tell Butler that "if we pursue the former course, we commit suicide; if the latter, according to your own policy and present position, we are mutineers against our party managers." For Tracy this was no choice at all; fusion had to be repudiated. Granberry, who as the manager of Austin's Alliance cotton yard had once been described as a "solid, cool, clear systematic businessman," agreed with Tracy, telling Butler pointedly that "many populists were led to support a democratic ticket one time but they can never be again."[3]

In truth, the events of the previous year had probably shattered the party beyond repair, no matter what strategy Populists pursued. But the fact that Butler and his fellow fusionists controlled the national committee—and hence the principal apparatus of the national party—virtually guaranteed that the People's Party's day as an independent political force was over. The only real source of Midroad strength at the national level was the National Reform Press Association, which had already fractured over fusion prior to the 1896 election, leaving it largely in the hands of Midroaders. The Midroad editors now rallied around their new president, Nebraskan Paul Vandervoort, a former commander of the Grand Army of the Republic veterans' group and a rather shady character. However, the real leader of the Midroaders, in terms of ability and influence, was Milton Park, the longtime editor of the *Southern Mercury*. Indeed, the staunchly antifusion Texans, constantly goaded on by Park and the *Mercury*, proved to be Vandervoort's main source of strength.[4]

When Marion Butler refused to call a meeting of the national committee in the spring of 1897 to begin reorganizing the party, the reform editors called one anyway. It convened in Nashville in July. Most of the leadership of the Texas People's Party initially opposed the meeting, fearing with good reason that it would lead to an open rupture in the national party. John B. Rayner, for example, who arguably had more to lose from the dissolution of Populism than any other major Texas Populist, counseled Butler to treat the Nashville meeting "with silent indifference," advice that Butler heeded. However, when it became apparent that the meeting would take place, most of the Texans decided to attend in hopes of moderating it. Among these was Joseph S. Bradley, the Abilene editor and associate of Henry Bentley. The delegates actually chose Bradley to chair the convention, a decision that party moderates quietly applauded. The influential Indianapolis editor Cuthbert Vincent communicated to Butler his belief that "Mr Bradley is a safe man I think and will be a good man for you to put a good measure of confidence in among the Texans." Hoping to downplay, if not heal, the internal divisions threatening party unity, Bradley and his fellow Texans Bentley, Tracy, and Charles H. Jenkins worked, in Jenkins's words, to give the meeting "a conservative tone." The efforts of Bradley and his colleagues were of course cheered on by the closet fusionist Cyclone Davis.[5]

Their efforts prevented a complete division of the national party, but just barely. The Midroad delegates instead created a so-called national organization committee, which in reality soon became a sort of shadow Populist national committee, with Park as its chair. Over the next months and years Park used the pages of the *Mercury* to assail the fusionists unmercifully, poisoning whatever chances might have existed to reconcile the two factions. Park's brand of Populism, like Cyclone Davis's, had always been tinged with racism and sexism in ways that much of the party avoided. And now that these two men, who were so alike in many ways, found themselves on opposite sides of the Populist divide and their party in crisis, the worst qualities of each man came to the fore. Davis complained bitterly to Butler about Park and the "Mercury crowd," charging that Park and the Midroaders were planning to start a new party in partnership with the nativist American Protective Association. Davis also grew increasingly obsessed with blaming his defeat in the 1896 congressional race on African Americans who voted Democratic, grousing that he wanted to move to "a warm country where the negro is not a factor in politics," later hinting that his choice might be South Africa.[6]

Davis notwithstanding, most Texans remained ideologically in the Middle of the Road as the 1898 elections approached, although they continued to disagree with one another over whether to try to wrest control of the national party away from Butler and the fusionists or to simply make the secession of the Park- and Vandervoort-led Midroaders formal and create a new party. The next act in this intraparty drama occurred in Omaha in June 1898, when Butler finally felt compelled to convene a meeting of the Populist National Committee. The meeting revealed what should have been predictable: Butler and the fusionists remained firmly in control of the party apparatus. In what the *Dallas Morning News* described as a "practical rout" of the Midroaders, the convention retained Butler as national chairman. The only concessions that Bradley, Bentley, Tracy, and the antifusion Texans were able to win were a vague statement opposing fusion and an agreement that the 1900 Populist National Convention would meet at least a month ahead of the two major parties, presumably to prevent a repeat of the 1896 endorsement of the Democratic nominee. (In a transparently fusionist proposal, Butler had wanted the Populists to meet concurrently with the Democrats.) Park's committee of ultra-Midroaders immediately called its own national nominating convention for September 1898, moving the party one step closer to a final rupture.[7]

In the meantime, back in Texas, Populists had a state ticket to nominate and an election campaign to conduct. For the sake of unity, the two wings of the state party sought common ground. Most members favored the renomination of Jerome Kearby for governor, but Kearby, whose health was failing, had made it known that he was not prepared to make another race. Some party moderates pushed the names of Charles Jenkins and Henry Bentley, but they likely would have been unacceptable to the hard-line Midroaders. Some in that faction favored Midroader J. M. Mallett to head the ticket, but Mallett lacked statewide name recognition, and support soon coalesced around Barnett Gibbs, the Dallas lawyer and former Democratic lieutenant governor who had been the Texans' floor manager in the 1896 St. Louis convention. Although he had been a Populist for only two years, Gibbs's wide popularity, political acuity, speaking skills, and personal wealth would enable him to mount a serious campaign.[8]

He had also attracted a great deal of attention in the months leading up to the convention by introducing and vigorously championing a new political cause: the construction of a state-built and -operated "relief railroad" from the Red River to the Gulf of Mexico. The proposal captured the imagination of Populists of all stripes, and it clearly reveals Populists' protoliberal ideas about activist government and the role of the state. All materials used in construction except the iron were to be produced in Texas. It would provide jobs for the unemployed. As Gibbs explained it, the line "would be a cornbread and bacon railroad with no expensive officials, attorneys or lobbyists." Since it would carry only freight and no passengers, the perennial problem of free passes for politicians would be obviated. And most important, operated as a nonprofit public utility whose freight rates would be regulated by law, the railroad would offer competition to commercial carriers, forcing down rates for everyone—an argument that Populists had long made in favor of government ownership of railroads. Indeed, Texas Populists believed that such a state railroad would stand as a model for what could be done on the major national trunk lines to bring down rates throughout the country. It was not a first step toward nationalization of all railroads; if it had been, it might have bolstered the arguments of those who saw Populists as quasi-socialists. Nor was it some harbinger of a system of "regional republicanism," wherein Populists were charting a more humane alternative to large-scale corporate capitalism. Essentially a market-based solution, it simply aimed to counterbalance and curb corporate power with power wielded by the people, which is to say, the voters. The relief railroad became the first plank in the 1898 state party platform.[9]

But the growing rift between Midroaders and those perceived as willing to cooperate with the fusionists in the national party was never far from the surface, and it took herculean efforts to keep these divisions from disrupting the state convention. Two proposed resolutions proved controversial. One endorsed the aforementioned actions of the state's national committeemen at the recent meeting of the Populist National Committee, a meeting that the ultra-Midroaders had boycotted. The other endorsed Milton Park as "president of reorganization of the national populists or anti-Butler party." Neither side could have been pleased with both of these resolutions, inasmuch as they were fundamentally incompatible. But in the interest of unity, both passed. As the nomination proceeded, some offices went to men identified as ultra-Midroaders and others to moderates: among the former, T. J. McMinn—still popular outside of his home region of South Texas—received the nod for the state supreme court; among the latter, Henry Bentley was nominated for state land commissioner. Then came an even more controversial moment: when the delegates were initially unable to agree on a nominee for attorney general, Harry Tracy took the floor and nominated Cyclone Davis for the office. "There was considerable growling over this," the *Dallas Morning News* reported, and it took three ballots for Davis to receive the nomination. Davis, of course, was the bête noire of Park and the Midroaders, and for good reason. Tracy's motives for nominating Davis are not entirely clear. Tracy knew as well as anyone how Davis had played footsie with Butler and the fusionists, how Davis had never been sound on greenback principles or on much else besides the political brand that was Cyclone Davis. Perhaps this sudden Tracy-Davis display of political affection was simply a temporary marriage of convenience; both men were part of the resistance to Park and the radicals, albeit with different ends in mind. Maybe it was simply another part of the campaign for party unity, a show of goodwill toward fusionists. And maybe Tracy thought that having Davis out on the hustings waging a campaign for statewide office would keep him busy and less likely to make mischief for those party leaders like himself who were still desperately trying to hold the party together *and* keep it in the middle of the road.[10]

In any case, it surely helped to accelerate the coming final break between Harry Tracy and his longtime associate and business partner in the *Southern Mercury*, Milton Park. At the Omaha meeting in June, Tracy had been reelected to the regularly constituted Populist National Committee; his acceptance of a place on Butler's committee would have made him anathema to Park, who was in the act of convening a rival Midroad national convention. Three weeks after the state convention, Marion Butler himself traveled to Texas to speak at a large gathering of Populists in Greenville, northeast of Dallas. Sharing the speakers' stand were Barney Gibbs, Jake and Lee Rhodes, Bill Farmer, Stump Ashby, Cyclone Davis, Harry Tracy, and Milton Park. It was likely the last time that all of these old Populist workhorses would share the same stage. When his time came to speak, the dapper US senator from North Carolina disingenuously declared that he opposed fusion and predicted that Bryan will be "politically obliterated" in 1900. He followed this declaration with "a short pause and with a side glance at Milton Park" and then swore to abide by the will of the party. Park knew that Butler's promises were meaningless, since fusionists allied with Butler clearly controlled the regular party apparatus. By engineering the secession of Midroaders from the national party, Park himself had done more than any man to ensure that the regular Populist organization would remain in Butler's hands. But as Park looked around him at the men sharing the platform that night, he would have seen that Butler, as chair of the party's regular national committee, still had far more allies there than he did, including his business partner Harry Tracy.[11]

Gibbs and the Populist state ticket went down in ignominious defeat that fall, polling less than half the vote that the Kearby-led ticket had garnered in 1896. In the meantime Park's splinter convention of Midroaders had met in Cincinnati and nominated a national ticket consisting of Wharton Barker of Pennsylvania and Ignatius Donnelly of Minnesota, hoping to preempt the regular party's actions by nominating a ticket a full two years in advance of the presidential-year election. Three weeks after the defeat in the 1898 state election, Tracy sold the *Mercury* to Park. In a public statement, Park says he and Tracy disagreed on policy but they remained "good friends, just as good friends as ever." If so, their friendship would not last much longer. By the time of the 1900 campaign, Park would be printing inflammatory denunciations of Tracy, such as one that read, "Harry Tracy and Jim Davis have gone back to the flesh pots of Egypt. Goodby, boys, we hope the Democrats will feed you on rotten eggs."[12]

When the Populist state convention met in Fort Worth in May 1900, the divisions that had afflicted the party for the past four years led to a new rupture. While the two warring wings of the state party had striven to paper over their differences in 1898, this time all pretense was cast aside. As we have seen, Tracy, Bentley, Bradley, Granberry, Jenkins, and their allies wanted Texas Populists to remain in the national party, send a delegation to the upcoming national convention in Sioux Falls, South Dakota, and fight for an honorable fusion that would maintain the People's Party as a viable political entity. To Milton Park and his allies, this constituted treason to the Populist cause. As the convention got under way, first Tracy and then Bentley "pleaded, begged, and insisted that they be allowed to explain the situation," but the convention refused to hear them, whereupon Tracy walked out of the convention. He was followed by his fellow national committeemen Bentley and Granberry, state chair Bradley, and a majority of the members of the state executive committee. The bolters then released a public statement charging Park and the Midroaders with seceding from Populism. Many of the Midroaders' backers, the statement contended, were not Populists at all but rather "avowed Socialists" who were "delighted at the victory they gained today."[13]

Whatever his shortcomings as a political strategist, Milton Park proved prescient about the course that the regular Populist party organization would pursue in 1900 under Butler's leadership. If Tracy, Bentley, Bradley, Granberry, and their allies had truly believed they could steer the party back to the middle of the road, they were sorely mistaken. As the 1900 election drew nearer, they found themselves forced to adopt a strategy that involved nominating William Jennings Bryan for president and a genuine southern or western Populist for vice president. Unlike in 1896, however, this time Bryan would be required to accept the nomination in writing, and the Democrats would have to accept the Populist vice presidential choice. In advocating such a plan, the Texans had clearly sacrificed much, but they saw it as the only realistic plan for maintaining a national Populist organization with any meaningful clout in national politics. In their minds, the middle of the road had disappeared, and they were now willing to swallow a fusion plan if it would not completely kill the People's Party.[14]

None of this went the way the Texans had hoped. When the national convention met in Sioux Falls, Bryan, as expected, was nominated by acclamation. But rather than nominate a Populist vice president, the convention nominated a silver Republican, Charles Towne of Minnesota. Much as he had done in 1896, Bryan ignored the Populist nominations, and when the Democrats nominated their own ticket of Bryan and Adlai Stevenson, Towne quietly withdrew, rendering the Populists' actions meaningless. Interviewed after the Populist National Convention, Midroader T. J. McMinn told a San Antonio reporter that true Populists could now say "I told you so" to the "fool fusionists" who had gone to Sioux Falls. "Of course the dupes were spat upon, as we mid-roaders had foretold, and I cannot say their fate was undeserved."[15]

Deserved or not, the fate of the moderate wing of the state party would soon be shared by the Midroaders. When the 1900 state convention met, it consisted only of some 250 Midroaders who nominated Jerome Kearby for governor, with no guarantee that he would accept. He declined, and later party leaders met and hastily replaced him with the likable but erratic McMinn, the San Antonio lawyer whose frustration over voter fraud in South Texas had led him to seek legal action to deny naturalization to Mexican immigrants in 1895. In a humiliating rout, McMinn garnered only 7 percent of the vote. At the state and national levels, Populism was effectively dead.[16]

~

As the People's Party in Texas dissolved into a squabbling shadow of its former self, the state's Democrats struggled to consolidate their power. Although the Populist threat had forced the Democrats to present a united front in 1894 and 1896 lest they lose power altogether, that unity was more apparent than real. The old divisions between the reform and conservative wings of the party, as personified in 1892 by Jim Hogg and George Clark, had never really gone away. The defeat of the Populists in 1896, propitious as it was from the Democratic perspective, only served to highlight two looming problems: Which wing of the party would emerge triumphant in a post-Populist era? And what was to guarantee that there might not be some sort of Populist resurgence, either under the old People's Party name or in some new guise?

The Hogg wing of the party, so dominant in 1890, had suffered from the rise of the Populists, as the People's Party siphoned off tens of thousands of reform-minded voters. If Reform Democrats were to regain that dominant position, they needed to wield the proverbial carrot and stick. For the carrot part of the equation, they needed to find ways to lure old Populists back into the party by promising Populist-style reforms and by negotiating terms under which Populists could honorably return to the Democratic Party. For the stick, they needed to find ways to permanently disrupt the Populist coalition. The challenge, of course, lay in doing both at the same time, for the carrot may not seem too appealing when offered by the hand that has just applied the stick.

In many locales in the years immediately following 1896, these dynamics played out in dramatic fashion. In those counties with a sizable African American population, the first order of business for Democrats was to disrupt local Populist organizations by mounting a concerted effort to end black voting. Here the Democrats had a template for what to do. In a few heavily black counties in the 1880s, biracial coalitions, operating either under Republican, independent, or sometimes even independent Democratic labels, had held power long after the end of Reconstruction, much to the distress of mainstream white Democrats. In one such county, Fort Bend (just west of Houston), local Democrats, under the guise of reform, organized a whites-only Democratic organ-

ization known as the Jay Birds. Their opponents, the entrenched biracial
coalition that included the local black Republican and independent Democratic
officeholders, gained the moniker of Woodpeckers. In 1889, despairing of ever
defeating the Woodpeckers, the Jay Birds mounted an armed siege of the Wood-
pecker leaders in the county courthouse. Gov. Sul Ross called out the state
militia and traveled to Fort Bend himself to negotiate a truce, but when all was
said and done, white-sponsored terrorism paid off, and the county was left in
the hands of the Jay Birds, who instituted a whites-only Democratic primary.
Most of the Woodpeckers fled the county. Democrats in neighboring Wharton County soon followed suit, eschewing the colorful name for a label that
more clearly indicated the nature of the organization; they called themselves
the White Man's Union. A few other Black Belt counties experimented with
white man's unions (or associations) in the mid-1890s, but in most places the
vitality of Populist organizations led to a *competition* for black votes between
Populists and Democrats rather than efforts to disfranchise them. Still, the
White Man's Union and a whites-only Democratic primary, backed by the implicit threat of violence, offered a potential model for other counties to follow.[17]

In the years after 1896, that is exactly what they did. With Populism now
greatly weakened, Democrats gradually concluded that black disfranchisement
held the key to the permanent defeat of Populism and the corresponding return of one-party Democratic rule at the county level. In 1898 white man's
unions (or in some cases, simply the regularly constituted county Democratic
Party) began promoting the exclusion of African Americans from county and
municipal Democratic primaries. They did so by portraying the move as a progressive, "good-government" reform aimed at ending corruption in local government and also ending voter fraud, which many whites blamed on blacks
or on other whites who manipulated the black vote. Here the motives of Democrats become complicated. In those counties where Populist or Populist-
Republican biracial coalitions had operated successfully in the 1890s, the white
primary aimed to pull enough of those coalitions' white voters away from Populists and back into the Democratic ranks to ensure victory for the Democrats. In counties where Populism had never been strong, conservative
Democrats—often of the planter class—had frequently held power through
their control of the black vote, either by effectively utilizing the power of patrons over dependents or by more blatant means of coercion or fraud. In either
case, Democrats claiming to be progressives stood to benefit by consolidating
all white votes under a new whites-only Democratic banner.

Using the handful of counties that had pioneered the idea in the late 1880s as models, in the years after 1896 county after county in regions with significant black populations witnessed the creation of white man's unions or primaries or both. Sometimes a county's white man's union conducted elaborate public relations campaigns to persuade voters to adopt a whites-only primary. In other places the county Democratic executive committee voted to simply close their party's primary to all but whites, requiring voters to pledge, "I am a white democratic voter" in order to cast a ballot. Both approaches proved effective. A partial list of counties where white primaries were created between 1897 and 1902 includes Bell, Dallas, Jackson, Grayson, Robertson, Milam, Burleson, Kaufman, Trinity, Rockwall, Houston, Harrison, and Gonzales. In some cases the white primary began in individual municipalities, as witnessed by its adoption in Beaumont, Houston, Mexia, Waxahachie, Hillsboro, Commerce, Temple, and Terrell. As early as July 1900, a Tyler newspaper reported with satisfaction that "the white primary appears to have been a winner all over Texas. Self-respecting people have endorsed it everywhere." Press coverage virtually never included accounts of the terrorism that sometimes accompanied black disfranchisement.[18]

In some cases white Populists were so demoralized over the events of 1896 that they simply accepted the proposition that a whites-only Democratic Party would bring reform. In these instances, their former black allies made for convenient scapegoats. Even before the fateful 1896 election, Milton Park had sounded the warning to African Americans, saying that "the negroes are miserably to be blamed" for letting Democrats steal or manipulate their votes. "If the negro does not qualify himself to be a freeman, and act like one," Park predicted, "the American people will become so thoroughly disgusted with this sort of thing after a while, that they may rise in their might and take the ballot away from him. Therefore, let the negro consider and be forewarned." At the time Park wrote these words in May 1896, Populists had desperately been trying to win black votes, and with the popular Jerome Kearby at the top of the state ticket, many African Americans enthusiastically supported the party. Four years later, though, growing numbers of previously sympathetic Populists were prepared to embrace disfranchisement. In April 1900 the party standard-bearer from the 1898 state election, Barnett Gibbs, pronounced his support for the white primary. His statement is worth quoting at length:

In Texas there can be but one white man's party and any of the numerous reforms needed will have to come from tickets selected in white primaries. The large negro vote traded in the State—one election to populists and the next to democratic leaders—forces the white voters into one primary to prevent the negro vote from having the balance of power. In some Southern states this vote has been disfranchised by conventional requirements; in this State by white primaries. Four years ago it was traded to populist leaders by republican leaders and not all delivered, because such leaders sold a large part of it to democratic leaders. Two years ago it was traded to democratic leaders solid, there being no other bid. Without white primaries this vote will be a menace to good State government based on issues presented, and can be fixed by the corporations and trusts to subserve their purposes. The white primaries eliminate it and force all State and county reforms to be sought there. There is no other escape in Texas.[19]

Gibbs and Park notwithstanding, there remained Populists, white and black, who refused to surrender to the Democrats or to the rising tide of white supremacy. Eight counties sent Populist state representatives to the 1897 legislature and six to the 1899 body. These included some East Texas districts where race would figure in major ways. By 1901 only one Populist, Benjamin A. Calhoun of Nacogdoches County in the Piney Woods, represented his party in the statehouse, and Edward Tarkington of Lavaca County would hold the distinction of being the final Populist legislator, elected in 1903.[20]

~

Even as the party seemed to be ebbing away, however, a few of the old People's Party strongholds continued to elect sheriffs, judges, clerks, and other local officials, much to the distress of Democrats eager to retake the reins of local power. In such places white Democrats frequently resorted to terrorism to rid their towns or counties of the stubborn Third-Party affliction. A practice known as "whitecapping" was typically employed where African Americans were a relatively small percentage of the population. It generally involved threatening blacks' lives unless they left the neighborhood, town, or county. For example, in 1898 in Bosque County south of Fort Worth, whitecappers posted a notice throughout the county that read: "Penalty, Death. To Mr. Nigger: All niggers in Meridian had better leave Meridian by July the 15th. If you don't leave, there will be a hot time. White Kaps." Whitecappers rarely revealed their motives, and clearly some instances were not directly related to politics. Nevertheless, in the immediate years after 1896 the practice proliferated, with cases reported in all parts of the state. Nor were African Americans the sole targets; in Atascosa and Caldwell Counties, Mexicans and Mexican Americans received whitecap threats. From the town of Lockhart in the latter county, a correspondent reported that "The Mexican population in the vicinity are terrorized, and do not know what to do."[21]

After a few years, the sort of ethnic cleansing envisioned by whitecappers provoked a public backlash, if only because it threatened the supply of cheap labor needed on farms and plantations. In the old North Texas Populist stronghold of Wise County, the local newspaper editor declared, "A large per cent of the negroes of Decatur are peaceful, industrious and law abiding. They have their rights as other human beings have. To drive them from the town, to make them give up their homes and sacrifice their property would be a deep-dyed wrong against humanity. Besides, they are useful. If they were gone many of our people would be very greatly inconvenienced. . . . The attempt of the whitecaps to cause a general exodus of the negroes by threatening letters is ill advised and wrong."[22]

On at least one occasion, in the southeast Texas town of Orange, the governor actually dispatched Texas Rangers to suppress whitecappers, but in most cases perpetrators went unpunished. Finally, in 1899, the state legislature felt compelled to take action, passing a bill making it a felony, punishable by two to five years in prison, for anyone to "post any anonymous notice or make any threats or signs, or skull and crossbones, or . . . by any other method post any character or style of notice or threat to do personal violence or injury to property on or near the premises of another . . . with the intention of causing such person to abandon such premises or precincts, or county."[23]

Even as the legislature debated the antiwhitecapping bill in the spring of 1899, events in one Texas county were about to demonstrate the lengths to which white Democrats would go to put down the Populist threat once and for all. Grimes County, a black-majority plantation county in the rich Brazos Valley northeast of Houston, had been a banner Populist county, sending Populists to the legislature and controlling the entire county government since 1896. There the local People's Party organization was led by Sheriff Garrett Lane Scott, a longtime resident and former Greenbacker. Scott could count as allies several prominent African American leaders, and Scott won their allegiance by treating black citizens fairly, a reputation made manifest by his employment of several black deputy sheriffs. Despairing of ever regaining control of the county, white Democrats in mid-1899 secretly organized a White Man's Union, modeled on those in some neighboring counties. The Union soon inaugurated a covert campaign of terror, paying midnight visits to the farms of black Populists and persuading many to give up on their political activism.[24]

By the beginning of 1900 the White Man's Union was strong enough to go public, and as the 1900 elections approached, it threw a series of elaborate public barbecues and rallies, attracting thousands of white citizens. It made no pretense about what its goals were: the elimination of African Americans from the county's politics. The White Man's Union openly applauded the methods used in a recent mayoral election in neighboring Bryan, where armed white Democrats had mounted a "show of force" and prevented blacks from voting. At one rally in Navasota, listeners applauded the reading of original poetry, one verse of which asserted,

> Twas nature's laws that drew the lines
> Between the Anglo-Saxon and African races,
> And we, the Anglo-Saxons of Grand Old Grimes,
> Must force the African to keep his place.

As these events unfolded, the campaign of violence and intimidation against African Americans accelerated. In July one of Scott's principal black allies, Jim Kennard, was gunned down in broad daylight on the main street of Anderson, the county seat. The assassin was alleged to be the Democratic candidate for county judge (and Union member) who had been defeated two years earlier. A few weeks later another leading black Populist, Jack Haynes, was killed by a shotgun blast while working on his cotton farm. Soon a black exodus from the county was under way. When election day arrived, the efficacy of the Union's work was apparent: from 1898, when 4,500 votes had been cast countywide, the vote now had declined to a mere 1,800. The Populists polled only 366 votes. In one heavily Populist precinct in south Navasota, the Third-Party vote dropped from 636 to 23.

Populism was destroyed in Grimes County, but for the triumphant Democrats, whose reign of terror had succeeded so dramatically, a landslide at the polls was not enough. The hated Garrett Scott was still sheriff until his term officially ended, and even after the new Democratic sheriff took his place Scott would still be in the county, a living symbol of the despised Third Party and a potential thorn in Democrats' sides. On the morning after the election, heavily armed members of the White Man's Union quietly began arriving at the county courthouse in Anderson. Shots were soon fired, and Garrett Scott's brother was killed. Scott himself was badly wounded in the hip. Retreating to the jail across the street from the courthouse, Scott and his deputies fought back, thus beginning a four-day-long siege of the jail by the White Man's Union members ensconced in the second floor of the courthouse. The siege came to an end only when a female relative took the train to Austin and demanded that the governor act. Troops were finally dispatched from Houston, a cease-fire was negotiated, and Scott, whose wound had developed gangrene, was placed on a mattress and loaded into a wagon. Several other wagons containing Scott's large extended family and all their worldly possessions joined the heavily guarded procession and were escorted from the county, never to return. Scott later sued the White Man's Union in federal court, prompting the Union's local officials to file murder charges against *Scott* in hopes of forcing his return to the county, where he almost certainly would have been convicted or killed, or both. Neither the lawsuit nor the spurious murder charge succeeded, and Scott died of his wounds four years later. Fully one-third of Grimes County's African Americans left the county over the next decade.[25]

~

If the stick in the carrot-and-stick approach of the Texas Democrats toward Populists was violence and a vicious white-supremacy campaign, then a promise of a renewed Populist-style reform agenda was the carrot. At the turn of the century, with the People's Party having siphoned off so many of the state's reform votes, the conservative wing of the Democratic Party had emerged triumphant at the state level. The first two governors of the new century, Joseph D. Sayers (1899–1903) and Samuel W. T. Lanham (1903–1907), were the last two Confederate veterans to hold the office, and both represented the traditional antigovernment, antitax, antireform style of southern Democratic politics. This wing of the party had little interest in courting former Populists. A party test banning all voters who had not voted a straight Democratic ticket in 1896 helped to keep former Populists on the sidelines in the 1898 primaries.[26]

Into this situation stepped the imposing figure of James Stephen Hogg. Ever since leaving office in 1895, the former governor had watched with dismay as Populists claimed the mantle of reform in Texas, and now he intended to do something about it. In 1900 Hogg introduced three reform measures, all aimed at his old nemesis the railroads. The Texas Railroad Commission, founded by Hogg in the early 1890s to regulate the railroads, had enjoyed only limited success, and now the ex-governor proposed constitutional amendments banning bankrupt corporations from conducting business in the state, keeping corporate money out of politics, and banning free passes for politicians. Milton Park's *Southern Mercury*, which for the past four years had angrily

spurned all overtures of Democrats toward Populists, came out enthusiastically in favor of the Hogg Amendments.[27]

Among the problems that Hogg and his reform-minded supporters faced
was the fact that their conservative opponents, aided by the machinations of
the wily wire-puller Col. Edward House, had mastered the art of manipulating the Democratic primaries in favor of the conservatives. The Hogg forces
gradually came to understand that electoral reforms would be necessary if the
reformers were to ever regain the ascendancy. In this realization they found
ready allies in Populists, who had long called for a "free ballot and fair count"
and who had themselves suffered from manipulation of the electoral process.
Hogg and his allies campaigned successfully for a relaxation of the rules keeping ex-Populists out of the Democratic primaries, and they also made the
adoption of a uniform statewide primary a cause célèbre. Encouraged by these
displays of good faith, many Populists swallowed their pride and returned to
the Democratic Party.[28]

In 1902 electoral reform took two forms: a poll tax amendment and the uniform statewide primary. Populists had steadfastly opposed a poll tax throughout the 1890s, but now they saw it as one important tool in cleaning up
government. Thanks to the White Man's Union and the local white primary,
black disfranchisement was already a fait accompli in much of the state, and
in most places the wedge had already been driven between white Populists and
their erstwhile black political allies. Seen by many Populists as an offer of fair
play by the Reform Democrats, the poll tax would deal a final blow to the conservative planters who marched their black tenants to the polls and to the party
bosses who otherwise manipulated and stole black votes. It would also serve
as a de facto system of voter registration. With the proceeds of the tax ear-
marked for education, some Populists no doubt saw it as a win-win proposition. Many Populists opposed it (correctly) on the grounds that it would
disfranchise many poor white farmers or on general grounds of justice and
constitutionality. As the editor of a Granbury Populist paper stated, the amendment "strikes at the foundation of civil liberty and our boasted constitution,
wherein it says that 'All men are created free and equal.'" The amendment's
prospects were bolstered, however, by the support of Cyclone Davis and Stump
Ashby, who now found themselves joined by Milton Park of the *Mercury*. In
the fall referendum it passed handily.[29]

The emerging coalition of ex-Populists and Reform Democrats did not
muster enough votes to capture the governor's office in 1902, but it did elect
enough legislators to ensure the enactment of their other major electoral

reform, the uniform state primary. In 1903 the legislature passed the Terrell Election Law, which set primaries for late July, when most farmers could participate, and guaranteed a standardized, secret ballot. A subsequent amendment to the law in 1905 added even more safeguards insuring the integrity of the voting process, albeit for a much-circumscribed electorate. The Hogg Amendments reining in the railroads still could not muster the legislative votes to secure their passage, but the enactment of these electoral reforms both signaled the arrival of the new reform coalition and further helped to augment it.[30]

Playing a key role in the reconstitution of the old 1890 Hogg coalition was a new farmers' organization. Founded in East Texas in 1902 by former Populist editor and Alliance organizer Newt Gresham, the Farmers' Educational and Cooperative Union of America—usually just called the Farmers' Union—was essentially the Alliance reborn. Like the Alliance, it promised to be nonpartisan, but it was clear that members were serious this time about not getting the organization involved in partisan politics. That said, their political orientation became fairly obvious when, in 1904, the Farmers' Union hired Jim Hogg as its lobbyist before the Railroad Commission. By 1905 the Union boasted 100,000 members, and, like the Alliance back in 1890 when Hogg was running for governor, it was a force that politicians ignored or alienated at their own peril. Former Populists active in the Farmers' Union included its founder, Isaac Newton Gresham; former Populist legislators Peter Radford (who was later a president of the Union), Lee Lightfoot Rhodes, Van Buren Ritter, and William Bye Whitacre; and former state executive committeemen William E. Moore, Samuel J. Hampton, and D. Evans Lyday (who was also a president of the Union). With farmers once again organized, the days of conservative Democratic dominance in Austin were numbered.[31]

In 1906 the reform forces nominated East Texas attorney Thomas Mitchell Campbell, a protégé of Hogg and a thoroughgoing progressive. Stump Ashby and Cyclone Davis endorsed him, with Davis calling Campbell "the nearest approach to old-time Populism that is now before the country." Backed by Hogg and no doubt bolstered by members of the Farmers' Union, Campbell swept to victory in a crowded Democratic primary field. In legislation that harkened back to the Alliance's 1886 Cleburne Demands, the legislature that convened the following year banned speculation in agricultural futures and gave farmers tax relief at the expense of banks, railroads, and other corporations. A state Department of Agriculture was created, and the Hogg Amendments cracking down on railroad abuses finally became law. The Campbell administration is remembered today as arguably the most progressive in the state's history.[32]

~

Among the legislators assembling in Austin in 1907 for that reform-minded legislature was a twenty-nine-year-old second-term state representative from remote Gillespie County in the Texas Hill Country. Cheered on by his Populist father, young Sam Ealy Johnson Jr. had also been encouraged to run in 1904 by his father *and* by his brother-in-law Clarence Martin, who had defeated Sam Sr. for the seat in 1892. Martin, whose politics apparently had moved considerably to the left since the 1892 race, told Sam Jr. that the "issue in the election . . . was 'whether the principles and tradition of a Republic shall be longer perpetuated, or whether we shall meekly surrender to the great trust combines the interests of the nation.'" In 1907 Sam Jr. enthusiastically supported Campbell's progressive legislative agenda, and before his career in the legislature was over, he had supported bills regulating utility rates, establishing a pure-food standard, levying a franchise tax on corporations, creating a juvenile court system, regulating the sale of securities, and establishing the eight-hour workday for railroad workers. He authored a bill that appropriated an unprecedented $3 million for drought relief and another that secured $65,000 for the state to purchase the Alamo property. During Campbell's 1906 campaign Sam had met a young Austin woman, Rebekah Baines, and when the 1907 session was over, the couple were married in Fredericksburg. A year later Rebekah gave birth to their first child, Lyndon. Like Stump Ashby, Harry Tracy, and so many of his father's other Populist comrades, Sam Jr. was now a Democrat, but the Populist heritage survived in Sam's belief that government's role was to help people help themselves, and that certain widely shared public problems demanded public solutions, especially in a modern capitalist society where unchecked corporations tended to exploit the people. Those fundamental beliefs would live on in his son, who sixty years later would find himself in a position to use them in fashioning what he termed a "Great Society."[33]

Conclusion · Toward Liberalism

Some [men] are whigs, liberals, democrats, call them what you please. Others are tories, serviles, aristocrats, &c. The latter fear the people, and wish to transfer all power to the higher classes of society; the former consider the people as the safest depository of power in the last resort; they cherish them therefore, and wish to leave in them all the powers to the exercise of which they are competent.
—Thomas Jefferson, 1825

The jig is up. The cat is out of the bag. There is no invisible hand. There never was. If the depression has not taught us that, we are incapable of education. . . . We must now supply a real and visible guiding hand to do the task which that mythical, non-existent invisible agency was supposed to perform, but never did.
—FDR advisor Rexford Tugwell, 1933

We must either protect labor or labor would be enslaved completely.
—US congressman and former Populist Joe Eagle, 1935

This is a book about Populism, and in looking at the People's Revolt in Texas, it argues that the movement constituted the first widespread elaboration of the major political ideas that later constituted twentieth-century liberalism. That said, this is not a book about twentieth-century liberalism. Few topics in American historiography have inspired such a large, diverse, sophisticated, and contentious body of published works, and the numerous scholars who have produced those works have rarely agreed even on a definition of modern liberalism, much less what its antecedents were. I have chosen to utilize a rather ecumenical definition of modern liberalism, fully understanding its limitations. I have defined liberalism as a coherent democratic ideology that seeks to promote life, liberty, and the pursuit of happiness. To achieve these ideals, it respects the rule of law and seeks to guarantee the rights of individuals, including their rights to join with other individuals to secure collective economic rights. It accepts capitalism as an economic system; however, it recognizes that concentrated power, in the form of an oppressive state *or* unrestrained corporations, threatens these ideals. Therefore it proposes to empower citizens, acting through their democratic institutions, to place restraints on that concentrated power. Liberalism requires compromise, and it exists in a perpetual state of creative tension between those policies that promote the common good and those that protect and encourage the pursuit of individual interest.

Scholars and other students of American history have generally identified three major landmarks in the development of twentieth-century liberalism: progressivism, the New Deal, and the Great Society.[1] No two observers agree entirely about the origins of these three movements, their essential natures, or their relationships to one another. The most basic common denominator was their willingness to exert state power in new and expansive ways in order to protect the rights of ordinary Americans and to share the benefits of corporate capitalism more equitably. This basic characteristic, I have suggested, they owed largely to the influence of Populism. But drawing a straight line from the Populists to the progressives to New Dealers and beyond quickly becomes problematic.

For its part, progressivism presents a problem because it differed from Populism in so many ways. First, progressivism took place across party lines; there were progressive Republicans, progressive Democrats, and third-party progressives. Moreover, the movement was characterized by what one historian termed a "vexatious variety": it stretched over a twenty-year period; it took place at the federal, state, and municipal levels; and it had a strong social component, as evidenced by the settlement house movement, education reforms, and the rise of social work as a profession. It had a decided urban and middle-class tilt to it, and in many ways it was elitist and even antidemocratic. It was usually overtly racist. As one perceptive modern scholar of progressivism, Sheldon Stromquist, notes, progressives believed that "neither individuals acting collectively nor the government acting through 'class legislation' should alter the fundamental structures of social power and property. By seeking to reinvent a society in which class had no enduring place, Progressives . . . lay the foundation for twentieth-century liberals' inability to see the world around them in class terms or conceive of social remedies that altered the social structures of class power." In this view, which dominated the scholarship on progressivism from the end of World War II into the 1980s, progressivism comes off as considerably more conservative, more elitist, and less egalitarian than Populism.[2]

That said, progressives did share one fundamental belief with Populists: a hostility to laissez-faire that manifested itself in a willingness to use the power of the state to counter the excesses of corporate capitalism. Theodore Roosevelt's efforts to combat the trusts, tame the political influence of corporations, and give new protections to workers, and Woodrow Wilson's large-scale federal planning and management of the economy during World War I, were made possible at least in part because of the ground that had been plowed in the 1890s by Populists, whose platforms had made such statist solutions a regular part of the national political dialogue. In other words, Populism had normalized anti–laissez-faire and made it a legitimate position for debate, a necessary precondition for the reforms of the Progressive Era. At the federal level, the Pure Food and Drug and Meat Inspection Acts (1906), the Hepburn Act regulating railroad rates (1906), the Federal Reserve Act (1913), the Clayton Antitrust Act (1914), and the constitutional amendments providing for the direct election of senators (1913), the graduated income tax (1913), and woman suffrage (1920) all constituted major achievements on which later liberalism would be built. They cannot be dismissed just because they lacked the class-based radicalism that many reformers at the time and since believed were necessary. Populists in the 1890s had championed most of these solutions, even while pressing for more thoroughgoing changes speaking the language of class in ways that progressives found antithetical. As political scientist Elizabeth Sanders has argued, "Most of the national legislative fruits of the Progressive Era had their unmistakable origins in the agrarian movements of the 1870s, 1880s, and 1890s," origins that she explicitly describes as "the afterlife of populism." Historian Robert McMath concurs, stating that "we may profitably view the entire period from the 1870s to the 1910s as a 'long agrarian moment' during which a populistic spirit and agenda always had to be reckoned with in the South."[3]

With some notable exceptions, as we will see below, the progressive impulse had largely run its course by the 1920s, at least at the national level. Though in many ways a progressive, Herbert Hoover famously campaigned in 1928 on a platform praising "Rugged Individualism" and promising "adherence to

the principles of decentralized self-government, ordered liberty, equal opportunity, and freedom to the individual." When the Great Depression swept the
Democratic Party back to power in 1933, relatively few of the old progressive
leaders had much of a role in shaping the New Deal order. Indeed, many of
them considered its redistributionist inclinations and its perceived pandering
to interest groups a dangerous betrayal of progressivism's attachment to individualism, a viewpoint that, as Otis L. Graham Jr. notes, only underscores "the
inherent conservatism of the predominant forms of progressive action."[4]

As for the New Deal itself, its chronological distance from the Populist era,
which meant that relatively few actual Populists were still alive and active, and
the massive changes that the country had undergone in the three ensuing decades, make it even harder to trace direct connections between the two reform movements. Furthermore, the New Deal itself was so far-reaching,
complicated, and often self-contradictory that Americans at the time and
scholars since have struggled to understand or even adequately describe it. If
Populism, as I have argued, developed a coherent ideology, and if the New
Deal, by contrast, was (in the words of Richard Hofstadter) "a chaos of experimentation," then any effort to trace some sort of actual intellectual lineage
from one to the other seems a dubious enterprise.[5]

Where, then, does this leave the Populists? How do we assess their role in
the construction of the circuitous course that American liberalism took in the
twentieth century? Definitively answering this question would require another
book, one more complicated than this one. With that admission, it still seems
worth the effort to provide a cursory examination of the paths taken by former Populists in the twentieth century and tentatively to suggest some of
the ways that the People's Revolt influenced the course of the modern liberal
project.

~

Like any great collective trauma, the collapse of the People's Revolt affected
its adherents in different ways. Some, like Jerome Kearby, simply gave up. Announcing that he was "done with politics" shortly after his defeat in the 1896
governor's race, the charismatic attorney died of kidney disease in 1904. Some,
like the indefatigable Henry Bentley, clung to the wreckage of Populism long
after it should have been clear that the movement was over. As late as 1908,
Bentley was serving as the self-appointed president of the National Federation
of People's Party Clubs and corresponding with Georgia's Tom Watson about
how best to resurrect the party. As late as 1915, a Texas newspaper article reported that he had "never voted in a democratic primary since leaving the party

thirty years ago" and that "he still claims to be a populist." Bentley, who had begun his career in independent politics in Austin in the 1870s defending the right of black and white workingmen to serve on juries, was never able to make his peace with the Democrats, although he surely agreed with many of their more progressive policies.[6]

More than a few of the party's radicals took the defeat of the People's Party as their signal to join the state's small but growing socialist movement. Of these, most came from the labor wing of the People's Party. Lee Rhodes, who had sat in the 1895 legislature, and his brother Jake, who had established a "Populist Institute" in East Texas, helped to found a Social Democratic Party in 1900, only to have the state's existing Socialist Labor Party bitterly denounce it as "the residual legatee of moribund Populism." The Rhodeses' party later morphed into the Texas Socialist Party, and one or the other Rhodes brother would be nominated for statewide office on its ticket in 1904, 1906, and 1908. As late as 1928 and 1930 Lee Rhodes would still be running for governor on the Socialist ticket. William E. "Bill" Farmer, the prominent Populist and Knights of Labor leader, chaired the 1902 Socialist Party state convention, and J. B. Gay, the Colorado County planter, state executive committeeman, and son of the respected female Populist leader Bettie Gay, likewise became a social-ist, as did the German American Populist leader E. O. Meitzen. At the height of the Socialist Party's influence in Texas, in 1910 and 1912, the former Baylor University president and Populist congressional nominee Reddin Andrews re-ceived the party's gubernatorial nomination. These high-profile ex-Populists-turned-socialists notwithstanding, one is struck not by how many former Populists turned to socialism but by how relatively few of them did. Although the Socialists briefly surpassed the Republicans as the state's second party in 1912 and 1914, at its peak the party never polled more than 12 percent of the statewide vote. If the Socialist Party had constituted a rebirth of the People's Party, it stands to reason that it would have polled a more robust vote. If the examples of the Rhodes brothers, Farmer, and Meitzen are instructive, then the more likely conclusion is that many of the ex-Populists who became so-cialists had always been more socialist than Populist. They certainly had little patience with what they considered to be the watered-down reforms and middle-class sensibilities that constituted progressivism.[7]

Not all old Populists, however, held the new progressive movement in such low esteem. A few of them, unwilling to cast their lot with the socialists but also unable to stomach the Democrats, found Theodore Roosevelt's brand of progressive reform attractive. Noah Allen, the Galveston attorney who had been a delegate to the Populist national conventions of 1892 and 1896 and a congressional nominee in 1896, moved to Houston around the turn of the century and won election to a local judgeship as a Roosevelt Republican. He later moved to Brownsville, where he ran for Congress as the GOP nominee and served as an assistant US attorney. But through it all, Allen retained an independent streak, and in 1912 he supported Roosevelt's third-party bid on the Progressive Party ticket, a move that cost him his federal appointment. Two years later the state's Bull Moosers nominated him for the state supreme court. Another old Populist, the Lamar County Alliance and People's Party leader James Washington "Buster" Biard, claimed to be a Populist long after the party had ceased to exist, but like Allen, he gravitated to the Bull Moose banner in the 1910s.[8]

Nevertheless, it remains true that for the vast majority of the Texans who voted the People's ticket in the 1890s and who wished to continue the fight for political reform in the new century, the progressive wing of the Democratic Party was the only viable option. For a more representative example of what became of former Populists politically in the years immediately following the People's Revolt, one might turn to the case of Charles H. Jenkins (plate 28). Jenkins in many ways could be considered the quintessential Texas Populist. He grew up and was educated in Dallas, where as a young man he served as city engineer. He soon turned his attention to the law, however, and in his mid-twenties he moved out to the west-central Texas town of Brownwood. He joined the Greenback-Labor Party in 1880 and went on to edit a Greenback newspaper, sit on that party's state platform committee in 1882, and serve as one of its presidential electors in 1884. He supported the various independent movements of the late 1880s and joined the People's Party as soon as there was a People's Party to join. He quickly became one of its highest-profile leaders. Over the next several years he represented his district on the state executive committee, including a stint as party chairman; served as a delegate to Populist national conventions of 1892 and 1896; ran twice as his district's congressional nominee, losing by only four hundred votes in 1894; and in 1898 accepted the party's nomination for state attorney general.[9]

Almost everyone—even his political opponents—liked and respected the courtly Jenkins. A civic leader in his adopted hometown, he served as alderman and mayor. In the 1880s he worked to negotiate a settlement between large ranchers and landless cattlemen in the so-called Fence-Cutting Wars in his home county. For twenty years he sat on his local school public board, serving as president for fourteen. He was also president of the local board of trade, vice president of the local fair association, trustee of Daniel Baker College, and an incorporator of the Texas Semi-Centennial Exposition. Like so many Populists, he belonged to the theologically liberal Disciples of Christ denomination; after his death a local newspaperman who had known him described him as "a free thinker." Although the historical record is mostly silent on his racial views, at least once he was a featured speaker at a Juneteenth celebration, where he shared a stage with a black minister. He always ably and vigorously defended his party's positions on the stump and in print, and did so with great dignity, leading one admirer to report that in a debate in his first congressional race he was "as gentle as a woman." In 1900 a Democratic editor paid him an extraordinary compliment by declaring that "Col. Jenkins is the cleanest public man the populists have in Texas since the death of Judge Nugent." Throughout the 1890s, when the party needed someone to explain Populist monetary policy, advocate for government ownership of the railroads and telegraph, or otherwise spread the Populist orthodoxy, Jenkins was always a popular and effective choice. At the 1896 Populist National Convention, along with Kearby, Ashby, Gibbs, Bentley, Rayner, and a handful of others, he fought the valiant— but ultimately losing—fight to keep the party in the middle of the road.[10]

Like many Populists, Jenkins remained faithful to the party until it was clear to him that it was irretrievably gone. But in 1900 he published an open letter explaining why he planned to vote for William Jennings Bryan and the Democrats that year. "I do not say that [the Democratic] platform comes up to the full standard of Populism," he wrote. "But the Democrats' embrace of free silver, their declaration against banks of issue," their recognition of "the sovereign power of the government to issue money," their endorsement of the direct election of US senators, their repudiation of "militarism and imperialism," and their adoption of the initiative and referendum were cause enough to support Bryan. Jenkins even believed that the Democratic Party's "declaration against trusts if honestly adhered to will lead it to government ownership of railroads and telegraphs." In short, though still a thoroughgoing Populist in his beliefs, Jenkins concluded that the newly progressive Democratic Party deserved a chance. If the election of 1896 had set in motion a realignment of American politics, as many scholars claim, then Jenkins stands as evidence of that realignment. In 1906, running as a Democrat, he won a seat in the state legislature and, as detailed in the preceding chapter, played a prominent role in perhaps the most reformist legislature in the state's history. Jenkins served two terms and then resigned to accept an appointment as associate justice of the Third Court of Civil Appeals, a position to which he was elected three more times. In 1915 he played a leading role in the state campaign for woman suffrage, and in 1916 he unsuccessfully sought the nomination for chief justice of the state supreme court. For several years in the 1920s he served as chair of a state commission charged with revising and codifying the laws of Texas, and in 1928, at age seventy-six, he was reelected to his old legislative seat, just in time to see the nation plunge into the Great Depression. He died in 1931, just missing the chance to watch Franklin Roosevelt launch the New Deal.[11]

Jenkins's story is recounted here not so much because of the details of his career as a Populist and then a progressive Democrat but because of what it tells us about the memory and the impact of Populism in the twentieth century. In 1914, shortly after Jenkins's first stint as a Democrat in the Texas legislature, the eminent University of Texas historian Eugene C. Barker, assisted by state librarian Ernest William Winkler, undertook to complete and publish a massive compendium of Texas history and biography begun by the late Frank W. Johnson some years earlier. Among the hundreds of biographical sketches that Barker and Winkler wrote for the multivolume work was a seventeen-hundred-word sketch of Jenkins. After presenting the facts of Jenkins's early life and education, the sketch devoted some eight hundred words to his career as an engineer, lawyer, and civic leader. Then, with scarcely a pause, the sketch segued to his election to the 1907 legislature, with another three-hundred-plus words detailing his career as a Democratic legislator and jurist. There is no hint of Jenkins's twenty-year career as a Greenbacker, independent, and Populist. It is unclear what sources Barker and Winkler used in drafting the sketch, but in a sense it matters little. Whether they solicited biographical details from Jenkins himself (which seems most likely) or relied on published sources or testimony of people familiar with Jenkins's life and career, Populism had been written out of the script entirely.[12]

Similarly, as Jenkins prepared a run for the state supreme court in 1916, the Austin Statesman prepared a feature on him bearing the headline, "C. H. Jenkins Is a Progressive in Democratic Politics." This was true enough, but the story misleadingly reported that "he was a member of the State platform committee at the State Conventions of 1896 and 1898" and "an alternate delegate to [the] Democratic National Convention" in 1896. "Since Bryan made his first race for the Presidency . . . Judge Jenkins has been associated with the progressive branch of the Democratic party." Of course, this was hogwash, and Texans who had followed state politics in the 1890s certainly would have known it; Jenkins was a dedicated Populist and not only a delegate to the *Populist* conventions of those years but Populist nominee for state attorney general in 1898. His years as a Populist are never mentioned in the story.[13]

A few years later, in the early 1920s, Jenkins himself had occasion to write a brief account of his political career. The precise circumstances behind the autobiographical sketch are not known, and it survives only because a Brownwood newspaper published excerpts from it two decades later. But Jenkins's choices about what to include and exclude are again instructive. "I was born a Democrat which means, if it means anything, that my father was a democrat," he began. "I voted for General Weaver in 1890 [James Weaver was actually the Populist presidential nominee in 1892] because I believed in full legal tender of paper money. . . . I was opposed to the demonetization of silver. I advocated the free coinage of silver, and believed in the quantitative theory of money as advocated by William Jennings Bryan. I have not changed my views as to those matters." In this account, Jenkins was willing to acknowledge only those elements of Populism that became popular with the advent of Bryan, and he entirely avoided mentioning the People's Party or Populism by name. The sketch then grows curiouser: "Beginning with 1888 I was a member of every Democratic precinct and Brown county Democratic convention, and of my state Democratic convention until I went on the bench at Austin in 1910, and thereafter without my solicitation I was elected to and attended all state Democratic conventions except two until I resigned from the Court of Civil Appeals. . . . I was a member of the platform committee . . . in the state conventions of 1908 and 1910, and also of the state conventions to select delegates to the St. Louis convention that nominated Alton B. Parker. . . . I was and am in favor of the United States becoming a member of the League of Nations. I believe that Woodrow Wilson was a wise statesman."[14]

Whether or not Jenkins's listing of 1888 as the starting date for his career as a Democrat was purposeful or just a typographical error, in this account Jenkins again chose to downplay his long career as a major third-party leader and emphasize his loyalty to the Democrats. If history is written by the victors, as the maxim attributed to Winston Churchill claims, then in the case of Populism those victors appear to have received a significant assist from the vanquished. Still, in Jenkins's case, as in those of many other Populists, the political realities of his post-Populist career remain indisputable: Jenkins remained a staunch champion of progressive causes, pushing the Democratic Party in directions that harkened back to Populist doctrine. The man who in 1894 had declared that he had "never been frightened by that scarecrow, strong government" never surrendered his belief "in a government strong enough to protect the lives, liberty and property of its citizens." Yet Jenkins was no radical—indeed, he was in many ways the very embodiment of the establish-

ment, a veritable pillar of his community to whom his fellow citizens repeatedly turned for civic and political leadership. Still, his prominence testifies to
the lasting influence of Populism on American politics, even when that influence may not be obvious to the casual observer.[15]

~

We do not know how many Charles Jenkinses there were in American politics in the decades following the collapse of Populism—that is, how many
actual former Populists continued to play an active role in political affairs and
successfully pushed elements of the Populist agenda. But the available evidence
from Texas suggests that there were more than a few who followed that trajectory. Stump Ashby, for example, moved sometime after 1902 to the Oklahoma
Territory, where he became president of his local Farmers' Union and then won
election to the newly created state's first legislature, eventually serving three
terms and aligning himself, according to his biographer, with the "progressive, social justice wing of the Democrats" in that state. S. O. Daws, whose work
as the Alliance's first "traveling lecturer" had saved the Alliance in 1884, also
moved to Oklahoma, where he became the president of the territorial Farmers'
Union. After statehood he served as Oklahoma's first state librarian for several
years but remained politically active as a Reform Democrat and was frequently
spoken of as a candidate for governor. In 1909 he was considering a run for
that office as an independent, but the state's primary rules kept him off the
ballot. Lewis N. Barbee, who represented Freestone County in the 1893 Texas
legislature and worked effectively to build a biracial Populist coalition in his
home county, likewise ended up serving in the Oklahoma legislature during
the Progressive Era. Barbee's Populist colleague in the 1893 legislature, Benjamin A. Calhoun of Nacogdoches, won a second term in the Texas House as a
Populist in 1900 but later served two terms in the 1910s as a progressive
Democrat. Former Populist state executive committeeman Charles K. Walter
served with Charles Jenkins in the reform-minded Thirtieth and Thirty-First
Texas Legislatures. James Madison Perdue, the principal author of the Cleburne Demands and one of the People's Party's most influential leaders, also
served two terms in the state legislature in the 1920s. The twentieth-century
careers of Jenkins, Ashby, Daws, Barbee, Calhoun, and Walter all seem to lend
credence to the observation made by historian Rebecca Edwards, that "for many
reasons, it makes sense to think of the Populists as early Progressives."[16]

Two prominent Texas Populists were destined to play roles on the national
political stage in the Progressive Era, and their stories are instructive. As we
have seen, Cyclone Davis had always been a rather singular figure among Texas

Populists. After the defeat of Populism, he held back from formally returning to the Democratic Party, choosing instead to endorse the Prohibitionists. But in 1906, like Charles Jenkins, he supported the candidacy of progressive Democrat Thomas Campbell for governor, declaring him the best available alternative to Populism. By 1912 Davis had formally returned to the Democratic Party and campaigned for Woodrow Wilson. In 1914 he finally realized his long-running ambition of becoming a congressman, winning Texas's sole at-large seat in the House. In Congress he enthusiastically supported farm legislation, including the landmark Hollis-Lever Federal Farm Loan Act, child-labor legislation, the Bankhead-Shackleford Federal Road Aid Act, funding for river and harbor improvements, a workman's compensation bill, and an unemployment insurance measure. When World War I began, he opposed America's participation and even introduced a bill—which, not surprisingly, went nowhere— "to draft millionaires' money as well as men in time of war."[17]

Davis's career as a progressive congressman proved short-lived; he was defeated for reelection in 1916. This time he could not do as he had done in his two failed congressional bids in the 1890s and blame his defeat on African Americans, since blacks in Texas had long since been effectively disfranchised by means of the poll tax, the white primary, violence, and intimidation. But Davis, in ways unmatched by virtually any other Populist or ex-Populist, remained a confirmed white supremacist, and if anything, his racism grew more virulent as the years passed. When the second Ku Klux Klan rose to prominence in Texas in the 1920s, he joined the order and became one of its most vocal defenders. "Thoughtful men," he intoned in one characteristic 1923 statement, "are now seeing the day in the not far distant future when the Jew and the Catholic, the negro and the alien enemies in our country will march in a solid column to the ballot box to take this country from the control of real Americans." Along with his famous counterpart in Georgia, Tom Watson, Davis and his twentieth-century racism, nativism, anti-Catholicism, and anti-Semitism did much to create the popular association of Populism with right-wing demagoguery. That Davis was nearly alone among major Texas Populist leaders in following this course has been largely lost to history.[18]

To place Davis in perspective, however, it is useful to examine the career of the other ex-Populist who went on to represent Texas in the US Congress. Joe Henry Eagle (plate 29), who had been the Populist congressional nominee in the Houston district in 1896 and 1898 (and chaired the 1898 state convention), returned to the Democratic Party after the turn of the century and won a seat in Congress, serving from 1913 to 1921. During his stint in the House, which overlapped with Davis's sole term, he championed the eight-hour workday for employees of interstate carriers, supported early efforts to create a system of unemployment insurance, and fought for appropriations to improve rivers and harbors. Like Davis, he strongly advocated affordable credit for farmers, which led to the passage of the Federal Farm Loan Act of 1916. He was instrumental in securing the Ellington Field air base for Houston and won a $4 million appropriation to deepen and widen the Houston Ship Channel. He was, by all accounts, a good progressive.[19]

But Eagle's career, in and out of politics, departed in significant ways from that of Davis. Davis always remained well outside the political establishment in Texas and grew more eccentric as the years passed; a 1922 *Austin Statesman* article aptly referred to the famous ex-Populist as a "political freak." By contrast, after the People's Revolt, Eagle was welcomed back not only into the Democratic Party but also into the mainstream of the social and business worlds of Houston. As a young lawyer he went into practice with the Houston attorney and timber magnate John Henry Kirby. He went on to represent the Kirby interests as they expanded into banking, railroads, and oil, and in 1919 Eagle proudly referred to the millionaire Kirby as his "best friend." He named one of his sons for Kirby. Both men were active in the Houston Yacht Club. Eagle's progressive Wilson-era congressional stint notwithstanding, he would seem a poor candidate for the "liberal" label, much less a champion of the common man.[20]

But Eagle never forgot his Populist roots. At the height of the Ku Klux Klan's popularity in 1922, he took a public stand against the hooded order, helping to spearhead a statewide effort to run an independent candidate against Klansman Felix Robertson in that year's Democratic US Senate primary. His biographer declared that he "vehemently condemned religious intolerance." A decade later, in January 1933, with the country in the grip of the Great Depression, he won reelection to his old House seat in a special election. He took office just as Franklin D. Roosevelt was preparing to launch the New Deal. For the next four years he supported Roosevelt's far-reaching plan to save the banking industry, restore business confidence, rescue agriculture, and provide relief to the millions of unemployed and destitute. Many of the major pieces of legislation in the New Deal's First Hundred Days passed on a voice vote, but on virtually every measure for which the yeas and nays were counted—the Agricultural Adjustment Act (AAA), the Tennessee Valley Authority Act (TVA), the National Industrial Recovery Act (NIRA), and others—Eagle voted with the president.[21]

Nor did Eagle's support of the new activist state cool after FDR's First Hundred Days. In 1934 he voted for the act that created the Securities and Exchange Commission, giving the federal government the first real power to regulate securities trading. The following year he helped to pass the Emergency Relief Appropriation Act, which among other things enabled FDR to create the Works Progress Administration (WPA), the Rural Electrification Administration (REA), the Public Works Administration (PWA), and the National Youth Administration (NYA). In April 1935 he voted for the landmark Social Security Act. Many of these bills, of course, garnered near-unanimous support from Democrats, but others were more controversial. The Public Utility Holding Company Act of 1935, an antimonopoly measure sponsored by his Texas colleague Sam Rayburn, either broke up or regulated large utility holding companies. It proved to be a bridge too far for eleven members of the Texas House delegation, but not for the old Populist. Perhaps the most telling sign of his enduring Populistic vision, however, came that same summer, when Congress debated the National Labor Relations Act, popularly known as the Wagner Act after its sponsor, Sen. Robert F. Wagner of New York.[22]

The Wagner Act embodied much of the spirit of the Populist labor platform. For the first time at the federal level, there would be meaningful legal guarantees of the right of workers to organize and collectively bargain. It prohibited unfair practices on the part of employers seeking to block unionization and provided a mechanism, the National Labor Relations Board, for enforcing its provisions. One leading historian of the era has called it "perhaps the most important law passed in the 1930s." In its codification of collective economic rights, it stands as arguably the most significant single departure in American history from Hoover's vaunted ethos of "rugged individualism."[23]

When the Wagner Act came to the floor for debate, Eagle publicly declared that he supported it "unreservedly" and "with all of my heart." A simple choice, he explained, confronted each representative: "He is either for giving bigger and bigger unreasonable dividends to capital at the expense of those who toil or he is in favor of taking care of the proper rights of those who toil before the larger dividend is passed on to capital." The Wagner Act actually passed the House by a voice vote, but individual legislators—especially those from the South—still had to face down serious opposition from conservative opponents of the legislation. Eagle learned this when he received a letter from an important constituent, Raymond E. Powell, the superintendent of Humble Oil's refinery outside Houston, bitterly complaining about Wagner's allegedly socialistic bill. Eagle, who sat on the House Labor Committee, not only answered Powell's letter but took the unusual step of entering the full text of his response into the *Congressional Record*. Eagle began by reassuring Powell that "every vote I have cast here has shown that I would not overtax and never confiscate capital or property. They show that I recognize as fully as any man living that our capitalistic system is the best system ever devised." The former Populist wanted it understood that he was no socialist. He then went on to voice a full-throated defense of the New Deal, pointing out that the administration's "first acts were to save the banks, the railroads, the building-and-loan companies, the insurance companies, and all legitimate big business enterprises." But no sooner had the New Deal saved capitalism, he argued, than an army of at-torneys and lobbyists had descended on Washington, "trying now to make us stop the new deal so that they can again make peons out of producers and make slaves out of labor." In language straight out of the 1890s, Eagle vowed that "we must either protect labor or labor would be enslaved completely." He passionately, if carefully, explained to the oil executive the need "to preserve minimum wages, maximum hours, the right of collective bargaining," and "the continued abolition of child labor." "I want to fix it so that labor must be treated with human justice by those who will otherwise oppress it, and so that [the] producer is not robbed for the benefit of manufacturer or anybody else. Then we will have justice and general prosperity and universal buying power, with consequent happiness in the land." Eagle closed his letter by saying, "Mine is an awful responsibility, Mr. Powell. If I could look at matters as a poli-tician, thinking first of myself, I would have far less trouble." He expressed the hope that "this does not result in any breach between you and me . . . but I must follow the right as I see the right." Near the end of his time in Congress, the American Federation of Labor gave Eagle a perfect score for his voting record on legislation that it deemed important.[24]

Nor was Eagle's liberalism restricted to labor issues. When he gave up his House seat to run for the US Senate in 1936, he ran on a platform supporting more generous old-age and veterans' pensions, unemployment insurance, ap-propriations to fight agricultural pests, and funding for the improvement of ports and waterways. Against the opposition of local heavyweights Jesse Jones and W. P. Hobby, he successfully rallied public opinion in Houston in favor of the city's participation in a PWA-sponsored public housing program.[25]

Eagle also supported a more progressive taxation system. In 1935 FDR called on Congress to enact a graduated corporate income tax, a tax on inheritances, and an increase on the personal income tax rate to 79 percent. As the bill was making its way through Congress, a constituent wrote to complain about it, and Eagle wrote (and published in the *Congressional Record*) a response that sounded very Populistic, very liberal, and very modern. It is worth quoting at length:

> To run the Government requires revenue, and that can only be raised by some form of taxation. I can assure you from long personal experience that each time any class are proposed to be taxed they assure the House and Senate that they cannot stand such taxation, that it is confiscatory, that it will ruin business, that their class are already overburdened while the other classes are not, and that such proposed taxation will result in their letting out men. . . . I think the sound principle is this: Taxation should be levied on the basis (1) of ability to pay, and (2) of benefits received on account of government. Applying those two simple fundamentals, my own conviction is that—granting money must be raised now by taxation—those who have vast or large or even considerable incomes net after all expenses and taxes and losses and depreciations can far better afford to pay than those who have not a dollar of fixed income. It is either to tax those who have the ability to pay or put a sales tax on the struggling, striving, disheartened masses on the necessities of life. As between these two extremes, I am never going to favor a sales tax.[26]

This same constituent likewise complained about FDR's "Brain Trust," the small group of Ivy League academic advisors who helped the president frame early New Deal policy. In their own time, the Populists' opponents had branded them as hicks and hayseeds, and in the twentieth and twenty-first centuries Populism became associated not only with demagoguery but also with anti-intellectualism. Eagle's reply to his constituent suggests the opposite:

> You speak of "brain trusters" somewhere in your letter. Of course, that is a term of opprobrium placed upon everybody connected with the new deal by the old thieving, reactionary gang that had been in power through the Republican Party for the previous 12 years. . . . Of course, also, if Roosevelt had put Wall Street men, representing Wall Street selfish financial interests, in all these departments, as his advisers, then that would have been all right with Wall Street and its kept press. But when he thought in terms of the general welfare and the common good and put in patriots in those capacities to help him who were not worshiping the golden calf, it became the unpardonable sin. I have never even met or come into contact with those the reactionary press has called "brain trusters." But I do think they have done a good job.[27]

But of course agriculture was the area of public policy most likely to capture the attention of a former Texas Populist, and Eagle, whose district was
primarily urban but relied heavily on the processing and transportation of cotton and other crops, devoted much of his energy to it. In 1933 he had supported the AAA, which paid farmers to take land out of production. He did so
as an emergency measure, believing that the nation was "within 30 days of a
bloody revolution." Emergency or not, he later declared that he did not regret
his vote. But the processors and distributors, who had suffered from the reduced volume of crops under the government's program, could not have been
satisfied with that vote. In 1935 Eagle proposed his own farm bill aimed at
addressing the supposed deficiencies of the AAA and a related bill, the Bank-
head Act. In the 1890s, Populists like Eagle had always argued that underconsumption, not overproduction, caused low crop prices. Eagle's legislation
would actually increase subsidies for farmers but would place no limits on
production, although only 40 percent of a farmer's crop would be eligible for
the subsidy. The plan was to be paid for by a broad-based "processing tax" on
"the whole American people," rather than the tax on processors themselves
under current policy. His bill, he argued, charted a middle course between
"two extremes—unlimited production, untaxed and unregulated, on the one
hand, which has ruined and will continue to ruin the producer; and, on the
other hand, a continuation of present policy which injures every branch of the
cotton industry except the producer."[28]

When the Supreme Court heeded the arguments of the processors and distributors and ruled the AAA unconstitutional the following year, Eagle had
further motivation to push his plan. Instead, Congress hurriedly passed substitute legislation, the Soil Conservation and Domestic Allotment Act, which
preserved many of the features of the AAA. Knowing that Congress's legislation was a stopgap measure, Eagle made his own plan a centerpiece of his race
for the US Senate, touting it as "a permanent program to maintain the cotton-
producing industry on a sound basis." The former Populist lost the Senate race,
and his bill never became law (Congress successfully enacted a new AAA in
1938 that passed constitutional muster), but his actions further indicate that
his Populist-inspired belief in an activist government remained alive and well.
Although his alternative to the AAA certainly would have helped the agricultural middlemen in his Houston district while still protecting producers, he
argued that it also would have addressed one of the principal flaws in the 1933
AAA (and, it turned out, in its 1938 successor): the AAA disproportionately
helped the large operators, often at the expense of small farmers and especially

tenants. In Eagle's words, the AAA had been injurious "to every other branch of the cotton industry—the cotton picker, the ginner, the transportation, the compressor, the warehouseman, the cotton merchants, and the innumerable laborers, clerks, and services connected with one and all of those branches." Whether his solution would have proven more egalitarian than the AAA, or even practicable, remains an open question. But what was not in doubt was the old Populist's continuing devotion to using government to help the people. As one New Deal scholar has put it, "In its basic farm legislation, the New Deal was, in effect, urging the farmer to participate in, rather than resist, the development of a collectivistic or organizational type of capitalism, a development that had started in the urban business world in the nineteenth century." Eagle had been part of that nineteenth-century world, an advocate of what Populists then had called "business methods" in government (because citizens, wielding the levers of government, needed to learn the power of collective effort, as business had). As a Populist he had discovered in the 1890s what Rexford Tugwell, one of the Brain Trusters whom Eagle admired, enunciated in 1933—that Adam Smith's theory of unfettered individualism in the marketplace working as an "invisible hand," magically regulating free markets, was unsuited for the modern world of corporate capitalism. As Tugwell so colorfully put it, "The jig is up. The cat is out of the bag. There is no invisible hand. There never was. If the depression has not taught us that, we are incapable of education. Time was when the anarchy of the competitive struggle was not too costly. Today it is tragically wasteful. It leads to disaster. We must now supply a real and visible guiding hand to do the task which that mythical, non-existent invisible agency was supposed to perform, but never did. . . . Laissez-faire exalted the competitive and maimed the cooperative impulses. . . . We are turning our back on the policeman doctrine of government and recapturing the vision of a government equipped to fight and overcome the forces of economic disintegration."[29]

~

Of course no one could argue that either progressivism or the New Deal rested entirely on the shoulders of actual ex-Populists like Eagle. Their numbers were already dwindling by the Wilson era, and only the youngest of them, such as Eagle, were still alive and politically active when FDR launched the New Deal. For Populism to have been anything other than a political aberration, an irrelevant movement that was ahead of its time, Populist *ideas* would have had to survive into the new century and be taken up by new generations of politicians. Tracing the genealogy of political ideologies or even of specific policies is always a challenging and inexact art. True, an individual political thinker's intellectual influences may be relatively easy to document. We know that Thomas Jefferson had studied the writings of various European Enlightenment figures and read the pamphlets from the seventeenth-century British Whig opposition. Lincoln had admired the antebellum Whig leader Henry Clay. FDR's liberalism bore the imprint of his cousin Teddy and his own experiences as a progressive political figure in the Wilson era. But relatively few politicians, and even fewer members of the public, devote much time to reading treatises on political philosophy or studying political history. Clearly, political ideas enter the public consciousness in less direct, or at least less apparent, ways.

One did not have to be a Populist to have become familiar with Populist ideas and to have been influenced by them. The careers of three Texas Democrats whose careers began in the Progressive Era and continued into the 1960s illustrate this point. Sam Rayburn, born in 1882, was too young to have been politically active during the heyday of Populism, but he grew up in northeast Texas where the movement had been strong. As his biographers state, "Through the period of Rayburn's boyhood, Texas's political thinking was strongly colored by the agrarian radicalism most colorfully exemplified in the populist movement." As a youth, Rayburn actually idolized the Democratic firebrand (and nemesis of Populists) Joseph Weldon Bailey, who, despite his well-deserved reputation for demagoguery, in his early career supported silver coinage, the progressive income tax, and railroad regulation. Elected to the state House in 1906 at the age of twenty-five, Rayburn served with Sam Ealy Johnson Jr., son of the old Populist, and both men sat in the famously progressive Thirtieth Texas Legislature, where they, along with ex-Populist Charles H. Jenkins and a majority of the House's Democrats, supported strengthening the state's antitrust law, banning free railroad passes for public officials, insuring bank deposits, and limiting working hours for railroad, telephone, and telegraph employees. Rayburn later served one term as Speaker of the state House, then won election to Congress. In the Wilson era he ardently supported the federal income tax amendment, the establishment of the Federal Reserve System, the passage of the Clayton Antitrust Act, and the creation of the Federal Trade Commission. He sponsored a bill to grant the Interstate Commerce Commission the authority to regulate the issuance of railroad securities and served as floor manager for a bill that gave insurance to soldiers for the first time.[30]

By the time Franklin Roosevelt took office in 1933, Rayburn had risen to the chairmanship of the powerful House Interstate and Foreign Commerce

Committee. From that position he played a key role in the passage of the Public Utility Holding Company Act, the Emergency Railroad Transportation Act, the Rural Electrification Act, and the legislation that created the Securities and Exchange Commission and the Federal Communications Commission. As majority leader starting in 1937, he was instrumental in shepherding much of the remainder of the New Deal through the House. Elected Speaker in 1940, he remained among the two or three most powerful men in Washington until his death in 1961. Although he was a pragmatist and has been described more as a "middle-of-the-roader" than a true liberal, he clearly believed in the constructive use of governmental power, particularly when it meant protecting common folk from exploitation by corporations. The influence of the People's Revolt of the 1890s on his political outlook was unmistakable.[31]

The career of Congressman Marvin Jones, born the same year as Rayburn (1882), tells a similar story of agrarian roots producing a lawmaker with progressive leanings. Jones grew up Cooke County in North Texas, where he heard his father complain that "the financial structure of this country is geared to the needs of industry and business" and not to the particular requirements of agriculture. Although not a Populist, his father argued that farmers and ranchers needed a separate credit structure, the same conclusion that Populists had reached when they championed the Subtreasury Plan. Moving to West Texas, Jones ran successfully for Congress in 1916 on a platform calling for government loans for agriculture and support for Woodrow Wilson. Appointed to the House Agriculture Committee, he became an expert on farm programs in the 1920s, and by 1931 he had risen through the ranks to become the committee's chair. Although Jones, like Rayburn, probably thought of himself as a pragmatist if not actually a conservative, he nonetheless enthusiastically embraced the New Deal's farm programs, including the Emergency Farm Mortgage Act and the Farm Credit Act of 1933, both of which he played a major role in drafting. Speaking in the small Texas Panhandle town of Pampa shortly after FDR's First Hundred Days, he contended that "the issuance of currency must be taken from the hands of 'international bankers'" and that "the solution must be public ownership of banks," positions that easily could have come from the mouth of a Populist in the 1890s. As the Dust Bowl grew worse, he fought hard for drought relief funds for hard-stricken farmers. As in the case of Rayburn, for Jones it seems clear that coming of age hearing the debates of the Populist era made it easy for him to embrace an activist government.[32]

Younger than Jones or Rayburn, a third twentieth-century Texas congress-man, Wright Patman, displays many of the same career patterns. Born in 1893 in Cass County in the far northeastern corner of the state, Patman, ac-cording to his biographer, was "schooled in the Populist tradition of protest." He was raised in the Primitive Baptist Church, a religious tradition that had nurtured many Populists, and when he won election to the Texas House in 1920, he found himself sharing a desk with Sam Ealy Johnson Jr., who surely regaled him with stories of his own Populist father. After two terms in which the main public issue was the resurgent Ku Klux Klan (which Patman, like Joe Eagle, staunchly opposed), Patman spent four years as a district attorney before winning election to Congress in 1928. In his election campaign and early congressional years he sounded many Populist notes, criticizing the con-centration of wealth, praising the common man, crusading against trusts, and championing the payment of a long-promised bonus to World War I veterans.[33]

As with Rayburn and Jones, Patman favored virtually all of FDR's New Deal agenda and cosponsored the Robinson-Patman Act of 1940, which prohibited anticompetitive pricing practices by large retail chains. He played a key role in creating the modern system of federal credit unions as a working person's alternative to banks, a cause that Texas Populists had championed in the 1890s. After World War II he sponsored the legislation that created the Small Busi-ness Administration. In what was perhaps his most Populistic crusade, he called for full government ownership and control of the Fed, and from his perch as chair of the House Banking Committee he strove for years to rein in large national banks. He was one of the first congressmen to call for an inves-tigation of the Watergate break-in. In his 1976 obituary the *New York Times* wrote, "To Wright Patman, the root of all evil was the concentration of eco-nomic power in the hands of a small number of bankers, business executives and government officials. He spent his life trying to expose the evils and re-strict the power, and his record contained many successes and many failures." It could have been the obituary of an 1890s Populist.[34]

Patman, Jones, Rayburn, Eagle, Jenkins, and countless other reform-minded politicians in the early twentieth century joined a national Democratic Party that itself had in large measure been remade in a Populist image. Most Texas Populists in 1896 had fiercely resisted the ill-fated fusion with the Bryan Demo-crats, and they rarely hesitated to remind their fellow Populists that Bryan was no Populist. Yet, even William Jennings Bryan had been schooled in the political ideas of the People's Revolt. As a young man in Nebraska he aligned

himself politically with the Farmers' Alliance, although as a lawyer he was ineligible for membership. In early 1890, before the birth of Populism in the
state, Bryan decided to run for Congress as a Democrat. That July, Nebraska
Alliancemen did create the People's Independent Party, and when Bryan failed
to dissuade the new third party from fielding a candidate in the race, he strove
successfully to position himself as an agrarian candidate. He thundered against
the trusts, championed free silver as a means of helping debt-strapped farmers, and proposed to ban nonresident aliens from speculating in land. Indeed,
as his recent biographer notes, "Nationalization of the railroads was the only
major Independent plank on which Bryan was silent." Of course Bryan never
endorsed the Subtreasury Plan or greenbackism either; to have done so would
have rendered him unacceptable as a Democratic candidate at the state or national level. Still, his embrace of many Populist planks in 1896 cost him the
support of the conservative wing of his own party, contributing heavily to William McKinley's victory. So tainted with Populism was Bryan that even the
reform-minded Princeton professor and lifelong Democrat Woodrow Wilson
could not bring himself to vote for the "Great Commoner" in 1896. Bryan, and
the Democratic Party that he led for the next twelve years, went on to support
the income tax, fairer labor laws, antitrust action, direct election of US senators, the initiative and referendum, civil service reform, and other Populistic
causes. Years later, Bryan himself even came out for government ownership
of the railroads, which was in some ways the banner Populist reform and certainly one of its most controversial. So great was the political shadow cast by
Bryan that as the New Deal took shape in 1933, none other than Herbert Hoover
branded it as "Bryanism under new words and methods."[35]

The influence of Bryan over the twentieth-century Democratic Party was
so great that some political scientists consider the 1896 election the catalyst
for a major national political realignment. They argue that the election marked
the shift of the Democratic Party from a conservative, probusiness, laissez-faire
party to a progressive or liberal party willing and ready to use the power of
government to promote opportunity and equality. For these realignment scholars, the influence of the Populists looms large. Political scientist E. E. Schattschneider was perhaps the first to propose that 1896 constituted a major
realignment of the national party system. He explicitly argued that the realignment resulted first "from the tremendous reaction of conservatives in both
major parties to the Populist movement," and second from the takeover of
the Democratic National Convention by "William Jennings Bryan and his

supporters" who "negotiated a Democratic-Populist fusion and nominated Bryan for the Presidency on a Populist platform."[36]

Of course many prominent twentieth-century progressives and liberals arrived at their ideological destinations without having been actual Populists like Charles Jenkins or Joe Eagle, or having come of age in an environment where agrarian protest had been strong and had driven the political debate, as did William Jennings Bryan, Sam Rayburn, Marvin Jones, and Wright Patman. Certainly neither Theodore Roosevelt, scion of a privileged New York City family, nor Woodrow Wilson, who spent the 1880s and 1890s at places like Johns Hopkins, Cornell, and Princeton, ever personally knew many Populists or heard many Populist stump speeches. Progressivism in the early twentieth century sprang from many sources, of which Populism was only one. Indeed, some historians now properly posit that there was no one thing called "progressivism" but rather multiple "progressivisms," and it remains true that while many progressive measures—the graduated income tax, direct election of senators, the initiative and referendum, and others—can trace their origins to Populist and Bryan-Democrat reforms, progressives like Teddy Roosevelt, William Howard Taft, and Wilson were often far less willing to flex the muscles of the national state than Populists were. Most notably, these progressives largely sought cooperation between big business and government, with publicity, mediation, and regulation the first steps in dealing with monopolies, and resorted to "trust-busting" only when other remedies had failed. Roosevelt, for example, famously declared that only "bad trusts" needed to be broken up—a far cry from the Populists' plans for a major restructuring of the nation's monetary, banking, transportation, and communication systems. Progressivism, as we have already noted, was also much more urban and middle-class than Populism, and its reforms often were aimed not so much at achieving social justice as quelling disorder and forestalling more radical remedies. On race, most progressives were unequivocally unprogressive, often embracing the latest junk science to justify overtly racist policies. On women's rights, however, they at least partially lived up to their label, supporting the successful push for a national suffrage amendment, a cause that many Populists had championed.[37]

Despite a policy legacy that seems to indicate an intellectual debt that the latter movement owed to the former, many progressives would have vigorously disputed any political or intellectual kinship with Populists. And yet, apart from the well-known national progressive legislation of the early twentieth century, some of the more far-reaching protoliberal Populist ideals survived in an unlikely and decidedly unsexy place: the United States Department of Agriculture (USDA). Starting around the turn of the century, accelerating in the 1910s, and continuing in the 1920s even as the rest of the progressive agenda waned, a quiet revolution of sorts—a revolution owing much to the People's Revolt—was taking place in the halls of the USDA and in the land-grant colleges, state legislatures, and countless farm communities that it served.[38]

If Populists had accomplished nothing else, they had awakened politicians of both parties to the existence of a large and potentially dangerous (in a political sense) bloc of voters, the nation's farmers. With Populism defeated, or at least suppressed, in the years after 1896, elected representatives in Washington pursued measures to help the long-beleaguered agricultural sector. They were pushed in doing so by farmers themselves, who had learned a thing or two about organization over the past several tumultuous decades. In Texas, for example, the Farmers' Union, composed largely of former Alliancemen and Populists, grew into a formidable voting bloc whose interests could not easily be ignored. The Union soon spread beyond Texas, and groups like it flourished in many parts of the country. The national economy improved somewhat in the years after 1896, but farmers often saw little of the alleged return of prosperity. In Texas and the Deep South, in fact, a dire new danger emerged with the appearance of the boll weevil, which devastated the region's cotton crops even as prices began to improve. Over much of the western part of Texas, another severe drought, coming on the heels of years of overgrazing, dealt ranchers a new blow.[39]

Remedies seemed available. In 1887 Congress had passed the Hatch Experiment Station Act, by which the USDA could provide federal funds to the states to conduct agricultural research. Land-grant colleges such as Texas A&M, with their existing agricultural departments, were the main means by which the state programs were implemented. Beginning around the turn of the century, the experiment station system and support staff in the USDA itself grew steadily. It could do so in an era when "limited government" had supposedly triumphed with the election of McKinley because of the federalistic nature of the program. Under the Constitution, states still had far more sweeping powers—if they chose to use them—than the federal government did, so funneling federal funds for agricultural research and education to states and counties was both constitutionally feasible and politically wise, as it served both to address farmers' issues *and* to steer them away from more radical solutions.

In an early example of this new federal concern for farmers, just outside the west-central Texas city of Abilene the USDA in 1898 established a Grass Experiment Station, intended to do research on how to improve the drought-ravaged and overgrazed pasturelands of the region. Two USDA scientists from the agency's Division of Agrostology traveled from Washington to oversee the leasing of a 640-acre tract and to design the experiments. Then the USDA appointed Henry Lewis Bentley, the longtime Populist leader, as "special agent in charge of grass experiments" to oversee the effort. The university-educated Bentley (plate 30) was another of Texas Populism's Renaissance men, having fought for the Confederacy, practiced law, served as district attorney, marketed Texas ranchland in Europe, farmed, managed the Populist state campaign in 1892, run for Congress in 1896, and edited a party newspaper. Over the next three years, with a missionary-like zeal, Bentley meticulously conducted fifteen hundred experiments on range restoration techniques and tested dozens of different varieties of grasses, publishing four technical treatises relating to the work. His research concluded that with proper husbandry and conservation techniques, including scientific plowing, the cultivation of native grasses, and periodic resting of pastures, grazing capacity on the depleted lands could be more than doubled.[40]

Populists such as Bentley were among the loudest advocates for the growing federal role in agriculture. In his final report before the experiment station was closed in 1901, the always upbeat Bentley noted that "the book farmer" had traditionally been "looked upon by the regulation or orthodox farmer as 'a crank,' a visionary sort of creature to be respected for his enthusiasm, but to be avoided in matters of business." He didn't bother to add that Populists, with their penchant for innovation and experimentation, had themselves long been dismissed as "cranks." Bentley contended, however, that in the modern world, "the farmer who reads, studies, experiments, and adopts scientifically correct methods is no longer sneered at by those who are less advanced than he." Although the world was "slow to adopt anything new," if it could "be demonstrated that it pays to do so . . . no people are more ready to take hold than are the farmers and stockmen of the United States." Subsequent events would prove him correct.[41]

In 1903, after the appearance of the boll weevil in Texas, the USDA dispatched Seaman A. Knapp, a respected agricultural reformer and former president of the Iowa State Agricultural College, to Texas to help farmers fight the pest. Working with local farmers, Knapp oversaw the creation of successful demonstration farms in Terrell and Greenville, and soon, with modest support from the state, the practice spread to other parts of the state. By 1906 a formal system of county agricultural extension agents was taking shape nationwide, a cooperative effort between the counties, the land-grant colleges (including Texas A&M), and the USDA. With the expanding network of experiment stations developing new seed varieties, cultivation techniques, and conservation practices, the expanding corps of county agents communicated their findings to actual farmers, stockmen, and timber growers. Finally, in 1914, with the full support of agrarian congressmen like Joe Eagle and Sam Rayburn, Congress passed the Smith-Lever Act, which for the first time provided large-scale federal matching funds for states to extend cooperative extension services. By 1917 the USDA was larger than any other department of the federal government other than the military, the Post Office, and the Treasury. Former Populists like Henry Bentley, long champions of a robust federal role in agriculture, undoubtedly looked on with approval. Indeed, in the aftermath of the passage of the Smith-Lever Act, Bentley himself received an appointment as a lecturer and state organizer for farmers' institutes and spent several years traveling the state and assisting in the work of government-funded agricultural education.[42]

World War I proved to be something of a golden age for American agriculture, as US farmers were called on to feed and clothe huge Allied armies and prevent widespread starvation in war-torn Europe. Farm incomes soared, and with the government's encouragement, millions of new acres were brought under cultivation. With the end of the war, however, the boom turned to bust. Agricultural prices by 1921 had collapsed to only 15 percent of their 1919 levels. It was the greatest crisis in American agriculture since the Populist era.[43]

Farm advocacy organizations, in which former Populists often played leading roles, were quick to respond in calling for government aid. Among these was the aforementioned Farmers' Union, a successor to the Farmers' Alliance founded by ex-Populists in East Texas in 1902. By 1919 the Union had grown to 140,000 members in thirty-three states. Even before the war was over, the national lecturer of the Union, former Texas Populist state legislator Peter Radford, had testified before Congress on the need for federal farm subsidies and price controls. Another, more radical organization, the Nonpartisan League, emerged in the northern plains and Midwest during the war years, focusing its attention on winning concessions from state legislatures. But the most potent farm organization proved to be the American Farm Bureau Federation (AFBF), founded during the war years by county agents with the active support and cooperation of the USDA. By 1921 it had nearly a million members.

The AFBF served as a sort of adjunct to the county extension agent system, but it also became a potent lobbying force in Washington. Working closely with its allies in the USDA (even though the AFBF was ostensibly a private organization), it soon came to wield enormous power over a group of farm-state legislators that became known as the "farm bloc."[44]

As the agricultural depression continued through the 1920s—even while big business "roared"—the farm bloc, responding to pressure groups like the AFBF and the Farmers' Union, developed a plan to save agriculture. The plan came to fruition in the McNary-Haugen Bill, which called for tariffs on foreign agriculture to raise prices for American farmers, with domestic surpluses to be sold overseas by the federal government. If the combined effect of these two actions did not cover the costs of production, then the government would make up the difference with a subsidy paid for by a tax on agricultural processors—the dreaded middlemen who had been such a target of Populist wrath. The goal was to achieve "price parity" for farmers, a benchmark based on the prices that farmers had enjoyed during the salad days of 1910 to 1914.[45]

Although differing from it in important details, McNary-Haugen embodied a major principle of the Populists' Subtreasury Plan in that it would creatively use large-scale federal intervention to ameliorate the uncertainties and insecurities of farming. It also met with the same hostile response from business interests, who stood to lose from the processing tax, and from politicians dedicated to low taxes and laissez-faire economics. Not surprisingly, conservative Republican president Calvin Coolidge vetoed the bill. But the fact that it passed both houses of Congress signaled the growing strength of an interest group composed of farmers, including, and in many cases led by, old Populists, with the congressional farm bloc ready and willing to do their bidding.

Through all of this, the power of the USDA quietly grew, both in the size of its workforce and the scope of its mission. The agency became a magnet for the nation's top scientists, creating, as historian Gary Gerstle has described it, "a university-like environment supportive of research, innovation, and autonomous inquiry." Ideas and personnel flowed freely between the department and the land-grant universities. The "scientific and intellectual culture" that emerged in the USDA led it to expand beyond just agriculturally related technical science; in the 1920s it began devoting resources to social-science research, an effort that included the creation of the Bureau of Agricultural Economics in 1922. The USDA gradually became a seedbed for new ideas in public policy. As early as 1906 it had flexed its muscles to help engineer the passage of Theodore Roosevelt's Pure Food and Drug Act, of which it also became the chief enforcer. That activist tradition continued with the agency's role in formulating the ideas that went into the stillborn McNary-Haugen Bill. As the farm crisis of the 1920s wore on, more and more of the policymakers inside the USDA—and its intellectual fellow travelers in academe and elsewhere—embraced various ideas involving central planning for the agricultural economy, planning that in some ways was inspired by the emergency measures enacted during World War I but which in its muscular use of federal power harkened back to the Subtreasury Plan and other Populist doctrine.[46]

Then came the Crash of 1929, followed by the onset of the Great Depression. In an era when the federal government overall remained relatively small, powerless, and ill-equipped to meet the exigencies of the unprecedented economic collapse, the USDA, its constituents in farm organizations and in the states, and its representatives in the congressional farm bloc stood uniquely prepared to meet the emergency. As Franklin Roosevelt prepared to take office, he assembled a group of agricultural experts that included Henry A. Wallace, an agricultural reformer whose father had directed the USDA in the Harding and Coolidge administrations, and Rexford G. Tugwell, a young Columbia University economics professor with a particular interest in farm policy. Working with FDR and the House Agriculture Committee chair (and Texan) Marvin Jones, among others, the advisors drew up a plan to save American agriculture. From Milburn L. Wilson, an Iowa native who had bounced back and forth between his job as an agricultural economics professor at Montana State College and a posting in the USDA, they took the idea of paying farmers to take land out of cultivation, a measure designed to shore up prices and restore farm income. From McNary-Haugen they borrowed the idea of "parity" as a goal, and of paying for the plan with a tax on processors. The act gave the USDA, which would administer the law, wide latitude in planning production and price targets. House agriculture chairman Marvin Jones never really agreed with the proposition that overproduction was the cause of the farm crisis, a philosophical position he shared with Texas Populists who had taken the same stance back in the 1890s. (They reasoned that when people were starving, underconsumption—not overproduction—must be the problem.) But believing it to be superior, overall, to any other viable alternative, he threw his weight behind the legislation. After a contentious two-month debate, Congress passed the Agricultural Adjustment Act (AAA), and it became one of the foundational programs of the New Deal. Commenting—not entirely approvingly—on the influence of agrarian ideas on the New Deal's farm legislation, historian David Kennedy declares that "in the crisis of the 1930s, [William Jennings] Bryan's avatars rose again. They rang all the changes of the same agrarian myth and won concessions beyond the Great Commoner's most sumptuous dreams. The New Deal laid the groundwork for a system of farm subsidies that in the end mocked the pieties of frontier individualism and made the agricultural sector a virtual ward of the state."[47]

Ward of the state or not, it is difficult to overstate the role that the agricultural sector—a sector owing much of its character and existence to Populism and ex-Populists—played in the making of New Deal liberalism. After the Supreme Court struck down the original AAA as unconstitutional, a new AAA, enacted in 1938, empowered the federal government to buy up and distribute surplus crops, releasing them onto the domestic market as needed. As Gary Gerstle has argued, "By the late 1930s, the New Deal system regulating agriculture looked a great deal like the ambitious subtreasury plan that the Populists had called for in the early 1890s. And true to the Populists' prediction, the vastly augmented regulatory role for the central government brought unprecedented stability and security to America's agricultural sector."[48]

Populist ideas, however, influenced the New Deal's liberalism far beyond just farm policy. As previously noted, New Deal labor legislation—most notably the Wagner Act—marked a fulfillment of the spirit, and much of the letter, of the Populist labor planks of the 1890s. Likewise, the bringing of banks, public utilities, and other corporations under greater federal regulation would have had old Populists nodding in approval as they read their newspapers in the 1930s. Even Populist ideas about monetary policy seemed to roar back to life under the changed circumstances of the Great Depression. Historian William Leuchtenburg has observed that "by the time Roosevelt took office, he and his advisers had developed, or familiarized themselves with, a body of theory a good deal more coherent than is commonly suggested." "From the Populists" he writes, came not only "a bevy of ideas for regulating agriculture" but also "a suspicion of Wall Street" that significantly influenced the architects of the New Deal. Not that all of his advisors, who otherwise championed the activist state, agreed with the Populist soft-money position. Rexford Tugwell, who found a congenial home in the USDA as an assistant secretary of agriculture but who exercised an outsized influence as a member of FDR's Brain Trust, related how in the early days of the New Deal FDR irritated his advisors "by persistently coming back to monetary devices taken by themselves. We were at heart believers in sound money. Greenbackism was part of the populist tradition that we hoped had been left behind. We knew well enough that it hadn't; its advocates were loud and growing louder; all the old schemes for cheapening money were apparently still alive, and there were many new ones. The Governor [FDR] wanted to know all about them. We shuddered and got him the information."[49]

It turned out that monetary policy, with distinctly Populist overtones, did indeed figure prominently in Roosevelt's thinking. The president knew that some of his policies would only add to the already severe problem of deflation, and debt-strapped farmers needed relief in any case. Like the Populists forty years earlier, he had made his peace with the principle of a currency controlled and managed by the government, even if many of his advisors had not. The rapid drain of American gold to other countries during the financial crisis only made the abandonment of the gold standard more pressing. Early in the New Deal, Burton K. Wheeler, a Montana congressman whose grandfather had been a Populist and who had himself mounted a third-party run for governor on the radical Nonpartisan League ticket and later for vice president with Robert La Follette on the Progressive ticket, introduced an amendment to re-monetize silver at the ratio of sixteen to one, the old Populist-Bryan nostrum. Although FDR supported a soft-money policy, it was alleged that his opposition to that specific inflationary tool was the only thing keeping the free-silver measure from passing Congress. Ultimately, however, a successful amendment to the Agricultural Adjustment Act by Sen. Elmer Thomas, an Oklahoma Democrat who had campaigned for Bryan in 1896, achieved much the same thing. The amendment authorized Roosevelt to remonetize silver, issue greenbacks, or reduce the gold content of the dollar. With the country about to abandon the hallowed gold standard, one conservative representative declared that we were now "on our way to Moscow," while the president's own budget director declared it "the end of Western civilization." But for politicians like Wheeler and Thomas, themselves products of the Populist era, abandoning the gold standard was an idea that had been debated all their lives, by people they knew and trusted. What for some loomed as the end of Western civilization to others seemed an idea whose time had come. FDR obliged, and effectively took the nation off the gold standard.[50]

Other links between Populism and New Deal liberalism are less obvious than farm programs, labor legislation, business regulation, or monetary policy. The rise of the welfare state is often seen as one of the sharpest breaks with the past to arise from the New Deal. Yet the idea that the government should play a role in relieving the misery of unemployment, natural disasters, or other unavoidable misfortunes was widely accepted by Populists. Going back as far as 1887, when Grover Cleveland had vetoed a $10,000 appropriation to provide seed for Texas farmers devastated by drought (Cleveland notoriously said that "though the people support the Government the Government should not support the people"), folks in Populist country had already departed from the dogma of absolute laissez-faire. Populists cheered on Coxey's "army" of the unemployed in its famous march on Washington in 1894, and the building of a state-owned railroad from the Red River to the Gulf of Mexico as a means of work relief for the unemployed formed the centerpiece of the Texas Populist platform in 1898. The relief programs of the Works Progress Administration and Public Works Administration and the old-age pensions provided by the Social Security Act certainly had precedents in the underlying philosophy, if not in the scope, of Populist programs. In the case of the AAA, the New Deal program perhaps most associated with its Populist antecedents, the USDA eventually was authorized to distribute the surplus crops purchased under the law to feed poor schoolchildren, a program that in 1946 received formal sanction as the National School Lunch Program, one of the twentieth century's most popular and effective welfare programs. It is difficult to imagine Populists disapproving.[51]

~

As with any broad topic in American history, no discussion of twentieth-century liberalism can fail to include race. Slavery was America's original sin, and racism has always been the nation's most intractable problem. As this book has shown, it was the greatest stumbling block for Texas Populists, the area in which they sometimes strove, but often failed, to live up to their professed democratic aspirations. If, as I have argued, the Populists numbered among the most important progenitors of modern American liberalism, then their shortcomings in the realm of race seem especially problematic. Even if many white Populists could be considered "ahead of their time" when it came to race—and certainly more enlightened than their major-party opponents—their inability to recognize that political and social citizenship could never truly be achieved while withholding social citizenship (what whites of the era called "social equality") guaranteed that their outreach to African Americans would be largely doomed to fail.

Our widely accepted national narrative about race in the twentieth century further complicates the association of Populism with modern liberalism. As that narrative goes, progressivism and the New Deal, for all practical purposes, excluded blacks and other racial minorities. Not until *Brown v. Board of Education* and the onset of the 1950s civil rights movement did the country confront its most egregious flaw, and only with the civil rights legislation and judicial decisions of the 1960s did it finally begin to live up to its liberal creed. In this narrative, then, liberalism's golden age coincides not with the New Deal but with the Great Society and its landmark civil rights legislation. If the People's Revolt of the 1890s only helped to fuel the largely racist impulses of progressivism and the New Deal, then its contribution to modern liberalism must have been, at best, half-hearted, hypocritical, and incomplete, just as liberalism itself was, and often is.[52]

The problem with this narrative is that it presents an oversimplified and bowdlerized version of the story of race and civil rights in the twentieth century. It is certainly true that Progressive Era reforms tended to be "for whites only," as C. Vann Woodward famously put it. Southern congressmen in that period, influenced by Populism or in some cases as former Populists themselves, played a prominent role in strengthening the regulation of interstate commerce, curbing the power of monopolies, and establishing the Federal Reserve System. As we have seen, they were instrumental in building up the power of the USDA and drafting ambitious farm legislation, both of which would serve as models for the New Deal. All of these things, by design, disproportionately benefited whites. Likewise, the New Deal itself would have been legislatively impossible without Populist-influenced southern Democrats like Sam Rayburn, Marvin Jones, Wright Patman, and the occasional actual ex-Populist like Joe Eagle, none of whom held enlightened views on race. In program after program, these southern representatives supported the burgeoning liberal economic state only under the condition that southern racial arrangements remain firmly under the control of state and local governments. Even as southern Democrats made possible the liberal state (and possibly kept the United States from following the path to fascism or communism), the New Deal, as historian Ira Katznelson has explained, "permitted, or at least turned a blind eye toward, an organized system of racial cruelty." Indeed, Katznelson asserts, "the New Deal did not just tolerate discrimination and social seclusion; its most notable, and noble, achievements stood on the shoulders of this southern bulwark." Franklin Roosevelt, whether by choice or by expediency, acquiesced in, if not actively abetted, this "southern cage" in which national policymakers were forced to operate. It is hard to dispute the conclusion that the liberalism of the Roosevelt administration "rested directly on its Faustian pact with the Southern Democrats."[53]

The traditional narrative, however, overlooks or discounts the law of unintended consequences. So while it is true that Populist-influenced southern congressmen eagerly created the liberal state on the often explicit condition that it would allow the perpetuation of black "discrimination and social exclusion," they were, as Katznelson argues, "ultimately creating conditions for their amelioration." By embracing the Populist doctrine of an activist state striving to give ordinary people a greater share of the benefits of the capitalist system, New Deal Democrats, in Katznelson's words, "helped save liberal democracy so successfully that they ultimately undermined the presuppositions of white supremacy."[54]

The best evidence for this undermining of white supremacy comes from the reinvigorated labor movement of the 1930s and 1940s. As detailed above, the Wagner Act of 1935 and subsequent prolabor New Deal laws and regulations ushered in a new day for organized labor. To be sure, southern congressmen made sure that these laws' provisions would not apply to farm or domestic workers, guaranteeing that the vast majority of African American laborers in the South would be unaffected. Even in manufacturing, blacks were usually consigned to only the dirtiest and most unskilled factory jobs, and many unions denied them membership. Nevertheless, by the 1940s a growing number of unions, particularly the new industrial unions affiliated with the Congress of Industrial Organizations (CIO), were cultivating African American membership. Such unions, many in the North but some in Texas and the South, "quickly became the most racially integrated institutions in American life," and their numbers were such that when they officially backed legislation to abolish the poll tax or punish lynching, their votes made a difference.[55]

During World War II, FDR issued an executive order banning "discriminatory employment practices because of race, color, creed, or national origin in government service, defense industries, and by trade unions." The order established the Fair Employment Practice Committee (FEPC) to investigate and redress grievances. The order elicited a harsh backlash from the South, and without congressional sanction or much funding, its achievements were limited. Southerners were instrumental in defeating a more robust FEPC law in 1946. Clearly, the gains of "civil rights unionism," as scholars now refer to it, remained limited, particularly in the South. But they constituted the most important part of the first phase of what is now called the "long civil rights movement," a corrective to the generally accepted narrative that no meaningful progress was made until the 1950s. Without the activist state first envisioned by Populists and made possible, however inadvertently, by southern support for the New Deal, the "classical phase" of the civil rights movement that began with the *Brown* decision would have played out very differently.

Black, brown, and working-class white union members, cooperating across the color line, had created much of the organizational infrastructure that made the boycotts, sit-ins, marches, and political organizing of the 1950s and 1960s possible. The Populist mindset that had helped legitimize the activist state in the first four decades of the century had much to do with making that possible.[56]

Finally, in the realm where Populists may have been the most ahead of their time—conceptions of gender—modern liberalism displays perhaps its most conspicuous debt to the People's Revolt. Populists, as we have seen, began the culturally difficult task of rejecting traditional forms of patriarchy. With a crucial assist from their evangelical churches, they started the process of replacing the long-treasured southern code of honor with a new code of dignity, which defined "manliness" as honesty, forthrightness, restraint, magnanimity, and independence rather than as physical power, martial attainments, and the ability to dominate one's dependent inferiors and secure their loyalty. More than simply supporting legal or political rights for women, the Populists helped to pioneer notions of the social, moral, and intellectual equality of men and women. In the twenty-first century, that project remains unfulfilled, but its proponents can point to the legacy of Populists as one its most important historical seedbeds.

~

There was a time, not too many decades ago, when many historians believed that American liberalism, its New Deal coalition augmented by the accession of newly enfranchised minorities in the 1950s and 1960s, had thoroughly triumphed over challengers from both the conservative right and the radical left. The historian Otis L. Graham Jr., writing from his vantage point in 1967, concisely summarized this liberal-consensus position: "The student of history sees in a longer perspective what any American observes in his lifetime, the inexorable democratization of our common life—the enlargement of political rights, material security, meaningful freedom. Liberalism is the name of the movement that, through ideas and political action, has sought to hasten this process." The liberalism that Graham celebrated, New Left historian Lawrence Goodwyn bemoaned. Indeed, Goodwyn, writing in the 1970s, believed that Populism in the 1890s had constituted the last "moment" for a more truly egalitarian America, an opportunity that was lost when protoliberals within the People's Party—the "shadow movement" of pro-Bryan fusionists—betrayed the fundamental principles of Populism. But whether one celebrated the triumph of liberalism (like Graham) or disapproved of it (like Goodwyn), there seemed to be broad agreement in the late 1960s and early 1970s that for better or worse, liberalism was here to stay. Even Richard Nixon, the bête noire of so many on the left during his lifetime, created the Environmental Protection Agency and the Occupational Safety and Health Administration, raised the minimum wage, called for universal health insurance, and supported affirmative action. America, it seemed, was liberal even when it was not.[57]

By the end of the twentieth century that all had changed. With the rise of Ronald Reagan and the New Right in the 1980s, students of American politics began proclaiming the end of the liberal era. Books with titles like *The Rise and Fall of the New Deal Order* (1989), *The End of Reform* (1995), *The Strange Death of American Liberalism* (2001), and *The Great Exception* (2016) suggested that rather than being a permanent ruling ideology, mid-twentieth-century liberalism had been more of a historical aberration, a relatively ephemeral exception to the general rule of American conservatism. The Democratic Party's retreat from liberalism under "New Democrat" Bill Clinton, eight years of Republican dominance under George W. Bush, and the GOP's capture of Congress and its hard veer to the right during the presidency of Barack Obama confirmed their worst fears. As if to emphasize the finality of liberalism's defeat, the radical scholar and social commentator Noam Chomsky declared in 2013—five years into the Obama presidency—that Richard Nixon had been the "last liberal president."[58]

If liberalism appeared to be dead or at least on life support in the early twenty-first century, the election in 2016 of Donald J. Trump seemingly confirmed that diagnosis. Significantly, many commentators loudly pronounced Trump *not* a conservative, despite the decidedly illiberal nature of many of his policies. Noam Chomsky has argued that Trump's GOP "is no longer a political party in the traditional sense" but rather "a 'radical insurgency,' one that has abandoned normal parliamentary politics." Chomsky gained an unlikely intellectual companion in the conservative former Speaker of the House, Republican John Boehner, who declared in 2018 that after a year of the Trump administration "there is no Republican Party." Indeed, in the aftermath of Trump's election, pundits of the right and the left rushed to pronounce the "death of conservatism," ironically echoing the epitaphs for liberalism coming from the left.[59]

If liberalism and conservatism have both had their obituaries written, then where does that leave American politics? In another great historical irony, the label most often affixed to Trump in his 2016 race and subsequent presidency was not "conservative" but rather "populist." Even before the rise of Trump, "populism" (with a lowercase *p*) had acquired mostly negative connotations. From the 1930s on, once most of the actual 1890s Populists had passed from the scene, virtually every antiestablishment politician who attacked out-of-touch, corrupt "elites" and made direct appeal to the "people" was labeled a populist. Applied to politicians such as Huey Long in the 1930s and George Wallace in the 1960s, the label often became associated with demagoguery. Attached to the billionaire third-party candidate Ross Perot in the 1990s, it could be a term of derision. In countries outside the United States, it has been used to describe figures of the far right (Marine Le Pen in France) as well as the far left (Hugo Chávez in Venezuela). A leading scholar of modern populism, Jan-Werner Müller, argues that apart from their antiestablishment political style, what unites modern populists of the right and left is their hostility to pluralism. Populism has thus acquired a strong association with racism, xenophobia, and ultranationalism. Only on rare occasions does it still get invoked in a positive manner, as in the 2016 US presidential race, when supporters of the social democrat Bernie Sanders labeled Trump a "fake populist," declaring that Sanders's liberal populism was the real thing. *New York Times* columnist David Leonhardt likewise bucked the trend and invoked the term in a positive manner, writing his own prescription for Democratic success in the approaching 2020 election: "It's the populism, stupid."[60]

In some cases, modern-day populists defy placement on either the political right or left. Displaying more style than substance, they may lack anything resembling a coherent ideology. Cultural historian Linda Schulte-Sasse, borrowing a metaphor that had been applied to Juan Perón by philosopher Slavoj Žižek, contended in the 1990s that the populism of Ross Perot, like that of Perón, constituted "an 'empty vessel' into which a variety of desires and 'feelings' can be poured." Much the same has been said of Trump. The fact that the populist label could be applied to such a wide range of different politicians suggests that the word functions like something of a Rorschach test, becoming whatever an observer thinks it is. Many contemporary observers probably define populism the way Justice Potter Stewart famously viewed obscenity: they know it when they see it.[61]

It remains to be seen whether the rumors of liberalism's demise are greatly exaggerated. Barack Obama's effort to enact government-subsidized universal health insurance, incomplete and flawed as it was, proved popular and surprisingly durable, given the vehemence of the Republican attacks against it. As this book goes to press, the rise of Trump appears to have done much to stir liberals from their torpor. Dismayed by the administration's attack on the social safety net, its rollback of environmental protections, its resurgent nativ-ism, and its aggressive assault on the civil rights of racial, ethnic, religious, and sexually nonconforming groups, American liberals are showing a level of energy not seen since the protests over the Vietnam War. Although many on the political left still prefer to call themselves "progressives," in 2018, for the first time in more than a generation, a majority of Democrats (51 percent) self-identified as "liberals."[62]

The rapid change in public attitudes in favor of gay, lesbian, and transgen-der rights has been little short of remarkable. A resurgent women's movement and protest movements against police brutality and mass incarceration have reinvigorated the left. It may be true that the era from the 1930s through the 1960s constituted, in historian Jefferson Cowie's reckoning, "the great excep-tion" in American history, a brief and fragile flowering of liberalism in an America otherwise committed to conservative individualism. Or it may be that the next era of liberal reform is simply awaiting another great national trauma to spur it into motion, much as the Great Depression triggered the New Deal. Trumpian "populism" may or may not prove to be that trauma.[63]

~

The real Populists of the 1890s would be dismayed at the fate of their move-ment's name; however, I think they would be heartened by the fact that their vision of government and society lives on, at least in some quarters. With rela-tively few exceptions, they knew what it meant to be a Populist, and it never meant unthinking or unscrupulous extremism. It meant placing enough power in the hands of citizens through the instrumentality of the ballot to curb concentrated power, whether that power resided in monopolistic corporations *or* a corrupt government. It meant campaigning with facts and appeals to rea-son and conducting those campaigns in a vigorous but dignified style. It meant a surprising degree of tolerance and acceptance of those different from themselves, certainly when compared to their opponents in the major parties. And above all, it signaled an abiding faith in the democratic instincts of ordi-nary people, who, with adequate education and their rights protected, would do the right thing. The Populists of the 1890s mostly lost the battles of their day, but their ideas lived on, shaping American politics to this day. Whether those ideas shall eventually prevail is a question we would do well to ponder.

APPENDIX

The Cooperative Movement

The following table lists all the Alliance cooperatives that I was able to identify with a reasonable degree of confidence. Records come primarily from the following sources: the annual credit-rating agency reports from R. G. Dun & Co. and from J. M. Bradstreet & Son; the Texas secretary of state's biennial reports; and various Texas newspapers, particularly the *Southern Mercury*. References from manuscripts or other miscellaneous sources are noted on the table. Although my use of the Bradstreet and Dun records was restricted to the holdings of the Library of Congress, which are incomplete, they do include most of the reports from the heyday of the cooperative movement, 1885 through 1891. The Texas secretary of state's reports, which list all enterprises that applied for a state charter, encompass most of the years from 1880 to 1900. Although it is true that some cooperatives secured state charters but never opened for business, I have assumed that in most cases Alliancefolk would not have gone to the trouble and expense of chartering their enterprises and then not following through. For the newspaper references, I included only those that were listed as operating or on the verge of opening their doors; this excluded many that were discussed or planned but may not have ever actually operated. As more Texas newspapers are digitized, keyword searches will undoubtedly make it possible to identify more cooperatives than are included here. The cited credit-rating agency reports and the secretary of state's reports are as follows:

Bradstreet's Commercial Reports of the Bankers, Merchants, Manufacturers and Others in the United States and British Provinces (New York: J. M. Bradstreet & Son) for Oct. 1886, Oct. 1887, Oct. 1888, Oct. 1889, Oct. 1890, July 1891, Apr. 1894.

Mercantile Agency Reference Book (New York: R. G. Dun & Co.) for Jan. 1885, Mar. 1886, Mar. 1887, Mar. 1888, Mar. 1889, July 1890.

Biennial Report of the Secretary of State of the State of Texas (Austin: State Printers) for 1879–1881, 1882, 1884, 1886, 1888, 1890, 1892, 1896, 1898, and 1900. The title and printers vary slightly from volume to volume. The date of publication for each report is the year immediately after the year of the report (e.g., the report for 1888 was published in 1889, etc.).

Table A.1. Alliance Cooperatives

County	City or Town	Type of Enterprise	Name of Sponsoring Alliance Entity (if known)	Source
Anderson	Neches	cotton yard		Southern Mercury
Anderson	Palestine	store	Alliance Co-op. Assoc.	J. M. Bradstreet
Anderson	Neches	wagon yard		Southern Mercury
Anderson	Neches	warehouse		Southern Mercury
Angelina	Burke	store		Southern Mercury
Austin	Bellville	cotton yard	Austin Co. Farmers' Alliance Co-op. Assoc.	R. G. Dun
Austin	Sealy	cotton yard		Southern Mercury
Austin	Bellville	lumberyard	Austin Co. Farmers' Alliance Co-op. Assoc.	R. G. Dun
Austin	Bellville	store	Austin Co. Farmers' Alliance Co-op. Assoc.	R. G. Dun
Austin	Shelby	store	Shelby Farmers' Alliance Store	J. M. Bradstreet
Austin	Wallis	warehouse		Albany Weekly News
Bastrop	McDade	cooperative assoc.	McDade Co-op. Alliance	R. G. Dun
Bastrop	Bastrop	cotton yard		Southern Mercury
Bastrop	Elgin	cotton yard		Southern Mercury
Bastrop	Bastrop	store		Galveston Daily News
Bastrop	Elgin	store	Alliance Co-op. Store	R. G. Dun
Bastrop	Paige	store		Southern Mercury
Bell	Temple	cotton yard		Fort Worth Gazette
Bell	Hackberry	gin	Hackberry Alliance Ginning Company	Secretary of State Report
Bell	Holland	preferred trade houses	Alliance Committee of Trade	Temple Times

County	Town	Type	Organization	Source
Bell	Belton	store	Farmers' Alliance Exchange	R. G. Dun
Bell	Heidenheimer	store	Heidenheimer Farmers' Southern Mercantile and Exchange Assoc.	Secretary of State Report
Bell	Temple	warehouse		*Fort Worth Gazette*
Belton	Bell	wagon yard		*Belton Journal*
Bexar	San Antonio	store		*Southern Mercury*
Bosque	Clifton	store		R. G. Dun
Bosque	Morgan	cotton yard		*Wise County Messenger*
Bowie	Texarkana	store		*Galveston Daily News*
Brown	Brownwood	cotton yard		*Southern Mercury*
Brown	Brownwood	gin		*Southern Mercury*
Brown	Brownwood	store		*Southern Mercury*
Burleson	Caldwell	store		*Brenham Weekly Banner*
Caldwell	Martindale	cooperative assoc.	Caldwell Co. Alliance Southern Mercantile Co-op. Assoc.	R. G. Dun
Caldwell	Lockhart	store		J. M. Bradstreet
Caldwell	Luling	store	Luling Alliance Co-op. Assoc.	J. M. Bradstreet
Caldwell	Prairie Lea	store		*Southern Mercury*
Callahan	Baird	gin		*Southern Mercury*
Callahan	Putnam	store	Putnam Farmers' Alliance & Co-op. Assoc.	J. M. Bradstreet
Cherokee	Wells	cooperative assoc.		*Austin Weekly Statesman*
Cherokee	New Birmingham	cotton yard		*Southern Mercury*

(continued)

Table A.1. Alliance Cooperatives (continued)

County	City or Town	Type of Enterprise	Name of Sponsoring Alliance Entity (if known)	Source
Cherokee	Alto	store	Alto (The) Cherokee Co. Farmers' Alliance Co-op. Assoc. (inc)	J. M. Bradstreet
Clay	Greenwood	gin		*Wise County Messenger*
Clay	Henrietta	store	Clay Co. Farmers' Alliance Co-op. Trade Assoc.	J. M. Bradstreet
Coleman	Coleman	store	Coleman Co. Alliance Co-op. Assoc. (inc)	J. M. Bradstreet
Collin	Farmersville	cotton yard		*Southern Mercury*
Collin	McKinney	cotton yard		*McKinney Democrat*
Collin	Saint Paul	gin		*Fort Worth Gazette*
Collin	Wylie	gin		*Brenham Banner*
Collin	McKinney	mill		*Austin Weekly Statesman*
Colorado	Columbus	store	Colorado Co. Farmers' Alliance Co-op. Assoc. (inc)	J. M. Bradstreet
Colorado	Weimar	store		*Colorado Citizen*
Comal	New Braunfels	woolen mill		*Southern Mercury*
Comanche	Comanche	cotton yard		*Southern Mercury*
Cooke	Marysville	gin	Farmers' Alliance Assoc. (not inc)	J. M. Bradstreet
Cooke	Gainesville	mill		*Fort Worth Gazette*
Cooke	Marysville	mill	Farmers' Alliance Assoc. (not inc)	J. M. Bradstreet
Cooke	Era	store	Alliance Co-op. Assoc. store	*Southern Mercury*, *Gainesville Hesperian*
Cooke	Gainesville	store	Alliance Co-op. Co.	J. M. Bradstreet
Coryell	Copperas Cove	store		*Fort Worth Gazette*

County	Town	Type	Name	Source
Dallas	Dallas	statewide exchange	Texas Alliance Exchange	*Southern Mercury*
Dallas	Pleasant Valley	gin		J. M. Bradstreet
Dallas	Cedar Hill	store		*Southern Mercury*
Dallas	Gibbs	store		R. G. Dun
Dallas	Dallas	mill	Alliance Milling and Manufacturing Company of Dallas County	Secretary of State Report
Dallas	Dallas	ag. implements mfg.	Dallas Branch Co-operative Manufacturing Alliance	Secretary of State Report
Dallas	Dallas	district exchanges	Farmers' Alliance Exchange of Texas (inc) (also Waco and Galveston)	R. G. Dun
Delta	Ben Franklin	store		R. G. Dun
Delta	Lake Creek	store		*Southern Mercury*
Delta	Cooper	cotton yard		*Cooper People's Cause*
Denton	Denton	cotton yard		*Southern Mercury*
Denton	Aubrey	gin		*McKinney Democrat, San Antonio Express*
Denton	Denton	gin		*Southern Mercury*
Denton	Flower Mound	gin		*Fort Worth Gazette, Handbook of Texas Online*
Denton	Mustang	gin	Mustang Alliance Corn Mill & Cotton Gin Co. (inc)	R. G. Dun
Denton	Denton	mill		*Southern Mercury, Handbook of Texas Online*
Denton	Mustang	mill	Mustang Alliance Corn Mill & Cotton Gin Co. (inc)	R. G. Dun
DeWitt	Cuero	preferred trade houses		*Southern Mercury*

(continued)

Table A.1. Alliance Cooperatives (continued)

County	City or Town	Type of Enterprise	Name of Sponsoring Alliance Entity (if known)	Source
Eastland	Cisco	cotton yard	District Alliance	*Southern Mercury*
Eastland	Cisco	mill		*Wise County Messenger*
Eastland	Cisco	store	District Alliance	*Southern Mercury*
Ellis	Ennis	mill		*Dallas Morning News*
Ellis	Ennis	store	Ennis District Alliance Agency	R. G. Dun
Ellis	Midlothian	store		*Galveston Daily News*
Ellis	Waxahachie	store	Ellis Co. Alliance Company	R. G. Dun
Ellis	Waxahachie	wagon yard		*Galveston Daily News*
Erath	Dublin	cotton yard		*Southern Mercury*
Erath	Stephenville	cotton yard		*Southern Mercury*
Erath	Alexander	lumberyard	Alliance Lumber Co.	R. G. Dun
Erath	Pleasant Home	preferred trade houses		*Southern Mercury*
Erath	Lingleville	school	Erath County Alliance High School	Secretary of State Report
Erath	Dublin	store	Erath County Farmers' Alliance (not inc)	J. M. Bradstreet
Erath	Dublin	warehouse		*Dublin Progress*
Falls	Marlin	cotton yard		*Southern Mercury*
Falls	Marlin	store		*Southern Mercury*
Fannin	Savoy	store		*Southern Mercury*
Fannin	Bailey	cooperative assoc.	White Rock and Grove Hill Alliance Ginning and Milling Company	Secretary of State Report

Fannin	Honey Grove	cooperative assoc.	Honey Grove Alliance Agricultural Assoc.	Secretary of State Report
Fannin	Bonham	cotton yard	Fannin County Alliance Agricultural Assoc.	Secretary of State Report
Fannin	Bonham	gin		*Dallas Morning News*
Fannin	Ladonia	gin	Rehobeth Alliance Ginning Co. (not inc)	J. M. Bradstreet
Fannin	Rohobeth	gin		*Fort Worth Gazette*
Fannin	Bonham	store	Fannin County Alliance Agricultural Assoc.	Secretary of State Report
Fayette	La Grange	cooperative assoc.	La Grange Farmers' Alliance Co-op. Assoc.	R. G. Dun
Fayette	Flatonia	store	Flatonia Southern Mercantile Co-Operative Assoc. of the Farmers' Alliance	*Fort Worth Gazette, Brenham Banner*
Fayette	Ledbetter	store		*Southern Mercury*
Fayette	Schulenburg	store	Fayette County Alliance Co-operative Assoc.	Secretary of State Report
Franklin	Mount Vernon	store		*Dallas Morning News*
Franklin	Winnsboro	cotton yard		*Wise County Messenger*
Galveston	Galveston	district exchange	Farmers' Alliance Exchange	J. M. Bradstreet
Gillespie	Fredericksburg	store	Gillespie County Farmers Alliance Co-operative Assoc.	Secretary of State Report
Goliad	Goliad	cotton yard		*Southern Mercury*
Gonzales	Gonzales	store		J. M. Bradstreet
Grayson	Van Alstyne	cotton yard		*Galveston Daily News*
Grayson	Choctow Grove	gin		*Southern Mercury*
Grayson	Collinsville	gin	Alliance Gin and Mill Assoc. of Collinsville	*Brenham Weekly Banner*
Grayson	Basin Springs	gin		*Southern Mercury*

(continued)

Table A.1. Alliance Cooperatives (continued)

County	City or Town	Type of Enterprise	Name of Sponsoring Alliance Entity (if known)	Source
Grayson	Collinsville	mill	Collinsville Alliance Gin & Mill Co. of the Farmers' Alliance (inc)	J. M. Bradstreet
Grayson	Denison	mill		*Fort Worth Gazette*
Grayson	Bells	store	Alliance Southern Mercantilee Assoc. (not inc)	J. M. Bradstreet
Grayson	Collinsville	store	Alliance Co-op. Assoc.	R. G. Dun
Grayson	Howe	store	Farmers' Alliance Co-op. Assoc.	J. M. Bradstreet
Grayson	Pink Hill	store		*Southern Mercury*
Grayson	Whitewright	store	Whitewright Farmers' Alliance Ag. Assoc.	J. M. Bradstreet
Grayson	Sherman	store		*Sherman Courier*
Grayson	Sherman	warehouse		*Southern Mercury*
Gregg	Longview	store		*Dallas Morning News*
Gregg	Longview	store	Colored Alliance	*Gainesville Hesperian*
Grimes	Navasota	store		*Galveston Daily News*
Guadalupe	Seguin	cotton yard		*Southern Mercury*
Guadalupe	Staples Store	gin		*San Marcos Free Press*
Guadalupe	Seguin	store		*Southern Mercury*
Harris	Houston	cotton yard	District Alliance Exchange of Southern Texas	*Southern Mercury*
Harris	Houston	store		*Galveston Daily News*
Hays	Kyle, San Marcos, Badina	cooperative assoc.	Western Texas Alliance Co-operative Assoc.	Secretary of State Report

County	Location	Type	Name	Source
Hays	Buda	gin		*Southern Mercury*
Hays	Buda	mill	Buda Milling and Ginning Assoc. of the Farmers' Alliance	Secretary of State Report
Hays	Kyle	cotton yard		*San Marcos Free Press*
Hays	Science Hall	preferred trade houses	Science Hall Suballiance	*San Marcos Free Press*
Henderson	Murchison	store		*Southern Mercury*
Henderson	Rusk	store		*Bryan Eagle*
Hill	Aquilla	store	Aquilla Alliance Co.	J. M. Bradstreet
Hill	Hillsboro	store		R. G. Dun
Hill	Hillsboro	warehouse		*Hillsboro Reflector*
Hood	Granbury	cotton yard		*Southern Mercury*
Hood	Contrary Creek	gin		*Granbury News*
Hopkins	Black Jack Grove	cotton yard	Alliance Mill & Gin Assoc.	J. M. Bradstreet
Hopkins	Sulphur Springs	cotton yard		*Southern Mercury*
Hopkins	Sulphur Springs	cotton yard		*Fort Worth Gazette*
Hopkins	Black Jack Grove	gin	Alliance Mill & Gin Assoc.	J. M. Bradstreet
Hopkins	Black Jack Grove	mill	Alliance Mill & Gin Assoc.	J. M. Bradstreet

(continued)

Table A.1. Alliance Cooperatives (continued)

County	City or Town	Type of Enterprise	Name of Sponsoring Alliance Entity (if known)	Source
Hopkins	Cumby	mill	Black Jack Grove Alliance Mill	*Fort Worth Gazette*
Hopkins	Black Jack Grove	store	Alliance Mill & Gin Assoc.	J. M. Bradstreet
Hopkins	Sulphur Springs	warehouse		*Southern Mercury*
Hopkins	Sulphur Springs	warehouse		*Fort Worth Gazette*
Houston	Crockett	cooperative assoc.	Houston County Alliance Co-operative Assoc.	Secretary of State Report
Houston	Weches	cotton yard		*Southern Mercury*
Houston	Weches	wagon yard		*Southern Mercury*
Houston	Weches	warehouse		*Southern Mercury*
Hunt	Wolfe City	cotton yard	Alliance Southern Mercantile Assoc. (not inc)	J. M. Bradstreet
Hunt	Wolfe City	cottonseed oil mill	Alliance Southern Mercantile Assoc. (not inc)	J. M. Bradstreet
Hunt	Celeste	gin		*Dallas Morning News*
Hunt	Floyd	gin	Orion Alliance Gin	*Fort Worth Gazette*
Hunt	Lone Oak	gin		*Galveston Daily News*
Hunt	Merit	gin		*Southern Mercury*
Hunt	Celeste	mill		J. M. Bradstreet
Hunt	Greenville	mill		*Fort Worth Gazette*
Hunt	Merit	mill		*Southern Mercury*

County	Town	Type	Name	Source
Hunt	Kinston	store		*Greenville Herald*
Hunt	Lone Oak	store		*Mineola Monitor*
Hunt	Wolfe City	store	Alliance Southern Mercantile Assoc. (not inc)	J. M. Bradstreet
Jack	Berwick	gin		*Wise County Messenger*
Jack	Berwick	mill		*Wise County Messenger*
Jack	Jacksboro	store		R. G. Dun
Jasper	Jasper	store		J. M. Bradstreet
Jasper	Jasper	tannery	Jasper and Newton Counties Farmers' Alliance Co-operative Tanning Assoc.	Secretary of State Report
Johnson	Alvarado	store		R. G. Dun
Johnson	Cleburne	store	Johnson Co. Alliance Stock Co. (inc)	J. M. Bradstreet
Johnson	Johnson City	store	Johnson City Alliance	J. M. Bradstreet
Johnson	Cleburne	cotton yard		*Southern Mercury*
Jones	Center Line	store		*Southern Mercury*
Jones	Anson	gin		*Fort Worth Gazette*
Kempner	Lampasas	gin		*Galveston Daily News*
Kimble	Junction	store	Kimble Co. Co-op. Assoc. of the Farmers' Alliance (inc)	J. M. Bradstreet
Lamar	Paris	store	Joint Agricultural Co-op. Assoc. (Alliance and Grange)	R. G. Dun
Lavaca	Hallettsville	store		R. G. Dun
Lee	Giddings	store		J. M. Bradstreet
Lee	Lexington	store	Farmers' Alliance Co-op. Assoc. (inc)	J. M. Bradstreet

(continued)

Table A.1. Alliance Cooperatives (continued)

County	City or Town	Type of Enterprise	Name of Sponsoring Alliance Entity (if known)	Source
Limestone	Groesbeck	cotton yard		*Southern Mercury*
Limestone	Mexia	cotton yard		*Southern Mercury*
Limestone	Kosse	store		*Galveston Daily News*
Limestone	Mexia	store		*Southern Mercury*
Limestone	Thornton	store		*Waco Daily Examiner*
Llano	Marble Falls	school	Marble Falls Alliance University	Secretary of State Report
Marion	Jefferson	cotton yard		*Clarksville Standard*
Marion	Jefferson	preferred trade houses		*Galveston Daily News*
Marion	Jefferson	warehouse		*Clarksville Standard*
Marlin	Waller	store		*Galveston Daily News*
Marlin	Falls	warehouse		*Galveston Daily News*
Mason	Fredonia	cooperative assoc.	Fredonia and Spice [Spy] Rock Alliance Co-operative Assoc.	Secretary of State Report
Mason	Mason	cooperative assoc.	Mason Co. Farmers' Alliance Co-op. Southern Mercantile Assoc.	R. G. Dun
Mason	Mason	store	Mason Co. Farmers' Alliance Coop. Southern Mercantile Assoc. (inc)	J. M. Bradstreet
McCulloch	Milburn	cooperative assoc.	McCulloch County Alliance Co-operative Assoc.	Secretary of State Report
McCulloch	Voca	store	Alliance Co-op. Assoc.	J. M. Bradstreet
McLennan	Mastersville	gin	Mastersville Alliance Gin and Mill Company	Secretary of State Report

County	Town	Type	Name	Source
McLennan	Bruceville	mill	Alliance Co-op. Assoc.	R. G. Dun
McLennan	Mastersville	mill		*Fort Worth Gazette*
McLennan	Bruceville	store	Alliance Co-op. Assoc.	R. G. Dun
McLennan	Mastersville	store	Alliance Co-op. Assoc.	R. G. Dun
McLennan	Waco	cotton yard		*Southern Mercury*
McLennan	Waco	store		*Galveston Daily News*
McLennan	Waco	manufacturing	Co-operative Manufacturing Alliance of Texas	Secretary of State Report
Medina	Hondo	store		*Galveston Daily News*
Menard	Menard	tannery		*Southern Mercury*
Milam	Cameron	cotton yard	Milam County Co-operative Cotton & Southern Mercantile Alliance (inc)	J. M. Bradstreet
Milam	Milano	gin		*Galveston Daily News*
Milam	Milano	mill		*Galveston Daily News*
Milam	Davila	store	Davilla Co-operative Southern Mercantile Alliance	Secretary of State Report
Milam	Maysfield	store	Milam County Co-operative Cotton & Southern Mercantile Alliance (inc)	J. M. Bradstreet
Milam	Rockdale	store		*Mineola Monitor*
Milam	Cameron	store	Milam County Co-operative Cotton & Southern Mercantile Alliance (inc)	J. M. Bradstreet
Mills	Goldthwaite	store		J. M. Bradstreet
Montague	Saint Jo	cooperative assoc.	Farmers Alliance Co-operative Assoc. of Montague County	Secretary of State Report

(continued)

Table A.1. Alliance Cooperatives (continued)

County	City or Town	Type of Enterprise	Name of Sponsoring Alliance Entity (if known)	Source
Montague	Nacona [near Bonita]	cotton yard		*Southern Mercury*
Montague	Illinois Bend	gin		J. M. Bradstreet
Montague	Bowie	store	Alliance (The) Farmers' Exchange & Coop. Assoc. (inc)	J. M. Bradstreet
Montague	Bowie	cotton yard		*Wise County Messenger*
Montague	St. Jo	store		J. M. Bradstreet
Montgomery	Conroe	store	Farmers' Alliance Coop. Assoc. of Montague Co. (inc)	R. G. Dun
Montgomery	Montgomery	store	Alliance Co-op. Assoc. of Montgomery	*Southern Mercury*
Montgomery	Willis	store		*Willis Index*
Morris	Daingerfield	store		*Fort Worth Gazette*
Morris	Station Belden	store	Farmers' Alliance Assoc. (not inc)	J. M. Bradstreet
Nacogdoches	Nacogdoches	cotton yard		*Southern Mercury*
Nacogdoches	Black Jack	store	Farmers' Alliance Co-op. Assoc.	J. M. Bradstreet
Navarro	Corsicana	cotton yard		*Southern Mercury*
Navarro	Corsicana	store		*Southern Mercury*
Navarro	Corsicana	warehouse		*Wise County Messenger*
Newton	Bleakwood	store		J. M. Bradstreet
Orange	Orange	cooperative assoc.	Orange County Farmers' Alliance Co-operative Assoc.	Secretary of State Report
Palo Pinto	Gordon	store		J. M. Bradstreet

County	City	Type	Name	Source
Panola	Carthage	cotton yard	Alliance Co-op. Southern Mercantile Assoc. of Panola Co.	J. M. Bradstreet
Panola	Rehobeth	gin	Alliance Ginning Company	Secretary of State Report
Panola	Carthage	store	Alliance Co-op. Southern Mercantile Assoc. of Panola Co.	J. M. Bradstreet
Parker	Weatherford	cotton yard	Farmers' Alliance Distributing Assoc. of Parker County	Moses P. Lamar Papers, UT–Arlington Special Collections
Parker	Weatherford	elevator	Alliance Mill & Elevator Co. (inc)	R. G. Dun
Parker	Reno	gin		*Fort Worth Gazette*
Parker	Springtown	gin		*Wise County Messenger*
Parker	Weatherford	mill		*Wise County Messenger*
Parker	Weatherford	store	Farmers' Alliance Co-op. Assoc. (inc)	J. M. Bradstreet
Polk	Corrigan	store	Corrigan District Co-operative Alliance Store No. 2	Secretary of State Report
Polk	Livingston	store		*Southern Mercury*
Polk	Livingston	tannery		*Southern Mercury*
Red River	Annona	cooperative assoc.	East Red River Co-operative Assoc. of the Alliance	Secretary of State Report
Red River	Clarksville	cooperative assoc.	Red River County Alliance Co-operative Assoc.	Secretary of State Report
Red River	Clarksville	cotton yard		*Clarksville Standard*
Red River	Clarksville	warehouse		*Clarksville Standard*
Red River	Fulbright	gin		*Fort Worth Gazette*
Rockwall	Rockwall	store		J. M. Bradstreet
Rusk	Henderson	store		R. G. Dun

(continued)

Table A.1. Alliance Cooperatives (continued)

County	City or Town	Type of Enterprise	Name of Sponsoring Alliance Entity (if known)	Source
Sabine	Geneva	store	Geneva Co-op. Assoc. (not inc)	J. M. Bradstreet
Sabine	near Shreveport	store		*Southern Mercury*
San Augustine	Macune	store	San Augustine Co. Farmers' Alliance Co-op. Assoc.	J. M. Bradstreet
San Augustine	Sharpsville	store		*Southern Mercury*
San Saba	San Saba	store		*Jasper Newsboy*
Shelby	Center	gin	Shelby Co. Coop. Store	*Southern Mercury*
Shelby	Center	mill	Shelby Co. Coop. Store	*Southern Mercury*
Shelby	Mt. Enterprise	preferred trade houses		*Southern Mercury*
Shelby	Center	store	Shelby Co. Coop. Store	*Southern Mercury*
Shelby	Joaquin	store		J. M. Bradstreet
Smith	Tyler	cooperative assoc.	Smith County Alliance Co-operative Assoc.	Secretary of State Report
Smith	Mount Sylvan	store	Mount Sylvan Alliance Co-op. Assoc. (inc)	J. M. Bradstreet
Smith	Tyler	store	Grange and Alliance Coop. Assoc.	J. M. Bradstreet
Stephens	Breckenridge	gin	Grover Alliance and Gin Mill Assoc.	Secretary of State Report
Stephens	Oak Grove	gin		*Austin Weekly Statesman*
Stephens	Oak Grove	mill		*Austin Weekly Statesman*
Stephens	Breckenridge	mill	Grover Alliance and Gin Mill Assoc.	Secretary of State Report
Tarrant	Smithfield	cooperative assoc.	Smithfield Alliance Trade Union	Secretary of State Report

County	Place	Type	Name	Source
Tarrant	Arlington	store		*Fort Worth Gazette*
Tarrant	Fort Worth	store		*Fort Worth Gazette*
Tarrant	Fort Worth	store	Negro Alliance Store (Colored Alliance)	*San Antonio Express*
Tarrant	Mansfield	store	Farmers' Alliance Co. (inc)	J. M. Bradstreet
Tarrant	Fort Worth	warehouse	District Alliance	*Fort Worth Gazette*
Taylor	Abilene	store	Abilene Alliance Assoc. (not inc)	J. M. Bradstreet
Taylor	Belle Plain	store		*Southern Mercury*
Taylor	Abilene	wagon yard		*Taylor County News*
Travis	Austin	cotton yard		*Southern Mercury*
Trinity	Groveton	cooperative assoc.	Farmers' Alliance Co-operative Assoc. of Trinity County, Texas	Secretary of State Report
Tyler	Chester	cooperative assoc.	Chester Alliance Co-operative Assoc.	Secretary of State Report
Tyler	Colmesneil	store	Tyler Co. Farmers' Alliance Co-op. Assoc.	J. M. Bradstreet
Upshur	Gilmer	store		*Dallas Morning News*
Van Zandt	Ben Wheeler	cooperative assoc.	Van Zandt County Farmers' Alliance Co-operative Assoc.	Secretary of State Report
Walker	Huntsville	cooperative assoc.	Alliance Co-operative Assoc.	Secretary of State Report
Walker	Sion	store	Bedias Alliance Store	J. M. Bradstreet
Waller	Hempstead	store		*Galveston Daily News*
Waller	Waller Station	warehouse		*Galveston Daily News*
Washington	Gay Hill	gin	Gay Hill Alliance Gin Co.	*Southern Mercury*
Washington	Gay Hill	mill	Gay Hill Alliance Gin Co.	*Southern Mercury*
Washington	Brenham	store		*Brenham Banner*

(continued)

Table A.1. Alliance Cooperatives (continued)

County	City or Town	Type of Enterprise	Name of Sponsoring Alliance Entity (if known)	Source
Washington	Chappell Hill	store		*Southern Mercury*
Williamson	Granger	cooperative assoc.	Macedonia Co-operative Alliance Assoc.	Secretary of State Report
Williamson	Bartlett	gin		*Williamson County Sun*
Williamson	Granger	gin		*Fort Worth Gazette*
Wilson	Floresville	cooperative assoc.	Wilson Co. Farmers' Alliance Coop. Assoc. (inc)	J. M. Bradstreet
Wise	Bridgeport	gin		*Paradise Messenger*
Wise	Brumlow	gin	Cottonwood Alliance Gin	*Wise County Messenger*
Wise	Cottondale	gin	Cottondale Alliance Gin and Mill Company	Secretary of State Report
Wise	Lucky Ridge	gin		*Wise County Messenger*
Wise	Willow Point	gin		*Paradise Messenger*
Wise	East Mound	gin		*Wise County Messenger*
Wise	Cottondale	mill	Cottondale Alliance Gin and Mill	*Galveston Daily News*
Wise	Decatur	mill		*Dallas Morning News*
Wise	Willow Point	mill		*Wise County Messenger*
Wise	Decatur	store		*Southern Mercury*
Wise	Decatur	cotton yard		*Wise County Messenger*
Wise	Alvord	cotton yard		*Wise County Messenger*
Wise	Rhome	cotton yard		*Wise County Messenger*
Wise	Decatur	fruit tree agent		*Wise County Messenger*
Wood	Mineola	cotton yard		*Southern Mercury*
Young	Farmer	cooperative assoc.	Farmers Alliance Co-operative Trade Assoc. of Young County	Secretary of State Report
Young	Graham	gin		*Dallas Morning News*

NOTES

Abbreviations

DMN   *Dallas Morning News*
FWG   *Fort Worth Gazette*
GDN   *Galveston Daily News*
HT   *Handbook of Texas Online* (see Digital Secondary Sources)
SM   *Southern Mercury* (Dallas)
TLPP   *Texas Legislators: Past and Present* (see Digital Primary Sources)
TSLAC   Texas State Library and Archives Commission (see Archival Collections)

Introduction

1. "Obama's Health Care Speech to Congress," *New York Times,* Sept. 9, 2009.

2. Ibid.; Kloppenberg, "Barack Obama and Progressive Democracy," 270–71.

3. Ronald Reagan, Inaugural Address, Jan. 20, 1981, http://www.reaganfoundation .org/pdf/SQP012081.pdf; Ryan, *On Politics,* 827 (quoting Sombart).

4. Starr, *Freedom's Power,* 3, 5–6, 16; Ryan, *Making of Modern Liberalism,* 23–26, 39; Fawcett, *Liberalism,* 21. There is a voluminous literature on the origins of Anglo-American political thought, including a vigorous debate between those who stress the importance of republicanism and those who emphasize classical liberalism. I tend to agree with James T. Kloppenberg, who argues that "attempts to disentangle the religious, liberal, and republican strands of the arguments woven during the eighteenth century are futile and counterproductive." See Kloppenberg, "Liberalism," 476. See also Kloppenberg, *Virtues of Liberalism,* 160–63.

5. Starr, *Freedom's Power,* 8–11, 96–99; Ryan, *Making of Modern Liberalism,* 10–12, 25–26; Kloppenberg, "Liberalism." Kloppenberg calls the distinction between positive and negative freedoms "empty and misleading" (476).

6. Kloppenberg, "Well-Tempered Liberalism," 673; Ryan, *Making of Modern Liberalism*, 25.

7. Kloppenberg, "Liberalism," 477–78; Starr, *Freedom's Power*, 96; Fawcett, *Liberalism*, 76–77.

8. Kloppenberg, "Liberalism," 479–80; Starr, *Freedom's Power*, 103–12. For an analysis of Progressive Era reformers who survived into the 1930s and their opposition to the New Deal, see Graham, *Encore for Reform*, esp. chap. 2.

9. Starr, *Freedom's Power*, 8–9, 85; Ryan, *Making of Modern Liberalism*, 459; Kloppenberg, "Well-Tempered Liberalism," 678.

10. Starr, *Freedom's Power*, 112, 126–27, 159–69; Katznelson, *Fear Itself*, passim but esp. 16–18. On the New Deal and the distinction between collective economic rights and individual rights, see Cowie, *Great Exception*.

11. Rawls, *Theory of Justice*; Ryan, *Making of Modern Liberalism*, 505–10 (quotation at 506).

12. Appleby, *Relentless Revolution*, 216–17.

13. Hicks, *Populist Revolt*; Woodward, *Tom Watson*. Woodward fully developed his ideas on Populism in *Origins of the New South*. For an excellent overview of Populist historiography through 1992, see Miller, "Centennial Historiography."

14. Hofstadter, *Age of Reform*; Ferkiss, "Populist Influences"; Miller, "Centennial Historiography," 58–59.

15. Miller, "Centennial Historiography," 59–60, 63–65; Pollack, *Populist Response*; Goodwyn, *Democratic Promise*. Another major example of a work influenced by Goodwyn is Palmer, *"Man over Money."*

16. Sanders, *Roots of Reform*; Lester, *Up from the Mudsills*. Book-length, state-level studies include Clanton, *Kansas Populism*; Larson, *New Mexico Populism*; Miller, *Oklahoma Populism*; Ostler, *Prairie Populism*; Beeby, *Revolt of the Tar Heels*; Rogers, *One-Gallused Rebellion*; Wright, *Politics of Populism*; Shaw, *Wool-Hat Boys*; Barnes, *Louisiana Populist Movement*; Cherny, *Populism, Progressivism*. The two synthetic works are Clanton, *Populism*; and McMath, *American Populism*.

17. Postel, *Populist Vision*, 5, 103, 106.

18. For a good general history of Texas that emphasizes the state's southern heritage, see Campbell, *Gone to Texas*. There have been two book-length studies of Texas Populism. Roscoe Martin's *People's Party in Texas* is a valuable foundational study by a political scientist writing in the progressive tradition of John Hicks. Donna Barnes's *Farmers in Rebellion* is an equally valuable sociological study employing mobilization theory to analyze the Alliance and Populism as a protest movement. However, it devotes only sixty pages to the actual politics of the People's Party.

19. In an influential 1980 article, James Turner, using Texas data, suggested that geographic and social isolation provided the best explanation for the appeal of Populism. In 2008 Worth Robert Miller and Stacy G. Ulbig, utilizing a massive database of precinct-

level election returns and sophisticated quantitative analysis, persuasively rebutted Turner's argument, finding that his argument had some validity for 1892 but that the Populists greatly broadened their appeal and expanded the electorate in the two subsequent statewide elections. My own interpretation is consistent with Miller and Ulbig's findings. See Turner, "Understanding the Populists"; Miller and Ulbig, "Building a Populist Coalition."

20. Kloppenberg, "Liberalism," 475–79; Ryan, *Making of Modern Liberalism,* 24; Starr, *Freedom's Power,* 32–52.

21. Fawcett, *Liberalism,* 25; Kloppenberg, "Liberalism," 479–80; Ryan, *Making of Modern Liberalism,* 33–34.

22. SM, July 11, Apr. 11, 1889; DMN, Dec. 23, 1894.

23. SM, June 9, 1892; TLPP, "J. B. Cone"; Daniell, *Personnel,* 121.

24. SM, Aug. 9, 1894; Ryan, *Making of Modern Liberalism,* 28; Fawcett, *Liberalism,* 25.

25. Kloppenberg, "Liberalism," 482; Starr, *Freedom's Power,* 16; Fawcett, *Liberalism,* 9. For a succinct overview of nineteenth-century patriarchy, see Edwards, *Gendered Strife and Confusion,* 6–8.

26. On Populism and restorationism, see Creech, *Righteous Indignation.*

27. Kazin, *Populist Persuasion.* For a perceptive examination of left- and right-wing populisms in a transnational perspective, see Postel, "American Populist and Anti-Populist Legacy."

28. On Bryan, Darrow, the Scopes Trial, and Populism, see Postel, *Populist Vision,* 246–47.

29. SM, Oct. 20, 1892.

1. The Roots of Texas Populism

1. Gillespie County Alliance Minutes, entry for April 1890. Descriptions of the Texas Hill Country in this chapter are from Caro, *Path to Power,* chap. 1. The information on Sam Johnson in this chapter is developed more fully in Cantrell, "Lyndon's Granddaddy."

2. Caro, *Path to Power,* 21–25.

3. Johnson, *Family Album,* 71; Gillespie County Alliance Minutes, entry for July 1889.

4. Gillespie County Alliance Minutes, entry for April 1890. It should be noted that federal subsidies to the transatlantic railroads eventually dwarfed even what the Subtreasury would have cost, but those monies were doled out piecemeal over time and in ways that largely escaped the public's attention. See White, *Railroaded,* 22–25; Davis, *Political Revelation,* 349.

5. Porter and Harris, *Webster's International Dictionary,* 848.

6. Cantrell, "Lyndon's Granddaddy," 134–36.

7. Ibid., 136–38.

8. Ibid., 138–40.

9. Johnson, *Family Album,* 71.

10. Ibid.; Creech, *Righteous Indignation,* 10–13; Cantrell, "Lyndon's Granddaddy," 138–39.

11. Cantrell, "Lyndon's Granddaddy," 139.

12. Ibid., 138; Jessie Johnson Hatcher interview with Edwin C. Bearss, quoted in Bearss, *Historic Resource Study,* 52.

13. Gillespie County Alliance Minutes, entry for July 1893, 106; Brooks, *Mental Science,* 1, 36–38; Cantrell, "Lyndon's Granddaddy," 150–51.

14. Cantrell, "Lyndon's Granddaddy," 143–50. Also see Chapter 2.

15. LBJ, quoted in Dugger, *Politician,* 55; Cantrell, "Lyndon's Granddaddy," 153–56.

16. Miller, "Farmers," 285; Campbell, *Gone to Texas,* 312.

17. Campbell, *Gone to Texas,* 290, 311.

18. Ayers, *Promise,* 195; Campbell, *Gone to Texas,* 311; White and Leonard, *Studies in Farm Tenancy;* Evans, "Texas Agriculture," 316–20.

19. Campbell, *Gone to Texas,* 310–12; Ayers, *Promise,* 44, 195–204; Spratt, *Road to Spindletop,* 56–60, 292, 295; Fite, *Cotton Fields,* 1–29; Ransom and Sutch, "Debt Peonage," esp. 651–58.

20. Spratt, *Road to Spindletop,* 292; HT, Cecil Harper Jr., and E. Dale Odom, "Farm Tenancy," accessed Feb. 9, 2019, http://www.tshaonline.org/handbook/online/articles /aefmu.

21. HT, Alice J. Rhoades, "Lampasas County," accessed Sept. 21, 2017, http://www .tshaonline.org/handbook/online/articles/hcl03. On the concept of the shatterbelt, see Ely, *Where the West Begins,* 8–16. Two classic treatments of this region can be found in Webb, *Great Plains,* and Fite, *Farmers' Frontier.*

22. McMath, *Populist Vanguard,* 3–16.

23. Hild, *Greenbackers,* 24–26; McMath, *Populist Vanguard,* 7–8; Goodwyn, *Democratic Promise,* 44–46. On the Grange, see Calvert, "Southern Grange."

24. *Burnet Bulletin,* Aug. 14, 1878, July 1, 1879; *Williamson County Sun* (Georgetown), Oct. 31, 1878; GDN, Apr. 16, 1879; *San Antonio Express,* July 12, 1881; *Austin Statesman,* Aug. 25, 1881.

25. HT, Jack W. Gunn, "Greenback Party," accessed Aug. 26, 2017, http://www .tshaonline.org/handbook/online/articles/wag01.

26. Campbell, *Gone to Texas,* 239–89; Barr, *Reconstruction to Reform,* 3–62.

27. Winkler, *Platforms,* 187–89; Hild, *Greenbackers,* 26; Hogg, "'Wash' Jones," 1–7, 9–11; HT, Thomas W. Cutrer, "Jones, George Washington," accessed Sept. 21, 2017, http://www.tshaonline.org/handbook/online/articles/fj049; Martin, "Greenback Party in Texas," 168–69; TLPP; Texas Legislature, *Legislative Manual,* passim; Kingston, Attlesey, and Crawford, *Texas Almanac's Political History,* 59–60.

28. McMath, *Populist Vanguard,* 8. For the Greenbacker affiliations of Bentley, Dohoney, Evans, Jenkins, and Perdue, see Winkler, *Platforms,* 199, 206, 229; for

Tracy, Kearby, and Evans, see their respective entries in HT. For more on Greenback-ers who became Populists, also see Chapter 2.

29. Goodwyn, *Democratic Promise*, 36–39; McMath, *Populist Vanguard*, 16–17. Daws's full name was Sir Outley Daws. His first name is spelled "Sire" or "Syre" in various sources, but apparently "Sir" was his actual name, based on a preponderance of the evidence, including the 1917 probate records of his estate in Greer County, OK, and his widow's Confederate pension record. It seems that he always went by his initials.

30. Goodwyn, *Democratic Promise*, 40–42, 48.

31. Ibid., 40–44; McMath, *Populist Vanguard*, 17–21; Barnes, *Farmers in Rebellion*, 60–66; HT, William F. Holmes, "Colored Farmers' Alliance," accessed Aug. 26, 2017, http://www.tshaonline.org/handbook/online/articles/aac01; Ali, *In the Lion's Mouth*, 48–50.

32. SM, Apr. 22, 1887, Aug. 29, 1889.

33. DMN, Oct. 30, 1885, Dec. 14, 1891; FWG, Oct. 30, 1886, May 10, 1887; GDN, June 9, 1887.

34. *Dallas Mercury*, Mar. 11, 1887; SM, Oct. 2, 1888, Apr. 4, Nov. 21, 1889, Mar. 29, 1890; *Austin Statesman*, Mar. 21, 1889, Aug. 13, 1891; *Gainesville Hesperian*, Apr. 21, 1888; FWG, Jan. 4, 12, June 21, 1888, Mar. 21, 1889, July 22, 1897; GDN, Feb. 26, 1891; *Dublin Progress*, Sept. 18, 1893. Also see the Appendix.

35. See the Appendix.

36. SM, Dec. 4, 1890; *Dallas Mercury*, Mar. 25, 1887.

37. DMN, Oct. 30. 1885; *Dallas Herald*, Oct. 3, 1885; McMath, *Populist Vanguard*, 19; SM, Jan. 3, 1889. In an influential 1983 article, Stanley B. Parsons and colleagues, in an explicit rebuttal to Lawrence Goodwyn, argued that Alliance cooperatives were too few in number, and the travel distance too great, for significant numbers of Alliancefolk to have taken advantage of them. Accordingly, the widespread "movement culture" that Goodwyn suggested had developed from the cooperative crusade could not have existed. The authors based their contention on the number of cooperatives they counted in Texas (which peaked, they argued, at 176) and also on their calculation that a farmer needed to live within seven miles of a cooperative. My own count places the number of cooperatives over 300, nearly double the number Parsons and colleagues counted (they used only the Dun reports), and the anecdotal evidence presented here clearly suggests that farmers did not feel constrained by a distance of greater than seven miles. See Parsons et al., "Role of Cooperatives," 866–85.

38. FWG, Oct. 4, 1890.

39. SM, April 22, 1887, Dec. 6, 1888, Jan. 3, 1889.

40. DMN, Dec. 7, 1894; *Dublin Progress*, Nov. 29, 1888; SM, Jan. 24, 1889.

41. SM, Jan. 31, 1889, July 5, 1894, Nov. 14, 28, 1889, Nov. 12, 1891; *McKinney Democrat*, Aug. 8, 1895.

42. SM, Apr. 22, 1887.

43. *Wise County Messenger*, Aug. 29, 1885.

44. Hild, *Greenbackers*, 67–70.

45. Ibid., 70–71; McMath, *Populist Vanguard*, 23; Goodwyn, *Democratic Promise*, 42–43; Allen, *Chapters*, 19–24, 45–88; *Wise County Messenger*, Aug. 8, 1885; FWG, Sept. 4, 1885.

46. Goodwyn, *Democratic Promise*, 56–57; McMath, *Populist Vanguard*, 23–24; FWG, Oct. 9, 1885; GDN, Feb. 23, 1886.

47. McMath, *Populist Vanguard*, 24; Goodwyn, *Democratic Promise*, 58–62.

48. Goodwyn, *Democratic Promise*, 63, 65; FWG, Nov. 2, 1888; Martin, *People's Party*, 32; Hild, *Greenbackers*, 75; *Brenham Banner*, Aug. 5, 1886; Calvert and Witherspoon, "Populism in Jack County," 32.

49. Daws, quoted in Goodwyn, *Democratic Promise*, 67.

50. Lightfoot, "Human Party," 28–35; HT, Bruce Palmer, "Gaines, Thomas," accessed Sept. 13, 2017, http://www.tshaonline.org/handbook/online/articles/fga5; HT, Bruce Palmer, "Jones, Evan," accessed Sept. 13, 2017, http://www.tshaonline.org/handbook/online/articles/fjo48; Hild, *Greenbackers*, 85; Goodwyn, *Democratic Promise*, 71; Wells, "J. N. Rogers," 48–54.

51. GDN, Aug. 4, 1886; *Waco Examiner*, Sept. 19, 1886; SM, Aug. 29, 1889; McMath, *Populist Vanguard*, 27; Hild, *Greenbackers*, 86; Goodwyn, *Democratic Promise*, 77–82; Winkler, *Political Platforms*, 234–37.

52. McMath, *Populist Vanguard*, 27; Goodwyn, *Democratic Promise*, 83.

53. Goodwyn, *Democratic Promise*, 83–89. On Macune, see Macune, "Wellsprings"; HT, Bruce Palmer and Charles W. Macune Jr., "Macune, Charles William," accessed July 15, 2018, http://www.tshaonline.org/handbook/online/articles/fmao9; Macune, "'The Last Shall Be First.'"

54. Macune, "Wellsprings"; Goodwyn, *Democratic Promise*, 84–94; McMath, *Populist Vanguard*, 28–35. Proceedings are in Dunning, *Farmers' Alliance History*, 48–55.

55. Cowden, "H. S. P. Ashby," 1–12; HT, Bruce Palmer, "Ashby, Harrison Sterling Price," accessed Sept. 13, 2017, http://www.tshaonline.org/handbook/online/articles/faso3.

56. Barnes, *Farmers in Rebellion*, 80–84; Goodwyn, *Democratic Promise*, 125–29.

57. Barnes, *Farmers in Rebellion*, 85–89; Goodwyn, *Democratic Promise*, 129–46. For a useful history of the Exchange by a contemporary, former *Mercury* editor Clarence N. Ousley, see SM, Mar. 29, 1890.

58. GDN, June 17, 24, Jul. 29, Oct. 13, Nov. 28, 1888; FWG, Apr. 27, June 11, Oct. 7, Nov. 2, 6, 8, 1888; *Austin Statesman*, Oct. 18, Nov. 15, 1888; *Waco Morning News*, Oct. 3, 1888; *Wise County Messenger* (Decatur), Sept. 1, 1888; *Corsicana Courier*, July 25, 1888; Winkler, *Platforms*, 266. Martin claimed that Red River County independents also employed the People's Party label in 1888, basing his claim on oral history interviews forty years later, but there is no evidence from the county's extant newspapers that such was the case. See Martin, *People's Party*, 33.

59. Barnes, *Farmers in Rebellion*, 99; SM, June 20, 1889.

60. SM, Jan. 31, 1889. The best account of the jute boycott is in Barnes, *Farmers in Rebellion*, 99–107.

61. FWG, Oct. 29, 30, 31, Nov. 1, 2, 3, 1888; *San Marcos Free Press*, Nov. 29, 1888; SM, Nov. 6, 22, 1888; DMN, Feb. 11, 1892.

62. McMath, *Populist Vanguard*, 90–92; Goodwyn, *Democratic Promise*, 171.

63. *National Economist* (Washington, DC), Dec. 14, 1889.

64. Dunning, *Farmers' Alliance History*, 124, 137.

65. Goodwyn, *Democratic Promise*, 391; SM, July 7, Aug. 28, Sept. 4, 1890.

66. Barnes, *Farmers in Rebellion*, 124–25; McMath, *Populist Vanguard*, 123–24.

67. HT, Robert C. Cotner, "Hogg, James Stephen," accessed Sept. 13, 2017, http://www.tshaonline.org/handbook/online/articles/fho17; Barr, *Reconstruction to Reform*, 118.

68. *Austin Statesman*, Jan. 22, 1891.

69. HT, Bruce Palmer, "Tracy, Harry," accessed Nov. 26, 2017, http://www.tshaonline.org/handbook/online/articles/ftro1; Goodwyn, *Democratic Promise*, 219; DMN, Mar. 31, 1915; "Jesse H. Tracy." The description of Tracy is from Dunning, *Farmers' Alliance History*, plate opposite p. 336.

70. Barnes, *Farmers in Rebellion*, 127; DMN, Mar. 6, 1891; GDN, Mar. 19, 1891; SM, Aug. 29, 1889, Apr. 23, 1891; FWG, Apr. 9, 1891.

71. Martin, *People's Party*, 26–27; Barr, *Reconstruction to Reform*, 121.

72. SM, Jan. 1, 1891; Dunning, *Farmers' Alliance History*, 152; Goodwyn, *Democratic Promise*, 227–32; McMath, *Populist Vanguard*, 107–9; Hild, *Greenbackers*, 137–39.

73. Goodwyn, *Democratic Promise*, 236–43.

74. Barnes, *Farmers in Rebellion*, 128–29; Goodwyn, *Democratic Promise*, 245–48; FWG, May 28, 29, June 28, 1891; GDN, May 21, 22, 28, 31, July 10, 1891; DMN, Apr. 16, 1894. On Davis, see Williams, "Political Career"; Ross, "Historical and Critical Study"; HT, Worth Robert Miller, "Davis, James Harvey [Cyclone]," accessed July 15, 2018, http://www.tshaonline.org/handbook/online/articles/fda41.

75. Martin, *People's Party*, 40; *McKinney Democrat*, May 28, 1891; DMN, June 8, 19, July 2, 3, 1891; GDN, July 4, 1891; FWG, Aug. 6, 1891; SM, June 18, July 9, 1891.

76. SM, Oct. 20, 1892.

77. SM, Nov. 21, 1889.

2. The Birth of the People's Party and the Election of 1892

1. McConnell, "Spiritualism in Dallas, Texas"; DMN, Aug. 7, 1887, June 30, 1889, Sept. 18, 1893, Sept. 26, 1894, Jan. 21, 1899; GDN, Feb. 18, 1880.

2. "History of Dallas City Hall Buildings," City of Dallas website, accessed Apr. 23, 2019, http://dallascityhall.com/government/citysecretary/archives/Pages/Archives_buildings.aspx; DMN, June 30, 1889.

3. DMN, Aug. 18, 1891; FWG, Aug. 18, 1891.

4. DMN, June 19, 1891. For Tracy's whereabouts during the Cincinnati convention, see SM, May 23, 1891; GDN, May 31, June 1, 1891. Nugent declared for the Ocala Demands in a speech in early July; see *Dublin Progress,* July 11, 1891. Kearby published a long letter endorsing Populist principles a week before the convention; see SM, Aug. 13, 1891.

5. DMN, July 2, 1891.

6. Ibid., Aug. 18, 1891.

7. Finley's action was precipitated by Dallas County's expulsion of county executive committeeman W. R. Cole for his pro-Subtreasury views. See Martin, *People's Party,* 39–40; Barnes, *Farmers in Rebellion,* 131–33; SM, Oct. 9, 16, Nov. 26, Dec. 3, 1891; *Abilene Reporter,* Mar. 4, 1892; *Velasco Times,* Apr. 1, 1892; GDN, Apr. 2, 1892.

8. DMN, Nov. 25, 1891, Feb. 11, Apr. 28, June 7, 1892; GDN, June 17, 1892; SM, Feb. 18, Apr. 14, May 12, 1892; FWG, Feb. 11, 1892; *Austin Statesman,* May 5, 1892. People in the 1890s often referred to the People's Party as the "Third Party," and I will use that term (capitalized) specifically to indicate the People's Party. Uncapitalized it will refer to a generic third party.

9. DMN, Feb. 3, 1892; FWG, Feb. 4, 1892.

10. SM, Feb. 13, 1892; DMN, Feb. 23, 1892; McMath, *Populist Vanguard,* 130–31.

11. *Dublin Progress,* Feb. 26, Mar. 11, June 3, 1892.

12. Alter, "Dirt Farmer Internationalists," 195–96 (including quotation from the *Halletsville Herald*).

13. SM, June 30, 1892; GDN, June 25, 1892.

14. Nugent, *Life Work,* 364.

15. GDN, June 24, 1892; DMN, June 25, 1892. Here and elsewhere I refer to the Dallas-Galveston *News* collectively because as sister papers owned by A. H. Belo, the *Dallas Morning News* and the *Galveston Daily News* shared much content. When I refer to them in this way, readers may assume that the same story appeared in both papers.

16. HT, Harold J. Weiss Jr., "McCulloch, Henry Eustace," accessed Oct. 28, 2017, http://www.tshaonline.org/handbook/online/articles/fmc35. For numerous examples of county conventions instructing for McCulloch, see GDN, June 6, 7, 12, 13, 1892.

17. HT, Weiss, "McCulloch, Henry Eustace."

18. HT, Worth Robert Miller, "Nugent, Thomas Lewis," accessed Oct. 28, 2017, http://www.tshaonline.org/handbook/online/articles/fnu02; Nugent, *Life Work;* Alvord, "T. L. Nugent: Texas Populist"; Taylor, "Thomas Lewis Nugent."

19. GDN, June 5, 9, 1892. As an indication of Nugent's low profile within Populist circles, the first significant mention of him in the *Southern Mercury* came when the paper published his Stephenville speech in its June 23 issue, the very day the Dallas convention began.

20. Ibid., June 14, 1892.

21. *McKinney Democrat,* June 30, 1892; DMN, June 24, 1892; GDN, June 25, 1892; SM, June 30, 1892; DMN, June 26, 1892.

22. GDN, June 25, 1892. Neither the Drake nor Clemmons nominations turned out well for the Populists, as Drake received and accepted the Republican nomination for Congress and Clemmons died before the election. Both had to be replaced on the ticket by the state executive committee. See GDN, July 13, Sept. 16, 1892.

23. DMN, Feb. 1, 1892.

24. GDN, June 25, 1892.

25. Ibid.; Winkler, *Platforms,* 271, 296, 299, 314–16. On the Single Tax, see Postel, *Populist Vision,* 228–33. Postel neglects to note the removal of the plank in the June convention.

26. Winkler, *Platforms,* 293–99, 314–16.

27. DMN, June 25, 1892; Winkler, *Platforms,* 315.

28. GDN, June 25, 1892.

29. Ibid., June 24, 25, 1892. Hayes of Tarrant and Jasper Crenshaw of Collin were the two black delegates chosen to go to Omaha. It is not clear why Crenshaw was the choice over Henry Jennings, the leader of the black Populists of Collin County, but Jennings's age—seventy-one—and his possible inability to pay for the trip may have been factors.

30. GDN, June 24, 1892; DMN, July 2, 3, 6, 1892; SM, July 14, 1892.

31. *Chicago Inter Ocean,* July 5, 1892.

32. DMN, July 9, 1892.

33. Barr, *Reconstruction to Reform,* 131; Northrup and DeZouche, "Turn Texas Loose."

34. Cotner, *James Stephen Hogg,* 270–71, 296.

35. Barr, *Reconstruction to Reform,* 131; Cotner, *James Stephen Hogg,* 277.

36. DMN, Aug. 9, 1892.

37. Ibid., Aug. 18, 19, 1892; Barr, *Reconstruction to Reform,* 134–36; Cotner, *James Stephen Hogg,* 300.

38. DMN, quoting the FWG, Aug. 3, 1892; SM, Aug. 18, 1892.

39. SM, April 7, 1892.

40. *Dublin Progress,* June 17, 1892; SM, Dec. 22, 1892.

41. *McKinney Democrat,* June 2, 1892; DMN, May 11, June 24, Sept. 12, Nov. 2, 1892; GDN, June 8, 1892; GDN, July 11, 1892; SM, May 5, 25, June 23, 1892. For an extensive discussion of Populist clubs, see Martin, *People's Party,* 146–48.

42. DMN, June 23, July 7, 12, Aug. 27, 1892; *McKinney Democrat,* July 7, 1892; SM, May 6, 26, June 23, 30, July 7, 14, 21, 28, Aug. 4, 11, 18, 25, Sept. 1, 8, 15, 22, 29, Oct. 6, 13, 20, 27, 1892.

43. DMN, Sept. 5, 1892. On Meitzen, see Meitzen, "Meitzens Make Texas Proud"; Alter, "Dirt Farmer Internationalists."

44. HT, Bruce Palmer, "Southern Mercury," accessed Oct. 28, 2017, http://www
.tshaonline.org/handbook/online/articles/ees12; HT, Palmer, "Tracy, Harry"; HT,
Cecil Harper Jr., "Park, Milton," accessed Oct. 28, 2017, http://www.tshaonline.org
/handbook/online/articles/fpa15; SM, Oct. 4, 1894. Chapter 8 of Martin, *People's
Party,* provides an excellent overview of the state reform press operation, and Wells,
"Reform Press," places Texas in the context of national Populism.

45. DMN, June 1, 1895. For the telegraphic sharing of news content by the two papers, see DMN, Oct. 10, 1885.

46. SM, May 11, 1893; GDN, Apr. 25, 1891; Martin, *People's Party,* 193–201. Martin
erroneously dates the founding of the state Reform Press Association to 1893. William Lamb, J. W. Erwin, Ward Coleman, Harry Tracy, Ed Moore, and Thomas Gaines
were the original officers of the association. According to newspaper industry data, in
1892 there were fourteen Alliance papers, four People's Party papers, and two Colored Alliance papers. These do not include T. L. Sanders's *Cleburne Tribune* and S. J.
Brownson and William Lamb's *Fort Worth Industrial Educator and Texas Independent*
(both listed as Labor); see N. W. Ayer, *N. W. Ayer* (1892), 712–39.

47. On Ashby, Nugent, Davis, Kearby, and Rayner as orators, see Martin, *People's
Party,* 116–18, 120–127; Cantrell, *Kenneth and John B. Rayner,* 209–10, 212, 226–29.
Physical descriptions of Wade can be found in GDN, Sept. 3, 1884; *McKinney Demo-
crat,* July 25, 1895. For a characteristic sampling of Wade's oratory, see DMN,
Nov. 29, 1892, Jan. 6, April 7, 1894, Feb. 1, June 3, 1896.

48. DMN, Aug. 6, 1892. The record for length of a Populist speech may have been
set by R. W. Coleman of San Antonio, who held forth for four hours and fifteen minutes at a camp meeting in Comanche County; see DMN, Aug. 23, 1892.

49. DMN, Aug. 19, 1892.

50. Ibid.

51. SM, Sept. 29, 1892.

52. Cotner, *James Stephen Hogg,* 268, 283, 302–3; Barr, *Reconstruction to Reform,*
122, 128; GDN, Sept. 19, 1892.

53. Cotner, *James Stephen Hogg,* 303–7; Barr, *Reconstruction to Reform,* 137–38;
Richardson, *Colonel Edward M. House,* 51–59; DMN, Nov. 4, 1892.

54. DMN, Oct. 2, 1892.

55. GDN, Sept. 1, 30, 1892.

56. Ibid., June 25, 1891, Sept. 12, Oct. 21, 26, 1892.

57. DMN, Nov. 11, 1892; GDN, Oct. 6, 9, 24, 26, 31, 1892.

58. Winkler, *Platforms,* 318; GDN, Sept. 10, 9, Oct. 2, 1892; DMN, Nov. 8, 1892.

59. For an extended discussion of the Populists and lynching, see Chapter 5.

60. SM, June 23, Oct. 6, 27, 1892; GDN, Aug. 8, Sept. 3, 20, 1892.

61. DMN, Aug. 19, 21, 1892; SM, Dec. 1, 1892.

62. SM, Oct. 13, 1892; DMN, Oct. 12, Nov. 2, 1892; *McKinney Democrat,* Oct. 13,
1892.

63. *Biennial Report . . . 1892*, 98; *Lampasas People's Journal*, Nov. 18, 1892; "Voter Participation in Texas," Texas Almanac.com, accessed Oct. 29, 2017, https://texasalmanac .com/sites/default/files/images/topics/prezturnout.pdf; Miller and Ulbig, "Building a Populist Coalition," 263; Cantrell and Barton, "Texas Populists," 662.

64. For analyses of geographic voting patterns in the 1892 election, see Miller and Ulbig, "Building a Populist Coalition," 270–78; Martin, *People's Party*, 58–70; Barr, *Reconstruction to Reform*, 139–40.

65. DMN, Nov. 18, 1892; *Lampasas People's Journal*, Nov. 11, 1892.

3. Ideology and Policy

1. This is the basic theme of Hicks, *Populist Revolt*, and of Martin, *People's Party*.

2. These themes have received their fullest treatment in the works of Robert C. McMath Jr., especially *American Populism*, 13, 17, 19–49 (quotation on p. 44). Also see McMath, "C. Vann Woodward," 752–53; McMath, "Another Look," 215–16.

3. White, *Railroaded*, 111–12.

4. The now sizable scholarly literature on republicanism begins largely with Bailyn, *Ideological Origins*; Shalhope, "Toward a Republican Synthesis"; Pocock, *Machiavellian Moment*; and Wood, *Creation of the American Republic*. For a collection of essays that elaborated on, and in some cases criticized, the concept, see the special issue of *American Quarterly* (Fall 1985). For a succinct summary of the relevant historiography, see Rodgers, "Republicanism."

5. Kloppenberg, "Virtues of Liberalism," 16–19.

6. Ibid., 24–25.

7. DMN, Nov. 13, 1891; SM, July 16, 1891, Apr. 14, 1892.

8. Luke 10:7. Also Matthew 10:10, I Timothy 5:18, II Timothy 2:6, and other passages.

9. SM, July 16, 1891; White, *Railroaded*, 111; McMath, *American Populism*, chap. 2, esp. 50–53.

10. Commons, *Documentary History*, 9:117–274; Powderly, *Thirty Years*, 112–20 (quotation on p. 118).

11. *Record of the Proceedings.*

12. *New York Times*, Feb. 23, 1878; Vincent, *Platform Text Book*, 81–82, 94 (quotations).

13. Winkler, *Platforms*, 199, 206, 229; HT, Palmer, "Tracy, Harry"; HT, David Minor, "Kearby, Jerome Claiborne," accessed Sept. 22, 2017, http://www.tshaonline .org/handbook/online/articles/fke02; HT, Aragorn Storm Miller, "Evans, Samuel," accessed Sept. 22, 2017, http://www.tshaonline.org/handbook/online/articles/fev32; Martin, "Greenback Party," 172; DMN, July 21, 1893.

14. Vincent, *Platform Text Book*, 118–19; Goodwyn, *Democratic Promise*, 101; Hild, *Greenbackers*, 113–14.

15. Vincent, *Platform Text Book*, 118–19; Goodwyn, *Democratic Promise*, 101; Hild, *Greenbackers*, 113–14. The Cleburne Demands can be found in Dunning, *Farmers' Alliance History*, 41–43.

16. GDN, Apr. 16, 1892, July 22, 1896; DMN, Apr. 27, 1896; Postel, *Populist Vision*, 235–36; *Shiner Gazette*, Aug. 4, 1897; *Weimar Mercury*, Oct. 26, 1895.

17. DMN, June 1, 1890, June 9, 1891; *Cameron Herald*, Dec. 5, 1895.

18. Nugent, *Life Work*, 176, 263, 266; DMN, July 30, 1893, Sept. 29, 1894.

19. Postel, *Populist Vision*, 228–33; Piott, *American Reformers*, chap. 2, esp. 34–36.

20. Winkler, *Platforms*, 271, 296, 299; DMN, June 24, July 7, 1892, Sept. 26, 1894; SM, May 11, 1893; *McKinney Democrat*, Mar. 15, 1894. Alsbury's obituary can be found in the GDN, Jan. 19, 1912.

21. Nugent, *Life Work*, 257–58, 263; *Texas Advance*, May 5, 1894.

22. Nugent, *Life Work*, 265. Readers of *Life Work* should read the section titled "Views on the Land Question" (110–20) with caution, because it was written by J. G. H. Buck, the ardent Populist Single Taxer from Hill County who attributes orthodox Georgeist beliefs to Nugent with little actual documentation. According to Buck, Nugent personally promised, if elected governor, to urge the state legislature to appoint a commission to study tax reform, which he hoped would incorporate George's theories. This may well be true, but we have to accept Buck's word for it. Some modern historians have described Nugent as a "Christian Socialist," a label with which I disagree. See Wilkison, *Yeomen, Sharecroppers, and Socialists*, 168; Alter, "Dirt Farmer Internationalists," 201.

23. *Wise County Messenger*, Aug. 1, 1885.

24. DMN, Feb. 28, Sept. 19, 1892.

25. SM, June 9, 1892, Jan. 3, 1895.

26. Ibid.

27. DMN, Dec. 23, 1894.

28. Ibid., July 9, Dec. 1, 1892, Mar. 5, July 13, 1895; SM, May 30, 1895, Jan. 16, 1896; Buck, Recording Ballot-Box; Bentley, Map.

29. *Wise County Messenger*, July 25, 1885; DMN, Aug. 7, 1892; SM, Oct. 27, 1892.

30. Nugent, *Life Work*, 172, 173, 247. Populists' use of the language of producerism has, I believe, led scholars to overemphasize its importance in Populist thought; see, e.g., Palmer, *"Man Over Money."* It has also had the effect of making the discontinuities between Populists and later reformers, particularly the progressives, seem greater than they may have been; see, e.g., Stromquist, *Reinventing "The People,"* esp. 13–22, 55, 57–59, 201–4.

31. DMN, Nov. 22, 1894; SM, Dec. 22, 1892; *Dublin Progress*, Mar. 17, 1893.

32. Cowie, *Great Exception*, 95; Hofstadter, *Age of Reform*, 46; Lasch, *True and Only Heaven*.

33. *McKinney Democrat*, May 17, 1894.

34. DMN, Jan. 17, 1896; *Dublin Progress*, June 23, 1893; SM, Aug. 6, 1896; Nugent, *Life Work*, 138.

35. White, *Railroaded*, xxiii, 4, 22–25, 50, 103, 221, 318, 419, 450, 492, 522.

36. Ibid., xxxi, xxxiv, 5–6, 119–20, 151–52, 160–62, 174–78, 282–316, 328–31, 492, 513.

37. *National Economist*, July 9, 1892; Winkler, *Platforms*, 315, 296, 297, 333, 334, 382, 383.

38. Nugent, *Life Work*, 137, 171, 174; SM, Mar. 21, 1895.

39. White, *Railroaded*, 331; SM, Feb. 11, 1892; *Mineola Alliance Courier*, Oct. 6, 1892.

40. DMN, July 10, 1892.

41. Ibid., July 31, 1892.

42. Ibid.; SM, Aug. 6, 1895.

43. SM, Feb. 11, 1892; DMN, Feb. 1, 1892; Winkler, *Platforms*, 398.

44. SM, July 7, 14, 1892, Mar. 21, 1895; DMN, July 10, 1892, May 14, 1894; *Texas Herald*, Mar. 31, 1898; Nugent, *Life Work*, 138, 155. On inflated bond values and over-capitalization, see, e.g., White, *Railroaded*, 189–200 and passim.

45. Tracy, in his appendix to Davis, *Political Revelation*, 332; DMN, Aug. 7, 1892, Feb. 29, 1896; SM, Oct. 20, 1892, Mar. 21, 1895; *Waco Evening News*, Sept. 6, 1892.

46. Chandler, *Visible Hand*, 204; Gallagher, *How the Post Office Created America*, esp. chap. 12.

47. Nonnenmacher, "History of the U.S. Telegraph Industry."

48. *Honey Grove Signal*, May 25, 1894; Fuller, "Populists and the Post Office."

49. SM, Aug. 3, 1893, Aug. 9, 1894, Mar. 5, 1896. All comparisons of Populism (or for that matter, liberalism) with socialism are complicated by the myriad definitions of what actually constitutes socialism. Socialism as a concept can encompass every-thing from a strict Marxism, in which private property has been largely or entirely abolished, to democratic socialism, in which a movement toward a socialist economy is achieved incrementally through peaceful and constitutional means, to systems of social democracy as practiced in certain Western European countries, which feature extensive state regulation of major industries but with only limited state ownership. Like twenty-first-century Americans, those calling themselves socialists in the Popu-list era could fall anywhere along this continuum. When Texas Populists criticized socialism and disclaimed any affinity for it (which was their usual position), they tended to use definitions of the Marxian or at least the democratic-socialist varieties; that is, they saw socialism as a replacement for capitalism. The reality is that most Populists in the 1890s, like most liberals in the twenty-first century, thought they knew what socialism was, and they did not believe that it described themselves, even if their own political ideology featured certain elements of practical socialism. A modern ob-server might equate 1890s Populism with social democracy today, and the compari-son would not be all wrong. Neither, however, are the comparisons between modern

476 NOTES TO PAGES 129–135

liberalism and social democracy all wrong; in modern usage the terms are virtually synonymous. When modern liberals hold up the Scandinavian countries as examples for the United States to emulate, they are touting social democracy; that is, they accept capitalism as an economic system but use both public ownership and government regulation to ameliorate its worst abuses and shortcomings. In the 2016 US elections, liberal Hillary Clinton (although she tended to call herself a progressive) and social democrat Bernie Sanders (who confusingly and inaccurately called himself a democratic socialist) differed only in details and degrees when it came to policy; they both supported a capitalist economy tempered by an activist state, and either could rightly be called either a liberal or a social democrat. Neither was much of a socialist. The point is that the 1890s Populists, in their understanding of the relationship between the individual, the state, and the economy, had much more in common with a Hillary Clinton or a Bernie Sanders than they did with any socialists, now or a century ago, who saw government ownership of the means of production as an end in itself. For a perceptive essay from the 2016 campaign that touched on these issues, see Tupy, "Bernie Is Not a Socialist."

50. Goodwyn, *Democratic Promise*, 222, 561–70.

51. Unlike the Populists' plans for government ownership of the railroads, much has been written about the Subtreasury Plan, a fact that reflects both the novelty and complexity of the plan as well as scholars' interest in it. Three foundational sources for in-depth study of the plan are Harry Tracy's 107-page treatise on the subject, published as an appendix to Davis, *Political Revelation*, 292–397; William P. Yohe, "An Economic Appraisal of the Sub-Treasury Plan," published as Appendix B of Goodwyn, *Democratic Promise;* and Hicks, "Sub-Treasury."

52. *Dublin Progress*, Sept. 12, 1891; Goodwyn, *Democratic Promise*, 135; McMath, *Populist Vanguard*, 134; Postel, *Populist Vision*, 154–55.

53. Ritter, *Goldbugs and Greenbacks*, 69–70, 285n15.

54. Postel, *Populist Vision*, 11–12, 34–38, 73–79, 153.

55. *Velasco Times*, Oct. 24, 1891; DMN, Aug. 15, 1892, Feb. 23, 1896.

56. *National Economist*, July 9, 1892; *Dublin Progress*, July 11, 1891; DMN, Oct. 12, 1892, Dec. 17, 1893, Jan. 17, 1896.

57. DMN, June 20, 1894; Winkler, *Platforms*, 333, 379–84; SM, Nov. 21, 1895, Feb. 6, 1896; "People's Party Platform, Adopted at St. Louis, July 24, 1896," in Edwards and DeFeo, *1896: The Presidential Campaign.*

58. SM, June 4, 1891, Feb. 12, 1892, Jan. 26, Apr. 13, 1893, May 30, 1895; DMN, June 20, 1894, June 1, 1895; Keynes, quoted in Steil, *Battle of Bretton Woods*, 75; Friedman, *Capitalism and Freedom*, 42; Lowenstein, *America's Bank.* One former Texas Populist, Joe Eagle, was a member of Congress when the Federal Reserve Act was passed, and he was one of its authors. He later took credit for proposing "those amendments to the original bill later adopted which made it more democratic and workable";

see "Joe H. Eagle, Candidate for Re-Election to Congress in Democratic Primary, July 27, 1940," campaign broadside in Eagle Papers, Box 4.

59. DMN, Feb. 25, 1896; SM, June 6, 1895.

60. My interpretation of the events of 1893 and the silver issue are drawn primarily from Ritter, *Goldbugs and Greenbacks*, 19–25, 39–47; Clanton, *Congressional Populism*, 45–58; Lewis L. Gould, "Party Conflict: Republicans versus Democrats, 1877–1901," in Calhoun, *Gilded Age*, 267–76; and esp. Williams, *Realigning America*, 21–39.

61. Quotations from *The Wonderful Wizard of Oz* in Ritter, *Goldbugs and Greenbacks*, 23; Williams, *Realigning America*, 36–38.

62. Pollack, "Origins of the Modern Income Tax," esp. 297, 299.

63. SM, Jan. 14, 1892, Mar. 23, 1893.

64. SM, Jan. 5, 12, 1893.

65. Ibid., Jan. 5, 12, 1893.

66. Pollack, "Origins of the Modern Income Tax," 302–6 (quote from Democratic congressman Uriel Hall on p. 304). On selective issue endorsement, see Barnes, *Farmers in Rebellion*, 44–45.

67. SM, Jan. 5, 1893, Apr. 9, 1896; "Pollack, "Origins of the Modern Income Tax," 307.

68. SM, Oct. 7, 1897.

69. Armstrong, *Little Statesman*, 9; SM, Oct. 7, 1897.

70. *National Economist* (Washington, DC), July 9, 1892; *McKinney Democrat*, Dec. 19, 1895; "1884 Democratic Party Platform," American Presidency Project, https://www.presidency.ucsb.edu/documents/1884-democratic-party-platform; Winkler, *Platforms*, 381; *St. Louis Post-Dispatch*, July 24, 1896. The *Post-Dispatch* of this date includes the entire platform as well as Kearby's role on the committee.

71. *Texas Triangle*, Oct. 7, 1898; *Dublin Progress*, July 14, 1893; SM, Dec. 22, 1892. By 1896, the state party had actually begun dividing its platform into six sections: National Politics, Taxation, Land, Schools, Labor, and General Demands; see Winkler, *Platforms*, 381–83. The party's education demands are treated extensively in Chapters 5 and 8.

72. *National Economist*, July 9, 1892.

73. SM, Aug. 2, 1894; DMN, July 2, 1896.

74. Winkler, *Platforms*, 315, 333–34, 382; Nugent, *Life Work*, 194, 195, 204.

75. SM, May 4, 1893, May 30, 1895. The party's legislative agenda at the state level is developed more fully in Chapter 8.

76. SM, June 15, 1893, May 4, 1893.

77. DMN, Sept. 23, 1894; SM, Feb. 11, 1892, Oct. 17, 1895.

78. For a particularly insightful Populist analysis of corporate limited liability, see W. E. Kimbrough's essay in SM, Jan. 7, 1892.

79. Nugent, *Life Work*, 183.

80. *National Economist* (Washington, DC), July 9, 1892. It should be noted that all of these reforms except the initiative and referendum became federal law in the twentieth century, and many states adopted the initiative and referendum.

81. Winkler, *Platforms*, 381, 382; *Texas Advance*, May 19, 1894; DMN, Feb. 2, 1896. See also Chapter 8.

82. SM, Mar. 24, 1892, Feb. 2, 1893, Oct. 4, Nov. 8, Dec. 18, 1894, Nov. 21, 1895, Jan. 2, 1896, Oct. 19, 1899; Winkler, *Platforms*, 334, 382, 398. See also Chapter 8.

83. Nugent, *Life Work*, 204–5.

84. *Cleburne Herald*, May 28, 1896.

4. The Religious World of Texas Populists

1. DMN, June 25, 1892.

2. Ryan, *Making of Modern Liberalism*, 30–31. For introductions to the topic of Texas Populists and religion, see McMath, "Godly Populists"; King, "Religious Dimensions"; and Locke, "Making the Bible Belt."

3. *Compendium of the Eleventh Census, 1890*, 2:265–72; Martin, *People's Party*, 84. Among the former states of the Confederacy, only Arkansas and Florida reported fewer communicants than Texas, but Texas's figures are roughly comparable to other, longer-settled states such as Pennsylvania (33%), Tennessee (31%), and Indiana (30%).

4. Creech, *Righteous Indignation*, 22–28 (quotation on p. 28).

5. Ibid., 5–6, 24–26.

6. Boyer, *When Time Shall Be No More*, 86–100; Phillips, *White Metropolis*, 47–51.

7. SM, Mar. 7, Apr. 11, Feb. 14, 1895; Moody, quoted in Phillips, *White Metropolis*, 50. Dwight L. Moody preached a series of revivals in Texas in 1895, and in his Dallas appearance shared the podium with Scofield; see DMN, Feb. 26, 1895. In the twentieth century, premillennial dispensationalism became a prominent feature of the new Protestant fundamentalism, which exercised significant influence over conservative politics from the 1920s down to the present day. The antipathy of Populism to dispensationalism's antireformist conservatism contradicts the arguments of those who find commonalities between the modern religious right and the Populists of the 1890s.

8. DMN, October 7, 1894, May 6, 1896; SM, Sept. 5, 12, 1895. On Jones, see Minnix, *Laughter in the Amen Corner*, esp. chap. 9.

9. For a perceptive account of the roots of southern evangelicalism, see Beeman, *Evolution of the Southern Backcountry*.

10. Hahn, *Nation*, 232–33.

11. DMN, Sept. 27, 1894; HT, Palmer, "Ashby, Harrison Sterling Price"; HT, Keith L. King, "Andrews, Reddin, Jr." accessed June 28, 2018, http://www.tshaonline.org/handbook/online/articles/fan49; *McKinney Democrat*, July 7, 1892; Cantrell, *Kenneth and John B. Rayner*; DMN, Sept. 27, 1894; King, "Religious Dimensions," 122–30.

The DMN article identifies John Wilson Biard as a preacher, but this is likely an error; there is no other record of his being a preacher, but his first cousin, James Monroe Biard, who was also an Allianceman, was a Disciples of Christ minister. All the Biards were Disciples.

12. DMN, Sept. 27, 1894.

13. *Christian Courier*, Mar. 28, 1894; GDN, Oct. 9, 1896; HT, Daniel A. Penick, "Dabney, Robert Lewis," accessed Oct. 5, 2017, http://www.tshaonline.org/handbook /online/articles/fda01. The conservative GDN, which opposed not only Populism but William Jennings Bryan as well, asked in 1896 whether "the evil work" of "getting church and state badly mixed" began with "Mr. Bryan's use of the crown and the cross at Chicago." See GDN, Sept. 13, 1896.

14. *McKinney Democrat*, July 26, 1894, Sept. 19, 1895; *Indiana State Journal*, June 23, 1897.

15. DMN, Apr. 24, 1894.

16. *McKinney Democrat*, Nov. 1, 1894, July 7, 1892, Jan. 16, 1896 (fourth and fifth quotations quoting the *Comanche Chief*), Apr. 16, 1896; *Mason County Herald* (quoting the *Texas Farmer*), July 9, 1892.

17. Creech, *Righteous Indignation*, 27.

18. Ibid., chap. 1, esp. pp. 17–18. The list of major Populists who were Disciples members is particularly striking: U. M Browder, E. L. Dohoney, Willis L. Harrison, Cyclone Davis, C. H. Jenkins, William B. Whitacre, W. L. Thurman, and John Wilson Biard, among many others.

19. On restorationism and Populism, see Creech, *Righteous Indignation*, xxiii–xiv, 10–14, 18–21, 100–101, 144–45, and passim. For an overview of restorationism with emphasis on the Christian Church, see Conkin, *American Originals*, chap. 1.

20. SM, Apr. 23, 1896; HT, Carl H. Moneyhon, "Wheelock, Edwin Miller," accessed Oct. 5, 2017, http://www.tshaonline.org/handbook/online/articles/fwh11. Wheelock's identity as a Populist is established by the obituary he wrote of Thomas L. Nugent in 1895, in which he referred to Nugent as "our standard bearer" and mentioned Nugent as a likely People's Party candidate for the vice presidency if he had lived; see Nugent, *Life Work*, 396.

21. *Rockdale Messenger*, Nov. 3, 1898; SM, Aug. 2, 1894, Feb. 28, June 13, 1895, Mar. 9, 1896.

22. SM, Sept. 19, 1894. For his denunciations of ministers and bishops, the Methodist Church eventually expelled Passmore from the ministry. See *Rocky Mountain News*, June 17, 1894; *Denver Evening Post*, Feb. 11, 1895; *Rocky Ford Enterprise*, Sept. 3, 1896; *Cheney Sentinel*, Sept. 3, 1896; *Appeal to Reason*, May 15, 1897.

23. DMN, Oct. 7, 1893; SM, June 24, 1897, Feb. 21, 1895; *San Antonio Express*, June 21, 1894; *Houston Chronicle*, Mar. 17, 1907.

24. References to Nehemiah can be found in DMN, July 22, 1892, Apr. 19, Sept. 21, 1894, Nov. 12, 1896.

25. DMN, Sept. 19, 21, 27, 1894; *Alliance Vindicator,* quoted in *Christian Courier,* Dec. 13, 1893; *McKinney Democrat,* Sept. 19, 1895.

26. SM, Nov. 12, 1896, June 16, 1892, Mar. 19, 1896; DMN, Apr. 19, 1894, June 12, 1892.

27. DMN, Feb. 2, 1895, July 28, 1892; SM, Feb. 4, June 16, Oct. 6, 1892.

28. *Dublin Progress,* July 7, 1893; *Texas Advance,* Apr. 7, 1894; GDN, Sept. 7, 1894.

29. *McKinney Democrat,* Sept. 26, 1895.

30. Postel, *Populist Vision,* 20–21, 246–49.

31. *McKinney Democrat,* July 2, 1896.

32. DMN, Apr. 19, 1894.

33. Ibid.

34. *Houston Chronicle,* May 9, 1909; John B. Rayner, "The Travail of the Soul, in Its Travel from Imperfection Back to Perfection," undated manuscript in Rayner Papers.

35. King, "Religious Dimensions," 161–63; DMN, Dec. 30, 1895, Dec. 5, 1897; GDN, Aug. 9, 1896; King, *John Counsellor's Evolution.*

36. GDN, Aug. 8, 1896; King, "Religious Dimensions," 163–64. For the results of Francisco's 1894 congressional race, see *Official Manual,* 79. The 1896 nomination for superintendent of public instruction was hotly contested, with Francisco emerging as something of a dark horse when delegates apparently became concerned that the prohibitionist views of the front-runner, E. L. Dohoney, would cost the party the German vote in Central Texas. An account of the nomination battle, along with an engraving of Francisco, can be found in the above-cited issue of the GDN.

37. Dohoney, *Average American,* 197; HT, S. S. McKay and Doug Johnson, "Dohoney, Ebenezer Lafayette," accessed Oct. 5, 2017, http://www.tshaonline.org/handbook /online/articles/fdoo7; King, "Religious Dimensions," 167–69.

38. HT, McKay and Johnson, "Dohoney, Ebenezer Lafayette"; Dohoney, *Average American,* 215–71; DMN, Aug. 8, 1896; Locke, "Making the Bible Belt," 32–33.

39. McConnell, "Spiritualism in Dallas, Texas," 149; DMN, June 30, 1889, Nov. 21, 1892, Sept. 18, Dec. 23, 1893, Jan. 20, July 16, Sept. 26, 1894; SM, July 25, 1895; Butler, "Freethinkers," 22–27; Texas Equal Rights Association Scrapbook, McCallum Papers, 25–26; Locke, "Making the Bible Belt," 54–56.

40. Postel, *Populist Vision,* 260; King, "Religious Dimensions," 169–72. For a recent study that reinforces the interpretation of Populist heterodoxy, see Postel, "Murder on the Brazos."

41. *Rockdale Messenger,* Jan. 26, Feb. 9, 23, Mar. 2, 16, 1899.

42. Nugent, *Life Work,* 313–14, 287, 307, 304–5, 310. Also see King, "Religious Dimensions," 154–56; Postel, *Populist Vision,* 254–55; Alvord, "T. L. Nugent"; Taylor, "Thomas Lewis Nugent."

43. SM, Nov. 3, 1892; DMN, Nov. 5, 1892.

44. Nugent, *Life Work,* 315–16.

45. *Dublin Progress*, June 8, 1894.

46. SM, Aug. 27, 1896; DMN, Aug. 31, 1898; King, "Religious Dimensions," 156–57.

47. *McKinney Democrat*, May 17, 1894; DMN, Mar. 15, 1894.

48. *Texas Advance*, Mar. 31, 1894; SM, May 4, 1893.

49. On the question of social and ideological discrimination against Jews by Populists, see Nugent, *Tolerant Populists*, esp. 109–21. The best-known case of a historian making the charge of anti-Semitism and anti-Catholicism is Hofstadter, *Age of Reform*.

50. DMN, May 23, 1895.

51. Nugent, *Tolerant Populists*, 107–16; *Mineola Alliance Courier*, Oct. 6, 1892.

52. Nugent, *Tolerant Populists*, 110–16. For examples of cartoons depicting Shylock or Rothschild, see Miller, *Populist Cartoons*, 27, 28, 37, 51, 66, 96, 98–100, 122, 128, 130, 148, 163; cartoons featuring the hayseed stereotype can be found on 30, 164, 175.

53. SM, June 25, 1896.

54. *Mason County Herald*, July 15, 1892; *Texas Advance*, Aug. 4, 1894. The *Herald* at this point had not yet moved into the Populist camp, but in mid-1892 it was the local Alliance organ and carried favorable stories about Populism, and later it would abandon the Democrats in favor of the Populists.

55. McMath, *Populist Vanguard*, 75–76; Martin, *People's Party*, 168–72.

56. SM, Aug. 8, 1895; *McKinney Democrat*, Aug. 8, 1895; GDN, July 24, 1892; DMN, Sept. 6, 1892.

57. SM, Aug. 8, 15, 1895; DMN, Aug. 31, July 6, 1894; GDN, July 6, 18, 24, 1892; *McKinney Democrat*, Aug. 20, 1896; *Honey Grove Signal*, Aug. 4, 1893.

58. DMN, July 13, 1894; GDN, July 24, 1892.

59. *McKinney Democrat*, Aug. 20, 1896; DMN, Aug. 7, Sept. 3, 1892; GDN, July 26, 1892.

60. *McKinney Democrat*, Aug. 8, 1895, Aug. 20, 1896; DMN, July 31, 1895; SM, Aug. 13, 1891, July 25, Aug. 8, 15, 1895; GDN, Aug. 18, 1895.

61. SM, Sept. 3, 1891, June 30, 1892; GDN, July 26, 1892.

62. GDN, Aug. 7, 1896.

63. Ibid.

5. Black Texans and the People's Party

1. HT, Alwyn Barr, "Wade, Melvin," accessed Oct. 30, 2017, http://www.tshaonline .org/handbook/online/articles/fwa99; DMN, July 5, 1889, Mar. 7, Oct. 8, 1891; *Dallas Times Herald*, Mar. 23, Oct. 31, Nov. 8, 1892, Aug. 9, 1903; FWG, Mar. 24, 1892; TLPP, "James K. Polk Record"; *John F. Worley & Co.'s Dallas Directory*, 522.

2. DMN, Aug. 18, 1891; FWG, Aug. 18, 1891.

3. DMN, Aug. 18, 1891. On Evans, see HT, Miller, "Evans, Samuel"; DMN, July 7, 1888; *Fort Worth Star-Telegram*, Jan. 2, 1905; *San Antonio Express*, Jan. 3, 1905.

4. DMN, Aug. 18, 1891; FWG, Mar. 7, 10, 1892; *Dublin Progress*, Mar. 11, 1892.

5. DMN, June 30, 1896. The ideas about citizenship, race, sex, and gender developed in this chapter are heavily influenced by Glenn, *Unequal Freedom*, chaps. 1–2, esp. pp. 19, 26–27; and Dailey, *Before Jim Crow*, chap. 3, esp. pp. 84–89. Also see Marshall, "Citizenship and Social Class," 93–112, esp. p. 94; Mazur, *Example for All the Land*, 8–11.

6. Dailey, *Before Jim Crow*, 87; *Mason County Herald*, July 9, 1892; GDN, July 2, 1894, quoting the *Livingston Pinery*.

7. DMN, Aug. 18, 1891; FWG, Aug. 18, 1891. Little is known about Hayes. Lawrence Goodwyn asserts that he had "teamed with Ashby and Evans" in an independent political movement in Fort Worth dating back to 1886—which is quite possible—but Goodwyn's footnotes fail to corroborate the assertion. The only pre-1890 sources on Hayes that I could find are both from 1888, and both have Hayes attending Republican meetings, although in one he is advocating fusion with the "non-partisan" movement. See FWG, Apr. 8, 1888, and DMN, Sept. 16, 1888.

8. DMN, Aug. 18, 1891. On "political manhood," see Chapter 7.

9. *McKinney Democrat*, June 16, 1892.

10. Winkler, *Platforms*, 293–97.

11. FWG, Aug. 27, Sept. 3, 1891.

12. Winkler, *Platforms*, 297–99; FWG, Feb. 3, 1892.

13. *McKinney Democrat*, June 6, 1894, June 16, 1892; SM, May 5, 26, July 7, 1892.

14. *McKinney Democrat*, July 7, 16, June 30, 1892.

15. Ibid., July 7, 1892.

16. SM, June 23, 30, 1892. Most likely the seventy-year-old Jennings was unable to attend the Omaha convention, and Crenshaw was selected in his place. The *Mercury* erroneously identified Crenshaw as being from Collin County, Henry Jennings's home county. Crenshaw was a prosperous farmer and prominent political leader from near Brenham in Washington County; see *Brenham Banner*, July 5, 1878, Feb. 24, Sept. 12, 1880, May 3, 1883, Aug. 9, 1885, Oct. 14, 1886, Dec. 1, 1887; GDN, May 4, 1893; *Houston Post*, Jan. 23, 1907.

17. SM, June 30, 1892.

18. Rice, *Negro in Texas*, 39–47.

19. DMN, Jan. 13, 1894. In May 1892, Wade was still saying that he "preferred to remain in the republican kitchen"; see GDN, May 7, 1892. Also see *Dallas Times Herald*, Apr. 29, 1892. In mid-June he was a "spectator" at a Dallas County Populist convention but also attended a Republican meeting two weeks later; see DMN, June 12, 26, 1892. The first record of him as a Populist is from the DMN, Aug. 11, 1892, where he is reported as a delegate to a Populist county convention. On Wade's fall campaigning for the Populists, see DMN, Aug. 14, Sept. 9, 1892.

20. DMN, Aug. 27, Sept. 14, 1892.

21. GDN, July 3, 1887. Unless otherwise noted, biographical information on Rayner is from Cantrell, *Kenneth and John B. Rayner.*

22. SM, Dec. 22, 1892; DMN, Aug. 19, 1893.

23. DMN, Aug. 20, 1893.

24. DMN, Nov. 22, Oct. 29, 1892; SM, Dec. 22, 1892; *McKinney Democrat,* June 6, Nov. 1, 1894.

25. Parker, *Historical Recollections,* 187, 160–61; SM, July 9, Oct. 15, 1891; *McKinney Democrat,* June 2, 1892; DMN, Sept. 2, Dec. 18, 1891, June 7, 24, 1892, Apr. 6, 1893, Feb. 24, Oct. 1, 1894, Feb. 28, Mar. 29, May 16, 1895, Oct. 24, 1910; Robertson County Tax Rolls, 1894. A photo of Peters can be found in DMN, Oct. 24, 1910. In my own biography of J. B. Rayner, I mistakenly identified J. K. P. Hanna as Peters's father-in-law rather than his brother-in-law; see Cantrell, *Kenneth and John B. Rayner,* 207.

26. Parker, *Historical Recollections,* 160–61; DMN, June 27, 1925; "J. K. P. Hanna"; SM, Oct. 4, 1894, Mar. 26, 1896.

27. GDN, Mar. 5, 1894; *Texas Advance,* Mar. 24, 1894.

28. SM, June 13, 1895; W. P. Laughler to Vachel Weldon, Oct. 1, 1894, Weldon Papers.

29. *Texas Advance,* Aug. 25, 1894.

30. *Houston Post,* July 29, 1894; *Texas Advance,* Aug. 25, 1894; DMN, July 30, 1894; *Hempstead News,* July 12, 19, Aug. 2, 1894.

31. *Waco Evening News,* June 20, 1894; DMN, June 21, 1894.

32. DMN, June 21, 22, 1894.

33. GDN, June 23, 22, 1894.

34. SM, Nov. 29, Nov. 15, 1894. For election results see Cantrell and Barton, "Texas Populists," 663. An estimated 26 percent of eligible African Americans did not vote.

35. Gammel, *Laws of Texas,* 10:628; DMN, Oct. 26, 1894; *Waco Evening News,* Apr. 13, 1894.

36. House Bills 112 and 132, 24th Leg., Reg. Sess. (1895), Bill files, Texas Legislature, TSLAC; *Austin Statesman,* Jan. 12, 13, 15, 1895; *Journal of House of Representatives,* 24th Leg., Reg. Sess. (1895), 13, 15, 22, 33, 34, 41, 66, 156, 157, 158, 225, 280; Gammel, *Laws of Texas,* 10:759–60.

37. Dailey, *Before Jim Crow,* 97–101.

38. Three other bills introduced in the Twenty-Fourth Legislature might be considered segregationist legislation. These were bills proposing the creation of a separate black insane asylum, reformatory, and state university. Unlike the waiting room bill, however, these were measures that would have enjoyed widespread support from the African American community—particularly in the case of the university bill. All three of these bills perished in committee with no roll-call vote ever having been taken, so it is impossible to say how the Populists voted. See *Journal of House of Representatives,* 24th Leg., Reg. Sess. (1895), 439, 506, 541, 654, 1058.

39. DMN, Oct. 28, 1922, Feb. 3, 1895; SM, Feb. 21, 1895; *Journal of House of Representatives*, 24th Leg., Reg. Sess. (1895), 201–2.

40. Carson apparently was responding to a Democrat, William B. Plemmons, who had inserted his own explanation of his vote into the record. Plemmons said, "I vote 'no' because I do not regard Fred Douglass as a true representative of his race, and because in my native state, North Carolina, the partisans of Douglass and his allies have recently cast a stigma upon that grand old State that I desire to rebuke." Plemmons was referring to a recent episode in North Carolina in which Democrats had refused a Republican motion to recess the legislature in honor of the death of Douglass. The Democrats sought to use the issue of Douglass's marriage to a white woman as a wedge to split North Carolina Populists from their Republican allies, thus sparking a bitter war of words in which the Democrats charged that the Populists favored social equality, while the Populists charged Democrats with cynically using the "scarecrow" of race to maintain power. See Beeby, *Revolt of the Tarheels*, 111–13.

41. Nugent, *Life Work*, 338–39; FWG, Oct. 7, 1892; *San Antonio Light*, Aug. 13, 19, 1892. My interpretation of Nugent's and the Populists' position on racial issues agrees in large measure with that put forth by Charles Postel, differing primarily in emphasis. Postel emphasizes that Populist support for segregation and other white supremacist measures was "part of the New South doctrine of progressive development" and that Populists "viewed white supremacy as scientific and modern"; see Postel, *Populist Vision*, chap. 6 (quotations on p. 175 and discussion of Nugent on pp. 193–95). I do not disagree with this assessment, but I think that Texas Populists viewed segregation not so much as a desired goal—a positive good to be actively promoted—but rather as a sort of fallback position, a perhaps impermanent solution to the race problem, made necessary as much by white intransigence as by black "backwardness." In any event, it was a position Populists *had* to take if they were to successfully navigate the dangerous political waters of the turn-of-the-century South, and their ambivalence or indifference to de jure segregation measures does suggest that most of them simply wished such issues would just go away.

42. *Houston Post*, Sept. 19, 1894; DMN, Nov. 23, May 14, 1894.

43. *Fairfield Recorder*, May 18, 1894; DMN, June 11, 1894; GDN, Oct. 4, 19, 1894; SM, Sept. 20, 1894; DMN, Oct. 10, 1894. The best account of the Nacogdoches jury controversy can be found in Borders, *Hanging in Nacogdoches*, 69–74, although my interpretation differs from that of Borders in some minor respects. Borders states (p. 70) that blacks did serve on juries in some Populist counties, a contention for which I can find no evidence. For further biographical information on Spradley, see Fuller, *Texas Sheriff*.

44. GDN, Oct. 27, 1894.

45. *Jacksonville Banner*, Nov. 2, 1894.

46. DMN, Oct. 20, 1894.

47. *Jacksonville Banner*, Nov. 2, 1894; Borders, *Hanging in Nacogdoches*, 74–75.

48. Walker, *Penology for Profit*, 114–16; *Austin Statesman*, Feb. 15, 1895.

49. DMN, Jan. 31, 1895; House Bill 507, 24th Leg., Reg. Sess. (1895), Bill files, Texas Legislature; *Journal of House of Representatives*, 24th Leg., Reg. Sess. (1895), 295, 334, 1049.

50. HT, John R. Ross, "Lynching," accessed Nov. 1, 2017, http://www.tshaonline.org /handbook/online/articles/jgl01; DMN, Feb. 15, Mar. 24, Dec. 16, 1893. For a typical expression of press approval of the lynching, see DMN, Feb. 9, 1893 (excerpting the FWG). For Hogg's message to the legislature proposing the antilynching bill, see *Journal of House of Representatives*, 24th Leg. (1895), Appendix A, 35–36; also see *New York Times*, Feb. 8, 1896. For a sketch of Hodges, see *Paris News*, July 28, 1959. Hodges did not receive the appointment.

51. Nugent, *Life Work*, 68, 67, 356, 249–50. Nugent's letter on the Paris lynching can also be found in the DMN, Feb. 17, 1893, and the *McKinney Democrat*, Feb. 23, 1893. For a major Populist who did denounce lynching, see the account of Jerome Kearby's statement on election eve, 1896, discussed at the end of Chapter 10.

52. DMN, Feb. 17, 1893. African American Republican Robert Lloyd Smith did introduce an antilynching bill in the 1895 legislature—a bill much stronger than Hogg's proposal—but the bill was immediately buried in committee and never saw the light of day. There is no record of how Populist legislators reacted to the bill.

53. DMN, Jan. 13, 1894. On civil rights unionism, see Hall, "Long Civil Rights Movement," 1245–48; Korstad, *Civil Rights Unionism*; Krochmal, *Blue Texas*.

6. The Election of 1894

1. SM, May 11, 1893.

2. The initial account of the election in DMN of Dec. 24, 1892, put the margin at twelve votes, but later stories reduced the number to seven.

3. DMN, Jan. 14, Dec. 24, 1892, Jan. 17, 31, Feb. 1, 5, 1893, Jan. 3, May 31, 1896; *Texas Advance*, July 28, 1894. R. A. Cain was still numbered among the Populist faithful in 1900; see DMN, Jan. 27, 1900.

4. LBJ, quoted in Dugger, *Politician*, 54. *San Antonio Express*, Oct. 26, 28, Nov. 2, 1892; *Austin Statesman*, Oct. 27, 1892; Cantrell, "Lyndon's Granddaddy," 146–50, 152.

5. DMN, Jan. 3, 1894; Crook, "William McEwin and Catherine Reynolds."

6. Williams, *Realigning America*, 25–29; Ritter, *Goldbugs and Greenbacks*, 45–46.

7. Williams, *Realigning America*, 25–35; Ritter, *Goldbugs and Greenbacks*, 34, 38–40.

8. Williams, *Realigning America*, 39.

9. DMN, Apr. 10, 1894; *Texas Advance*, Mar. 10, 1894.

10. DMN, Nov. 8 (quoting the *Greenville Alliance Echo*), Dec. 31, 1892.

11. *Texas Advance*, Jan. 6, 1894.

12. DMN, Oct. 28, 1894, Feb. 28, 1896; HT, Thomas W. Cutrer, "Walton, William Martin," accessed Nov. 7, 2017, http://www.tshaonline.org/handbook/online/articles /fwa47; Walton, *Epitome*, 94.

13. DMN, Dec. 10, 1894, Feb. 3, 1896.

14. *A Memorial and Biographical History of Johnson*, 434–35; *Texas Advance*, Mar. 17, 1894; DMN, Jan. 10, 1894, quoting the *Boerne Post*.

15. SM, May 11, 1893; DMN, Jan. 4, June 20, 1894; Cantrell, "'Our Very Pronounced Theory,'" 679; *American Newspaper Directory*, 946; Alter, *Dirt Farmer Internationalists*, 220.

16. SM, Dec. 22, 1892.

17. Ibid.

18. DMN, Apr. 25, 28, June 21, July 2, 18, 24, 1894; FWG, May 1, June 21, 1894; *San Antonio Light*, Apr. 27, 1894; *Waco Evening News*, June 20, 1894; SM, July 12, 1894.

19. DMN, Sept. 15, 1894. For further evidence of Park's illiberality, see his comments about woman suffrage in Chapter 7 and his attacks on fellow Populists in Chapter 11.

20. SM, Jan. 26, 1894.

21. *Houston Post*, Jan. 19, 1894.

22. SM, Mar. 19, 1896.

23. DMN, May 11, Aug. 16, Sept. 16, 1894.

24. DMN, Apr. 1, May 6, Nov. 1, 1894.

25. *Fairfield Recorder*, May 18, 1894; Cantrell, *Kenneth and John B. Rayner*, 210.

26. DMN, Sept. 7, 1894.

27. DMN, Apr. 24, 1894.

28. *Dublin Progress*, Dec. 8, 1893.

29. DMN, June 17, 1894; *Dublin Progress*, July 20, 1894; SM, Apr. 13, 1893.

30. Ayers, *Promise of the New South*, 35–37.

31. SM, July 2, 1891; DMN, Aug. 19, 1892.

32. SM, Jan. 5, 1893.

33. SM, Apr. 21, May 12, 1892; *Rockdale Messenger*, Oct. 18, 1898; DMN, Feb. 29, 1896.

34. *McKinney Democrat*, Dec. 17, 1896; DMN, June 3, 1896.

35. DMN, Feb. 4, Mar. 18, 1894.

36. Ibid., Jan. 31, 1894.

37. Ibid., June 20, 21, 22, 24, 1894; *Waco Evening News*, June 20, 21, 1894; *McKinney Democrat*, June 28, 1894.

38. SM, June 28, 1894; *Waco Evening News*, June 20, 1894; DMN, June 21, 1894. On Johnson's role in the 1875 convention, see Williams, "Of Rutabagas and Redeemers."

39. DMN, June 22, 1894.

40. Ibid., June 24, 1894.

41. Ibid., June 22, 1894; Winkler, *Platforms*, 332–35, McGirr, *War on Alcohol*, 15–23.

42. DMN, June 22, 1894; Winkler, *Platforms*, 332–35.

43. DMN, June 21, 22, 24, 1894.

44. DMN, Apr. 17, 1894, quoting the Bryan *Texas Factotum*. On Texas Democratic "harmony," see DMN, Mar. 19–22, 1894; Barr, *Reconstruction to Reform*, 154–55.

45. DMN, Mar. 31, 1894.

46. SM, Sept. 20, Oct. 11, 1894; Barr, *Reconstruction to Reform*, 156–57; Butts, "Architect of the American Century," 22–29.

47. DMN, Aug. 11, Sept. 22, 1894; SM, Sept. 19, 1894; Winkler, *Platforms*, 341. For efforts to woo the urban labor vote in Dallas, see Rodriquez, "'Of Whom Shall the Third Party Be Composed?'"

48. DMN, June 22, Oct. 16, 1894; Katznelson, *Fear Itself*, 266–72.

49. Hild, *Greenbackers*, 86–87; *Dublin Progress*, June 1, 1894; DMN, Jan. 26, 1896.

50. Case, *Great Southwest Strike*, 179, 180–81; DMN, Apr. 8, 1886, July 4, 1891, Feb. 3, 1892; FWG, Feb. 3, 1892; Winkler, *Platforms*, 298, 418, 442; *Waco Evening News*, June 21, 1894; *McKinney Democrat*, Aug. 20, 1896.

51. *New York Times*, Mar. 9, 29, 1886; DMN, Mar. 28, 1886, Sept. 26, 27, 30, 1894; GDN, Mar. 28, Apr. 28, May 9, 1886, Sept. 7, 1893, Sept. 4, Oct. 14, 1894, Feb. 11, 1915; US Department of the Interior, Census Office, *Twelfth Census, 1900*, Galveston, Galveston County, TX, series T623, roll 1637, p. 115 , s.v. "John Dyer"; *Waco Evening News*, June 21, 1894; SM, Aug. 2, 1894.

52. DMN, July 4, 13, 1894; FWG, July 4, 1894.

53. *Blossom Monitor*, Oct. 5, 1894; *McKinney Democrat*, Oct. 25, 1894.

54. SM, Oct. 18, 1894; *Texas Advance*, Aug. 4, 1894.

55. DMN, Oct. 30, Nov. 4, 1894; SM, Sept. 20, 1894; *Honey Grove Signal*, Sept. 7, 1894.

56. *Blossom Monitor*, Oct. 5, 1894; DMN, Oct. 21, 1894.

57. DMN, Nov. 14, 1894; SM, Nov. 8, 1894; Miller and Ulbig, "Building a Populist Coalition," 280–83; Texas Secretary of State, *Biennial Report . . . 1894*, 252.

58. Cantrell and Paschal, "Texas Populism," 58; Texas Secretary of State, *Biennial Report . . . 1894*, 245–48.

59. DMN, Apr. 19, 1895.

60. Miller and Ulbig, "Building a Populist Coalition," 280–83.

61. Cantrell and Barton, "Texas Populists," 672.

62. Barnes, *Farmers in Rebellion*, 32–50.

63. Ibid., esp. 43–47.

64. SM, Nov. 8, 1894.

7. Women, Gender, and Populism

1. DMN, July 15, 22, Aug. 1, 2, 1894; *Johnson County Review*, July 6, 1894; *Waxahachie Enterprise*, July 6, 27, 1894.

2. DMN, Aug. 2, 3, 1894; *Dallas Times-Herald*, Aug, 3, 21, 1894; *Johnson County Review*, Aug. 10, 1894; *Terrell Times-Star*, Aug. 10, 1894.

3. *Dallas Times-Herald,* Aug. 22, 23, 1894; DMN, Aug. 22, 23, 1894.

4. *Johnson County Review,* Sept. 7, 1894; DMN, Aug. 30, 31, 1894.

5. Baker, "Domestication of Politics," 628–30; Edwards, *Angels in the Machinery,* 25.

6. Scott, "Gender," 1067.

7. Edwards, *Angels in the Machinery,* 4–38.

8. Ibid., 19–35. For examples of Democrats' accusations that the Subtreasury Plan was "paternalistic," see SM, Feb. 2, 1896; DMN, Feb. 23, 1896.

9. Edwards, *Angels in the Machinery,* 22–23, 92, 122–27.

10. Ayers, *Vengeance and Justice,* 26–33; Creech, *Righteous Indignation,* 12, 17, 22–24, 31–33, 184–85, 155.

11. Ayers, *Vengeance and Justice,* 9–33.

12. Glenn, *Unequal Freedom,* 15; Ayers, *Vengeance and Justice,* 24; Creech, *Righteous Indignation,* 31–32.

13. DMN, May 28, 1895; *Texas Advance,* Mar. 17, 1894; *Houston Post,* June 4, 1900.

14. SM, Oct. 10, 1895, Apr. 7, 1892; DMN, June 25, 1892.

15. *McKinney Democrat,* June 30, 1892 (quoting the FWG); DMN, Jan. 22, 1895.

16. *Rockdale Messenger,* Nov. 3, 1898; *McKinney Democrat,* June 16, 1892, Oct. 25, 1894; SM, Oct. 18, 1894, Apr. 7, 1892, June 25, 1896, Feb. 26, 1891.

17. SM, Sept. 20, 1894.

18. *Houston Post,* Oct. 22, 1896.

19. *Karnes City Reformer,* May 17, 1894; DMN, June 6, 1895, June 11, 1896; SM, Feb. 4, 1896.

20. HT, Bob C. Holcomb, "Bailey, Joseph Weldon," accessed Nov. 9, 2017, http://www.tshaonline.org/handbook/online/articles/fba10; Holcomb, "Senator Joe Bailey," 11–16; *Honey Grove Signal,* Aug. 17, 1894; *McKinney Democrat,* May 31, Nov. 1, 1894.

21. Holcomb, "Senator Joe Bailey," 90–92, 272–80; DMN, Oct. 2, 1894.

22. HT, A. Elizabeth Taylor, "Woman Suffrage," accessed Nov. 9, 2017, http://www.tshaonline.org/handbook/online/articles/viw01.

23. Mary M. letter, June 28, 1888, in Barthelme, *Women in the Texas Populist Movement,* 134.

24. Ibid.; Ann Too letter, June 28, 1888, and Poor Gal letter, Aug. 21, 1888, both in Barthelme, *Women in the Texas Populist Movement,* 135, 162–63. For an account that illustrates the typical election-day scene at the polls, see *Whitney Messenger,* Nov. 10, 1894.

25. Ann Other letter, May 31, 1888, in Barthelme, *Women in the Texas Populist Movement,* 108–11.

26. Karbach, "Ellen Lawson Dabbs"; HT, Melissa G. Wiedenfeld, "Dabbs, Ellen Lawson," accessed Nov. 9, 2017, http://www.tshaonline.org/handbook/online/articles/fda66; Winkler, *Platforms,* 298; GDN, Nov. 30, 1891, Nov. 10, 1895, Aug. 17, 1896; SM, Feb. 4, 1892; DMN, June 24, 1892, June 27, 1906. For notice of a Dabbs appearance at an 1894 Populist encampment where she "delivered a strong plea in advocacy of better government," see DMN, July 7, 1895. Also see GDN, Aug. 12, 26, 1893,

Mar. 3, Apr. 4, 29, May 28, 1894, Aug. 27, Sept. 26, 1896. Dabbs's residence in Oklahoma is noted in GDN, June 27, 1906.

27. GDN, May 12, 1893, Aug. 6, 1896; DMN, May 9, 1893, Mar. 31, June 6, 7, 8, 9, Aug. 12, 1894; SM, Dec. 1, 1892, Mar. 14, 1895; Karbach, "Ellen Lawson Dabbs," 188–90; Wiedenfeld, "Women," 47–49; HT, Wiedenfeld, "Dabbs, Ellen Lawson"; HT, Mary M. Standifer, "Danforth, Grace," accessed Nov. 9, 2017, http://www.tshaonline.org /handbook/online/articles/fda75. For examples of TERA members speaking at Populist and Alliance gatherings, see DMN, July 5, 1896 (Sarah L. Trumbull), Aug. 19, 1897 (Alice McAnulty), GDN, Mar. 11, 1894 (Ellen Lawson Dabbs), Aug. 24, 1895 (Margaret L. Watson). For the TERA, see Taylor, "Woman Suffrage," 196–201; HT, Judith N. McArthur, "Texas Equal Rights Association," accessed Nov. 9, 2017, http://www.tshaonline .org/handbook/online/articles/vito2; Brannon-Wranosky, "Southern Promise," 86–131.

28. DMN, May 22, 1893 (quoting the *Bryan Eagle*), Oct. 29, 1895, May 19, 1893 (quoting the *Brenham Herald*). For other examples of the use of the term "hen convention" to denigrate women's meetings, see GDN, Aug. 11, 1893, July 27, 1897.

29. The list of TERA charter members can be found in Texas Equal Rights Association, Minutes of the First Session, May 10, 1893, pamphlet in Equal Rights Assn. Scrapbook—starting 1893, folder 1, box 34, McCallum Papers (hereinafter referred to as TERA Scrapbook). On Dohoney, see HT, McKay and Johnson, "Dohoney, Ebenezer Lafayette"; Dohoney, *Average American;* Winkler, *Platforms,* 293, 298, 314, 332, 335. On Russell, see GDN, June 18, 1892, Nov. 3, 1893, Aug. 20, 24, 1894, Apr. 7, 1895. On Bristol, see DMN, Aug. 11, Nov. 21, 1892, Sept. 18, Oct. 7, Dec. 12, 1893, June 30, Sept. 26, 1894, July 24, 1896. On Jones, see DMN, June 13, 1894, Apr. 11, 1898, May 26, 1906. On Lincoln, see DMN, June 13, Oct. 6, 1894. On Roebuck, see DMN, Feb. 9, 1896, Nov. 10, 1998; "Ellis County Doctors."

30. HT, Christopher Long, "Biard, John Wilson," accessed July 20, 2018, http:// www.tshaonline.org/handbook/online/articles/fbicd; Winkler, *Platforms,* 335; GDN, Feb. 2, 18, Nov. 29, 1892, May 26, 1893, June 9, 1894; SM, July 28, 1892, Sept. 1, Dec. 1, 8, 1892, May 11, 1893, Dec. 5, 1901; *Taylor County News,* Oct. 21, 1892; *Dublin Progress,* Mar. 10, 1893; *Linden Alliance Standard,* May 16, 1893; DMN, June 9, 1894; undated clipping (ca. June 9, 1894) from *Fort Worth Gazette* in TERA Scrapbook, 23. Care must be taken not to confuse John Wilson "Earthquake" Biard with his brother James Washington "Buster" Biard. Both were Alliancemen and Populists (Buster was party chairman in his home county of Lamar), although John Wilson was much more prominent as a Populist. Both commonly were identified by their initials "J. W." in the press. James Washington lived all his life in Lamar County, while James Wilson moved first to Lenore (Jones County); then to Luling (Caldwell County), where he ran for Congress in 1896; to Brazoria (Brazoria County); and finally to Oklahoma, where he died in 1913. If this is not confusing enough, their first cousin, James Monroe Biard (commonly referred to as J. M. Biard), was also an Allianceman and served one term in the state legislature, 1887 to 1889. He was a prominent Disciples of Christ

minister. The press occasionally confused the two brothers and their cousin; for example, one account had John Wilson as a Disciples minister, probably confusing him with his cousin James Monroe, and another story had James Washington as the Disciples minister, also likely confusing him with his cousin James Monroe. See, in addition to the sources cited above, Smith, *Biard Family*, 22–23, 30–31, 34–35; DMN, Sept. 27, 1894, June 10, 1900; SM, Aug. 10, 1899, Feb. 1, Mar. 22, 1900; *Paris News*, Jan. 24, 1938; F. A. Battey & Company, *Biographical Souvenir*, 80–81.

31. FWG, June 9, 1894; DMN, June 9, 1894; GDN, Aug. 9, 1896.

32. Nugent, *Life Work*, 378, 33, 323, 324, 305.

33. DMN, Mar. 31, June 8, Aug. 12, Oct. 16, Nov. 18, 1894; clipping from *Fort Worth Gazette*, June 7, 1894, TERA Scrapbook, 21; undated clipping from *Williamson County Sun*, TERA Scrapbook, 32.

34. DMN, Feb. 1, 1892, June 17, Aug. 15, 1894.

35. DMN, July 5, 1893; *Waco Evening News*, June 20, 1894; SM, June 30, 1892.

36. For the party's instructions to local Populist clubs, see *Dublin Progress*, June 17, 1892.

37. DMN, May 6, Aug. 2, 1894. For further information on Hallie and her husband W. W. Dunklin, see GDN, May 8, 1874, Oct. 13, 1876, Apr. 4, 1877, Feb. 20, 24, Mar. 3, 5, 1878, July 11, 20, 1880, June 28, 1882, Nov. 20, 1886, Jan. 4, 1897; DMN, Mar. 11, 1897, Mar. 9, 1899, Jan. 8, Nov. 24, 1901, Apr. 21, 1902, Oct. 25, 1904, May 24, 1916; *New York Times*, Apr. 14, 15, 1924. Around 1902, Dunklin moved to New York City, where she remained active in women's clubs and social affairs until her death in 1924.

38. DMN, Jan. 17, 1896. Hunt County Populists must have been particularly receptive to women's participation in politics, because in 1895 news that Mary Elizabeth Lease of Kansas would speak in the county reportedly evoked "considerable enthusiasm" at a local Populist meeting; see DMN, May 23, 1895.

39. DMN, Mar. 20, 1894.

40. Ibid.

41. Ibid.

42. Ibid.

43. Ibid.

44. Ibid.; DMN, Aug. 6, 12, 1894.

45. Clipping from unidentified paper dated Sept. 30, 1894, TERA Scrapbook, 5. The Godkin quotation, and a fuller explication of the ideas presented here, can be found in Stanley, "Conjugal Bonds" (quotation on p. 474).

46. Wright, *Politics of Populism*, 190, 198–99; SM, Nov. 22, Dec. 6, 1894.

47. HT, Harper, "Park, Milton"; HT, Keith L. King, "Dixon, Samuel Houston," accessed Nov. 26, 2017, http://www.tshaonline.org/handbook/online/articles/fdi31; SM, May 28, 1896.

48. SM, Dec. 20, 1894.

49. Ibid.

50. HT, Melissa G. Wiedenfeld, "Gay, Bettie Munn," accessed Nov. 26, 2017, http://www.tshaonline.org/handbook/online/articles/fga60; Postel, *Populist Vision*, 73–75; SM, Feb. 26, 1891, Jan. 17, 1895, Aug. 6, 1896; *Philadelphia North American*, Aug. 8, 1892.

51. SM, Jan. 17, 1895.

52. Ibid.

53. DMN, Nov. 25, 1894.

54. GDN, Jan. 6, 1895; Dunlap, "Reform of Rape Law," 358. According to the *New York Times* of Oct. 15, 1895, five states actually had lower ages of consent than Texas, including Delaware, where the age was seven.

55. GDN, Feb. 1, 1895.

56. For biographical information on Harrison (whose first name is frequently misrendered as "William" rather than "Willis"), see Loughery, *Texas State Government*, 62–63; TLPP, "William Lyman Harrison"; DMN, Feb. 19, 1915. He represented Bell, Lampasas, Coryell, Hamilton, and Bosque Counties in the Senate; DMN, Sept. 3, 1894. For the text and progress of Harrison's bill, see Senate Bill 59, 24th Leg., Reg. Sess. (1895), Bill files, Texas Legislature. On Cureton, see Pool, "Westward I Go Free"; HT, William C. Pool, "Cureton, Calvin Maples," accessed Nov. 11, 2017, http://www.tshaonline.org/handbook/online/articles/fcu26. Information on Cureton's bill can be found in House Bill 127, 24th Leg., Reg. Sess. (1895), Bill files, Texas Legislature. Also see *Journal of House of Representatives*, 24th Leg., Reg. Sess. (1895), 1033.

57. GDN, Jan. 30, 1895.

58. GDN, Mar. 2, 1895, quoting the *Lockhart Register*; *San Antonio Light*, Feb. 13, 1895.

59. *Austin Statesman*, Feb. 5, 1895.

60. *San Antonio Light*, Feb. 13, 1895; *Austin Statesman*, Feb. 10, 1895; GDN, Apr. 29, 1894. The *Statesman* noted that Helen Stoddard, the president of the Texas WCTU who had helped to organize the campaign and who had led the women's delegation to the legislature, had lived in Texas sixteen years, and that the women in the Senate chamber that day were all Texans "without an exception as far as they know."

61. *Journal of Senate*, 24th Leg., Reg. Sess. (1895), 50, 60, 70, 90, 126–27, 132–34, 136, 146, 173–75, 506, 509, 535; GDN, Feb. 8, 20, 1895. The provisions allowing the victim's status as a "female of bad character for chastity" or "a common prostitute" to be introduced as evidence were ultimately deleted from the bill. In the House, where roll-call votes were even rarer than in the Senate, we have little hard data on how Populists voted, except for one instance in which all twenty-two of them voted against an amendment to lower the age from fifteen to fourteen. But the fact that a consent bill (House Bill 127) was introduced by William Cureton, and Thomas L. Nugent came

out publicly in favor of raising the age to sixteen, along with the fact that the Populists maintained remarkable solidarity on almost all legislative measures, suggests with fair certainty that they all endorsed raising the age to sixteen or higher. See *Journal of House of Representatives*, 24th Leg., Reg. Sess. (1895), 40, 700, 782; GDN, Feb. 12, 1895. The Populists' willingness to compromise on an age lower than eighteen probably was reinforced by a statement by Nugent, who was willing to set the age at sixteen; see GDN, Feb. 12, 1895.

62. *Austin Statesman*, Feb. 2, 1895; Glenn, *Unequal Freedom*, 7, 13–14; Dunlap, "Reform of Rape Laws," esp. 353–54. The two Populists on the committee (House Judiciary Committee No. 2) were John A. O'Connor of San Antonio and T. R. Watkins of Corsicana. The bill would have defined "unlawful intercourse" as "the carnal knowledge of a female not less than twelve nor more than eighteen years of age, with her consent, such female being other than the wife of the person having such carnal knowledge," and it carried a punishment of fines between $25 and $1,000 and/or jail terms between one month and two years. For the full text of the bill and the majority and minority reports, see House Bill 252, 24th Leg., Reg. Sess. (1895), Bill files, Texas Legislature.

63. *Austin Statesman*, Feb. 7, 1895.

64. DMN, June 30, 1896.

65. DMN, Feb. 6, Apr. 9, 1894; *Austin Statesman*, Feb. 9, 1894; *Journal of Senate*, 24th Leg., Reg. Sess. (1895), 200; Gammel, *Laws of Texas*, 10:834; Dunlap, "Reform of Rape Law," 362.

66. House Bill 718, 24th Leg., Reg. Sess. (1895), Bill files, Texas Legislature; *Journal of House of Representatives*, 24th Leg., Reg. Sess. (1895), 661, 1059. Further reform of Texas's law on the age of consent beyond the age of fifteen would have to wait until 1918, when the legislature raised the age to eighteen—yet another Populist cause that came to fruition in the Progressive Era. It would later be lowered to seventeen, where it remains today. Populists continued to agitate for sex-law reform after the failed campaign of 1895. In 1896, for example, Ellis County Populists passed a resolution calling for the age to be raised to twenty, along with a penalty of five to twenty years in prison for violating the state's seduction laws; see GDN, Feb. 24, 1896.

67. In keeping with his un-Populist-like attitude toward suffrage, the *Southern Mercury*'s Milton Park ridiculed the age-of-consent issue and other social reforms then being debated in the legislature, saying, "All of this reform is of a social nature. It is socialistic, and does not reach the finances of the state or throw a protecting arm around the hard earnings of the people." Except for this one brief mention, the *Mercury* never mentioned the age-of-consent debate, and Park's is the only Populist voice anywhere in the historical record that I can find expressing disapproval of the bill. See SM, Mar. 24, 1895.

68. *McKinney Democrat*, Sept. 22, 1892.

69. Ibid.

8. Legislating Populism

1. *Biennial Report . . . 1894*, 249–52, 295–98.

2. DMN, Jan. 9, 1894.

3. My own analysis of the personnel of the Twenty-Second Legislature (1891) reveals that it contained sixty-four lawyers, sixty-two nonlawyers, and sixteen whose professions were unknown. I used this legislature because a biographical directory exists for that year, containing many (but not all) of its members' names; see TLPP, "22nd Legislature Members." A press account of the Twenty-Fourth Legislature confirms this conclusion, identifying fifty-one lawyers in the House, which would be well over half of the Democrats; see *Linden Alliance Standard*, Mar. 5, 1895.

4. This data on the individual Populists of the Twenty-Fourth Legislature comes from a very wide variety of sources, including newspapers, biographical directories, census and tax records, and genealogical websites, which are cited as individual legislators mentioned in this chapter.

5. HT, Gregg Cantrell, "Townsen, James Madison," accessed Nov. 26, 2017, http://www.tshaonline.org/handbook/online/articles/fto60; TLPP, "S. T. Foster"; FWG, July 30, 1886, Apr. 15, May 16, 1888; SM, Apr. 30, 1891.

6. TLPP, "William Whitacre"; *Texas Miner* 2 (June 29, 1895): 8; *History of Texas . . . Central Texas*, 569–71; *Dublin Progress*, Apr. 29, 1910.

7. HT, Jonathan Perry, "Seago, Tillman Kimsey," accessed Nov. 27, 2017, http://www.tshaonline.org/handbook/online/articles/fse40; Johnson, *History of Texas*, 3:1310; *Palo Pinto Tribune*, Apr. 5, 1895; HT, Charles G. Davis, "Lamesa, TX (Dawson County)," accessed Nov. 27, 2017, http://www.tshaonline.org/handbook/online/articles/hel04; *Comanche Pioneer-Exponent*, July 5, 1888.

8. Hunter, *Trail Drivers*, 53–56; "William E. Cureton," Vertical Files, Briscoe Center; *History of Texas . . . Central Texas*, 29–30; Loughery, *Texas State Government*, 152; HT, Pool, "Cureton, Calvin Maples."

9. *Mexia Weekly Herald*, Apr. 9, 1914; "Peter Radford," Vertical Files, Briscoe Center; *Abilene Reporter*, Aug. 4, 1911; GDN, Dec. 10, 1912; *Wichita Daily Times*, Dec. 5, 1913; *Commerce Journal*, Dec. 12, 1913; *San Antonio Light*, Feb. 14, 1915; *Weatherford Weekly Herald*, Dec. 5, 1918. The State Warehouse Commission, which sought at the state level to embody several of the major principles of the old Alliance Subtreasury Plan, was established in 1913; see *Journal of Senate*, 33rd Leg., 1st Called Sess. (1913), 292–310.

10. HT, Jonathan Perry, "Darwin, James Lewis," accessed Nov. 27, 2017, http://www.tshaonline.org/handbook/online/articles/fda65; *Memphis Daily Appeal*, Feb. 7, 1870; *N. W. Ayer & Son's Newspaper Annual* (1896), 748; DMN, Nov. 22, 1894; GDN, Nov. 8, 1896; *Claiborne Guardian* (Homer, LA), July 9, 30, Aug. 13, 27, 1879, Aug. 25, 1880, Jan. 9, 1883; *Colfax* (LA) *Chronicle*, Oct. 2, 1880; *Clarksville Standard*, July 26, 1888; FWG, Apr. 39, Nov. 8, 1894, Feb. 21, 22, Mar. 7, 27, 1895; US Dept. of the Interior, *Twelfth Census, 1900*, Red River County, Precinct 4, SD 1, ED 107, Sheet 3.

11. HT, Brooke Wibracht, "Huddleston, Martin Luther," accessed July 20, 2018, http://www.tshaonline.org/handbook/online/articles/fhuad.

12. Loughery, *Texas State Government*, 157; *Brownsville Herald*, June 13, 1904; HT, Wibracht, "Huddleston, Martin Luther"; "Diary of Martin Luther Huddleston," Anderson County Genealogical Society; HT, Michael Green, "Rhodes, Lee Lightfoot," accessed Nov. 27, 2017, http://www.tshaonline.org/handbook/online/articles/frhod; SM, Dec. 19, 1895; *McKinney Democrat*, July 18, 1895, quoting the *Jefferson Jimplecute*.

13. *Austin Weekly Statesman*, Aug. 25, 1892; DMN, July 11, 1891, Feb. 21, 1896, Nov. 23, 1900; FWG, Apr. 30, 1887, Feb. 2, 1892, Mar. 1, 1895; GDN, Feb. 19, 1892, Oct. 13, 1893, Oct. 28, 1895; *Memorial and Biographical History of Navarro*, 520–21; Brooke Wibracht, "Ritter, Van Buren," accessed Nov. 27, 2017, http://www.tshaonline.org/handbook/online/articles/fri66; SM, Apr. 23, 1891, Sept. 15, 1892, Aug. 24, 1893.

14. Loughery, *Texas State Government*, 62–63; W. L. Harrison Confederate Service Record, Compiled Service Records, Twenty-Eighth Cavalry, NARA M323; Scott, *Texas Pulpit*, 170–82, 383; TLPP, "William [sic] L. Harrison"; GDN, Oct. 28, 1895.

15. TLPP, "James Rogers Cocke"; HT, Jennifer Eckel, "Cocke, Frederick Bird Smith," accessed Nov. 27, 2017, http://www.tshaonline.org/handbook/online/articles/fcolc; Patterson, *Nixon*, 8.

16. HT, Brooke Wibracht, "Carson, James W.," accessed Nov. 27, 2017, http://www.tshaonline.org/handbook/online/articles/fcabi.

17. GDN, May 4, 1889, Aug. 20, 1890, Apr. 16, June 7, 1892, July 28, 1895; *Austin Statesman*, Feb. 27, 1890.

18. Loughery, *Texas State Government*, 105–6; *Morrison & Fourmy's General Directory*, 64; *City Directory of Austin*, 17; *Austin Daily News-Tribune, Industrial Review Edition: Austin, Capital City of Texas*, Feb. 1906; SM, July 12, 1906.

19. Johnson, *History of Texas and Texans*, 5:2248; GDN, Oct. 14, 1894; Loughery, *Texas State Government*, 87–88; DMN, Jan. 20, 22, 1895.

20. Fire Insurance Map from Austin, Travis County, TX, Sanborn Map Company, Jan. 1894, http://www.loc.gov/resource/g4034am.go8415003/?sp=16; Augustus Koch, "Austin, State Capital of Texas, 1887," Texas Bird's-Eye Views, accessed Mar. 1, 2015, http://www.birdseyeviews.org/zoom.php?city=Austin&year=1887&extra_info=; photo of Congress Avenue looking north toward the capitol, ca. 1895, "Austin Streets," Austin History Center, Austin Public Library, accessed Mar. 1, 2015, http://www.austinlibrary.com/ahc/streets/congress.htm; TSHA, *Texas Almanac . . . 1910*, 168.

21. Stewart and Bowen, *History of Wages*, 227; HT, William Elton Green, "Capitol," accessed Nov. 12, 2017, http://www.tshaonline.org/handbook/online/articles/ccc01.

22. Message of Gov. Charles A. Culberson to the Legislature, Jan. 16, 1895, *Journal of Senate* (1895), 39–45.

23. DMN, Jan. 12, 1895.

24. Ibid., Jan. 8, 1895.

25. Ibid., Jan. 22, 1895.

26. Ibid., Jan. 8, 1895.

27. *San Antonio Light*, Jan. 23, 1895.

28. DMN, Jan. 27, 1895.

29. Ibid., Jan. 25, 26, 1895.

30. Ibid., Feb. 2, 1895.

31. DMN, Feb. 2, 1895.

32. Bill files for HBs 402, 484, 515, and 204, TSLAC.

33. Winkler, 315, 333; FWG, Feb. 1, 1895; Bill file for HB398, TSLAC; GDN, Jan. 26, 1895. After the session, when all of the lien-law bills had failed, the Dallas Trades Council would harshly condemn Governor Culberson for his failure to include either the lien law or the convict-labor law (see below) in his call for a special session; see GDN, Oct. 8, 1895.

34. Bill file for HB613, TSLAC.

35. Bill file for HB507, TSLAC; also see *Austin Statesman*, Feb. 25, 1895.

36. Bill file for HB 475, TSLAC.

37. Bill file for HB 216, TSLAC.

38. *Journal of Senate* (1895), 165–66; Bill file for SB194, TSLAC.

39. Mason, *From Buildings and Loans to Bail-Outs*, 12, 21–22, 27, 28 (quotations on p. 22).

40. Ibid., 28, 30–32; US Bureau of Labor, *Ninth Annual Report*, 14, 300, 302, 682.

41. FWG, Dec. 16, 1894; Mason, *From Buildings and Loans to Bail-Outs*, 32–25.

42. US Bureau of Labor, *Ninth Annual Report*, 333; FWG, Dec. 16, 1890; Mason, *From Buildings and Loans to Bail-Outs*, 20; Bill file for SB194, TSLAC.

43. FWG, Apr. 10, 1895; DMN, Apr. 13, 17, 1895; TLPP, "Robert Roy"; GDN, Apr. 21, 1895.

44. GDN, Apr. 23, 1895. On the subsequent history of Nugent's B&L, see Paddock, *History of Texas*, 4:402. Thrifts would not come under meaningful federal regulation until the 1930s; see Mason, *From Buildings and Loans to Bail-Outs*, 69–99.

45. *Abilene Reporter*, Mar. 22, 1916.

46. For this list, and for one of the best explanations of how the system led to corruption, see Crow, "Fee System," 8–9, 56.

47. Message of Gov. Hogg, *Journal of House of Representatives*, Appendix A, 24.

48. *San Antonio Light*, May 1, 1895.

49. Message of Gov. Hogg, 24.

50. Message of Gov. Culberson, 54.

51. Winkler, *Platforms*, 315, 333.

52. Bill file for HB128, TSLAC; DMN, Jan. 14, 1895; *Austin Statesman*, Jan. 14, Feb. 7, 1895.

53. *San Antonio Light*, Mar. 2, 1895; FWG, Mar. 31, 1895. The full text of HB707 can be found in DMN, Apr. 4, 1895.

496 NOTES TO PAGES 313-318

54. *San Antonio Light*, Mar. 2, Apr. 8, 9, 13, 1895; GDN, Jan. 28, Mar. 5, Apr. 11, 12, 1895; FWG, Apr. 8, 10, 12, 1895. Elmendorf's charge seems plausible on the face of it, as O'Connor had been supported by Elmendorf's opponent, Democratic boss Bryan Callaghan. Callaghan surely believed that his defeat was only a temporary setback, which proved to be the case when he retook the mayoralty in 1897. If O'Connor's goal had been only to strike a political blow at Elmendorf, then permanently taking San Antonio's municipal services out of the hands of both Republicans *and* Democrats would be a strange and possibly counterproductive strategy. Indeed, O'Connor's ally Callaghan had built much of his power base through clever manipulation of local patronage, and he would defeat Elmendorf at the next election.

55. Bill file for HB 378, TSLAC; FWG, Mar. 10, 1895. The full text of Ward's consolidation bill can be found in GDN, Jan. 26, 1896. On Ward, see Loughery, *Texas State Government*, 125-26.

56. Winkler, *Platforms*, 295, 297, 315, 333.

57. Bill file for HB8, TSLAC.

58. See Chapter 7.

59. See Chapter 5.

60. Bill files for HB332, HB350, HB508, TSLAC; Gammel, *Laws of Texas*, 10:87; *Burnet Avalanche*, Mar. 10, 1892. There is no bill file for the telegraph-wire bill, HB672, but the *Journal of House of Representatives* provided a brief synopsis of the bill; see *Journal of House of Representatives* (1895), 514. There is also no bill file for the railroad-intersection bill, HB435, but the provisions of the bill can be found in GDN, Feb. 5, 1895.

61. Bill files for HB442, HB494, TSLAC; *Journal of House of Representatives* (1895), 514.

62. Bill file for HB183, TSLAC. Bill files for McNeill's HB654 and 655 are both missing. In the case of HB655, neither the newspapers nor the legislative journals give a detailed text of the bill, so the precise nature of the prescribed "requisites" is not known. Given McNeill's staunch record on legislation seeking to impose higher educational standards in general, it is safe to assume that the bill tightened lax standards in this case; see *Journal of House of Representatives* (1895), 492.

63. Bill file for HB577, TSLAC.

64. *Brownsville Herald*, Apr. 8, 1895; *Austin Statesman*, Apr. 2, 1895. Both of these papers place the estimated number of Reform Democrats at forty.

65. DMN, Apr. 14, 16, 18, 23, 1895; *Fort Worth Mail-Telegram*, quoted in GDN, Apr. 2, 23, 1895; *Austin Statesman*, Apr. 2, 1895; FWG, Apr. 3, 1895.

66. DMN, Apr. 18, 1895.

67. *Journal of Senate* (1895), 7; Loughery, *Texas State Government*, 34-36; Bill file for SB1, TSLAC; *Austin Statesman*, Apr. 18, 1895. For papers supporting the bill, see *Temple Times*, Feb. 15, 1895; *Abilene Reporter*, Mar. 15, 1895; *Brenham Banner*, Apr. 13, 1895; *San Antonio Light*, Feb. 16, 1895; *Comanche Chief* and *Fort Worth Mail-Telegram*, both quoted in GDN, Apr. 2, 1895.

68. GDN, Apr. 13, 1895.

69. DMN, Apr. 12, 1895.

70. SM, Apr. 25, 1895.

71. Ibid., Apr. 18, 1895.

72. Gardner, "Texas Antitrust Law," 16–24, 33–42.

73. Ibid., 23–26, 43–44; *Journal of Senate* (1895), 35.

74. Bill file for HB404, TSLAC; *Journal of House of Representatives* (1895), 472–73.

75. *Journal of Senate* (1895), 533–34, 539, 549; DMN, Apr. 19, 1895; Gardner, "Texas Antitrust Law," 42–48. The bill's author in the House, Armistead, eventually agreed to a number of amendments, which, while not restoring the agricultural exemption, apparently made the bill more palatable to Populists, and in the vote on final passage of the bill, the Populist delegation was split almost evenly over the measure; see *Journal of House of Representatives* (1895), 588–89, for roll-call vote.

76. *Journal of House of Representatives* (1895), 670.

77. DMN, Apr. 18, 21, 1895; *San Antonio Light*, Apr. 17, 20, 22, May 7, 1895; SM, May 2, 1895.

78. DMN, Apr. 27, 1895.

79. DMN, May 3, 1895. The three minor Populist bills were a bill to restore to Delta County a local court that Democrats had taken away when the Populists won the county in 1892; a bill to create a better road system in Parker County; and a bill authorizing the State Orphans' Home to sell surplus water from its artesian well.

80. The "cooperative commonwealth" trope is Goodwyn's and has been used by many other scholars; the "regional republicanism" model, invoked by Gerald Berk, posits that Populists and other agrarians envisioned "a more decentralized, less hierarchical, and more public alternative" to the large-scale corporate capitalism that emerged in the late nineteenth century. See Berk, *Alternative Tracks*, 4.

9. The Problem of the Border

1. Portions of this chapter were reproduced and modified with permission from Gregg Cantrell, "'Our Very Pronounced Theory of Equal Rights to All': Race, Citizenship, and Populism in the South Texas Borderlands," *Journal of American History* 100, no. 3 (2013): 663–90, published by Oxford University Press on behalf of the Organization of American Historians. Readers are urged to consult that article for further details and documentation.

2. In this chapter I use the terms "Mexican Americans" and "Tejanos" interchangeably to refer to Texas-born people of Mexican ancestry. I use "ethnic Mexicans" or "Mexicanos" to refer to people of Mexican ancestry regardless of their country of birth. "Chicano," "Latino," and "Hispanic" are terms of more recent vintage, and I have chosen not to use them.

3. GDN, Apr. 17, 1886. The only scholar to write much about Populism in South Texas, Roscoe Martin, focused his analysis on the eleven counties with Mexican

majorities, all but three of which (Bexar, Nueces, and San Patricio) lay along the Rio Grande or contiguous to the river counties. His analysis was therefore weighted heavily toward those counties where the Democratic machines controlled local politics and where there was little tradition of political opposition. Martin concluded, then, that "the People's Party drew almost no support from the Mexicans," which he believed explained "the fatal weakness of Populism" in South Texas. But the Populists did have significant success in recruiting Mexican supporters in many of the counties north of the Rio Grande Valley where Mexicans comprised a sizable share of the population, if not a majority; see Martin, *People's Party,* 99–102. For a treatment of the boss system in South Texas that touches on the 1890s but mostly emphasizes the twentieth century, see Anders, *Boss Rule.* For a contemporary account of fraudulent manipulation of the Mexican vote in South Texas immediately preceding the era discussed in this chapter, see *San Antonio Express,* Nov. 20, 1888.

4. *Texas Advance,* July 28, 1894; J. W. Sansom to Vachel Weldon, Oct. 10, 1894, Weldon Papers; SM, May 14, 1896.

5. GDN, May 26, 1892, Sept. 21, 1893, May 2, Sept. 21, 23, 1894; *San Antonio Light,* Nov. 15, 1893; Louis d'Autin Zubaga to Vachel Weldon, Oct. 15, 1894, A. R. Stevenson and V. F. Carvajal to Vachel Weldon, Oct. 19, 1894, both in Weldon Papers; "Vicente F. Carvajal," Wilson County Historical Society, accessed May 7, 2019, http://wilsoncounty history.org/Moments/VICENTE%20F.%20CARVAJAL.pdf; Hunter, *Trail Drivers of Texas,* 549–51.

6. On O'Connor, see Johnson, *History of Texas and Texans,* 5:2248; Loughery, *Texas State Government,* 87–88; GDN, Oct. 14, 1894; *San Antonio Express,* Jan. 23, 1897. On machine politics in San Antonio and Bexar County, see Waller, "Callaghan Machine"; Baum and Miller, "Ethnic Conflict," 63–84.

7. DMN, Oct. 6, 14, 1894. The 1894 race in the Eleventh District can be followed in great detail in the Weldon Papers. On Terrell's withdrawal and the fusion arrangement, see undated clippings from unidentified newspaper containing open letter from the Eleventh District Populist Executive Committee to the Populists of the Eleventh Congressional District, Oct. 13, 1894, Ben Terrell to Whom It May Concern (n.d.), Capt. Joseph Sheley to Whom It May Concern, Oct. 13, 1894, H. S. P. Ashby to the Eleventh District Populist Executive Committee, Oct. 8, 1894, and Henry E. McCulloch to the Eleventh District Populist Executive Committee, Oct. 12, 1894, all in Weldon Papers. For a concise summary of the election and especially Rayner's role in it, see Cantrell, *Kenneth and John B. Rayner,* 217–21.

8. R. J. Shelton to Vachel Weldon, Oct. 1, 1894, Weldon Papers.

9. R. B. Rentfro to A. S. Crisp, Oct. 14, 1894, and V. F. Carvajal to Vachel Weldon, Oct. 26, 1894, both in Weldon Papers; HT, Eleanor Russell Rentfro, "Rentfro, Robert Byron," accessed Nov. 30, 2017, http://www.tshaonline.org/handbook/online/articles /fre29. Wealthy Republican rancher Dennis O'Connor related to Weldon the infor-

mation about funding from the Democratic National Committee, saying, "This one of my school mates & a Crain man gave me to understand." See Dennis O'Connor to Vachel Weldon, Oct. 29, 1894, Weldon Papers.

10. V. F. Carvajal to A. S. Crisp, Oct. 26, 1894, and R. B. Rentfro to Vachel Weldon, Nov. 12, 1894, Weldon Papers; *Biennial Report . . . 1894*, 246–47.

11. N. H. McGirk to Vachel Weldon, Nov. 20, 1894, R. B. Rentfro to Vachel Weldon, Nov. 14, 27, 1895, A. J. Carothers to Vachel Weldon, Nov. 8, 1894, Weldon Papers.

12. HT, S. W. Pease, "Taylor, Henry Ryder," accessed Nov. 30, 2017, http://www.tshaonline.org/handbook/online/articles/fta18; DMN, June 19, 1896; *San Antonio Express*, Feb. 7, 1895; Waller, "Callaghan Machine," 77–78, 90.

13. *San Antonio Light*, May 15, 1896; *Texas Advance*, Aug. 4, 1894. A slightly more generous press estimate of how many immigrants had taken out final papers was "less than 100" out of 10,000. See "Noonan's District," DMN, May 23, 1896.

14. For the Hidalgo County and Starr County statistics, see Publication 7RA211, Index to Naturalization Records. For a more complete explanation of this analysis, including a graph illustrating the issue, see Cantrell, "'Our Very Pronounced Theory,'" 672–73.

15. Cantrell, "'Our Very Pronounced Theory,'" 665–66.

16. GDN, Oct. 8, Nov. 15, 1894; *San Antonio Express*, Oct. 21, 24, 28, 31, 1888.

17. T. J. McMinn to Vachel Weldon, Dec. 5, 1894, Weldon Papers.

18. DMN, Feb. 6, 1895; *Journal of House of Representatives*, 24th Leg., Reg. Sess. (1895), 353–55.

19. *Journal of House of Representatives*, 24th Leg., Reg. Sess. (1895), 724–25; Texas Legislative Council, *Amendments to the Texas Constitution*, 74.

20. On Ricardo Rodriquez, his application for citizenship, and the case surrounding it, see In re Rodriguez, May 3, 1897, District Court, W.D. Texas, Westlaw 81 F. 337; De León, "In re Ricardo Rodriquez."

21. *San Antonio Express*, Nov. 21, 1888; In re Rodriguez; *San Antonio Light*, May 19, 1896.

22. In re Rodriguez; HT, "Maxey, Thomas Sheldon," accessed Dec. 1, 2017, http://www.tshaonline.org/handbook/online/articles/fma86.

23. Haney López, *White by Law*, 49–67, 202–3; Padilla, "Early Chicano Legal Recognition," 566–71.

24. In re Rodriguez, 347; *San Antonio Light*, Jan. 17, 1897.

25. *San Antonio Express*, Oct. 31, 1888.

26. *San Antonio Express*, May 12, 1896; *San Antonio Light*, May 12, 1896; DMN, May 14, 1896.

27. *El Regidor*, May 14, June 18, July 2, Aug. 13, 1896. For an overview of Cruz and *El Regidor*, see Martinez, "Pablo Cruz." Ayer's *American Newspaper Annual* lists *El Regidor*'s political affiliation as "Populist," but it is more accurate to say that the paper was independent, as it always endorsed eclectic slates of candidates in the 1890s. The

main criterion Cruz had for endorsing candidates at the local level was the extent to which they treated Mexican Americans fairly and supported their causes. For the paper's list of 1896 endorsements, see *El Regidor,* Oct. 29, 1896.

28. *San Antonio Express,* May 12, 1896; *El Regidor,* July 16, 1896. Born in 1865, Deutschmann emigrated from Germany to Texas in 1879. He worked variously as a printer's devil, fruit stand owner, shoestring salesman, sheepherder, rubber stamp manufacturer, clerk, and newspaper reporter before passing the bar in 1895 and becoming a lawyer; see the biographical sketch in *San Antonio Express,* May 20, 1915; Bushick, *Glamorous Days,* 92, 96–97. His prominence in the local People's Party was sufficient to get him elected as a delegate to the 1896 Populist state convention; see *San Antonio Light,* June 14, 1896.

29. *San Antonio Express,* May 13, 1896; *San Antonio Freie Presse für Texas,* May 13, 1894.

30. *San Antonio Express,* May 14, 1896.

31. *San Antonio Light,* May 16, June 14, 21, 1896; *San Antonio Express,* May 28, 1896; GDN, May 27, 1896; *El Regidor,* May 28, 1896.

32. *San Antonio Light,* June 21, 1896. Little else is known about Montalbo, except that he worked as a printer at the firm of Guessaz and Ferlet and was a politically active Tejano, receiving the Populist nomination for weigher in Bexar County in 1894. The *Express* referred to him as "one of the most prominent citizens of the Queen City" in an 1898 obituary of his son. See *San Antonio Light,* Oct. 1, 1894; *San Antonio Express,* July 8, 1898; Appler, *General Directory,* 435.

33. *Brownsville Herald,* July 4, 1896, reprinting undated article from the *San Antonio Express.*

34. *El Regidor,* May 14, July 2, 30, Aug. 6, 1896.

35. Ibid., July 30, 1896; *San Antonio Light,* June 14, July 29, 1896; GDN, July 16, 1896.

36. *San Antonio Express,* Aug. 8, 1896; Winkler, *Platforms,* 382.

37. *San Antonio Express,* May 25, 1896.

38. DMN, Aug. 9, 1896.

39. *Brownsville Herald,* Oct. 13, 1896; *San Antonio Express,* Oct. 9, 1896; *San Antonio Light,* Oct. 10, 1896.

40. *El Regidor,* Aug. 27, 1896.

41. Ibid., Oct. 1, 22, Nov. 5, 1896. On McRae, see *Fort Worth Telegram,* June 12, 1904.

42. *San Antonio Light,* Nov. 12, 1896; In re Rodriguez, 354–55. Thomas Paschal, the only one of the amici curiae who actually supported Rodriguez's application, was more skeptical than his colleagues about definitively declaring Rodriguez a full-blooded Indian, pointing out that over three centuries the "aboriginal" inhabitants of Mexico had "so freely intermingled" their blood with the Spaniards that "the pure stock of either . . . is seldom met with." And though he referred to the "hair-splitting, technical, and meaningless consideration of who are meant by 'white people,'" he nonetheless based his legal opinion on factors other than race, saying,

"the spirit of the law must be present, whatever may be its letter." See In re Rodriguez, 342–43.

43. *Brownsville Herald*, May 6, 1897; *San Antonio Express*, May 7, 1897, June 9, 1898; *El Regidor*, Oct. 13, 1898.

44. *San Antonio Express*, June 9, 1898, Oct. 31, 1888; *Victoria Advocate*, Sept. 29, 1900.

45. *San Antonio Light*, May 31, Oct. 10, 1896; DMN, June 19, 1896.

46. DMN, Jan. 20, May 14, 1896; Miller, "Harrison County Methods."

10. The Election of 1896

1. DMN, Nov. 11, 1892; SM, Nov. 24, 1892, Jan. 24, 1895; *Dublin Progress*, May 26, 1893.

2. DMN, Apr. 26, June 9, 1895, Feb. 23, 1896.

3. Ibid., May 28, 1895, Feb. 25, 26, 27, Mar. 2, 1896.

4. Ibid., Sept. 3, 4, 1895; SM, Sept. 12, Oct. 3, 1895.

5. *Dublin Progress*, Dec. 8, 1893; SM, June 6, 1895.

6. DMN, Oct. 18, 1894; Feb. 3, 1896; HT, Cutrer, "Walton, William Martin."

7. DMN, May 31, June 30, 1895, Feb. 25, 1896; SM, Apr. 23, 1896.

8. SM, June 6, 189; DMN, July 15, 1895. For a sketch of Alsbury (which mistakenly refers to him as "Edward"), see DMN, Aug. 9, 1896.

9. Argersinger, "Taubeneck's Laws"; Watts, "Taubeneck"; DMN, Dec. 11, 1894, Jan. 4, 1895, Feb. 22, 1896; SM, Jan. 5, 1895.

10. Argersinger, "Taubeneck's Laws," 100. Milton Park charged that "not one-fifth of the regular elected national executive committee were present" at the St. Louis meeting but that fusionists "held proxies enough to declare a quorum present and dictate the policy"; see SM, Nov. 12, 1896. The committee had 114 members; the day before the meeting the press estimated that fewer than fifty would attend. See *Raleigh News and Observer*, Jan. 17, 1896. This was presumably due to the relative poverty of many members. When the meeting actually convened, only "forty delegates and proxies answered to the roll call," and it was noted that "the old guard was not represented as strongly as in former meetings"; see *San Francisco Call*, Jan. 18, 1896. The *Topeka Daily Capital* alleged that Taubeneck "came to the convention with enough proxies to pack it," see *Topeka Daily Capital*, Jan. 22, 1896. Peter Argersinger, who has done the most comprehensive research on the question of the January meeting, agrees that the proxies were deftly manipulated and finds that Taubeneck and his fusionist allies controlled 51 of 87 total votes (apparently 27 of the 114 members did not assign proxies); see Argersinger, *Limits of Agrarian Radicalism*, 128.

11. For their 1892 Omaha convention, the Populists had modified the traditional formula by setting the basis of representation at eight delegates at-large from each state, plus four from each congressional district, a formula which, apparently by design,

resulted in 1,776 delegates for the July 4 convention (although something under 1,400 actually attended). After the first day of the St. Louis meeting, the press reported that the basis of representation would be fixed at one delegate at-large from each state and one for each 1,000 votes cast by Populists at the last election. This new formula would have given Texas, with its 178,000 Populist votes in 1894, 179 delegates, which would have likely produced a Midroader delegate majority. But the committee reversed itself on the second day of its meeting, resulting in the final decision that reduced Texas's delegate count to 103. See Hicks, *Populist Revolt*, 200; *San Francisco Call*, Jan. 18, 1896; *Topeka Advocate*, Jan. 22, 1896; Thurston, "How Presidents Are Nominated."

12. Beeby, *Revolt of the Tarheels*, 74; *Raleigh News and Observer*, July 21, 1896; Hunt, *Marion Butler*, 104. The statistics in this paragraph are determined as follows: in the 1894 election, fusionist chief justice candidate William T. Faircloth received 148,000 votes; given that the Republican candidate for governor in 1892 had polled 95,000 votes, it seems safe to assume that the GOP probably contributed about that many votes to the fusion coalition in 1896, meaning that something in the range of 50,000 votes constituted actual Populist strength. Election returns are from Dubin, *United States Gubernatorial Elections*, 17; *Statistician and Economist*, 84.

13. SM, Oct. 10, 1895.

14. SM, Jan. 30, Feb. 6, 1896; DMN, Feb. 25, Mar. 6, 1896.

15. DMN, Feb. 29, Mar. 6, 7, 1896; SM, Mar. 12, 26, 1896; *McKinney Democrat*, Mar. 12, 1896.

16. SM, Mar. 19, 26, 1896.

17. DMN, June 26, 1892, July 2, Nov. 28, 1896; *McKinney Democrat*, Oct. 17, 1895; SM, Oct. 17, 1895.

18. In 1891 Gibbs had called for the establishment of banks of circulation under the provisions of the National Bank Act, where the banks would make low-interest loans to farmers by issuing legal tender notes, redeemable in coin or 2 percent, twenty-year US bonds, to be secured by a mortgage on agricultural lands on a basis of half their market value. See *Granbury News*, 1891; HT, Worth Robert Miller, "Gibbs, Barnett," accessed Dec. 1, 2017, http://www.tshaonline.org/handbook/online/articles /fgi42.

19. DMN, Jan. 8, 9, 11, 17, 19, 25, 26, 29, Feb. 2, 9, 23, Mar. 8, 9, 1896.

20. Ibid., Feb. 29, Mar. 2, 8, 1896.

21. Ibid., Nov. 28, 1896.

22. Ibid., June 9, Nov. 28, Dec. 5, 1895, June 14, 1896; SM, Dec. 5, 1895; *McKinney Democrat*, Jan. 16, 1896; Cantrell and Paschal, "Texas Populism."

23. DMN, May 2, 1896.

24. Ibid.; HT, Worth Robert Miller, "Gore, Thomas Pryor," accessed Dec. 1, 2017, http://www.tshaonline.org/handbook/online/articles/fgo46.

25. DMN, June 3, 16, July 2, 13, 14, 1896; *McKinney Democrat*, May 7, 1896; HT, Jonathan Perry, "Calhoun, Benjamin A.," accessed Dec. 1, 2017, http://www.tshaonline

.org/handbook/online/articles/fca88; HT, Alwyn Barr, "Eagle, Joe Henry," accessed Dec. 1, 2017, http://www.tshaonline.org/handbook/online/articles/fea01; *Bartlett Tribune*, Apr. 8, 1924; *Clay Center Times*, July 13, 1893; GDN, Sept. 6, 25, 1894, Jan. 21, May 31, June 15, 21, July 12, Aug. 7, 1896, June 3, 1917; *Laredo Weekly Times*, June 10, 1917; Lee, *Farmers vs. Wage Earners*, 76.

26. SM, Aug. 29, 1889, Feb. 18, 1892; DMN, July 4, 1891, Feb. 3, 1892, Feb. 23, Nov. 11, Sept. 27, 1894, Jan. 8, 1896, Sept. 4, 1898; *Mineola Alliance Courier*, Oct. 6, 1892; FWG, Feb. 3, 1892; Winkler, *Platforms*, 298.

27. DMN, Mar. 22, Apr. 2, 8, 12, July 18, 1896. Wood went on to serve as a Populist presidential elector in 1896, and in 1898 he finally received the congressional nomination; see *Denton County News*, Oct. 31, 1896; DMN, Sept. 4, 1898.

28. DMN, Mar. 21, May 22, June 17, 21, 1896; SM, Oct. 17, 1895.

29. DMN, Apr. 22, May 27, 1896; *Austin Weekly Statesman*, May 7, 1896; *St. Louis Globe-Democrat*, July 23, 1896.

30. Williams, *Realigning America*, 62–93.

31. Kazin, *Godly Hero*, 56–62.

32. *Dublin Progress*, Aug. 7, 1896; *McKinney Democrat*, July 18, 1896.

33. *San Francisco Call*, July 22, 1896. On the Southern Hotel, see Cooper, "Lecture Tour: St. Louis," Oscar Wilde in America, accessed Dec. 2, 2017, http://www.oscarwildeinamerica.org/lectures-1882/february/0225-st-louis.html.

34. GDN, July 28, 1896, quoting the *New York Sun*.

35. *Indianapolis News*, July 22, 1896.

36. *St. Louis Globe-Democrat*, July 22, 1896; DMN, July 21, 1896.

37. *St. Louis Republic*, July 22, 1896; DMN, July 19, 1896.

38. *St. Louis Post-Dispatch*, July 22, 1896; *St. Louis Republic*, July 22, 1896.

39. *St. Louis Republic*, July 22, 26, 1896. For a particularly clear explanation of the plan, by delegate Charles H. Jenkins, see SM, July 23, 1896. Also see *Arkansas Gazette*, July 22, 1896.

40. *San Antonio Light*, July 22, 1896; *Official Proceedings of the Eleventh Republican National Convention*, 22–23; DMN, July 22, 23, 1896; *Dallas Times Herald*, July 22, 1896; Durden, *Climax of Populism*, 32–33; *St. Louis Globe-Democrat*, July 23, 25, 1896; *Raleigh News and Observer*, July 23, 1896; *St. Louis Republic*, July 23, 1896.

41. *St. Louis Republic*, July 24, 1896; *St. Louis Globe-Democrat*, July 24, 1896; DMN, July 24, 1896.

42. *St. Louis Republic*, July 24, 1896; *Dallas Times Herald*, July 24, 1896; Bryan, *First Battle*, 264–70; *St. Louis Globe-Democrat*, July 24, 1896.

43. *St. Louis Globe-Democrat*, July 24, 1896. The fullest account of the meeting and Gibbs's role in it comes from the DMN, July 25, Aug. 2, 1896; *St. Louis Globe-Democrat*, July 24, 1896; *Houston Post*, July 25, 1896.

44. DMN, July 25, Aug. 2, 1896; *St. Louis Globe-Democrat*, July 24, 1896; *Houston Post*, July 25, 1896; *St. Louis Republic*, July 26, 1896.

45. *St. Louis Globe-Democrat,* July 26, 1896; *San Antonio Light,* July 25, 1896; *St. Louis Post-Dispatch,* July 25, 1896; *Dallas Times Herald,* July 24, 1896.

46. *Nebraska State Journal,* July 25, 1896; *St. Louis Globe-Democrat,* July 25, 1896.

47. DMN, July 25, 1896; Jones, *Presidential Election,* 259.

48. *Houston Post,* July 25, 1896; DMN, July 25, 1896; *St. Louis Republic,* July 25, 1896.

49. *St. Louis Globe-Democrat,* July 25, 1896; DMN, July 25, 1896.

50. *St. Louis Globe-Democrat,* July 22, 26, 1896; *St. Louis Republic,* July 25, 26, 1896; *Dallas Times Herald,* July 25, 1896; *Houston Post,* July 26, 1896.

51. GDN, Aug. 4, 1896; *Houston Post,* Oct. 29, 1896.

52. DMN, July 28, 1896. Marion Williams, one of the most outspoken Midroaders at St. Louis, made the same prediction as Jones; see *McKinney Democrat,* July 30, 1896.

53. Arthur Sewall to William J. Bryan, July 25, 1896, James S. Hogg to William J. Bryan, July 28, 1896, both in Bryan Papers.

54. Hunt, *Marion Butler,* 112–16; Durden, *Climax of Populism,* 52–56; Williams, *Realigning America,* 124–26; GDN, Aug. 3, 1896.

55. DMN, Aug. 5, 1896.

56. GDN, Aug. 6, 1896; DMN, Aug. 6, 1896; *Dallas Times Herald,* Aug. 5, 1896.

57. DMN, Aug. 7, 1896.

58. *Dallas Times Herald,* Aug. 7, 1896; DMN, Aug. 8, 1896.

59. DMN, Aug. 8, 1896.

60. Ibid., Aug. 9, 1896; *Austin Weekly Statesman,* Aug. 13, 1896.

61. Goodwyn, *Populist Moment,* 26; *Austin Weekly Statesman,* Aug. 13, 1896.

62. GDN, Aug. 20, 1896; SM, Aug. 27, 1896.

63. SM, Oct. 1, 1896.

64. GDN, Oct. 17, 1896.

65. *Houston Post,* Aug. 15, 26, Sept. 3, 13, Oct. 14, 17, 20, 24, 1896; GDN, Aug. 22, Oct. 6, 8, 12, 14, 1896; *Austin Weekly Statesman,* Oct. 8, 1896.

66. *McKinney Democrat,* Sept. 17, 1896; *Houston Post,* Oct. 17, 1896; DMN, Oct. 16, 20, 21, 1896.

67. *Houston Post,* Oct. 20, 1896; *Denton County News,* Oct. 8, 1896; DMN, Oct. 21, 1896; *Abilene Reporter,* Oct. 30, 1896.

68. DMN, Aug. 19, Oct. 13, 1896; GDN, Aug. 19, 20, 21, Oct. 9, 1896; *Denton County News,* Oct. 8, 1896; *Brenham Daily Banner,* Sept. 3, 1896.

69. Davis, *Memoir,* 56; *St. Louis Republic,* July 26, 1896.

70. DMN, July 30, 1896; GDN, Aug. 2, 1896; Davis, *Memoir,* 39.

71. *McKinney Democrat,* Oct. 15, 29, 1896; Miller, "Harrison County Methods"; DMN, Sept. 26, Oct. 7, 1896.

72. SM, Oct. 29, Dec. 24, 1896; see also *Abilene Reporter,* Oct. 31, 1896; *Dublin Progress,* Dec. 5, 1896; *McKinney Democrat,* Jan. 14, 1897.

73. GDN, Nov. 2, 1896; *Houston Post*, Oct. 30, Nov. 3, 1896; *Denton County News*, Oct. 31, 1896; *Gainesville Hesperian*, Nov. 3, 1896; SM, Nov. 4, 1897, Sept. 22, 1898.

74. *Cooper People's Cause*, Oct. 30, 1896.

75. DMN, Nov. 3, 1896.

76. Ibid. For a more pro-Democratic perspective, see *Houston Post*, Nov. 3, 1896.

77. DMN, Nov. 3, 1896.

78. GDN, Nov. 4, 1896; SM, Feb. 4, 1897.

79. McCarver and McCarver, *Hearne on the Brazos*, 27; Parker, *Historical Recollections*, 48–49; GDN, Nov. 7, 19, 1896; *Bryan Eagle*, Nov. 12, 1896; clipping from the *Houston Press*, Feb. 18, 1931, photocopy in author's possession, original in possession of Otis D. Cannon. See also St. Clair, "History of Robertson County," 154–56.

80. SM, Dec. 17, 1896.

81. Barr, *Reconstruction to Reform*, 171–72; Cantrell and Barton, "Texas Populists," 685–89; Miller and Ulbig, "Building a Populist Coalition," 290–94.

82. SM, Dec. 17, 1896.

11. The Collapse of Texas Populism

1. *San Antonio Express*, Oct. 16, 1892; SM, Sept. 6, 1894; GDN, June 21, 1896; DMN, Aug. 7, 1896; Bentley, *Cattle Ranges of the Southwest*; Bentley, *Report upon the Grasses*; Bentley, *Forage Plants*; *Big Spring Herald*, Aug. 24, 1933; H. L. Bentley to Marion Butler, Mar. 10, 1897, Butler Papers.

2. J. H. Davis to Marion Butler, Mar. 30, 1897, Butler Papers.

3. Harry Tracy to Marion Butler, Mar. 23, 1897, Butler Papers; SM, Dec. 12, 1888; S. C. Granberry to Marion Butler, Mar. 27, 1897, Butler Papers; Jacobus, *Granberry Family*, 46–57.

4. Vandervoort had led a corruption-tainted career in GOP politics and was an avowed nativist, lending some credence to historians' later charges of Populist nativism. He later founded La Gloria, an American colony in Cuba. He died in 1901. See Wells, "Most Interesting and Picturesque Fraud."

5. Milton Park et al. to Marion Butler, Apr. 8, 1897, J. B. Rayner to Marion Butler, Apr. 27, 1897, Joseph S. Bradley to Marion Butler, Mar. 20, 1897, Cuthbert Vincent to Marion Butler, Apr. 8, 1897, C. H. Jenkins to Marion Butler, June 2, 1897, C. H. Jenkins to Marion Butler, June 2, 1897, all in Butler Papers. The best account of the post-1896 factionalism in the party is Barnes, *Farmers in Rebellion*, 189–94, although Barnes's chronology of events is sometimes difficult to follow.

6. J. H. Davis to Marion Butler, Mar. 26, 1897, J. H. Davis to Marion Butler, July 12, 1897, both in Butler Papers.

7. DMN, June 18, July 2, 1898.

8. SM June 16, July 7, 14, 21, 28, Aug. 4, 1898; DMN, June 8, July 9, 1898; *Dublin Progress*, July 8, 1898; *Stephenville Empire*, July 28, 1898; Barnes, *Farmers in Rebellion*, 190.

9. DMN, Jan. 23, Feb. 6, Mar. 20, 1898.

10. Ibid., July 29, 1898.

11. Ibid., Aug. 20, 1898.

12. Ibid., Dec. 1, 1898; SM, May 17, 1900.

13. Ibid., May 5, 1900.

14. *Houston Post*, Apr. 1, 1900. For an excellent contemporary account of Populist factionalism in early 1900, including the complicated Populist fusion plan, see *Rockdale Messenger*, Jan. 25, 1900. See also DMN, Feb. 8, 1900.

15. *San Antonio Express*, July 12, 1900.

16. Barnes, *Farmers in Rebellion*, 194; *Houston Post*, July 24, 25, Sept. 2, 1900.

17. Barr, *Reconstruction to Reform*, 197–99; Yelderman, *Jay Birds*, esp. chaps. 2 and 3. Other counties with early White Man's Unions included Colorado, Matagorda, and Brazoria.

18. Barr, *Reconstruction to Reform*, 200; *Houston Post*, Mar. 9, 14, Jul. 23, Nov. 23, 1898, Jan. 16, 1900; SM, Sept. 15, 1898, Oct. 6, 1901, Feb. 8, Mar. 2, 1902; *Victoria Advocate*, Aug. 12, 1899; *McKinney Democrat*, Feb. 1, 1900; DMN, Mar. 18, 1900, June 16, 1902; *Rockdale Messenger*, May 17, 1900; *Bryan Eagle*, May 13, Aug. 30, 1900; *Shiner Gazette*, June 18, 1902; *Fort Worth Register*, Jan. 14, 1902; *San Antonio Express*, Mar. 20, 1902; *Fort Worth Register*, July 19, 1900.

19. SM, May 28, 1896; *Cass County Sun*, Apr. 3, 1900.

20. TLPP, "Benjamin A. Calhoun," "Edward Tarkington."

21. *Houston Post*, Dec. 24, 1897, July 6, 1898. For reports of whitecappers' activities, see *Bryan Eagle*, Sept. 2, 11, 1897, Mar. 11, May 28, June 16, 1898, Aug. 3, 1899; *Austin Statesman*, Sept. 2, 1897; *Brenham Banner*, Sept. 30, Nov. 25, 1897; *El Paso Herald*, Jan. 21, Dec. 14, 1898; *Brownsville Herald*, Feb. 23, 1898; *Shiner Gazette*, June, 1, 1898; Evans, "Texas Agriculture," 320–21.

22. *Wise County Messenger*, Sept. 13, 1901.

23. *Weimar Mercury*, Aug. 26, 1899; *Houston Post*, May 5, 1899; *Bryan Eagle*, May 5, 1899; *El Paso Herald*, May 26, 1899; Gammell, *Laws of Texas*, supp., 215.

24. Except where otherwise indicated, the accounts in this paragraph and the next three are drawn from Goodwyn, "Populist Dreams."

25. Information on Scott's life after the siege is from *Houston Post*, Feb. 18, 1902, Jan. 22, 1903, Oct. 14, 1904. Goodwyn did not write about the lawsuit or the murder charges.

26. Miller, "Building a Progressive Coalition," 163, 165.

27. Ibid., 164, 167.

28. Ibid., 168–71.

29. Ibid., 172–74; *Granbury Graphic-Truth*, Aug. 22, 1902.

30. Miller, "Building a Progressive Coalition," 175; Barr, *Reconstruction to Reform*, 235–36.

31. Miller, "Building a Progressive Coalition," 176–77; HT, Patrick Cox, "Farmers Union," accessed Dec. 6, 2017, http://www.tshaonline.org/handbook/online/articles/aafo4; HT, Worth Robert Miller, "Gresham, Isaac Newton," accessed Dec. 6, 2017, http://www.tshaonline.org/handbook/online/articles/fgrab; *Fort Worth Star-Telegram*, Aug. 17, 1917.

32. Schmelzer, *Our Fighting Governor*; Miller, "Building a Progressive Coalition," 178–81 (Davis quotation on p. 179). For a more comprehensive account of the role of Populists in the rise of the progressive wing of the Democratic Party, see Miller, "Populist Return."

33. Dallek, *Lone Star Rising*, 21–23; HT, Dayton Kelley, "Johnson, Samuel Ealy, Jr.," accessed Dec. 7, 2017, http://www.tshaonline.org/handbook/online/articles/fjo24.

Conclusion

1. There are exceptions even to this broad generalization. Intellectual historian Nancy Cohen, for example, traces the roots of twentieth-century liberalism back to the writings of Gilded Age economists, journalists, and social scientists who, though dedicated to individual freedom and laissez-faire economics, championed an administrative state as an alternative to Populist-style popular democracy; see Cohen, *Reconstruction of American Liberalism*.

2. Graham, *Encore for Reform*, 9; Stromquist, *Reinventing "The People,"* 4. For a sample of major works on progressivism, see Hofstadter, *Age of Reform*; Link, *Woodrow Wilson and the Progressive Era*; Wiebe, *Search for Order*; Harrison, *Congress, Progressive Reform, and the New American State*; McGerr, *Fierce Discontent*; Stromquist, *Reinventing "The People"*; Flanagan, *America Reformed*. For a perceptive historiographical analysis of the trend outlined in this paragraph, see Johnston, "Re-democratizing the Progressive Era," 72–77.

3. Cowie, *Great Exception*, 64–67, 88–89, 226; Sanders, *Roots of Reform*, 149; McMath, "C. Vann Woodward," 744.

4. Cowie, *Great Exception* (quoting Hoover), 87; Graham, *Encore for Reform*, esp. 66–73, 174 (quotation on p. 73).

5. Hofstadter, *Age of Reform*, 307.

6. SM, Dec. 17, 1896; Henry L. Bentley to Thomas E. Watson, Feb. 20, 1908, Watson Papers; *Cameron Herald*, Apr. 29, 1815; *Austin Weekly Statesman*, Oct. 10, 1878; *Austin Daily Democratic Statesman*, Oct. 23, 25, 30, 1878.

7. Winkler, *Platforms*, 418, 420, 442, 470, 483, 513, 527, 564, 590; HT, Green, "Rhodes, Lee Lightfoot"; HT, Alwyn Barr, "Socialist Party," accessed Feb. 28, 2018, http://www.tshaonline.org/handbook/online/articles/waso1. On the relationship between Populism and Socialism in Texas, see Wilkison, *Yeomen, Sharecroppers, and Socialists*; Alter, "Dirt Farmer Internationalists."

8. Winkler, *Platforms*, 554, 597; GDN, Nov. 10, 1910, Feb. 27, 29, Dec. 22, 1914; DMN, Feb. 13, 1912; *Cameron Herald*, Apr. 29, 1915; *Austin American*, Apr. 24, 1916; *Austin Daily Statesman*, Aug. 19, 1912; *Houston Post*, Aug. 2, Sept. 7, 1912; *Bryan Eagle*, Aug. 2, 1912, Aug. 12, 1914, June 6, 1916; *Laredo Weekly Times*, June 10, 1917.

9. Orton, "Charles H. Jenkins"; HT, Worth Robert Miller, "Jenkins, Charles H.," accessed Feb. 28, 2018, http://www.tshaonline.org/handbook/online/articles/fje03; Johnson, *History of Texas and Texans*, 4:1870–71; HT, John Leffler, "Brown County," accessed Feb. 28, 2018, http://www.tshaonline.org/handbook/online/articles/hcb17.

10. FWG, Nov. 29, 1883; DMN, Jan. 26, Apr. 8, 1896; White, *Promised Land*, 105; *Austin Weekly Statesman*, June 27, 1889; SM, Aug. 9, Sept. 9, 1894, July 2, 1895; *Comanche Chief*, quoted in the *Brenham Daily Banner*, Aug. 9, 1900; *Dublin Progress*, Aug. 5, 1892.

11. *Dublin Progress*, Aug. 7, 1900; *Austin American*, Jan. 28, 1915, June 14, 1916; *Houston Post*, June 11, Aug. 8, 1916; Orton, "Charles H. Jenkins."

12. Johnson, *History of Texas and Texans*, 4:1870–71.

13. *Austin Statesman*, Apr. 30, 1916.

14. White, *Promised Land*, 104–6.

15. SM, Aug. 9, 1894.

16. HT, Palmer, "Ashby, Harrison Sterling Price"; Cowden, "H. S. P. Ashby," 128–38; Jim Bissett, "Indiahoma Farmers' Union," *Encyclopedia of Oklahoma History and Culture*, accessed May 31, 2018, https://www.okhistory.org/publications/enc/entry.php ?entry=IN003; *Indian Journal*, Feb. 9, 1906; *Shawnee News*, Aug. 12, 1907, Aug. 20, 1910; *Daily Oklahoman*, Oct. 17, 1901; *Guthrie Daily Leader*, Mar. 25, 1916; *Cordell Beacon*, Mar. 30, 1916; HT, Jonathan Perry, "Barbee, Lewis N.," accessed May 31, 2018, http://www.tshaonline.org/handbook/online/articles/fbaao; HT, Perry, "Calhoun, Benjamin A."; TLPP, "Charles K. Walter"; Winkler, *Platforms*, 297; TLPP, "James M. Perdue." Edwards was agreeing in the main with Charles Postel on the links between Populism and progressivism; see Edwards, in Miller, "*The Populist Vision*: A Roundtable Discussion," 27.

17. HT, Worth Robert Miller, "Davis, James Harvey [Cyclone]," accessed June 1, 2018, http://www.tshaonline.org/handbook/online/articles/fda41; Miller, "Building a Progressive Coalition," 179; Voting records, 64th Congress, Govtrack, https://www.govtrack.us/congress/votes.

18. *McKinney Courier-Gazette*, Sept. 4, 1923.

19. *Ferris Wheel*, July 30, 1898; SM, Aug. 4, 1898; *Texas Triangle*, Oct. 7, 1898; HT, Barr, "Eagle, Joe Henry"; Voting records, 63rd–66th Congresses, Govtrack, https://www.govtrack.us/congress/votes.

20. *Austin American*, Aug. 14, 1922; *Houston Post*, Apr. 25, 1919; HT, Dora (Sam) Akkerman, "Houston Yacht Club," accessed June 1, 2018, http://www.tshaonline .org/handbook/online/articles/xsh01; Ragan, "Joe Henry Eagle." Kirby actually was reasonably progressive early in his career, subscribing to a sort of Texas version of An-

drew Carnegie's "Gospel of Wealth." But Kirby grew increasingly conservative as he got older, and in the 1930s he was a rabid anti–New Dealer; see Morgan, "Gospel of Wealth."

21. *Austin American*, Sept. 16, 1922, Jan. 31, 1933; Voting records, 64th Congress, Govtrack, https://www.govtrack.us/congress/votes. In his biographical sketch of Eagle, Ragan claimed that Eagle gave only "lukewarm" support for the New Deal, but this appears to be a misreading of Eagle's actual record; see Ragan, "Joe Henry Eagle."

22. Voting records, 73rd, 74th Congresses, Govtrack, https://www.govtrack.us/congress/votes.

23. McElvaine, *Great Depression*, 258–59; Cowie, *Great Exception*, 111–14.

24. 79 Cong. Rec. 7779, 9713 (1935); Katznelson, *Fear Itself*, 357–59; *Big Spring Herald*, July 7, 1936.

25. HT, Barr, "Eagle, Joe Henry"; *Marshall News Messenger*, Apr. 26, 1836; Fairbanks, "Public Housing," 417.

26. W. Elliott Brownlee, "Taxation," in Graham and Wander, *Franklin D. Roosevelt*, 416; 79 Cong. Rec. 12,447 (1935).

27. Elliot A. Rose, "Brains Trust," in Graham and Wander, *Franklin D. Roosevelt*, 40–41; 79 Cong. Rec. 12,447 (1935).

28. 79 Cong. Rec. 4536, 12,446 (1935).

29. Richard S. Kirkendall, "Agricultural Adjustment Act," in Graham and Wander, *Franklin D. Roosevelt*, 1–2; 79 Cong. Rec. 4536 (1935); *Denison Press*, Apr. 19, 1936; Kirkendall, "Great Depression," 156–57; Tugwell, "Design for Government," 330–31.

30. Hardeman and Bacon, *Rayburn*, 24, 27, 46–53, 73–78, 93–94.

31. Ibid., 150–61, 167–203; HT, Anthony Champagne and Floyd F. Ewing, "Rayburn, Samuel Taliaferro," accessed June 2, 2018, http://www.tshaonline.org/handbook/online/articles/fra49.

32. May, *Marvin Jones*, 8–10, 23, 49–79, 98–129; HT, Irvin M. May Jr., "Jones, John Marvin," accessed June 2, 2018, http://www.tshaonline.org/handbook/online/articles/fjo82.

33. Young, *Wright Patman*, 6, 11–19, 24–25, 26, 34–35, 49–60, 65–78; HT, Philip A. Grant Jr., "Patman, John William Wright," accessed June 3, 2018, http://www.tshaonline.org/handbook/online/articles/fpa62.

34. Grant, "Patman, John William Wright"; Young, *Wright Patman*, 62–72, 167–69; *New York Times*, Mar. 8, 1976.

35. Kazin, *Godly Hero*, 26; Cooper, *Woodrow Wilson*, 73; Hoover, quoted in Edwards, *New Spirits*, 207.

36. See Schattschneider, *Semisovereign People*, 78–80.

37. Flanagan, *America Reformed*; Johnston, "Possibilities of Politics," 100; Gould, *Presidency*, 28, 212, 279; Frank Wagner, "Boll Weevil," accessed June 3, 2018, http://www.tshaonline.org/handbook/online/articles/tebo1; Lowry, "Study of Droughts," 13–14; Bentley, *Cattle Ranges of the Southwest*, 6–10.

38. Gerstle, *Liberty and Coercion*, 193–97; Gilbert, *Planning Democracy*, 25–79.

39. HT, Cox, "Farmers Union"; Fisher, *Farmers' Union*.

40. Gerstle, *Liberty and Coercion*, 190–92; Bentley, *Cattle Ranges*; Bentley, *Experiments in Range Improvement*; Bentley, *Progress of Experiments*; Bentley, *Report upon the Grasses*; HT, Juanita Daniel Zachry, "Range Conservation Experimental Station at Abilene," accessed May 18, 2018, http://www.tshaonline.org/handbook/online/articles/ncr01.

41. Bentley, *Experiments in Range Improvement*, 11–12.

42. HT, David Minor, "Knapp, Seaman Asahel," accessed May 19, 2018, http://www.tshaonline.org/handbook/online/articles/fkn02; HT, Irvin M. May Jr., "Texas Agricultural Extension Service," accessed May 19, 2018, http://www.tshaonline.org/handbook/online/articles/amtpw; HT, Steve Hill, "Texas Agricultural Experiment Station," accessed May 19, 2018, http://www.tshaonline.org/handbook/online/articles/kct14; Gerstle, *Liberty and Coercion*, 194–96; *Austin Statesman*, Mar. 20, 1915; GDN, Mar. 20, 1915; *Waco Morning News*, June 16, 1915; *Abilene Daily Reporter*, July 9, 1915. On Rayburn, see Shanks, "Sam Rayburn," 68. The 177–9 vote in the House was not recorded, but it seems safe to assume that the ex-Populist Eagle was among the majority. For the vote, see 64 Cong. Rec. 2001 (1914).

43. Gerstle, *Liberty and Coercion*, 197–98.

44. US Congress, *Food Production*, 157–75; Gerstle, *Liberty and Coercion*, 198–99; Lansing, *Insurgent Democracy*; Fisher, *Farmers' Union*, 16.

45. Gerstle, *Liberty and Coercion*, 199–201; Volanto, *Texas, Cotton, and the New Deal*, 12–16.

46. Gerstle, *Liberty and Coercion*, 192–93.

47. Kennedy, *Freedom from Fear*, 202.

48. Gerstle, *Liberty and Coercion*, 205.

49. Leuchtenberg, *Franklin D. Roosevelt*, 33; Tugwell, quoted in Kennedy, *Freedom from Fear*, 129.

50. David D. Webb, "Thomas, John William Elmer, (1876–1965)," *Encyclopedia of Oklahoma History and Culture*, accessed May 19, 2018, https://www.okhistory.org/publications/enc/entry.php?entry=TH008; McElvaine, *Great Depression*, 148–49; Wheeler, *Yankee from the West*, 41, 250–66, 279.

51. Grover Cleveland, "Veto Message," Feb. 16, 1887, American Presidency Project, http://www.presidency.ucsb.edu/ws/?pid=71489; Gerstle, *Liberty and Coercion*, 205.

52. Hall, "Long Civil Rights Movement," 1233–35.

53. Ibid.; Woodward, *Origins*, 369; Katznelson, *Fear Itself*, 16, 18; Cowie, *Great Exception*, 125.

54. Katznelson, *Fear Itself*, 18, 23.

55. Ibid., 172–75; Hall, "Long Civil Rights Movement," 1245–58.

56. Katznelson, *Fear Itself,* 186–88; Hall, "Long Civil Rights Movement," 1245–48. For fuller treatments of civil rights unionism, see Korstad, *Civil Rights Unionism* and Krochmal, *Blue Texas.*

57. Graham, *Encore for Reform,* 181; Goodwyn, *Democratic Promise;* Fund, "Nixon at 100."

58. Fraser and Gerstle, *Rise and Fall;* Brinkley, *End of Reform;* Brands, *Strange Death;* Cowie, *Great Exception;* Conetta, "Noam Chomsky."

59. Chomsky and Barsamiam, "Noam Chomsky"; Jennifer Rubin, "John Boehner: 'There Is No Republican Party,'" *Washington Post,* May 31, 2018. For a sample of commentators declaring the death of conservatism, see Richard North Patterson, "Donald Trump and the Death of Principled Conservatism," *Boston Globe,* July 10, 2017; E. J. Dionne, "It's Time to Say Last Rites over American Conservatism," *Washington Post,* Feb. 26, 2018; Stan, "How Trump Broke Conservatism"; Walther, "Conservatism Is Dead"; Coaston, "Conservatism Is Dead."

60. Kazin, *Populist Persuasion;* Müller, *What Is Populism?,* 3; Marans, "Bernie Sanders." Also see Postel, "What We Talk About"; Leonhardt, "Secret to Winning."

61. Schulte-Sasse, "Meet Ross Perot," 91–92.

62. Valencia, "Most Democrats."

63. Cowie, *Great Exception.*

BIBLIOGRAPHY

Archival Collections

Bill Files, Texas Legislature. Texas State Library and Archives Commission, Austin, Texas.

Bryan, William Jennings. Papers. Library of Congress.

Butler, Marion. Papers. Southern Historical Collection. University of North Carolina.

Compiled Service Records of Confederate Soldiers Who Served in Organizations from the State of Texas. National Archives and Records Administration.

Eagle, Joe H. Papers. Houston Metropolitan Research Center, Houston Public Library.

Gillespie County Alliance Minutes. Briscoe Center for American History, University of Texas at Austin.

Huddleston, Martin Luther. Diary. Anderson County Genealogical Society, Palestine, TX.

Index to Naturalization Records Found in Federal, State, and County Courts in Texas, ca. 1846–1939. Records of District no. 14 (San Antonio). National Archives RG 85.5.9.

Lamar, Moses P. Papers. Special Collections. University of Texas at Arlington.

McCallum, Jane Y. Papers. Austin History Center, Austin Public Library.

Rayner, John B. Papers. Briscoe Center for American History, University of Texas at Austin.

Texas County Tax Rolls. Texas State Archives and Library Commission.

Weldon, Vachel. Papers. Briscoe Center for American History, University of Texas at Austin.

Newspapers

All are Texas newspapers unless otherwise noted.

Abilene Reporter
Albany Weekly News

Appeal to Reason (Girard, KS)
Arkansas Gazette (Little Rock, AR)
Austin American
Austin Daily News-Tribune
Austin Statesman
Bartlett Tribune
Belton Journal
Big Spring Herald
Blossom Monitor
Brenham Banner
Brownsville Herald
Bryan Eagle
Burlington Evening Gazette (IA)
Burnet Avalanche
Burnet Bulletin
Cameron Herald
Cass County Sun (Linden)
Cheney Sentinel (KS)
Chicago Inter Ocean (IL)
Christian Courier (Dallas)
Claiborne Guardian (Homer, LA)
Clarksville Standard
Clay Center Times (KS)
Cleburne Herald
Colfax Chronicle (LA)
Comanche Chief
Comanche Pioneer-Exponent
Commerce Journal
Cooper People's Cause
Cordell Beacon (OK)
Corsicana Courier
Daily Oklahoman (Oklahoma City, OK)
Dallas Herald
Dallas Mercury
Dallas Morning News
Dallas Times Herald
Denison Press
Denton County News (Denton)
Denver Evening Post (CO)
Dublin Progress

El Paso Herald
Fairfield Recorder
Ferris Wheel
Fort Worth Gazette
Fort Worth Register
Fort Worth Star-Telegram
Gainesville Hesperian
Galveston Daily News
Granbury Graphic-Truth
Granbury News
Greenville Herald
Guthrie Daily Leader (OK)
Hempstead News
Hillsboro Reflector
Honey Grove Signal
Houston Chronicle
Houston Post
Indianapolis News (IN)
Indiana State Journal
Indian Journal (Eufala, OK)
Jacksonville Banner
Jasper Newsboy
Johnson County Review (Cleburne)
Karnes City Reformer
Lampasas People's Journal
Laredo Weekly Times
Linden Alliance Standard
Marshall News Messenger
Mason County Herald (Mason)
McKinney Courier-Gazette
McKinney Democrat
Memphis Daily Appeal (TN)
Mexia Weekly Herald
Mineola Alliance Courier
Mineola Monitor
National Economist (Washington, DC)
Nebraska State Journal (Lincoln, NE)
New York Times (NY)
North Texas Farmer (Paris)
Palo Pinto Tribune

Paradise Messenger

Paris News

Philadelphia North American (PA)

Raleigh News and Observer (NC)

El Regidor (San Antonio)

Rockdale Messenger

Rocky Ford Enterprise (CO)

Rocky Mountain News (Denver, CO)

St. Louis Globe-Democrat (MO)

St. Louis Post-Dispatch (MO)

St. Louis Republic (MO)

San Antonio Express

San Antonio Freie Presse für Texas

San Antonio Light

San Francisco Call (CA)

San Marcos Free Press

Shawnee News (OK)

Shiner Gazette

Southern Mercury (Dallas)

Stephenville Empire

Taylor County News (Abilene)

Terrell Times-Star

Temple Times

Texas Advance (Dallas)

Texas Herald (Paris)

Texas Triangle (Paris)

Topeka Advocate (KS)

Topeka Daily Capital (KS)

Velasco Times

Victoria Advocate

Waco Evening News

Waco Examiner

Waco Morning News

Waxahachie Enterprise

Weatherford Weekly Herald

Weimar Mercury

Whitney Messenger

Wichita Daily Times (Wichita Falls)

Williamson County Sun (Georgetown)

Willis Index

Wise County Messenger (Decatur)

Print Primary Sources

American Newspaper Directory. New York: George P. Rowell, 1896.

Appler, Jules A, compiler. *General Directory of the City of San Antonio, 1895–'96*. San Antonio: Jules A. Appler, 1895.

Armstrong, K. L., ed. *The Little Statesman: A Middle-of-the-Road Manual for American Voters*. Chicago: Schulte Publishing, 1895.

Barthelme, Marion K., ed. *Women in the Texas Populist Movement: Letters to the Southern Mercury*. College Station: Texas A&M University Press, 1997.

Bentley, H. L. *Cattle Ranges of the Southwest: A History of the Exhaustion of the Pasturage and Suggestions for Its Restoration*. Washington, DC: Government Printing Office, 1898.

———. *Experiments in Range Improvement in Central Texas*. Washington, DC: Government Printing Office, 1902.

———. Map. US Patent filed September 21, 1899, issued May 8, 1900. Portal to Texas History, University of North Texas Libraries. https://texashistory.unt.edu/ark:/67531/metapth513548/.

———. *Progress of Experiments in Forage Crops and Range Improvement in Abilene, Tex.* Washington, DC: United States Department of Agriculture, Division of Agrostology, 1899.

———. *A Report upon the Grasses and Forage Plants of Central Texas*. Washington, DC: Government Printing Office, 1898.

Brooks, Edward. *Mental Science and Methods of Mental Culture*. Lancaster, PA: Normal Publishing, 1883.

Bryan, William Jennings. *The First Battle: A Story of the Campaign of 1896*. Chicago: W. B. Conkey, 1896.

Buck, James G. H. Recording Ballot-Box. US Patent 224385 filed October 8, 1879, issued February 10, 1880. Portal to Texas History, University of North Texas Libraries. https://texashistory.unt.edu/ark:/67531/metapth169958/.

City Directory of Austin with Street Directory of Residents. Austin, TX: J. B. Stephenson, 1907.

Commons, John R., Ulrich B. Phillips, Eugene A. Gilmore, Helen L. Sumner, and John B. Andrews, eds. *A Documentary History of American Industrial Society*. 10 vols. Cleveland, OH: Arthur H. Clark, 1910.

Davis, James H. (Cyclone). *A Political Revelation*. Dallas, TX: Advance Publishing, 1894.

Davis, James Harvey Cyclone. *Memoir*. Sherman, TX: Courier Press, 1935.

Dohoney, Ebenezer Lafayette. *An Average American*. Paris, TX: self-published, 1907.

Dubin, Michael J., ed. *United States Gubernatorial Elections, 1861–1911: The Official Results by State and County*. Jefferson, NC: McFarland, 2010.

Dunning, N. A., ed. *The Farmers' Alliance History and Agricultural Digest*. Washington, DC: Alliance Publishing, 1891.

F. A. Battey & Company. *Biographical Souvenir of the State of Texas*. Chicago: F. A. Battey & Company, 1889.

Gammel, H. P. N. *The Laws of Texas*. 10 vols. plus supp. Austin, TX: Gammel Book Co., 1898.

"Jesse H. Tracy." *Confederate Veteran* 23 (1915): 420.

"J. K. P. Hanna." *Confederate Veteran* 36 (Oct. 1928): 287.

John F. Worley & Co.'s Dallas Directory for 1901. Dallas, TX: John F. Worley, 1901.

Johnson, Rebecca Baines. *A Family Album*. New York: McGraw-Hill, 1965.

King, Thomas Benton. *John Counsellor's Evolution: Or, a Real Experience of the Second Coming*. St. Louis, MO: John Counsellor Publishing, 1903.

McConnell, Letta V. "Spiritualism in Dallas, Texas." *Carrier Dove* 9 (May 1892): 149.

Morrison & Fourmy. *Morrison & Fourmy's General Directory of the City of Austin, 1900–1901*. Galveston, TX: Morrison & Fourmy, 1901.

Nugent, Catharine, comp. *Life Work of Thomas L. Nugent*. Stephenville, TX: privately published, printed by Laird and Lee, Chicago, 1896.

N. W. Ayer & Son. *N. W. Ayer & Son's American Newspaper Annual*. Philadelphia: N. W. Ayer & Son, 1892, 1896.

Official Manual of the State of Missouri for the Years 1895–96. Jefferson City, MO: Tribune Printing, 1895.

Official Proceedings of the Eleventh Republican National Convention. Pittsburgh, PA: James Francis Burke, 1896.

Porter, Noah, and W. T. Harris, eds. *Webster's International Dictionary of the English Language, Being the Authentic Edition of Webster's Unabridged Dictionary, Comprising the Issues of 1864, 1879, and 1884*. Springfield, MA: Merriam, 1907.

Powderly, Terrence V. *Thirty Years of Labor*. Columbus, OH: Excelsior Publishing, 1890.

Record of the Proceedings of the General Assembly of the Knights of Labor, Held at Reading, Pennsylvania, January 1–4, 1878. Reading, PA: The Assembly, 1878.

Scott, Laurence W., ed. *Texas Pulpit by Christian Preachers*. St. Louis, MO: Christian Publishing, 1888.

Statistician and Economist. San Francisco: L. P. McCarty, 1895–96.

Texas Legislature. House of Representatives. *Journal of House of Representatives During the Regular Session Twenty-Fourth Legislature, Begun and Held at the City of Austin, Texas, January 8, 1895*. Austin, TX: Ben C. Jones, 1895.

————. Senate. *Journal of Senate of Texas Being the First Called Session of the Thirty-Third Legislature, Begun and Held at the City of Austin, July 21, 1913, to August 19, 1913*. Austin, TX: Von Boeckmann-Jones Co., 1913.

————. Senate. *Journal of Senate of Texas Being the Regular Session Twenty-Fourth Legislature, Begun and Held at the City of Austin, Texas, January 8, 1895*. Austin, TX: Ben C. Jones, 1895.

————. *Legislative Manual for the State of Texas . . . 1879–1880*. Austin, TX: E. W. Swindells, 1879.

Texas Miner. (Magazine). Thurber, TX.

Texas. Secretary of State. *Biennial Report of the Secretary of State of the State of Texas, 1892.* Austin, TX: Ben C. Jones, 1893.

———. *Biennial Report of the Secretary of State of the State of Texas, 1894.* Austin, TX: Ben C. Jones, 1895.

Tugwell, Rexford. "Design for Government." *Political Science Quarterly* 48 (Sep. 1933): 321–32.

US Bureau of Labor. *Ninth Annual Report of the Commissioner of Labor, 1893: Building and Loan Associations.* Washington, DC: Government Printing Office, 1894.

US Congress. *Congressional Record.*

———. House of Representatives. Committee on Agriculture. *Food Production, Conservation, and Distribution: Hearings before the Committee on Agriculture, House of Representatives, on H.J. Res. 75, H.R. 4125, H.R. 4188, and H.R. 4630.* 65th Cong., 1st sess. Washington, DC: Government Printing Office, 1917.

US Department of the Interior. Census Office. *Compendium of the Eleventh Census, 1890.* 3 Pts. Washington, DC: Government Printing Office, 1892–1897.

———. *Twelfth Census of the United States, Taken in the Year 1900.* Washington, DC: United States Census Office, 1901.

Vincent, Cuthbert, ed. *The Platform Text Book.* Omaha, NE: Vincent Publishing, 1900.

Walton, William Martin. *An Epitome of My Life.* Austin, TX: Waterloo Press, 1965.

Wheeler, Burton K., with Paul F. Healy. *Yankee from the West: The Candid, Turbulent Life Story of the Yankee-Born U.S. Senator from Montana.* Garden City, NY: Doubleday, 1962.

Winkler, Ernest William, ed. *Platforms of Political Parties in Texas.* Austin: University of Texas, 1916.

Digital Primary Sources

The American Presidency Project. https://www.presidency.ucsb.edu/.

"Congress: Voting Records." Govtrack. https://www.govtrack.us/congress/votes.

Edwards, Rebecca, and Sarah DeFeo. *1896: The Presidential Campaign. Cartoons and Commentary.* Vassar College, 2000. http://projects.vassar.edu/1896/1896home .html.

Familysearch.com. https://www.familysearch.org.

Legislative Reference Library of Texas. *Texas Legislators: Past and Present.* http://www .lrl.state.tx.us/legeLeaders/members/lrlhome.cfm.

Northrup, Theo. H. (music), and C. C. DeZouche (words). "Turn Texas Loose." Galveston: Thos. Goggan & Bro., 1892. In Lester S. Levy Sheet Music Collection, Johns Hopkins University, Sheridan Libraries and University Museums. http:// levysheetmusic.mse.jhu.edu/collection/016/077.

Reagan, Ronald. Inaugural Address. January 20, 1981. Reagan Foundation. https:// www.reaganfoundation.org/media/128614/inaguration.pdf.

Texas Legislative Council. *Amendments to the Texas Constitution since 1876.* Texas Legislative Council, Austin. May 2018. http://www.tlc.state.tx.us/docs/amendments/Constamend1876.pdf.

Texas State Historical Association. *Texas Almanac.* https://texasalmanac.com.

Thomas E. Watson Papers Digital Collection. Southern Historical Collection, University of North Carolina at Chapel Hill. https://docsouth.unc.edu/watson/.

Wilson County Historical Society. "Vicente F. Carvajal." Accessed May 12, 2019. http://wilsoncountyhistory.org/Moments/VICENTE%20F.%20CARVAJAL.pdf.

Print Secondary Sources

Ali, Omar H. *In the Lion's Mouth: Black Populism in the New South, 1886–1900.* Jackson: University Press of Mississippi, 2010.

Allen, Ruth. *Chapters in the History of Organized Labor in Texas.* Austin: University of Texas, 1912.

Alter, Thomas E., II. "Dirt Farmer Internationalists: The Meitzen Family, Three Generations of Farmer-Labor Radicals, 1848–1932." PhD diss., University of Illinois at Chicago, 2016.

Alvord, Wayne. "T. L. Nugent: Texas Populist." *Southwestern Historical Quarterly* 57 (July 1953): 65–81.

Anders, Evan. *Boss Rule in South Texas: The Progressive Era.* Austin: University of Texas Press, 1982.

Appleby, Joyce. *The Relentless Revolution: A History of Capitalism.* New York: W. W. Norton, 2010.

Argersinger, Peter H. *The Limits of Agrarian Radicalism: Western Populist and American Politics.* Lawrence: University Press of Kansas, 1995.

———. "Taubeneck's Laws: Third Parties in American Politics in the Late Nineteenth Century." *American Nineteenth Century History* 3 (Summer 2002): 93–116.

Ayers, Edward L. *The Promise of the New South: Life after Reconstruction.* New York: Oxford University Press, 1992.

———. *Vengeance and Justice: Crime and Punishment in the 19th-Century American South.* New York: Oxford University Press, 1984.

Bailyn, Bernard. *The Ideological Origins of the American Revolution.* Cambridge, MA: Harvard University Press, 1967.

Baker, Paula. "The Domestication of Politics: Women and American Political History, 1780–1920." *American Historical Review* 89 (June 1984): 620–47.

Barnes, Donna A. *Farmers in Rebellion: The Rise and Fall of the Southern Farmers Alliance and People's Party in Texas.* Austin: University of Texas Press, 1984.

———. *The Louisiana Populist Movement, 1881–1900.* Baton Rouge: Louisiana State University Press, 2011.

Barr, Alwyn. *Reconstruction to Reform: Texas Politics, 1876–1906*. Austin: University of Texas Press, 1971.

Baum, Dale, and Worth Robert Miller. "Ethnic Conflict and Machine Politics in San Antonio, 1892–1899." *Journal of Urban History* 19 (Aug. 1993): 63–84.

Bearss, Edwin C. *Historic Resource Study: Lyndon B. Johnson National Historic Site, Blanco and Gillespie Counties, Texas*. Denver: National Park Service, 1971.

Beeby, James M. *Revolt of the Tarheels: The North Carolina Populist Movement, 1890–1901*. Jackson: University Press of Mississippi, 2008.

Beeman, Richard R. *The Evolution of the Southern Backcountry: A Case Study of Lunenburg County, Virginia, 1746–1832*. Philadelphia: University of Pennsylvania Press, 1984.

Berk, Gerald. *Alternative Tracks: The Constitution of American Industrial Order, 1865–1918*. Baltimore, MD: Johns Hopkins University Press, 1994.

Borders, Gary B. *A Hanging in Nacogdoches: Murder, Race, Politics, and Polemics in Texas's Oldest Town, 1870–1916*. Austin: University of Texas Press, 2006.

Boyer, Paul. *When Time Shall Be No More: Prophecy Belief in Modern American Culture*. Cambridge, MA: Belknap Press of Harvard University Press, 1992.

Brands, H. W. *The Strange Death of American Liberalism*. New Haven, CT: Yale University Press, 2001.

Brannon-Wranosky, Jessica. "Southern Promise and Necessity: Texas, Regional Identity, and the National Woman Suffrage Movement, 1868–1920." PhD diss., University of North Texas, 2010.

Brinkley, Alan. *The End of Reform: New Deal Liberalism in Recession and War*. New York: Alfred A. Knopf, 1995.

Bushick, Frank H. *Glamorous Days*. San Antonio, TX: Naylor, 1934.

Butler, Stephen R. "Freethinkers: Religious Nonconformity in Dallas, 1879–1904." *Legacies: A History Journal for Dallas and North Central Texas* 24 (Fall 2012): 16–29.

Butts, Robert. "An Architect of the American Century: Colonel Edward M. House and the Modernization of United States Diplomacy." PhD diss., Texas Christian University, 2010.

Calhoun, Charles W., ed. *The Gilded Age: Perspectives on the Origins of Modern America*. 2nd ed. Lanham, MD: Roman & Littlefield, 2007.

Calvert, Robert Arnold. "The Southern Grange: The Farmer's Search for Identity in the Gilded Age." PhD diss., University of Texas, 1969.

Calvert, Robert, and William Witherspoon. "Populism in Jack County, Texas." *Southern Studies* 25 (Spring 1986): 31–66.

Campbell, Randolph C. *Gone to Texas: A History of the Lone Star State*. 3rd ed. New York: Oxford University Press, 2017.

Cantrell, Gregg. *Kenneth and John B. Rayner and the Limits of Southern Dissent*. Urbana: University of Illinois Press, 1993.

————. "Lyndon's Granddaddy: Samuel Ealy Johnson Sr., Texas Populism, and the Improbable Roots of American Liberalism." *Southwestern Historical Quarterly* 118 (Oct. 2014): 133–56.

————. "'Our Very Pronounced Theory of Equal Rights to All': Race, Citizenship, and Populism in the South Texas Borderlands." *Journal of American History* 100 (Dec. 2013): 663–90.

Cantrell, Gregg, and D. Scott Barton. "Texas Populists and the Failure of Biracial Politics." *Journal of Southern History* 55 (Nov. 1989): 659–92.

Cantrell, Gregg, and Kristopher B. Paschal. "Texas Populism at High Tide: Jerome C. Kearby and the Case of the Sixth Congressional District, 1894." *Southwestern Historical Quarterly* 109 (July 2005): 30–70.

Caro, Robert A. *The Years of Lyndon Johnson: The Path to Power.* New York: Alfred A. Knopf, 1982.

Case, Theresa A. *The Great Southwest Strike and Free Labor.* College Station: Texas A&M University Press, 2010.

Chandler, Alfred D., Jr. *The Visible Hand: The Managerial Revolution in American Business.* Cambridge, MA: Harvard University Press, 1977.

Cherny, Robert W. *Populism, Progressivism, and the Transformation of Nebraska Politics, 1885–1912.* Lincoln: University of Nebraska Press, 1981.

Clanton, Gene. *Congressional Populism and the Crisis of the 1890s.* Lawrence: University Press of Kansas, 1998.

————. *Kansas Populism, Ideas and Men.* Lawrence: University Press of Kansas, 1969.

————. *Populism: The Humane Preference in America, 1890–1900.* Boston: Twayne, 1991.

Cohen, Nancy. *The Reconstruction of American Liberalism, 1865–1914.* Chapel Hill: University of North Carolina Press, 2002.

Conkin, Paul K. *American Originals: Homemade Varieties of Christianity.* Chapel Hill: University of North Carolina Press, 1997.

Cooper, John Milton, Jr. *Woodrow Wilson: A Biography.* New York: Alfred A. Knopf, 2009.

Cotner, Robert C. *James Stephen Hogg: A Biography.* Austin: University of Texas Press, 1959.

Cowden, Frances Kay. "H. S. P. Ashby: A Voice for Reform, 1886–1914." PhD diss., University of Oklahoma, 1996.

Cowie, Jefferson. *The Great Exception: The New Deal and the Limits of American Politics.* Princeton, NJ: Princeton University Press, 2016.

Creech, Joe. *Righteous Indignation: Religion and the Populist Revolution.* Urbana: University of Illinois Press, 2006.

Crow, Carl. "The Fee System: An Inheritance from the Dark Ages." *Saturday Evening Post* 183 (Nov. 19, 1910): 8–9, 56.

Dailey, Jane. *Before Jim Crow: The Politics of Race in Postemancipation Virginia.* Chapel Hill: University of North Carolina Press, 2000.

Dallek, Robert. *Lone Star Rising: Lyndon Johnson and His Times, 1908–1960*. New York: Oxford University Press, 1991.

Daniell, Lewis E. *Personnel of the Texas State Government*. Austin, TX: City Printing, 1887.

De León, Arnoldo. "In re Ricardo Rodriguez: An Attempt at Chicano Disfranchisement in San Antonio, 1896–1897." In *En Aquel Entonces: Readings in Mexican-American History*, edited by Manuel G. Gonzales and Cynthia M. Gonzales, 57–63. Bloomington: Indiana University Press, 2000.

Dugger, Ronnie. *The Politician: The Life and Times of Lyndon Johnson: From the Frontier to Master of the Senate*. New York: W. W. Norton, 1984.

Dunlap, Leslie K. "The Reform of Rape Law and the Problem of White Men: Age-of-Consent Campaigns in the South, 1885–1910." In *Sex, Love, Race: Crossing Boundaries in North American History*, edited by Martha Hodes, 352–72. New York: New York University Press, 1999.

Durden, Robert F. *The Climax of Populism: The Election of 1896*. Lexington: University Press of Kentucky, 1966.

Edwards, Laura F. *Gendered Strife and Confusion: The Political Culture of Reconstruction*. Urbana: University of Illinois Press, 1997.

Edwards, Rebecca. *Angels in the Machinery: Gender in American Party Politics from the Civil War to the Progressive Era*. New York: Oxford University Press, 1997.

———. *New Spirits: Americans in the "Gilded Age," 1865–1905*. 3rd ed. New York: Oxford University Press, 2015.

Ely, Glen Sample. *Where the West Begins: Debating Texas Identity*. Lubbock: Texas Tech University Press, 2011.

Evans, Samuel Lee. "Texas Agriculture, 1880–1930." PhD diss., University of Texas, 1960.

Fairbanks, Robert B. "Public Housing for the City as a Whole: The Texas Experience, 1934–1955." *Southwestern Historical Quarterly* 103 (April 2000): 403–26.

Fawcett, Edmund. *Liberalism: The Life of an Idea*. Princeton, NJ: Princeton University Press, 2014.

Ferkiss, Victor. "Populist Influences on American Fascism." *Western Political Quarterly* 10 (June 1957): 350–57.

Fisher, Commodore B. *The Farmers' Union*. Lexington: University Press of Kentucky, 1920.

Fite, Gilbert C. *Cotton Fields No More: Southern Agriculture, 1865–1980*. Lexington: University Press of Kentucky, 1984.

———. *The Farmers' Frontier, 1865–1900*. New York: Holt, Rhinehart, and Winston, 1966.

Flanagan, Maureen A. *America Reformed: Progressives and Progressivisms, 1890s–1920s*. New York: Oxford University Press, 2007.

Fraser, Steve, and Gary Gerstle, eds. *The Rise and Fall of the New Deal Order, 1930–1980*. Princeton, NJ: Princeton University Press, 1989.

Friedman, Milton. *Capitalism and Freedom*. 40th anniversary ed. Chicago: University of Chicago Press, 2002.

Fuller, Henry C. *"A Texas Sheriff": A. J. Spradley of Nacogdoches County, Texas*. Nacogdoches, TX: Baker Printing, 1931.

Fuller, Wayne. "The Populists and the Post Office." *Agricultural History* 65 (Winter 1991): 1–16.

Gallagher, Winifred. *How the Post Office Created America*. New York: Penguin, 2016.

Gardner, Brennan. "Texas Antitrust Law: Formulation and Enforcement, 1889–1903." MA thesis, Texas Christian University, 2013.

Gerstle, Gary. *Liberty and Coercion: The Paradox of American Government from the Founding to the Present*. Princeton, NJ: Princeton University Press, 2015.

Gilbert, Jess. *Planning Democracy: Agrarian Intellectuals and the Intended New Deal*. New Haven, CT: Yale University Press, 2015.

Glenn, Evelyn Nakano. *Unequal Freedom: How Race and Gender Shaped American Citizenship and Labor*. Cambridge, MA: Harvard University Press, 2002.

Goodwyn, Lawrence. *Democratic Promise: The Populist Moment in America*. New York: Oxford University Press, 1976.

———. "Populist Dreams and Negro Rights: East Texas as a Case Study." *American Historical Review* 76 (Dec. 1971): 1435–56.

———. *The Populist Moment: A Short History of the Agrarian Revolt in America*. New York: Oxford University Press, 1978.

Gould, Lewis L. *The Presidency of Theodore Roosevelt*. Lawrence: University Press of Kansas, 1991.

Graham, Otis L., Jr. *An Encore for Reform: The Old Progressives and the New Deal*. New York: Oxford University Press, 1967.

Graham, Otis L., Jr., and Meghan Robinson Wander, eds. *Franklin D. Roosevelt: His Life and Times: An Encyclopedic View*. New York: Da Capo, 1990.

Hahn, Stephen. *A Nation under Our Feet: Black Political Struggles in the Rural South from Slavery to the Great Migration*. Cambridge, MA: Harvard University Press, 2003.

Hall, Jacqueline Dowd. "The Long Civil Rights Movement and the Political Uses of the Past." *Journal of American History* 91 (Mar. 2005): 1233–63.

Haney López, Ian. *White by Law: The Legal Construction of Race*. New York: New York University Press, 1996.

Hardeman, D. B., and Donald C. Bacon. *Rayburn: A Biography*. Lanham, MD: Madison Books, 1987.

Harrison, Robert. *Congress, Progressive Reform, and the New American State*. Cambridge: Cambridge University Press, 2004.

Hicks, John D. *The Populist Revolt: A History of the Farmers' Alliance and the People's Party*. Minneapolis: University of Minnesota Press, 1931.

———. "The Sub-Treasury: A Forgotten Plan for the Relief of Agriculture." *Mississippi Valley Historical Review* 15 (Dec. 1928): 255–373.

Hild, Matthew. *Greenbackers, Knights of Labor, and Populists: Farmer-Labor Insurgency in the Late-Nineteenth-Century South.* Athens: University of Georgia Press, 2007.

History of Texas, Supplemented with Biographical Mention of Many Families of the State . . . Together with Biographical Sketches of Many of the Families of Central Texas. Chicago: Lewis Publishing, 1896.

Hofstadter, Richard. *The Age of Reform: From Bryan to F.D.R.* New York: Alfred A. Knopf, 1955.

Hogg, Kerek Darren. "'Wash' Jones: The Life of George Washington Jones, 'Economic Radical' and Political Dissenter." MA thesis, Texas Tech University, 1993.

Holcomb, Bob Charles. "Senator Joe Bailey, Two Decades of Controversy." PhD diss., Texas Technological College, 1968.

Hunt, James L. *Marion Butler and American Populism.* Chapel Hill: University of North Carolina Press, 2003.

Hunter, J. Marvin, comp. and ed. *Trail Drivers of Texas.* 2nd ed. Nashville, TN: Cokesbury Press, 1925.

Jacobus, Donald Lines, comp., based on data collected by and for Edgar Francis Waterman. *Granberry Family and Allied Families Including the Ancestry of Helen (Woodward) Granberry.* Hartford, CT: Edgar F. Waterman, 1945.

Johnson, Frank W., ed. *A History of Texas and Texans.* 5 vols. Chicago: American Historical Association, 1914.

Johnston, Robert D. "The Possibilities of Politics: Democracy in America, 1877 to 1917." In *American History Now,* part 1, edited by Eric Foner and Lisa McGirr, 96–124. Philadelphia: Temple University Press, 2011.

———. "Re-democratizing the Progressive Era: The Politics of Progressive Era Political Historiography." *Journal of the Gilded Age and Progressive Era* 1 (Jan. 2002): 68–92.

Jones, Stanley L. *The Presidential Election of 1896.* Madison: University of Wisconsin Press, 1964.

Karbach, Ruth Hosey. "Ellen Lawson Dabbs: Waving the Equal Rights Banner." In *Texas Women: Their Histories, Their Lives,* edited by Elizabeth Hayes Turner, Stephanie Cole, and Rebecca Sharpless, 176–200. Athens: University of Georgia Press, 2015.

Katznelson, Ira. *Fear Itself: The New Deal and the Origins of Our Time.* New York: Liveright Publishing, 2013.

Kazin, Michael. *A Godly Hero: The Life of William Jennings Bryan.* New York: Alfred A. Knopf, 2006.

———. *The Populist Persuasion: An American History.* Ithaca, NY: Cornell University Press, 1998.

Kennedy, David. *Freedom from Fear: The American People in Depression and War, 1929–1945.* New York: Oxford University Pres, 1999.

King, Keith Lynn. "Religious Dimensions of the Agrarian Protest in Texas, 1870–1908." PhD diss., University of Illinois, 1985.

Kingston, Mike, Sam Attlesey, and Mary G. Crawford. *The Texas Almanac's Political History of Texas.* Austin, TX: Eakin Press, 1992.

Kirkendall, Richard S., "The Great Depression: Another Watershed in American History?" In *Change and Continuity in Twentieth-Century America,* edited by John Braeman, Robert H. Bremner, and Everett Walters, 45–89. Columbus: Ohio State University Press, 1964.

Kloppenberg, James T. "Barack Obama and Progressive Democracy." In *Making the American Century: Essays on the Political Culture of Twentieth Century America,* edited by Bruce J. Schulman, 267–87. New York: Oxford University Press, 2014.

———. "Liberalism." In *The Princeton Encyclopedia of American Political History,* vol. 1, edited by Michael Kazin, 475–84. Princeton, NJ: Princeton University Press, 2010.

———. *The Virtues of Liberalism.* New York: Oxford University Press, 1998.

———. "The Virtues of Liberalism: Christianity, Republicanism, and Ethics in Early American Political Discourse." *Journal of American History* 74 (June 1987): 9–33.

———. "A Well-Tempered Liberalism: Modern Intellectual History and Political Theory." *Modern Intellectual History* 10 (2013): 655–82.

Korstad, Robert Rodgers. *Civil Rights Unionism: Tobacco Workers and the Struggle for Democracy in the Mid-Twentieth-Century South.* Chapel Hill: University of North Carolina Press, 2003.

Krochmal, Max. *Blue Texas: The Making of a Multiracial Democratic Coalition in the Civil Rights Era.* Chapel Hill: University of North Carolina Press, 2016.

Lansing, Michael J. *Insurgent Democracy: The Non-Partisan League in North American Politics.* Chicago: University of Chicago Press, 2016.

Larson, Robert W. *New Mexico Populism: A Study in Radical Protest in a Western Territory.* Boulder: Colorado Associated University Press, 1974.

Lasch, Christopher. *The True and Only Heaven: Progress and Its Critics.* New York: W. W. Norton, 1991.

Lee, R. Alton. *Farmers vs. Wage Earners: Organized Labor in Kansas, 1860–1960.* Lincoln: University of Nebraska Press, 2006.

Lester, Connie L. *Up from the Mudsills of Hell: The Farmers' Alliance, Populism, and Progressive Agriculture in Tennessee, 1870–1915.* Athens: University of Georgia Press, 2006.

Leuchtenberg, William E. *Franklin D. Roosevelt and the New Deal.* New York: Harper & Row, 1963.

Lightfoot, B. B. "The Human Party: Populism in Comanche County, 1886." *West Texas Historical Association Year Book* 31 (1955): 28–40.

Link, Arthur S. *Woodrow Wilson and the Progressive Era, 1910–1917.* New York: Harper & Row, 1954.

Locke, Joseph. "Making the Bible Belt: Preachers, Prohibition, and the Politicization of Southern Religion, 1877–1918." PhD diss., Rice University, 2012.

Loughery, E. H. *Texas State Government: A Volume of Biographical Sketches and Passing Comment.* Austin, TX: McLeod & Jackson, 1897.

Lowenstein, Roger. *America's Bank: The Epic Struggle to Create the Federal Reserve*. New York: Penguin, 2015.

Lowry, Robert L., Jr. "A Study of Droughts in Texas." *Texas Board of Water Engineers, Bulletin 5914*. [Austin?]: Texas Board of Water Engineers, 1959.

Macune, Charles W. "'The Last Shall Be First, and the First Last': The Agrarian Revolt, the Press, and C. W. Macune (1851–1940)." Paper presented at the Southwestern Social Science Association Annual Meeting, Corpus Christi, TX, March 1998.

Macune, Charles W., Jr. "Wellsprings of a Populist: Dr. C. W. Macune before 1886." *Southwestern Historical Quarterly* 90 (Oct. 1986): 139–58.

Marshall, T. H. "Citizenship and Social Class." In *The Citizenship Debates: A Reader*, edited by Gershon Kafir, 93–112. Minneapolis: University of Minnesota Press, 1998.

Martin, Roscoe C. "The Greenback Party in Texas." *Southwestern Historical Quarterly* 30 (Jan. 1927): 161–77.

———. *The People's Party in Texas: A Study in Third Party Politics*. Austin: University of Texas Press, 1933.

Martinez, Ana Luisa R. "Pablo Cruz, *El Regidor*, and Mexican American Identity in San Antonio, 1888–1910." PhD diss., Texas Tech University, 2003.

Mason, David L. *From Buildings and Loans to Bail-Outs: A History of the American Savings and Loan Industry*. New York: Cambridge University Press, 2004.

May, Irvin M., Jr. *Marvin Jones: The Public Life of an Agrarian Advocate*. College Station: Texas A&M University Press, 1980.

Mazur, Kate. *An Example for All the Land: Emancipation and the Struggle over Equality in Washington, D.C.* Chapel Hill: University of North Carolina Press, 2010.

McCarver, Norman L., and Norman L. McCarver Jr. *Hearne on the Brazos*. San Antonio, TX: Century Press, 1958.

McElvaine, Robert S. *The Great Depression: America, 1929–1941*. New York: Times Books, 1993.

McGerr, Michael. *A Fierce Discontent: The Rise and Fall of the Progressive Movement in America, 1870–1920*. New York: Free Press, 2003.

McGirr, Lisa. *The War on Alcohol: Prohibition and the Rise of the American State*. New York: W. W. Norton, 2016.

McMath, Robert C., Jr. *American Populism: A Social History, 1877–1898*. New York: Hill and Wang, 1993.

———. "Another Look at the 'Hard Side' of Populism." *Reviews in American History* 36 (June 2008): 209–17.

———. "C. Vann Woodward and the Burden of Southern Populism." *Journal of Southern History* 67 (Nov. 2001): 741–68.

———. "The Godly Populists: Protestantism in the Farmers' Alliance and People's Party of Texas." MA thesis, North Texas State University, 1968.

———. *Populist Vanguard: A History of the Southern Farmers' Alliance*. New York: W. W. Norton, 1975.

A Memorial and Biographical History of Johnson and Hill Counties, Texas. Chicago: Lewis Publishing, 1892.

A Memorial and Biographical History of Navarro, Henderson, Anderson, Limestone, Freestone and Leon Counties, Texas. Chicago: Lewis Publishing, 1893.

Miller, Worth Robert. "Building a Progressive Coalition in Texas: The Populist-Reform Democrat Rapprochement, 1900–1907." *Journal of Southern History* 52 (May 1986): 163–82.

———. "A Centennial Historiography of American Populism." *Kansas History* 16 (Spring 1993): 54–69.

———. "Farmers and Third-Party Politics." In *The Gilded Age: Perspectives on the Origins of Modern America,* 3rd ed., edited by Charles W. Calhoun, 283–306. New York: Rowman & Littlefield, 2007.

———. "Harrison County Methods: Election Fraud in Late Nineteenth-Century Texas." *Locus: Regional and Local History* 7 (Spring 1995): 111–28.

———. *Oklahoma Populism: A History of the People's Party in the Oklahoma Territory.* Norman: University of Oklahoma Press, 1987.

———. *Populist Cartoons: An Illustrated History of the Third-Party Movement of the 1890s.* Kirksville, MO: Truman State University Press, 2011.

———. "The Populist Return to the Democratic Party and Their Influence on the Progressive Era in Texas, 1896–1906." MA thesis, Trinity University, 1977.

———, ed. *"The Populist Vision: A Roundtable Discussion." Kansas History: A Journal of the Central Plains* 32 (Spring 2009): 18–45.

Miller, Worth Robert, and Stacy G. Ulbig. "Building a Populist Coalition in Texas, 1892–1896." *Journal of Southern History* 74 (May 2008): 255–96.

Minnix, Kathleen. *Laughter in the Amen Corner: The Life of Evangelist Sam Jones.* Athens: University of Georgia Press, 1993.

Morgan, George T., Jr. "The Gospel of Wealth Goes South: John Henry Kirby and Labor's Struggle for Self-Determination, 1901–1916." In *Texas Labor History,* edited by Bruce A. Glasrud and James C. Maroney, 141–52. College Station: Texas A&M University Press, 2013.

Müller, Jan-Werner. *What Is Populism?* Philadelphia: University of Pennsylvania Press, 2016.

Nugent, Walter T. K. *The Tolerant Populists: Kansas, Populism and Nativism.* Chicago: University of Chicago Press, 1963.

Orton, Susan J. "Charles H. Jenkins (1852–1931): A Biographical Sketch." Unpublished manuscript.

Ostler, Jeffrey. *Prairie Populism: The Fate of Agrarian Radicalism in Kansas, Nebraska, and Iowa, 1880–1892.* Lawrence: University Press of Kansas, 1993.

Paddock, B. B., ed. *History of Texas: Fort Worth and the Texas Northwest Edition.* 4 vols. Chicago: Lewis, 1922.

Padilla, Fernando V. "Early Chicano Legal Recognition: 1846–1897." *Journal of Popular Culture* 13 (Spring 1980): 564–74.

Palmer, Bruce. *"Man over Money": The Southern Populist Critique of American Capitalism.* Chapel Hill: University of North Carolina Press, 1980.

Parker, Richard Denny. *Historical Recollections of Robertson County.* Salado, TX: Anson Jones Press, 1955.

Parsons, Stanley B., Karen Toombs Parsons, Walter Killilae, and Beverly Borgers. "The Role of Cooperatives in the Development of the Movement Culture of Populism." *Journal of American History* 69 (Mar. 1983): 866–85.

Patterson, Cyril Leone. *Nixon (Gonzales County), Texas: A Progressive Diversified Agricultural Haven.* San Antonio, TX: Sid Murray & Son, 1938.

Phillips, Michael. *White Metropolis: Race, Ethnicity, and Religion in Dallas, 1841–2001.* Austin: University of Texas Press, 2006.

Piott, Steven L. *American Reformers, 1877–1920: Progressives in Word and Deed.* Lanham, MD: Rowman & Littlefield, 2006.

Pocock, J. G. A. *The Machiavellian Moment: Florentine Political Thought and the Atlantic Republican Tradition.* Princeton, NJ: Princeton University Press, 1975.

Pollack, Norman. *The Populist Response to Industrial America.* New York: W. W. Norton, 1962.

Pollack, Sheldon D. "Origins of the Modern Income Tax, 1894–1913." *Tax Lawyer* 66 (Winter 2013): 295–330.

Pool, William C., ed. "Westward I Go Free: The Memoirs of William E. Cureton, Texas Frontiersman." *Southwestern Historical Quarterly* 81 (Oct. 1977): 155–90.

Postel, Charles. "The American Populist and Anti-Populist Legacy." In *Transformations of Populism in Europe and the Americas: History and Recent Tendencies,* edited by John Abromeit, Bridget Maria Chesterton, Gary Marotta, and York Norman, 116–35. London: Bloomsbury Academic, 2015.

———. "Murder on the Brazos: The Religious Context of the Populist Revolt." *Journal of the Gilded Age and Progressive Era* 15 (2016): 197–219.

———. *The Populist Vision.* New York: Oxford University Press, 2007.

———. "What We Talk About When We Talk About Populism." *Raritan* 37 (Fall 2017): 133–55.

Ransom, Roger L., and Richard Sutch. "Debt Peonage in the Cotton South after the Civil War." *Journal of Economic History* 32 (Sept. 1972): 641–69.

Rawls, John. *A Theory of Justice.* Cambridge, MA: Harvard University Press, 1971.

Rice, Lawrence D. *The Negro in Texas, 1874–1900.* Baton Rouge: Louisiana State University Press, 1971.

Richardson, Rupert Norval. *Colonel Edward M. House: The Texas Years, 1858–1912.* Abilene, TX: Hardin-Simmons University, 1964.

Ritter, Gretchen. *Goldbugs and Greenbacks: The Antimonopoly Tradition and the Politics of Finance in America.* Cambridge: Cambridge University Press, 1997.

Rodgers, Daniel T. "Republicanism: The Career of a Concept." *Journal of American History* 79 (June 1992): 11–38.

Rodriquez, Alicia E. "'Of Whom Shall the Third Party Be Composed?'" In *Populism in the South Revisited,* edited by James M. Beeby, 56–81. Jackson: University Press of Mississippi, 2012.

Rogers, William Warren, Sr. *The One-Gallused Rebellion: Agrarianism in Alabama, 1865–1896.* Baton Rouge: Louisiana State University Press, 1970.

Ross, Chapin. "A Historical and Critical Study of the Public Address of James Harvey 'Cyclone' Davis (1853–1940) of Texas." PhD diss., University of Southern California, 1969.

Ryan, Alan. *The Making of Modern Liberalism.* Princeton, NJ: Princeton University Press, 2012.

———. *On Politics: A History of Political Thought from Herodotus to the Present.* London: Penguin Books, 2013.

Sanders, Elizabeth. *The Roots of Reform: Farmers, Workers, and the American State, 1877–1917.* Chicago: University of Chicago Press, 1999.

Schattschneider, E. E. *The Semisovereign People: A Realist's View of Democracy in America.* New York: Holt, Rhinehart, and Winston, 1960.

Schmelzer, Janet. *Our Fighting Governor: The Life of Thomas M. Campbell and the Politics of Progressive Reform in Texas.* College Station: Texas A&M University Press, 2014.

Schulte-Sasse, Linda. "Meet Ross Perot: The Lasting Legacy of Capraesque Populism." *Cultural Critique* 25 (Autumn 1993): 91–119.

Scott, Joan. "Gender: A Useful Category of Historical Analysis." *American Historical Review* 91 (Dec. 1986): 1053–75.

Shalhope, Robert E. "Toward a Republican Synthesis: The Emergence of an Understanding of Republicanism in American Historiography." *William and Mary Quarterly* 29 (Jan. 1972): 49–80.

Shanks, Alexander G. "Sam Rayburn in the Wilson Administrations, 1913–1921." *East Texas Historical Journal* 6 (1968): 63–76.

Shaw, Barton. *The Wool-Hat Boys: Georgia's Populist Party.* Baton Rouge: Louisiana State University Press, 1984.

Smith, Maud Biard. *The Biard Family.* Paris, TX: self-published, 1954.

Spratt, John Strickland. *The Road to Spindletop: Economic Change in Texas, 1875–1901.* Dallas, TX: Southern Methodist University Press, 1955.

Stanley, Amy Dru. "Conjugal Bonds and Wage Labor: Rights of Contract in the Age of Emancipation." *Journal of American History* 75 (Sep. 1988): 472–500.

Starr, Paul. *Freedom's Power: The True Force of Liberalism.* New York: Basic Books, 2007.

St. Clair, Lawrence Ward. "History of Robertson County." MA thesis, University of Texas, 1931.

Steil, Benn. *The Battle of Bretton Woods: John Maynard Keynes, Harry Dexter White, and the Making of a New World Order.* Princeton, NJ: Princeton University Press, 2013.

Stromquist, Shelton. *Reinventing "The People": The Progressive Movement, the Class Problem, and the Origins of Modern Liberalism.* Urbana: University of Illinois Press, 2006.

Taylor, A. Elizabeth. "The Woman Suffrage Movement in Texas." *Journal of Southern History* 17 (May 1951): 194–215.

Taylor, Jon Edward. "Thomas Lewis Nugent: Portrait of a Populist Leader." MA thesis, Baylor University, 1992.

Thurston, John M. "How Presidents Are Nominated." *Cosmopolitan* 39 (May 1900): 194–200.

Turner, James. "Understanding the Populists." *Journal of American History* 67 (Sep. 1980): 354–73.

Volanto, Keith J. *Texas, Cotton, and the New Deal.* College Station: Texas A&M University Press, 2005.

Walker, Donald R. *Penology for Profit: A History of the Texas Prison System, 1867–1912.* College Station: Texas A&M University Press, 1988.

Waller, Randall Lionel. "The Callaghan Machine and San Antonio Politics, 1885–1912." MA thesis, Texas Tech University, 1974.

Watts, Tim J. "Taubeneck, Herman E." In *Encyclopedia of Populism in America: A Historical Encyclopedia,* vol. 2, edited by Alexandra Kindell and Elizabeth S. Demers, 699–702. Santa Barbara, CA: ABC-CLIO, 2014.

Webb, Walter Prescott. *The Great Plains.* New York: Ginn, 1931.

Wells, Jeff. "J. N. Rogers, the Jacksboro Rural Citizen, and the Roots of Farmers' Alliance Journalism in Texas, 1881–1886." *Southwestern Historical Quarterly* 121 (July 2017): 28–55.

Wells, Robert Jeffrey David. "The Reform Press: The Journalists of the Farmers' Alliance and People's Party." PhD diss., Texas Christian University, 2014.

White, E. V., and William E. Leonard. *Studies in Farm Tenancy in Texas.* Austin: University of Texas, 1915.

White, James C. *Promised Land: A History of Brown County, Texas.* Brownwood, TX: Brownwood Banner, 1941.

White, Richard. *Railroaded: The Transcontinentals and the Making of Modern America.* New York: W. W. Norton, 2011.

Wiebe, Robert H. *The Search for Order, 1877–1920.* New York: Hill and Wang, 1967.

Wiedenfeld, Melissa Gilbert. "Women in the Texas Farmers' Alliance." MA thesis, Texas Tech University, 1983.

Wilkison, Kyle G. *Yeomen, Sharecroppers, and Socialists: Plain Folk Protest in Texas, 1870–1914.* College Station: Texas A&M University Press, 2008.

Williams, Marshall L. "The Political Career of Cyclone Davis." MA thesis, East Texas State Teachers College, 1937.

Williams, Patrick G. "Of Rutabagas and Redeemers: Rethinking the Texas Constitution of 1876." *Southwestern Historical Quarterly* 106 (Oct. 2002): 230–53.

Williams, R. Hal. *Realigning America: McKinley, Bryan, and the Remarkable Election of 1896*. Lawrence: University Press of Kansas, 2010.

Wood, Gordon S. *The Creation of the American Republic, 1776–1787*. Chapel Hill: University of North Carolina Press, 1969.

Woodward, C. Vann. *Origins of the New South, 1877–1913*. Baton Rouge: Louisiana State University Press, 1951.

——. *Tom Watson: Agrarian Rebel*. New York: Macmillan, 1938.

Wright, James Edward. *The Politics of Populism: Dissent in Colorado*. New Haven, CT: Yale University Press, 1974.

Yelderman, Pauline. *The Jay Birds of Fort Bend County*. Waco, TX: Texian Press, 1979.

Young, Nancy Beck. *Wright Patman: Populism, Liberalism, and the American Dream*. Dallas, TX: Southern Methodist University Press, 2000.

Digital Secondary Sources

Chomsky, Noam, and David Barsamiam. "Noam Chomsky Diagnoses the Trump Era." *Nation*, Oct. 3, 2017. https://www.thenation.com/article/noam-chomsky-diagnoses-the-trump-era/.

Coaston, Joan. "Conservatism Is Dead, and Trump Killed It." MTV News, Dec. 12, 2016. http://www.mtv.com/news/2962840/conservatism-is-dead-and-trump-killed-it/.

Conetta, Christine. "Noam Chomsky: Richard Nixon Was 'Last Liberal President.'" Huffington Post, Feb. 21, 2014. https://www.huffingtonpost.com/2014/02/21/noam-chomsky-richard-nixon_n_4832847.html.

Cooper, John. "Oscar Wilde in America." 2018. http://www.oscarwildeinamerica.org/lectures-1882/february/0225-st-louis.html.

Crook, Tory. "William McEwin and Catherine Reynolds." RootsWeb. Accessed Apr. 12, 2019. http://freepages.genealogy.rootsweb.ancestry.com/~tory/bobskin/mcewin.html.

"Ellis County Doctors." Ellis County TXGenWeb. Sept. 10, 2018. https://sites.rootsweb.com/~txellis/_pioneers/Ellis_County_Doctors.html.

Fund, John. "Nixon at 100: Was He 'America's Last Liberal'?" *National Review*, Jan. 11, 2013. https://www.nationalreview.com/2013/01/nixon-100-was-he-americas-last-liberal-john-fund/.

"History of Dallas City Hall Buildings." City of Dallas. Accessed Apr. 12, 2019. http://dallascityhall.com/government/citysecretary/archives/Pages/Archives_buildings.aspx.

Leonhardt, David. "The Secret to Winning in 2020: It's the Populism, Stupid." *New York Times*, Dec. 18, 2018. https://www.nytimes.com/2018/12/16/opinion/democrats-2020-election-economic-populism.html?rref=collection%2Fbyline%2Fdavid-leonhardt.

Marans, Daniel. "Bernie Sanders Says Trump Budget Exposes President as Fake Populist." Huffington Post, May 23, 2017. https://www.huffingtonpost.com/entry/bernie-sanders-donald-trump-fake-populist_us_5924947de4b0ec129d301869.

Meitzen, John Edward. "The Meitzens Make Texas Proud." Labor History from Texas, 2001. http://www.labordallas.org/hist/meitzen.htm.

Nonnenmacher, Tomas. "History of the U.S. Telegraph Industry." In *EH.net Encyclopedia of Economic and Business History,* edited by Robert Whaples. Economic History Association. Aug. 14, 2001. http://eh.net/encyclopedia/history-of-the-u-s-telegraph-industry/.

Oklahoma Historical Society. *Encyclopedia of Oklahoma History and Culture.* Accessed Apr. 12, 2019. https://www.okhistory.org/publications/encyclopediaonline.

Ragan, Cooper K. "Joe Henry Eagle." *Houston Lawyer* 13 (Mar. 1976): 28–32. In Barbara Jordan Scrapbook, March–December 1976. Portal to Texas History, University of North Texas Libraries. Accessed June 1, 2018. http://www.texashistory.unt.edu/ark:/67531/metapth616562/m1/15/?q=barbara%20johe%20henry%20eagle.

Stan, Adele M. "How Trump Broke Conservatism." *American Prospect,* Mar. 7, 2018. http://prospect.org/article/how-donald-trump-broke-conservatism.

Texas State Historical Association. *Handbook of Texas Online.* https://tshaonline.org/handbook.

Tupy, Marian. "Bernie Is Not a Socialist and America Is Not Capitalist." *Atlantic,* Mar. 1, 2016. https://www.theatlantic.com/international/archive/2016/03/bernie-sanders-democratic-socialism/471630/.

Valencia, Janie. "Most Democrats Now Identify as 'Liberal.'" FiveThirtyEight, Jan. 11, 2019. https://fivethirtyeight.com/features/most-democrats-now-identify-as-liberal/.

Walther, Matthew. "Conservatism Is Dead." *The Week,* Nov. 27, 2017. http://theweek.com/articles/739147/conservatism-dead.

Wells, Jeff. "The Most Interesting and Picturesque Fraud in the State of Nebraska: Paul Vandervoort and Gilded Age Nebraska." Nebraska State Historical Society Brown Bag Lecture Series, Oct. 28, 2016. https://www.youtube.com/watch?v=uJvj9oVJZTE.

INDEX

Page numbers in italics refer to figures.

Democratic Party (cont.)
398–99; as against Populist Party,
17–18, 101, 112, 114, 125, 132, 141,
155–56, 184, 198–99; racial views of,
192, 198, 211–12, 218; Reform
Democrats, 87–88, 300, 308, 311,
316–20, 331; and Subtreasury Plan,
55–57, 64–65, 66–68; violence of,
207, 265–66, 399–404; and woman
suffrage, 276–78. *See also* Subtreasury Plan
Democratic Promise (Goodwyn), 9
Denison, Tex., 267
Department of Labor, 6
Deutsche Anzieger, Der, 232
Deutschmann, Selig, 335–36, 337–38,
340–41, 343, 500n28, plate 22
Dewey, John, 6, 7
Dibrell, Joseph B., 289
Dimmit County, 325
Dixon, Samuel, 54–55, 280
Dohoney, Ebenezer L.: and 1896
elections, 360; as a Greenbacker, 37;
and People's Party founding, 64; and
prohibition, 74–75, 171, 480n36;
religious views of, 182; and third-
party politics, 68; and woman
suffrage, 271–73
Donnelly, Ignatius, 58, 114, 142, 145,
313, 396
Dornblaser, Owen Franklin, 68, 262,
374–75, 381
Douglass, Frederick, 213, 221, 484n40
Douthit, William F., 358, 381
Drake, C. C., 74, 471n22
Drinkard, Allen, 296, 311
Dublin Progress, 68, 132
Dumas, A. W., 164, 165, 168
Dunklin, Hallie Milburn, 275,
490n37
Dunlap, Andrew, 45, 48

Dunning, Nelson A., 54
Dwyer, John "Johnnie," 249–50

Eagle, Joe Henry, plate 29; congressional
career of, 418–24, 432, 476–77n58,
509n21, 510n42; oratory of, 262,
408; as a Populist, 353–54, 358, 380,
429; racial views of, 419, 427, 438
East Texas, 55, 94, 106, 206, 214, 296,
358, 401
education. *See* African Americans;
legislation
Edwards, Rebecca, 417, 508n16
Edwards, Thomas L., 293, 295
Ellis County, 41, 86, 240, 492n66
Elmendorf, Henry, 312
El Paso Times, 107
Erath County, 39, 47, 50, 68, 71
Erwin, J. W., 472n46
Evans, Andrew Jackson, 333–35, 337,
339, 341–42
Evans, Rufus, 210
Evans, Sam, 37, 50, 52, 104, 105,
189–90, 193, 196
experiment stations, 430–32

Faircloth, William T., 502n12
Fair Labor Standards Act, 249
Farmer, William E. "Bill": and 1896
elections, 358–59, 381; and 1898
elections, 396; on *Dallas News,* 84;
as a Greenbacker, 37, 104; and
Knights of Labor, 45, 46, 50,
249–50; on monetary policy, 134;
post-Populism, 412; and third-party
politics, 52, 59
farmers: agricultural conditions of,
32–33, 110, 430, 432–35; financial
conditions of, 29–32, 42, 131–3, 296,
305–6; and transportation, 23–24.
See also Panic of 1893

Greer, J. L., 212
Gresham, Newt, 406
Gresham's Law, 349
Grimes County, 172, 221, 236, 402–4

Hampton, Samuel J., 406
Hampton, Wade, 34
Hanna, James K. P., 66, 204–5, 208, 236
Hanna, James Scott, 204–5
Hanna, Marc, 372
Hanson, C. H., 104
Harrison, Narnie, 275–76
Harrison, William Henry, 228
Harrison, Willis Lyman, plate 18; and
    age-of-consent campaign, 284–85,
    286–88, 314; and banking legisla-
    tion, 306–7, 314, 321; morality of,
    292, 297; and religion, 155, 479n18
Harrison County, 95, 344, 383, 388,
    400
Harvey, William H., 136
Hawkins, Perry, 278
Hayek, Friedrich von, 4
Hayes, R. H.: background of, 482n7;
    and Omaha convention (1892), 200,
    471n29; and People's Party founding,
    190; and Populist executive commit-
    tee, 77, 193–97, 200; as Populist
    organizer, 202, 204; and St. Louis
    convention (1892), 67
Haynes, Jack, 403
health care, 1–3, 22, 442
Hempstead News, 207
Hendricks, Thomas A., 34
Henry, O. (William Sidney Porter), 295,
    329
Hepburn Act, 410
Hicks, John D., 8, 13
Hidalgo County, 330
Hill Country, 11, 23–24, 94, 177, 193.
    See also Central Texas

Hill County, 258
Hillsboro, Tex., 258, 400
Hobby, W. P., 421
Hodges, Jake, 218, 277
Hofstadter, Richard, 8, 411
Hogg, James Stephen, plate 5; and 1892
    elections, 79–81, 86–94, 98, 224,
    242, 246; and Bryan, William J., 373;
    and Farmers' Alliance, 55–56; as
    governor, 113, 250, 254; and Hogg
    Amendments, 404–4; on lynching,
    218–20; as Reform Democrat, 203,
    210, 247, 255, 398, 405–6; on woman
    suffrage, 278
Hoover, Herbert, 410, 420, 428
Hopkins County, 41–42, 236
House, Edward M., 89, 247, 405
Houston, Sam, 261, 334
Houston, Tex.: conditions in, 228, 248;
    immigration to, 177; political
    conventions in, 80, 81, 87, 91, 214;
    politics in, 265, 312, 358, 380, 400,
    418–19, 421, 423
Houston County, 94, 265, 387, 400
Houston Post, 88, 265, 385
Howard, Milford, 371
Huddleston, Martin Luther, 296
Hughes, Charles Shelley, 221–22
Humphrey, Richard M., 50, 58
Hunt County, 275–76, 490n38
Huntington, Colis P., 120

Illinois, 21, 250, 370
Imboden, W. M., 216
immigration: federal policies regard-
    ing, 331, 333, 334, 343; and Populism,
    21; and religion, 151, 177; in Texas,
    29, 323, 327, 329, 332, 383. *See also*
    Germans; Mexicanos
Indiana, 156–57, 478n3
Industrial Brotherhood, 103–4

a Greenbacker, 37, 104–5; and labor,
249; and Mexicanos, 335, 338–39;
monetary views of, 135, 349; oratory
of, 85–86, 183, 323, 343, 355, 372,
386–87; and People's Party founding,
65, 70; policies of, 97, 141, 144, 342;
as Populist leader, 118–19, 355–56,
365; religion and, 167, 176; and
Subtreasury Plan, 132; and third-
party politics, 50, 52
Kennard, Jim, 403
Kennedy, David, 435
Keynes, John Maynard, 134
King, Alice, 273
King, Thomas B., 73, 169–70, 238, 273,
348
Kirby, John Henry, 419, 508–9n20
Kittrell, Norman, 278
Kloppenberg, James, 5, 463n4
Knapp, Seaman A., 431
Knights of Labor: activism of, 134, 142,
233, 249–50; and code of dignity,
262; cooperative spirit of, 13, 307; and
farmer-labor movements, 13, 51, 251,
261; and Farmers' Alliance, 44–47,
49, 59, 61, 68; and Mallory steamship line, 44–45, 250; and McAnulty,
Alice, 270, 274; and People's Party
inspiration, 22, 103, 104, 225, 348;
and Populist leaders, 15, 296, 304,
358, 412; in South Texas, 323; and
third-party politics, 52, 57
Ku Klux Klan, 387, 418, 419, 427

labor activism, 12, 13, 61, 102–3,
142–43, 233, 249, 299
La Follette, Robert, 6, 436
Lamar County, 41
Lamb, William Robert: and 1894
elections, 243; and African American

leadership, 188–90; background of,
37; and cooperative movement, 38;
and Farmers' Alliance leadership, 55,
59, 60; moderation of, 124, 273–74;
oratory of, 74; and People's Party
founding, 64–66, 67, 69, 77; as
publisher, 84–85, 269, 472n46; and
third-party politics, 43–46, 47, 48, 50,
52, 57, 67, 68
Lampasas County, 32–34, 36, 42, 50,
72, 95–100
Lanham, Samuel W. T., 404
Laughler, W. P., 206, 207
Lavaca County, 325
Lease, Mary Elizabeth, 183, 490n38
Lee, Robert E., 390
legislation: age-of-consent, 283–84,
286–87, 314, 321, 491–92n61,
492n66; alien suffrage, 332; antitrust, 319–20, 497n75; banking,
306–9; civil service reform, 312–13,
496n54; debt relief, 305; education,
315–16; electoral reform, 313–14,
405–6; fee system, 309–12, 320;
labor, 304–5, 495n33; libel, 317–18;
prison reform, 217, 305; public safety,
314–15; railroad, 304, 404–5; rape,
289–90, 314; segregation, 212;
whitecapping, 402
Lester, Connie, 10
liberalism: American, 2, 16, 88, 411,
437, 440; classical, 4–6, 12, 14, 59,
99–100, 102, 109–10, 112, 152,
309, 410, 428; and conservatism,
3–4, 9, 150, 441; in contemporary
politics, 440–43; history of, 4–7,
150, 408–9, 507n1; modern, 4–8,
12, 16, 18–19, 26, 408–9,
437–38, 440; and Populism, 7–8,
12–16, 19

Midroad Populists: and 1896 elections, 377–78, 382, 392–93; and 1898 elections, 394, 396–97; definition of, 9; and Gibbs plan, 369–71; at St Louis convention (1896), 350–52, 363–65, 367–68, 372, 376; in Texas, 350, 352, 394–95
Midwest, 7, 57, 58, 432
Milam County, 106, 169, 172–73, 201, 400
Mill, John Stuart, 5, 7
Mills, Roger Q., 89
Mills, Seth Phineas, 301
Mississippi, 48, 367
Missouri, 312
Moley, Ray, 117
monetary policy: and 1894 elections, 237–39; and 1896 elections, 361–62; fiat currency, 130, 134–35; New Deal and, 435–36; Populism and, 104–5, 130–33; Populist conflict surrounding, 348–50, 352, 359–60; Populist oratory regarding, 164, 179; and Populist recruitment, 229–30, 348; and state politics, 247. *See also* gold standard; Populist thought
monopoly: antimonopolism, 46, 100–102, 108, 110, 112–14, 129, 131, 159, 319, 420; cooperative responses to, 59; corporate power and, 2, 14, 30, 43, 145; Democrats and, 51, 100; government as remedy for, 60, 114, 116, 127–29, 147; Populist opposition to, 101–2, 110–12, 118, 130, 162, 166, 176, 256, 319, 349, 443; railroads and, 102, 121, 123, 304; regulation of, 116, 147, 429, 438. *See also* corporations; Populist thought
Montalbo, Adrés Lopéz, 338–41, 343, 500n32

Montesquieu, 4, 100
Montgomery County, 235
Moody, Dwight L., 152–53, 154, 160, 167, 213, 478n7
Moore, Ed, 472n46
Moore, J. M., 88
Moore, William E., 406
Morgan, W. Scott, 54, 353
Morris, J. S., 45
Morse, Charles, 278

Nacogdoches County, 215–17, 221, 484n41
Nash, A. F., 265, 387
Nation, The, 279
National Economist, 25, 28, 53, 55
National Farmers' Alliance and Cooperative Union. *See* Southern Alliance
National Labor Relations Act, 420, 435, 439
National Labor Union (NLU), 102–4
National Order of Videttes, 52
National Reform Press Association. *See* Reform Press Association
Native Americans: attacks by, 99, 111; Comanche, 32, 49, 284; Populists portrayed as, 362–63; Mexicanos and, 331, 333–34, 336, 343
Navarro County, 50, 257
Nebraska, 68, 77, 370. *See also* Bryan, William Jennings
Nelms, W. W., 377
New Deal: and labor laws, 249; and modern liberalism, 6–7, 8, 409, 411; Populist influence on, 321–22, 424–27, 428, 434–43; and Populists, 415, 419, 421–22. *See also* race
New York, 228, 351
New York Herald, 180